Competency	Chapter
Human Behavior (7)	
Practice Behavior Examples...	
Understand human behavior across the life course; the range of social systems in which people live; and the ways social systems promote or deter people in maintaining or achieving health and well-being	7, 8, 13
Apply theories and knowledge from the liberal arts to understand biological, social, cultural, psychological, and spiritual development	10
Utilize conceptual frameworks to guide the processes of assessment, intervention, and evaluation	
Critique and apply knowledge to understand person and environment	3
Policy Practice (8)	
Practice Behavior Examples...	
Understand that policy affects service delivery and they actively engage in policy practice	
Know the history and current structures of social policies and services; the role of policy in service delivery; and the role of practice in policy development	4, 7
Analyze, formulate, and advocate for policies that advance social well-being	2, 6,12
Collaborate with colleagues and clients for effective policy action	13
Practice Contexts (9)	
Practice Behavior Examples...	
Keep informed, resourceful, and proactive in responding to evolving organizational, community, and societal contexts at all levels of practice	13
Recognize that the context of practice is dynamic, and use knowledge and skill to respond proactively	
Continuously discover, appraise, and attend to changing locales, populations, scientific and technological developments, and emerging societal trends to provide relevant services	1, 5, 11
Provide leadership in promoting sustainable changes in service delivery and practice to improve the quality of social services	2
Engage, Assess, Intervene, Evaluate (10)	
Practice Behavior Examples...	
Identify, analyze, and implement evidence-based interventions designed to achieve client goals	
Use research and technological advances	
Evaluate program outcomes and practice effectiveness	
Develop, analyze, advocate, and provide leadership for policies and services	
Promote social and economic justice	

CSWE's Core Competencies and Practice Behavior Examples in this Text

Competency	Chapter
A) ENGAGEMENT	
substantively and effectively prepare for action with individuals, families, groups, organizations, and communities	
Use empathy and other interpersonal skills	6, 9
Develop a mutually agreed-on focus of work and desired outcomes	
B) ASSESSMENT	8
collect, organize, and interpret client data	
Assess client strengths and limitations	12
Develop mutually agreed-on intervention goals and objectives	
Select appropriate intervention strategies	2
C) INTERVENTION	
Initiate actions to achieve organizational goals	
Implement prevention interventions that enhance client capacities	
Help clients resolve problems	
Negotiate, mediate, and advocate for clients	
Facilitate transitions and endings	
D) EVALUATION	
Critically analyze, monitor, and evaluate interventions	

Just when you thought the *Connecting Core Competencies Series* couldn't get any better... it did.

Each book has been enhanced with these features:

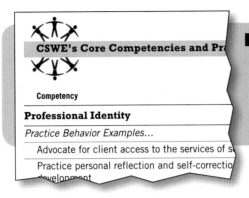

CSWE's Core Competencies and Pr...

Competency

Professional Identity

Practice Behavior Examples...

Advocate for client access to the services of s...

Practice personal reflection and self-correctio...

■ A grid indicates where **competencies** and **practice behaviors** are highlighted in the text

Policy Practice

Practice Behavior Example: Analyze, formulate, and advocate for policies that advance social well-being

Critical Thinking Question: Generalist social workers develop strategies that may include interventions at many system levels including the level of social policy. What questions should be considered when determining whether a social policy should be targeted for intervention in a specific client situation?

■ Highlighted **core competencies,** throughout the text, with:

• a Practice Behavior example for that competency

• a Critical Thinking Question to help students apply the competency through a critical thinking lens

■ **Chapter Review** questions build on each other with three types of questions. Students go from —

1. assessing basic knowledge, to
2. understanding larger themes and concepts, to
3. applying the concepts and themes with mini-case study questions.

■ **MySearchLab Connections** indicate correlated chapter-specific online videos, cases, assessment, and more.

Learn more about MySearchLab on the next page…

MySearchLab

MySocialWorkLab has become MySearchLab!

MySearchLab provides engaging experiences that personalize, stimulate, and measure student learning.

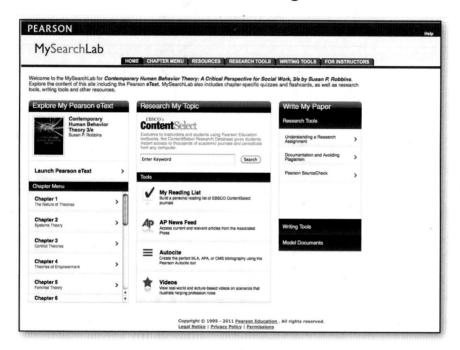

Features in MySearchLab include:

- **A complete eText—** Just like the printed text, you can highlight and add notes to the eText online or download it to your iPad.

- **Assessment—**chapter quizzes, topic-specific assessment and flashcards offer immediate feedback and report directly to your grade book.

- **Chapter-specific learning applications—**ranging from videos to case studies, and more.

- **Writing and Research Assistance—** A wide range of writing, grammar and research tools and access to a variety of academic journals, census data, Associated Press newsfeeds, and discipline-specific readings help you hone your writing and research skills.

Students: if your text did not come with bundled with MySearchLab, you can purchase access at: www.mysearchlab.com

Instructors: Your students will get access to MySearchLab at no extra cost only when you use the bundle ISBN. See back cover for ISBN to give to your bookstore.

www.mysearchlab.com

MySearchLab Connections in this Text

In addition to the outstanding research and writing tools and a complete etext in **MySearchLab**, this site contains a wealth of resources for social work students.

Below is a listing of the assets, keyed to the text chapter, you'll find in **MySearchLab**.

VIDEOS

* Professional Roles and Boundaries (1)
* Applying Critical Thinking (1)
* The Ecological Model Using the Friere Method (2)
* Participating in Policy Changes (2)
* Building Self-Awareness (3)
* Understanding Forms of Oppression and Discrimination (3)
* Keeping Up with Shifting Contexts (4)
* Building Alliances (4)
* Engagement (5)
* Learning From the Client to Co-create an Action Plan (6)
* Developing an Action Plan that Changes the Internal and External (6)
* Advocating for the Client (7)
* Developing an Action Plan That Changes the Internal and External (7)
* Advocating for the Client (8)
* Providing Leadership to Promote Change to Improve Quality of Social Services (8)
* Tolerating Ambiguity in Resolving Conflicts (9)
* Contracting with the Client to Select an Evidence-Based Therapy (9)
* Assessment (9)
* Professional Demeanor (10)
* Engaging the Client to Share Their Experiences of Alienation, Marginalization, and/or Oppression (11)
* Engaging in Research Informed Practice (11)
* Building Alliances (11)
* Demonstrating Effective Oral and Written Communication (12)
* Attending to Changes and Relevant Services (12)
* Managing Personal Values: The Code of Ethics (13)
* Advocating for Human Rights and Social and Economic Justice (13)
* Intervention (13)
* Evaluation (13)

* = CSWE Core Competency Asset
Δ = Case Study

MySearchLab   Connections in this Text

READINGS

Δ Ethical Dilemas (1)
Δ Please Don't Let Our Mother Die (2)
Δ Travis (Adoption) (2)
Δ A Puzzling Case Involving a Cambodian Patient (3)
Δ Travis: A Case of Working with Children in Juvenile Detention (3)
Δ Chelsea Green Space and the Power Plant (4)
Δ Crisis and Kinship in Foster Care (5)
Δ Melinda: a Child Sexual Abuse Case (5)
Δ The Lathe Family (5)
Δ Military Veteran Justice Outreach and the Role of a VA Social Worker, Part I (6)
Δ The Leon Family (6)
Δ Annie (7)
Δ Bob and Phil (7)
Δ Mrs. Smith and Her Family (7)
Δ Lost in a Foreign Land (8)
Δ Carrie (9)
Δ Frank (9)
Δ Oliver (9)
Δ A Qualitative Inquiry to Adult Child–Parent Relationships and Their Effects on Caregiving Roles (10)
Δ End-of-Life Decisions in an Intensive Care Unit (10)
Δ Resident's Rights to Intimacy in an Assisted Living Residence (10)
Δ Faith Harper (11)
Δ Military Veteran Justice Outreach and the Role of a VA Social Worker (11)
Δ Sarah and Robert (12)
Δ Stephanie and Rose Doer (12)
Δ Adventures in Budgets and Finances (13)
Δ Community to Community (13)
Δ Professional Decision Making in Foster Care (13)
Δ The Boyds (13)
Δ The Morgan Family (13)

★ = CSWE Core Competency Asset
Δ = Case Study

The Social Work Experience

An Introduction to Social Work and Social Welfare

Mary Ann Suppes
Mount Mary College, Milwaukee, WI

Carolyn Cressy Wells
University of Wisconsin, Oshkosh, WI

PEARSON

Boston   Columbus   Indianapolis   New York   San Francisco   Upper Saddle River
Amsterdam   Cape Town   Dubai   London   Madrid   Milan   Munich   Paris   Montreal   Toronto
Delhi   Mexico City   São Paulo   Sydney   Hong Kong   Seoul   Singapore   Taipei   Tokyo

Editorial Director: Craig Campanella
Editor in Chief: Dickson Musslewhite
Executive Editor: Ashley Dodge
Editorial Project Manager: Carly Czech
Editorial Assistant: Nicole Suddeth
Vice President, Director of Marketing:
  Brandy Dawson
Executive Marketing Manager: Jeanette Koskinas
Senior Marketing Manager: Wendy Albert
Marketing Assistant: Dasle Kim

Media Editor: Felicia Halpert
Production Manager: Meghan DeMaio
Creative Director: Jayne Conte
Cover Designer: Karen Noferi
Cover Image: ©ImageZoo/Alamy
Interior Design: Joyce Weston Design
Editorial Production and Composition Service:
  Ravi Bhatt/PreMediaGlobal
Printer/Binder: Edwards Brothers
Cover Printer: Lehigh-Phoenix Color

Credits appear on page 493, which constitutes an extension of the copyright page.

Library of Congress Cataloging-in-Publication Data

Suppes, Mary Ann.

 The social work experience : an introduction to social work and social welfare /
  Mary Ann Suppes, Carolyn Cressy Wells.—6th ed.
    p. cm.
  Includes bibliographical references and index.
  ISBN-13: 978-0-205-81996-6
  ISBN-10: 0-205-81996-6
 1. Social service—United States. 2. Social service—Vocational guidance—United States.
  I. Wells, Carolyn Cressy.   II. Title.
  HV10.5.S97 2011
 361.3'202373—dc23

                                                                              2011034319

10 9 8 7 6 5 4 3 2 1 EB 15 14 13 12 11

                                                    Student Edition
                                                    ISBN-10: 0-205-81996-6
                                                    ISBN-13: 978-0-205-81996-6

                                                    Instructor Edition
                                                    ISBN-10: 0-205-82000-X
                                                    ISBN-13: 978-0-205-82000-9

                                                    à la Carte Edition
                                                    ISBN-10: 0-205-06443-4
                                                    ISBN-13: 978-0-205-06443-4

Contents

2. Theoretical Perspectives for Social Workers   40

5. Family and Children's Services   123

8. Social Work in the Schools   235

Preface

Developing this text has been an absorbing project for its two authors for many years. The venture began one beautiful, crisp fall day in Wisconsin when two friends, both experienced social work educators, set off by car for a conference 200 miles to the north. We were those friends, and our conversation during that drive sparked the ideas that resulted in the first edition of *The Social Work Experience*. Both of us were teaching introductory courses in social work that semester and, because our roots were in social work practice, we were frustrated by the lack of well-developed, contemporary case study materials. Authentic, current case material, we were convinced, would help students to identify with the real people who are served by social workers, and with the social workers themselves.

It occurred to us that we could create those materials from our own professional practice experiences and from the field learning experiences of our students. Our case studies could portray diverse populations in both client and social worker roles. Some could illustrate baccalaureate-level social work students in fieldwork settings. We could synthesize real-life situations of people we had known and thus avoid exact duplication of any actual cases. With these ideas and commitments, the book emerged.

In the sixth edition, the primary focus remains entry-level generalist social work practice, but the linkage between generalist and specialist practice is presented as well. The professional practice competencies required by contemporary CSWE baccalaureate accreditation standards are highlighted throughout. The common themes of the previous editions remain integrated into every chapter: generalist practice, research, ethics and values, and human diversity. Augmenting the human diversity theme, poverty, populations at risk, and social justice issues are also integrated throughout. Case studies continue to reflect our concern for special issues relevant to women and other vulnerable populations. New case studies highlight contemporary concerns such as the unexpected fall into poverty of many middle-class families in the years following the economic crash in 2008, plus issues and concerns in the international community.

Today, as we put the finishing touches on the sixth edition, we wish to express appreciation to some of the many people who assisted us in this project. We wish to thank Crystal Parenteau, Jennifer Nonenmacher, and Ravi Bhatt of PreMediaGlobal—to Crystal for keeping us on-task and reasonably sane during technology crises, to Jennifer for the photographs and contemporary cartoons that enrich each chapter, and to Ravi for amazing patience and good humor during the editing process. Our gratitude is also expressed to those who provided materials for or helped to design our composite case studies: Isaac Christie, Jason Dietenberger, Joe Dooley, Linda Ketcher Goodrich, David Kucej, Julie Kudick, Maureen Martin, Melissa Monsoor, Malcolm Montgomery,

Dolores Poole, Wanda Priddy, Nicholaus P. Smiar, Rachel Fox, Sara Stites, Delores Sumner, Jody Searl Wnorowski, and Ellen Zonka. We are grateful to Roberta Ephraimson, Ana Marin-Sanchez, Beth Reed, and Heidi Walter for their technical assistance. We both owe enormous gratitude to our husbands, Dennis Loeffler and Fritz (Fred) Suppes, for their patience, support, and contributions to our research and resource exploration and for stimulating and nurturing our thinking on social issues.

We continue to be indebted to two prominent theorists, Betty L. Baer and Ronald C. Federico, whose vision of generalist social work practice remains alive today in baccalaureate social work education and within the pages of this book. It is our sincere hope that faculty and students alike will find our book helpful in their professional journeys.

Get Connected with **MySearchLab**

Provided with this text, MySearchLab provides engaging experiences that personalize, stimulate, and measure student learning. Pearson's MyLabs deliver proven results from a trusted partner in helping students succeed.

Features available with this text include:

- A **complete eText**—just like the printed text, you can highlight and add notes to the eText online or download it to your iPad.
- **Assessment**—chapter quizzes, topic-specific assessment, and flashcards offer and report directly to your grade book.
- Chapter-specific **learning applications**—ranging from videos to case studies, and more.
- **Writing and research assistance**—a wide range of writing, grammar, and research tools and access to a variety of academic journals, census data, Associated Press newsfeeds, and discipline-specific readings help you hone your writing and research skills.

MySearchLab can be packaged with this text at no additional cost—just order the ISBN on the back cover. Instructors can also request access to preview MySearchLab by contacting your local Pearson sales representative or visiting www.mysearchlab.com.

1

The Social Work Profession

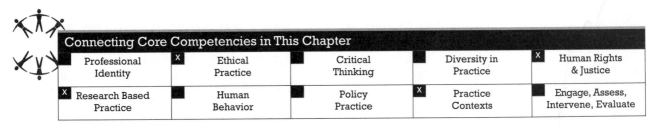

Connecting Core Competencies in This Chapter				
Professional Identity	X Ethical Practice	Critical Thinking	Diversity in Practice	X Human Rights & Justice
X Research Based Practice	Human Behavior	Policy Practice	X Practice Contexts	Engage, Assess, Intervene, Evaluate

Susan Dunn

The telephone rang shrilly at the women's shelter at about 6:15 in the evening. The caller's voice was urgent, frightened, and intense, although little louder than a whisper. "I just called the crisis telephone line that was advertised on the radio," the woman began, "and the person who answered told me to try you. I need a safe place to stay, right now. Can you take me?"

"We may be able to," the social worker replied. "It depends on your situation. Our agency has been set up to help women who have been physically abused. Can you tell me something about yourself? What makes you need a place to stay just now?"

"I can't talk very long because I'm so afraid he'll come back soon," the caller responded, her voice slightly louder this time. "My husband just beat me up again, but he ran out when I threatened to call the police. The children saw the whole thing. I've decided I've had enough. But I don't know where to go. My friends are afraid to get involved. I've got two kids who have to go with me. I don't have any money of my own."

"Sounds like you're in a tough spot. My name is Pamela Wright. I'm a social worker here. Tell me if you need to stop talking. Call me back if you have to hang up. If you're in danger right at this moment, I can take your name and address and call the police for you."

"Oh no," the woman said. "The reason I didn't call the police in the first place is that I don't want to get my husband in trouble. I make him upset. Calling the police would embarrass the whole family. I couldn't possibly do that."

"You said your husband hurt you. Do you have injuries that may need immediate medical attention?" "When he hit my face I tried to defend myself. I didn't want my face covered with bruises again. I put my hands up to my face. My right arm and shoulder hurt pretty badly now. I don't think I need to see a doctor or go to the hospital. I just need to get away from here."

"Do you feel it is safe for you to talk with me for a few minutes now?"

"Yes. The last time my husband got mad at me and left, he stayed away for a couple of hours. I'm pretty sure he'll do that again this time."

"Well," Pamela Wright said gently, "from what you say, this isn't the first time your husband has physically abused you. I take it that you want to be gone this time when he gets home?"

"Yes. He might come home drunk and hit me again. That's what happened last time. If it weren't for the children, I might take a chance and wait for him, because he might come home sorry and ready to make up. But the kids are awfully upset and scared. I want to get out of here this time."

"Have you any relatives who might be able to take you and the children tonight? You might feel a lot better if you had some family members around you to support you and help with the kids this evening. We'd be happy to help you here even if you were staying somewhere else. You could come in tomorrow, in fact, to talk with one of our counselors about things you could think about doing to deal with the physical abuse by your husband."

"I haven't got any family of my own around here. My parents live in another state, and so does my sister. My in-laws live near here, and they're good to me, but they would break down and tell my husband where I was. Then he'd come, and he might beat me up again. So I don't want anybody to know where I am."

Recognizing that this was an emergency situation, Pamela Wright said quickly, "We do have a room available in our shelter right now. I think that it is important for you to leave your home as quickly as possible. Will you be able to get yourself over here on your own if I give you the address?"

"Oh, I don't think I can. I don't have a car. My arm really hurts. I don't think I can carry anything. My 6-year-old can make it on her own, but the 2-year-old is too much trouble to take on the bus the way my arm hurts. And I'll need to bring some clothes and things."

"Have you any money at all right now?" Pamela asked. "We do have some special funds to send a cab in emergency situations, but those funds are very tight. Could you pay for a cab to get yourself and the kids over here?" "Well, I have about $15 in my purse. My husband always keeps the checkbook with him, and he just gives me cash a little bit at a time. But if I spend what I have on a cab, I won't have any money at all to pay for my stay with you, or for anything else, for that matter." "Our services are free. We can supply you with a small room for yourself and your children. We also provide meals. You can stay with us for up to a month. We will help you to decide what to do next. There will be rules about sharing household tasks and some other things, but I can explain more when you get here. You need to know, though, that we may want you to get checked out by a doctor. Sometimes people are more seriously injured than they initially think they are. Do you think you want to come?" After a moment's hesitation the caller whispered, "Yes, I do. Can I come with the kids right away?"

"Certainly," Pamela said. "But how bad is your arm? Will you be able to manage?"

"I think I can. I'll just have to pack with one hand. My 6-year-old can help. Is there anything in particular that we should bring?"

"Just bring the routine stuff—you know, toothbrushes, pajamas, toys, extra clothes, anything to keep you and the children as comfortable as possible."

"Okay. Thank you very much. I hope I'll be there soon."

"Fine. I'll give you our address. You are asked to tell it to no one but the cab driver, because for safety reasons we need to keep it secret." Pamela gave the woman the address of the shelter. "Now," she continued, "if your husband comes home before you get a chance to leave in the cab, do call the police right away, the minute you see him approaching. Or call us, and we'll call the police. Don't take the chance of another beating. Now, what is your name and address? I need to take your phone number, too, just in case." The address that the caller, Susan Dunn, gave turned out to be from a rather affluent suburban subdivision.

When Susan Dunn and her two children arrived at the shelter, their appearance betrayed some of their trouble. Susan's left eye was swollen and turning black. She held her sore right arm awkwardly, and several fingers were bleeding and discolored. The eyes of both children were red from crying. Susan's clothes were rumpled and torn. She carried a small suitcase, and her 6-year-old daughter was wearing a backpack full of school supplies.

The newcomers entered the shelter, a crowded house in a busy city neighborhood, quite hesitantly and looked anxiously about the first-floor hallway with its worn brown rug and cheerful, hopeful posters. A dark-eyed child of 5 or 6 ran up to greet them. Pamela Wright introduced herself and the child, waiting for Susan to introduce herself in turn along with her own children: Martha and Todd.

As Pamela Wright completed the introductions, Susan slumped into a chair and tears streamed down her face. She apologized, saying how grateful she was to be there. Pamela asked again about her injuries, and this time Susan replied, "Maybe I do need to see a doctor. My arm and my fingers hurt so much. Maybe something really is broken." Pamela immediately unloaded the children's and Susan's few belongings. "Would it be OK if Sara, our student social worker, helped the children get settled in with something to eat while I take you over to the emergency room to get checked out?" Susan reached for 2-year-old Todd and hugged him to her. She brushed away her tears and said, "I'd really like to get the children comfortable first, then I think it would be a good idea to get my arm checked out."

An hour later, with the children in Sara's gentle care, Pamela drove Susan to the hospital. In the car, Susan talked more about her husband, Jason, a recent college graduate who was building his future in the business world but with increasing stress and growing reliance on alcohol. X-rays demonstrated that Susan's right arm and two fingers were fractured. Pamela stayed at Susan's side as the medical staff attended to her fractures. Then the police were contacted by the hospital staff, and reports were filed. The ride back to the shelter was a quiet one. Pamela tried to help Susan understand that she was doing the right thing for herself and her family by taking action to stop the abuse. Susan smiled weakly through her pain and tears.

SOCIAL WORK: A UNIQUE PROFESSION

As the case study of Susan Dunn ends, you can probably imagine Pamela Wright's quick glance at Susan and Pamela's observation of the painful way Susan was moving her body and the grim, anxious expression on Susan's face. In her professional practice, this social worker had come to know well the terror and panic that threatened to overwhelm the women that arrived at the door of the shelter. Pamela's heart went out to Susan. She looked so frightened, so unsure of her decision. But, as a social worker, Pamela also had a good intellectual understanding of the dynamics of domestic abuse and the vulnerability faced by adults and children in at-risk situations. Pamela would review quickly in her mind the information she would need to obtain from Susan and the decisions that might need to be made quickly. She would prepare to use her social work expertise to listen to Susan's story and to offer Susan emotional support. Pamela, a baccalaureate-level social worker **(BSW),** was proud of her profession and confident in her ability to work with the people served by the shelter.

The Susan Dunn case was designed to introduce readers to this book and also to the profession of social work. Following Chapter 1, each of the chapters in the book will begin with a case study that will further illustrate the many dimensions of the profession, the diversity of the people social workers serve, and the social welfare system that forms the context for social work practice. We begin our exploration of this profession with a definition of **social work:**

> The major profession that delivers social services in governmental and private organizations throughout the world, social work helps people prevent or resolve problems in psychosocial functioning, achieve life-enhancing goals, and create a just society.

This definition underscores several important aspects of the profession. First, social work emerges out of the governmental and private organizations of nations; therefore, it is grounded in the human social welfare systems of countries. In conjunction with its focus on preventing and resolving problems in psychosocial functioning, the profession seeks to empower people and to identify and build on the strengths that exist in people and their communities. The social justice focus of social work is distinctive among the professions.

The ultimate goal of the social work profession is social justice.

While there are areas of overlap between social work and other human service professions, there are several ways in which social work is unique. Its dual focus on both the social environment and the psychological functioning of people differentiates social work from professions such as psychology and psychiatry. The social work approach of building on strengths within people and their communities further differentiates social work from these and other professions. The social work profession defines key values that, taken together, are unique among professions. The values guide and define the ethical practice of social workers. These values include belief in the dignity and worth of all persons, commitment to service, and the ultimate goal of social justice, among others. The values appear in the *National Association of Social Workers (NASW) Code of Ethics* (National Association of Social Workers [NASW], 2010a). The code is referred to frequently throughout this book because it is so essential to social work practice. It can be obtained online at http://www.socialworkers.org.

Social work, then, is a profession that provides an opportunity for people who want to make a difference in their world. Social workers make this difference by helping individual persons, families, and communities, large and small. Social workers are employed by private nonprofit organizations, faith-based agencies, governmental organizations, for-profit organizations, and sometimes have their own private practices. While some social workers function primarily out of their offices, others work primarily in the field. This profession provides challenge, excitement, and splendid opportunities to work with very diverse populations. It also requires courage, ability to see strengths in difficult situations, and willingness to advocate for vulnerable people. As a profession, social work is uniquely committed to the fight for social justice.

PROFESSIONAL SOCIAL WORKERS

Using this basic understanding of the uniqueness of the social work profession as a frame of reference, we will next explore the different levels of professional practice in social work. We will begin with the baccalaureate level, the BSW. This book will emphasize social work at the baccalaureate level; therefore, more substantial information will be provided about BSW practice than the two more advanced areas, the master's **(MSW)** and doctorate degree levels of the profession.

Generalist BSW Social Workers

The BSW is the first or entry level into the profession. The degree is generally referred to in conversation as a BSW, but the actual degree awarded by colleges and universities ranges from a BA, BS, BSSW, to the BSW degree. All of these baccalaureate degrees are of equal value, assuming that the social work educational program in which the degree is earned is accredited by the Council on Social Work Education (CSWE). The BSW can be completed in 4 years of college or university work, longer if the student is enrolled on a part-time basis. The BSW social worker, like Pamela Wright in the chapter case study, is professionally prepared as a generalist. What is a generalist? The authors of this book define the **generalist social worker** as:

> A professional social worker who engages in a planned change process—to arrive at unique responses to prevent or resolve problems involving individual persons, families, groups, organizational systems, and communities. Generalist social workers view clients and client systems from a strengths perspective to build upon the innate capabilities existing in

all people and communities. They respect and value human diversity. Generalist social work practice is grounded in ethical principles and guided by the NASW Code of Ethics. It is committed to improving human well-being and furthering the goals of social justice.

Another way of understanding generalist practice is to look at what it is *not*. A generalist social worker is not a specialist in psychotherapy (treatment of mental disorder) with individuals or families. Nor is she or he an expert in working with groups, nor primarily a community worker. Yet a generalist social worker must often counsel with individuals and families; will often facilitate groups; and must often track down and mobilize, or even create, appropriate community resources.

The CSWE, the organization that accredits social work education programs in the United States, requires that baccalaureate programs prepare students to become entry-level professionals in generalist practice. As a generalist with a 4-year baccalaureate degree, there are certain competencies that Pamela Wright must have achieved.

The Professional Competencies and Practice Behaviors of the BSW Social Worker

BSW social workers are well prepared to begin practice when they graduate from college. The courses and fieldwork they complete provide them with knowledge and skills—expertise—in specific areas. The CSWE has identified 10 core competencies that are critical to professional BSW social work education and practice. These competencies are identified in the front of this book. They will be a prominent feature of your classes and fieldwork if you are a social work major. You will encounter them frequently throughout this book. In every chapter an icon (emblem) in the margin will call your attention to competencies as they emerge in the chapter content. If you haven't already discovered the competencies in the front of this book, take a look at them now. The first of the competencies relates to professional identity. The final one relates to the social work practice processes of engagement, assessment, intervention, and evaluation. Notice the bullet points under each of the 10 competencies. These are the practice behaviors of social workers that characterize the competency.

Let's look at how Pamela Wright, in the chapter case study, demonstrated her professional competence and required practice behaviors. As the case study began, Pamela's calm, professional presence and her telephone communication skills (Competency 1) enabled her to quickly determine if Susan could be helped by the shelter. Using her critical, careful thinking skills (Competency 3), Pamela assessed Susan's crisis situation (Competency 10) and determined that Susan could be admitted to the shelter. Notice how Pamela used engagement skills (Competency 10) as she began to work with Susan. She communicated concern, caring, and respect, yet she obtained necessary information. On the telephone and in welcoming Susan to the shelter, Pamela showed no discrimination based on Susan's age, socioeconomic class, culture, or any other factor.

Pamela's professional competence enabled her to understand the abuse and oppression that Susan had experienced as a woman. Her social work knowledge and skills also enabled her to understand and respect other women at the shelter who were single parents, very poor, disabled, lesbians, or of diverse religions or cultures (Competency 4). Will Pamela Wright tell Susan to divorce her husband and never return to him again? Undoubtedly Pamela wants Susan and her children to be safe and to have a good quality of life, but Pamela would be violating one of the ethics (Competency 2) of the social work profession if she took away Susan's right as a legally responsible adult to make her own decisions.

Pamela enjoyed working with families (Competency 10). Often she helped children and their mothers find ways to talk to each other about what was happening in their lives. Each evening Pamela conducted group sessions (Competency 10) where the women talked about their day-to-day struggles and triumphs. Susan, for example, was astounded to learn in a group session about the exciting ways other residents were building new lives around jobs, further education, and reconnecting to family members. Individuals, families, and groups are three of the social systems (Competency 7) that generalists work with.

Sometimes in group sessions at the shelter, issues emerged about the rules or procedures of the shelter. Pamela would advocate with the shelter's staff, executive director, or even the board of directors on behalf of the residents to get needed changes made. It was on the basis of her awareness of a growing number of Hispanic residents (Competency 9) that special efforts were made (Competency 5) to increase the Hispanic volunteers and staff members at the shelter and to develop educational materials on domestic violence in the Spanish language.

Susan Dunn and the other residents were grateful that the shelter existed, but Pamela and the other staff were deeply concerned that their shelter often had to turn people away. Pamela and the agency director, an MSW social worker who was her supervisor, formed a committee, which included several residents, to conduct research (Competency 6) to identify factors related to the increase in domestic violence and possible solutions. Questions about the effectiveness of the current shelter program and the community domestic violence prevention programs were also researched. Pamela was one of the committee members who volunteered to study the changing social welfare policies (Competency 8) that limited access to education for women receiving temporary financial assistance. This committee work excited Pamela. She felt especially good to be working toward goals that would further the quality of life of many people in her community. This ability to help individual people and also to make a difference in the larger community was exactly why Pamela chose social work as a career.

The Baccalaureate Social Work Curriculum: How Competence and Expertise Evolve

When Pamela was a sophomore student in college, she declared social work as her major. At that time she did not realize that the course of study for the major had been designed to be consistent with the standards of the CSWE. In fact, since 1974 CSWE has required BSW programs to design a professional curriculum, one that is built on a liberal arts base. If a college or university's program is to be accredited, it must adhere to the educational policies set by CSWE.

Generally, students begin the social work major with just a few social work courses in the freshman and sophomore years. These courses usually introduce the social work profession and focus on social welfare, its history, current policies, and the impact of political decisions on the people whom social workers seek to help. The first and second years of the social work major are primarily taken up with liberal arts courses, which may include introductory courses in psychology, sociology, biology, college writing, philosophy, literature, and the arts—all courses that provide content that will be used later as professional courses unfold.

Important concepts for professional development appear in the introductory social work and social welfare courses taken in the first year or two of college. Professional ethics and values are among these concepts. Social workers' values significantly affect their practice. So, what are values? In general, *values* can be thought of as the philosophical concepts that we cherish as individuals, within our families, and as a nation. The NASW Code of Ethics discusses the profession's core values that are taught in social work classes. Why are values important pieces of the social work curriculum? Well, society in the United States and in many other countries holds contradictory values concerning the needy. Some values found in society guide people toward helping the poor; others guide people away from helping the poor, either because poor people are viewed as unworthy or because they are viewed as potential competitors. Because we are all products of our society, an honest assessment of our own personal values may reveal that we have absorbed some quite negative values about certain people—the poor, for example. Yet that clearly conflicts with the profession's valuing of social justice.

Ethical Practice

Practice Behavior Example: Recognize and manage personal values in a way that allows professional values to guide practice

Critical Thinking Question: How might personal values impact on a social worker's practice?

Probably persons who do not relate to these values will drop out of social work courses as students or will leave the profession early in their careers. By contrast, persons who value human diversity and respect the dignity of others are more likely to be good candidates for a career in social work. Future chapters in this book will frequently refer to the NASW Code of Ethics. The code guides social work practice and helps both the profession and civil courts to assess conduct when ethical issues emerge. The code comprises six major standards including more detailed substandards for each. The Code of Ethics is based on social workers' responsibilities in the six areas of responsibility:

- To clients
- To their colleagues and coworkers
- In their work in organizations and practice settings
- Within their professional roles
- To the profession itself
- To communities of all sizes from local neighborhoods to global social systems (NASW, 2010a)

The discussion of social work ethics and values becomes much deeper and more complex in the junior- and senior-year courses. This is where the professional curriculum dominates the courses students are enrolled in. Building on earlier liberal arts and social work courses, students in the junior and senior years develop their knowledge of human behavior. Studying the phases of human development promotes understanding of why people behave as they do. Learning about social systems and how they interact to promote or deter human well-being adds other important dimensions to the social worker's knowledge base.

To work effectively on behalf of the people they serve, social workers also need to understand the basic structures of local, state, national, and even international social welfare systems. Social workers are social change agents, and they want to be a part of the evolution that is constantly under way in the social welfare system. **Policy practice** is the term used for the conscious effort to effect change in the laws, regulations, and provisions of services of governmental and nongovernmental policies and programs.

In junior- and senior-year courses, social work majors also study practice theory. In these courses they learn how to interview effectively; how to develop respectful, effective relationships with the people they serve; and how to use the planned change process that is at the heart of generalist social work practice. Students learn how to uncover strengths in people and their environments; assess the problem situations faced by their clients; and work collaboratively with clients, not imposing their own solutions but engaging people in discovering new and more effective means for dealing with difficult situations. Research is interwoven in the curriculum, often in practice courses that help social work majors learn how to use systematic approaches for gathering data from interviews **(qualitative research)** and/or to use statistical, numerical data gathering and analysis to arrive at valid, reliable conclusions **(quantitative research)**. Research skills will help students evaluate the effectiveness of their own practice and also the effectiveness of social programs. Students learn to appreciate the necessity of using research findings to inform their practice, and as they achieve practice skills, they increasingly see how their understanding of social work practice can make them better as researchers.

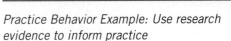

Research Based Practice

Practice Behavior Example: Use research evidence to inform practice

Critical Thinking Question: In what ways might the social worker in the chapter case study use research to improve her practice?

Respect for human diversity and growing understanding of the amazing diversity of the people they serve is another thread that weaves its way through social work courses. Students learn about cultures, lifestyles, physical and mental health factors, socioeconomic differences, gender orientation, age-related issues, and spiritual values and practices that differ from their own. Understanding and valuing differences is not enough, however. Social workers must learn how to actively explore diversity in practice because it affects every phase of the intervention or problem-solving process. Because social justice is the ultimate goal of the profession, social work education provides special attention to populations that are most at risk of poverty, discrimination, and oppression. These are the unloved people of our society. Social work students need to learn strategies that will be effective in assisting individuals, families, and often whole communities of people. Advocacy strategies can be learned to attain social and economic justice for an individual **(case advocacy)** or whole groups of people **(cause advocacy).**

Field education generally occurs in the junior and/or senior year, when most, if not all, of the other required social work courses have been completed. This is the part of the curriculum that students look forward to most eagerly. BSW students spend a minimum of 400 hours working with clients in one or more supervised field placements. The settings for field placements range widely but may include courts; child or adult protection settings; health care organizations such as hospitals, home health care, or nursing homes; adoption or foster care agencies; community centers; youth-serving organizations; domestic violence shelters; or mental health facilities. Field education is closely monitored and evaluated by social work faculty. By the time students complete field education, they have demonstrated all of the competencies and required practice behaviors of the generalist social worker. In other words, they are ready to begin professional practice!

Advanced Practice: Social Workers
with MSW and PhD Degrees

Advanced and specialized social work practice usually requires additional education. The MSW is designed as a 2-year degree following completion of a baccalaureate degree. Actually, however, an MSW can be completed in as little as 1 year for students who are awarded advanced standing because they have already completed a BSW. The MSW prepares social workers for advanced professional practice in an area of concentration. Although they differ among MSW programs, concentrations include various methods of practice (such as group work, administration), fields of practice (clinical social work or health care), social problem areas (poverty, substance abuse), or special populations (older adults, a cultural group such as Hispanic Americans). Advanced generalist practice is also an area of concentration for some MSW programs.

The domestic violence shelter in the case study employed an MSW social worker as well as Pamela Wright, BSW. Amy Sacks, MSW, received specialized training in working with individuals, families, and groups. Such a concentration is fairly common at the graduate level and may be called direct practice or clinical social work. Amy's work is rather narrowly defined. It is structured by appointments for individual and family therapy, regularly scheduled group sessions, and staff meetings. Amy is responsible for overseeing the shelter's program in crisis couples' counseling and for the batterers' intervention program, where she works with groups designed specifically for people like Susan Dunn's husband who abuse their partners. In batterers' groups, which are sometimes court-ordered, members must confront their patterns of response to stress and explore new, nonviolent ways of expressing their needs and emotions. These group experiences may be difficult and extremely emotional and are sometimes confrontational; the group process is aimed primarily at personality change rather than at emotional support, which is the main goal for the evening women's groups at the shelter. In therapy groups and in couples' counseling, where personality change is a primary goal, specialized training for the leader or therapist is very important.

Pamela Wright's role at the shelter is broader and more flexible than Amy's. She too counsels individuals, families, and groups, but usually in a less formal manner, often as needed and not necessarily by appointment. In addition, she responds to crisis calls, intervenes in problems among the residents, trains volunteers, and supervises the myriad tasks involved in running a residential facility. She does not live at the shelter but coordinates the schedules of evening staff and occasionally receives calls at night from staff for help during emergencies.

The fact that the BSW is educated to be a generalist does not mean that on occasion she or he does not develop or learn specialized skills in a particular field of practice (or, for that matter, that the MSW cannot be a generalist). In the real world, where funding may not provide the means to hire enough professionals to do a given job, both BSWs and MSWs may end up doing approximately the same thing, but the MSW curriculum provides its students with specialized knowledge in an area of concentration that allows them to work at an advanced practice level. MSWs are also more likely to be promoted to administrative positions, especially in larger organizations. The work of the BSW is usually more diverse and more flexible, and it usually involves mobilizing a wide variety of skills and resources.

Doctorate degrees are also offered in social work. Doctorates are the highest degrees awarded in education. In social work, a doctorate could take 3 to

5 years to complete beyond the master's degree. The doctoral degree in social work, usually a PhD or a DSW, prepares people for teaching in colleges and universities, for specialized advanced practice, or for research and organizational administrative positions.

THE ENVIRONMENT AND CONTEXT OF PRACTICE

Regardless of the degree they receive—BSW, MSW, or PhD—social workers practice their profession in a remarkably wide array of settings. By contrast, teachers tend to be employed in schools, physical therapists and nurses in health care organizations, and psychologists in mental health settings. A misconception about social work, held by some people, is that all social workers are employed by governmental organizations and work with the poor or in child welfare, where they take children away from their parents. Social workers do have special concerns about poverty and social injustice, but people of all income levels are clients of social workers. Social workers do not work only in governmental offices. And social workers make every possible effort to keep families together.

There are so many misunderstandings about the profession of social work! Many people would be surprised to learn about the range of settings in which social workers are found. To begin with, while most social workers are employed by organizations, some social workers are in private practice similar to the private practice of doctors. Like many other professionals (e.g., teachers, lawyers, rehabilitation therapists), some social workers are government employees; however, a declining number of social workers are employed in federal, state, or local tax-supported organizations. Increasingly, social workers are likely to be employed by nonprofit private agencies (such as the American Red Cross), denominational (church-sponsored) organizations, or for-profit businesses (most nursing homes fall into this category). A sampling of the amazing variety of social work practice environments is shown in Box 1.1.

New environments for social work practice constantly evolve. Genetic counseling, for example, has grown in recent years. Social workers who once specialized in child adoption placement now find themselves helping people

---

Box 1.1 Social Work Practice Settings: Selected Examples

Hospitals, emergency rooms, nursing homes, home health care, hospices

Police departments, probation and parole offices, juvenile detention facilities

Child welfare: foster care, adoptions, child safety services

Group homes or residential facilities that care for runaway children, persons with disabilities, or frail elderly persons

Legislative offices at all levels of government

Employee assistance programs, victim/witness programs

Senior centers, older adult day care, planning councils for older adult programs

Immigrant and refugee centers, disaster relief services

Schools, after-school group and counseling programs, gang prevention programs

Mental health hospital and outpatient services, substance abuse programs

locate their birth parents. War, terrorism, natural disasters, and even home or apartment building fires have resulted in a need for social workers who can help people get their basic needs met and deal with physical as well as psychological trauma.

Where do most social workers spend the majority of their working hours? Social work is an active profession. Many social workers go wherever people are experiencing problems—to the places where people live, work, study, and play. Social workers who make home visits know that entering into the natural environment of people, entering into their world, often makes people more comfortable and is much less threatening than an office visit. Sometimes social workers meet their clients in a coffee shop, in a school or hospital, or even on the streets if they are doing outreach work to persons who are homeless. When working with children in foster care or detention or in contested custody cases, social workers may spend hours in court. Meetings in the community occur frequently as groups of professional people, including social workers, come together to advocate for new legislation, for example.

Regardless of their settings, social workers have offices where, generally, some clients, family members, or other professionals meet with them. Here, too, social workers have access to telephone, fax, files, and computers. Even those social workers who primarily do outreach work or home visits need to spend time in their offices. Students doing an internship or field placement would also use the office as a home base.

A BROADER ECOLOGICAL PERSPECTIVE

Today the profession is beginning to awaken to the significance of our global physical environment. Natural disasters such as earthquakes, floods, and hurricanes destroy homes and communities, and they seem to be occurring with increased frequency throughout the world. War and industrial pollution claim victims in many parts of the world. Our asthma-infected children and health threats from toxic contamination of the produce being sold in our supermarkets have given many Americans a renewed concern about the physical environment.

Social workers are increasingly interested in the relationship between human social welfare and ecology. The NASW publication, *Social Work Speaks,* describes ecological contexts of special concern to American social workers:

> The inextricable links among poverty, environmental degradation, and risk to human well-being cannot be denied.... The relationships and subsequent health disparities are clear in polluted inner-city neighborhoods where children of color suffer from high rates of asthma; in crop lands where poor migrant workers carry agricultural pesticides home to their families on their work clothes; in low-income Louisiana parishes along the industrial "Cancer Alley" stretch of the Mississippi River; and in the unsanitary, crowded, and hastily and poorly constructed maquiladoras that house Mexican plant workers along the United States–Mexico border. (2009, p. 122)

What this means for social workers is that as students and practitioners, we need to be invested in building a

Practice Contexts

Practice Behavior Example: Continuously discover, appraise, and attend to changing locales, populations, scientific and technological developments, and emerging societal trends to provide relevant services

Critical Thinking Question: What environmental hazards exist for poor people in your community?

healthy environment for all people. We need to develop our understanding of the relationship between poverty and the risks emanating from degraded environments. In our daily social work practice, we need to take special care not to further endanger people by placing them in unsafe housing, and we need to work with landlords, volunteer groups, neighborhoods, and communities to clean up degraded areas and create environments that can nurture children, families, and older adults. Of great importance is the advocacy that we engage in together with other environmental activists. Whether we are working with individual clients, families, or groups, or within organizations or communities, our professional behaviors must reflect a sense of responsibility for environmental concerns.

SELECTING A CAREER IN SOCIAL WORK

College students typically experience a great deal of pressure to select a major and begin a career path. Selecting a career is surely one of life's most exciting and most difficult challenges. Fortunately, many resources are available to help with decisions about the choice of career. Career counseling centers in colleges and universities offer a variety of aptitude and interest tests. The Internet and libraries offer resources such as the *Occupational Outlook Handbook* of the U.S. Bureau of Labor Statistics. Professors and advisers are yet another source of career advice and information. In the end, however, the choice is a very personal one.

Selecting a career is surely one of life's most exciting and most difficult challenges.

Many college students know very little about the profession of social work, yet some might think that social work could potentially be a career that would enable them to accomplish their desire of helping others. This book seeks to help you determine if a social work career is right for you.

You will find that every chapter in this book begins with a case study describing social workers in action. In the next several paragraphs, you will learn about the paths taken by several of the case study social workers as they launched their careers. This book is primarily focused on professional social work at the baccalaureate level, so the three social work career tracks introduced are of BSW social workers. (Please note that the people in the case studies are actually fictitious.) We will begin with Pamela Wright from this chapter's case study.

Pamela Wright

Pamela Wright entered college directly from high school. She had years of volunteer experience in the grade school where her mother was a teacher, and she knew the inner workings of hospitals through her father's employment as an accountant in a local hospital. Pamela knew that she wanted to be a social worker, and, while in college, she selected elective courses in some of the liberal arts areas that would enhance her social work competence: courses in psychology, Spanish, and political science. Her senior-year social work field placement was with an inner-city shelter for homeless families. As Pamela told her dorm roommate, she just loved her work at the shelter, especially her work with abused women and their children. Following graduation, Pamela was immediately employed by the shelter that provided emergency care for Susan Dunn and her children.

Alan Martin

In Chapter 11 you will meet Jamie Sullivan's parole agent, Alan Martin. The 2 years Alan spent working on the family farm after high school convinced him that farming was not his calling in life. Accounting, bank financing, and crop planning necessitated a lot of paperwork, allowing for minimal interaction with people. After his father's death, Alan and his mother sold the farm to pay off Alan's father's medical expenses. When Alan enrolled at the state university branch campus, he was not sure what major to declare, but he was certain that he wanted to work with people. At the start of his sophomore year, Alan enrolled in an Introduction to Social Work course. A guest speaker for his class, a social worker who was a probation/parole agent for the state, especially intrigued him. Neither Alan's student field placement nor his first job following graduation was in the criminal justice field. In his substance abuse position, however, several of Alan's clients were on probation, and his contacts with their probation agents reawakened Alan's interest in the criminal justice system. Alan decided to take the exam for a probation/parole agent position. Six months and several interviews later, Alan received notice that he had been approved for a position, and, luckily, it was with the office that served youths in the rural western part of the state. The best of both worlds! Alan really preferred living in a rural area. He also especially enjoyed working with youths. His new position was with the juvenile probation and parole unit. By the time Jamie Sullivan, an adolescent convicted of armed robbery, met with Alan for the first time, Alan had 4 years' experience in juvenile justice work.

Madeleine Johnson

Unlike Alan Martin, Madeleine Johnson grew up in a middle-class, primarily African American suburb of a large metropolitan city. Along with her two older sisters, Madeleine was involved in volunteer work with her church's youth groups. Madeleine's mother's volunteer service at a church was the inspiration for her first career. Madeleine completed an associate degree in nursing and worked in various hospitals for 5 years. Following her divorce and a period of personal unhappiness, Madeleine decided to pursue a second career. When she returned to college, she found that it would take a total of 3 more years to earn a social work degree, but Madeleine was determined to do this. Her life experience proved to be a real asset, making courses in history, philosophy, and research much more interesting than she had expected. Madeleine really enjoyed the role-play exercises in the social work courses; she could understand how clients might feel, yet she could also sense compatibility with the role of the social worker. Because of her nursing background, Madeleine was initially interested in a hospital field placement but was challenged by the social work faculty to explore new areas. After careful thought, she selected a public social service agency. Here, Madeleine was given experience with nurturing groups for teen parents and with intensive, in-home services to families where child abuse had occurred. The panel that interviewed Madeleine when she applied for a position with the Salvation Army after graduation was impressed with her years of volunteer work, her experience as a nurse in health care, and her field placement with the public family and children's agency. You will learn about Madeleine Johnson's work with Dan Graves at the Salvation Army in Chapter 9.

The case studies introduce some social workers who struggled with career decisions, just as readers of this book may be struggling. "I want to help people.

Which profession should I pursue? Am I in the right major?" These questions are asked over and over again by college students. Social work is an exciting career. There are few "dull moments" in a day for social workers. It is a career that enables people to make a difference in the lives of others. It offers opportunities to transform the world. But it isn't the right profession for all people. Students are encouraged to talk with social workers, to do volunteer work, or perhaps to test their ability to work with others through a part-time job in the broad area of human services. Taking an introductory course in social work or social welfare is a very useful way for students to further explore their suitability for a career in social work. We hope this book will increase our readers' understanding of social work as a profession. We hope, too, that it will provide a sense of the remarkable opportunities this profession offers to people who sincerely want to make a difference in our world.

EDUCATION AND THE SOCIAL WORK CAREER LADDER

In selecting a career, it is important for college students to understand the concept of the career ladder, which includes a progression of career advancement opportunities within a single, recognized profession. A **career ladder** is constructed of the steps one must take to progress upward and therefore to advance in a profession or occupation. The notion of a career ladder is based on the assumption that it is possible to begin at a low level and then to move from one position to another, continuously progressing toward the top of the ladder.

In some occupations or professions, obtaining an entry degree enables a person to progress up the ladder without returning to school for graduate or postgraduate degrees, advancing based primarily on performance. In other professions, the career-ladder concept is viable only if additional academic credentials are obtained. Social work reflects an interesting mix. As Figure 1.1 shows, there are multiple educational levels within the profession. Each is explained next, along with typical responsibilities.

At the lowest rung of the ladder is the *preprofessional* (also referred to as paraprofessional) *social work* or *human service aide*. Although they do not have access to membership in NASW or to professional status, persons with bachelor's degrees in areas related to social work (e.g., psychology, sociology, and behavioral science majors) and persons with associate degrees are employed in human services. They assist clients by helping with complicated paperwork or performing tasks such as assisting chronically mentally ill persons, frail elderly people, or persons with disabilities to obtain needed resources. Some preprofessional staff members are hired without regard for their academic credentials but, instead, for their extensive firsthand knowledge of the community served by the agency.

The BSW is the basic entry level. The academic credential for this category is precisely defined: a bachelor's degree from a college or university social work program that is accredited by the CSWE. The basic professional level social worker has been prepared as a generalist and is able to engage in practice with individuals, families, groups, organizations, and communities. In this chapter's case illustration, a distinction is made between the responsibilities of Pamela Wright, the BSW, and those of Amy Sacks, who has an MSW degree. Pamela conducted intake interviews for the domestic violence shelter, worked with the children as well as the client herself, and ran group sessions with all

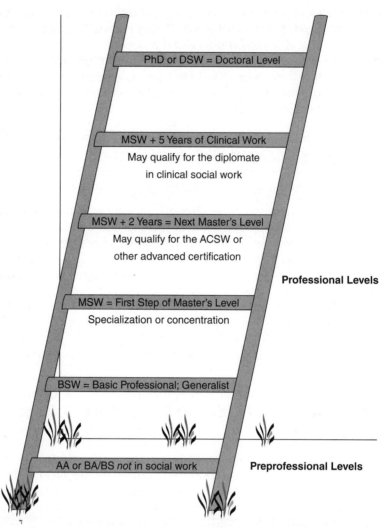

PhD or DSW = Doctoral Level

MSW + 5 Years of Clinical Work

May qualify for the diplomate

in clinical social work

MSW + 2 Years = Next Master's Level

May qualify for the ACSW or

other advanced certification

Professional Levels

MSW = First Step of Master's Level

Specialization or concentration

BSW = Basic Professional; Generalist

AA or BA/BS *not* in social work   **Preprofessional Levels**

Academic credentials are a significant component of the social work career ladder. Experience alone does not necessarily provide access to the next rung of the career ladder in social work.

Figure 1.1

The Social Work Career Ladder and Professional Education

the women in the shelter. As a recognized professional person, Pamela was able to engage clients, do an assessment of strengths as well as the problem situation, design and carry out an intervention plan, and then terminate and evaluate the intervention. Amy Sacks, in contrast, functioned at the MSW professional level.

The master's degree in social work, the MSW, must also be from a program accredited by the CSWE. The curriculum of master's degree programs builds on generalist content to develop a concentration in a practice method or social problem area; some master's degrees focus on advanced generalist practice. The MSW social worker should be able to engage in generalist social work practice and also function as a specialist in more complex tasks. Amy Sacks, the MSW social worker at the shelter in the case study, received specialized graduate training in clinical social work. At the shelter Amy's role is more focused, and the service she provides is in greater depth than Pamela Wright's. Amy does individual, family, and group therapy, usually by appointment. In addition, Amy is the executive director of the shelter.

At the top of the professional education classification system is the *social work* doctorate. Some doctoral programs have a research or teaching focus, whereas others prepare for advanced clinical practice or for careers in planning and administration.

EMPLOYMENT OPPORTUNITIES

Unfortunately, it is rather difficult to find research that accurately describes the full scope of employment of social workers. One very plausible reason for this is that social workers are so often employed under other titles. In some states, too, it is still possible for persons without degrees from accredited social work programs to obtain licensure or certification as social workers; research that included these persons would not provide a true picture of social work employment in that state. Researching the NASW membership base also fails to provide a clear picture of social work employment because not all social workers, whether BSWs, MSWs, or PhDs, hold membership in the social work national organization. While not providing a truly comprehensive survey of the profession, selected studies can provide useful data about employment in social work.

A Research Question: Where Do Social Work College Graduates Find Jobs?

Fortunately a valuable set of research data on the employment of social work college graduates is available. It is collected annually from BSW social work programs by the Association of Baccalaureate Social Work Program Directors Inc. (BPD). This research is part of a nationwide effort to assess the outcomes of BSW education and to determine if BSW programs meet the needs of their graduates as well as the needs of employing agencies.

Persons who graduated 2 years previously responded to the survey reflected in Box 1.2. The graduates' responses about employment provide an answer to one of the most frequently asked questions about social work: Where do social work majors get jobs after graduation? As Box 1.2 shows, child welfare settings accounted for the largest percentage (21 percent) of these social workers' primary fields of practice, followed by mental health and aging/gerontological services. A pattern that emerged from this study was that no single type of employment setting accounted for much more than 20 percent of the social workers' practice settings. (This finding may reflect one of the purposes of BSW education: to prepare generalist social workers who can competently work in a wide variety of settings.) However, if clusters of similar settings were combined, it would be apparent that close to one-third of BSW social workers were employed in child and family services (child welfare and family services), and a similar portion were employed in health care (mental health; health/medical; and alcohol, drug, or other substance abuse) (Buchan et al., 2010). The BPD survey findings related to fields of practice are not new. The surveys conducted by this organization have produced remarkably similar findings for nearly 20 years.

Box 1.2 Primary Fields of Practice (Percent) of BSWs, 2010	
Child welfare/child protection	21.0
Mental/behavioral/community mental health	16.2
Aging/gerontological/adult protective services	11.0
Family services	8.5
Health/medical care/rehabilitation	8.1
Mental retardation/developmental disabilities	5.1
Corrections/criminal justice/violence/victim services	4.8
Alcohol, drug, or substance abuse	4.4
Crisis intervention/information and referral services	4.3
School social work	3.8
Other	12.8

Source: Adapted from The Annual BEAP Report, February 24, 2011, 28th Annual BPD Conference, Cincinnati, Ohio, by Vicky Buchan, Tobi DeLong Hamilton, Brian Christenson, Roy (Butch) Rodenhiser, Ruth Gerritsen-McKane, Marshall Smith. Reprinted by permission of the authors.

Another way of looking at jobs for BSWs is to consider the auspices, public or private, of their employing organizations. The data from the BPD survey of graduates shown in Box 1.3 are especially interesting because they demonstrate that an overwhelming portion of BSWs are not employed by governmental agencies, as is often assumed. In fact, in the survey population, two-thirds of the graduates were employed in the private sector. This is a considerable shift! In 1999 just over half of BSW program graduates were employed by governmental agencies, and for at least the preceding 10 years survey data showed that 50 percent of BSW graduates were employed by governmental agencies. Box 1.3 also reflects private, for-profit sector employment of BSWs; this is a new and growing trend (Buchan et al., 2010).

Box 1.3 Employment Auspices (Percent) of BSWs, 2010	
Private nonprofit nonreligious	37.5
Private nonprofit religious	15.2
Private for-profit	13.9
Total private sector	66.6
Public state	18.0
Public county, municipal, or town	12.1
Public federal non-military	2.8
Public federal military	0.5
Total public sector	33.4
	100

Source: Adapted from The Annual BEAP Report, February 24, 2011, 28th Annual BPD Conference, Cincinnati, Ohio, by Vicky Buchan, Tobi DeLong Hamilton, Brian Christenson, Roy (Butch) Rodenhiser, Ruth Gerritsen-McKane, Marshall Smith. Copyright © 2011. Reprinted by permission of the authors.

The largest employer of BSWs, as shown in Box 1.3, is the private, nonsectarian sector (the American Red Cross would be one example). The largest governmental employer in the BPD study proved to be state government. This could include state child welfare, aging, mental health, or probation and parole programs.

Employment Patterns for MSWs

An NASW membership workforce survey provides a picture of social work practice of persons who hold primarily the MSW degree (Whitaker, Wilson, & Arrington, 2009). The NASW study has somewhat different categories, but it is interesting to compare Figure 1.2, the primary practice areas of the NASW social work survey population, with Box 1.2, which illustrates the primary practice areas of BSWs. The largest portion of BSWs was employed in child welfare, whereas the largest percentage of the NASW, primarily MSW group, worked in mental health (the second strongest area for BSW employment). Child welfare, by contrast, was only minimally represented among the mainly MSWs surveyed. MSWs were scattered widely across the many areas of social work practice.

Private practice emerges as a strong area for MSWs, especially solo practice where social workers work independently out of their own offices. Psychotherapy is likely to be the service provided by most of these practitioners. Private sector employment is growing significantly for BSW practitioners too, although not as psychotherapists (a role that is appropriate only to MSWs or doctoral professionals). Many of these privately funded organizations do seek out and use considerable amounts of governmental funds to conduct their programs. A nonprofit child welfare organization may actually contract with a

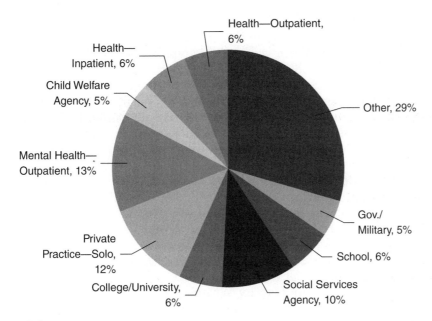

Figure 1.2

Primary Practice Areas of MSWs

state or county public welfare office to provide the child protection services that, in the past, the county had provided. Religious denominational organizations, too, often seek grants or contracts with public agencies to support their programs. For BSWs, the for-profit sector is a relatively new practice setting. These organizations, as the name implies, must provide services in a way that ensures that the corporation will earn a profit for its owners. Counseling positions in mental health, house manager and group facilitation positions in group homes, telephone crisis and referral jobs in employee assistance programs—these are all examples of the kinds of for-profit employment opportunities that are increasingly available to BSWs.

Salaries and Demand for Social Workers

In recent years there has been a very uneven job market for social workers. In some urban areas of the United States it has been difficult for social workers to find employment. At the same time, however, states such as Texas, Iowa, and Arkansas were seeking social workers. Rural areas were so desperate for social work staff that they employed uncredentialed people because they were unable to attract professionally trained social workers.

The job search experiences reported in the BPD studies, however, are quite positive. Although some BSW respondents elected to go to graduate school after receiving their degrees and a small number sought employment in another field or were not successful in finding social work jobs, more than 75 percent consistently obtained social work employment. Salary data are another important consideration.

When looking at salary data, however, it is important to consider several factors. First, it is very important to keep in mind that social work salaries tend to increase every year. The salary information that we provide in this book is outdated as soon as the book is published, so the salary information we provide here is very likely to be *less* than the salary that social workers in the field are earning when you read this report, and the data reported here are likely to be considerably lower than the salaries students are likely to earn when they graduate. Social work salaries vary immensely by region of the country, years of experience, field of practice and auspice, and highest degree earned. Another important factor to remember is that commitment to vulnerable populations is a stronger motivation for some social workers than salary, and many accept employment with seriously underfunded organizations that pay extremely small salaries. This, then, tends to skew the earnings data on social work employment and to give an impression of lower salaries than the salaries that may, in fact, be available from other organizations. The Bureau of Labor Statistics' *Occupational Outlook Handbook* is a reliable source for current general salary information. It tracks median annual salaries for social workers according to their field of practice, as shown in Box 1.4. This makes it possible to compare salaries according to areas of particular interest to students or beginning social workers.

An NASW study reported by Whitaker and Wilson (2010) provides additional interesting data about social work salaries. In their survey, the median income for the study group (comprised primarily of MSWs but including some BSWs) was $55,000, compared with $47,640 for a similar NASW study population just four years earlier (Whitaker, Weismiller, & Clark, 2006). Considering that some social workers choose to work in underfunded

Box 1.4   U.S. Bureau of Labor Statistics: Social Work Median Annual Wages, 2008

	Lowest 10 Percent	Top 10 Percent	Median
Child, family, and school social workers	$25,870	$66,430	$39,530
Elementary and secondary schools			$55,860
State government			$39,600
Individual and family services			$34,450
Medical and public health social workers	$28,100	$69,090	$46,650
General medical and surgical hospitals			$51,470
Home health care			$46,930
Nursing care facilities			$41,080
Mental health and substance abuse social workers	$21,770	$61,430	$37,210
Outpatient care centers			$36,660
Individual and family services			$35,900
Residential facilities			$33,950
All other social workers	$27,400	$74,040	$46,220
Local government			$51,700
Individual and family services			$36,660
Community food and housing and emergency and other relief services			$31,890

Source: Adapted from "Social Workers." Occupational Outlook Handbook, 2010–11 Edition, U.S. Department of Labor, Bureau of Labor Statistics, (2009). Retrieved from http://www.bls.gov/oco/ocos060.htm.

organizations because of the vulnerable populations they wish to serve, it was not surprising that there were some fairly low salaries reported, even among MSWs. What might be surprising for some people is the fact that some salaries exceeded $100,000. The annual base pay of 17,851 social workers in the 2010 NASW study is depicted in Table 1.1. The base pay data exclude any overtime, bonuses, or extra pay of any kind. If the data in the $40,000–$59,000 and the $60,000–$79,000 categories in Table 1.1 were combined, it would show that 60 percent of these social workers were earning $40,000 to nearly $80,000. The employment settings that demonstrated the highest base pay were those of solo (private) practice, government sector, and school social work; the lowest base pay was in group practice and hospice settings (Whitaker & Wilson, 2010).

Again, a reminder: both MSW and BSW salaries tend to increase each year, so the salary information in these exhibits probably won't be a true representation of social work salaries when you read them, and they will be even less representative of social work salaries by the time you graduate from college. Salaries also vary considerably across the different geographic regions of the United States.

Table 1.1	**NASW Workforce Studies: Social Workers Annual Base Pay (Percent), 2009**
Under $20,000	6
$20,000–$39,000	18
$40,000–$59,000	34
$60,000–$79,000	26
$80,000–$99,000	9
$100,000 and above	8

Source: Workforce Trends Affecting the Profession 2009. Copyright 2009 by National Association of Social Workers. Reproduced with permission of National Association of Social Workers in the format Textbook via Copyright Clearance Center.

Future Employment Opportunities for Social Workers

Economic conditions, the political climate, social welfare policy decisions made by the U.S. government, even changing demographics, and technological advances—all of these factors affect employment prospects in social work and other fields. Replacement needs as some social workers retire or leave for other reasons also influence the number of positions available.

"Landmark Study Warns of Impending Labor Force Shortages for Social Work Profession" was the headline for an NASW press release announcing findings from the study of Whitaker et al. (2006). NASW's sense of urgency was repeated in 2009 with special concern about a looming challenge—a time when the profession may be unable to meet the challenges of increased demand (Whitaker & Wilson, 2009). Concern persists regarding:

- The number of new social workers providing services to older adults is decreasing, despite projected increases in the number of older adults who will need social work services.
- The supply of licensed social workers is insufficient to meet the needs of organizations serving children and families.
- Workload expansion plus fewer resources impede social worker retention.
- Agencies struggle to fill social work vacancies. (Nadelhaft & Rene, 2006, pp. 1–2)

Already there are reports of shortages in social workers, not just in the United States but also in other parts of the world. As early as 2001 a *Social Worker Today* article, reporting on a California state assembly hearing, cited "a severe shortage of trained social workers and the lack of a candidate pool to fill employment positions" as well as an insufficient number of social work students graduating from state schools (Harvey, 2001, p. 20). In 2006, Hawaii's Department of Human Services reported a shortage of social workers for its child welfare department, and Kaui Castillo of the Queen Liliuokalani Center told a reporter: "We are seeing this in child welfare, gerontology, mental health, the criminal justice system, schools and health in general" (Lee, 2006, p. 1). In Capetown, South Africa, the Minister of Social Development stated that "a critical shortage of social workers [is] inhibiting the provision of welfare services.... The extent to which we are able to provide social welfare services is fundamentally influenced by critical shortages in the supply of social workers and other social service professionals" (News 24, 2006, p. 1). Reports from Scotland and the United Kingdom also showed serious shortages of social workers (Community Action, 2005, p. 1). In Scotland, the Minister of Education expressed grave concern that children's welfare was potentially being jeopardized as a result of the social work shortage. She asked that the social work profession seek out new methods to recruit social workers in order to stop even a greater crisis to occur within social work departments across the country (SNP: It's Time, 2005).

Returning to the U.S. Department of Labor for data, we find that 642,000 social work jobs existed in 2008, a considerable increase from 468,000 in 2000 (Bureau of Labor Statistics, 2009d). Table 1.2 tracks the remarkable growth of social work positions since 2004 and then forecasts employment in social work for the year 2018.

The *Occupational Outlook Handbook* reported that there does tend to be more competition in cities for social work jobs. This is especially likely in cities where professional educational programs are present. In rural areas, however, the need for social workers is often very great and shortages of social workers are very apparent. In fact, rural areas appear to have great difficulty attracting and retaining social workers. Given all of these facts, what employment projection does the U.S. Department of Labor make for social workers? "Employment for social workers is expected to grow faster than the average for all occupations through 2018" (Bureau of Labor Statistics, 2009d, p. 3). This prediction is a remarkably strong statement!

The U.S. Department of Labor categorizes social work, along with psychology and other human service professions, within the professional and related occupations area. The Labor Department's *Occupational Outlook Handbook* predicts that from 2008 to 2018, total employment in the United States will increase by 25.1 million, a growth rate of about 10.7 percent. The professional and related occupations group, however, is expected to add the most new jobs (5.2 million) of all other major occupational groups (Bureau of Labor Statistics, 2009b).

The employment outlook for some professions within the general category of professional and related occupations is not as positive as that for others. Employment positions in psychology, for example, are expected to increase

Table 1.2   U.S. Bureau of Labor Statistics: Social Work Employment Trends and Projections

Occupational Title	Employment in 2004	Employment in 2008	Projected Employment in 2018	Change from 2008 to 2018 Number	Percent
Social workers	562,000	642,000	745,400	103,400	16
Child, family, and school social workers	272,000	292,600	328,700	36,100	12
Medical and public health social workers	110,000	138,700	169,800	31,100	22
Mental health and substance abuse social workers	116,000	137,300	164,100	26,800	20
Social workers, all other	64,000	73,400	82,800	9,400	13

Source: Adapted from "Social Workers," *Occupational outlook handbook, 2010–11 Edition*, U.S. Department of Labor, Bureau of Labor Statistics (2009). Retrieved from http://www.bls.gov/oco/ocos060.htm.

by 12 percent (from 170,200 in 2008 to 190,000 in 2018) compared with a 16 percent increase (from 642,000 in 2008 to 745,400 in 2018) for social workers (Bureau of Labor Statistics, 2009c,d). The Labor Department also notes that in psychology, a doctorate degree is required for most clinical work, although the master's degree is acceptable for some positions in schools and industry. Few opportunities are projected for persons holding only a bachelor's degree in psychology (2009c).

Why will social work positions increase in the future? The increasing population of older persons is one compelling reason. The U.S. Department of Labor anticipates that job prospects will be especially favorable in areas involving social work with older adults. A rapidly growing aging population plus the aging baby-boomer generation will require services—services to assist with the stresses that accompany midlife crises related to career as well as personal issues. Increased demand for social workers is also expected in adult protective services, adult day care centers, home health care, assisted living, and hospice programs. The number of older adults with serious mental health and substance abuse problems is expected to put stress on existing services, which may exceed the number of available social workers (Bureau of Labor Statistics, 2009d). Fortunately, a whole new generation of social work students is being prepared for effective, compassionate work with older adults, thanks to the historic partnership of the Hartford Foundation and the CSWE beginning in 1998. Over 200 BSW and MSW schools of social work and well over 1,000 students have participated in and continue to be involved in gero-enriched curricula, field placements, and research. As a result, students who never imagined themselves working with older adults have become inspired by this field of practice (Hooyman, 2009).

In addition to employment opportunities with older adults, the Bureau of Labor Statistics foresees continued growth in the private social service sector. Increasing student enrollments will likely create demand for more school social workers. The mental health and substance abuse social work fields are also anticipated to grow especially as persons who abuse substances are increasingly being placed in treatment programs rather than given prison sentences. Additional growth is also expected in health care. These social work employment projections are driven by anticipated growth in programs and also by the need for replacement workers for those persons who will be retiring from the profession of social work (Bureau of Labor Statistics, 2009d).

LEGAL REGULATION OF THE PROFESSION

State Licensure and Certification

Can doctors practice their profession without being licensed? Can pharmacists? Dentists? How about social workers? While there are some situations in which doctors, pharmacists, and dentists may practice without a license, these are relatively few. Medicine, pharmacy, and dentistry were among the first professions to be legally regulated in the United States (Biggerstaff, 1995). The term **legal regulation** refers to governmental authority for the practice of selected professions and occupations. Today doctors, pharmacists, and dentists are licensed by the states in which they practice.

Social workers, too, are legally regulated in all states in the United States. The first statute providing for the legal regulation of social workers was passed in Puerto Rico in 1934 (Thyer & Biggerstaff, 1989). There are several different forms of legal regulation governing social work. In most states social workers are licensed, generally at both the BSW and MSW levels. In a few states social workers are certified, not licensed. Canadian provinces generally use the term *registration* instead of licensure or certification for their legal regulation.

Licensure and certification in the United States are very similar. Both are created through the passage of state law, so they are born out of the political process. State boards of regulation and licensing are responsible for administering licensing and certification of all professions. Only persons with appropriate credentials (usually degrees from CSWE-accredited schools) are permitted to take the social work competency examinations that are required. A national organization, the Association of Social Work Boards, provides examinations to the states; each state determines its own passing score. There is one important difference between certification and licensure. While certification protects the title *social worker*, it doesn't prohibit uncertified people from practicing social work. Uncertified people simply may not legally call themselves social workers. Certification is not considered to be as strong a form of legal regulation as licensure.

Although states determine the categories of social workers they will license or certify, the four categories most commonly seen and the academic degree and practice experience required are as follows:

Bachelor's: a baccalaureate degree in social work
Master's: an MSW degree; no experience required
Advanced generalist: an MSW degree plus 2 years of supervised experience
Clinical: an MSW degree plus 2 years of clinical practice (Association of Social Work Boards, 2006)

Renewal of a state license or certification, which may occur every 2 years, usually requires documentation of completed continuing education. Earning a degree in social work is truly not the end of a social worker's education!

NASW Certification of Professional Achievement

There is a growing demand by consumers and insurance companies for the affirmation of experienced professionals beyond the entry level and even beyond state licensure. NASW has met this challenge by creating specified credentials for social workers. NASW sustains authority over their affirmation process; it is not a form of governmental regulation such as licensing, although it often incorporates requirements for state licensing.

The ACSW was the first advanced practice credential offered by NASW. Developed in 1960, it is still the most respected and recognized social work credential. The **ACSW** designates membership in the Academy of Certified Social Workers. It is available to members of NASW who have an MSW degree, 2 years of additional MSW-supervised social work practice, professional evaluations that confirm their practice skills and values, and 20 hours of related continuing education (NASW, 2010b).

Following the development and broad acceptance of the ACSW, NASW created the Diplomate in Clinical Social Work (DCSW) and the Qualified Clinical Social Worker (QCSW). They, too, have been very successful. Both are advanced practice credentials. The diplomate, which requires 5 years of post-MSW or postdoctorate clinical practice, is the highest professional level authorized by NASW. The QCSW requires 2 years of clinical practice following receipt of an MSW or doctorate in social work, plus attainment of state licensure. Note that the ACSW, the diplomate, and the QCSW are all designated by NASW as professional credentials.

In more recent years, NASW has responded to the need for additional acknowledgment of specialized expertise. It created specialty certifications to recognize specific practice expertise, as compared with the broader areas of the advanced practice credentials described earlier. Three new certifications recognize special expertise in practice with older adults: the Clinical Social Worker in Gerontology (CSW-G) and the Advanced Social Worker in Gerontology (ASW-G) at the master's level, and the Social Worker in Gerontology (SW-G) at the baccalaureate level. The ASW-G denotes practice expertise in macro and administrative practice with people who are elderly in contrast to the clinical focus of the CSW-G. The SW-G certificate affirms professionalism in care and case management in BSW practice. In general, all three of these certificates require membership in NASW, a minimum of 2 years (3,000 hours) of experience, 20 hours of continuing education related to practice with older adults, appropriate references, and attainment of state license or certification within the appropriate category (NASW, 2010b). Clearly, the aging demographics surfacing in the United States and internationally are creating a market for social workers, especially social workers with recognized practice expertise with older adults.

A range of additional certificates offered by NASW include those designated for practice in children, youth, and family social work; in health care; in the field of substance abuse; in case management; and in school social work. The specific requirements for all of these certificates are similar to those described in the preceding paragraph (NASW, 2010b). They can be accessed online in the "Practice & Professional Development/Social Work Credentials" area on the NASW website: http://www.socialworkers.org.

Credentials that testify to expertise in specialized areas of practice can provide a competitive advantage in the job market. They are also a way of alerting potential clients or referral sources to the knowledge and practice expertise of the social worker.

Social workers and students attend NASW social policy conference in Washington, DC.

PROFESSIONAL SOCIAL WORK ORGANIZATIONS

This chapter has already referred to NASW and CSWE numerous times. Hopefully this signifies the remarkable importance of the two national social work organizations for the profession and for social workers. NASW and CSWE are, indeed, the most prominent, but many other professional social work organizations also exist.

The National Association of Social Workers

NASW has become the major professional membership organization in the United States. There are approximately 150,000 members of NASW (NASW, n.d.). NASW is located in Washington, DC. It was founded in 1955 when seven existing but quite separate social work organizations (such as the American Association of Medical Social Workers) joined together. The NASW has four major functions:

1. Professional development
2. Professional action
3. Professional standards
4. Membership services

Graduates of schools of social work that are accredited by the CSWE are eligible for full membership in the NASW. Students in CSWE-accredited programs are eligible for student membership at reduced rates. NASW's journal, *Social Work*, is a respected source for research findings in various fields of practice (useful for writing term papers). The monthly publication of the national office, *NASW News*, provides information regarding new developments, social policy discussions, and updates on legislation of interest to social workers and their clients; it also advertises social work professional positions. All 56 chapters publish newsletters, keeping chapter members abreast of statewide developments. At the national level, NASW employs a lobbyist to represent members' views on policy issues known to Congress. Through the Political Action for Candidate Election (PACE) wing of NASW, candidates for national as well as state offices are endorsed, and information about their positions is disseminated.

NASW's strong commitment to service is dramatically evident in its online resource, *Social Workers: Help Starts Here* (http://www.helpstartshere.org). This beautifully designed website provides stories of people who have experienced very difficult times but discovered organizations, experts (sometimes social workers), or even their own inner strength that enabled them to get through a problem or crisis. Helpful, readable, current information on subjects as varied as health and wellness, family problems, and issues facing older adults is offered. Readers are invited to share their own story about how a social worker helped them or a loved one. Under the heading of "Find a Social Worker," a link is provided that provides an electronic connection with a social worker. This anonymous electronic resource is offered as a public service.

The Council on Social Work Education

Like NASW, the CSWE is a private, nongovernmental organization. It is located in Alexandria, Virginia; it has a membership of more than 3,000 individuals as well as institutional memberships of colleges and universities. CSWE is the only organization in the United States that is authorized to accredit social work educational programs. CSWE's mission is to provide and sustain high quality in social work education through developing and maintaining standards for social work education in the United States (CSWE, 2010).

CSWE has accredited MSW programs since its creation in 1952. In 1974 accreditation was expanded to include baccalaureate programs. Currently, 200 MSW programs and 470 BSW programs are accredited (CSWE, 2010). To date, doctoral programs in social work are not accredited by CSWE.

CSWE conducts a number of other activities in addition to accreditation. An annual conference, for example, showcases presentations of scholarly papers and current research. CSWE also publishes a scholarly journal (*Journal of Social Work Education*). A recent and ongoing project aims at strengthening the competence of social workers for work with the growing population of older adults. Through its members, the CSWE also seeks to influence social policy and funding, both governmental and private, to support social work education.

The National Association of Black Social Workers

The National Association of Black Social Workers (NABSW), like NASW, is a membership organization located in Washington, DC, but unlike NASW its membership is open to any Black person who is employed in social work or human services; it does not specify academic credentials. NABSW was created in 1968 to address issues pertaining to the recruitment and education of Black social workers and the delivery of social welfare services to Black people (NABSW, n.d., History section).

The Code of Ethics speaks eloquently to the mission and purpose of this organization. It states, in part:

> I hold myself responsible for the quality and extent of service I perform and the quality and extent of service performed by the agency or organization in which I am employed, as it relates to the Black community.
>
> I accept the responsibility to protect the Black community against unethical and hypocritical practice by any individuals or organizations engaged in social welfare activities.
>
> I stand ready to supplement my paid or professional advocacy with voluntary service in the Black public interest.
>
> I will consciously use my skills, and my whole being, as an instrument for social change, with particular attention directed to the establishment of Black social institutions. (NABSW, n.d., Code of Ethics section, p. 1)

The NABSW has several publications, including *The Black Caucus Journal.* More than 100 chapters of NABSW exist throughout the United States with affiliate chapters in other countries such as South Africa, Canada, Ghana, and the Caribbean. Student units also exist on college and university campuses. National conferences are held annually in key cities in the United States and are open to both members and potential members. Summer international conferences offer exciting opportunities to "experience African culture, heritage, and social institutions" in Ghana, South Africa, and globally where people of African descent live and have communities (NABSW, n.d., History section).

The National Association of Puerto Rican & Hispanic Social Workers

Founded in 1983, the National Association of Puerto Rican & Hispanic Social Workers (NAPRHSW) offers membership to social workers, students, and other professionals in the field of human services. Like the NABSW, it does not restrict membership to credentialed social workers. It seeks to organize social workers and others to enhance the general welfare of Puerto Rican/Hispanic families and communities. The organization's objectives, found at its website (http://www.naprhsw.org), are:

> To advocate in the interest of Latinos at the local, state and nationwide levels in private and public sectors.
>
> To establish connections with other community resources that further and solidify the position of the Latino population in addressing policy issues that impact the community.
>
> To disseminate knowledge for professional growth to its membership and increase the academic foundation for providing assistance towards that end.
>
> To be a resource to the Latino Community for information and advocacy.
>
> To continue efforts to recruit and encourage Social Workers and Human Service students in their professional aspirations. (NAPRHSW, 2010, Mission section, p. 1)

Members of the NAPRHSW have opportunities to attend conferences dealing with such issues as strengths and diversity of the Latino family, immigration reform, ethnic sensitive practice, substance abuse, and domestic violence. The organization also shares information on employment opportunities and engages members in political, educational, and social activities (NAPRHSW, 2010, Membership section).

Other Professional Organizations

There is a wealth of other professional organizations serving social workers. In addition to the NAPRHSW, there is a Latino Social Workers Organization that sponsors annual conferences and offers committee membership to students as well as professional social workers. Some of the emphases of this organization are training in cultural competency and recruitment and retention strategies. Founded in 1970, the National Indian Social Workers Association seeks to support Native American people, including Alaska Natives. It also provides consultation to tribal and other organizations. Other groups exist for gay and lesbian social workers, Asian American social workers, and American social workers who live and work in other countries. In addition there are practice-related organizations such as the National Association of Oncology Social Workers, the National Federation of Societies of Clinical Social Workers, and the North American Association of Christians in Social Work.

International Social Work Organizations

Social workers in countries outside the United States also have professional organizations. Some examples are the Australian Association of Social Workers; the Canadian Association of Social Workers; the Nederlands Instituut voor

Box 1.5   Aims of the International Federation of Social Workers (IFSW)

The Constitution of the IFSW provides that the aims shall be:

- To promote social work as a profession through international cooperation, especially regarding professional values, standards, ethics, human rights, recognition, training, and working conditions.
- To promote the establishment of national organisations of social workers or professional unions for social workers and when needed national coordinating bodies (collectively "Social Work Organisations") where they do not exist.
- To support Social Work Organisations in promoting the participation of social workers in social planning and the formulation of social policies, nationally and internationally, the recognition of social work, the enhancement of social work training and the values and professional standards of social work.

In order to achieve these Aims the Federation shall:

- Encourage cooperation between social workers of all countries.
- Provide means for discussion and the exchange of ideas and experience through meetings, study visits, research projects, exchanges, publications, and other methods of communication.
- Establish and maintain relationships with, and present and promote the views of Social Work Organisations and their members to international organisations relevant to social development and welfare

Source: From International Federation of Social Workers, Aims. November 11 Edition, © 2005, p. 1. http://www.ifsw.org. Reprinted by permission.

Zorg en Welzijn (The Netherlands); the Chinese Association of Social Workers; and national associations of social workers in Ghana, Nigeria, and Israel, among others.

One social work organization, the International Federation of Social Workers (IFSW), was initiated in 1956 to help social workers learn about the experience of their counterparts in other countries. Currently, the IFSW represents 80 countries and half a million social workers around the world. Although membership in the IFSW is limited to national social work organizations, individuals may join the Friends of IFSW. The organization publishes a newsletter and it is a sponsor of the journal *International Social Work* (IFSW, 2005 Publications). The aims of the IFSW are listed in Box 1.5.

Just as international trade has developed globally in the past decade so, too, have international efforts to improve the health and welfare of all people. Hopefully, the future will bring increasing cross-national and international social welfare development and advocacy efforts especially to war-torn and economically devastated areas. What a challenge for the next generation of social workers!

COMPARING RELATED OCCUPATIONS

To meet the challenges of the present as well as the future, social workers need to understand and develop cooperative working relationships with the professions and occupational groups that work alongside us in the social welfare arena. Currently, a great deal of overlap exists in the responsibilities and tasks of professions. In hospitals, for example, nurses as well as social workers assist patients with discharge planning. In mental health the overlap appears even greater. Psychiatrists, psychologists, social workers, and professional counselors all engage in psychotherapy with individuals, groups, and families. Each profession, however, has its own area of expertise. This can be confusing. In the paragraphs that follow, we will try to identify and compare roles and responsibilities across several professions or occupations.

Sociology

We will begin by looking at sociology, an academic area that is closely related to social work. In fact, social work students are likely to be required to take some sociology courses early in their social work major. Sociology is an academic discipline that examines society and the behavior and beliefs of specific groups in society. Sociologists study characteristics of all types of groups: ethnic minorities, families, children, men, women, gays, the elderly, juvenile delinquents, and many others. Sociologists also examine the class structure of society. Through careful research, they attempt to sort fact from fiction regarding the mythology surrounding various social groups. Sociologists develop theory regarding how and why people become what they are, and in particular they study the influence of the social environment on thought, behavior, and personality.

What students of sociology learn to do is to observe carefully, think systematically, develop theory, and perform research to test theory. Sociological knowledge is useful to the social worker, and many social workers developed their initial interest in social work by taking sociology courses. Hence there is often confusion regarding the two disciplines. Also confusing is the fact that there are branches of sociology developing today called *applied* and *clinical* sociology. Applied sociology involves the use of sociological research methods for community needs assessment and program evaluation. Clinical sociology involves the application of sociological theory to social intervention. Their domains and methods are not yet clearly defined. Because sociologists specialize in the study of various types of groups, however, it is likely that applied and clinical sociologists will focus on the applications of sociological theory to behavior in groups, organizations, and communities.

Although they need to study sociology, social workers are expected to apply their knowledge to working with people to solve problems. Sociology normally teaches students to observe and to research social problems, but it is social work that teaches interpersonal skills and techniques and that provides an analytical approach to problem solving. Sociologists with advanced degrees often apply their education by researching and teaching.

Psychology

Psychology is another field closely related to social work. Psychologists study individuals and try to understand how they develop as they do and the important internal factors that influence a person's mind and behavior. Many psychologists study perception and learning in the laboratory setting and try to understand the inner workings of the mind through experimental means. Like sociologists, many psychologists spend their careers researching, testing theory, and teaching. One branch of psychology is applied, so that some psychologists also counsel individuals and families and conduct IQ tests, personality tests, and the like. Psychologists who wish to specialize in psychotherapy usually earn a doctorate degree.

Social workers must study both sociology and psychology. They must utilize information from both of these fields to assess the problems of their clients appropriately and to develop workable intervention plans. Social workers cannot focus solely on the individual, as psychologists tend to do, or on the social environment, as sociologists do. Instead, they must examine aspects of both, and how they interact, to engage in constructive problem solving.

The U.S. Department of Labor lists multiple specializations for psychology. The primary ones are licensed clinical psychologist and counseling psychologist. Both require a doctorate degree. Other specialization areas are school psychology; industrial–organizational psychology; and developmental, social, and experimental or research psychology (Bureau of Labor Statistics, 2009c). School psychologists may need only a master's degree.

Counseling

Counseling is another profession that overlaps social work in many ways: counselors, too, serve the social and emotional needs of people in schools, mental health settings, and other settings where social workers are employed. Most counselors hold master's degrees from university programs in education or psychology, although some doctorates are also available in counseling. There is a confusing array of areas in this field, including mental health counseling; educational, vocational, or school counseling; rehabilitation counseling; substance abuse and behavioral disorder counseling; and gerontological counseling. The vast majority of counselors, more than 275,000, are employed as educational, vocational, or school counselors (Bureau of Labor Statistics, 2009a). Recent legislation allowing some counselors to be reimbursed by insurance companies has increased the growth of private practice among counselors. Like social workers, counselors work with people who have personal, family, or mental health problems; however, counselors often have special expertise in helping people with educational or career planning.

Marriage and Family Therapy

This is another professional area that is somewhat confusing because persons from a number of different professions can be certified as marriage and family therapists (MFTs). To qualify for certification in most states, evidence must be presented of completion of a master's or doctoral degree in marriage and family therapy or in a program with equivalent content. In addition, at least 2 years of clinical experience (or 3,000 hours) are required. MSW social workers, psychologists, psychiatrists, and some nurses may qualify. According to the American Association for Marriage and Family Therapy, MFTs treat a wide variety of personal and mental health problems. The focus, even for an interview with a single person, is on the relationships in which the person is most significantly involved (American Association for Marriage and Family Therapy, 2002). Marriage and family therapy emphasizes short-term treatment.

Psychiatry

Psychiatry is related to social work, but psychiatry is a specialization of medicine. An MD (medical degree) must first be earned, and then the aspiring psychiatrist must complete a postdoctoral internship. Psychiatrists' primary focus on the inner person is grounded in their knowledge of physiology and medical practice. They may practice psychotherapy, but most do so very infrequently. Instead, their focus is on prescribing medications such as antidepressants and antipsychotics, the drugs used to treat psychoses (severe forms of mental illness). Psychiatrists frequently see people for 15-minute medication monitoring sessions.

Human Services

In its broadest definition, human services includes all occupations and professions seeking to promote the health and well-being of society: lawyers, firefighters, social workers, teachers, and so on. The narrower definition includes only those people who have completed an educational program with a major in human services or people who have been hired to work in the broad human services area without academic credentials. Human service academic programs generally offer a 2-year associate degree, although sometimes they involve 4-year, master's, or even doctoral degrees. While knowledge development is not ignored, the human service field emphasizes task completion and skill development. Graduates seek employment across multiple paraprofessional and professional job areas; these positions sometimes offer only minimal opportunities for advancement.

In the 1980s, a National Commission for Human Service workers was initiated to credential and certify human service workers, but it has since disbanded. Recently, the National Organization for Human Services announced the creation of a new credential for practitioners who have a minimum of a 2-year associate degree in human services. This new credential is not yet well known to employers nor recognized by state departments of regulation and licensing (National Organization for Human Services, 2009).

HOW PROFESSIONS RELATE

How might some of these professions become involved in a case such as that of the Dunn family in the case study at the beginning of this chapter? A sociologist might study the social problem of battered women or battering families; he or she might interview the Dunn family to learn what they have to say about the phenomenon from their personal experience. The sociologist, as a result of this study, might publish research that might result in decreased domestic violence. The sociologist, however, probably would not be involved in direct assistance to members of the Dunn family. The professional person that the Dunn family is most likely to encounter in a domestic violence shelter is a social worker.

Through the counseling they receive from social workers while in crisis, Susan Dunn and her husband could decide there is enough hope for change for themselves that they will begin living together again. With encouragement, they may follow up on the social worker's recommendation that they attend longer-term marriage and family counseling with a family service agency. The Dunn's counselor at the family service agency might be an MSW social worker, a PhD psychologist, or possibly a counselor. A consulting psychiatrist would be retained on the staff of the agency, to whom the Dunns could be referred if the primary counselor felt medication was required.

There could be several outcomes to this case. Let us say, for purposes of speculation, that as counseling progresses, Susan's husband voluntarily enters a group for batterers conducted by a professional counselor; a social worker or psychologist could also facilitate this group. Although he often feels like dropping out of the group, he continues with it as well as the family counseling. Over the months, several episodes of angry outbursts occur, but there are no further episodes of physical abuse. Gradually, both parents learn healthier ways of communicating with each other. Meantime, Susan Dunn has established a better relationship with her own family and begun to make routine visits back home. With the help of a vocational counselor, she has enrolled in a computer class at the local community college and has acquired several women friends from class. Susan now has a safety plan involving family and friends, in the event that she should need it. If Susan's husband continues to work very hard with the batterers group and no longer uses violence as a way of dealing with his frustrations, the future looks reasonably promising for this couple.

What would happen if, instead, Susan Dunn remains in clear physical danger? Let us say, for example, that her husband refuses to attend any kind of counseling with her and openly threatens future abuse. Susan might still choose to go home, believing that, if she behaves more carefully, she will be able to avoid causing her husband to physically abuse her. She is likely to have at some point another crisis requiring her to flee again to the shelter. At least this time she will know where she is going. If her husband is drinking or becomes violent at work and loses his job, Susan may find herself becoming involved with the government's financial assistance program called Temporary Assistance for Needy Families (TANF). The staff she encounters with this program will probably not have professional training in social work. Their role is a more clerical one that may also involve some employment counseling and referral to other resources.

Although Susan Dunn comes from a middle-class background and has remained a member of the middle class because of her husband's occupation, once she leaves her husband she is at risk of poverty. Almost overnight she could become a poor, single mother. The social worker at the shelter might be able to help her locate an inexpensive apartment. She might also file a legal restraining order through the district attorney's office, prohibiting her husband from threatening or even contacting her. She might file for divorce and child support; however, legal action against her husband could be very difficult without money. If fortunate, she might be able to secure inexpensive legal assistance from a legal aid society. Waiting lists for such programs are often long, however. Susan's social worker will help her assess her evolving situation and take whatever steps are necessary to ensure that Susan and her children are safe from harm. Susan's decisions, however, will be respected by the social worker.

The story of Susan Dunn and her family introduced readers of this chapter to the profession of social worker. The remainder of this book will delve into the work of social workers in much greater detail. Other social work clients will also be introduced as the chapters unfold. First, however, we can get a better grounding in the evolution of the profession by taking a brief look at the history of the social work profession.

HISTORY OF SOCIAL WORK: LINKAGE TO SOCIAL JUSTICE

Social work is an evolving, relatively young profession, but it has a longer history than some fields such as counseling. As Morales and Sheafor (2002) point out, the profession of social work grew out of and has sustained commitment to a threefold mission: caring, curing, and changing society. All three components are intrinsically related to social justice. From its earliest beginnings, the predecessors of social work have cared for the most vulnerable groups of people in society. Sometimes the caring was (and still is) prompted by humanitarian concerns; at other times it was mixed with less noble objectives. Persons who were not valued by society because they were too ill, too old or too young, too disabled, or otherwise not productive tended to be the very persons that social workers recognized as needing services and assistance. But social workers also have a history of helping people change, grow, and develop new skills. Persons with mental health

Human Rights and Justice

Practice Behavior Example: Advocate for human rights and social and economic justice

Critical Thinking Question: How does the history of the social work profession reflect commitment to social justice and human rights?

or behavioral disorders have been helped through counseling and psychotherapy, immigrants have been helped to acquire citizenship, and prisoners have been empowered to rebuild their lives following incarceration. Some of the earliest social workers were reformers who advocated for human rights through labor laws, political action, and community development.

The Civil War in the United States is probably responsible for the first paid social work–type positions. These jobs were created in 1863 by the Special Relief Department of the U.S. Sanitary Commission to assist Union Army soldiers or their families with health and social problems related to the war. The impact of these workers and other humanitarians, such as Clara Barton who later founded the American Red Cross, helped pave the way of the future social work profession. Three subsequent social movements arising in the late 1800s, however, significantly contributed to the development of the profession. One major movement was the Charity Organization Society (COS); it began in England and took hold in Buffalo, New York, in 1877. Its most famous leader was Mary Richmond. Volunteers for the COS initially viewed the abject poverty of many urban dwellers, especially immigrants, to be the result of personal character defects. "Friendly visitors," usually wealthy women who were not permitted by social norms of the time to be employed, visited people in their homes to provide "moral uplift." Only as a last resort was material aid offered.

A second major movement contributed a strong social justice thrust to the developing young social work profession. This was the settlement house movement, which, like the COS, began in England. In the United States, Jane Addams was its most famous leader. Addams established Hull House in Chicago in 1889. Settlement workers brought a more compassionate view of poor people than the COS volunteers. They believed that poverty resulted from unjust and unfortunate social conditions. Settlement workers lived among the poor. They assisted in developing needed services such as day care for children of factory workers through mutual aid. They also advocated for better working conditions and protective legislation through various governmental bodies.

A third movement, more diffuse and often not recognized for its historical impact on the development of the profession, was the child welfare movement. This began with the Children's Aid Society founded in New York in 1853 and was strengthened by the Society for the Prevention of Cruelty to Children that was founded in 1875, also in New York City (Popple, 1995). The child welfare movement, over time, evolved into the entire area of foster care, adoptions, child protective services, and juvenile court services.

A growing desire for professionalization emerged by the late 1890s. Charity organization work and settlement house work were increasingly salaried, but as yet there was no name for this profession. By the early 1900s the broad field of applied philanthropy began to be called social work or social casework. The New York School of Philanthropy, established in 1904, was the first professional education program. Mary Richmond, leader of the COS, was among the original faculty. The school is now known as the Columbia University School of Social Work.

With increasing confidence in their new profession, social workers invited Abraham Flexner to address the 1915 National Conference of Charities and Correction. Flexner's critique of the medical profession was renowned for dramatically improving that profession's status and quality of care. Flexner's pronouncement that social work was not yet a real profession startled the social work world but unleashed new energy directed at rectifying the deficiencies he identified (Popple, 1995). As Flexner's criticisms were attended to, large numbers of persons flocked to the profession expanding social work practice into new areas such as schools and hospitals. The theory base of the profession was developed, and research began to be published. Freudian theory was widely adopted in the 1920s. The Great Depression turned public attention to the economic and social forces causing poverty. The result was the passage of the Social Security Act in 1935, legislation in which social workers played a prominent role. From its earliest days, then, the profession of social work embodied emphases both in social reform and in the psychosocial problems of individuals, families, and communities.

World wars I and II further increased social workers' involvement in mental health as psychiatric casualties of the wars brought large numbers of social workers into military social work. Social workers with master's degrees dominated the profession by the early 1950s, but they tended to work in specialization areas such as child welfare, medical social work, or psychiatric social work. In a remarkable move toward unity, seven specialty areas merged to found the NASW in 1955. Until 1970, when BSWs were added, NASW membership was exclusively limited to MSWs. The founding of NASW and enactment of the NASW Code of Ethics to ground the practice of all social workers firmly established social work as a profession.

In the years since the birth of the profession, social work has grown dramatically in numbers, in areas of practice, in the people it serves, and in status. In recent years it has achieved legal regulation (licensure or certification) in every state. The profession has struggled to retain its social reform legacy by lobbying against discriminatory legislation and by supporting social policies that promote human welfare and well-being. Social work and social welfare, therefore, remain intertwined today. Because of its commitment to social and economic justice and its mission to work on behalf of people who are discriminated against, the profession of social work is sometimes not well understood nor even well accepted. Its values make social work a truly unique profession.

SUMMARY

The case of Susan Dunn and her family, who are in need of social services from a shelter following an episode of domestic violence, introduces the chapter and also the profession of social work. A definition of social work is offered. The ways in which social work is unique among human service professions, its strengths perspective and social justice commitment, for example, are identified. Because the generalist perspective is a basic ingredient of all social work practice and lies at the heart of baccalaureate practice, the concept of generalist practice is explored. The generalist social worker is presented as one who engages in a systematic planned change process with a variety of social systems, including individual people, families, groups, organizations, and communities. The competencies that comprise generalist practice are carefully explained as they will continue to be woven into the content of the entire book.

Social work educational programs prepare social workers at the baccalaureate (BSW), master's (MSW), and doctoral (PhD or DSW) levels. The chapter provided information about the curriculum at the baccalaureate level. Less information was presented about the MSW or doctoral curricula because they vary depending on the area of concentration offered by the program.

Pamela Wright was the social worker who assisted Susan Dunn and her family in this chapter's case study. Each chapter in this book will begin with a case study showing how social workers utilize their competencies as they engage people and work with them to solve problems across many different social agency and community practice settings. Most people who consider a career in social work do so because they want to help people. Like Pamela Wright, they want their lives to make a difference. The chapter offers information about career options and employment opportunities in a profession that is devoted to making a difference—social work.

Social work, like most other professions, is legally regulated by state licensing boards to protect consumers from unethical and uncredentialed practice. Unfortunately, because states' social work license laws are not consistent, there remains much work to be done to ensure that persons who deliver social services and claim to be social workers really are social workers. Some states still have no licensure or certification for BSW social workers. It remains possible for persons without academic degrees in social work to obtain social work positions in a few states. NASW has led the effort to achieve social work licensure at all levels and in all states. This chapter explains some of the other ways in which NASW serves its members and also tries to protect clients. Other social work professional organizations, such as the CSWE and the IFSW, are also introduced in this chapter.

The primary profession that is devoted to making a difference: social work!

Social work is sometimes confused with other professions. Students often wonder, for example, whether they should major in psychology or social work, not knowing that social workers carry some of the same responsibilities for counseling and therapy as persons with degrees in psychology. Yet, while professions such as psychology and social work do overlap, all professions are unique and have their own areas of expertise. The chapter compares several related professions and highlights the uniqueness of the social work profession.

In the Chapter 2 case study you will meet another social worker, Stephanie Hermann, who applies her social work practice skills and knowledge to the problems faced by so many people that successful intervention required response from an entire community. The Stephanie Hermann case study leads to an exploration of the theories on which generalist social work practice is grounded. Inextricably connected to the theory of practice is an understanding of political perspectives and how they influence the well-being of people.

PRACTICE TEST The following questions will test your knowledge of the content found within this chapter. For additional assessment, including licensing-exam type questions on applying chapter content to practice behaviors, visit **MySearchLab.**

1. The 10 Core social work competencies are _____
   a. only evaluated through the field experience
   b. required to be mastered for BSW graduation
   c. emphasized in both social work class and field
   d. not covered in all BSW social work programs

2. The _____ has the legal authority to regulate and monitor social worker's professional practice.
   a. State licensing/regulations agency
   b. School/Department of Social Work
   c. Council on Social Work Education
   d. National Association of Social Workers

3. The National Association of Black Social Workers _____.
   a. is affiliated with CSWE
   b. is only open to Social Workers in Washington, DC
   c. Is a subsection of NASW
   d. accepts any African American who is working in social services

4. The difference between human services and social work is that human services _____.
   a. is limited to those with an associates degree
   b. includes paraprofessionals without academic credentials
   c. workers are not regulated
   d. offers a wide array of advancement opportunities

5. The Social Justice mission of social work includes _____, _____, and _____.
   a. helping, healing, honoring
   b. counseling, teaching, advocating
   c. casework, collaboration, comfort
   d. caring, curing, changing society

6. In the case of Susan Dunn, Pamela Wright, the social worker _____.
   a. insisted that Susan never return to her abusive husband in order to stay at the shelter
   b. focused on the immediate needs of Susan and her children
   c. lectured Susan on the dangers to herself and her children if she stayed with an abusive partner
   d. dropped Susan off at the Emergency Room at the hospital in order to protect her privacy

7. During her freshman year, Sarah volunteered at the local literacy council to help low-income adults learn to read. She worked with a young woman who had recently been released from prison for a drug-related crime. This experience inspired her to seek a social work degree. What advice would you give her to facilitate successful employment as a social worker when she graduates? Review Pamela's professional competence as a social worker. Identify the behavioral indicators of her practice behavior competence indicated in the case study.

Reinforce what you learned in this chapter by studying videos, cases, documents, and more available at **www.MySearchLab.com**.

Watch and Review

Watch these Videos

* Professional Roles and Boundaries
* Applying Critical Thinking

Read and Review

Read these Cases/Documents

Δ Ethical Dilemmas

Explore and Assess

Explore these Assets

The Social Work History Station—http://www.boisestate.edu/socwork/dhuff/xx.htm

Newfoundland & Labrador Association of Social Workers—http://www.nlasw.ca/

National Association of Social Workers—http://www.socialworkers.org

Assess Your Knowledge

Assess your knowledge with a variety of topical and chapter assessment.

Conclude your assessment by completing the chapter exam.

* = CSWE Core Competency Asset
Δ = Case Study

Theoretical Perspectives for Social Workers

2

Connecting Core Competencies in This Chapter				
Professional Identity	Ethical Practice	X Critical Thinking	Diversity in Practice	Human Rights & Justice
Research Based Practice	Human Behavior	X Policy Practice	X Practice Contexts	X Engage, Assess, Intervene, Evaluate

The case study for this chapter introduces a community-level problem requiring social work intervention and then describes how a particular person,
Sandra McLean, is affected. It illustrates how persons and environments interact and how social welfare policy influences social work practice. While the
events described in this case took place a number of years ago, the generalist
practice skills demonstrated by social worker Stephanie Hermann remain contemporary and impressive.

The Several Roles of Stephanie Hermann, BSW

Stephanie Hermann, BSW, waited impatiently for the mail that morning, for her
boss had told her to expect an important memo. Stephanie worked as an assistant
administrator in a regional office of the Division of Community Services, a part of
her state's Department of Health and Social Services (DHSS). The office interpreted
new DHSS policies pertaining to health and social service agencies in the region,
both public and private. Stephanie consulted with agency administrators to clarify
state policies and to document agency compliance.

Recently, the state DHSS office had received notice from the Federal Health Care
Administration that people with developmental disabilities (DD) would soon lose
eligibility for Medicaid funding in nursing homes. The intent of this policy was to
encourage the development of community-based living settings for people with disabilities. A survey had been conducted around the state, and 2,025 adults with disabilities were found to be living in nursing homes. Among them was Sandra McLean,
whose story will be a focus of this chapter.

This large number worried DHSS officials. They did not believe there were existing alternative community placement options that could care for anywhere near this
number of people. Stephanie's boss had described the memo that was on its way as
"at least trying to head us off from a bigger problem later."

The expected memo arrived: "The Department of Health and Social Services finds
that an emergency exists. . . . This order amends the department's rules for nursing
homes . . . to prohibit the admission of any person with a developmental disability,
including mental retardation, to a nursing home for intermediate nursing care unless the nursing home is certified . . . as an intermediate care facility for the mentally
retarded (ICF/MR)."

The memo explained that to obtain certification as an ICF/MR, a nursing home
must identify staff skilled in working with persons with developmental disabilities
and describe specific internal programs, supplementary services from other agencies, admission policies, and individual care plans for each resident. The DHSS
memo defined developmental disability as follows: "mental retardation or a related
condition such as cerebral palsy, epilepsy, or autism, but excluding mental illness
and the infirmities of aging."

Stephanie was excited by the new policy. She had long believed that most persons with disabilities should be placed in family-like settings. But few such places
of residence currently existed. Adult family care homes (foster homes for adults)
required families willing to take in persons with disabilities; small group homes required paid staff. Apartment living required monitoring and support. All required
funding and neighbors willing to accept persons with disabilities.

Brockton Manor. When Stephanie received the emergency order from the state
DHSS, she decided to consult with every county in her region. At this point only new
DD clients were prohibited from receiving Medicaid funding for nursing home care,
so Stephanie believed that new placement options could be developed gradually.

She also consulted with nursing homes that were currently caring for persons with disabilities, to assist them in developing state-certified ICF/MR programs.

However, only 2 weeks after the state's emergency ruling, Brockton Manor, a large nursing home in Stephanie's region, decided to phase out its services for people with disabilities. Administrators believed they could easily fill their beds with elderly people, who are less costly to serve. Brockton Manor offered to cooperate with county and state officials in developing alternative living arrangements so that each of its 49 residents with developmental disabilities would have a place to go.

Now Stephanie had an immediate situation to deal with. A worst-case scenario would be 49 new street people. But fortunately, Medicaid regulations required individual assessments and specific discharge plans, including places to live and **active treatment.** Active treatment involved individualized plans for training, therapy, and services to help achieve the highest possible level of functioning. But how did one find or develop such resources?

Critical Thinking

Practice Behavior Example: Social workers demonstrate effective oral and written communication in working with individuals, families, groups, organizations, communities, and colleagues

Critical Thinking Question: In what ways does Stephanie Hermann use her communication skills in her work with the Brockton Manor case?

Stephanie determined that she would need to play several roles. The first would involve coordinating the efforts of various community agencies. Brockton Manor's major responsibility would be to provide individual plans of care for each DD resident; each county's primary responsibility would be to develop alternative living arrangements, and the state's responsibility would be to provide funding, with federal assistance through Medicaid.

A second community-organizing role would be to involve private voluntary organizations, such as the Association for Retarded Citizens (ARC), in planning efforts on behalf of Brockton Manor's DD clients. For example, the ARC might organize informational meetings and help locate alternative living settings.

Third, Stephanie knew she would have to mediate disputes among various county and state offices. Thirty-five of the forty-nine residents with developmental disabilities at Brockton Manor originally came from different counties. Their counties of origin were likely to refuse to resume responsibility because of the cost. Fourth, Stephanie planned to help assess the needs of DD residents of Brockton Manor and to help develop appropriate discharge plans.

Stephanie began to carry out her organizing role immediately. She arranged a meeting of representatives from all the key agencies that would be involved in relocating the DD residents, including Brockton Manor staff, county officials responsible for finding new living arrangements, administrators from the state DHSS offices, and members of Stephanie's own regional office. A Subcommittee on Relocation was established that met biweekly for more than a year. The subcommittee set up teams to assess all residents with disabilities at Brockton Manor. It also conducted a study to determine the probable cost of **community placement** for each resident.

Funding complications soon became apparent. Besides encouraging development of more family-like settings, community placement was intended to cut costs. Medicaid thus funded community care at only 60 percent of the institutional-care reimbursement rate for the same DD person. Yet the money was supposed to cover active treatment as well as room, board, and assistance in daily living tasks. Many of the people at Brockton Manor required 24-hour care and supervision.

Still, the subcommittee pressed on. It organized a large stakeholders meeting for all agencies and individuals who might be willing to get involved. Videotapes of several residents were prepared to educate the community and to enhance the human-interest side of the story. The meeting spearheaded a flurry of community activity. Several voluntary organizations collected supplies for new apartments, the Kiwanis Club developed a proposal for public housing for people with disabilities, county departments of social service advertised for adult family care homes, and Brockton Manor solicited foster parents from its own staff. Two private social service agencies developed small group homes. Funding for these homes required creative planning; half the residents had to be taken from costly state institutions, because the Medicaid funding available for community placement for these persons was higher.

Through the development of small group homes and new **family care homes,** 15 of Brockton Manor's residents were soon placed into the community. One of these persons was Sandra McLean.

Sandra McLean: The Effects of Institutionalization. Sandra McLean's mother had a long and difficult labor, and finally forceps were used in delivery. The forceps injured Sandra's skull. The result was mental retardation and grand mal epileptic seizures, commonly known as convulsions.

Mr. and Mrs. McLean raised Sandra at home until she was about 8 years old, by which time she was toilet trained, could walk, and could say "Mama" and "Papa." Then they sent her to public school. This was before the days of special education, however, and they soon decided they could educate her better at home. They were able to teach Sandra to bathe, dress, and feed herself.

When Sandra was about 10, her parents had a second daughter, a normal, healthy infant named Susan. After Susan's arrival, the McLeans did not have quite so much time for Sandra, but by then she was more independent. When Sandra was in her late teens, an activity center for people with disabilities was established in a nearby community. Her middle-class parents could afford the moderate fee, and so she was enrolled. To the McLeans' delight, Sandra blossomed. She began to talk and smile more. She was a favorite among the staff.

The blow struck when Sandra was 27 years old. First, her father died of a heart attack. Shortly thereafter, her mother had a stroke. Partially paralyzed, Sandra's mother was no longer able to care for Sandra. Susan was ready to go to college, and Mrs. McLean did not want to hold her back. The family doctor suggested that Sandra be placed in a state institution. Mrs. McLean, seeing no other option, reluctantly agreed. At the institution, Sandra was medicated heavily to control her seizures. There wasn't enough staff to provide her with the compassionate care she had received at home or to respond immediately if she were to have a seizure. She spent her days strapped into a wheelchair, eyes glazed, drooling.

Several years later, Sandra was transferred to Brockton Manor, and several years after that, she was referred for community placement by Stephanie Hermann's team. Stephanie arranged for Sandra's mother, then very frail, to visit. The team listened with amazement as Mrs. McLean described Sandra as a young girl, able to walk and talk. Stephanie contacted Sandra's sister, Susan, and heard the same story. Mrs. McLean talked about the activity center Sandra had participated in years before, so staff members there were contacted as well. A therapist who had known Sandra visited and was shocked to see her current condition. The therapist described the smiling person she used to know, who enjoyed socializing and who could walk, talk, feed, and toilet herself. Stephanie and the assessment team called in a physician skilled in working with people with disabilities. The physician was willing to prescribe different medications. The assessment team then held a joint meeting with all the professional staff at Brockton Manor involved with Sandra's care. They explained that Sandra might begin to have seizures again, and they discussed how to deal with them. They suggested that occasional grand mal seizures might not be too high a price to pay if the young woman were able to learn to walk again and to communicate with people, at least in a limited way. The nursing home staff agreed.

The plan worked. Sandra did begin to have seizures again, but they were not too difficult to handle. With physical therapy she learned to walk again, and with occupational therapy she learned to dress and feed herself. The nurses taught her how to toilet herself again. Sandra became a social person once more and began to use limited words. She clearly recognized her mother and sister. Everyone felt deeply rewarded. Now the time had come to develop community-based living arrangements.

Although Mrs. McLean would have loved to have her daughter return home, she was not physically able to care for her. Sandra's sister, Susan, explained to Stephanie Hermann, with obvious distress, that she worked full-time and had two children to care for. She frequently helped her mother with routine household chores. She did not feel able to take on her sister's care as well. But both mother and daughter welcomed the idea of a family care home for Sandra.

A potential home was located and licensed by social workers from the county Department of Social Services. The foster parents, a childless couple in their mid-30s, had learned of the need through newspaper advertisements. They visited Sandra several times at Brockton Manor and took her home for a trial overnight visit before making a final decision. The Brockton Manor staff taught them about Sandra's special needs, especially about what to do during seizures. Arrangements were made for Sandra to attend the local activity center for people with disabilities during the day, once she was living in her foster home. She enjoyed the social and recreational opportunities, such as exercise classes, educational games, and other small group activities very much. The placement worked out so well that her foster family took in a second adult with a disability.

Ongoing Challenges of Community Placement. An adult family care home was provided for Sandra McLean by the Department of Social Services because federal funding through Medicaid and Supplemental Security Income (to be discussed in Chapter 4) was sufficient to pay all her bills, including foster care and active treatment at the local activity center. However, funding was not sufficient to permit community placement of residents who needed more care, and eventually many of them had to be transferred to different nursing homes that met the new federal requirements.

SOCIAL WORK AND SYSTEMS THEORY

As illustrated by this chapter's case study, social work is a profession that requires working with systems of many sizes. For example, Stephanie Hermann was employed by a large state organization, the DHSS. The DHSS was, in turn, strongly affected by the policies of an even larger organization, the federal government. Stephanie, by publicizing and interpreting new federal and state policies, affected the operations of the social service organizations and agencies in her entire region, both public and private. She provided professional assistance to help these organizations and agencies meet changing requirements. She also educated citizens' groups about new regulations and solicited their aid in developing new resources to meet community needs.

Besides working with larger systems, Stephanie worked with smaller ones. For example, she helped establish a formal task group, the Subcommittee on Relocation, which managed the job of finding and developing alternative living arrangements for disabled residents of Brockton Manor. She met with this group for more than a year. She also worked with a team of staff at Brockton Manor to assess the needs of each resident with a disability.

As part of her work in assessing the needs of individual residents at Brockton Manor, Stephanie worked with a yet smaller system, the individual named Sandra McLean (among others). To help gain a better understanding of Sandra's potential capabilities and needs, Stephanie met with part of Sandra's family system as well, Mrs. McLean and Susan. These family meetings led Stephanie to contact another system or organization, the activity center that Sandra had attended many years before.

Practice Contexts

Practice Behavior Example: Social workers provide leadership in promoting sustainable changes in service delivery and practice to improve the quality of social services

Critical Thinking Question: Why is social work leadership more likely to be successful if all relevant systems are involved?

As is obvious from Sandra McLean's story, improving the life of just one person can involve skills in working with systems of many sizes. For this reason, social work is a complex practice. It requires the guidance of a broad theoretical framework to help organize and analyze large amounts of information. For many social workers, systems theory provides that theoretical framework. Systems theory helps the social worker attend to and understand the dynamic interactions among the many biological and social systems that affect ongoing practice (Sheafor, Horejsi, & Horejsi, 2000).

Applying systems theory requires familiarity with certain basic concepts. A few will be introduced here. The term **system** has been defined in many ways, but perhaps the simplest is that a system is a whole consisting of interacting parts. These parts are so interrelated that a change in any one part affects all the others.

Let us consider an example of a biological system, the human body. The body is composed of many interrelated, interacting parts, including the skeleton, muscles, blood, and so on. What happens when one part is disturbed in some way? Let's say a piece of the skeleton is broken. Every other part of the system is affected. Muscles tighten, and blood circulation increases in the area of the broken bone. Nerves carry impulses to the brain that are translated as pain, which affects every other part of the body.

Each of the major parts of the system called the human body can itself be considered a system: skeletal system, muscle system, blood system, nervous system, for example. These smaller systems are themselves made up of parts even smaller: organs, molecules, atoms, and particles of atoms. Sometimes smaller systems within larger systems are called *subsystems*. Whether something is considered a system or a subsystem depends only on where the observer decides to focus attention. The important point to keep in mind with respect to systems theory is the concept of interrelationships: a change in one part of a system affects all the other parts in some way. Smaller systems that are parts of larger systems affect each other and the larger system as a whole. Any change in the larger system (or *suprasystem*) affects all the systems and subsystems within.

The human body is an example of a biological system, and humans, as biological organisms, are part of a larger physical environment. But people are also social systems and parts of larger social environments. Both physical and social environments are made up of systems of various sizes to which people must adapt.

Box 2.1	**Important Systems for Social Workers**
Change agent system	Social workers and their agencies of employment
Client system	People who have requested social work services or who have entered into a formal or informal contract with a social worker
Target system	People who need to change in order for social work clients to meet their goals
Action system	All those who work cooperatively with the social worker to accomplish desired changes
Professional system	Social work education programs, professional organizations, and the social work professional culture, including values and ethics

Consider the human family. The family constitutes a certain type of social system, a whole consisting of interacting parts, so that while its form may vary, family members know who belongs and who does not. A change in one part affects all others: people cannot join or withdraw without other family members responding in some way. In the McLean case, having to send Sandra to an institution undoubtedly affected her mother's well-being in a negative way. Research has even shown that if one family member is physically injured in the presence of another, the physical body of the observer will be affected (stress hormones will be released, muscles will tighten, and so on). For this reason, systems theory has been adapted for use in medicine, social science, social work, and other professions (Wells, 1998).

Compton and Galaway (1999) have identified five systems of special importance to social workers:

- Change agent system
- Client system
- Target system
- Action system
- Professional system

The change agent system includes social workers and their agencies of employment. The client system includes people who have requested social work services or who have entered into a formal or informal contract. The target system includes people who need to change in order for clients to meet their goals, and the action system includes all those who work cooperatively with the social worker to accomplish desired changes. The last system, the professional system, is made up of social work education programs, professional organizations, and the professional culture, including values and ethics (see Box 2.1).

THE ECOSYSTEMS PERSPECTIVE

Social workers have long promoted a person-in-environment perspective. General systems theory, proposed by biologist Ludwig Von Bertalanffy in the late 1960s, was adopted by many social workers as an overall framework for practice very much because it was congruent with their ongoing experience.

The theory helped social workers remember and pay attention to the interactions between larger and smaller systems and thus provided a useful framework for analysis. However, according to Germain and Gitterman (1995), some theorists felt that systems theory was too abstract for practical use. They adopted instead a closely related outlook from biological science, which was itself derived from the basic assumptions of systems theory, the ecological or **ecosystems perspective** (Sommer, 1995). Many social workers now use an ecosystems or ecological perspective to guide their practice.

The ecosystems perspective encourages social workers to maintain simultaneous focus on person and environment, much as workers have done since the birth of the profession. Now, however, the practice is supported and strengthened by a theoretical model. The ecosystems' focus on interactions between person and environment is perhaps a simpler way of expressing major concepts in general systems theory (such as the importance of interactional effects). The concept of *environment* as presented from the ecosystems perspective is virtually synonymous with the concept of a large or suprasystem from systems theory; *person* is simply an example of a smaller or subsystem (see Box 2.2).

Useful concepts for social workers who use an ecosystems perspective include person/environment fit, life stressors, and adaptation, among others. The *person/environment fit* is the actual fit between human wants and needs and the environmental resources available to meet them. *Life stressors* include issues and needs that exceed environmental resources. *Adaptations* are the processes people use to try to improve the fit between themselves and their environments (Johnson & Rhodes, 2005).

To apply ecosystems concepts to the situation of Sandra McLean, consider how Sandra's environment affected her personally. Her life became completely different in the institutional setting from what it had been at home or at the activity center. Sandra's experience and behavior became so changed that she

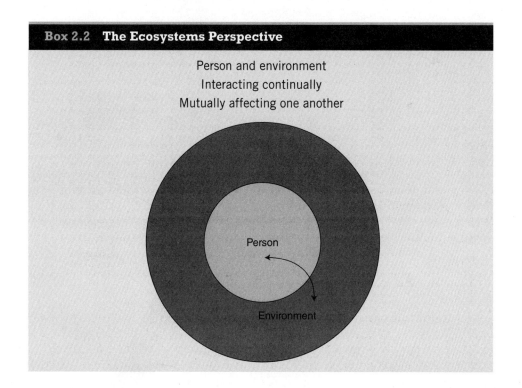

Box 2.2   The Ecosystems Perspective

Person and environment
Interacting continually
Mutually affecting one another

Person

Environment

Only when federal policy changed, and Sandra was viewed as a whole person with human rights despite her disability, did she have a chance to live a more normal life.

might as well have been a different person. The heavy dose of drugs that was administered to control her seizures acted as a physiological stressor that suppressed her capacity to adapt, and she essentially became a human vegetable. Only when federal policy changed, and Sandra was viewed as a whole person with human rights despite her disability, did she have a chance to live a more normal life. In her case, that required changes in state and local social policy, which led in turn to changes in the medical and social services available to her. Sandra couldn't live a fulfilling life of her own until new opportunities were created in the wider environment by changed social policies and by professional practices committed to carrying out those policies.

Changes in Sandra herself also affected her environment. For example, her new abilities affected various medical professionals, who were astounded at what she could accomplish and who then were willing to consider modifying medications for other people with disabilities as well. Sandra's new opportunities also affected the people who became her foster parents and those whom they later took in with her. Sandra's good fortune affected staff at the activity center, who rejoiced for her and were inspired to develop new activities to assist in her recovery. Her mother and sister rejoiced also: a family tragedy had been transformed by what seemed like a miracle (see Box 2.3).

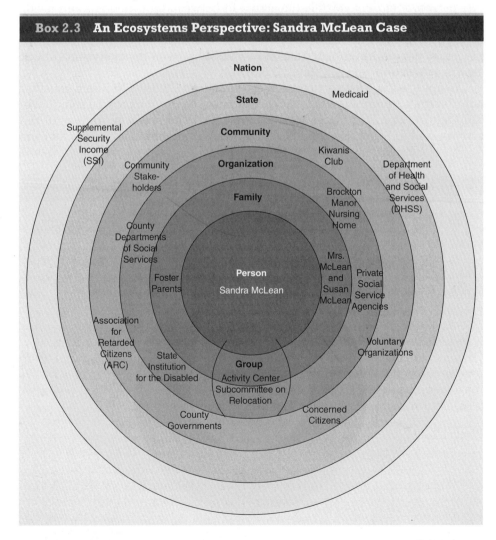

Box 2.3   An Ecosystems Perspective: Sandra McLean Case

THE GENERALIST APPROACH

The **generalist approach** to social work practice is strongly rooted in systems theory and its descendant, the ecosystems perspective. As described earlier, systems theory and its attention to systems interactions served as a useful guide for social work practice soon after biologist Von Bertalanffy published his ideas in the 1960s. The ecosystems perspective that developed out of systems theory provided the conceptual framework for the development of the generalist approach to social work practice. Thus, the generalist approach involves attention to multiple **levels of intervention** (discussed in the next section); the term *level*, as used in this context, is virtually synonymous with the term *system*.

The ecosystems perspective helps the social worker recognize that intervening on one systems level will prompt all other systems levels to adapt in some way. The worker must assess these adaptations because she or he may then have to intervene on multiple levels (individual, family, group, organization, community, etc.) to achieve the desired result. A generalist practitioner such as Stephanie Hermann, as she begins to intervene at a large system level (the community), is guided by the ecosystems perspective to attend to changes occurring on smaller systems levels due to adaptation processes (Brockton Manor, the McLean family, Sandra McLean as an individual, etc.).

The generalist approach, in addition to an ecological perspective and attention to multiple levels of intervention, requires a careful problem-solving or planned change process (to be discussed later). While each CSWE-accredited baccalaureate social work program develops its own definition of generalist practice according to accreditation guidelines, the following is typical:

> The generalist approach to social work practice, supported by concepts drawn from social systems theory and using an ecological perspective, is attentive to person and environment and their interactions. Generalist practice is based on research-guided knowledge and uses a planned change or problem-solving process to determine the level or levels of intervention—individual, family, group, organization, and/or community—appropriate to addressing the issues presented. It recognizes the profession's dual purpose and responsibility to influence social as well as individual change.

Levels of Intervention

Note that the preceding definition explains that the generalist approach involves not only an ecological perspective but the use of multiple levels of intervention and a planned change process. The planned change process will be discussed further on. At this point, let us describe the various levels (systems) of intervention identified in the definition of generalist.

Individual

Intervening at the individual level involves working one-on-one, either to help a person better adapt to his or her environment or to modify the environment so it better meets the needs of the person. In this chapter's case study, Stephanie Hermann worked with Sandra McLean individually to help assess her abilities and needs.

Family

Intervening at the family level may involve working with whole families or parts of a family, such as a mother and child or a pair of parents. Stephanie Hermann worked with members of Sandra's family in planning for her care. Some types of family work can be much more intensive. Family therapy, for example, assists families in overcoming interpersonal conflicts and power imbalances among members.

Group

Intervening at the small group level may involve working with many different types of groups. Stephanie Hermann developed and worked with a task group, the Subcommittee on Relocation, at Brockton Manor. The activity center where Sandra received services ran activity groups and support groups for its clients.

Organization

Intervening at the organizational level involves assessing needs within an organization and planning and coordinating efforts to meet those needs. For example, Stephanie alerted Brockton Manor about new federal regulations regarding care for residents with disabilities. When the nursing home administration decided not to serve these clients any longer, Stephanie helped coordinate the organization's efforts to develop responsible discharge plans.

Community

Intervening at the community level involves evaluating community needs and planning and coordinating efforts to meet those needs. Stephanie Hermann helped her region of the state to evaluate its capacity to provide family-like care for citizens with disabilities and coordinated the efforts to expand resources and options (please review Box 2.3).

Some social workers prefer to talk of micro-, mezzo-, and macropractice rather than practice with individuals, families, groups, organizations, and communities (Zastrow, 2007). Professionals differ, however, in their understanding of which levels of intervention these terms include. This text, to simplify, will refer to specific levels of intervention: individual, family, group, organization, and community. However, we must remember that as our world shrinks and we all become more interdependent, our concept of community must extend to include the whole planet (see Box 2.4).

Global, Environmental, and Spiritual Considerations

While the generalist approach to social work practice traditionally encompasses individual, family, group, organization, and community levels of intervention, the profession is awakening to the increasing impact of wider environmental

Box 2.4   Social Work Levels of Intervention
Community
Organization
Group
Family
Individual

issues. These issues extend beyond any particular community—they are global, affecting everyone on earth today and future generations as well. Social workers need to be aware of global and environmental issues because they affect absolutely everyone, not only ourselves and our clients. Spiritual awakening can help empower people as they struggle to save planet earth, currently under siege.

As an illustration of the magnitude of the environmental problem, Bauerlein (2006) writes:

> According to the vast majority of government and other scientists,...the past few years have brought overwhelming evidence that pollution at currently permitted levels is sickening and killing thousands of people....For example, 30,000 people die each year from power-plant pollution alone, according to a study by a firm that trains EPA (Environmental Protection Agency) staffers—almost twice as many as are killed by drunk drivers and 50% more than are murdered. As in Chicago, the study found that simply enforcing air-quality laws would save two-thirds of those lives. (p. 58)

Michael Lerner (2006) issues another powerful warning:

> We live in an Age of Extinctions. This is the sixth great spasm of extinctions in the history of our planet. We are driving biodiversity back 65 million years, to its lowest level of vitality since the end of the Age of Dinosaurs. Climate change, ozone depletion, toxic chemicals, habitat destruction, and invasive or infectious species are five of the principal drivers of this Age of Extinction. (p. 543)

For students who are already socially and politically aware, looking toward the future can be frightening at this time in human history. Preceding generations have been exceedingly short-sighted, and many economic institutions today have built in pressures to remain short-sighted. (For example, the stock market responds to short-term profits, regardless of how those profits are made. Most corporations, therefore, do whatever they can to increase short-term profits, regardless of the affect on planet earth. Few investors are willing to invest in a company that does not show a profit, so that clearly, we are all culpable at some level.)

Lerner notes that health issues continue to increase worldwide due to the factors he identifies in the preceding extract (ozone depletion, toxic chemicals, etc.). He also finds that "the impact of poverty on health is an overwhelming reality, especially in developing countries" (2006, p. 545). Poor people simply do not have access to the health care that might help protect them or the political clout that might enable them to prevent waste dumps from being established in their neighborhoods, as one example. However, Lerner is not a pessimist. He believes that there is a path to saving the planet and its people and that this path is already being blazed by a growing environmental health movement. He believes that mothers who want to breast-feed their babies with milk that is toxin-free, health professionals who care about their clients, environmental justice groups who want to save endangered species, religious groups who literally want to save human souls, and many other potential allies will recognize the power of joining forces. Out of this alliance, Lerner believes a movement can arise strong enough to stop the race toward the destruction of our good earth. The task is incredibly challenging, and one in which the social work profession can and hopefully will play an important role.

Progress will not come easily. The United Nations Climate Change Conference in Copenhagen, Denmark, in December 2009 made only slight progress toward a sustainable future. While the United States, guided by the new Obama administration, was willing to negotiate seriously, the powerful nation of China was not. Although small island nations predicted by climate change data to disappear beneath the rising sea urged strong action, they were unable to prevail. The Copenhagen conference produced only a nonbinding agreement to keep the maximum temperature rise below two degrees Celsius, and initiated a list of emission reduction targets for the developed countries ("Closing press briefing," 2009). Small additional steps toward reducing the rate of global climate change were taken in 2010 at the UN conference in Cancun, Mexico; thankfully, the UN continues to organize global environmental conferences as much more needs to be done to avoid irreversible damage.

It is possible that the strongest force to save humanity from extinction will come not from politics but from spiritual strength and religious conviction. Theologians Tucker and Grim reflect that:

It is possible that the strongest force to save humanity from extinction will come not from politics but from spiritual strength and religious conviction.

> It must be recognized that the world's religions, through intolerance and exclusive claims to truth, have often contributed to tensions between peoples, including wars or forced conversions. It is also the case that religions have often been at the forefront of reforms, such as in the labor movement, in immigration law, in justice for the poor and oppressed. The movements of non-violence for freedom in India and for integration in the Unites States were inspired by religious principles and led by religious leaders.

How to adapt religious teachings to this task of revaluing nature so as to prevent its destruction marks a significant new phase in religious thought. Indeed, as the historian of religions, Thomas Berry, has so aptly pointed out what is necessary is a comprehensive reevaluation of human–earth relations if the human is to continue as a viable species on an increasingly degraded planet. In addition to major economic and political changes, this will require adopting worldviews that differ from those that have captured the imaginations of contemporary industrialized societies that view nature as a commodity to be exploited. How to utilize the insights of the world's religions is a task of formidable urgency. Indeed, the formulation of a new ecological theology and environmental ethics is already emerging from within several of the world's religions. Clearly, each of the world's religious traditions has something to contribute to the discussion (Tucker & Grim, 2009).

A hopeful development is that even some members of the conservative evangelical Christian movement are calling for awareness of the dangers of today's environmental degradation, particularly global warming. For example, Reverend Richard Cizik, former Washington spokesperson for the National Association of Evangelicals, has urged national action toward reducing global warming based on the biblical demand for "creation care" or stewardship of the land provided by the Creator (Lampman, 2006). Cizik developed his concern after talking with an Evangelical scientist based at Oxford University who laid out the scientific consensus on the issue.

In addition, there is evidence that even some of the most serious polluters on the planet, American corporations, now understand that global warming is increasing at such a rapid rate, and is so hazardous to human life, that government regulation is necessary. General Motors, for example, in 2007 joined a list of companies urging federal policies to tighten standards on vehicle emissions. This is finally taking place because some chief executive officers (CEOs) have truly "gotten religion" on what they see as major threats to the ecosystem and the economy; others, more pragmatic, want to "have a seat at the table" when policies are written and to have advance knowledge of what regulations are likely to involve (Trumbull, 2007).

However, many large national and multinational corporations have yet to "find religion." The terrible explosion of British Petroleum's oil rig in the Gulf of Mexico in 2010, killing eleven workers and spewing thousands of gallons of oil into the sea every day for months, provides ominous evidence that many corporations need not only national but international regulation. Otherwise, the profits they crave may drive most of the species of the earth (including humans) to extinction (see Figure 2.1).

Hopefully, social workers and students today will recognize that their work must extend beyond traditional forms of service and include efforts to achieve ecological sanity, so that plants, animals, and people can survive on this earth and in its waters. Efforts directed toward developing a sustainable world are needed if we are to leave a habitable planet to our children.

"Can't we just dye the smoke green?"

Figure 2.1

Policy Practice

Practice Behavior Example: Social workers analyze, formulate, and advocate for policies that advance social well-being

Critical Thinking Question: How can improving environmental policies—local, national, and international—help social workers as well as clients?

The Intervention Process

To continue our more mundane discussion of the generalist approach to social work practice, the third major component (besides the ecosystems perspective and the use of multiple levels of intervention, as previously described) is the intervention, problem-solving, or planned change process. This third component has traditionally been known as the **problem-solving process**, and that terminology continues to be used today by many social workers. The terms *intervention process* and *planned change process*, however, are sometimes preferred because some think they better encompass the idea of preventive work. For example, parents who wish to maintain a safe neighborhood may request assistance in developing a community center for teens who might otherwise become involved in gangs. However, many social workers point out that problem solving can also encompass preventive work.

Regardless of the terminology used, a careful, step-by-step process must be employed in professional social work practice. It is all too easy for a caring person to hear about a situation that needs to change and immediately jump in to try to "do something," unintentionally causing serious complications.

An explicit intervention process alerts responsible social workers to think carefully before acting and provides guidelines regarding how to think critically. This text will usually use the terms **problem-solving process or intervention process** to describe the painstaking methodology employed in professional social work practice. Acting after hearing just one person's side of a story neglects other people's experience and points of view. The intervention process involves several steps, as described in the CSWE Educational Policy and Accreditation Standards (CSWE, 2008):

> Professional practice involves the dynamic and interactive processes of engagement, assessment, intervention, and evaluation at multiple levels. Social workers have knowledge and skills to practice with individuals, families, groups, organizations, and communities. Practice knowledge includes identifying, analyzing, and implementing evidence-based interventions designed to achieve client goals; using research and technological advances; evaluating program outcomes and practice effectiveness; developing analyzing, advocating, and providing leadership for policies and services; and promoting social and economic justice.

Obviously, this process is involved and requires expertise! To translate for beginning students (see Box 2.5), the generalist social worker usually begins with a *situation in which change is desired*. Let us use this chapter's case study as an example. Government officials in the state where Stephanie Hermann worked desired to change the situation in which people with developmental disabilities were routinely placed in nursing homes. Stephanie's job as a social worker in her regional government office was to assist the desired change to come about. She entered into *engagement* processes with her client system, in this case the social service providers in her region, by alerting them to the coming policy changes. She used her interpersonal skills to help prepare them for action.

As part of *assessment* processes, Stephanie helped her clients collect and organize relevant data: for example, how many nursing home clients would be affected? What alternative placements might be available for them? How

---

Box 2.5   The Intervention Process: Council on Social Work Education Policies

Educational Policy 2.1.10(a)—Engagement

Social workers

- substantively and effectively prepare for action with individuals, families, groups, organizations, and communities;
- use empathy and other interpersonal skills; and
- develop a mutually agreed-on focus of work and desired outcomes.

Educational Policy 2.1.10(b)—Assessment

Social workers

- collect, organize, and interpret client data;
- assess client strengths and limitations;
- develop mutually agreed-on intervention goals and objectives; and
- select appropriate intervention strategies.

Educational Policy 2.1.10(c)—Intervention

Social workers

- initiate actions to achieve organizational goals;
- implement prevention interventions that enhance client capacities;
- help clients resolve problems;
- negotiate, mediate, and advocate for clients;
- facilitate transitions and endings.

Educational Policy 2.1.10(d)—Evaluation

Social workers critically analyze, monitor, and evaluate interventions.

_____

Source: Quoted from Educational Policies 2.1.10(a)–2.1.10(d), Educational Policy and Accreditation Standards, Council on Social Work Education (2008).

---

could new placements be financed? When Brockton Manor announced that it wanted to seek alternative placements for all its residents with developmental disabilities, Stephanie, in collaboration with the nursing home and various other community agencies and organizations, helped develop goals, objectives, and strategies to implement this plan. The work involved developing mutually agreed-on responsibilities and roles for a number of community stakeholders.

As part of *intervention* processes, Stephanie helped implement the mutually determined plans of action using the best knowledge and technological advances available (involving, e.g., medical evaluations and video services). She displayed leadership in developing new resources (e.g., new group homes and family care homes). She also advocated for individual clients with developmental disabilities (such as Sandra McLean) to assure that their needs were met.

Engage, Assess, Intervene, Evaluate

Practice Behavior Example: Social workers select appropriate intervention strategies

Critical Thinking Question: In what ways were Stephanie's intervention strategies appropriate and effective?

Stephanie used *evaluation* processes on an ongoing basis, continually monitoring outcomes throughout her intervention efforts. When circumstances improved to her clients' satisfaction, she facilitated the transition of leadership from herself to the community organizations and regional social service providers involved.

The problem-solving process helps the generalist social worker determine which level or levels of intervention to involve in resolving the issue or concern at hand. In Stephanie's case, resolving the issue included working at every level of intervention: the community (Stephanie's region of the state); the social service agencies and voluntary organizations within that region; and several families, small groups, and individuals like Sandra McLean. On the other hand, generalist intervention may involve working only with a single individual or a particular family, group, or organization. The important point is that the plan of action determined by the generalist worker depends on the nature of the circumstances and careful implementation of the planned change process. The plan of action is not determined according to a method that simply happens to be preferred by the worker—for example, one-on-one counseling or group work.

VALUES, ETHICS, AND HUMAN DIVERSITY

The trend toward community placement of people with developmental disabilities was a welcome one for the social work profession. Social work values, as identified in Chapter 1, include the dignity and worth of each person. It is easy to recognize the dignity and worth of fortunate individuals with no apparent disabilities, who can live independently as expected in our society. But what about persons like Sandra McLean, who, no matter how hard they may try, will require ongoing assistance throughout their lives? A basic ethical principle in social work requires that social workers respect the inherent worth and dignity of all. Sandra, despite her disabilities, was a whole person who deserved respectful treatment designed to meet her special needs, treatment that would help maximize her potential.

Sandra was a member of a population at risk: people with disabilities. The dignity and worth of people with disabilities is frequently overlooked, as is their right to self-determination (another basic social work value). In fact, **ableism** is identified by Berg-Weger (2005, p. 104) as a practice in which people without disabilities exclude and/or oppress those who do. Sadly, the worth and dignity of the disabled person may be overlooked by the wider community because that community simply wants to spend the least amount of money for care possible. Self-determination may never even be considered, so many people with disabilities are drugged to unconsciousness to make them easier to manage, as was Sandra McLean. Yet in many instances, people with disabilities are able to make many decisions for themselves, and in all cases, worth and dignity should be honored. Fortunately, respectful care often leads to skilled, professional treatment, which can turn out to be less expensive than warehousing in institutions, as in this chapter's case example.

SOCIAL JUSTICE AND POPULATIONS AT RISK

As will be discussed in more detail in Chapter 3, certain populations in this society are especially at risk of poverty, discrimination, and oppression. People with disabilities are among the populations at risk. Social workers can serve as advocates to assist them to live happy, productive lives. Social work values and ethics challenge us to work with people with disabilities: a major professional value promoted by the National Association of Social Workers is **social justice**, with the related ethical principle of challenging social injustice. People with disabilities are often treated unjustly and require active intervention and advocacy. They do not choose their disabilities, and they do not deserve to be ignored, isolated, and oppressed because of their disabilities. Instead, social workers should provide assistance in achieving their goals, which are as varied as the goals of people without disabilities. They may range from simply enjoying the love and companionship of others to engaging in a professional career, depending on the individual situation.

The Strengths Perspective: Resilience and Empowerment

Dennis Saleebey pioneered what has become known as the strengths-based approach to social work practice. He reminds us that it is of great importance to seek and identify strengths in all client systems. Focusing only on problems and deficits tends to discourage workers and clients alike. Saleebey (2006) notes that despite the difficulties our clients may have experienced, they have also developed many skills and attributes that have helped them to meet and overcome difficult challenges. People often exhibit remarkable resiliency in the face of adversity.

Glicken (2004) points out that the strengths perspective always views clients in a hopeful and optimistic way, regardless of the complexity of their issues. Like Saleebey, Glicken believes that all clients have innate strengths and abilities. Social workers can enhance these strengths when they focus on positive and successful client behaviors, which can be found in even the most difficult situations. Glicken counsels social workers to do a conscious asset review of a client's many positive behaviors and qualities.

The strengths-based approach is especially appropriate in working with clients with disabilities. The focus can and should be on strengths and abilities, not on deficits. Consider the example of Sandra McLean. Despite being warehoused in institutions for many years, this remarkable woman rebounded courageously when given a chance. She turned out to be an amazingly resilient human being. She relearned how to walk, talk, feed, and toilet herself, and she was especially talented in the area of social relations.

Assisting clients to discover and honor their own strengths and powers of **resilience** may be our very best service to them as individuals. In addition, many external environments, even seemingly the poorest and most harsh, offer important resources that can make a difference in our clients' lives. The practitioner's challenge is to help find these resources and assist clients to utilize them.

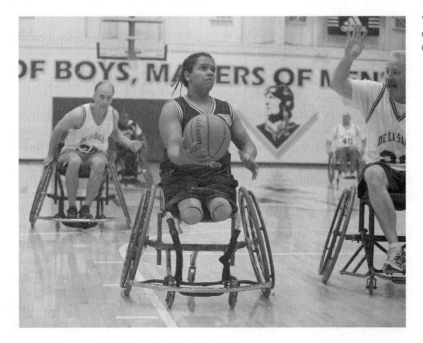

Young person with disability displays courage and determination.

A **strengths perspective** leads naturally to the idea of empowering clients; recognizing and honoring strengths is a firm foundation for **empowerment**. According to Dubois and Miley (2011), empowerment involves both personal and political aspects. *Personal empowerment* involves one's sense of competence, control, mastery, socioeconomic security, and the like. *Political empowerment* involves resource accessibility and the power to make choices. Genuine options must be available in the wider environment, and people need the power to choose them (or not) to have political empowerment.

POLITICAL PERSPECTIVES

The concept of empowerment leads to a discussion of political perspectives and their importance to social workers and their clients. Remember that the impetus for Stephanie's region to provide community placements for people with disabilities came from changing *government policies* at the *federal* level. These policy changes were a result of political action by various groups of people with disabilities and their advocates, including social workers. It was a positive result of long years of work by those who wanted people with disabilities to have the option to live in family-like settings in order to lead more fulfilling lives. It was an achievement that helped empower many people with disabilities. However, even if enough family care and small group homes were available to care for all, many disabled people would be unable to pay for them. That is because people with disabilities are especially at risk of poverty and discrimination. Without government help, many people with disabilities are simply unable to secure the financial resources to pay for community care.

Helping poor people achieve their needs and goals is considered a legitimate government function by some in the United States today, but not by others.

Helping poor people achieve their needs and goals is considered a legitimate government function by some in the United States today, but not by others. The political parties differ markedly in their views on this matter. Thus, it makes sense for students considering the social work profession to become informed voters. Social work clients frequently belong to populations at risk who experience poverty and other ongoing challenges. Government assistance can be crucial in allowing them to obtain the resources necessary to improve their lives. One way social workers can help their clients is by voting for the candidates whose policies will genuinely assist the poor and disadvantaged. Even better, professional social workers can develop active political careers themselves.

To help students make thoughtful choices in the voting booth, this chapter will discuss political perspectives known as **conservative, liberal, or progressive**, and **radical**. It will also briefly describe **neoconservative** and **neoliberal** views. The discussion here will be very basic; students are encouraged to read as much as possible from additional sources and to examine Box 2.6, "Up for Debate."

The Political Spectrum

Political parties in the United States today fall along a political spectrum, described as *right* to *left*. Those on the right are considered relatively conservative; those on the left are considered relatively liberal or progressive. The major conservative political party in the United States today is the Republican Party, and the major liberal party is the Democratic Party. There are parties

Box 2.6 Up for Debate	

Proposition: Should the federal government develop programs designed to assist poor people?

Yes	No
People are naturally industrious and will use such assistance responsibly to better their lives.	People are naturally lazy, and government assistance will only make them more lazy and irresponsible.
Environmental conditions such as discrimination may hold a person back unless government assists to "level the playing field."	Individuals are autonomous and achieve according to their inborn talents; they have complete free will.
Government programs are necessary to help meet basic human needs for all.	The free market economy is the best way to fulfill individual needs.
A free market economy needs intervention and regulation by government to ensure that competition is fair.	Government's role should be to support, not regulate, the free market.

even further right (or more conservative) than the Republican, however, and parties further left than the Democratic.

Webster's Dictionary defines *liberal* as "favoring reform or progress, as in religion, education, etc.; specifically, favoring political reforms tending toward democracy and personal freedom for the individual; progressive" (Guralnik, 1984, p. 814). It defines *progressive* as "favoring, working for, or characterized by progress or improvement, as through political or social reform" (Guralnik, 1984, p. 1135). *Webster's* defines *conservative* as "tending to preserve established traditions or institutions and to resist or oppose any changes in these (conservative politics, conservative art)" (Guralnik, 1984, p. 302). These definitions are useful in understanding basic differences in perspective between liberals or progressives and conservatives in the United States.

People who find themselves on different ends of the political spectrum tend to have very different attitudes regarding the proper role of government with respect to the economic market (Popple & Leighninger, 2005; Karger & Stoesz, 2010). We will discuss some of these differences next.

Conservative Perspectives

The term *conservative* is derived from the verb to *conserve* or to *save*. So it should come as no surprise that people who are conservative tend to want to keep things as they are and to resist change. People want to keep things as they are for many good reasons, but perhaps the simplest is that these individuals tend to be "haves" who want to keep what they have or who believe that the current system will provide them with the best opportunity to become haves.

In particular, conservatives believe that government should not interfere with the free market forces of supply and demand. They want to preserve the traditional free market economic system because this is the system that got them where they are or else it is the system they believe can best take them where they want to go. Given these perspectives, it follows that conservatives do not believe that government should use its powers to help poor people. They worry that government assistance might increase what they perceive as a tendency to be lazy. Government should, instead, provide tax breaks for the rich, because wealthy people invest money in the economic market. New investment theoretically could lead to new jobs for poor people, who would be better off with more work. This perspective is popularly known as the *trickle down theory* or, more formally, as *supply-side economics*. Conservatives do not oppose all help to the poor, but they believe aid should be offered only through the private sector (as charity) (Karger & Stoesz, 2010).

The conservative orientation goes beyond economics. Preservation of social traditions such as the nuclear family is also strongly promoted. Thus, political conservatives generally oppose such potential public services as government day care programs because, from this perspective, child care should be provided only by a wife within the family household. Single parenthood, sex outside of marriage, abortion, homosexuality, and so on, are also generally opposed by conservatives because these practices are not considered traditional. This type of conservatism, sometimes called **cultural conservatism**, results in major contradictions, however. While conservatives insist that government take a hands-off (laissez-faire) position with respect to intervention in the economic market, many conservatives push hard for government intervention restricting reproductive choice, access to sex education in the schools, and the like.

The major conservative political party in the United States today is the Republican Party, as mentioned earlier: that of Presidents Nixon, Ford, Reagan, George H. W. Bush, and George W. Bush. Within the Republican Party, as this chapter is being revised, is a new faction known as the Tea Party, even further to the right than the general membership. Other conservative parties include the Traditionalists, who believe that Christian doctrine should become the law of the nation, and the Libertarians, who oppose virtually all government regulation (including taxation), except when one individual threatens the physical safety of another (Karger & Stoesz, 2005, 2010).

Liberal or Progressive Perspectives

The liberal or progressive **worldview** is quite different from that of the conservative. First of all, the conception of human nature is more optimistic. Liberals believe that people are naturally good and do not need to be controlled or forced to work. Rather, they need to be protected from corrupting influences in the wider environment (Popple & Leighninger, 2005). Liberals believe that people are industrious by nature and will take pleasure in hard work and personal accomplishment if conditions are humane.

Liberals believe that conditions in the social environment strongly affect people's chances to develop their talents and achieve a fulfilling life. From this viewpoint, if people are poor, it is in large part due to lack of opportunity, societal discrimination, oppression, and the like—problems that lie in the external environment. Liberals or progressives support government intervention in the workings of the economic market to try to level the playing field for groups they believe are disadvantaged. For example, they tend to support government social welfare programs that provide monetary assistance to poor children and their families. They tend to support affirmative action programs to provide better access to jobs for women and ethnic minorities. They support national programs such as Head Start, which provides early environmental and educational enrichment for poor children to give them a better chance to fully develop their talents (see Box 2.7).

Box 2.7   The Political Spectrum

Liberal or Progressive Perspectives	Conservative Perspectives
Change can make the world a better place	Change should be resisted; tradition should be maintained
People are naturally good and industrious	People are naturally lazy, corrupt, and irresponsible
People are strongly influenced and shaped by their environment	People are autonomous and guided entirely by free will
Family is an evolving institution; family forms may change	The traditional family should be upheld; programs designed to help nontraditional families should be opposed
The social system needs regulation; government should intervene in the economic market to assist disadvantaged populations	The social system functions correctly as is; government regulation threatens individual liberty and smooth functioning of the economic market

Source: Popple, Philip R. & Leighninger, Leslie. Social Work, Social Welfare, and American Society, 6th Edition, © 2005. Reprinted by permission of Pearson Education, Inc., Upper Saddle River, NJ.

The major political party in the United States today that supports a liberal or progressive perspective is the Democratic Party, that of Presidents Kennedy, Johnson, Carter, Clinton, and Obama. There are other parties more liberal than the Democratic in the United States; they are much smaller, however. The Green Party is an example. It promotes environmental sustainability, community-based economics, grassroots democracy, nonviolence, respect for diversity, feminism, and social justice, among other progressive policies. The party began in Germany and is now a worldwide movement (Karger & Stoesz, 2005, 2010).

Neoliberalism and Neoconservatism

Confusing to many students today is the fact that there are *neoconservative* and *neoliberal* perspectives, which are also important forces on the political scene. While a great deal could be said about them, it will be stated here only that both are to the *right* of their parent movements, the conservative and the liberal. American politics in general shifted greatly to the right toward the end of the 20th century, and the momentum has been strong enough that many liberals have tried to distance themselves from the term *liberal*, using the term *progressive* instead. For neoconservatives, the shift to the right has involved adopting stands that are strongly culturally conservative, such as opposing reproductive choice for women, banning gay people from the military, and banning gay marriage. Their stance could be described as *reactionary*, opposing any policy empowering minorities. For neoliberals, the shift to the right has involved adopting favorable policies toward big business.

American politics in general shifted greatly to the right toward the end of the 20th century.

Bill Clinton was among the founders of the neoliberal movement, believing that a more favorable attitude toward big business would help him get elected. This attitude may have been what persuaded him, as President, to sign the bill (to be discussed in a later chapter) known as the Personal Responsibility and Work Opportunity Act, which, in 1996, ended the entitlement of all poor children in the United States to public welfare. To be sure, the bill was passed by a Congress largely composed of Republican neoconservatives. *Neos*, especially neoconservatives, strongly oppose public welfare programs for the poor, or any increase in minimum wages, because they fear such assistance to the poor might interfere with the workings of the free market by limiting corporate profits.

Radical Perspectives

The radical perspective, which may be described as *left* of the liberal, is held by a much smaller number of people in the United States than either the conservative or liberal, but it is still influential. The radical view of human nature parallels that of the liberal or progressive—that people are inherently good and naturally industrious. They will work hard and take pride in their achievements given reasonable working conditions. Like liberals, people who take a radical perspective believe that environmental influences may prevent people from achieving their full potential. But while liberals believe that the environment can potentially be made fair *within* the capitalist system by enlightened government intervention, radicals believe that capitalism itself is the problem. They believe that a wealthy and powerful elite make decisions that further their own interests at the expense of others, so that fairness is not possible under this system. Instead, society must be entirely restructured to redistribute wealth and power among all the people (Popple & Leighninger, 2005; Karger & Stoesz, 2010).

Probably the major party in the United States today that most nearly reflects the radical perspective is the Socialist party, although it is very small (see Box 2.8).

The Political Spectrum and Social Welfare Policy

Liberal and conservative positions fall toward opposite ends of the political spectrum, as described earlier. Conservatives oppose government intervention in the workings of the free market, except to bolster big business, and liberals support intervention to correct imbalances and empower citizens who fall outside the mainstream. By the late 20th century, these positions had polarized. A Democratic majority elected to both houses of Congress in 2006 helped limit the power of the then-neoconservative executive branch, but discourse continued to be strident. Our greatest challenge in the future may be finding a way for people of differing political perspectives to enter constructive dialogue.

When President Obama was elected in 2008 along with a strongly Democratic Congress, he clearly hoped to work collaboratively across party lines. However, not a single Republican would support any controversial bill

Box 2.8 The Political Spectrum

Left				Right
Radical	Liberal	Neoliberal	Conservative	Neoconservative

←- →

Socialist	Green	Democratic		Republican Libertarian

This exhibit portrays where the author believes certain political parties lie today along the "left–right" political spectrum. This illustration is made according to the author's best understanding, but other views may differ. In some ways, it is incorrect to place Libertarian to the "right" of Republican, as Libertarians strongly promote individual liberties, including those of the less powerful, so they do not promote legislation limiting women's right to choice, gay marriage, etc.

proposed by the Democrats. Republicans even opposed a health care bill intended to assist millions of Americans lacking health insurance. Obama was finally able to get the Affordable Health Care Act passed in 2010 by personally leading the effort, but he was unable to save a "public option" component, which would have provided a government-run health insurance plan. Such a plan would have posed serious competition to the huge American private insurance industry that continues to drive up health care costs today. Portions of the Affordable Health Care Act are being challenged in court as the chapter is being revised.

While the Obama administration has worked hard to provide average Americans more opportunities—for example, programs to assist homebuyers nearing foreclosure, a stimulus bill to help retain and restore jobs, increases in college student loans, restoration of family planning funds lost under G. W. Bush, new protections for women against pay discrimination (to be discussed in Chapter 3)—still, the wars in Iraq and Afghanistan continue to gorge on public funds that might otherwise be available to assist American citizens. In addition, in 2011, the United States engaged in war with Libya.

To return to our chapter's case study regarding a politically powerless but personally plucky individual like Sandra McLean, would there be any way that people from both ends of the political spectrum might be willing to assist her? Remember that it was a policy change at the *national* level that prompted reassessment of her care in the *local* nursing home and her subsequent rehabilitation and foster home placement. What could a conservative approach do for Sandra? Under what conditions might the free market have an interest in helping her? Should Sandra be helped even if the free market has no interest in her, given economic recession, a cost-cutting goal by the government, and the fact that she is unable to work? If so, why? If not, why not? Students are requested to keep such questions in mind as they read further in this text and others.

TURNING TO EACH OTHER

Dr. Margaret Wheatley, an organizational consultant, author, and international speaker with a strong orientation toward systems theory (described earlier in this chapter), believes that Americans may ultimately have to turn to each other to meet today's challenges. Wheatley, who works with organizations all over the world including the United Nations, believes that the recession that became worldwide in 2008 was *not a* financial crisis. It was, instead, a global crisis that occurred because the world has become organized according to economic values. These values place cost-cutting, not service provision to persons in need, as the primary goal. Economic values are espoused by virtually every corporation, organization, and nation on earth today. The result has been a disaster for millions.

Wheatley asserts that we live in a culture that is still based on Social Darwinism, a powerful theory that arose out of Charles Darwin's 1859 book *On the Origin of Species*. The theory presents life as a struggle for survival, in which each individual must compete against every other, and only the fittest can survive. This perspective leads to the belief that if you "make it" in this world you are "fit," but if you don't, you are defective and should be allowed to perish (Social Darwinism will be discussed in more detail in Chapter 4).

To the contrary, Wheatley notes life's building blocks are relationships, not competitive struggles. People survive only in community. She describes healthy communities as ones that identify themselves as community, preserve and learn from their histories, involve their youth in significant ways, invite a diversity of voices into conversation, and expect leadership from everyone.

Wheatley notes that relationships are crucial not only for physical survival but also for emotional and spiritual well-being. Due to the intense competitiveness of our times, many people rush about without time for meaningful relationships. Wheatley reports that sadly, loneliness, and alienation have resulted in suicide being the second leading cause of death among adolescents in the United States. Clearly, many young Americans do not have a sense of belonging.

Wheatley reports that even in the hard sciences, including physics, relationships have been recognized as being the key to existence. She writes:

> In the quantum world, relationships are not just interesting; to many physicists, they are *all* there is to reality. One physicist, Henry Stapp, describes elementary particles as, "in essence, a set of relationships that reach outward to other things" (in Capra, 1983, 81). Particles come into being ephemerally through interactions with other energy sources. We give names to each of these sources—physicists still identify neutrons, electrons, and other particles—but they are intermediate states in a network of interactions. Physicists can plot the probability and results of these interactions, but *no particle can be drawn independent from the others*. (Wheatley, 2009, 35)

In truth, no person is fully independent—imagine an infant or toddler trying to survive without a caretaker. Everyone has been an infant and a toddler. Instead, we, like quanta, are enmeshed in webs of relationships instrumental to our survival. We need relationships to affirm our very being. If crucial components of the webs to which we belong, such as our governments, do not value us enough to consider our needs to be of primary importance, but focus instead on economic values and cost-cutting, the result is likely to be widespread misery. Wheatley has found reason to hope, however. Her studies of natural disasters, such as the flooding of New Orleans in 2005 and the earthquake in Haiti in 2010, demonstrate the remarkable resilience of ordinary people working together. It was the people of New Orleans, the "Cajun Navy," who first rescued each other from rooftops, risking their lives in rickety boats. And although rescue workers reached Haiti in a much more timely fashion than they reached New Orleans, it was the Haitian people who first helped each other by searching for loved ones under piles of rubble, maintaining courage by literally singing together in the streets.

Wheatley believes that the best hope for the world rests on people turning to one another and pulling together. She observes that anyone can be a leader. All it takes is genuine caring and a willingness to help. In times of great need, she finds, communities respond; people help each other. Wheatley has learned through her work that there is no power greater than a community discovering what it cares about (Wheatley, 2009, 2010).

Fortunately, the profession of social work is made up of a remarkable number of people such as those Wheatley describes—people who care about and will assist others in times of need. They work with individuals, families, groups, organizations, and communities, depending on where the need or opportunity arises. Not only professional practitioners, but social work students are helping all over the world today, making a difference.

SUMMARY

This chapter begins with the case study of Sandra McLean, a young woman who suffered a head injury at birth and cannot live independently. Sandra's situation is used to help illustrate the importance of two major types of theoretical perspectives necessary for competent social work practice: those that guide daily practice and those that guide social welfare policy decisions and strongly affect practice.

With respect to social work practice theory, the chapter discusses the influence of systems theory and an ecosystems perspective on today's generalist approach to practice. Levels of intervention included in the generalist approach are discussed as well as the systematic planned change or intervention process. The importance of a strengths-based orientation and recognition of client resilience is discussed. The chapter notes that appropriate levels of social work intervention today may extend beyond former notions of community to include global, ecological, and environmental considerations.

The chapter then discusses basic political theory to help social work students understand different views on government action that will strongly impact practice with clients, who often fall outside the mainstream. Conservative perspectives are contrasted with liberal or progressive and radical viewpoints. Neoconservative and neoliberal points of view are introduced.

Information on basic political theory is followed by a discussion of the political spectrum and how it affects social welfare policy decisions. Social work students are challenged to think about which political perspective might best assist their clients and to attempt to find ways to encourage people who fall on opposite ends of the political spectrum to work together to improve the lives of all.

The chapter concludes with thoughts and observations regarding the importance of ordinary people (including social workers) pulling together in community to achieve mutual goals.

PRACTICE TEST

The following questions will test your knowledge of the content found within this chapter. For additional assessment, including licensing-exam type questions on applying chapter content to practice behaviors, visit **MySearchLab.**

1. The Ecosystems perspective _____.
   a. was proposed by Ludwig Von Bertalanffy
   b. originated in the biological sciences and guides social work practice
   c. was viewed as controversial by Germain and Gitterman
   d. is clearly distinct from general systems theory

2. "Global practice considerations" refers to _____.
   a. interventions developed by the United Nations
   b. current international political issues
   c. issues that impact the wider environment and future generations
   d. traditional religious missionary activities

3. A hallmark of the neoliberal political perspective is _____.
   a. the promotion of policies that favorably impact big business
   b. commitment to culturally conservative ideas
   c. commitment to nongovernmental solutions to community problems
   d. that capitalism is inherently problematic

4. The generalist approach _____.
   a. is informed by ecological systems theory
   b. primarily focuses on large system interventions
   c. primarily focuses on individual changes
   d. is not relevant for intervening with global problems

5. According to Dubois and Miley, empowerment involves _____.
   a. the power of individuals and families
   b. community organizing and coalition building
   c. obtaining financial independence
   d. both personal and political aspects of power

6. The case study of Sandra McLean points out the importance of which social work value?
   a. integrity
   b. respect for the inherent worth and dignity of all people
   c. morality
   d. service

7. Effective administrative social work practice in policy implementation requires a range of competencies. The case study at the beginning of the chapter identifies practice behaviors from three of the expected CSWE competencies. Identify these three specific competencies, and list at least one practice behavior exemplar associated with each competency. Link these practice behavior exemplars with specific illustrations from the case study.

MySearchLab CONNECTIONS

Reinforce what you learned in this chapter by studying videos, cases, documents, and more available at **www.MySearchLab.com**.

Watch and Review

Watch these Videos

* The Ecological Model Using the Friere Method
* Participating in Policy Changes

Read and Review

Read these Cases/Documents

Δ Please Don't Let Our Mother Die

Δ Adoption: Travis

Explore and Assess

Explore these Assets

Canadian Research Institute for Social Policy—http://www.unb.ca/crisp/index.php

Assess Your Knowledge

Assess your knowledge with a variety of topical and chapter assessment.

Conclude your assessment by completing the chapter exam.

* = CSWE Core Competency Asset
Δ = Case Study

3

Social Justice, Poverty, and Populations at Risk

Connecting Core Competencies in This Chapter									
X	Professional Identity		Ethical Practice		Critical Thinking	X	Diversity in Practice	X	Human Rights & Justice
	Research Based Practice	X	Human Behavior		Policy Practice		Practice Contexts		Engage, Assess, Intervene, Evaluate

Juanita Chavez

Juanita cheered when she was offered the job as a social worker at Urban Neighborhood Center. A recent BSW graduate, Juanita knew she was competing for the position with more experienced workers. But she had an important skill: she spoke both Spanish and English fluently. Moreover, as part of the requirements of her social work major, she had served her senior-year field placement in an alternative school where Spanish was the first language of many of the students. Urban Neighborhood Center was located in an area where many residents were of Hispanic origin. Juanita hoped her bilingual abilities would help her get the job. They did.

Juanita had now been working for several months. She felt she was developing a broad understanding of the needs of the neighborhood as a whole that surrounded the agency. As part of her job, she was expected to help identify major needs of community residents, to inform residents about the services available at the center, and to provide them with information concerning community resources that might help meet their needs. The Center provided after-school recreational programs for school-age children, limited tutoring services, and a food pantry staffed by volunteers. Lately, however, the food pantry had been short on supplies, and hungry people had been sent home empty-handed. That bothered Juanita very much. While she liked the fact that her position gave her a broad perspective of the neighborhood in which she worked—indeed of the midsized city of which the neighborhood was a part—that knowledge could be disturbing. She now knew that resources needed by many of the poorer residents were frequently not available.

Professional Identity

Practice Behavior Example: Social workers demonstrate professional demeanor in behavior, appearance, and communication

Critical Thinking Question: How does Juanita's behavior on her new job demonstrate her professional identity?

Juanita's first crisis call on the job related to Temporary Assistance for Needy Families (TANF, to be discussed in more detail later in the chapter). She remembered the phone call well. A volunteer helping supervise a recreational program had called Juanita just as the new social worker was trying to organize her tiny office. Two children much too young for the agency's after-school programs, and much too young to be out on the streets alone, had been brought in by a school-age child who regularly came to the agency. The child said she had found the toddlers on the sidewalk, crying and apparently lost. Juanita soon encountered the young children, ages approximately 2 and 3, who said their names were Tomas and Tomacita. They could not provide an address or last name. They said they had been put to bed for a nap by their mother, but when they awakened, she was gone. Frightened, they began to search for her.

Juanita decided that she would have to call Protective Services to report abandoned children. Because the situation was not perceived as an emergency by the city's overburdened department, however, no worker arrived at Urban Neighborhood Center for several hours. Toward the end of the day, one of the longtime agency social workers returned after having made some home visits. By good fortune, this worker recognized Tomas and Tomacita and knew that they were siblings of a teenage girl who sometimes attended tutoring programs at the agency. There was a family telephone number on file. A call was made immediately, and a distraught mother answered. She had had to report to job training that day under the rules of the TANF program, she explained. Her older daughter, who usually babysat, was involved in a field trip with her school class, and the mother had not wanted her to miss it. The neighbor who had promised to substitute had been unavailable at the last minute. The children's mother didn't dare miss her job training as she could then be eliminated from the TANF program. That would take away her only source of money for food and rent. She knew people who had missed a single day of training due to lack of child care who had already been dismissed. So Tomas and Tomacita's mother had opted to take a serious risk, leaving her children alone after putting them to bed for a nap, hoping against hope that they would remain asleep.

The children's mother and the Protective Services worker arrived at Urban Neighborhood Center at almost the same moment. Only the advocacy of the agency social worker who knew the mother prevented the children from being taken into the foster care system then and there. Had that happened, months might have passed before Tomas and Tomacita were returned home. Their mother promised, of course, never to leave the children again without a babysitter. The Protective Services worker scolded her for not taking advantage of child care that was supposed to be provided by the TANF program. The mother explained that she had applied for child care months before but that it hadn't come through yet.

Juanita learned later that child care, while theoretically available to poor mothers enrolled in TANF in her city, in reality involved a long waiting list. While her state permitted child care assistance for poor mothers under an option allowed by federal TANF legislation, funding was inadequate to meet the need. Tomas and Tomacita's older sister missed school regularly so that the mother could attend job training. The ability to secure a pay check to purchase food and shelter was naturally perceived by this family as more important than education.

Juanita soon became aware that many other families who lived near Urban Neighborhood Center were in the same situation. Many parents, languishing somewhere on TANF waiting lists for child care, depended on older children to babysit so they could go to work. Others with regular jobs earned wages too low to afford child care and also depended on their older children, especially teenage girls, to babysit. These helpful teens risked truancy proceedings, adding to family difficulties.

Juanita began to collect data on a number of high school girls in her area who were routinely missing school to babysit for younger siblings. She hoped eventually to influence legislators to appropriate more funds for child care. Juanita also hoped to see a Spanish-speaking day care center established by her agency because none yet existed in the city. She even made an appointment to speak with her agency's board of directors about establishing such a service. She was excited when the board appointed a special committee to study the situation and appointed Juanita a member. The committee then authorized Juanita to conduct a door-to-door survey to find out how many families would take part in a Spanish-speaking day care center if one were available. In this way, the social worker became engaged in community organization work, along with her other responsibilities at the neighborhood center.

As Juanita walked up the steps of a tiny, single-family cottage one day collecting data for her survey, she noticed that one of the special school vans that transport students with disabilities was pulling up to the door. The driver honked and then asked Juanita to knock, since he needed to deliver a child. No one answered the door, however, and the driver explained that he would have to take the child back to school. Juanita could see the sad face of a little girl peering out of the side window of the bus. Her head was misshapen and too large for her features. The driver muttered something about irresponsible mothers, shook his head, and drove away.

Juanita returned to the cottage later that day. This time her knock was answered by a young woman who appeared to be in her early 20s. Juanita explained who she was and why she had dropped by earlier. The woman looked blank, and then said haltingly, with a heavy accent, "I no speak English." Juanita then greeted the young woman in Spanish. Her reward was an enormous, engaging smile. When Juanita mentioned the incident with the bus, however, the young woman's face took on an alarmed expression. She invited Juanita inside. She introduced herself as Carla Romero. "You say you are a social worker from Neighborhood Center?" she asked in Spanish. Juanita nodded. "Maybe you can help me, then," Carla continued.

"Tell me how I can assist," Juanita replied in Spanish, and the young woman began her story.

Carla told Juanita that her young daughter, Maria, was physically and cognitively disabled due to complications of birth that had resulted in permanent swelling of the brain. Now 6 years old, Maria functioned at a 12-month level. She had to be constantly supervised. But Carla had to work to support herself and the child. Her ex-husband, father of the child, kept in touch but had returned to Puerto Rico from where the couple had come. Child support checks were few and far between. Carla went to work when Maria began public school at the age of 3. The little girl received skilled service at school: occupational, physical, and speech therapy. Lately, however, there had been an embarrassing problem. The school nurse had sent Maria home with head lice. Carla had bought a number of products from the neighborhood pharmacy and used them carefully, but a few nits, or eggs, seemed to persist no matter what Carla did. The child continued to be sent home.

Carla, since she could not speak English, had already had a neighbor call the school to explain that she was doing all she could. The neighbor asked politely if the child could remain in school in spite of a few nits because her mother, Carla, had to work to provide food and shelter for the family. But the school nurse insisted that Maria could not attend school unless she was nit-free. The next day Juanita called the nurse. She got the same story: no exceptions. Juanita called the health department for assistance. There she learned that certain strains of lice were currently resisting all remedies available in the store. The health department had effective treatments, a nurse there told her, but due to funding cuts, the staff could no longer provide services to help with this problem. Lice were no longer considered a "communicable disease" under current funding definitions! The nurse suggested taking the child to a doctor and fumigating the house.

Carla was fortunate in that, while her job paid very low wages and did not provide any benefits such as health insurance, she was nevertheless able to take her daughter to the doctor and to save enough money to pay for fumigating the house. That was because Maria qualified for both Medicaid and Supplemental Security Income (SSI) (programs authorized under the Social Security Act) as a severely disabled child. The doctor told the young mother, however, that he did not know of any better treatment for lice or nits than the over-the-counter remedies she was already purchasing in the local stores. Carla then bought another standard treatment at the neighborhood pharmacy. She also had the house fumigated. But the problem continued.

Carla called Juanita at Urban Neighborhood Center in desperation after her daughter was sent home from school for the third month in a row. Her neighbor was babysitting regularly now, but she was not happy about it, and the cost was taking up most of Carla's food budget. The young mother frequently had to turn to Neighborhood Center's food pantry, but sometimes even the pantry was out of supplies. Juanita called the health department again, explaining that Carla had done everything she could but still her child was being sent home from school. The department continued to insist that it had no staff to deal with the problem. In desperation, Carla shaved Maria's head. Even that did not work! Tiny nits persisted, and Maria continued to be sent home. Juanita had angry words with the school nurse, explaining that the little girl, through no fault of her own, was missing out on valuable therapies at school and that her physical condition was deteriorating as a result. But the nurse, perhaps understandably, was unmovable.

Then Juanita had an inspiration. She called the social worker at the school Maria attended. That worker was aware of the problem and had already tried to intervene with the school nurse, but to no avail. But this worker and Juanita agreed that both of them would make impassioned pleas to the health department. The health department refused once more, pleading budget cuts. Finally, the school social worker had her supervisor call the health department. That worked. At last, a public health nurse visited the Romero home. Juanita was present at the appointment, serving as translator and family advocate. The nurse promptly diagnosed Maria's strain of lice precisely and provided an effective remedy. Little Maria went back to school. But she had lost out on 4 months of education and therapy at an important developmental stage.

The Romero family's problem was not unique, of course. In Juanita's rounds of the neighborhood to collect information for her survey, she found that little Maria was not the only child missing school because of resistant strains of head lice. She also found several teenage girls at home taking care of babies, sometimes their younger siblings but sometimes their own children. Unable to afford the child care that would have enabled them to stay in school, and lacking any hope of reaching the top of the TANF waiting list for child care, they dropped out. The teen mothers were lucky if their parents let them continue to live at home, because most jobs available to people without high school degrees paid too low a wage to cover rent, food, clothing, and child care.

Human Behavior

Practice Behavior Example: Social workers critique and apply knowledge to understand person and environment

Critical Thinking Question: How did Juanita's knowledge of environmental conditions shape her understanding of the behavior of teenage girls in the neighborhood where she worked?

In addition, Juanita found several children in the neighborhood who stayed out on the streets after school because their parents had to work long hours and could not be home to supervise. Local schools offered a few sports programs for boys, but similar programs for girls were lacking. She also learned to her surprise that many of the families who used the agency's food pantry included full-time workers; some of the larger families included two full-time working adults, yet they still could not make ends meet. Wages were simply too low to cover expenses for a family, so cupboards stood empty at times.

Juanita decided to take the results of her survey back to the committee who had appointed her and to the full Urban Neighborhood Center board of directors as well. Now, besides a Spanish-speaking day care center for young children, she was interested in developing an after-school sports program for girls, as none currently existed in the area. Perhaps she could work with neighborhood schools to this end. Juanita also wondered if there might be a way to increase the supplies in her agency's food pantry. She hoped that, with a number of caring minds working on the problems she documented, effective solutions might be generated, including ways to raise funds to finance new programs. The agency's budget was limited, she knew. But as a social work professional, Juanita believed she could make a difference, especially if she could combine her problem-solving efforts and energies with those of other dedicated people committed to the agency and the surrounding community.

SOCIAL JUSTICE, POVERTY, AND POPULATIONS AT RISK

Little Tomas and Tomacita and Carla and Maria Romero belonged to a population at risk, or a population likely to suffer poverty in the United States. In fact, they belonged to several. Tomas, Tomacita, and Maria were children; Tomacita,

Carla, and Maria were female; all were members of the ethnic minority group known as Hispanic or Latino. Children, women, and ethnic minorities are all populations at risk in the United States. **Prejudice** against populations at risk, particularly against ethnic minorities and women, is common. **Poverty**, a basic issue of social and economic justice, is a common experience for members of these groups. *Poverty* may be defined broadly as the lack of resources to achieve a reasonably comfortable standard of living.

Social and economic justice and populations at risk are intertwined in the real world. Social welfare policies and programs have been developed in many times and many places to help promote social and economic justice, to help improve the lives of people at risk. Sometimes these efforts have been successful, sometimes not. Some programs, unfortunately, seem to have been designed more to control people who are poor than to alleviate poverty or promote other forms of social or economic justice.

Social and Economic Justice

Let us begin with a discussion of **social and economic justice.** If social and economic justice were to be realized, members of diverse population groups would have an equal chance to achieve a reasonably comfortable standard of living. There would be fairness among people so that one's gender, race, ethnicity, sexual preference, and so on, would not act as handicapping conditions getting in the way of obtaining a good education, rewarding employment, fulfilling leisure opportunities, quality medical care, and other aspects of a comfortable standard of living. This is an ideal condition, of course, which would require vision and social cooperation to accomplish. Economic justice is part of the larger concept of social justice, relating specifically to people's right to an adequate income to secure the basic necessities of life (food, shelter, clothing, medical care, etc.).

Human Rights and Justice

Practice Behavior Example: Social workers engage in practices that advance social and economic justice

Critical Thinking Question: In what ways do you think social workers can help advance human rights and social and economic justice?

The United Nations' Universal Declaration of Human Rights, adopted in 1948, is an inspirational document comprising 30 articles that outline important elements of social justice. Hodge (2007) notes that this is still the most widely accepted human rights declaration in the world today. Article 1 affirms that "all human beings are born free and equal in dignity and rights. They are endowed with reason and conscience and should act towards one another in a spirit of brotherhood." Many other articles specify conditions necessary for the attainment of social justice as an overall ideal. Article 25 relates most specifically to economic justice (UN, 1948):

> Everyone has a right to a standard of living adequate for the health and well-being of himself and of his family, including food, clothing, housing and medical care and necessary social services, and the right to security in the event of unemployment, sickness, disability, widowhood, old age or other lack of livelihood in circumstances beyond his control.
>
> Motherhood and childhood are entitled to special care and assistance. All children, whether born in or out of wedlock, shall enjoy the same social protection.

Cynthia Rocha and Andrea McCarter (2003/2004) note that students need assistance to understand how social and economic justice relates to trends in the economy and social welfare policies and programs. This text will try to

Figure 3.1

One in Eight Americans on Food Stamps

Source: The *Christian Science Monitor*, Dec. 20, 2009, p. 27

further that understanding. This chapter's case study, for example, illustrates how poverty can result in young children left without parental supervision, lost educational opportunities, entire families experiencing hunger, and mothers forced to work outside the home although badly needed within. It introduces some of our national poverty programs purporting to ease the plight of the poor. But do our current policies and programs advance social and economic justice? Do they provide adequate "special care and assistance" to poor mothers and children as advocated by the United Nations' Declaration of Human Rights?

Although the United States is the wealthiest nation in the world today, poverty is widespread. More than one child in five lives in poverty, and the number is growing. Nearly 40 million Americans live in poverty, and that number is also growing. Approximately 49 million Americans suffer food insecurity (not enough food for healthful living; hunger), and more than 16 million of them are children (22.5 percent of all children). The United States, to its shame, has the highest child poverty rate of any industrialized nation in the Western world (Brown, 2010; The state of America's children, 2008; Hunger in the US, 2009). What does it say about a nation's commitment to social and economic justice when so many people, especially children, suffer poverty and malnutrition (see Figure 3.1)?

What does it say about a nation's commitment to social and economic justice when so many people, especially children, suffer poverty and malnutrition?

The Impact of Poverty

What is the matter with being poor? After all, some believe that poverty is beneficial, motivating family members to work hard, pull together, and practice frugality. Indeed, self-help efforts have assisted many poor people to survive. However, poverty is almost always harmful, because it substantially limits people's choices. Where it is severe, the means for securing necessities such as food and shelter are lacking, so that poverty can literally steal people's lives.

As noted by Irons (2009):

> Unemployment and income losses can reduce educational achievement by threatening early childhood nutrition; reducing families' abilities to provide a supportive environment (including adequate health care, summer activities, and stable housing); and by forcing a delay or abandonment of college plans. (p. 6)

Childhood poverty is of particular importance in terms of social policy, not only because children suffer disproportionately to other groups, but also because their experiences in childhood will have implications for their adult lives: childhood lays the foundations for adult abilities, interests, and motivations and, hence, is the keystone for assuring equal opportunities for adults.

A nation's social policies, if that nation so wills, can prevent child poverty and lay the foundations for a fulfilling, competent adulthood. This has been proven by the experiences of other countries, particularly the Scandinavian and some of the other European nations. But policies that create social and economic justice and eliminate poverty require an aware populace with the value base, political savvy, and determination to bring them about.

Policies that create social and economic justice and eliminate poverty require an aware populace with the value base, political savvy, and determination to bring them about.

POPULATIONS AT RISK

Everyone in the world is, to some degree, at risk of poverty and other hazards. But not everyone is at risk to the same degree. Those people who fall into the categories that research has found most likely to experience poverty, for reasons beyond their own control but not due to chance or laziness, are known as **populations at risk**.

Members of populations at risk make up the clientele with whom social workers do most of their work. Tomas, Tomacita, Carla, and Maria of this chapter's case study are members of various populations at risk; Sandra McLean of Chapter 2 is at risk because she is female, and further at risk because she has a disability. Susan and Martha Dunn of Chapter 1 are at risk because they are female, and Martha and Todd Dunn are at risk because they are children. Members of two or more categories of risk, such as children who are female or members of ethnic minorities, suffer increased risk.

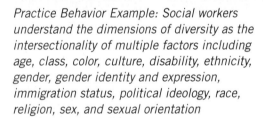

Diversity in Practice

Practice Behavior Example: Social workers understand the dimensions of diversity as the intersectionality of multiple factors including age, class, color, culture, disability, ethnicity, gender, gender identity and expression, immigration status, political ideology, race, religion, sex, and sexual orientation

Critical Thinking Question: Many diverse populations are "at risk" in the United States. Of what are they at risk, and why?

Children

Sadly, children comprise the United States' largest population at risk. During the 1980s, growth in child poverty rates led to the coining of the term **juvenilization of poverty.** The child poverty rate today is higher than it was 40 years ago; more than a third of all persons living in poverty in the United States today are children (Shierholz, 2009). In the last few years, child poverty has been rising even among working families. Between 2008 and 2010, for example, the poverty rate for children under the age of 18 rose from 19 percent to 22 percent (more than one child in five, over 14 million; US Census Bureau News, 2009; income, poverty and health Insurance in the United States: 2009—Highlights; About poverty – Highlights, 2011). Nearly 1 child in

12—more than 6 million—lived in extreme poverty or below half the poverty line (The state of America's children, 2008; Suitts, 2010). These figures, serious as they are, belittle the problem, because the United States' formula for determining the poverty line (to be discussed later in the chapter) severely underestimates the number of people who actually experience poverty.

While the poverty rate among all children is high, the proportion of poor children who are members of ethnic minorities is even higher. They suffer myriad undeserved privations. An interview with a Hispanic teen in Harlem illustrates how children raised in deprived urban environments feel about their value in this society (Kozol, 1996, p. 38):

> "Think of it this way," says a 16-year-old named Maria ———. "If people in New York woke up one day and learned that we were gone, that we had simply died or left for somewhere else, how would they feel?"
>
> "How do you think they'd feel?" I ask.
>
> "I think they'd feel relieved. I think it would lift a burden from their minds. I think the owners of the downtown stores would be ecstatic. They'd know they'd never need to see us coming in their doors, and taxi drivers would be happy because they would never need to come here anymore. People in Manhattan could go on and lead their lives and not feel worried about being robbed and not feel guilty and not need to pay for welfare babies."
>
> "It's not like, 'Well, these babies just aren't dying fast enough,' " Maria says. " 'Let's figure out a way to kill some more.' It's not like that at all. It's like—I don't know how to say this—." She holds a Styrofoam cup in her hands and turns it slowly for a moment. "If you weave enough bad things into the fibers of a person's life—sickness and filth, old mattresses and other junk thrown in the streets and other ugly ruined things, and ruined people, a prison here, sewage there, drug dealers here, the homeless people over there, then give us the very worst schools anyone could think of, hospitals that keep you waiting for 10 hours, police that don't show up when someone's dying, take the train that's underneath the street in good neighborhoods and put it above where it shuts out the sun, you can guess that life will not be very nice and children will not have much sense of being glad of who they are. Sometimes it feels like we've been buried six feet under their perceptions. This is what I feel they've accomplished."

Clearly, in the United States we do not enjoy the situation often piously described as "women and children first." Children especially often come last, and if the interview just quoted is evidence, they apparently know it. Children often feel unappreciated and unloved as well as poor and deprived. However, the situation is not necessary or inevitable, but the result of choices our elected representatives have made in major social policy decisions (see Box 3.1).

Women

Women compose another population at risk. Although progress has been made over the past two decades, that progress, unfortunately, may be less than what most people believe. Part of the problem is lack of access to high-paying professions. Women's limited ability to earn is shown by the disparity in average earnings between female and male full-time workers in the United States. Nearly half a century after the passage of the Fair Pay and Equal Pay Acts, the

Box 3.1 Poverty Kills

Poverty kills. It also maims and stunts the growth and eclipses the dreams of hundreds of millions of children around the world. Yet the fact that more than 20,000 people worldwide will die in extreme poverty will not make tomorrow's headlines. Similarly disregarded is the irony that America's poorest residents continue to be worse off than those of almost any other country in the developed world.

Poverty in America is a political problem, caused less by a lack of resources than by a failure to come to terms with reality. It is universally understood that food, shelter, health care, and other basics are crucial to the well-being of children and families. What is largely ignored by our leaders, the news media, and the public, however, is the fact that millions of families do not have adequate income to provide these necessities.

Source: From The State of America's Children® 2005. This material was created by the Children's Defense Fund online at http://www.childrensdefense.org/.

average woman worker in 2009 earned only 77 cents for every dollar earned by a man with similar work efforts, a penny lower than that in 2007 (Income, poverty and health insurance coverage in the United States, 2009). The disparity was even greater for women of color. College-educated women, who outperform men in every field of education including math and science, earn only about 80 percent of what their male peers earn. Ten years after graduation, college-educated women make only 69 percent of what their male counterparts earn (Oliver, 2007).

That gender discrimination is perceived to be a serious issue by many women today is illustrated by a number of recent class action sex discrimination lawsuits against several large employers such as Walmart and Morgan Stanley (Navetta, 2005). Achieving equality through legal action is not easy, however. For example, in May 2007, the U.S. Supreme Court ruled against a female employee, Lilly Ledbetter, of Goodyear Tire and Rubber Company. After being employed by Goodyear for many years, Ledbetter learned via an anonymous letter that she was earning several thousand dollars per year less than her male counterparts. She filed a legal challenge within a month of receiving the letter, but the Supreme Court ruled against her on the grounds that she had not filed within 180 days of original employment.

Ruth Bader Ginsburg, the only woman then on the Court, wrote a powerful dissent to the conservative Ledbetter ruling, calling on Congress to enact legislation to correct the "high court's parsimonious reading of pay inequity claims" (Terzieff, 2007). One of the bright spots in progress toward gender equity for American women took place in fall 2008 when a Democratic Congress passed the Lilly Ledbetter Fair Pay Act. This was the first act President Obama signed into law, on January 29, 2009. It stipulates that pay discrimination claims accrue with every discriminatory pay check an employee receives, not only when a discriminatory pay decision or practice is adopted (Lilly Ledbetter Fair Pay Act, 2009). However, in another regressive conservative decision in 2011, the U.S. Supreme Court ruled against women employees in their class action suit against Walmart.

While many women have branched out into nontraditional professions (women have increased their representation since 1989 in 106 of 497 occupations tracked by the U.S. Labor Department), most remain clustered in lower-paying jobs such as sales workers, secretaries, cashiers, nurses, elementary school teachers, hairdressers, receptionists, and so on (Francis, 2001). Gabriel and Schmitz (2007) conclude from their study of gender differences in occupational distribution that women are overrepresented in service, clerical, professional, and technical occupations because these occupations offer more "nonwage amenities" such as flexible work arrangements.

Women often require flexible work arrangements because they provide the bulk of the caregiving for children, elders, and other dependent persons. The average woman now spends 12 years out of the paid workforce caregiving ("You can't save," 2008). However, our economic system undervalues caregiving work. It completely overlooks the fact that caregiving *is* work when provided in the home. Because wages are not involved, caregiving work at home does not qualify a woman for her own Social Security benefits or for unemployment insurance if she is "fired" by her husband. It no longer entitles her to public assistance under the Social Security Act when she is a single parent with dependent children, even though women shoulder most of the burden of child rearing in cases of divorce or birth out of wedlock.

Outside the home, caregiving is poorly paid, exposing many female wage earners to poverty. It is not surprising that in 2008, nearly 38 percent of female-headed families lived in poverty, and the number continues to grow (Shierholz, 2009). The substantial poverty of women has led to the coining of the term **feminization of poverty.**

There is some good news for women—the Obama administration appointed over 1,000 women to government positions within the first year. One of these appointments was the Secretary of the U.S. Department of Health and Human Services, Kathleen Sebelius ("Women Appointees Celebrated," 2010). Empowerment of women can be significantly enhanced through such government actions.

Older Adults

Older adults compose another population at risk. There is some good news, however, for this group as well. Social Security amendments passed in the 1960s and 1970s (primarily Medicare and SSI, to be discussed later in the chapter) helped reduce poverty rates for people over age 65 from more than a third to 8.9 percent in 2009, the lowest rate among all age groups. It remained statistically unchanged at 9% in 2010 (Income, poverty and health insurance in the United States: 2009—Highlights; About poverty – Highlights, 2011). However, if a revised formula proposed by the National Academy of Sciences were used, the poverty rate for older Americans would be greater than 18 percent ("General information on Social Security," 2005; "Hidden pockets of elderly," 2009).

If older adults enjoy a poverty rate lower than that for the population as a whole, how can they be considered at risk? The fact is that the overall figures hide wide discrepancies among older people. Older women and ethnic minorities have a much higher poverty rate than the average. Social Security is the principal source of income for almost half of older Americans and pulls more than a third above the poverty line who otherwise would be desperately poor (Caldera, 2009). The G. W. Bush administration tried to privatize Social Security, but fortunately this effort failed as privatization most likely would have resulted in reduced benefits for many.

Elderly people in financial need frequently face discrimination in the workplace, and elderly women and members of ethnic minority groups are even more likely to face it. For those fortunate enough to receive a pension upon retirement, the pensions are almost always less than wages earned previously. Many people do not receive pensions at all. Companies are not legally required to offer pension plans, and those that do may go bankrupt and be unable to honor their commitments. Some older adults lose their pensions because they are intentionally laid off just before reaching retirement age. Today, many pension plans have been replaced by tax-sheltered annuity options, which involve substantial employee contributions and financial risk.

The percentage of older adults who are considered to live in poverty would rise significantly if the standard for measuring poverty were updated, critics believe. The poverty line used as today's standard was established in the early 1960s. It resulted from surveys taken from 1955 through 1961 that indicated that the ratio of food consumption to all other household expenditures was 1:3. A basic food budget was then generated by the Department of Agriculture and was multiplied by 3 to determine the **poverty line**. The food budget developed for the elderly was lower than that for younger people, so the official poverty line for the elderly was also lower. In 2009 it was $10,289 for a single older adult as compared with $11,161 for a younger person ("Poverty thresholds for 2009," 2010). The percentage of older adults who are recognized to be poor today would go up considerably if the poverty line used were the same as that for younger people. Moreover, the formula for determining the poverty line has not changed since the 1960s except to account for inflation, yet food now comprises only about one-seventh of average family expenditures (Karger & Stoesz, 2010). For this reason organizations such as the National Academy of Sciences have proposed updated means of measurement, so far without success.

Racial and Ethnic Minority Groups

Racial and **ethnic minority groups**, those with distinct biological or cultural characteristics different from the majority, are other major populations at risk. Groups that are considered minorities differ from country to country and from region to region. For example, although Hispanics are a minority group in the United States, that is not the case in Mexico or Latin America. The term *race* usually refers to physical or biological characteristics. In the United States, four racial **minority groups** are usually distinguished: Native Americans, African Americans, Hispanics, and Asian Americans. This can be confusing, because not all members of these groups are people of color. Persons who consider themselves Hispanic, for example, include both Whites and non-Whites. Thus Hispanics can more accurately be considered an ethnic group rather than a race.

Ethnic groups share certain cultural characteristics that distinguish them from others, such as customs, values, language, and a common history. An ethnic group may contain members of different races, as in the example of Hispanics, or it may differ culturally from the race it most resembles physically.

Racial and ethnic minority groups, earlier in U.S. history, were expected to become part of a national melting pot. Minority groups were thus pressured toward giving up cherished aspects of their cultural identities. Today, however, a new paradigm, or model for understanding, is emerging: **cultural pluralism** and ethnic diversity, in which difference is expected, acknowledged, tolerated, and even celebrated. This paradigm is increasingly embraced by social workers, and **cultural competency**, or the skill of communicating competently with people of contrasting cultures, is becoming an increasingly important expertise in social work practice (Lum, 2007). One simple reason: almost one in three Americans today, more than 100 million persons, are members of racial and ethnic minority groups (Bernstein, 2007).

Persons of ethnic minority heritage encounter increased risk of poverty and homelessness.

What minority groups have in common in the United States is that they have less power than the majority group. Lack of power renders minority group members vulnerable to discrimination and devaluation. (In this sense, females are considered a minority group, even though they constitute a numerical majority.) Discrimination in the United States influences the amount minorities are likely to earn so that they suffer a greater risk of poverty. For example, in 2010, while the poverty rate for non-Hispanic Whites was 9.9 percent, the rate for Asian Americans was 12.1 percent. The rate for Hispanics was 26.6 percent and for African Americans 27.4 percent (Income, poverty and health insurance in the United States: 2009—Highlights; About poverty – Highlights, 2011). The poverty rate for Native Americans was even higher; among women and children it was nearly one person in two (Racuya-Robbins, 2010).

Sometimes a person's racial or ethnic heritage affects where he or she can live more directly than income alone. Those who succeed financially despite discrimination may find themselves unwelcome and may be actively harassed in areas predominantly inhabited by persons of European background. Fortunately, due to civil rights activism and legislation in the 1960s, such harassment is no longer legal (see Box 3.2).

Arizona passed a law in 2010 that may reinstitute legal harassment of ethnic minorities, however. The law allows police to stop anyone "reasonably" suspected of being an illegal immigrant. Arizona has a large number of undocumented immigrants living in the state, and most are Hispanic. The law prohibits "racial profiling," but it seems more than likely that darker-skinned people will be the ones suspected of being illegal. Following Arizona, Utah, Indiana and Georgia passed similar laws, and in 2011, Alabama passed one that was even harsher, making it illegal for anyone even to assist an undocumented immigrant. Challenges to these laws continue as this chapter is being revised but sadly, other states are considering similar legislation (Reeves, 2011).

In some cases, the cultural heritage of a minority group has been actively suppressed, not only in historical times but also in the present. In the worst-case

---

Box 3.2   The Segregation Conundrum

Despite the election of an African American president in 2008, segregation persists in the United States. Even with significant civil rights legislation and widespread open housing laws, whole sections of cities, especially in the north, serve mainly Whites, whereas other sections, usually poorer ones, house African Americans. Some neighborhoods are inhabited mostly by Latinos and/or other ethnic minorities. Why should this be so? The answer to this conundrum seems to be as much custom and prejudice as economics. That is because, prior to learning habits of intolerance, children of different races can frequently be seen playing happily together in preschool settings, holding hands and skipping along merrily. Perhaps if all American youngsters could play together with youngsters of different races in their *very* earliest formative years and could continue to do so throughout their childhoods and on into adulthood, a new generation of Americans would view racial difference as nothing but an interesting fact of life. Then the enduring social custom of segregation might be transformed.

---

scenario, sometimes members of majority groups try to exterminate others entirely. The example of the Holocaust against Jewish people, Gypsies, homosexuals, and the disabled under Germany's Nazi regime during World War II is a case in point. In the United States, hundreds of thousands of Native Americans were exterminated during the migration of White people across the continent. Millions of people in Tibet were massacred by the Chinese in the 1960s and 1970s. The recent ethnic cleansings in Bosnia, Rwanda, Kosovo, Darfur, and other areas of the world, including Iraq, provide chilling evidence that people still have not learned that the example we set today plants seeds for the future.

Since the terrorist attacks in New York City and Washington, DC, in the fall of 2001, the United States has experienced a powerful new challenge relating to minority ethnic groups. Because the men who hijacked the planes crashing into the World Trade Center and the Pentagon were of Middle Eastern origin, people of that ethnic group immediately became suspect. Thousands, including students, were arrested without delay. Congress soon passed the USA Patriot Act, legislation that diminishes many cherished American civil liberties. For example, student records can now be subpoenaed if a judge agrees they might obtain information pertinent to terrorist investigations, and any person's residence can now be searched without that person's knowledge or consent. All phone records are now routed and stored in a national data bank for possible review.

The fear that understandably arose from the 2001 attacks was used by President G. W. Bush to declare war on Afghanistan and then Iraq, despite strongly expressed disagreement by the United Nations and most other nations of the world. Bush then declared, as America's commander-in-chief, that people captured in these wars were enemy combatants without any legal rights, as opposed to prisoners of war protected under the Geneva Convention.

Torture was used against the prisoners at Guantanamo Bay, and other terrorist suspects were kidnapped all over the world and taken to nations where torture was widespread, a practice called *extraordinary rendition* ("Anti-torture efforts on Capitol Hill," 2006). The purpose was to extract information from prisoners in ways that would not normally be legal in the United States under its Constitution. The U.S. Supreme Court overturned certain aspects of the Bush administration's policies (Civil liberties and human rights, 2004), and the United Nations Committee Against Torture called upon the United States to close the detention camp at Guantanamo Bay (Richey & Feldman, 2006).

The Obama administration began releasing carefully screened prisoners from Guantanamo Bay immediately after President Obama's inauguration in 2009, and he ordered that torture be halted. The camp, however, remains open as this chapter is being revised. Certain prisoners have no country willing to take them, and some are considered (at least by a vocal minority) too dangerous to release even to prisons in the United States.

Early in 2006, information was leaked to the press that the federal government under G. W. Bush was routinely tapping, without judicial warrants, the telephone conversations of all persons suspected of communicating with suspected terrorists (telephone conversations with any persons overseas); it was also collecting telephone records of every citizen in the United States. This practice continues today.

Many Americans agree that national security concerns should trump human rights, but legal and humanitarian protections lost to one are lost to all. If the President can remove legal protections and thus dehumanize anyone by declaring that person an "enemy combatant," who among us, besides the President, is free?

As noted by Grier (2001):

> Once bullets begin to fly, government officials must judge how much danger the nation is in, where those dangers lie, and whether the defense against them requires some abridgement of much-cherished individual rights—all under the pressure of onrushing time. History shows that they don't always get it right. The World War II internment of those of Japanese ancestry is today widely seen as a blot on the nation's honor. (p. 8)

People with Disabilities

People with disabilities are another population at risk, because people who do not have disabilities may hold negative attitudes toward those who do. An extreme example of the inhumane treatment that may result took place in Nazi Germany, where many were sent to concentration camps and exterminated. In the United States, historically, many people with disabilities were sent to public institutions and sterilized so they could not reproduce.

Today, persons with disabilities may find themselves subject to social ostracism, ridicule, job discrimination, and the like. The civil rights movement in the United States in the 1950s and 1960s helped develop an awareness of social justice issues for the disabled, and they and their families began to advocate for legal rights and protections. Legislation important to persons with disabilities in the United States will be discussed in Chapter 12.

Societal definitions of disability differ with time and are hotly debated; the consequences are serious because certain protected populations can benefit from legislation from which others are excluded. For example, tens of thousands of poor children lost their federal disability benefits as part of 1996 welfare reform legislation simply because of changes in the legal definition of disability.

Persons with disabilities experience many barriers, both social and economic, to full participation in today's world. Many suffer unemployment or underemployment. For this reason, many qualify for SSI, as did little Maria in this chapter's case example, but SSI rarely lifts a person with a disability above the poverty line. The Americans with Disabilities Act of 1990 was designed to help people with disabilities improve their chances of escaping poverty. It has had mixed results and will be discussed in more detail in Chapter 12.

Many Americans agree that national security concerns should trump human rights, but legal and humanitarian protections lost to one are lost to all.

Gay and Lesbian Persons

Discrimination is a fact of life for most gay and lesbian persons, and, unlike other groups who suffer this problem, federal civil rights protections have not yet been extended to include them. The reason seems to be that many people, because of their personal or religious values, do not accept those whose sexual orientation is toward persons of the same gender. While people have the right to choose their own values, discrimination against gays and lesbians is nevertheless discrimination against our fellow human beings.

Without civil rights protections, people who are gay and lesbian can be fired from their jobs, denied home mortgages, refused apartment rentals, and so on, without legal recourse. To protest these and other discriminatory practices, hundreds of thousands of gays, lesbians, and other civil rights activists marched on Washington in 1993, seeking to obtain civil rights protection under the law. The efforts failed to obtain their immediate objective, but gay rights did gain recognition as a national issue.

In 1994, a Republican Congress was elected, slowing progress toward equality considerably. Concerned that the state of Hawaii was about to legalize gay marriages, Congress responded by passing the Defense of Marriage Act of 1996. This act permitted states not to accept as legal gay marriages performed in any other state.

In 2000, gays and lesbians won a joyful victory in Vermont, when the state legislature approved civil unions for same-sex couples, legally equivalent to marriage (Marks, 2000). Another step forward was taken when the Massachusetts Supreme Court ruled in 2003 that barring persons to marry solely because those persons wanted to marry persons of the same sex violated the Massachusetts constitution (Paulson & Stern, 2003).

As of this writing, six states, Connecticut, Iowa, Massachusetts, New Hampshire, New York, and Vermont, plus Washington, DC, have legalized gay marriage. In addition, Maryland recognizes same-sex marriages from other states. Several states recognize domestic partnerships and/or civil unions: California, Colorado, Delaware, Hawaii, Illinois, Maine, Nevada, New Jersey, Oregon, Rhode Island, Washington, and Wisconsin. These arrangements confer many or all of the legal rights of marriage to committed same-sex couples. But the majority of states specifically ban gay marriage. Ironically, Hawaii, the first state to legalize gay marriage through a court decision, now bars it via constitutional amendment, although civil unions are permitted; and voters in Maine and California overturned court decisions that had legalized gay marriage in those states (Farrell, 2010; "State by state," 2009; Same-sex marriage, 2011).

Gays and lesbians have responded with courage to discrimination against them. When the state of Colorado passed a ban against antidiscrimination protection laws for gays and lesbians, activists scored a victory when they appealed the ban to the Supreme Court. In the 1996 case of *Romer v. Evans,* the Supreme Court ruled that Colorado's prohibition was unconstitutional (Segal & Brzuzy, 1998).

Despite the fact that President George W. Bush proposed constitutional amendments to ban gay marriage throughout the country virtually every year of his administration, progress has been made in recent years. Gay marriage became legal in Iowa in 2009, thanks to the decision of the Iowa Supreme Court. A move to initiate a constitutional amendment to ban gay marriage in the Iowa legislature failed, although it may be reintroduced in the future. In 2009, the Vermont legislature legalized gay marriage, and Washington, DC, did so the same year. New York approved gay marriage in 2011. Gay marriage activists in California filed a lawsuit challenging the constitutionality of California's voter-approved ban on gay marriage in 2008; in 2010 a federal court ruling by U.S. District Judge Vaughn Walker found that the state's amendment was unconstitutional. The issue seems likely to end up in the U.S. Supreme Court (Heining, 2010).

To help protect gay and lesbian persons from violence, President Obama in 2009 signed into law federal legislation that includes acts of violence against gay and lesbian persons under the list of federal hate crimes. He then began working to modify the "don't ask, don't tell" policy requiring gays in the military to remain "in the closet" if they wanted to remain in military service. Obama was successful: in late 2010, with his urging, a lame duck Congress passed legislation permitting gays and lesbians to serve openly in the military.

POTENT FORMS OF DISCRIMINATION IN THE UNITED STATES

Although Americans proclaim an overall belief in equal justice for all, and although various social movements have produced important legislation to protect the rights of minority groups, a marked discrepancy still exists between principle and practice today. Certain potent societal isms are clearly still in evidence.

Isms are prejudices common to large segments of society that relegate people who are perceived as different to a lower social status. Isms in the United States stem from cultural teachings such as White is better, male is better, young is better, and heterosexual is better. Isms have many consequences, including the fact that minority populations are at risk. Risk can vary from milder forms of social discrimination such as lack of access to certain jobs and lower pay to attempted extermination of the devalued population. Sadly, people who suffer discrimination often take their poor treatment to heart, and so they suffer loss of self-esteem as well.

Racism

Racism is the belief that one race is superior to others, a belief that tends to justify exploiting members of other races. In the United States, the majority race includes a variety of white-skinned ethnic groups of European origin, who tend to consider themselves superior to people with darker skin. Racism leads to discrimination against people of color perpetrated by both individuals and social institutions such as governmental bodies and private organizations. Institutional racism, or patterns of racial discrimination entrenched in law and custom, lives on in many subtle forms today. It was far more blatant, of course, before the civil rights movement of the 1960s and early 1970s. The civil rights movement was sparked in 1955 by Mrs. Rosa Parks's courageous refusal to obey a White man's demand that she give up her seat on a Montgomery, Alabama, bus, as required by racist laws.

Today, overtly racist laws have been ruled unconstitutional, but subtler institutional racism and personal affronts continue. Ongoing racism is clearly illustrated in the United States today by the residential segregation visible throughout most of the nation.

Sexism

Sexism is the belief that one sex is superior to the other, usually that males are superior to females. This belief tends to justify exploiting females economically and sexually. Sexism is undergirded, unfortunately, by various organized religions that cite ancient texts alleging the superiority of the male. However, modern scholars have found substantial evidence indicating that these texts were selectively edited over time to conceal the value of female roles and to stifle women's leadership potential. Whole books have been written about this fascinating subject, including *The Gnostic Gospels* by Elaine Pagels (1979), *Beyond Belief* by the same author (2003), and *The Chalice and the Blade* by Riane Eisler (1987).

Although numerous laws have been adopted in recent times to help create equal opportunity for females, a constitutional amendment, stating simply, "Equal rights under law shall not be denied or abridged by the United States or by any State on account of sex," was never ratified. Many women helped fight to maintain gender inequality, fearing loss of certain legal protections such as exemption from military draft. However, it is unlikely that the draft, if reinstated in the future, would exclude women anyway. Women's contributions to the paid labor force are simply too important to ignore today.

Discrimination against females has important effects. Girls and young women tend to limit their aspirations to the types of positions they perceive they can get. Unskilled women, for example, tend to fill service positions, while educated women disproportionately select service professions like nursing, teaching, and social work. Women are characteristically paid less than men, even with the same education, the same job position, and the same number of years of paid work experience. This injustice forces many women to remain economically dependent on men (Navetta, 2005).

Ageism

Ageism is the belief that youth is superior to age, that old people have outlived their usefulness and therefore are of little value. Ageism involves such stereotypes as that the majority of old people are senile, old-fashioned, and different. These stereotypes tend to justify discrimination against the elderly.

Robert Butler (1994), the social scientist who originally coined the term *ageism,* pointed out a peculiar irony many years ago that is still true today. Most people dream of a long life, and in general this hope is being realized. However, instead of celebrating the possibility of longer years for themselves, younger people view the elderly as potential economic burdens. They resent older adults' access to Social Security benefits at the same time that they fear that the Social Security system will be bankrupt by the time they are old enough to collect. Butler pointed out that this fear is greatly exaggerated because, due to the falling birthrate, the total dependency–support ratio (ratio including dependents both below 18 and over 64 to working adults in a given family) has been steadily declining since 1900. It will continue to do so until 2050.

Myths that most older adults are senile and physically debilitated are simply that: myths. Most older people describe their health as reasonably good. Memory loss is associated more with stress than with age, and it is usually reversible. The exception is memory loss caused by medical factors, such as Alzheimer's disease (see Chapter 10). Younger people, however, can also be victims of this disease. Various studies have shown that what appear to be characteristics of aging, such as decreased mobility and memory loss, can also afflict younger people. These difficulties can often be reversed even among the very old with proper health and mental health care.

Heterosexism and Homophobia

Heterosexism is the belief that heterosexuals are superior to homosexuals. **Homophobia** is the fear, dread, or hatred of people who are homosexual. Both lead to social and economic discrimination against people who are gay or lesbian. There was a time when homosexuality was viewed as a mental disorder. However, research has led to the knowledge that sexual orientation has nothing to do with one's mental health (except, of course, that discrimination can result in fear and depression). For this reason, homosexuality is no longer listed as a pathology in the *Diagnostic and Statistical Manual of Mental Disorders, Fourth Edition, Text Revision (DSM-IV-TR)* used by mental health professionals. Gays and lesbians are similar to other people in every way except their sexual orientation. No one understands the causes of homosexuality, but it generally is not considered a personal choice; hence, most gays and lesbians prefer to speak of **sexual orientation** rather than "sexual preference."

SOCIAL JUSTICE ISSUES IN THE 21ST CENTURY

Discriminatory treatment, as discussed earlier, tends to result in ongoing poverty by a disproportionate percentage of populations at risk. Poverty directly causes many other problems, such as hunger and homelessness. These remain important social justice concerns in the 21st century. The following issues are of great concern to the profession of social work.

Poverty Programs That Maintain Poverty

Most U.S. financial assistance programs leave beneficiaries far below the poverty level. For example, consider the poverty suffered by Tomas and Tomacita and their mother in our chapter's case example. The mother worked hard, albeit in a state Temporary Assistance to Needy Families (TANF) program. But she was not paid even the equivalent of the federal minimum wage—rather, she received a stipend of $800 per month, or about $13,200 per year counting food stamp assistance. Her budget looked roughly like this:

Income:	$800	Income from TANF
	300	Food stamps
Total	$1,100	
Expenses:	$490	Rent (heat included)
	350	Food for three
	60	Electricity
	35	Laundry
	60	Transportation to TANF program
	65	Clothes (including diapers)
	40	Telephone
Total	$1,100	

By comparison, the 2009/2010 Federal Poverty Guidelines list $18,310 as "100% of poverty" for a family of three ("FY 2009/2010 federal poverty guidelines," 2009), many thousands of dollars more per year than what this family was trying to survive on. No wonder the mother couldn't afford a babysitter. No wonder she and many other TANF participants in her neighborhood frequently relied on Urban Neighborhood Center's food pantry to help keep body and soul together. Note that there was no room in this budget for child care, miscellaneous items, emergencies, or recreation. It seems as if we like to punish the poor just for being poor, as if they have no right to enjoyment or security of any kind.

Most U.S. financial assistance programs leave beneficiaries far below the poverty level.

Poverty Line Determination Method

As mentioned earlier, the method of determining the nation's poverty line has not been revised or updated for many years, except for inflation. When developed in the 1960s, it was based on the price of food. The Department of Agriculture's least expensive food plan was multiplied by 3, because an earlier study showed that the average family at that time spent about one-third of its income on food (Fisher, 1998). Today, however, housing, utilities, child care, and medical care make up a much higher proportion of the average family's budget. Many experts believe that a true analysis of modern costs of living would require a much higher poverty line.

Poverty and the Minimum Wage

U.S. social policy seems to be based on the idea that anyone can find a job and that, by working, people can pull themselves and their families out of poverty. The problem is that this idea does not represent reality for large numbers of Americans today. Many people simply do not possess the educational qualifications or the technical skills required to get the jobs that are available. And in many places today, jobs that pay wages that can lift a family out of poverty simply do not exist.

Many people who work full-time remain in poverty. This problem is rooted in government policy. The federal minimum wage in 1968 was set so that a worker employed full-time at that wage could maintain a family of three (husband, wife, and child) at 120 percent of the poverty line. The minimum wage, however, has never been indexed to inflation. It remained at $5.15 per hour for a full 10 years, from 1997 until early 2007, when a new Democratic Congress was able to pressure President Bush into signing an increased minimum wage law. The minimum wage rose to $5.85 in the summer of 2007, to $6.55 in the summer of 2008, and to $7.25 in the summer of 2009 (Federal Minimum Wage Increase for 2007).

Even when the minimum wage finally reached $7.25 per hour in 2009, a full-time employee earning that wage still took home less than a poverty level income for a family of three. The Children's Defense Fund pointed out that if the minimum wage had increased at the same rate as the pay of CEOs between 1990 and 2005, the minimum wage would have been $23.03 per hour, not $5.15 per hour, in 2005! The low minimum wage has had devastating effects on children and their families (The state of America's children, 2005).

Affirmative Action Policies: Under Attack

Affirmative action policies are designed to try to "level the playing field" for populations at risk. Due to historical exploitation, prejudice, discrimination, and the isms discussed earlier in this chapter, members of populations at risk suffer economic hardships through no fault of their own. There are two main approaches in the United States to address this injustice: **nondiscrimination** and **affirmative action**. Nondiscrimination laws simply ban discrimination. The Civil Rights Act of 1964 was the first powerful national legislation to bar discrimination, carrying with it the power of the courts. Title VII of this act, as amended in 1972, prohibits employment discrimination on the basis of race, color, religion, sex, or national origin. Today, age and disability are also protected categories.

Despite the Civil Rights Act, discrimination remained widespread, so courts began to require companies who lost discrimination cases to engage in affirmative action efforts to improve compliance with the law. Affirmative action required targeted outreach toward minorities.

This approach has always been controversial, because a member of a protected minority might be recruited ahead of an equally qualified member of a nonprotected category. Such instances have led to accusations of *reverse discrimination*. Court decisions since 1978 have been inconsistent, sometimes upholding affirmative action efforts and sometimes not. In general, with conservative political trends, affirmative action is under attack and policies have become weaker. A recent assault on affirmative action came with the Supreme Court decision in 2007 not to allow race as a deciding factor in assigning students to certain schools. Many public school systems had used race as a factor in school assignment to maintain racially integrated school populations. The decision was 5–4; had Sandra Day O'Connor not left the Court, to be replaced by President Bush's choice of an ideologically conservative justice, Samuel Alito, the decision would likely have gone 5–4 the other way (Richey, 2007) (see Box 3.3).

Social Policy and the Growing Gap between Rich and Poor

The old saying "the rich get richer and the poor get poorer" has been the reality for the United States over the past several decades. Wealth in America (the value of everything a family owns, minus debts) has

---

Box 3.3   Up for Debate

Proposition: Affirmative action programs should be maintained to assist in provision of equal opportunity for all.

Yes	No
Affirmative action programs help correct past discriminatory hiring practices by seeking qualified applicants of color and women.	Affirmative action programs may discriminate against people who are white, especially white males.
Affirmative action programs help ensure that jobs are genuinely and equally accessible to qualified persons without regard to sex, race, or ethnicity.	Affirmative action programs may hire women and people of color rather than others who are equally or sometimes more qualified.
Affirmative action programs help ensure that qualified persons of merit gain employment, even if minority or female, rather than applicants who simply happen to be white and male.	Affirmative action programs may help qualified minorities and females gain employment rather than white males who may be equally qualified.
In a democratic, multiracial society, integrated institutions can provide higher levels of service than agencies run entirely by one sex and race.	The most qualified applicants should always be hired, even if they all happen to be white and male.

increasingly been concentrating in the hands of the privileged few. The top 1 percent owns approximately 34.6 percent of all private wealth; the next level (managerial, small business, and professional), about 19 percent of the population, owns 50.5 percent; while the majority at the bottom, the wage and salary workers who comprise 80 percent of the population, own only 15 percent (Domhoff, 2009).

The gap between the rich and the poor is growing in large part due to deliberate social policies at the national level justified by conservative ideology. The shamefully low minimum wage is one such policy. The George W. Bush administration's personal income tax reduction tremendously favoring the rich is another. But perhaps even more devastating is a tax policy that has led to the decrease of manufacturing jobs in the United States, a policy that allows U.S.-owned multinational corporations to avoid paying taxes on profits earned in other countries (Rocha & McCarter, 2003/2004). As a result, large numbers of these companies have moved their operations abroad, and thousands upon thousands of Americans have lost jobs that paid union wages. New jobs have primarily been available in the service and retail sectors of the economy, in which wages are much lower (and benefits much poorer, if available at all).

Health Insurance Accessibility

A huge number of Americans under the age of 65—nearly 47 million in 2005—lacked health insurance, and the number was continuing to grow at a frightening rate when President Obama was elected in 2008. More than 8 in 10 of the uninsured came from working families with jobs that did not provide benefits (National Coalition on Health Care, 2007). Nine million of the uninsured were children, and millions more children were underinsured ("Nine million uninsured children," 2007).

Good news finally arrived in 2010—after a full year of squabbling in Congress, where Republicans refused all support, the Obama administration was finally able to pass the Affordable Health Care Act. Many compromises had to be made in order to secure the Democratic votes needed (no Republican would vote for the bill). The new law promises affordable health care coverage to the majority of Americans. Time will tell how the law unfolds, as it is being challenged in court as this chapter is being revised, but in its current form its provisions allow students to remain on their parents' health insurance policies up to the age of 26. It denies insurance companies the right to exclude children with preexisting conditions, and forbids insurance companies from excluding adults with preexisting conditions beginning in 2014. A time-limited government program insures adults with preexisting conditions until 2014. The Act forbids insurance companies from placing lifetime caps on benefits.

Administrative Barriers to Aid

A different type of concern is that the U.S. welfare system often discourages even eligible categories of people from applying for aid. Forms are lengthy and complicated; they are especially confusing to people with limited education or whose first language is other than English. Work requirements under new TANF programs can be confusing and discouraging to people who lack child care provisions, adequate clothing for work, or transportation. Even if needy people decide to apply anyway, they may end up languishing on waiting lists, like Tomas and Tomacita's mother in this chapter's case example, who was still waiting for child care assistance. Such complications are known as administrative barriers to aid.

Social Welfare Policy and Social Justice

Social justice remains a major, even a growing, issue today. However, many organized attempts have been made to alleviate the suffering of poor people over the past centuries. Assistance is sometimes informal: for example, private acts of charity have been carried out by individuals, families, and religious groups from time immemorial. But in recent centuries, social justice issues have also led to government legislation creating formal public social welfare policies and programs designed to assist at least some of the poor.

Social welfare policy establishes the goals and procedures that enable social welfare programs to commence and to operate. Such policy is often established by government legislation. For a glimpse of public social welfare programs sanctioned by government social welfare policy in the United States today, let us consider this chapter's case example.

While many families living near the Urban Neighborhood Center were very poor, a few public programs were available that assisted them to some degree, even though these programs did not lift the families out of poverty. As discussed earlier, Tomas and Tomacita's mother was enrolled in the **TANF** program. Maria Romero was assisted by SSI and Medicaid because she was a severely disabled child. TANF is a cash benefit program (requiring work or work training) run by the county but established under state law according to federal guidelines. SSI is a cash benefit program for certain categories of poor people administered by the federal government, and Medicaid is a federal program administered by the state that provides medical care for certain categories of poor people.

These programs are all part of the U.S. system or institution of social welfare. They help families survive, but, sadly, are not designed to lift poor people out of poverty. Hence efforts by voluntary organizations and private charities to help poor Americans remain essential for basic survival. The next chapter will focus on the development of social welfare policies and programs in the United States today, both public and private.

SUMMARY

The cases of Tomas and Tomacita and of Carla and Maria Romero dramatize the predicament of people who are dependent on a variety of income maintenance and social service programs in the United States. The introduction of programs such as TANF, replacing Aid to Families with Dependent Children, along with limited funding for other public programs such as public health, powerfully affects the lives of poor children and families.

Populations at high risk of poverty in the United States are identified and discussed, along with various isms that increase this risk through stigma and an undermining of political strength. These populations include children, women, older adults, racial and ethnic minorities, people with disabilities, and gays and lesbians. They are the ones usually in most need of assistance from the social work profession.

Major social justice issues facing the nation are examined. For example, poverty programs in the United States leave their beneficiaries in poverty; application processes for very limited assistance are complicated and time consuming. The measure used to determine the poverty line is outdated and does not reveal the true extent of poverty in this country. The national minimum wage leaves a family of three below the poverty line even if a parent works full time. The populations at risk identified in this chapter face discrimination and lower wages in the job market. The wealth gap between the rich and the poor in America is huge and growing. All of these issues are of concern to the social work profession.

PRACTICE TEST The following questions will test your knowledge of the content found within this chapter. For additional assessment, including licensing-exam type questions on applying chapter content to practice behaviors, visit **MySearchLab.**

1. The Defense of Marriage Act_____.
   a. prohibits same-sex marriage in Hawaii
   b. prohibits domestic partnerships
   c. legalizes same-sex marriage in Iowa
   d. was passed by the U.S. Congress in 1996

2. The U.S. constitutional amendment providing equal rights to both genders was_____.
   a. never ratified
   b. ratified by Congress in 1979
   c. vetoed by the U.S. President in 1920
   d. an example of cultural competency

3. Historically, U.S. policy allowed public institutions to_____.
   a. restrict disability benefits for residents
   b. sterilize residents who had a disability
   c. exterminate individuals who had a disability, just like Nazi in Germany
   d. have no control over residents with a disability

4. Cultural pluralism refers to_____.
   a. communicating competently with people from contrasting cultures
   b. the acknowledgment, tolerance and expectation of ethnic diversity in social interactions
   c. creation of a national melting pot of minority groups
   d. racial differences between minority groups

5. Economic justice refers to_____.
   a. provision of free education for all individuals
   b. provision of free medical care for all individuals
   c. establishment of an equal opportunity to secure the basic necessities of life
   d. mandating fairness in employment decisions

6. _____ and _____ are forms of oppression and discrimination.
   a. Civil rights laws, residential segregation
   b. Respect for the wisdom gained with age, retirement
   c. White male privilege, paying women less for the same job done by a man
   d. Homophobia, domestic partnership benefits

7. Community agency social workers wear many hats and fill many roles within a community-based agency. In the case of Juanita Chavez, identify the various social work roles that she fulfilled and discuss how her actions demonstrated competency as an identified professional social worker.

Reinforce what you learned in this chapter by studying videos, cases, documents, and more available at **www.MySearchLab.com**.

Watch and Review

Watch these Videos

* Building Self-Awareness
* Understanding Forms of Oppression and Discrimination

Read and Review

Read these Cases/Documents

Δ A Puzzling Case Involving a Cambodian Patient

Δ Travis: A Case of Working with Children in Juvenile Detention

Explore and Assess

Explore these Assets

Toberman Neighborhood Center—http://www.toberman.org/

East Side House Settlement—http://www.eastsidehouse.org/

Influencing State Policy—http://www.statepolicy.org/

Poverty Guidelines, U.S. Department of Health and Human Services—http://aspe.hhs.gov/poverty/index.shtml

Assess Your Knowledge

Assess your knowledge with a variety of topical and chapter assessment.

Conclude your assessment by completing the chapter exam.

* = CSWE Core Competency Asset
Δ = Case Study

4

Social Welfare Policy: Historical Perspectives

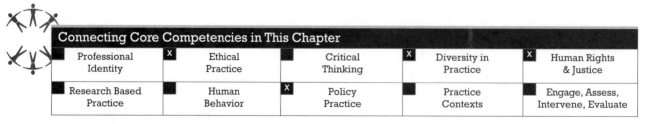

Connecting Core Competencies in This Chapter									
	Professional Identity	X	Ethical Practice		Critical Thinking	X	Diversity in Practice	X	Human Rights & Justice
	Research Based Practice		Human Behavior	X	Policy Practice		Practice Contexts		Engage, Assess, Intervene, Evaluate

Donna Rudnitski

Donna Rudnitski, BSW, put down her local newspaper with a sigh and turned to her husband. "Ray," she said, "things are getting pretty bad around here. The newspaper says that our county's unemployment rate is over 13%."

"I didn't know it was that bad," Ray replied, "but with the furniture factory closing down two years ago and the sports equipment store going bankrupt last year, I'm not surprised. The cutlery factory moved to China last year, too, and that sure didn't leave much work for people around here."

"Most people who are laid off can get unemployment benefits for awhile," Donna mused, "and usually some food stamps. Food pantries can help a little also, but now a lot of people are losing their homes because they can't pay the mortgage. They have no place to go."

"I thought people who got foreclosed on by the banks were getting sent down to the city," Ray replied, "so they could stay in shelters there."

"True," Donna responded, "they are. But the city shelters are overflowing, from what I hear at work."

Donna worked in the foster care section of her local human services department. She had already placed children in foster care because the parents had lost their homes and didn't want the children living on the streets. Donna hated this part of her job, because she felt something should be done to help these families stay together.

Her concern growing, Donna made an appointment to talk with the director of her human services department. She found that the director too was alarmed about the local homeless situation. He had already spoken with the mayor of the town to see if there were any funds available for emergency housing. But no money was accessible. Tax revenues were down because of unemployment, and budget allocations were being cut.

Donna and Ray talked the problem over again a few days later, when they read in the newspaper that another local business, a building supply store, was going under. That would mean more breadwinners would lose their jobs. What would happen to them and their families?

"If public agencies can't help, what about our church," Ray asked? "We have a parish hall that could house a few homeless families."

"But that would get in the way of the Sunday school, the women's club meetings, the scout meetings, 4-H—I don't think our pastor would allow it," Donna said slowly. "But it couldn't hurt to find out."

The next Sunday morning Donna asked her pastor, Reverend Jonas, if she could talk with him privately after church. The pastor readily agreed, thinking that Donna wanted to consult about a family problem. What he heard, of course, was about a multiple-family problem. Reverend Jonas was already aware of the growing issue of local families losing their homes. Some of the newly homeless belonged to his church.

"Well," the man said thoughtfully, "we could probably take several families in for a short while, but a few will need shelter for months—we can't give up church space for that long." He looked sympathetic but started to shake his head.

Donna had an idea. "What if other churches in town would join us?" she asked. "Maybe the churches could take turns, so that each one would only have to give up space for a short time?"

And so the Compassionate Council of Churches was born. Eight local churches plus four more in nearby towns agreed to shelter homeless families for 1 week each on a rotating basis. Each church agreed to find volunteers to help with cooking, cleaning, and transporting children to school.

One of the churches donated an old, unused parsonage to serve as a day center for adults. The Council decided to hire a social worker to run the day center and to assist adults in finding work and more permanent shelter. Donna Rudnitski applied for the job, even though she knew it would involve a cut in pay.

The Rutherford Family. Katherine and George Rutherford considered themselves comfortably middle class. Now in their early 40s, they were proudly helping their two children, Tina, 20, and Anthony, 19, attend college. To help with the college expenses, they had recently taken out a substantial second mortgage on their home. Mortgage payments were something of a stretch, but they paid every month on time. Kathy worked part time on the cleaning staff of a nearby motel, and George worked for a local building supply store.

When disaster struck it took place so fast the family could hardly understand what was happening. First, Kathy felt a lump in her right breast. A biopsy showed that she had cancer and needed immediate surgery. The day after this frightening diagnosis, George was laid off from his job. The faltering economy had harmed the building supply business. Now the family had no health insurance, formerly provided by George's employer.

Kathy and George had a small savings account, which could cover their normal bills for about 2 months, but the cost of Kathy's cancer surgery was well beyond their means. At first the couple hoped they could continue their health insurance temporarily through a government-mandated program called COBRA, but George's former employer was too small to be covered. The couple then anxiously called several hospitals to try to locate the least expensive surgery available. The lowest they could find was an operation costing $25,000, not including follow-up care.

If Kathy were to live, she had to have that surgery. But in addition, she needed chemotherapy and radiation in follow-up. Kathy went ahead with the surgery, quitting her job just beforehand because she knew the operation would make it too painful for her to do the lifting and bending required (the motel where she worked part time was so small that it did not offer sick days or sick pay). While recovering from surgery, Kathy decided to forgo the follow-up treatments for her cancer because of the cost. She knew she was gambling with her life, but she felt she had no choice.

Soon Kathy and George were struggling with medical bills piling up unpaid. They got behind on their mortgage. George's unemployment benefits helped somewhat, but they paid far too little to cover expenses. Embarrassed, the couple found themselves applying for food stamps and seeking additional help at a local food pantry.

Desperate, Kathy and George advised their son and daughter that they could no longer help with college costs, but they urged Tina and Anthony to do whatever possible to continue their education. The resourceful students applied for loans and work study funds and were able to stay in school, but they were not able to help their parents financially. They grieved for their parents and for themselves as well, because they knew they might lose their childhood home.

Soon, Kathy and George decided that they had to file for bankruptcy. The procedure allowed them to keep their house, but they still could not meet the mortgage payments. Kathy was not feeling well enough to work, and George could not find a new job. While the recession was severe everywhere, the couple lived in an area where unemployment was even higher than the national average. They fell further and further behind financially, and after a few months, the bank foreclosed.

What to do? Where to go? It was the Rutherford's pastor, Reverend Jonas, who urged the couple to consider staying temporarily in the shelter organized by the Compassionate Council of Churches. He apologized that they would have to share space with many other people including young children and would have to move sleeping quarters every week. He was glad to be able to tell them, however, that there was a day center that stayed in one place.

In better times, the Rutherfords had contributed to the shelter fund through their church, never dreaming that they would need to make use of it themselves. Fearful but grateful, they moved in. The next morning, at the day center, they met social worker Donna Rudnitski, who had recently been hired for the new position. Donna welcomed them warmly and offered support by listening with empathy to the Rutherford's ongoing ordeal.

Donna soon realized that, in addition to housing, a pressing need for Kathy Rutherford was additional medical treatment. President Obama had recently succeeded in shepherding his health care bill through Congress, even though not a single Republican had voted for it. Donna knew there was a provision in the bill providing a high-risk pool insurance program for people with preexisting medical conditions, but she doubted that it could help someone like Kathy, who had no income to purchase it. Donna wondered if she could possibly find free care for Kathy, given the life-threatening situation.

SOCIAL WELFARE POLICY

What is **social welfare**? Social welfare is a system, sometimes referred to as an institution, comprising a wide variety of policies, programs, and services that help people meet their basic needs. These needs may be economic, social, health-related, and/or educational. The institution of social welfare not only helps individuals to survive but ideally promotes harmony and stability in the wider society. Is social welfare the same as social work? Not exactly, although the two are certainly related. Social work, as described in Chapter 1, is a profession with the purpose of assisting people to improve their lives. The profession frequently makes use of the programs and services provided by the social welfare system. Social work is really only one profession among many that can be considered part of the U.S. institution of social welfare. Other professions that also contribute to helping people meet social, economic, educational, and health needs are medicine, education, library science, and law, to name only a few.

Because many of the decisions and referrals a social worker makes rely on familiarity with the various programs available within the social welfare system, we will focus on them before turning to the fields of practice explored in the coming chapters.

Social work is really only one profession among many that can be considered part of U.S. institution of social welfare.

SOCIAL WELFARE POLICY IN THE OLD WORLD

Social Welfare Concepts: Residual versus Institutional

Wilensky and Lebeaux (1965) pointed out more than 50 years ago that the United States holds two dominant conceptions of social welfare: residual and institutional. These distinctions are valid today.

Those who endorse the residual approach to social welfare believe that people should normally be able to meet all their needs through their own family or through the job market. Only after the family and the job market have failed should the formal social welfare system get involved. Under these circumstances the assistance is considered *residual;* it is activated only as a temporary, emergency measure. Services are accompanied by the stigma of charity, as they imply personal failure. The intent is that they be short term, lasting only for the duration of the emergency.

Box 4.1   Residual and Institutional Concepts of Social Welfare

Residual Approach	Institutional Approach
• Needs are to be met through family and job market.	• Social welfare system is viewed as part of first line of defense.
• Aid from welfare system is considered abnormal.	• Aid from government welfare system is considered normal.
• Aid is offered after family and job market have failed.	• Aid is offered before family breakdown, for preventive purposes.
• Aid is temporary, emergency, and as little as possible.	• Aid is preventive, ongoing, and adequate to meet needs.
• Stigma is attached.	• No stigma is attached.

Policy Practice

Practice Behavior Example: Social workers know the history and current structures of social policies and services; the role of policy in service delivery; and the role of practice in policy development

Critical Thinking Question: Which approach to social policy do you think would best meet current human needs, the residual or the institutional? Why?

Under the institutional conception, social welfare services are viewed as "normal, first line functions of modern industrial society" (Wilensky & Lebeaux, 1965, p. 138). According to the institutional view, social welfare services should be offered routinely as part of normal, nonemergency, problem-solving processes; they should be available without stigma to help prevent further problems. This approach assumes that in a complex society, everyone needs assistance at times. For example, even the best workers may lose their jobs when a company downsizes.

The social welfare system in the United States today reflects both the residual and the institutional approaches. Historically, the residual approach is older. Developments during and after the Great Depression of the 1930s pulled the social welfare system strongly toward the institutional concept, however. Then, during the 1970s, conservative politicians and presidential administrations began to pull it back toward the residual approach. This pull is extremely powerful today. The two concepts of social welfare are outlined in Box 4.1.

Now, let us examine the historical roots of the social welfare system in the United States, because what happened in the past has shaped what the system looks like today.

Old World Historical Roots

Social welfare policy is controversial today, and perhaps it always has been. Questions inevitably arise about whom to help and how much. We may think we want to help our neighbor, but how much? And are we interested in helping a stranger at all?

The earliest form of assistance for the needy was probably mother caring for child. Mutual aid among adults familiar with each other would be another example of help for the needy in early times, when reciprocal helping was provided by extended family members or members of one's tribe.

Only when more formal institutions had developed could a concept like *aid to the stranger* arise. One of the earliest known forms of aid to the stranger was provided by religious groups. The idea that services to the poor should be provided by *faith-based organizations* clearly goes back a long way!

In Judeo-Christian tradition, almsgiving was commonly practiced. The commandment "Love thy neighbor," accentuated in the New Testament but based on early Scripture, motivated people to give of what they had. Many believed that aiding the needy would provide a means of salvation in the next world. Some religious groups established formal tithes, with a portion of the money raised being used for assistance to the poor. Such assistance was residual in nature, because it was offered as temporary charity in times of emergency.

England provided the model for social welfare provisions in its colonies in America, and so we will focus on the social welfare history of that country. Responsibility for the poor in England remained primarily a function of the church until the arrival of the Black Death (bubonic plague) from continental Europe in 1348. So many people died that a labor shortage resulted. In 1349, a law was passed called the Statute of Laborers, which forbade able-bodied people to leave their parishes and required them to accept any work available. Alms were forbidden to the able-bodied (Karger & Stoesz, 2010). Such a law clearly reflected the interests of the ruling class. Since the time of the plague, many secular laws relating to the poor have been designed to control the labor supply at least as much as to relieve the suffering of the destitute.

Throughout the 1500s the Commercial Revolution grew, and feudalism declined. Tenants were evicted from the land, sometimes to make room for sheep, whose wool was increasingly valuable in the manufacture of cloth. Large numbers of destitute people went looking for work in the cities, where they found themselves crowding into urban slums. The resulting poverty and social need led to government assumption of more responsibility for social welfare. In England, legislation culminated in the famous Elizabethan Poor Law of 1601 (Whitaker & Federico, 1997). The Elizabethan Poor Law was brought by the first colonists to America. Its concepts still influence current thinking about provisions for the poor in the United States and, hence, affect current law.

The Elizabethan Poor Law and the Act of Settlement

The Elizabethan Poor Law of 1601 was the first public legislation establishing a governmental system to meet the needs of the poor. The law established which unit was responsible to assist whom. By establishing which categories of people were eligible for what kind of assistance, the law was also geared toward social control (Segal & Brzuzy, 1998).

The local governmental unit, usually the parish (a geographic area similar to a county), was to maintain its own poor, and taxes could be levied for this purpose. An overseer of the poor—a public official, not a member of the clergy—was to be appointed. Families were to take care of their own members (reflecting the residual concept of social welfare). Whenever possible, grandparents were responsible for the care of children and grandchildren, and similarly, children and grandchildren were responsible for parents and grandparents.

Poor people were divided into categories, and relief was provided according to the category. Two of the categories, the impotent poor and dependent children, were considered *deserving* and so were offered aid. Children were to be indentured or placed in the service of whoever would charge the parish the least amount of money for their care (the *lowest bidder*). The impotent poor (the old, the blind, and people otherwise disabled) were to be either put into an **almshouse (indoor relief)** or offered aid in their own homes **(outdoor relief)**, depending on which plan would be least expensive to the parish.

Box 4.2   A Workhouse Experience

Q: And, in your opinion, many of the old people in your union would rather die than go to the workhouse?

A: Very many of them; they would rather, sir . . .

Q: Did you find that work severe?

A: No, not severe; monotonous. You did not know what to do. You could not go out to write a letter, or to read, or to do anything: you had no time of your own; in fact, it was a place of punishment, and not relief. . . .

Q: Would you state any other objections you have to the treatment of the aged poor?

A: I think the taskmaster is very much more severe than he should be.

Q: In what way?

A: Well, when you go to dine, or to breakfast, or anything like that, he says, "come quicker," and pushes you partly into the seat; that is a very trifling thing. I had a sore throat, and he objected to my wearing a scarf around my throat and he said, "I will pull those rags off you when you come back here again." That is, if I went back again. "You must not wear such things as this." I said, "I have a sore throat," and he says, "I don't care whether you and your father and your grandfather had sore throats." My father died of starvation through his throat growing together, and he suffered with sore throat. I suffered with sore throat, but not much; still, sufficient.

Q: Did you complain to the master of the workhouse of the language and treatment by the man you call the taskmaster?

A: No, my lord, not the slightest good in doing that.

Q: Why?

A: Whatever the taskmaster wished the master to say, the master would say. They were all under one control, even the doctor, and everybody was the same.

Source: Quoted from Jill Quadagno. (1982). *Aging in early industrial society: Work, family, and social policy in nineteenth century England.* New York: Academic Press, pp. 107–110.

The category of able-bodied poor was not considered deserving. These people were treated punitively. Alms were prohibited. People who came from outside the parish **(vagrants)** were to be sent away. Able-bodied poor who were residents were to be forced to go to a **workhouse**, where living conditions were hard and work was long and tedious. If they refused, they were to be whipped or jailed or put in stocks (Trattner, 1999; Federico, 1984).

The intent of the Elizabethan Poor Law of 1601 was that almshouses and workhouses should be separate institutions, with the almshouses meeting the special needs of the deserving sick and infirm. In practice, most communities that built such facilities combined them into one building for the sake of expense. Records indicate that people dreaded going into such places (see Box 4.2).

Quadagno (1982, p. 95) writes that "overseers, conscious of the desire of rate-payers to keep rates down, did all they could to prevent paupers from becoming chargeable to the parish." The Settlement Act of 1662 required every person to be enrolled as a resident in some parish somewhere. Procedures establishing residency were complex. Persons who could not prove legal residence in the parish where they were living could be declared vagrants and sent away, in order that they not become financial burdens on the parish in the future.

Minor adjustments to the law were made over the years, but the Settlement Act of 1662 increased parish control over poor people.

New Concepts in Poor Law

Two acts were passed in England in 1795 that temporarily improved the condition of the poor. One act forbade parishes to drive nonresidents away unless they actually applied for relief. The other, the Speenhamland Act, introduced new concepts into poor law. This act was a humane response to the rising price of wheat. Rather than force poor able-bodied people into workhouses after they were destitute, the law established a wage supplement to help prevent destitution. The size of the supplement was determined according to both the number of children in a family and the price of bread.

Improvement of the condition of the poor was temporary under this act because the law did not include a requirement for a minimum wage. The gentry tended to lower the wages they paid, and the difference was picked up through the wage supplement that was financed by taxes paid by small farmers (Quadagno, 1982). Hence, before long, taxpayers strongly opposed the law.

In 1834 the New Poor Law reinstated most of the provisions of the Elizabethan Poor Law and introduced a new principle known as **less eligibility**. This was based on the idea that "pauperism was willful and the condition of the pauper who was relieved should be worse than the condition of the poorest, independent, self-supporting laborer" (Quadagno, 1982, pp. 97–98).

Today, as a similar example, the United States has a minimum wage law, but the minimum wage, even with the increase that began in summer 2009 ($7.25 per hour), leaves a family of three with an income below the poverty level. A full-time worker with a family thus may qualify for public relief such as food stamps and/or the Earned Income Tax Credit (EITC; discussed later). Taxpayers' anger tends to focus on people who receive such assistance rather than on employers who increase their profits by providing very low wages.

POOR RELIEF IN THE UNITED STATES

Each colony in America enacted its own version of the Elizabethan Poor Law of 1601; Plymouth Colony was the first, in 1642. Ideas such as settlement and less eligibility, although codified under English law after the original colonization of America, continued to influence colonial attitudes.

After the American Revolution, the U.S. Constitution separated functions of state and federal governments, and assistance to the poor became a state prerogative. The federal government did not become involved until the end of the Civil War, in 1865, when the first national agency for social welfare was established: the Freedmen's Bureau. Through the Freedmen's Bureau, federal taxes supported free educational programs and financial assistance for former slaves for a few short years (Lieby, 1987). The bureau was disbanded in 1872 as a result of political infighting.

Values

Values strongly affected American poor law, and like the law itself, the major religious and cultural values of the United States originated in the Old World. Religious doctrines of various traditions taught that rich and poor alike should give what they could for others, motivated by love and compassion, not fear.

During the Protestant Reformation of the 16th century, many of these teachings were questioned. A Protestant ethic of salvation by hard work challenged the older notion of salvation by helping people in need. Puritan Calvinists, for example, "decreed one either saved or damned, a member of the elect or not. Charitable works could not alter this decision, for it was made eternally by God. One could, however, find out or at least seek indications of one's future celestial status" (Tropman, 1989, p. 134). While no one could know for sure, many people came to believe that prosperity indicated one was among the elect and that poverty meant one was not among the elect. From this point of view, why help the poor?

Also in conflict with older religious and humanitarian ideals to help the unfortunate were new ideas from philosophy and economics. In *The Wealth of Nations* (1776), Adam Smith argued in favor of the principle that became known as laissez-faire: that government should not interfere in the "natural functioning" of the market by imposing interference such as taxes. The market should be allowed to perform solely according to the influences of supply and demand. Taxation to support poor people interfered with the rights of the wealthy and only created dependency among the poor, according to Smith's argument.

Thomas Malthus, an economic philosopher and clergyman, published *An Essay on the Principle of Population* in 1798. In it, he argued that relief for the poor contributed to overpopulation and that surplus population would result in disaster. Also contributing to reluctance to help the poor was Herbert Spencer's philosophy known as *social Darwinism.* Influenced by biological theories of evolution discussed in Charles Darwin's book *On the Origin of Species* (1859), Spencer preached that only the fittest people should survive. Poor people should be allowed to perish as they are demonstrably unable to compete (Karger & Stoesz, 2010). Such an argument overlooked the fact that no individual member of the human species could survive without the cooperation, as opposed to the competition, of others. For example, not a single person could survive infancy without the assistance and cooperation of others.

Do any of these arguments for or against aid to poor people sound familiar? Although some are centuries old, these ideas and values still affect societal responses to poor people today. Obviously, the value base underlying the social welfare system is complicated and conflicting. Conflicting values in social and political arenas affect what happens in social welfare legislation; social welfare legislation affects the resources available to social workers and their clients.

Conflicting values in social and political arenas affect what happens in social welfare legislation; social welfare legislation affects the resources available to social workers and their clients.

The Charity Organization Society and the Settlement House Movement

The effects of values on approaches to social welfare in the United States are seen particularly clearly in two movements in private charity that strongly affected relief measures beginning in the 1880s. These movements, the Charity Organization Society and the settlement house movement, were introduced in Chapter 1 and are discussed more fully here because they, along with a more scattered child welfare movement, led to the birth of the social work profession. The two movements differed markedly in philosophy and methods.

The Charity Organization Society (COS) began in England in 1869; its first office in the United States opened in Buffalo, New York, in 1877 (Popple, 1995). Leaders of the COS believed that many poor people were unworthy, so applicants for aid should be carefully investigated. Records were to be kept about each case, and a central registry was developed to ensure that no person received aid from more than one source. The principal form of help to be offered should be "moral uplift," which was to be provided by "friendly visitors." Most of the visitors were women recruited from the upper class. Not only were these the persons who had the most time to volunteer, but, due to the patriarchal nature of the era, church-related, unpaid work was among the few outlets for these women's talents.

The methods developed by the COS were used as models for local public agencies; organization, investigation, and written records proved very useful in welfare work. Mary Richmond, a well-known leader of the COS movement in the United States, taught in the first social work training school, the New York School of Philanthropy (now the Columbia University School of Social Work), begun in 1898. The COS replaced most friendly visitors with paid staff by the early 1900s, partly because there were not enough volunteers and partly because volunteers were found to lack appropriate expertise (Popple, 1995).

The settlement movement, in contrast, involved concepts of self-help and mutual aid rather than moral uplift. Jane Addams, one of the movement's most famous leaders, established Hull House in Chicago in 1889. Settlement work arose in response to continuing pressures of the Industrial Revolution, which brought large numbers of immigrants to American cities, where they were forced to work long hours in factories under dangerous, unhealthful conditions.

Settlement houses brought idealistic young people, including many women of upper-class backgrounds, into the slums to live and work with less fortunate people. Settlement staff assisted immigrants in organizing into self-help groups and established **mutual aid** services ranging from day nurseries to garbage collection to organization of cultural events. In addition, settlement house staff and neighborhood participants became involved in political processes, advocating for better working conditions in the factories, better sanitation in the cities, and protective legislation for women and children (see Box 4.3).

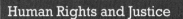

Human Rights and Justice

Practice Behavior Example: Social workers understand that each person, regardless of position in society, has basic human rights, such as freedom, safety, privacy, an adequate standard of living, health care, and education

Critical Thinking Question: Which do you think was more effective in advancing human rights and justice, the Charity Organization Society or the settlement movement? Why?

Box 4.3 Comparison of Charity Organization Society and Settlement House Movement	
Charity Organization Society	**Settlement House Movement**
LEADER	
Mary Richmond	Jane Addams
TYPE OF WORKER	
Friendly visitors	Volunteers who lived among poor
TYPE OF AID OFFERED	
Central registry of poor	Mutual aid
Short-term charity	Self-help
Moral uplift	Social and political action
PRIMARY LEVEL OF INTERVENTION	
Casework with individuals and families	Group work; work with families, organizations, and communities

SOCIAL WELFARE IN THE UNITED STATES IN THE 20TH CENTURY

The history of social welfare in the United States in the 20th century revealed, according to James Lieby, an increasing role over time for both public and private nonsectarian agencies (agencies not affiliated with particular religious groups). Lieby (1987) believes:

> It is helpful to analyze this general trend in three periods: 1900–1930, when the action was at the level of local and state governments and local private agencies organized under the Community Chest; 1930–1968, when the federal government took important initiatives; and since 1968, when the progress of the "welfare state" has seemed to stop if not turn back. (p. 765)

Lieby made this observation many years ago; it is clear today that he was right—progress toward the welfare state has indeed turned back. That trend was highlighted by the passage of the Personal Responsibility and Work Opportunity Act (PRWOA) in 1996, which will be discussed later. Then, in the early 21st century, the Republican administration of President George W. Bush engaged in an attack on the poor that was not limited to mothers and their children, but targeted the elderly and disabled as well, via a push to privatize Social Security. See the time line in Box 4.4.

Box 4.4	Time Line: Major Historical Events in Social Welfare and Social Work
1348	Black death. Feudal system begins to break down
1349	Statute of Laborers (England)
1500s	Accelerated breakdown of feudal system (Commercial Revolution)
1601	Elizabethan Poor Law (England)
1642	Plymouth Colony enacts first colonial poor law, based on English Poor Law
1662	Settlement Act (England; idea migrates to colonies)
1795	Speenhamland Act (England)
1834	New Poor Law (England)
1865	Freedmen's Bureau (the United States—ends in 1872)
1869	First Charity Organization Society (COS), London, England
1877	First COS in the United States, Buffalo, New York
1884	First settlement house (Toynbee Hall, London)
1886	First settlement house in the United States (Neighborhood Guild, New York City)
1889	Hull House, Chicago
1898	First formal social work education program (summer training by COS in New York City; evolves into New York School of Philanthropy, later Columbia School of Social Work)
1915	Flexner's report concluding social work is not a full profession
1917	First organization for social workers, National Workers Exchange
1919	American Association of Schools of Social Work (AASSW) formed
1921	American Association of Social Workers formed (from National Social Workers Exchange)
1928	Milford Conference; determines social work is a single profession

Box 4.4	Time Line: Major Historical Events in Social Welfare and Social Work (Continued)
1929	Stock market crash leads to Great Depression International Council on Social Welfare (ICSW) founded in Paris
1933	President Franklin D. Roosevelt launches "New Deal" program
1935	Social Security Act signed into law
1936	National Association of Schools of Social Administration (NASSA) established
1952	Council on Social Work Education (CSWE) forms, merging AASSW and NASSA; accredits MSW programs
1955	National Association of Social Workers (NASW) forms, merging seven separate social work organizations; accepts MSW only
1956	International Federation of Social Workers (IFSW) established; membership consists of national social work organizations
1957	Greenwood article declares social work a full profession
1964	President Lyndon Johnson launches the War on Poverty
1967	The Work Incentive Program (WIN) established under the Social Security Act
1970	NASW admits baccalaureate social workers as members
1974	CSWE begins accreditation of baccalaureate social work education programs; Supplementary Security Income program established under the Social Security Act for the aged, blind, and disabled; category of poor children omitted
1981	WIN program eliminated under the Reagan administration
1988	Family Support Act; parents receiving aid for dependent children under the Social Security Act must work when child is 3 years old
1996	Personal Responsibility and Work Opportunity Act signed into law by President Bill Clinton; eliminates right of poor children and parents to aid under Social Security Act; establishes Temporary Assistance to Needy Families (TANF) program
2000	Push by President George W. Bush to privatize formerly public assistance programs and provide federal funding to "faith-based" programs
2004	Medicare Part D signed into law by President George W. Bush, providing limited assistance to older adults in purchasing prescription drugs; law prohibits government from negotiating drug prices
2010	Affordable Health Care Act signed into law by President Obama, providing access to affordable health insurance to the majority of Americans, including those with preexisting conditions.

The Progressive Years, 1900–1930

The early 1900s were a time of reform in the United States. World War I slowed down reform efforts but did not entirely eliminate them. Women, for example, first gained the vote after the war, in 1920. A few women began to go to college, and some started to use ways to plan their pregnancies. Magazines designed to appeal to women appeared, such as *Good Housekeeping,* helping women begin to relate to other women. Activists such as those involved in the settlement house movement advocated, and in many cases secured, laws for the protection of women and dependent children, for better sanitation, and for better safety conditions in the factories. Forty states enacted mother's pensions, although only for those considered fit: the widowed mothers (Bartkowski & Regis, 2003). By 1920, 43 states had passed workers' compensation laws.

Federal guidelines were soon established; today all states have workers' compensation laws that meet federal guidelines. National leadership in protective legislation for children was provided by the Children's Bureau, established in 1909 as part of the U.S. Department of Labor.

Voluntary organizations also expanded during this period. Examples include the establishment or significant growth of the Boy Scouts and the Girl Scouts, the American Cancer Society, the National Association for the Advancement of Colored People, the National Urban League, and the Red Cross.

Federal Initiatives, 1930–1968

A great economic depression followed the stock market crash of 1929. Voluntary organizations and state and local governments did what they could to meet what seemed like unending financial need. But soon local treasuries were empty, including both private charities and relief-giving units of local government. People turned to the federal government for help. President Herbert Hoover was a proponent of laissez-faire economic theory and a political conservative. He believed that the federal government should not interfere with the economic market. Desperate Americans, however, began to perceive the widespread and rapidly increasing poverty as a **public issue** (an issue affecting so many people that it is considered beyond the fault of each affected individual) rather than a **private trouble**. Franklin D. Roosevelt was elected president in 1932 because he promised to involve the federal government in solving the crisis.

Roosevelt ushered in a series of emergency programs on the federal level to meet immediate needs for **income maintenance** and employment. His overall program was known as the New Deal. The New Deal offered temporary cash assistance and work-relief programs to needy people regardless of race. Roosevelt's major long-term proposal was the Social Security Act, passed by Congress in 1935. Since 1935, almost all additional federal social welfare policies have been adopted as part of this act (Segal & Brzuzy, 1998).

The Social Security Act is a complex piece of legislation that has been amended many times. The 1935 law established three types of federal provisions: (1) **social insurance**, (2) **public assistance**, and (3) health and welfare services.

Social insurance and public assistance are quite different. Insurance programs require the payment of taxes (in this case, the Social Security, or FICA, tax) earmarked for a special fund available only to the insured. Following rules relating to the amount of money contributed, benefits cover the expected problems of a modern industrial society, such as the death of a breadwinner.

Public assistance programs, on the other hand, are funded out of general tax revenues, usually income tax revenues, and people may receive benefits even if they have never paid taxes themselves. One qualifies according to whether one fits a specified category (e.g., elderly person) and in addition meets a **means test** or has an income below a certain level specified by law. A stigma is often attached to public assistance benefits, because they are considered unearned.

The social insurance provisions of the original Social Security Act were Old Age and Survivors Insurance (OASI) and unemployment insurance. OASI was intended to provide income for retired workers, widows, and minor children of deceased workers. Later, in 1957, coverage was extended to include disabled persons. In 1965, Title XVIII, Medicare, was added to the act. (Medicare and Medicaid, Title XIX, will be examined in detail in Chapter 7.)

Three categories of people were originally eligible for aid under public assistance: the blind, the aged, and dependent children. Later, Aid to Dependent Children was expanded to include the mother and in some cases the father; the program became known as **Aid to Families with Dependent Children (AFDC)**. A fourth category of people eligible for aid, the permanently and totally disabled, was added in 1950 (McSteen, 1989). In 1965, Title XIX, Medicaid, was added to the act.

Initially, most Black Americans were barred from Social Security benefits because of the power of southern Democrats, who insisted that domestic and agricultural workers be excluded from the law. They argued that such benefits would undermine the work ethic of their servants and laborers of whom, respectively, African Americans comprised 50 and 60 percent (Tyuse, 2003). It was not until 1950 that agricultural and domestic workers were finally included.

In 1974, to equalize benefits nationwide and to help remove stigma, public assistance income maintenance programs for the blind, the aged, and the disabled were combined into one program known as Supplemental Security Income (SSI). SSI is funded and administered by the federal government, and people apply for benefits through federal Social Security offices, not local welfare offices.

AFDC was not included in the SSI program. Why? The answer seems to be that some categories of poor people are still considered undeserving of aid. Political passion can be inflamed by criticizing poor single mothers or men who for whatever reason fail to provide. Their children suffer accordingly. AFDC remained a poor relation of SSI, with benefits that varied from state to state but, on the average, maintained recipients well below the poverty line, until 1996. In August of that year, the Personal Responsibility and Work Opportunity Act (PRWOA) ended the AFDC program and all entitlement of poor children and their mothers to government assistance. The PRWOA will be discussed more fully later in this chapter.

Young single mother with baby to care for, forced to find paying work.

Reflecting the rescinding of all legal right to assistance in the United States for poor children and their mothers, Bartkowski and Regis (2003, p, 58) note: "The compassion of the maternalistic state manifested in the early decades of the 1900s had, by century's end, given way to the discipline and austerity of paternalistic governance."

General Assistance

One category of people has never been eligible for assistance under the Social Security Act, able-bodied adults between the ages of 18 and 65 (age 60 for widows) who have no minor children. Sometimes able-bodied adults in need can receive help from local programs known as general assistance or poor relief. These programs varied widely across localities in the past, but in most places today they have simply been eliminated. Conservative ideologies focus on decreasing taxes rather than helping the poor. General assistance, in those very rare places where it still exists, is strongly residual: aid is temporary and carries a stigma. Repayment is usually required.

Food Stamps/SNAP and Other Federal Voucher Programs

The food stamp program was established by Congress in 1964; today the program is called SNAP (Supplemental Nutrition Assistance Program). The program is administered by the U.S. Department of Agriculture, but state and local welfare departments process the applicants and provide the stamps. The program is means-tested, and allotments are based on family size and income. Food stamps are **vouchers** that may be used to buy most food items available at the supermarket. Today they look similar to debit cards.

Originally, many poor adults who qualified for no other aid could receive assistance in the form of food stamps. But in 1996, the Personal Responsibility and Work Opportunity Act (PRWOA) enacted large cuts in food stamp availability, cutting the program's funding by nearly $28 million over the 6-year period to follow.

From a high of 27.5 million people in 1994, only 17.3 million received food stamps in 2001. By 2011, however, 40.3 million people were receiving them, indicating a very high level of need. This increase occurred despite complicated application processes and an average per person benefit of only $ 133.79 per month ($289.61 per household) ("Annual summary of food and nutrition service programs," 2011).

In addition to food stamps, the federal government offers other voucher programs, such as fuel assistance, rent subsidies, and infant nutritional supplements. The Women, Infants, and Children (WIC) program is one of the best known of the latter. It provides supplemental foods to pregnant and breast-feeding women and their children up to age 5. The program is means-tested; applicants with pretax incomes up to 185 percent of the poverty line are eligible. Coupons or vouchers for specific food items are provided for purchases at grocery stores. The program is not an entitlement; funds may not be available to serve every woman who meets eligibility criteria. Yet WIC is very important, serving over 91 million women and children in 2011 ("WIC program participation," 2011).

Post-Depression Trends

The Great Depression came to an end in the 1940s, when World War II provided full employment. The nation began to look at poor people as unworthy again. The 1950s set the stage for the social activism of the 1960s, however. Women who had worked full-time in paying jobs during World War

II were sent back home to make room in the job market for returning veterans. Although returning to the home was more a philosophical idea than a reality for many women (especially for the poor and those from ethnic minorities, who often had no choice but to work outside the home), the 1950s gave rise to feminist activism based on women's loss of status and access to employment equality. The decade also harbored the beginning of the civil rights movement, sparked by Rosa Parks's refusal to give up her seat to a white man on a bus in Montgomery, Alabama, in 1955.

Then in the 1960s came the War on Poverty, under the leadership of presidents Kennedy and Johnson. This movement was stimulated by Michael Harrington's book, *The Other America,* originally published in 1962, which exploded the myth that people in poverty deserve their own misery. Much liberal legislation was initiated in the 1960s, furthered by the civil rights movement as well as by renewed understanding of societal causes of poverty. The AFDC-UP (Unemployed Parent) program, the food stamp program, WIC, the Head Start program, educational opportunity programs, college work-study programs, job training programs, Peace Corps, Vista (Volunteers in Service to America), Medicare, and Medicaid all were instigated during this period (Champagne & Harpham, 1984; Karger & Stoesz, 2006).

Increasing welfare rolls led to new public outcry, which led to the passage of the Work Incentive (WIN) program in 1967. The WIN program was designed to encourage welfare recipients to take paid employment. Those who could find jobs were allowed to keep part of their welfare grant up to a certain earnings level. The program was unable to reduce welfare costs, however, as not enough jobs were available, and funds were lacking to provide adequate job training. In addition, day care facilities and inexpensive transportation were lacking (Champagne & Harpham, 1984).

Cutting Back the Welfare State, 1968 to the Present: Earned Income Tax Credit and Welfare Reform

Earned Income Tax Credit

Major efforts to reform the welfare system were made by Nixon's Republican administration from 1969 to his resignation in 1974 and by the Democratic Carter administration from 1977 to 1981, but their plans were not accepted by Congress. However, President Gerald Ford (Republican, 1974 to 1977) signed into law an important provision of the tax code, the Earned Income Tax Credit (EITC), which has become the largest means-tested income transfer in the United States today. Low-income families with children can receive an earnings supplement of up to 40 percent, to a maximum of about $4,000 for families earning under $12,000. Depending on the number of children in a family, the EITC phases out so that families earning slightly over $30,000 no longer qualify. The EITC is popular today because benefits go only to the working poor, perceived as worthy (Bane, 2003; Segal & Brzuzy, 1998). Yet, in effect, through this legislation taxpayers pay wages for employers who can increase their profits in this way. There is a danger that, as in the time of the Speenhamland Act, the public will eventually instigate a tax revolt and repeal the wage supplement, rather than insist that employers pay a wage sufficient to support an average family (see Box 4.5).

Welfare Reform. The president who was able to get major welfare reform proposals accepted was Ronald Reagan (Republican, 1981 to 1989). President Reagan was elected in 1980 with an apparent public mandate to lower taxes

Box 4.5   Issues with EITC

The EITC can be considered a guaranteed income support for poor working families with children. In contrast, there is no longer a federal guarantee for those outside the labor market, since Congress eliminated the entitlement of impoverished children to AFDC in 1996. One critical issue concerning the U.S. family policy is the absence of a major public safety net for the most impoverished group of children whose parents are not attached to the labor force. In addition, this group excluded from the public safety net is more likely the children of unmarried/never married parents. Through welfare reform and the EITC expansion, the nation has created two subclasses of children within the low-income class—one with and the other without a public safety net, based solely on the parents' employment and marital status. The assumption underlying this discriminatory treatment is that children of the nonworking and/or unmarried are unworthy and undeserving of public support. That is, the public value of children is determined by their parents' employment status and lifestyles. The nation appears to believe that the children of this "underclass" have no vested value for America's future.

Source: Copyright © 2001 Routledge. Reprinted by permission.

and inflation and to repair the budget deficit. Elected with massive financial support from right-wing conservatives, he and his administration were politically committed to investing in the military. Cutting taxes while building up the military obliged President Reagan to drastically reduce federal expenditures for income maintenance programs. The savings thus incurred were very small compared with the massive amounts of new money being poured into the military. The budget deficit became astronomical during Reagan's two terms of office. (President Reagan did not accomplish these deeds alone, but with the sanction of a Democratic Congress.)

The political agenda of the 1980s involved forcing able-bodied people, including the working poor, off welfare. The concept of aid returned to the old residual idea to assist helpless children on a temporary, emergency basis and only as a last resort (an approach popularly called the *safety net*). The result was the 1981 Omnibus Budget Reconciliation Act. The financial incentive built into the WIN program (described earlier) was eliminated. Most of the working poor opted to keep their jobs despite the loss of welfare benefits, but their financial circumstances were severely hurt, especially as many lost eligibility for Medicaid as well.

President Reagan signed another major welfare bill in 1988, the Family Support Act, just before he left office. This one was designed to force mothers who had remained on AFDC into the job market. All parents with children over 3 years old (1 year at states' option) were required to work or enter job training programs (if available) under this bill. However, it wasn't until 1996 that poor children lost all entitlement to aid under the provisions of the Social Security Act. The Personal Responsibility and Work Opportunity Act (PRWOA) was signed into law by President Clinton, a Democrat, in August of that year, ending 6 decades of guaranteed government aid for economically deprived children and their families. Clinton's acceptance of this law, proposed and passed by a Republican Congress, was seen by many liberals as a betrayal of the poor. The former AFDC program was eliminated by this bill. In its place, a new program called Temporary Assistance for Needy Families (TANF) was established. TANF was to be funded by federal block grants to the states. Block grant funding is very different from the former open-ended funding for AFDC;

each state receives a fixed sum of money for TANF and no more, regardless of need (Tyuse, 2003).

Under TANF, no family or child is entitled to assistance. Each state is free to determine who can receive assistance and under what circumstances. If a state runs out of money in a given year, it can simply stop providing aid, and poor families will have to wait until the following year for assistance. Besides the fact that assisting needy families is optional for states, regulations are complex and confusing under TANF. Some of the most significant requirements are that states are not allowed to assist anyone for longer than 5 years. States must require parents to work after 24 months of assistance. When parents work, the state may, but is not required to, provide child care assistance. Minor parents may not be assisted unless living at home and attending school. Assistance must be eliminated or reduced if the family is uncooperative with respect to child support–related requirements (e.g., if the mother does not name the father). Assistance may be denied to children born into families already receiving public assistance. Karger and Stoesz (2006) describe TANF legislation as a type of "welfare behaviorism," or social engineering. The law is designed to force poor parents to work outside the home regardless of suitability of jobs available or adequacy of wages. If they do not comply, punishment is severe (hunger, homelessness, loss of children to foster care, etc.).

The law is designed to force poor parents to work outside the home regardless of suitability of jobs available or adequacy of wages.

While this law was touted as a way of ending welfare dependency, no national programs were created to help address the many external factors keeping poor people on the welfare rolls (e.g., lack of affordable day care, lack of a family-supporting minimum wage, lack of educational opportunities, lack of adequate job training programs, lack of jobs in the skill range of many recipients or in the geographic areas where they live, and lack of affordable transportation to places where jobs are available).

Fortunately, Medicaid was not included in the TANF block grant, and poor families who meet the previous income guidelines continue to be eligible for this program. Saving eligibility for Medicaid for many poor families required dedication and persistence by many legislators of liberal persuasion.

SOCIAL WELFARE POLICY IN THE 21ST CENTURY

As noted by Goldberg (2002b), if any nation has the means to lift its poor out of poverty, it is the United States. Instead, however, welfare provisions for poor Americans have steadily eroded over recent decades. The trend toward diminishing social welfare policies and programs apparent in the beginning of the 21st century began, of course, in the 20th. Aid for poor families today is work-based and thoroughly residual, forcing mothers to take jobs outside the home at paltry wages, with no attempt on the part of the nation to develop decent employment opportunities. "In the post-welfare era," Bane (2003, p. 57) writes, "the old poor law system has made a comeback … Welfare reform legislation of 1996 … has thrust us back into the Elizabethan past of poor laws and local oversight—if not local overseers."

A few of the major 21st century welfare programs are summarized in the following sections.

Temporary Assistance for Needy Families

TANF, as discussed earlier, is not an entitlement program. No needy child or poor parent in the United States has a legal right to aid today, and aid under TANF, where provided, is limited to 5 years in a given parent's lifetime. Amendments hard-fought by organizations advocating for the poor, such as the National Association of Social Workers (NASW) and the Children's Defense Fund, have resulted in some ameliorating provisions, thankfully. For example, states may now opt to allow battered women to postpone employment for a time. States may also opt to provide child care assistance for longer than 5 years, as child care is not classified as a cash benefit. However, conservatives in Congress and the White House increased work requirements under this program during the G. W. Bush administration. The assistance level remains terribly low. For example, although Alaska, California, New York, Vermont, and Wisconsin provide the most generous benefits, they are just above *half* the poverty line. Mississippi, with the lowest benefit, allows approximately 13 percent of the poverty line ("The State of America's Children," 2008).

The Working Poor and the Earned Income Tax Credit

The federal government and several of the states provide earned income tax credit programs. The EITC lifts more children and families out of poverty today than any other federal program—far more than TANF. Yet millions of Americans remain poor today, and the number is growing due to unemployment and the low minimum wage. In 2010 the U.S. child poverty rate reached 22 percent, and the poverty rate of all families grew to a shocking 15.5 percent (About poverty- Highlights, 2011). While the EITC does help many poor families, it also helps businesses by allowing them to keep wages low and thus reap higher profits at the expense of the average taxpayer.

Privatization

Privatization involves shifting the provision of social services and financial benefits from publicly operated government programs to private organizations, either nonprofit or for-profit. For example, many states now contract with private agencies and organizations to operate TANF programs.

The political philosophy behind privatization is conservative, that government should have a minimal role in promoting the public welfare especially when it involves provision of economic assistance to the poor, as this might interfere with the economic market. (Workers might be unwilling to labor long hours for low wages if given an alternative.) This philosophy asserts that competition among private businesses is the most economical way to provide services and benefits.

The Faith-Based Trend

"Charitable choice" language first appeared in the 1996 Personal Responsibility and Work Opportunity Act (PRWOA). This legislation permitted public funds to be used for religiously oriented social service programs. While denominationally sponsored social service programs had been eligible for public funds for many years, these earlier faith-based programs separated their social services from religious proselytizing. By contrast, charitable choice language in the PRWOA broadened eligibility to allow public funding for church-sponsored programs that incorporated pervasive religious content. The G. W. Bush administration strongly promoted transferring public social service programs to private, religious organizations.

Promoting the provision of social services by faith-based groups comes at a risk. Religious organizations, for example, are exempt from employment nondiscrimination laws. Stoessen (2004, p. 4) noted in the *NASW News* that the Salvation Army "has come under scrutiny due to some of its policies about hiring and providing services to lesbian, gay and bisexual people."

In other organizations, beneficiaries in great need may find themselves required to espouse certain religious beliefs before they can receive food or shelter. But in a court case that could serve as an important precedent, a federal district judge in Iowa ruled in 2006 that a faith-based prison ministry program that required participating inmates to attend weekly revivals, religion classes, and prayer services where Jesus Christ was presented as the sole means of salvation overstepped the hazy line governing church-state relations (Paulson, 2006).

There is another important concern, however. The provision of social services by faith-based groups can allow the federal government to bow out of any responsibility to care for its poorest and most vulnerable citizens and divert its tax revenue instead to huge increases in military spending. That is exactly what happened under the administration of President George W. Bush. The Democratic Obama administration is making increased attempts to assist poor Americans (e.g., increasing student loans, mortgage assistance, extending unemployment benefits), but ongoing wars continue to divert funds to for-profit corporations that produce weaponry.

Most faith-based organizations are not capable of providing widespread services to large numbers of people in need over long periods of time. It was the inability of faith-based and other voluntary organizations to meet the public need during the great depression that led to the passage of the Social Security Act in 1935. Due to the severe recession, charitable giving in America declined by about 6 percent in 2009 (Whittle & Kuraishi, 2009), and there was great concern that the decrease would continue due to economic uncertainty. People strapped by their own financial circumstances simply cannot give as generously as they might like to.

Still, faith-based programs remain an important part of U.S. efforts to help the poor. Consider our chapter's case example. Without the assistance of the churches in their area, Mr. and Mrs. Rutherford would have become street people. And yet the churches could provide only a highly inconvenient form of shelter—the Rutherfords would have to move to a different church every week. The churches themselves suffered as well, having to give up space normally used for religious services and/or religious education for those weeks.

Ethical Practice

Practice Behavior Example: Social workers have an obligation to conduct themselves ethically and engage in ethical decision making

Critical Thinking Question: What can social workers do when their employing agency has policies that are professionally unethical?

Most faith-based organizations are not capable of providing widespread services to large numbers of people in need over long periods of time.

AN INTERNATIONAL PERSPECTIVE

How does the United States compare with other advanced nations of the world with respect to promoting the common welfare of its citizens? A rather sobering assessment has been compiled by the Children's Defense Fund. In its data sheet

"How America Ranks Among Industrialized Countries" (2008), this important advocacy organization notes that the United States ranks:

First in gross domestic product
First in the number of billionaires in the world
First in health expenditures
First in military technology
First in defense expenditures
First in military weapon exports
Sixteenth in maternal mortality rates
Twenty-first in 15-year-olds' science scores
Twenty-second in low birth weight rates
Twenty-third in neonatal mortality rates
Twenty-fifth in 15-year-olds' math scores
Twenty-seventh in infant mortality rates
Last in relative child poverty
Last in the gap between the rich and the poor
Last in adolescent (age 15 to 19) birth rates
Last in protecting the children against gun violence
Worst in the number of persons incarcerated

Diversity in Practice

Practice Behavior Example: Social workers recognize the extent to which a culture's structures and values may oppress, marginalize, alienate, or create or enhance privilege and power

Critical Thinking Question: Members of diverse populations suffer discrimination and neglect. What are some documented results?

The same data sheet also notes that only the United States and Somalia have failed to ratify the U.N. Convention on the Rights of the Child. (The Obama administration revived efforts to have the United States sign the treaty [Heilprin, 2009], but little progress has been made). The United States is the only major industrialized country that does not guarantee prenatal care to women who are pregnant. Black women in the United States are more likely to die of prenatal and birth complications than mothers in Azerbaijan, Turkmenistan, and Uzbekistan. Over 100 nations have lower percentages of low-birth-weight births, including Algeria, Botswana, and Panama (see Box 4.6).

Americans have always liked to think of themselves as a people who care about human life, especially children. What do the preceding numbers suggest about this idea? With fewer tax dollars coming into the federal Treasury because of huge tax cuts enacted under the G. W. Bush administration (mainly benefiting our richest citizens) and later to the recession that struck heavily at the end of that administration, and with billions and billions of dollars still going out in military spending, what does that mean for the ordinary citizen? Certainly there will be fewer resources to help people who are in need. President Obama's 2010 budget called for an increase in many important federal initiatives such as child nutrition, Head Start, support for low-income college students, American Indian education and health services, the Peace Corps, housing assistance, and health care, yet due to the growing deficit many of these aims were thwarted.

"Guns or butter" is an old saying in U.S. common folk wisdom. Can the United States really be secure when millions of its citizens, especially children, lack access to basic necessities? Are guns a better collective investment than food, shelter, education, and health care for all American citizens? That is perhaps the most crucial question for the future (see Figure 4.1).

The United States is not the only nation where welfare has been diminishing in recent years—this unfortunate situation has been occurring even in

Box 4.6   Up for Debate

Proposition: Medical care should be provided in a free, single-payer government program

Yes	No
All Americans need medical care, and so it should be freely available to all.	People would abuse the system and demand medical care they didn't need.
Physicians could help all in need, not just those who could purchase insurance or pay out of pocket.	Physicians might receive less income than they are accustomed to.
Prenatal care for all pregnant mothers would reduce infant mortality and low birth weights.	Women who cannot afford medical care should not get pregnant.
Hospitals in poor areas would be more financially solvent if they received payment for all their patients.	Hospitals in financial trouble should limit their care to those who have purchased insurance or can pay out of pocket.
In the long run, medical expenditures would be lower in the United States if all Americans could receive treatment when first needed.	Short-run costs for medical care would be too high to justify providing medical care for all.
A single-payer government system would provide more actual health care per dollar spent, since administrative costs of Medicare are under 5%, but administrative costs of private insurance are nearly 40%.	People are accustomed to private insurance, and it meets most needs of those who can afford to purchase it.

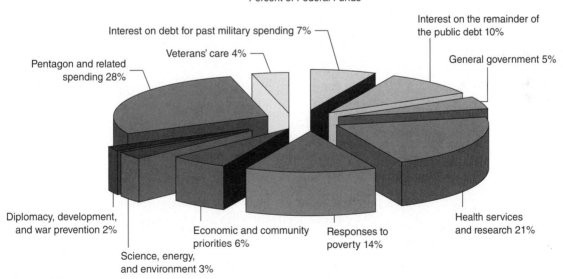

FY 2011 Federal Budget Proposal
Percent of Federal Funds

Interest on debt for past military spending 7%

Interest on the remainder of the public debt 10%

Pentagon and related spending 28%

Veterans' care 4%

General government 5%

Diplomacy, development, and war prevention 2%

Economic and community priorities 6%

Responses to poverty 14%

Health services and research 21%

Science, energy, and environment 3%

Figure 4.2

Where do our Income Taxes go?

Source: "Where do our Income Taxes Go?" From Friends Committee on National Legislation, Washington, DC. http://fcnl.org/assets/issues/budget/FY2011PieChart.pdf. Reprinted by permission.

nations with generous, long-established policies of social provision, such as Sweden. An excellent book examining this phenomenon, *Diminishing Welfare* (2002) by Gertrude Goldberg and Marguerite Rosenthal, finds that wherever governments have failed to defend full employment policies, social welfare programs have been cut back. This is because without full employment, a nation's tax base isn't broad enough to provide adequate resources for a strong social welfare system. At the same time, sadly, without full employment more people need assistance. So, many must go without.

The trend toward diminishing welfare among industrial nations seems to relate to the increasing power of international corporations. Corporations do not usually favor full employment policies or comprehensive social welfare programs because they prefer cheap labor. Corporations use their considerable assets to lobby against social welfare provisions nation by nation and to convince the general public through advertising that social welfare programs cause budget deficits (obscuring the real culprits: tax cuts favoring rich individuals and rich corporations, along with increased military spending). Ordinary citizens without political savvy and without ready access to jobs and/or adequate social welfare provisions do not have the information or clout to fight for better jobs or better wages. And unemployed and underemployed citizens cannot provide the tax base necessary to support a generous social welfare system.

Sweden

While Sweden has cut back its social provisions in recent years, its system is still extremely generous by American standards. This nation invests nearly twice the percentage of gross domestic product in social expenditures as the United States (Goldberg, 2002a). The following are social programs benefiting Swedish citizens, which are only a dream to Americans:

- A universal children's allowance, with child support advances to single parents in situations where an absent parent fails to pay.
- Parental leave for birth and adoption with salary replacement of 80 percent for 360 days as long as each parent takes at least 30 days' leave (note encouragement of shared parental responsibility). An additional 90 days leave are covered on request at a lower rate of salary replacement.
- Sixty days' annual leave for sick child care, with a wage replacement of 80 percent.
- Highly subsidized child care centers utilized by 80 percent of two-parent families and 90 percent of single-parent families.
- Highly subsidized, publicly owned housing so that substandard housing and homelessness are virtually unknown.
- Generous funding of apartment renovations for older adults to help maintain independence; assistance with transportation and shopping available; many subsidized adult day care centers.
- Universal, virtually free health care. A small co-pay has recently been introduced, but total payment is limited to $125 per year. All health care is free for children under 20. Most prescription drugs are free.
- Free dental care for children under 20.
- Social assistance programs (means-tested general assistance programs) are available to all unemployed adults, without any time limit, when unemployment insurance has been exhausted. Retraining programs are provided (often required) by the government.

Truly, life for a Swede is not nearly as insecure as for an American. Poverty is rare. However, program cuts in recent years mean that poverty is no longer unknown. Pensions for the elderly have been especially weakened in the past decade. They are now based on each individual's lifetime earnings, instead of providing a universal amount for everyone (some credit is given for years of study and child care). A 2.5 percent payroll tax is earmarked for investment in private accounts, providing no guarantee of future yield (a policy proposed in the United States by the Bush administration).

Japan

Japan is the most advanced industrialized country outside of Europe and North America and has the seventh largest population in the world. Yet it spends an even smaller proportion of its gross domestic product on social welfare programs than the United States (Goldberg, 2002a).

While Japan does have a few public welfare programs, Nomura and Kimoto (2002) estimate that less than a 10th of the eligible population actually receives benefits. They list three reasons:

1. Nearly one-third of Japan's labor force works in large firms or government units that provide welfare services such as housing, medical care, and pensions. This circumstance has its roots in World War II, when conditions were so terrible that strong labor unions arose. Organized labor demanded and won many benefits.

2. Nearly one-fifth of Japan's labor force is self-employed or family employed. While this percentage of the population is lower than that in the past, it is still politically strong. The national government, to maintain loyalty, provides protection via implementing policies such as restricting competition from large-scale retail chains.

3. The agricultural sector is organized and has political clout, and farmers have won protection by the government from outside competition. Thus, small family businesses and farms usually earn an income adequate to maintain a decent standard of living. In return, families are expected to support their own members.

In Japanese families today, the wife of the eldest son is expected to care for his parents for life, and nearly half of Japan's elderly do live with family members. Full-time work among women outside the home is discouraged by a tax policy in which the husband loses a tax deduction if his wife earns over a certain limited amount, and the wife then has to contribute to the public pension system. Full-time homemaking for women is encouraged by a tax policy in which she may receive a basic public pension (described later in this chapter) without contributing any money to the fund.

Government assistance to single mothers involves a severe means test and carries a strong stigma, so most women in this situation must get a job. Japan has had a children's allowance since the early 1970s, but it is not intended to fully support a child. There is so strong a social stigma against single-parent families that they are virtually nonexistent (only 1.3 percent of households). Nearly all pregnant teens get abortions. The divorce rate is very low and the remarriage rate high.

With respect to health care, all Japanese workers must purchase medical insurance, and there are different programs for different categories of workers. Those who work in large businesses receive most of their care from company programs. Japan's pension system for the elderly has three tiers. The first tier is a basic program for all the insured, partially funded by the state. Full-time housewives are eligible. Beyond the basic program, additional tiers are funded by large employers in both private and governmental sectors. Benefits relate to a worker's before-retirement income. Despite these programs, fully one-quarter of elderly Japanese over 65 today work out of necessity. Beginning in 2000, all Japanese have contributed to a system of nursing care insurance for the elderly. The program is designed to supplement family care, not replace it.

Japan's unemployment program targets full-time workers and provides short-term benefits. Only about one-third of part-time workers are assisted. As in the United States, when unemployment benefits run out, there is no further assistance offered. Families are expected to provide. In some situations, subsidies for tuition for retraining programs are available.

Japan thus has very limited national social welfare programs. Its tax and protectionist policies for small family firms and farms, however, assist families to provide for the basic needs of their members to a much greater extent than their counterparts in the United States.

Progress of Social Justice Today

The United Nations' Declaration of Human Rights, parts of which have been quoted in Chapter 3, states that everyone has the right to a decent standard of living, including food, housing, medical care, and security in the event of unemployment, illness, and the like. The Declaration asserts that motherhood and childhood should receive special care and assistance.

This Declaration was made more than a half century ago. Has progress been made toward achieving its goals? The answer varies according to the nation under consideration. Sweden, for example, has achieved a good deal more (despite recent cutbacks) than the United States or Japan.

Unfortunately, overall commitment to social justice seems to have decreased worldwide in recent years. Assistance to poor people has diminished at the very time that economic insecurity has grown. Goldberg and Rosenthal's research (2002) indicates that even the long-established programs of social provision in nations such as Sweden have diminished. This trend continues in the 21st century, placing heavy burdens on international organizations such as the United Nations that try to assist the poor. According to the Food and Agricultural Organization of the United Nations, nearly 1 billion people in the world were undernourished in 2010, a slight decline from the prior year but still far too many, and there were concerns that the number would increase again due to rising food prices (Global hunger declining, 2010).

The National Association of Social Workers (NASW) finds it increasingly important to advocate for poor people in these times. To that end, it has developed guiding principles and programs to advance human rights, some of which are discussed here. It has also allied itself with other organizations committed to achieving social justice in the United States and throughout the world.

NASW and Ongoing Human Rights Efforts

As part of its efforts to help achieve humane social policy in the United States, the NASW has developed several policy statements. One regards the "Role of Government, Social Policy, and Social Work" (see Box 4.7).

The NASW Social Work Congress of March 2005 adopted 12 "Social Work Imperatives for the Next Decade." Several are listed here:

- Take the lead in advocating for universal health care.
- Address the impact of racism, other forms of oppression, social injustice, and other human rights violations through social work education and practice.

Box 4.7 Role of Government, Social Policy, and Social Work

Although social agencies and social work professionals can help shape policies and practices, the nature of the service delivery system and the legitimacy of social work as a profession is established by public social policy, and in many ways the current policy is antithetical to social work values. There is a shift from blaming victims to punishing them. The category of "undeserving poor" has expanded to include almost everyone, even those formerly protected, such as children, veterans, elderly people, and people with mental and physical illnesses. Restructuring and limiting government responsibility has profoundly altered the availability and the delivery of social work services and the role and status of social work as a profession. NASW's position is that the federal, state, and local governments must play a role in developing economic justice, improve the quality of life for all people, and enhance communities. Among other issues, these policies and programs should address entitlements to help eliminate poverty; access to comprehensive health care; adequate minimum wage; adequate, affordable housing, and quality education for all.

Source: Social work speaks: National Association of Social Workers policy statements, 2009- 2012 by National Association of Social Workers. Copyright 2010. Reproduced with permission of National Association of Social Workers in the formats Textbook and Other Book via Copyright Clearance Center.

- Mobilize the social work profession to actively engage in politics, policy, and social action, emphasizing strategic use of power.
- Continuously acknowledge, recognize, confront, and address pervasive racism within social work practice at the individual, agency, and institutional levels.
- Strengthen social work's ability to influence the corporate and political landscape at the federal, state, and local levels.

To help promote social justice, the NASW has also established a Human Rights and International Affairs Department. This department houses the organization's efforts on behalf of women, gays and lesbians, and racial and ethnic groups. It addresses such issues as diversity, discrimination, affirmative action, and cultural competence. The NASW has also become part of an alliance of U.S.-based international and humanitarian nongovernmental organizations called InterAction, the American Council for Voluntary International Action. This alliance comprises more than 160 organizations working to advance social justice around the world, and it includes many well-known advocacy organizations such as CARE, Oxfam America, and Save the Children (Association Joins Global Coalition, 2005).

Clearly, social justice throughout the world can be achieved only by committed, intensive, long-term, cooperative efforts.

SUMMARY

The case example of Donna Rudnitski and the Rutherford family illustrates how important community organizational work is for the average social worker. Ms. Rudnitski's after-hours community work led to the development of a coalition of churches that found a way to shelter homeless families on a temporary basis. Our case example also illustrates how a middle-class family can fall into poverty, and even become homeless, in a very short time. Unemployment and medical expenses can and often do bankrupt normally hard-working people and their families.

To understand why our income maintenance programs operate as they do, helping only certain categories of people and generally keeping recipients well below the poverty level, we must begin with the Old World background. The

Elizabethan Poor Law of 1601 was the law that English settlers brought to the colonies in America. The U.S. system has gradually evolved under the influence of values, policies, issues, and concerns stemming out of the American experience.

A history of social welfare movements and income maintenance programs in the United States reveals a shifting political impact of two ways of thinking about U.S. social welfare system: the residual and the institutional. Residual services dominated the colonies and the nation as a whole up until the Great Depression (1929). Experiences during the Great Depression brought about the temporary dominance of the institutional approach to social welfare, and national programs such as Social Security were developed that lifted many people out of poverty. The trend of the 1980s and 1990s toward the residual view, which accelerated under the George W. Bush administration in the early years of the 21st century, has meant less aid for poor people and fewer resources to sustain the social worker's referral system of financial and material aid. The Obama administration partly halted the trend through new governmental programs such as the Affordable Health Care Act, but overall the social welfare system in the United States remains strongly residual. The United States is the only nation in the western industrialized world where poor children have no entitlement to assistance.

Issues for the future involve a rethinking of the nation's institution of social welfare. A contemporary, contrasting model from Sweden is introduced for consideration, as is a model from Japan not unlike that of the United States in many ways, except that tax policies in Japan are clearly designed to help small family businesses and farms to flourish, so as to be able to support family members adequately.

The NASW has issued many policy statements. Its statement on the role of government urges the United States to stop punishing its poor citizens and to address needed access to adequate income, health care, housing, education, and other basic needs. The United States needs to determine how much interference in the free market is appropriate to alleviate poverty, which continues to deepen among children, women, and other populations at risk.

PRACTICE TEST The following questions will test your knowledge of the content found within this chapter. For additional assessment, including licensing-exam type questions on applying chapter content to practice behaviors, visit **MySearchLab.**

1. The two dominant philosophies regarding social welfare in the United States are _____.

   a. the religious and secular perspectives

   b. the indoor and outdoor perspectives

   c. the residual and institutional perspectives

   d. the moral uplift and self-help perspectives

2. The settlement house movement promoted _____.

   a. service provision by volunteer friendly visitors

   b. careful investigations of poor families

   c. development of public agencies to provide case management

   d. self-help and mutual aid

3. "Charitable Choice" refers to _____.

   a. permitting public resources to be used for religiously oriented social service programs

   b. the tax credit for contributions to charities

   c. a United Way campaign to encourage more donations

   d. an option for private individuals to contribute to public social services

4. Since the Middle Ages, laws enacted to regulate the poor have been designed to _____.

   a. keep families together

   b. provide medical and housing assistance

   c. assure that all families are maintained at or above the "povety level"

   d. control the labor supply and relieve suffering

5. Privatization of social welfare services

   a. is governed by federal statutes

   b. rarely occurs

   c. is the management and provision of public social and financial benefits by private contractors

   d. is common in European countries

6. In the "Donna Rudnitsky" case study she considered the impact of ____ and ____ when looking for solutions to the rising homelessnes problem.

   a. contributing her own funds, opening up her own home

   b. starting a college fund, the cost of school loans

   c. health care policies, studying to become a nurse

   d. decreasing tax revenues, collaborative efforts

7. After reading Chapter 4, consider the case of Kathy and George Rutherford within three different historical contexts, a) during the enactment of the Elizabethan Poor law, b) during the Charity Organization Society movement, and c) as an African American family during the 1960's. Provide an analysis of the likely course of events and outcomes for Kathy and George based on the social welfare policies and traditions of each period.

MySearchLab CONNECTIONS

Reinforce what you learned in this chapter by studying videos, cases, documents, and more available at **www.MySearchLab.com**.

Watch and Review

Watch these Videos

* Keeping Up With Shifting Contexts
* Building Alliances

Read and Review

Read these Cases/Documents

Δ Chelsea Green Space and the Power Plant

Explore and Assess

Explore these Assets

Influencing State Policy—http://www.statepolicy.org/

U.S. Department of Health and Human Services—http://www.dhhs.gov/

Assess Your Knowledge

Assess your knowledge with a variety of topical and chapter assessment.

Conclude your assessment by completing the chapter exam.

* = CSWE Core Competency Asset
Δ = Case Study

5

Family and Children's Services

Connecting Core Competencies in This Chapter									
	Professional Identity	X	Ethical Practice		Critical Thinking	X	Diversity in Practice		Human Rights & Justice
X	Research Based Practice		Human Behavior		Policy Practice	X	Practice Contexts		Engage, Assess, Intervene, Evaluate

LaTanya Tracy

LaTanya Tracy's great-grandmother, Ruby Bell Lowe, called Protective Services in a panic early one morning. Ruby had become exhausted from trying to care for LaTanya, an infant of only 9 months. The baby had been crying all night, and Ruby had gotten little sleep. In her mid-80s, the elderly woman had been caring for LaTanya single-handedly for the past 3 weeks, ever since Natasha Tracy (Ruby's granddaughter and LaTanya's mother) had asked her to babysit late one evening. Ruby had felt uneasy accepting at that hour, suspecting that Natasha planned to go out drinking, but she had agreed for the baby's sake.

Natasha had not returned the following morning as promised, and LaTanya was keeping Ruby awake night after night. Exhausted and angry, Ruby remembered that a social worker from the County Department of Protective Services had been helpful a few years before when Natasha neglected her parental responsibilities to her son, Martin, because of a drinking habit. The intake worker with whom Ruby spoke at Protective Services checked the computer files and found that Natasha Tracy, 24 years old, had indeed been referred to the department previously. At that time, Natasha's young son, Martin, had been placed temporarily in foster care due to **neglect**, or failure to provide appropriate care, brought on by Natasha's drinking. (For reasons of confidentiality, the worker did not relay this information to Ruby, although Ruby probably already knew.) Martin had been returned to his mother after 8 months, and the case had been closed. That was because Natasha had entered an alcohol treatment program and had followed all court orders carefully. There had been no further referrals for child neglect until Ruby's anxious telephone call. The intake worker at Protective Services, on consultation with her supervisor, accepted the case for investigation and referred it to the social worker who had worked with Natasha previously, an experienced professional named Lauren White.

Lauren White, BSW, like Natasha, was a woman of African American descent. She knew from personal as well as professional experience that Black families have many strengths. In times of difficulty, for example, extended family members such as Ruby frequently pitch in to help care for young children. Grandparents, great-grandparents, aunts, uncles, older siblings, and even neighbors frequently help out when needed. Lauren checked Natasha's files to assist in recalling the facts of the former case. Four years before, the paternal grandmother had called to report neglect of Natasha's then-infant son, Martin. At that time Natasha was abusing alcohol, marijuana, and cocaine. A single parent, she was trying to cope with a baby with no assistance from that baby's father.

The case with Martin had a satisfactory ending, at least at the time. Once the little boy had been placed in foster care, Natasha had been willing to work hard to meet the conditions required by the court to get him back: regular participation in an alcohol and drug abuse treatment program and in a parenting class. Once court conditions had been met, Martin had been returned home, and the case had been closed shortly thereafter.

Lauren White's first step was to call Ruby Bell Lowe. She remembered the great-grandmother from her previous work with Natasha. Besides, no current telephone number had been given for Natasha, and the number on file was no longer working. From Ruby, Lauren learned that Natasha's telephone had been disconnected. Ruby could not take the bus to visit Natasha to talk with her as she was too frail to climb the vehicle's steep steps with an infant in her arms. She could not afford a cab.

Diversity in Practice

Practice Behavior Example: Social workers recognize and communicate their understanding of the importance of difference in shaping life experiences

Critical Thinking Question: How did Lauren White's personal experiences as an African American assist her in her professional work with Natasha Tracy? How did her knowledge of the strengths of African American families help make the intervention be successful?

Ruby told Lauren that she didn't think she could keep LaTanya much longer. The baby had severe asthma attacks that frightened the old woman and sometimes kept her up many hours of the night. Ruby gave Lauren Natasha's address. She explained that she believed her granddaughter was abusing alcohol and possibly other drugs again. When Lauren asked where Natasha's son, Martin, was currently staying, Ruby didn't know.

Natasha Tracy opened the door of her apartment hesitantly at Lauren's knock, wearing an old bathrobe and smelling of alcohol although it was early in the afternoon. She recognized her former worker and invited her in with an embarrassed smile. She offered Lauren a seat on an ancient sofa and sank into a nearby chair with a sigh. "I know," she said, "I'll bet my grandmother called you."

Lauren replied that the elderly woman had done just that. "Ruby is very worried about you, Natasha," the worker continued sternly, "and LaTanya is hard for her to care for, as you can imagine. What has happened that you felt you had to leave LaTanya with your grandmother?"

Thus began a long, hesitant conversation in which Natasha seemed almost grateful to have someone to talk with, even if that someone was a social worker from Protective Services with the power to take away her children. Natasha explained that things had gone well enough for a couple of years after her son, Martin, had come home. But then she had become involved with an abusive boyfriend, LaTanya's father. This man frequently struck her when he was angry and ridiculed her when she cried. Then, just before LaTanya was born, the boyfriend had been arrested for armed robbery. He was now serving a long prison sentence. That solved the **abuse** problem, at least temporarily, but left Natasha alone with a young son and an infant with severe asthma. After LaTanya's father went to prison, Natasha applied for Temporary Assistance for Needy Families (TANF; see Chapter 4). Under her state's program, TANF required Natasha to find a job right away since LaTanya was more than 12 weeks old by then. The young mother complied but soon felt exhausted by her dual responsibilities— sole parent to a baby and full-time employee at a fast-food restaurant. Even worse, the child care promised by TANF did not come through. There was a substantial waiting list for this service. Most of LaTanya's relatives and friends were also working outside their homes, many of them required to do so by the same TANF program. They could only occasionally help Natasha. Soon, Natasha lost her new job because she was absent caring for LaTanya too often. Discouraged, the young mother began to drink again. Eventually, realizing she was unable to care for her children properly, she took LaTanya to her grandmother's house and Martin to the home of his paternal grandmother. That was 3 weeks earlier. Now, Natasha's drinking was completely out of control, and she was in debt to her landlord for her rent, facing eviction.

Lauren White realized that here was a young woman with multiple problems but that she and her extended family had many strengths. First, there were two elderly grandmothers willing to help as long as possible. Probably other relatives could also be found to help from time to time. Second, Lauren knew from past experience that Natasha was a good mother when she was not drinking. She had even been responsible enough to find other caretakers for her children when she realized her drinking was getting out of control again.

Gently, Lauren asked the young mother what she wanted for herself and her children. Did Natasha want to continue in the direction she was now heading, addicted to alcohol and in danger of losing her children, or was she willing to accept assistance toward recovery? Lauren *asked* Natasha because

Ethical Practice

Practice Behavior Example: Social workers know about the value base of the profession, its ethical standards, and relevant law

Critical Thinking Question: Ethical practice is important with all clients, including those who are involuntary. How does Lauren White demonstrate this aspect of professional competence?

self-determination is a core social work value, to be implemented to the greatest extent possible even with involuntary clients. Clients who feel heard and respected will usually work harder to meet their goals.

Natasha's eyes filled with tears as Lauren asked her what she wanted to do with her life. She admitted that she had a substance abuse problem and said she was ashamed that she wasn't caring for her children. She knew she needed help.

Lauren had her work cut out for her to find resources to assist Natasha, but she was successful. An aunt was able to help Ruby Bell Lowe care for LaTanya until Natasha felt ready to take the baby home again. The paternal grandmother was willing to care for Martin a little longer. Family members loaned the young woman enough money to pay her back rent. Lauren was able to arrange counseling for Natasha at the Islamic Family Center. While Natasha was not a Black Muslim, the Islamic Family Center was willing to accept her as a client even though Natasha's only way to pay was through Medicaid, a health insurance program for certain categories of poor people, which has a very low payment schedule (see Chapter 4). Natasha's counselor at the Islamic Family Center connected her with an Alcoholics Anonymous (AA) group that met in her neighborhood. Partly motivated by the provisions of a court order that Lauren White secured, and partly motivated (and increasingly empowered) by the encouragement and support she now received in counseling, Natasha attended her AA group faithfully. She regained control of her drinking.

Within a few weeks, Natasha stopped drinking entirely. After that, she was able to bring her children home under Lauren White's supervision. She found another job and was able to work regularly enough to keep it. She was able to work regularly this time because, as a Protective Services client, she was eligible for immediate child care services through a Protective Services program. Natasha continued counseling at the Islamic Family Center and attending her AA group. After a few months passed, Lauren knew that Natasha was ready for release from supervision from Protective Services. She was worried, however, because once Natasha ceased to be a Protective Services client, funding for child care through that agency would stop. Lauren realized that she would need to become involved in advocacy for Natasha with the TANF program to assist her in being readmitted and to help ensure continuity in child care. Without that, Natasha would be right back in the situation that precipitated her previous substance abuse. Lauren knew that her task would not be easy, but she was willing to go beyond the call of duty to do what she could to ensure a decent future for LaTanya, Martin, and Natasha Tracy.

HISTORICAL PERSPECTIVES ON FAMILY AND CHILDREN'S SERVICES

Children and families in need have been helped by family members and other members of their villages or tribes since well before written history. Otherwise, we could not have survived as a species. Given that human infants are born almost totally helpless, it is cooperation among various members of humankind, not competition, that has enabled humanity to survive. Early human beings foraged for food and shelter at the mercy of an unpredictable environment. Survival was precarious, as it still is today in impoverished areas of the United States and other parts of the world.

Formal services to help those in need are a relatively recent invention. In earlier times, infanticide and abandonment were the primary means available for families to deal with infants they couldn't care for. In the ancient Greek city of Athens, a child's birth was recognized socially only 5 days after the biological event. Before that, he or she could be disposed of. In situations of great poverty today, families still occasionally resort to infanticide or abandonment.

As recently as the middle of the 18th century, nearly half the children born in London died of disease or hunger before they were 2 years old. In 18th-century France, two-thirds of all children died before they reached age 20 (Kadushin & Martin, 1988). A high death rate is probably a major reason why rates of childbirth were so high in the past and remain high in poorer countries even today: adults have multiple offspring in the hope that one or two will survive.

Both Jewish law from the Old Testament and early Christian teachings stressed the importance of caring for needy children and families. The Catholic Church, in particular, exhorted the sanctity of all human life and taught (as it still does) that not only infanticide but also birth control and abortion were unacceptable. By preaching against all methods of regulating family size, the church obligated itself to help needy parents care for mouths they otherwise could not feed. A portion of church revenues was set aside for this purpose as early as the 2nd or 3rd century. Infants were often abandoned at church gates (Kadushin & Martin, 1988).

Under secular law, in early Europe there was no recognition of the rights of the child; the father had absolute control and no obligation to protect or maintain a child. Many babies were abandoned. The first known asylum for abandoned infants was founded in Milan in the year 787. After that, many other orphanages were established, among them the London Foundling Hospital, opened in 1741, "to prevent the murders of poor miserable children at birth and to suppress the inhuman custom of exposing newborn infants to perils in the streets, and to take in children dropped in churchyards or in the streets or left at night at the doors of church wardens or overseers of the poor" (Kadushin & Martin, 1988, p. 43).

Other mutual aid groups that helped children and families were the guilds (small groups of merchants and craftsmen that generated basic income to meet family economic needs of their members). However, with changes in technology, guilds ceded their function to factories, which were large, impersonal places of work with no sense of obligation to those who labored. Secular law began to provide some assistance to replace or supplement informal charity by church or guild. Life was still very hard, and assistance was extremely limited in kind and form. By the mid-1500s the average human life span was only about 30 years, and children were earning their own living by age 7 or 8. An English statute of 1535 reads, "Children under 14 years of age and above 5 that live in idleness and be taken by begging may be put to service by the government of cities, towns, etc., to husbandry or other crafts of labor" (Kadushin & Martin, 1988, p. 47).

The English Poor Law of 1601 codified many previous laws dealing with the needy. As described in Chapter 3, aid was usually offered only in almshouses or workhouses. The death rate in these institutions was extremely high because the sick and insane were usually housed with everyone else. Destitute families were separated, as children were apprenticed out to whoever offered to take them for the least cost to the parish.

English poor laws were brought to the New World in the 1600s, and help for needy children and families in America through the mid-1800s remained roughly the same: the almshouse for most destitute people, with children being apprenticed out as soon as possible. Death rates and sheer human misery were high. Some towns did offer temporary "outdoor relief" (assistance in one's own home), but this practice was rare.

In 1853 Reverend Charles Loring Brace took an innovative approach to helping poor children with the founding of the New York Children's Aid Society. Brace developed training schools, workshops, and living quarters for the city's destitute children, but the magnitude of their needs and the growing problem of juvenile delinquency alarmed him. He responded by devising a plan to ship the children out of the city to farmers in the West who could use their labor. He viewed this as a way of finding foster homes for the children and also to "drain the city" of a serious problem. Beginning in 1854, more than 50,000 children were sent west on Brace's *orphan trains*. They were generally turned over to anyone who would take them. Many people opposed the plan, of course, including parents who hated to see their children go but were too poor to support them. Charity workers sometimes called the program "the wolf of indentured labor in the sheep's clothing of Christian charity." The westward transport continued, however, for more than 25 years (Trattner, 1999, p. 118). A positive legacy was a growing public interest in foster care for needy children.

Beginning in 1854, more than 50,000 children were sent west on Brace's orphan trains. They were generally turned over to anyone who would take them.

The federal program that assisted African American and destitute White families in the South for a brief period after the Civil War (between 1865 and 1872), the Freedmen's Bureau, was almost revolutionary in concept. It was the first federal program to aid the poor. As discussed earlier, it provided education, work, land, and relief directly to families in the home setting. Unfortunately, this remarkable program fell victim to partisan politics after only 7 years of operation.

In the late 1800s, the settlement house movement, originating in England, came to the United States. Inner-city settlement houses began to offer services to poor families with children by helping to organize cooperative child care and other self-help programs. Jane Addams, as noted in Chapter 4, founded the famous Hull House of Chicago in 1889.

Partly due to activists in the settlement movement, laws began to be passed in the United States in the late 1800s against the use of "mixed almshouses," institutions in which destitute young children were housed with the sick and the elderly. One result was that more orphanages began to be established. Unfortunately, most excluded African American children, so Black people were forced to continue to rely on a strong network of extended family, friends, African American churches, and other African American voluntary organizations for basic survival.

Also in the late 1800s a major organization committed to helping families stay together in times of need, the Charity Organization Society, took shape, first in England and then in the United States. Mary Richmond was the major leader of the movement in the United States. "Friendly visitors" were sent into poor people's homes to counsel parents toward better ways of living. The distribution of material aid to people's homes was centrally coordinated. Early friendly visitors believed poverty could be relieved by "moral uplift" of the poor. Later on, as workers became more knowledgeable about causes of poverty (such as low wages and poor health), they began to advocate for social reform in collaboration with settlement house workers. (The Charity Organization Society, the forerunner of today's family service agencies, and the settlement house movement were discussed in Chapter 4.)

The Child Welfare Movement and Protective Services Programs

The child welfare movement was a major contributor to the birth of the social work profession. Its roots can probably be traced to Charles Loring Brace's founding of the New York Children's Aid Society in 1853. While the practice of shipping children west became controversial, as it divided families and subjected children to serious trauma, Brace's efforts publicized the plight of poor children and orphans. Many Children's Aid Societies were founded in other cities. By the 1870s, some of these societies began to board impoverished children in family homes instead of sending them west, the beginning of foster care and adoption programs in the United States (Karger & Stoesz, 1998).

Public debate arose around the use of orphanages versus foster homes for needy children. This question was resolved, at least in theory, with the 1909 White House Conference on Children. The conference was attended by Jane Addams, famous leader of the settlement house movement. It recognized the importance of families and unequivocally recommended foster rather than institutional care. Although many children continued to be placed in large institutions due to funding considerations and lack of available homes, the 1909 conference focused national attention on the plight of poor children. It was so successful that the conference has reconvened every 10 years except during the Reagan administration.

The need for protective services, the type of social services mobilized in the LaTanya Tracy case described in this chapter, formally came into recognition around 1875. The catalyst for protective services for children was a 10-year-old girl named Mary Ellen Wilson (see Box 5.1).

Because of increased public awareness of abuse to children as a result of the Mary Ellen case, many societies for the prevention of cruelty to children were created throughout the country in the late 1800s. These were private, voluntary agencies. In some parts of the nation they still exist; in other parts they have merged with various other social agencies serving children.

Formalized public services to protect children were not mandated by law in the United States until the passage of the Child Abuse Prevention and Treatment Act of 1974. Federal funds were provided to the states for this purpose,

---

Box 5.1 The Case of Mary Ellen

Mary Ellen Wilson was badly abused by a woman to whom she had been indentured at 18 months of age. The woman later admitted in court that Mary Ellen was the illegitimate daughter of her deceased first husband. Neighbors tried to help the girl because she was beaten regularly and kept as a virtual prisoner in her home. In 1874, they enlisted the help of a visitor to the poor, who appealed for assistance to the police and various charitable societies. As no assistance was forthcoming, the visitor then appealed to the president of the New York Society for the Prevention of Cruelty to Animals (SPCA), who sent an investigator. Due to conditions documented by the SPCA, a court order was obtained to temporarily remove the child from the home. The president of the SPCA then took Mary Ellen's case to court as a private citizen. He called it to the attention of the *New York Times* as a means of publicizing the problem of cruelty to children. The newspaper story succeeded in arousing widespread public concern. Mary Ellen was removed from the abusive home permanently, and her foster mother was sentenced to a year in prison.

Source: Based on Sallie A. Watkins. (1990, November). The Mary Ellen myth: Correcting child welfare history. *Social Work, 35(6),* 501–503.

and a national Center on Child Abuse was established. Title XX of the Social Security Act was also passed in 1974 and provided block grants to the states, which helped finance child abuse programs (Segal & Brzuzy, 1998; Samantrai, 2004). Some states had provided these services on their own initiative for a number of years, but all states created protective services programs by 1978.

Establishment of protective services programs was accompanied by new laws requiring certain categories of professionals, such as doctors and social workers, to report suspected child abuse to designated authorities, a requirement known as *mandated reporting*. Mandated reporting, not surprisingly, resulted in a great increase in reports of suspected child abuse and neglect. Unfortunately, however, most protective services programs are seriously underfunded and understaffed, so workers generally can provide service only in situations of crisis proportions (Karger & Stoesz, 1998; Samantrai, 2004).

Families who are reported to protective services units are often referred for more intensive counseling to private family service agencies, those connected historically with the Charity Organization Society. These agencies provide remedial services such as counseling to help improve conditions for neglected or abused children. They also usually provide preventive and educational programs. For example, all member agencies of Family Service of America provide family counseling, family life education programs, and family advocacy services.

The Family Preservation and Support Services Act was passed as part of the Omnibus Budget Reconciliation Act of 1993. This law aims to strengthen families by providing funds to states to develop new family support and preservation services. Responsibility for developing plans for specific programs rests with the states, which must target services in areas of greatest need and utilize community-based strategies that involve community groups, residents, and parents in the planning process (Samantrai, 2004).

Children's Rights as International Law

The idea that children have rights is rather new. The United Nations, in November 1954, proclaimed through the General Assembly's Declaration of the Rights of the Child that children all over the world have certain rights (see Box 5.2). These rights became international law in 1990 as the Convention on the Rights of the Child. Ninety-six percent of the world's children now live

---

Box 5.2   United Nations Declaration on the Rights of the Child

Every child in the world has rights.

Every child has the right to have a name and a country.

Every child has the right to have enough food to eat, a place to live, and a doctor's care.

Every child who is handicapped has the right to special treatment and care.

Every child has the right to grow up in a family feeling safe, loved, and understood.

Every child has the right to go to school and to play.

Every child has the right to be watched over and taken care of in times of danger.

Every child has the right to be protected from cruelty or unfair treatment.

Every child has the right to grow up without fear and hatred and with love, peace, and friendship all around.

Source: From the Convention on the Rights of the Child, 1990. Reprinted by permission of the Secretary of the Publications Board, United Nations. Quoted in C. S. Ramanathan and N. J. Link. (1999). *All our futures, principles, and resources for social work practice in a global era.* Belmont, CA: Brooks/Cole, p. 10.

in countries that have ratified the convention, but unfortunately the children of the United States are not among them. The United States signed the convention in 1995, but, except for Somalia, is the only nation in the world that has refused to ratify it. The Bush administration believed that the convention would infringe on U.S. sovereignty (Steinberg, 2006); the Obama administration favors ratification (Heilprin, 2009), but has made little progress as this chapter is being revised.

Underscoring the importance of children's rights, the International Federation of Social Workers developed a specific policy supporting the Convention on the Rights of the Child. Hopefully, the United States will ratify the convention in the foreseeable future.

CHALLENGES OF AFRICAN AMERICAN FAMILIES: A BRIEF HISTORY

As noted in the chapter-opening case study, both Natasha Tracy and Lauren White were of African American descent—members of a minority group that has suffered immense challenges in the United States both historically and in contemporary times. Many, like Natasha, still struggle to meet basic needs. Others, like Lauren, have secured the education that allows them to enter the professional world. Lauren's path was easier, of course: she did not have two young children to provide and care for.

As is well known, African Americans have endured a history of slavery in the United States, enriching others at terrible cost to themselves. But the first African Americans came to the colonies in 1619 not as slaves but as indentured servants. The institution of slavery did not take firm hold in the United States until the late 1600s, when the South developed an agricultural economy dependent on slave labor (Lum, 1992).

The legacy of slavery is profound and reaches to the present day. Africans were different from other immigrant groups because the vast majority, including most of the indentured servants, were brought to the United States as captives against their will. Unlike other immigrant groups, they had no stable community of free kinsmen or countrymen to turn to for assistance upon arrival. Instead, slave traders systematically separated families and tribal members and sold them apart from one another to reduce chances of coalition and revolt. Native languages and religious traditions were forbidden. Every attempt was made to suppress the spirit of the slaves. Laws denied them the right to marry, to maintain families, to assemble in groups, to learn to read and write, or to sue for redress of grievances. Slaves were legally not persons but property.

Slavery existed at first in both northern and southern states and territories. Rhode Island was the first state to free its slaves, in 1784, a few years after the American Revolution (Quarles, 1987). By the time of the Civil War there were approximately half a million free Blacks in the nation (Logan, Freeman, & McRoy, 1990). They were strictly regulated, however. All had to carry special papers certifying their free status, and they could be sold back into slavery if their papers were lost or stolen. In most states they were denied the right to vote, hold public office, or testify in court.

The Civil War from 1860 to 1865 freed the slaves, but at great cost. One in four died from disease and deprivation related to the terrible conflict (Logan et al., 1990). The first federal social welfare agency, the Bureau of Refugees, Freedmen, and Abandoned Lands, known as the Freedmen's Bureau, was established 2 months before the end of the war, in anticipation of the enormous human need that would follow. The Freedmen's Bureau distributed food, clothing, and medical supplies to starving Blacks and Whites alike. It also established 46 hospitals, several orphan asylums, and more than 4,000 schools for African American children. It established institutions of higher learning for African Americans, including Howard, Atlanta, and Fisk universities (Axinn & Levin, 1992). Unfortunately, the Freedmen's Bureau was terminated in 1872. Had it been allowed to continue, the conditions for African Americans as a whole today would be much improved.

After slavery, all former states of the Confederacy except Tennessee passed *Black Codes* that limited the property rights of African Americans and forbade them to hold skilled jobs such as craftsman or mechanic. In Georgia, unemployed African Americans could be rounded up and put on chain gangs as criminals. State and local welfare programs for Blacks were inferior to those for White people. Orphaned Black children in Mississippi, for example, were apprenticed, and their former masters were given preference. No guarantees for adequate food, clothing, or education were written into the terms of indenture, as were included for White children (Axinn & Levin, 1992).

Under such difficult conditions, mutual aid and self-help were crucial for the survival of African Americans. The extended family rescued thousands of orphaned children, and churches organized orphanages, day care centers, and kindergartens. Churches also helped care for sick and elderly members and arranged for the adoption of children. African American lodges like the Masons and the Odd Fellows raised funds and provided needed services, as did various women's organizations (Logan et al., 1990).

African Americans make up about 12.6 percent of the U.S. population, comprising about 39 million persons ("USA QuickFacts," 2010). They constitute the second largest minority group, after Hispanics. Among the many strengths of African American people is the fact that mutual aid extends beyond nuclear family boundaries. Aid is routinely offered to extended family members, friends, and neighbors, permitting the survival of many in need. Aid from the extended family network was crucial to the survival of LaTanya Tracy and her family in this chapter's case study.

It is important for social workers to remember that there is no single African American family structure. African American families may be nuclear (including two biological parents or blended in a variety of ways) or single parent; they may be wealthy, middle income, or poor. However, because of the realities of discrimination and limited opportunity, a disproportionate number are poor, increasing the chances of involvement with the social service system.

A significant percentage of child and family services are offered by professional social workers. Workers with this background can be instrumental in improving the quality of service.

SERVICES AND THEIR PROVIDERS: A CONTINUUM OF CARE

A significant percentage of child and family services are offered by professional social workers. The 1980 Adoption Assistance and Child Welfare Act recommends a minimum of a baccalaureate-level degree in social work (but unfortunately does not require it). While this important work is often performed by people without appropriate training or experience, the social work degree remains the best professional preparation for the field. Workers with this background can be instrumental in improving the quality of service.

Least Restrictive Environment

Services to children and families, like services to other populations at risk, should be offered in the **least restrictive environment**, the setting that provides the least interference with normal life patterns yet provides the most important and needed services. The least restrictive environment for children is normally the biological family home.

Services offered to children in need can be classified in several ways, but one of the simplest is to divide them into two major categories: in-home (the least restrictive environment) and out-of-home. (Be careful not to confuse these contemporary service categories with *indoor* and *outdoor relief* as offered under historic English poor laws.) A continuum of care from least restrictive environment to most restrictive is illustrated in Box 5.3.

In-Home Services

In-home services (see Box 5.3) are provided to a family to help members live together more safely and harmoniously in their own homes. They are preventive in orientation. Paradoxically, some (like day care) may be offered outside the home, but the goal is to assist families to stay together. In-home services are described in this section. A discussion of out-of-home services appears further on. There is some overlap between in-home and out-of-home services,

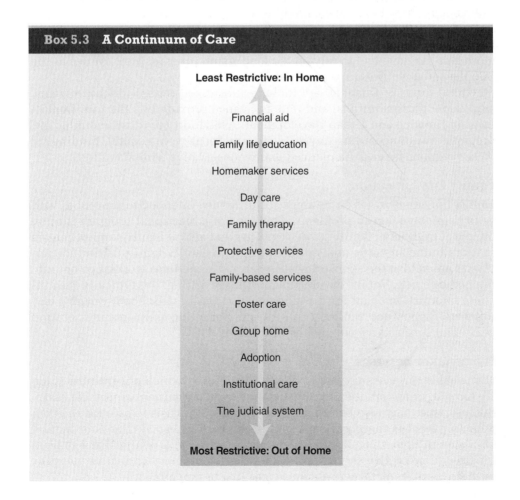

Box 5.3   A Continuum of Care

Least Restrictive: In Home

Financial aid

Family life education

Homemaker services

Day care

Family therapy

Protective services

Family-based services

Foster care

Group home

Adoption

Institutional care

The judicial system

Most Restrictive: Out of Home

of course. For example, adoption, while classified here as an out-of-home service because it removes children from their biological homes permanently, also *provides* needy children with homes.

Financial Aid

Many families require financial aid to survive. The major programs available were described in Chapter 4 and will be reviewed briefly here. The federally administered Social Security program provides income to families in which a breadwinner who has paid sufficient Social Security taxes has died, become disabled, or retired.

States *may* provide limited financial aid to poor families for no more than 5 years in a given parent's lifetime under the Temporary Assistance for Needy Families (TANF) program. This option is authorized under the federal Personal Responsibility and Work Opportunity Act (PRWOA) of 1996. TANF replaced Aid to Families with Dependent Children (AFDC), a program previously *entitling* poor children to aid under the Social Security Act.

Medicare and Medicaid programs provide funding for medical care for many families in need. They are authorized by amendments to the Social Security Act. Medicare primarily provides funds for elderly and disabled people. Medicaid is available to certain categories of poor people who pass a means test. Most people who qualify for TANF also qualify for Medicaid.

Food stamps provide financial assistance to families in voucher form (the voucher now looks like a credit or debit card). The amount of aid given depends on the number of people in a household and on the combined household income. Since the economic recession beginning in 2008, more and more families have had to rely on the food stamp program (now known as the Supplemental Nutrition Assistance Program).

Other forms of financial aid include subsidized school lunch programs, surplus food distributions, and rent assistance provided by the U.S. Department of Housing and Urban Development. Availability of these and other aid programs varies according to year, state, and locality. In general, funding for these programs tends to be reduced under conservative administrations.

Family Life Education

Family life education is an in-home social service intended to prevent as well as to help solve family problems. This type of educational program is often offered at traditional family service agencies and also at family support centers that are found in some areas of the country. Usually family life education classes are held at the sponsoring agencies, but sometimes workers go out into the home setting. Topics covered vary with the setting, but typically they include information about the developmental stages of childhood, weaning and toilet-training issues, building self-esteem, parenting skills, communication skills, and constructive methods of discipline.

Homemaker Services

Homemaker services may be provided to families in which one member is too ill, too old, or too emotionally unstable to carry out normal household tasks. Such services may also be provided on a short-term basis to care for children when a parent is temporarily absent because of physical illness or mental breakdown. Sometimes a homemaker is assigned to a family that has been reported to protective services for neglect, as a temporary corrective measure. In these cases, homemakers assume a teaching or modeling role.

The provision of homemaker services can allow families to stay together in their own homes under circumstances that might otherwise break them up. Services may include cleaning, shopping, cooking, laundry, and child care. They are offered at low cost to eligible families that meet a means test, through both public and private social service agencies. In most cases, services are provided by aides rather than social workers.

Day Care

Day care is considered an in-home social service, even though it is often provided outside the home. This service permits a working parent who has no partner, or two working parents, to maintain young children as part of the household.

Too common are "latchkey children," who spend part of their day in school and part at home alone, having let themselves in. Even this arrangement, however, is not feasible for families with infants and toddlers; without day care, these very young children would require foster care. For this reason, many states and counties have established programs in which day care is publicly subsidized, and a sliding fee is charged according to the income of the parent(s). The replacement of AFDC by TANF makes subsidized day care programs particularly imperative today since most poor mothers have to work outside the home. Yet there is no national requirement for such a service.

Day care centers that serve special populations of children are probably most likely to have social workers on staff. For example, some centers offer care for children with developmental disabilities or for those adjudicated by the courts as **children at risk**. At-risk children usually come through the recommendation of protective services social workers, who have determined that these children would be reasonably safe at home if their parents were relieved of child care responsibilities during all or part of the day.

Family Therapy

Family therapy is a service available to families experiencing many different kinds of distress. Although it usually is conducted in professional offices, it is considered an in-home service because it assists family members to live together more safely and harmoniously.

Family therapy is a practice concentration within the social work profession, and it requires a master's degree. Family therapy may be provided by members of related professions as well, such as psychologists or psychiatrists. Sometimes family therapists work in teams in which a psychologist administers psychological tests, a psychiatrist administers medication, and both serve as consultants to the social worker, who usually provides the ongoing counseling.

Protective Services

Protective services are designed to shield children from maltreatment, including both abuse and neglect. Lauren White of the LaTanya Tracy case was a protective services worker. The Child Abuse Prevention, Adoption, and Family Services Act of 1988 provides a general federal definition of maltreatment (quoted in Gustavsson & Segal, 1994, p. 75):

> The physical or mental injury, sexual abuse, or exploitation, negligent treatment or maltreatment of a child by a person who is responsible for the child's welfare, under circumstances which indicate that the child's health or welfare is harmed or threatened thereby, as determined in accordance with regulations prescribed by the Secretary of the Department of Health and Human Services.

While each state has its own definition of child maltreatment, the preceding federal definition specifies that it may be physical, mental (including emotional), or sexual, and it may involve active abuse or negligence.

Protective services workers usually begin by investigating and monitoring a referred child's own home. They counsel both children and parents; inform parents of legal requirements; and use as motivation for positive change both skillful professional relationships and sanctions, or penalties for noncompliance, provided by the court. In situations of extreme risk (and when such resources exist), protective services workers may mobilize family preservation teams for intensive in-home intervention as described later. Where safety issues remain serious, children may be placed in foster care (Reich, 2005). Children removed from parental homes are ideally placed in homes of relatives, as in the LaTanya Tracy case.

The primary goal of protective services programs under the Adoption Assistance and Child Welfare Act of 1980 was to preserve families while providing safe environments for children at risk. This law emphasized rehabilitation of parents so that children could leave the limbo of foster care and return to their own homes (McKenzie & Lewis, 1998; Reich, 2005). However, despite the good intention of this law, many children then remained in the limbo of foster care awaiting parental rehabilitation, in situations where the parents indicated little or no interest in change. The Adoption and Safe Families Act, signed into law by President Clinton in November 1997, acknowledges the importance of family preservation and support services but also encourages more timely **permanency placement**, recognizing children's developmental need to have a permanent home. The bill authorizes bonuses to states to increase adoptions of children and also speeds up timelines for holding hearings initiating proceedings to terminate parental rights (Adoption and Safe Families Act, 1997). States receive "report cards" on performance factors such as the number of adoptions completed and the shortness of stay in foster care (Samantrai, 2004).

Family-Based Services

Family-based services were prompted by the federal Adoption Assistance and Child Welfare Act of 1980, which required states to maintain children in the least restrictive environment possible (Smith, 1998). Later, in 1993, additional legislation entitled "Family Preservation and Family Support Services" was added to the Social Security Act. The purpose was to help keep families together, healthy, and safe. In 1997 the program's scope was expanded and reauthorized as the "Promoting Safe and Stable Families Program."

Practice Contexts

Practice Behavior Example: Social workers continuously discover, appraise, and attend to changing locales, populations, scientific and technological developments, and emerging societal trends to provide relevant services

Critical Thinking Question: How does the "least restrictive environment" principle, which reflects a societal trend, shape social work practice with minor children at risk?

Family support services are generally designed to promote the stability and well-being of families and to prevent family problems from escalating to a crisis point where out-of-home placement might be required. These services are usually targeted toward at-risk families—those where there is increased risk of abuse or neglect—and may include a variety of health, mental health, social, and educational benefits. Usually no time limit is imposed.

Family preservation services are designed specifically to help families that have been reported to public authorities for problems of neglect and abuse, when the children are at immediate risk of placement outside the home. Crisis workers may spend many hours per week in the family home on a short-term basis, focusing on parenting skills. Family preservation services are usually employed only after all other assistance has failed (Samantrai, 2004).

Out-of-Home Services

Sometimes, regardless of the amount of effort invested by protective and other supportive services, family circumstances still remain unsuitable for the upbringing of a child. In these cases, **out-of-home services** must be substituted, short or long term depending on the circumstances (see Box 5.3).

Foster Care

The type of foster care provided to LaTanya and Martin Tracy was perhaps the very earliest form available: care in a relative's home. Placement may be informal, purely a family matter. However, placement by a government agency such as a department of child welfare involves a foster home licensing process. Requirements for licensing include such factors as the amount of space in a house compared with the number of people living there, the number of bedrooms, and compliance with building codes and fire safety regulations. In addition, prospective foster parents must be investigated with respect to character, reliability, and parenting skills. Usually, social workers are the professionals who conduct foster home studies and recommend acceptance or rejection.

Once a foster home is accepted, social workers supervise the home. They visit on a regular schedule and talk with both foster parents and children to make sure that a constructive relationship is developing. When there is a problem, social workers become involved in solving it. Some foster homes are specialized; they are licensed to care for children who have unusual needs, such as physical or mental disabilities, behavioral disturbances, or emotional illness.

Normally, while a child is in foster care, the social worker works with the biological as well as the foster parents. The purpose of this work is to enable the natural parents to prepare for the successful return of their child, wherever possible.

Group Homes

Group homes are usually licensed to house eight people, a number large enough so that residents can have a variety of others to meet and talk with but small enough so that they can receive individual attention. Homes for children usually have a stable staff of youth care workers, often BSWs, supplemented by a housekeeping staff and child care aides. The aim is to make the setting as family-like as possible.

This type of out-of-home service meets several needs. First of all, given the shortage of licensed foster homes, group homes can provide shelter when regular foster homes are not available. In some cases, group home care may meet a particular child's needs better than a foster home can. For example, some teenagers cannot make the emotional investment necessary to develop close relationships with foster parents. They may be much more willing to relate to peers in a group home.

Shelters for runaways have emerged in many cities over the past two decades. Originally founded by volunteers, many shelters have become licensed as foster group homes. Runaway shelters usually provide bed, board, and crisis counseling, and their ultimate goal is to reunite families under conditions that are safe for the children.

Shelters for battered women and their children, which were introduced in Chapter 1, can be thought of as another type of group home for family members who are "running away from home." These shelters provide short-term bed and board. In addition, most provide information and referral services and crisis counseling. Usually, shelters are more widely available for battered women than for battered men. This is because women are most often the victims of battery and because women activists (including social workers) have usually been the driving force behind the creation of the shelters.

Adoption

Sometimes out-of-home substitute care goes beyond the temporary and becomes permanent by adoption. Adoption benefits needy children by providing a permanent plan of care. It provides children and their adoptive parents the same legal rights and responsibilities with respect to one another as are available to biological parents and their children. Children become available for adoption only when the rights of both natural parents have been terminated. Occasionally parental rights are terminated involuntarily by court order—for example, in circumstances of extreme, documented battery to the child. More often, biological parents themselves decide that they are not in a position to provide the kind of parenting they wish for their child.

The Adoption and Safe Families Act of 1997, as discussed earlier, encourages increased recognition of children's need for permanent homes. To this end, incentives are offered to speed up adoption procedures in situations where evidence is persuasive that the biological parents cannot provide suitable homes.

Social workers often provide counseling for people trying to reach the difficult decision of whether or not to place a child for adoption or even, in recent times, whether or not to continue a problem pregnancy. Termination of pregnancy is potentially an option in many circumstances, although the U.S. Supreme Court's 1989 Webster decision provided states with more regulating power. In recent years, more and more states have used this power to enact restrictive laws, and in early 2006 the U.S. Supreme Court overturned a nationwide injunction aimed at preventing violence at abortion clinics (Roth, 2006). Thus, women can be intimidated by extremist groups from trying to obtain abortions.

Children who have special characteristics or needs (such as those who are older, part of a sibling group, of mixed race, or disabled in some way) are hard to place and may spend their lives in foster homes. These are the children that single people or older couples are encouraged to adopt. An important task for social service agencies is the recruitment of adoptive placements for children who might otherwise never find permanent homes.

States are authorized under the Adoption Assistance and Child Welfare Act of 1980 to provide adoption subsidies for hard-to-place children. The medical costs of raising physically fragile children, for example, can be exorbitant. Subsidies make adoption a more realistic choice for many families (Gustavsson & Segal, 1994).

Adopted children may want to try to find their biological parents at some point in their lives. In recent years laws have been changed in many states, allowing adopted persons (after becoming adults) to obtain some of their social service agency records or, as in New Hampshire, to obtain copies of their original birth certificates (Collins, 2005). Parents who terminate their rights and place a child for adoption today may opt, in some states, to note in the records that they would be willing for the adult child to contact them.

Institutional Care

Institutional placement is another out-of-home option for the care of minor children. In the recent past, children who lost their parents were often placed in large institutions known as orphanages. Most such facilities have now been closed, replaced by foster homes and small group homes. Where large child care institutions still exist, they usually provide specialized treatment or short-term emergency shelter for children awaiting placement in less restrictive environments.

Some children are placed for a year or more at a type of institution known as a residential treatment center. These children usually have been determined by professional evaluation to be seriously emotionally disturbed; they often are referred by courts in an effort to control delinquent behavior. Residential treatment centers often provide a comprehensive range of services that include behavior modification programs (an approach sometimes called milieu therapy), individual counseling, family therapy, and instruction by teachers skilled in working with the emotionally and behaviorally disturbed.

The children who are placed in residential treatment facilities usually have been referred first to special education services in their respective community schools. Federally mandated special education policy requires treating children in the least restrictive environment possible. Only if less restrictive interventions fail will a child be referred to a residential treatment center, and only then if the community is willing to accept the expense (or, in rare cases, if parents can afford the expense).

The Judicial System

If a child has committed frequent and/or severe-enough crimes, he or she may be sentenced by the court to what amounts to a jail for minors. Pending a court hearing for an alleged offense, a child may be held temporarily in a detention center. This step is truly a last resort, and it usually represents the failure of other services. This is what is likely to happen when a child needed residential or other treatment earlier in life, but the care was not provided because of monetary cost. Attention to short-term budgetary concerns without consideration of long-term costs, both human and monetary, has been tragically characteristic of social planning in the United States (see Box 5.4).

Box 5.4   Child Welfare in the United States: Milestones

1642   Plymouth Colony enacts poor law similar to Elizabethan Poor Law of 1601.
Destitute children and orphans are apprenticed.

1790   First publicly funded orphanage in the United States: Charleston, South Carolina.

1853   Reverend Charles Loring Brace founds Children's Aid Society, New York City.

1865   Freedmen's Bureau founded, first federal welfare agency; in action until 1872.

1877   Society for Prevention of Cruelty to Children founded in New York City.
First Charity Organization Society in the United States founded in Buffalo, New York.

1886   First Settlement House in the United States founded in New York City.

1889   Hull House founded in Chicago by Jane Addams.

1909   White House Conference on Children.

1912   U.S. Children's Bureau founded.

1935   Social Security Act: Dependent children who are poor receive entitlement to aid.

1974   Child Abuse Prevention and Treatment Act.

1993   Family Preservation and Support Services Act.
Family and Medical Leave Act.

1996   Personal Responsibility and Work Opportunity Act ends entitlement of poor children to aid under Social Security Act. Establishes Temporary Assistance for Needy Families (TANF) program *at states' option.*

1997   Adoption and Safe Families Act.
Promoting Safe and Stable Family Program

CLIENT SELF-DETERMINATION AND PROFESSIONAL DECISION MAKING

The social work profession holds as an important principle the right of clients to make their own decisions. A major principle of the social work Code of Ethics deals specifically with **self-determination.** It requires social workers to respect clients' right to self-determination unless their actions create a serious risk for themselves or others.

The LaTanya Tracy case is a good example of a situation in which a social worker, Lauren White, in her professional role as a protective services worker, determined that Natasha Tracy's actions were posing a serious risk to herself and her children. Thus, while the principle of self-determination would normally guide a social worker to honor a client's own decisions, Natasha's substance abuse presented a substantial enough risk to justify Lauren's intervention ethically as well as legally. However, Lauren maximized her profession's ethical principle of self-determination to the greatest extent possible under the circumstances. She listened respectfully to Natasha; helped the young mother identify the many problems in her life that needed addressing; helped her sort out her own goals, which included caring for her children; and assisted in developing a plan of action that would solve many of the problems and permit the children to return home.

WOMEN, CHILDREN, AND ETHNIC MINORITY GROUPS: POPULATIONS AT RISK

In the United States, we are so accustomed to thinking of child rearing as a family responsibility that we forget that the nation as a whole benefits. In addition to what children add to the tapestry of human experience, their survival is essential to carrying on the fundamental tasks of the economic market. Today's productive adults will grow old and die; they will need replacement. Thus, despite superficial appearances, it is in the national interest, not just the interest of the individual family, to provide for children so that they can grow up to be emotionally stable, well educated, and capable of contributing to the common good (see Box 5.5).

Box 5.5   Should Single Mothers Be Forced to Work Outside the Home?

Poor single mothers already shoulder a double burden in parenting; should social policy require them to perform yet another job? The issue is not whether women with care giving responsibilities should enjoy full opportunity and equality in the labor market. Of course they should. The issue is coercion. Why should poor single mothers—and *only* poor single mothers—be forced by law to work outside the home?

Care giving, especially for young children—and 63 percent of mothers on welfare have children under age 5—involves more than baby sitting. It includes managing a household; doing housework; and most important, nurturing, loving, and comforting. Meeting the basic challenges of family work—nutritious meals with very little money, schlepping to the laundromat without a car, attending to a child's schedule of needs, cleaning, mending, caring—takes time, effort, energy, and responsibility (the very skills and sacrifices assigned economic value in the outside labor market). For a solo care giver who is poor, it can be a labor-intensive, full-time job.

Source: From *Welfare's End* by Gwendolyn Mink. Copyright © 1998 Cornell University Press.

Because we don't seem able to recognize the value of raising children in America, however—to recognize child rearing as valid work—we do not consider the task worth paying for (if provided by the mother). The Personal Responsibility and Work Opportunity Act (PRWOA) rescinded any national responsibility to assist poor parents in their child rearing job. Thus, as described in our chapter's case example, when the men in Natasha Tracy's life abandoned her to raise their two children alone, so did the nation. She then faced an impossible dilemma. Natasha needed to hold a paying job to feed herself and her two children, but her paycheck wasn't large enough to purchase child care. She needed to purchase child care to keep her paying job. This dilemma is experienced by millions of poor women today. The TANF program (see Chapter 4) can help for a time, if it is offered, but it requires a mother to work outside the home. In many states, even where a TANF program is provided, assistance with child care is not available.

Has the PRWOA and its TANF program helped poor people in the United States, as trumpeted enthusiastically by supporters? It was supposed to reduce welfare "dependency," thus producing "proud, self-supporting mothers" previously labeled "too lazy and dependent" to work outside the home. After the PRWOA was passed, welfare caseloads did drop significantly, which was touted as a great national success.

However, the reduction in caseloads has meant that millions of poor people, mostly women and children, have simply lost access to assistance. Only about 60 percent of the adults forced off welfare found jobs, and only about half of those earned enough to pull their families above the poverty line. Rarely did the jobs they found provide decent pay or benefits such as health insurance. Only a third of the newly employed were able to work continuously for a full year. Many who enrolled in TANF were forced off the program due to **sanctions** (Hays, 2007). Many were sanctioned as they were unable to meet TANF work or training requirements due to child care needs.

It is clear that TANF can help some young parents—perhaps 10 to 15 percent are in a better position now than they would have been if the PRWOA law had not been passed. Some have been provided with valuable training, work clothes, bus vouchers, child care subsidies, and income supplements, at least for a time (Hays, 2007). However, many others have been unable to meet TANF requirements and have experienced what happened to Natasha Tracy and her children—they were simply dropped from the program.

States have various options under the PRWOA. For example, they may require a mother to work outside the home before her child reaches the federally mandated age of 24 months. Natasha's state required her to work outside the home when LaTanya was only 12 weeks old. States may institute a lifetime policy benefit shorter than the federal limit of 5 years; they may deny additional benefits to children conceived by women receiving assistance; and they may choose weak, moderate, or strong sanctions for recipient infractions such as missing work due to child care needs.

A team headed by Soss (2004) wondered if state policy choices would follow a color line. Specifically, the team hypothesized that tougher policies would be adopted in states where Blacks and/or Hispanics made up a higher proportion of the welfare caseload when the PRWOA was passed. Sadly, their study confirmed the hypothesis. States with higher percentages of Black and Hispanic clients were significantly more likely to adopt harsher policies, especially stricter family caps and stricter time limits for assistance.

How are poor people faring since the passage of the PRWOA? Not very well. Hunger in the United States has been increasing every year. A survey by Feeding America in 2010 found that the program was feeding 37 million people annually in emergency feeding centers ("Hunger in America," 2010). The National Coalition for the Homeless found that in 50 cities, the number of homeless people greatly exceeded the number of emergency shelter and transitional housing spaces. Numbers of homeless at any given time are approximate, but estimates suggest that there are between 2 and 3 million every year, and nearly 40 percent are children ("How Many People Experience Homelessness?" 2009, July).

TANF caseloads *fell* in 22 states during the course of a 16-month study following the onset of the severe economic recession that began in December 2007. To be sure, there was a small *average* increase in state caseloads of 1.8 percent (not counting California), but this increase was much smaller than the real need for assistance indicated by a 20.2 percent increase in the number of food stamp recipients. According to the Women's Legal Defense and Education Fund, these caseload figures "underscore the urgent need for federal action to make TANF more accessible and responsive" (Casey, 2009) (see Box 5.6).

Attachment Theory and Emotional Bonding

Forcing poor mothers of infants and young children to work outside the home in order to ward off starvation and homelessness can have serious consequences with respect to emotional bonding or attachment between the child and the mother. The first attachment theorist, psychologist John Bowlby, described attachment as a long-term psychological connection between people. He believed that the very earliest bond between an infant and a

---

Box 5.6   Up for Debate

Proposition: Poor children should be entitled to public assistance

Yes	No
Children, especially young children, need a parent to care for them at home for consistent parental bonding, supervision, and a sense of security.	Even in many intact, middle-class families today, both parents have to work to make ends meet.
Day care services affordable to poor parents who have to work outside the home are likely to be unregulated and of poor quality, putting poor children at increased disadvantage.	Day care services may be available in centers offering a sliding fee. Besides, babysitting for other people's children can provide welfare mothers a means of earning an income.
Poor parents usually have been disadvantaged with respect to education; they often must accept jobs at or near minimum wage, which is too low to raise their families out of poverty.	If public assistance is offered to poor children, their parents may opt not to work outside the home, thus depriving potential employers of low-wage workers.
Many studies, both national and international, have shown that good welfare programs do not increase birth rates in single-parent families. Besides, regardless of the circumstances of their birth, all children deserve a minimum standard of living even if their biological parents cannot provide.	Assisting poor children may encourage poor, single mothers to have more children whom society does not want.

primary caregiver has enormous importance, influencing a person's entire life. Attachment theory holds that caregivers who are consistently available and responsive to their infants' needs create secure foundations for their children to begin to explore the world. Such infants are described as having secure attachments. But where caregivers are not dependably responsive to their infants' needs, secure attachments will not be achieved.

Psychologist Mary Ainsworth expanded on Bowlby's theory. In her study of children 12 to 18 months old, she found that those who were "securely attached" exhibited little distress when separated from their caregivers. When frightened, they returned with confidence to their caregivers for comfort and reassurance. However, children who were not securely attached demonstrated very different behaviors. Those with "ambivalent attachment" became exceedingly upset when separated from caregivers. Ainsworth's research data suggested that ambivalent attachment resulted from poor maternal availability. Those with "avoidant attachment" tended to avoid their parents or caregivers; when offered a choice, they showed no preference between caregivers and strangers. Data suggested that abuse or neglect could cause this type of attachment.

What happens to children who do not form secure attachments? Research suggests that their behavior is negatively affected throughout their entire lives. They are frequently diagnosed with oppositional defiant disorder, conduct disorder, and post-traumatic stress disorder (Cherry, 2010). Could these disorders help explain why the United States puts such a high percentage of its population behind bars? Could this be a very costly downstream solution to the problem of poverty?

Can a single mother who is forced to work outside the home be consistently and reliably available to meet her infant's or young child's needs? While parents with a partner may also work outside the home, there are two responsible adults available to share parenting, breadwinning, and housework tasks. Two parents can also provide emotional security for one another. By contrast, the single parent must struggle alone and may need to hold more than one job to make ends meet. Thus, it seems unlikely that such a parent could provide a child with the kind of dependable, ongoing attention required to develop secure attachment. TANF requirements force her to get a paying job instead.

Reproductive Rights and Single Parenting

Ironically, at a time when the nation is abandoning its poor children, it continues to deny poor mothers the means to terminate unwanted pregnancies. In 1973, the Supreme Court ruled that women have a constitutional right to safe and legal abortions *(Roe v. Wade),* but the Hyde Amendment of 1976 denied Medicaid funding for abortions to poor women. That amendment remains in force today. Since the 1973 ruling, all women have found it increasingly difficult to get an abortion, poor or not. Many states have passed restrictions such as parental notification for minors and mandatory waiting periods. More than a hundred clinics have been shut down by disruptive demonstrations and threats on people's lives. The National Organization for Women secured a court injunction preventing demonstrators from blocking clinic entrances, but the Supreme Court overturned the injunction in early 2006 (Roth, 2006).

The Supreme Court also made abortions more difficult to obtain by allowing a late-term abortion ban in 2007. It was a 5–4 decision, extremely dangerous to women as it allowed no exception to safeguard a woman's health. Justice Ruth Bader Ginsberg, the only woman then on the court, blasted the majority for using "flimsy and transparent justifications" for upholding the ban (Richey, 2007).

A hopeful development is the approval granted by the U.S. Food and Drug Administration (FDA) in 2006 allowing nonprescription sale of an emergency contraception pill to women over 18. This pill can prevent fertilization of the woman's egg "the morning after" unplanned intercourse. However, minors who need the pill must procure a physician's prescription (Erickson, 2006a).

While the FDA's decision was an advance for the United States, other nations are not nearly so conservative. For example, public health clinics across the nation of Chile freely distribute the morning-after pill to women and girls age 14 and older. This policy was instituted by President Michelle Bachelet, a woman, because a very high percentage of Chilean girls were becoming pregnant by age 14. Bachelet's policy was strongly opposed by the Catholic Church, but a ruling by Chile's Supreme Court permitted distribution centered on the fact that the pill is not abortive, but works to inhibit ovulation, thus preventing fertilization (Ross, 2006). Interestingly enough, at the end of Bachelet's term in office, her approval rating was over 70 percent in Chile in large part due to her support of mothers and children's education programs (Llana, 2010).

No one knows for certain what the future will bring with respect to reproductive rights in the United States, but neoconservative President George W. Bush appointed two judges to the Supreme Court whose records are not promising for women (e.g., the subsequent late-term abortion ban). Reproductive rights are clearly in jeopardy. Hostility of lawmakers toward women who become pregnant out of wedlock may help explain the government's paradoxical refusal both to fund abortions for poor women who want them and to help them finance raising the children that Medicaid policies force them to bear. After all, lawmakers in the United States are overwhelmingly male (see Box 5.7).

One goal of welfare reform was to encourage single women to marry, in part by making marriage more economically imperative. However, research has found that the number of marriages per year actually declined after the 1996 PRWOA was passed. We have much to learn about factors that lead to marriage (Campbell, 2004). Economic desperation by legislation does not seem to be sufficient incentive.

Ecological Issues

Ecological research alerts us that not only are poor people at risk on this good earth, but all people are—in large part because the population is exploding (Nadakavukaren, 2006). The population of the United States reached nearly 309 million in 2010. The population of the world reached more than

Box 5.7   Welfare Reform to Punish Nontraditional Families?

The drive to reform welfare that began in the early 1980s and culminated with the PRWOA in 1996 was never about welfare alone. In fact, the attack on welfare helped to fulfill other political agendas. Liberal politicians bashed welfare and the poor to establish their conservative credentials. Business and industry turned against welfare arguing that it undercut their profits. The social conservatives used welfare reform to promote their own version of family values that ruled out all but the two-parent, heterosexual household.

Source: Quoted from M. Abramovitz. (2000). *Under attack, fighting back, women and welfare in the United States.* New York: Monthly Review Press, p. 17.

6.8 billion in 2010 and will reach 9 billion by 2050. Alarmingly, people have consumed more food than farmers have been able to produce over most of the past decade, leading to a tripling of the price of wheat and corn and a fivefold increase in the price of rice. There were food riots in over two dozen countries between 2005 and 2008 (Bourne, 2009; "US & World Population Clock," 2010; "World POPClock Projection," 2010).

In addition to the danger of people outgrowing the food supply as farm lands succumb to housing and industry, the natural environment is in grave danger. Climate change is accelerating, due in part to high carbon emissions into the atmosphere from human use of fossil fuels. The ice caps are melting, glaciers are receding, and large chunks of ice are dropping into the oceans, threatening to redirect the course of the Gulf Stream. Temperatures in the Northern Hemisphere have been significantly warmer in the last 30 years than at any time since the U.S. government began collecting data in 1895 (Kaufman, 2007). In addition, a vast hole in the ozone layer is growing because of chlorine atoms emitted by consumer goods such as hair spray, refrigerants, pesticides, plastics, and fire retardants (Ornes, 2007). Climate change is projected to lead to hotter growing seasons and increasing scarcity of water worldwide (Bourne, 2009).

The ice caps are melting, glaciers are receding, and large chunks of ice are dropping into the oceans, threatening to redirect the course of the Gulf Stream.

What must be done to save the environment, so that the human species can survive along with it? Scientists have documented the issue, but many politicians are avoiding their counsel; the most responsible nations are pointing fingers at each other without taking serious steps to solve the problem. Certainly the United States needs to cooperate with international treaties designed to reduce emissions (see Figure 5.1).

Population stabilization measures are desperately needed, not only in the United States but around the world (Nadakavukaren, 2006). Family planning

"SORRY BILLY,,, HAPPY PONY IS ON,,, AND I'M _NOT_ MISSING HAPPY PONY!"

Figure 5.1

services that include voluntary termination of pregnancy need to be available to all. A sound education for all children is imperative, along with programs alerting all to the need for conservation. American children are in special need of conservation education: the average American consumes 20 times as much energy as the average African (Francis, 2006).

Education and family planning services hopefully can allow world population to stabilize through voluntary means. Many studies have shown that women with access to family planning services, educational opportunities, and rewarding careers decrease their family size voluntarily. The alternative has been demonstrated in China, where a burgeoning population led the government to restrict families to a single child. Involuntary abortion, increased voluntary abortion and infanticide (abortion and infanticide especially of female babies), and an alarming imbalance in the ratio of males to females are among the results. Chinese families restricted to a single child tend to keep the male, as the male child is expected to marry a wife who is expected to care for her husband's parents. But where will the wives come from now?

Gay and Lesbian Families

According to Savin-Williams and Esterberg (2000), research has found that children who are raised by lesbian or gay parents exhibit no differences from those raised by heterosexuals with respect to gender identity, sex-role behavior, self-concept, intelligence, personality characteristics, or behavioral problems. They are also no more likely to suffer any kind of sexual abuse.

Given this research knowledge, the National Association of Social Workers (NASW) defends gay families and frequently files legal briefs in defense of gay and lesbian foster or adoptive families. For example, when the Central Baptist Family Services Agency in Illinois tried to take over guardianship of a foster child placed by the Department of Children and Family Services in the home of a lesbian couple, simply because the couple was lesbian, the NASW filed a legal brief defending the foster family. The Central Baptist Family Services Agency planned to return the child to grandparents who had previously fractured his skill and tibia and had inflicted a number of other serious wounds.

Fortunately, the NASW brief helped prevent the child from being sent back to such a dangerous environment (Stoessen, 2005). But the fact that the Baptist Family Service Agency considered a home with severely abusive grandparents superior to a safe and loving home with lesbian foster parents indicates the extent of prejudice in some places against gays and lesbians.

Many gays and lesbians share parental responsibilities with committed partners who may try legally to adopt the biological children of their mates. Such adoptions have been difficult to obtain in court, although spouses in heterosexual marriages where children have been conceived through alternative means (e.g., artificial insemination) are automatically considered the legal parents of these offspring. Legal marriage for gays and lesbians would provide a child conceived by alternative means two legal parents, but so far only six states and Washington, DC, have provided this opportunity. Sadly, backlash movements threaten the law in even these states. Misinformed, frightened, and prejudiced citizens have passed constitutional amendments forbidding gay marriage in most states.

How to become parents presents practical problems for both lesbian women and gay men. Adoption is a possibility for some, although many programs discriminate against people of same-sex orientation. Those who want to become biological parents face a different challenge. Some women may ask male friends to consider becoming sperm donors, while others may turn to sperm banks. The use of medically administered sperm banks eliminates the potential danger of later court battles for parental rights (donors in medically controlled donor insemination programs waive parental rights and responsibilities), so many women prefer this option. Gay men, on the other hand, unless they or their partners have custody of children from prior heterosexual relationships, must find surrogate mothers. For them, the risk that a surrogate may later sue to gain custody is a real concern.

Sperm banks have been available for decades, but people have become more aware of them in recent years, and some interesting questions have arisen. For example, are multiple women inseminated by the same man? Is it likely their children might meet in the future? Do children conceived in this way want to locate their fathers?

According to Engbur and Klungness (2000), most sperm banks have developed policies to limit the likelihood of encounter with half siblings. Sperm from a given donor may be used for only a limited number of pregnancies, and sperm is shipped all over the nation, not just to a local area. Thus, the likelihood of a child later entering a relationship with a half sibling is extremely small.

When the practice of artificial insemination was first begun, secrecy was practiced. Donor records were destroyed to protect the privacy of the adults involved. However, similar to adoptive children, some children conceived through artificial insemination wish to meet their biological fathers. Many sperm banks today provide an option for donors to be contacted by children once they have turned 18. Some require potential donors to grant grown children that right.

Unfortunately, heterosexism and homophobia are still very much alive in the United States. It is important that social workers maintain not only a broad cultural perspective but an understanding of the conditions in their own communities. While self-disclosure may help many gays and lesbians create a more integrated life, it can expose others to real danger (Pardess, 2005). Social workers who counsel **gay** and **lesbian** persons need to understand the challenges this minority faces and consider both empowerment and safety issues.

Multiracial Families

Multiracial families are now a part of the American scene, although as yet a fairly small part. For the first time in 2000, the U.S. census permitted people to classify themselves in more than one racial category. Approximately 2 percent took advantage of the opportunity (Belsie, 2001). Interracial marriage is one way to form a multiracial family; another is to adopt a child of a different race. Each process presents its own opportunities and challenges.

According to Diller (1999), children raised in multiracial families are quite capable of developing healthy ethnic identities. They can integrate different cultural backgrounds into a single sense of self, and they tend to welcome the opportunity to discuss who they are ethnically with other people. Children may meet special challenges in school, where the question "what are you" requires a skillful response. Teens especially may be pushed by peers to adopt part of their racial identity and reject another; their single-race parents may have difficulty understanding the pressures involved. Still, supportive parents can make an important difference in helping interracial children cope with a complex, sometimes hostile world.

The modern family may be multi-racial.

Interracial couples face special challenges; it is common for at least one set of in-laws to reject the chosen partner, for example. Interracial couples may find themselves socially isolated not only from families of origin but from former friends. In response, many associate mostly with other interracial couples. Moreover, each partner brings different cultural expectations to the marriage, so role expectations may require skillful negotiation. Many couples meet these challenges successfully, however.

Intercultural adoptions involve a different set of challenges. They are usually opposed by people of color, especially African Americans and Native Americans, who believe that White parents cannot provide minority children appropriate exposure to their cultural heritage or teach them how to cope with discrimination in the wider society. Many children of color adopted by White parents in the United States today come from overseas. Special efforts must be made to help these children learn about their cultural heritage.

Immigrant Families

Like multiracial families, immigrant families face myriad challenges although they differ in nature. Fathers often find that the vocational and educational skills they worked so hard to achieve in their nation of origin are not transferable to the United States; former professionals may find themselves performing unskilled labor, earning incomes too meager to adequately support a family. Financial need may require the wife, who probably did not work in the nation of origin, to find a job to supplement the family income. In the new work setting she may learn that gender roles in the United States allow more freedom to women and that she has new legal rights. She may begin to challenge the gender roles of her nation of origin, leading to marital strife. Men may begin to feel a loss of power and self-esteem while the wife gains more power and authority (Delgado, Jones, & Rohani, 2005).

Children in immigrant families can also feel the strain. They are likely to learn English much faster than their parents, for example. Serving as translators for parents can burden children by exposing them to adult issues before they are ready, leading to premature independence and a power shift in the family. Children taking on adult roles prematurely can virtually skip their own childhood. They can lose confidence in their parents as they see them changing from competent caretakers to overwhelmed individuals dependent on translation services of their children. They are likely to challenge their parents' authority at an early age.

Language may also become a serious communication barrier within immigrant families. Children may adopt English as their first language and forget what they ever knew of their language of origin, whereas members of the grandparent generation, who may have immigrated with the family, never learn English at all. Children may become ashamed of members of their extended family who cannot speak English and who maintain customs from their nation of origin (Delgado et al., 2005). Family therapy could help family members appreciate each other's strengths, but immigrant families rarely seek out such services. This may be due to lack of information as well as cultural norms that teach that family issues should remain within the family.

DIVERSE FAMILY STRUCTURES AND SOCIAL WORK'S ETHIC OF CULTURAL COMPETENCE

Social workers today frequently work with families to help strengthen the relationships among members, foster nonviolent parenting skills, assist in finding financial and material resources, help protect abused and neglected children, help arrange foster care, provide home studies for adoption, and the like. For this reason, it is very important that workers recognize, understand, and respect family diversity, whether ethnic, cultural, lifestyle, socioeconomic, or whatever. The social work Code of Ethics specifically instructs social workers to learn about differences among people and to recognize that certain groups may suffer oppression through no fault of their own. Advocating for justice for these groups is also an important provision of the Code.

Carter and McGoldrick (2005) point out that diverse groups have very different cultural expectations relating to the family, including the importance attributed to different life-cycle transitions, intergenerational relationships, gender roles, and the like. For example, the Irish place great emphasis on the wake, viewing death as the most important life-cycle transition. African Americans also emphasize funerals. But Italian and Polish families place greatest emphasis on the wedding; Jewish families emphasize the bar mitzvah and bat mitzvah, the transition to adulthood for boys and girls, respectively. With respect to intergenerational relationships, families of British heritage may feel they have failed if their children do *not* move away from the home as adults. Italian families may feel they have failed if their children do move away! Italian and Greek children are taught at an early age that it is their responsibility to care for their parents in old age. But older adults of British heritage tend to consider dependence on adult children a tragic situation.

Because expectations relating to the family differ markedly among diverse cultural groups, it is important for social workers to educate themselves about the characteristics of the populations they serve. There are variations *within* populations as well, so that the worker's knowledge must constantly be refined and updated. Diversity will only increase in the future. It is estimated that by 2042, racial minority populations combined will comprise a majority in the United States, and many people of color embrace minority ethnic traditions (van Gelder, 2010).

SPIRITUALITY, RELIGION, AND SCIENCE

Social work literature has reflected an increasing interest in spiritual issues in recent years, and many social workers on the front lines have felt a growing need for a vision of society and the human person that transcends the material. In the United States, a person's worth is often measured in dollars only, and those who serve the less fortunate may experience a hunger to find a measure of human worth providing more dignity and hope.

Spirituality can be defined most simply as the universal search for meaning and purpose. It is an aspect of humanity common to all.

Some find solace in traditional religions, but others look toward what can perhaps be a more all-embracing source of strength, **spirituality**. Spirituality can be defined most simply as the universal search for meaning and purpose. It is an aspect of humanity common to all: atheist, Christian, Jew, Buddhist, Muslim, traditional Native American, whomever. It involves a loving appreciation for all that exists, allowing almost mystical new perspectives, increasing one's understanding and ability to cope with human suffering (Lindsay, 2002).

Most Western educational institutions (with the possible exception of theological schools and departments) avoid any discussion of spiritual issues in the classroom. After all, Western science has "proven" that people are material only, that one's life ends at death, that the soul is a fictional concept, and so on. This worldview, espoused by Western science, is known as materialism. Meantime, sadly, traditional religions often battle one another trying to impose their particular nonmaterialistic interpretations of reality on others.

Spirituality shares much in common with religion, but does not claim any particular truth nor does it try to impose anything on others. Instead, spiritual seekers remain open to new understandings involving human capabilities and our place in the universe. Such seekers may or may not affiliate with a particular religious group.

Oddly enough, new understandings involving human capabilities are emerging from an unexpected source: Western science! To be more specific, they are deriving from the work of a few courageous scientists who use Western scientific methods to prove that the Western scientific worldview of materialism is inadequate. These are the researchers into psychic phenomena (a field known as parapsychology). As asserted by psychologist (and parapsycholgist) Dr. Charles Tart, one can both be a serious scientist and maintain a strong interest in psychic research. He writes, "... you can take a basically scientific stance toward life and still legitimately claim that, using rigorous kinds of scientific procedures, the human mind shows properties that underlie what we think of as spiritual" (Tart, 2009, p. 36).

Psychic research has been ignored and/or ridiculed by mainstream science, because psychic phenomena are considered impossible according to the Western worldview. Research funding is thus extremely limited. Still, an impressive amount has been accomplished. Tart considers research evidence for what he calls the "basic five" psychic phenomena, telepathy, clairvoyance, precognition, psychokinesis, and psychic healing, so strong that he describes them as "basic possibilities for humans" (Tart, 2009, p. 12).

A series of books by Dr. Larry Dossey, physician of internal medicine, describes a number of modern, controlled, double-blind research studies that provide highly statistically significant evidence that prayer and human intention promote healing—not only in humans (where a placebo effect, or the power of expectation, might confound these experiments) but in a variety of animals, bacteria, fungi, cancerous tissues, and enzyme preparations. Prayer has even been demonstrated to make plants grow faster (Dossey, 1989, 2003, 2008).

Dr. Dean Radin, laboratory director at the Institute of Noetic Sciences in Petaluma, California, has conducted several studies demonstrating, with overwhelming statistical significance, that the human mind can affect matter. For example, human intention can increase growth in brain cells cultured in the laboratory and can even slightly modify the output of numbers produced by random number generating machines (Radin, 2006).

On an entirely different track, Dr. Gary Schwartz, who received his PhD in psychology from Harvard University and is now a professor at the University of Arizona and director of its Laboratory for Advances in Consciousness and Health, has been investigating a phenomenon considered impossible by most Western scientists—survival of consciousness after death. He has tested several well-known psychic mediums under laboratory-controlled conditions to find out if they can give accurate information about loved ones who have died (information consistent among independent mediums and confirmed by knowledgeable family and friends). He has found evidence strong enough to convince himself, his team, and many others (Schwartz, Simon, & Chopra, 2002).

Most of the preceding research has been ignored by mainstream scientists as it lies outside the Western paradigm of thought. But Dr. Marilyn Schlitz, president of the Institute for Noetic Sciences, known for her double-blind experiments on the power of human intention to promote physiological changes in other humans (and having produced statistically significant evidence that it can), finds herself pondering the meaning of Schwartz's work (see Box 5.8).

An important reason that Western scientists ignore scientifically controlled studies such as those by Tart, Schwartz, Schlitz, and Radin is that no one has any idea how humans could possibly produce the effects shown in such experiments. Yet the quality of experiments dealing with healing has

---

Box 5.8   Hope for the Bereaved?

Does this mean that we can communicate with the dead? No. But we also don't know that we can't. As studies of mediums are combined with other efforts, such as investigations of reincarnation, out-of-body experiences, and near-death experiences, scientists are formulating a new image of death. We are moving from an image of the grim reaper, cutting us off from our loved ones, to what psychiatrist Raymond Moody described as "the being of light." From this perspective, death is seen as a continuum rather than an either-or condition. By reframing death, we may engage in levels of transpersonal growth that can provide us with connections to the subtle, causal, and ultimate realms of reality.

This exploration of the possible survival of consciousness, even in the absence of definitive answers, can offer comfort to the bereaved. The burden of grief, the lingering fears and doubts, may be tempered by hope and possibility. Through this process, we may move outside a limited paradigm of separateness and finality and toward a larger sense of self and our connections to the whole.

Source: From M. Schltz, T. Amorok, & M. Micozzi (Eds.). *Consciousness and healing, integral approaches to mind body medicine.* St. Louis, MO: Elsevier, pp. 222–223. Copyright © 2005, Elsevier Science, Inc. Reprinted by permission.

been independently assessed, and rated as *B* or *good* overall (Dossey, 2008). Is it possible that the materialistic world view needs to be updated? Is there more to humanity than materialism recognizes?

Dr. Lawrence LeShan points out that maintaining a materialistic world-view is leading us to destroy life on our planet. If we are merely random conglomerations of elements and chemicals, why not take whatever we want for ourselves, with no thought for others or for the future? As he notes: "unless we can change the way we regard and define human beings, we will not be able to stop killing each other and poisoning our only planet. Psychic research has the data to give us a new way to view ourselves and each other" (LeShan, 2009, p. 18).

FAMILY POLICY, DOMESTIC AND INTERNATIONAL: RESEARCH RAISES QUESTIONS

Is the United States meeting the needs of its children and families? While lip service is given to family values in the United States, few governmental supports exist to provide assistance to those in need. The result is unfortunate: for example, research data reveal that the United States falls far down on the list of comparative infant mortality rates among industrialized nations—it is 25th. The United States ranks 22nd among industrialized nations in low infant birthweights. Since the year 2000, child poverty rates have continued to increase; more than one child in five lives below the poverty level, and poverty rates are much higher in families of ethnic minority heritage than in White families ("About Poverty—Highlights," 2011; "Income, Poverty and Health Insurance in the United States," 2009) (see Box 5.9).

How do other nations help keep their children out of poverty? Many different approaches are taken, but virtually all Western industrialized nations

---

Box 5.9   Children at Higher Risk in Red States

Michael R. Petit, the president and founder of Every Child Matters Education Fund and an NASW member, has released a book with statistics showing that the well-being of children living in "red states" (those that voted Republican for President, e.g., for Bush) is worse than that of children living in "blue states" (those that voted Democratic for president, e.g., for Gore or Kerry). . . .

Petit's book, *Homeland Insecurity,* offers data showing that anti tax and anti government policies place children at greater risk for low birth weight, infant mortality, premature death, child abuse, lack of health insurance, and poverty. . . .

Petit used U.S. Census data and other governmental sources to compare and rank states on outcomes for children. He developed a "child vulnerability index," based on 11 statistical measures, such as the percentage of uninsured children, child mortality rates, child abuse fatailties, juvenile incarceration rates, child welfare spending, and other factors.

For overall child vulnerability rankings, based on the 11 measures, 9 of the 10 best-ranked states were blue states. All of the 10 worst-ranked states were red states.

Petit also compared the United States with other developed countries. The United States has higher rates of incarceration, homicides, and firearm deaths than the United Kingdom, Canada, Germany, Italy, France, or Japan. The United States also has the lowest life expectancy and the hightest infant mortality rate among these countries.

except the United States provide universal health care. Many nations also provide universal, non-means-tested children's allowances to help keep families out of poverty in the first place, recognizing that children bring additional expenses to every family. Some countries provide an additional stipend if a noncustodial parent fails to keep up with child support payments. Many nations provide universal day care, either free or on a sliding scale. Others provide paid maternity and/or paternity leaves for as long as a full year, with the guarantee that one has a job when one is ready to return to work. Unfortunately, however, all these benefits are in jeopardy because of intense international competition from global corporations and trends in privatization of social services (Ford, 2005).

Research Based Practice

Practice Behavior Example: Social workers use research evidence to inform practice

Critical Thinking Question: What does international research tell us about the types of policies that can prevent childhood poverty?

The good news is that government programs can make a difference to children and can help strengthen families. A distinct low point in U.S. child poverty rates was achieved in 1969, and it was not due to any accident, but rather was the result of the combined effects of important programs in the War on Poverty at that time. The War on Poverty was not lost because it could not be won, but rather because the money was diverted to the military budget and the conflict in Vietnam (Van Wormer, 1997).

The bad news is that the United States continues to use a huge proportion of its tax revenues to support the military and military action. "Guns vs. butter" has been the subject of persistent debate: which is more important, military action or humanitarian aid at home and abroad? In recent years, guns have clearly trumped butter; the United States spends more on its military than *all* the other nations in the world *combined.* As a result, hunger and homelessness have been growing here, and the refugee population among displaced persons in the world has also been growing.

In the United States, a network of emergency food providers has arisen to try to meet the ever-increasing need, such as Feeding America, mentioned in an earlier section (see Figure 5.2). Other organizations such as the National Coalition for the Homeless have been trying to provide shelter in many places. Coalitions of churches have been working hard to try to meet hunger and shelter needs, as described in our chapter's case study. But while the work of voluntary organizations is impressive, that so many people are so poor today is quite an indictment of the values of the leadership of this country, currently the wealthiest nation in the world.

Research thus indicates a growing need for basics such as food and shelter for poor citizens in the United States. When President Obama was elected along with a Democratic House and Senate in 2008, an opportunity seemed to open to change our nation's priorities. But with a huge budget deficit inherited from the Republicans; declining tax revenues due to the recession; and two ongoing, very expensive wars, the new administration started out with a huge handicap. President Obama was able to pass health care legislation in 2010 to help average Americans, but the country remained mired in war in Afghanistan and Iraq, and Obama later engaged in another war as well, this time in Libya. Given the enormous ongoing costs of war, and with Congress unwilling to raise taxes on the superrich to pay for them, average Americans may increasingly be on their own trying to provide for themselves and their families. Will they be able to meet their needs in the workplace?

Figure 5.2

HOW FAMILY-FRIENDLY IS THE AMERICAN WORKPLACE?

Given that the shrinking of government programs is forcing more and more parents to work outside the home, the question of whether the workplace is family-friendly becomes increasingly important. Studies show, unfortunately, that the workplace in the United States has a long way to go in this area.

A study by the Center for WorkLife Law at the University of California–Hastings found that pregnancy discrimination lawsuits in the United States rose from a mere 97 in 1996 to 481 in 2005 (Gardner, 2006). By 2007, they had increased to over 5,500 (Shellenbarger, 2008). Discrimination lawsuits continue to increase today because a woman is all too likely to be transferred or terminated if she becomes pregnant, especially if she requests family leave. Men have also been terminated for requesting family leave. Employers frequently refuse to consider women for promotion if they are pregnant or have young children. Few firms allow flexible schedules, crucial for parents with young children, or allow a new parent to phase in the return to work. Nevertheless, such provisions are increasingly necessary given that the majority of women in the workforce have young children.

The United States is unique in the Western industrialized world in that it does not require employers to provide paid parental leave under law. Recognizing the need, the state of California passed an innovative public policy designed to help families in 2004. While the California law does not guarantee time off for new parents, it does provide parents whose employers grant family leave with 55 percent of their regular salaries for up to 6 weeks. The program is operated through the state disability system and is financed entirely by employees. Young parents find this provision tremendously helpful in meeting their new parental responsibilities (Gardner, 2006).

In 2007, the state of Washington adopted a paid parental leave act, but it has never been implemented due to lack of funding. New Jersey adopted a paid parental leave program in 2009, funded by a small worker contribution of about $18 per year, and it is operating successfully. The Obama administration has proposed allocating $23 million to the states to implement paid parental leave programs, but the proposal has not been enacted as of this chapter's revision. Research has shown that lack of paid parental leave leads to increased postpartum depression, early termination of breast feeding, and family debt ("Paid Parental Leave Lacking," 2011).

A former president of the NASW, Elvira Craig de Silva, reminded social workers in 2006 that the United Nations adopted two covenants in 1966 involving human rights, the International Covenant on Civil and Political Rights and the Covenant on Economic, Social and Cultural Rights. These include rights to liberty, health, and education and the right to work, protect one's family, and earn a decent standard of living. Because the United States has not lived up to these covenants, the NASW has become a partner of the ONE Campaign, a worldwide movement to end poverty (de Silva, 2006).

The National Organization of Women (NOW) is also trying to move the United States toward meeting the terms of these UN covenants, trying to achieve a more just nation and a more family-friendly workplace. When the United States filed a report with the United Nations claiming compliance with the International Covenant on Civil and Political Rights in October 2005 (10 years late), circumventing many issues such as prisoner abuse, domestic wiretapping, and infringement of civil liberties in the guise of fighting terrorism, this report asserted that American women have full protection under the law from sex discrimination. Disputing this assertion, NOW Foundation filed a "Gender Shadow Report" with the United Nations in July 2006, asserting that:

- The U.S. government has failed to adopt effective laws that address persistent pay inequity for women.
- Laws against sexual harassment and discrimination in employment and education in the United States are inadequate and poorly enforced.
- Family support policies are seriously lacking in the United States, and their absence makes it nearly impossible for women to achieve equality in the workforce. Family and medical leave provisions are among the most unfriendly of all developed nations, providing only unpaid leave and requiring only about half of all employers to provide even this.

The effort to highlight U.S. problems such as these to the United Nations was successful: the UN Human Rights Commission's concluding observations on U.S. compliance, after considerable subsequent investigation, was that the commission was "especially concerned about the reported persistence of employment discrimination against women" (Erickson, 2006b, p. 17).

Employment discrimination against women in the workplace remains ongoing in the United States today. Few, if any, changes have taken place since the UN Human Rights Commission expressed its concern, with the exception of the Lilly Ledbetter Law that President Obama signed in 2009, strengthening the legal groundwork for gender equity in pay.

The absence of family support policies is especially harmful. Someone has to care for infants, transport young children to day care, attend parent–teacher conferences, take children to medical appointments, care for the sick, and the like—the father can do this as well as the mother, of course, but usually it is she who is expected to perform these tasks. The United States remains an exception among industrialized countries in that it does not honor the needs of parents by requiring employers to provide paid parental leave. Many nations require paid leave for *both* parents.

ASSISTING FAMILIES AROUND THE WORLD

Fortunately, many of the best minds on earth today are concerned about worldwide issues of grave concern to the family. The United Nations has provided a forum where many of these minds can meet and work together. In 1990, a special committee composed the UN Millennium Declaration and set 2015 as a target date to achieve eight millennium development goals. These goals are as follows:

- Eradicate extreme poverty and hunger
- Achieve universal primary education
- Promote gender equality and empower women
- Reduce child mortality
- Improve maternal health
- Combat HIV/AIDS, malaria, and other diseases
- Ensure environmental sustainability
- Develop a global partnership for development

Imagine the positive effects on family life if these goals were met? By 2009, according to a report commissioned by UN Secretary General Ban Ki-moon, limited but measurable progress had been made. The developmental goals triggered worldwide efforts to alleviate poverty, hunger, disease, and environmental destruction. Extreme poverty was reduced to slightly more than one-quarter of the world's population from nearly half in 1990. Hunger was substantially reduced, and 88 percent of young children were enrolled in primary school and receiving important immunizations. Deaths of children under 5 had declined. Secretary Ban Ki-moon thus affirmed that the right policies and actions, backed by adequate funding and political commitment, can indeed have a positive impact.

However, the global economic crisis that took hold in 2008 reversed some of the progress and plunged millions back into poverty. Secretary Ki-moon urged that "efforts to restore economic growth should be seen as an opportunity to make some of the hard decisions needed to create a more equitable and sustainable future" (Ki-moon, 2009, p. 3).

CURRENT TRENDS IN THE UNITED STATES

A major concern of the American family today is the fact that many middle- and working-class families struggle to make ends meet. Unemployment is high, and wages have stagnated, so that breadwinners lucky enough to find work may need to hold more than one job to support their families.

National economic policy strongly affects family welfare. For example, when G. W. Bush took office as President in 2001, he had major political obligations to wealthy businessmen, the religious right, and the National Rifle Association, among other conservative constituencies that financed his campaign. Thus he proposed and was able to pass substantial tax cuts favoring the wealthiest of Americans, while at the same time cutting child care subsidies for low-income families (Gardner, 2001). He reinstated the *gag rule* so that federally funded family service agencies could not inform pregnant women of their option for abortion. He presided over a substantial build-up in military spending, a major benefit for big business, well before the events of September 11, 2001. His spending on war-related efforts exploded over the years, creating an enormous budget deficit.

As a result of the G. W. Bush policies favoring big business, income inequality grew at an alarming rate during his administration. The top 1 percent of households tripled their income, and gained ownership of one-third of the wealth and 40 percent of all financial assets in the United States (Yule, 2006; "Economic Inequality," 2009). Taking into consideration a different measure, the ratio of CEO to worker compensation in the United States in 1980 was 42:1; in 2005 it was 411:1. The average American worker thus labored for more than a year at that time to earn what the average CEO made in a day (Trumbull, 2007, February 2). By comparison, Mexico, the country with the next highest inequality record, had a CEO to worker compensation ratio of "only" 60:1. The ratio in Japan was 11:1, a situation considerably more equitable (Trumbull, 2007, January 4).

By 2010, according to an AFL–CIO analysis of 299 companies, a CEO of a Standard & Poor's (S&P) 500 Index company received, on average, $11.4 million in total compensation every year ("Executive Paywatch," 2011.) By comparison, a full-time worker earning minimum wage received about $15,000 for a year's work, usually with no benefits.

Disturbingly, the top 5 percent of Americans own over 60 percent of the nation's net wealth, and the top 20 percent earn over half the country's income. Since the major investment of the middle and working classes tends to be in their homes, the downturn in home values during the recession beginning in 2008 (a consequence of deregulation of the banks that began during the Clinton administration and accelerated under G. W. Bush) almost certainly increased the alarming disparity in wealth between the classes ("Economic Inequality," 2009).

Poverty today is no longer an issue primarily of the inner cities. According to a study by the Brookings Institution of Washington, DC, the population of poor people jumped by 15 percent during the G. W. Bush administration, but the increase was even larger in the suburbs, where poverty increased by 25 percent. By 2008, one-third of the nation's poor lived in the suburbs. Many suburbs lack services to cope with hunger and homelessness because they are not accustomed to dealing with such issues. They lack important resources such as public housing and public transportation (Guarino, 2010, February 14).

When President Obama took office in 2009, the Democratic President and Democratic Congress made some immediate important changes: for example, child care subsidies were increased for low-income families, emergency aid was made available for struggling homeowners, increased loans were made available to university students, and the *gag rule* was quietly removed from federally funded family service agencies (allowing workers to discuss abortion with pregnant women as a possible option). Congress passed and Obama signed the Lilly Ledbetter Law, bolstering the possibility of improving pay equity between men and women. The Affordable Health Care Law was passed. Military spending, however, continued to increase when President Obama decided to build up the war in Afghanistan and later to enter a war in Libya.

Given the enormous and growing national debt and the ongoing wars, it is unlikely that American families will see legislative changes that can benefit them very soon. A tax increase on the wealthiest Americans would help manage the debt, but powerful political interests continue to prevent that from happening.

Many families are aided by limited government programs such as food stamps and school lunches, but much need is unmet. Voluntary organizations, often assisted by grants from both governmental and nongovernmental sources, continue to work to provide emergency food and shelter for poor Americans. These small programs, such as the one helping the Rutherford family in Chapter 4's case study, can be tailored to meet specific needs of specific communities. However, such efforts are fragmented, without dependable funding, and not available to all who need them. What is required today is a nationwide, coordinated effort to address the causes of poverty that are robbing so many American families of their dreams.

SUMMARY

This chapter's case study describes the circumstances of LaTanya Tracy, an infant who has been left in the care of her great-grandmother. Unable to cope, the great-grandmother calls for help from her local protective services program. The case study illustrates how the problem was successfully resolved through the skilled intervention of a baccalaureate social worker, Lauren White.

The social work value of self-determination guides and challenges Lauren White in working with the Tracy family. Ms. White's primary client is an infant whose mother has become neglectful due to substance abuse. How can the value of self-determination be applied in a situation like this? The social worker skillfully finds ways to work with the mother, maximizing her self-determination and thus her cooperation, in this way best protecting the interests of the child.

A historical context is provided for family and children's services. Mutual aid among family members came first, supplemented later on an emergency basis by churches. Secular law eventually provided certain kinds of assistance, such as the categorical aids under the Elizabethan Poor Law of 1601. Formal assistance to families beyond the financial and material aspects came even later. For example, the first protective services case was not taken to court until 1875, and then it was brought by the president of the SPCA, a private organization to help animals. Not until the 1970s did the federal government, through Title XX of the Social Security Act, require all states to provide protective services for children. Legislation requiring protective services did not mandate adequate funding, however, so many neglect and abuse cases reported today are never investigated.

It is believed that services to assist families should be offered in the least restrictive environment; the least restrictive environment for families is usually the home. In-home services available to meet special needs of children and families in the United States today include (extremely limited) financial aid, family life education, homemaker services, day care, family therapy, protective services, and family-based services. Among out-of-home substitute services are foster care, group homes, adoption, institutional care, and the judicial system.

Research reveals that public assistance to families is decreasing in the United States and many other nations, although aid is especially limited in the United States. The possible relationship of family diversity to the curtailment of public assistance in the United States is considered. Data revealing mixed results of welfare reform are discussed. Social policies and services that assist families in other industrialized countries are compared with those in the United States. Findings indicate that families in the United States receive many fewer supports than families in other industrialized nations.

Ecological issues such as pollution and global warming and their relationship to population growth are explored. Family planning policy and its impact on population growth is examined. Research finds that women limit family size voluntarily when family planning services are available along with educational and vocational opportunities. Mandatory limits in childbearing as practiced in China today have resulted in a skewed gender ratio toward males, portending future problems.

Spirituality is explored as a resource for both social workers and clients in our increasingly challenging world. A spiritual orientation is introduced as a means of developing strength in these complex and difficult times. Research demonstrating efficacy of prayer and human intention in double-blind scientific studies is introduced, along with a discussion as to why this research is largely overlooked.

Finally, trends in family policy are discussed. Family supports have been decreasing in the United States in recent decades, although there are signs of hope. Among the first actions of the Democratic Congress that took office in 2007 was an increase in the minimum wage, assisting many poor Americans. The Obama administration signed a bill supporting gender equality in salaries early in 2008 and provided financial supports to families such as additional child care subsidies, aid to struggling home owners, and loans to university students. But widening budget deficits, ongoing wars, and economic recession have made help for American families increasingly challenging.

PRACTICE TEST   The following questions will test your knowledge of the content found within this chapter. For additional assessment, including licensing-exam type questions on applying chapter content to practice behaviors, visit **MySearchLab.**

1. Federal child protection policies were mandated in the year _____.
   a. 1784
   b. 1875
   c. 1974
   d. 1978

2. The _____, filed by the National Organization of Women, asserted that the United States has failed to adequately address pay inequity, sexual harrassment, and family support needs.
   a. International Covenant on Civil and Political Rights
   b. Gender Shadow Report
   c. millennium development goals
   d. Covenant on Economic, Social, and Cultural Rights

3. The _____, a federal social welfare agency, distributed food, clothing, and medical supplies to the poor following the Civil War.
   a. Freedmen's Bureau
   b. Mason's
   c. Odd Fellows
   d. Charity Organization Society

4. Early social workers, from the _____, who worked with low-income families were concerned about the "moral uplift" of the poor.
   a. public welfare agency
   b. settlement house movement
   c. Healthy Families Program
   d. Charity Organization Society

5. Population stability and control is most ethically and effectively achieved through _____.
   a. mandatory child bearing and birth control laws
   b. access the family planning services, educational opportunities, and rewarding career opportunities for women
   c. male sterilization
   d. teen pregnancy prevention programs

6. Which of the following interventions offers the least restrictive approach to meeting family preservation needs?
   a. child protection investigation
   b. foster care
   c. family life education
   d. adoption

7. Consider the child protection agency expectations of poor parents, like Natasha Tracy, who are also receiving public economic assistance (TANF). Identify at least three policies and/or practices noted in the chapter that put poor families at risk of losing their parental rights and responsibilities and foster poor outcomes for children.

MySearchLab CONNECTIONS

Reinforce what you learned in this chapter by studying videos, cases, documents, and more available at **www.MySearchLab.com**.

Watch and Review

Watch these Videos

* Engagement

Read and Review

Read these Cases/Documents

Δ Crisis and Kinship in Foster Care

Δ Melinda a Child Sexual Abuse Case

Δ The Lathe Family

Explore and Assess

Explore these Assets

Interactive Cases for Practice: Child Welfare

The Collaborative on Health and the Environment—http://www.healthandenvironment.org/

The Gay and Lesbian Alliance Against Defamation (GLAAD)—http://www.glaad.org/

Children's Rights—http://www.childrensrights.org/

Children's Welfare League of America—http://www.cwla.org/

Casey Family Programs—http://www.casey.org/

Assess Your Knowledge

Assess your knowledge with a variety of topical and chapter assessment.

Conclude your assessment by completing the chapter exam.

* = CSWE Core Competency Asset
Δ = Case Study

Social Work in Mental Health

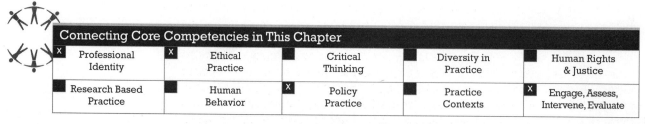

Connecting Core Competencies in This Chapter				
X Professional Identity	X Ethical Practice	Critical Thinking	Diversity in Practice	Human Rights & Justice
Research Based Practice	Human Behavior	X Policy Practice	Practice Contexts	X Engage, Assess, Intervene, Evaluate

David Deerinwater

Roberta Sholes, a BSW (baccalaureate-level social worker) with several years of experience at the Oklahoma State Mental Health Center, had just returned from vacation in the eastern part of the state, where she had visited Oklahoma Indian country. Now she would be working with a newly admitted Cherokee man who was from that area. Psychiatric **staffings** (multidisciplinary patient care meetings) always excited Roberta's interest, but today she was especially eager to meet David Deerinwater, her new client.

Sadly, the first of the five persons discussed by the team was a young woman who was critically ill following an aspirin overdose. Next was a 55-year-old attorney who had been readmitted following an episode of frenetic behavior; he had discontinued taking the medication prescribed for his bipolar disorder. Following him were two elderly women who had been admitted with severe depression. Then the psychiatric resident who had admitted David Deerinwater began by sharing what he knew about his case.

David Deerinwater had come to Tulsa from a ranch in the Goingsnake District of Oklahoma about 10 years ago, in search of employment. Living in a series of one-room, inner-city apartments, he sustained himself with odd jobs and some janitorial service work; he had few social contacts, although he seemed to identify strongly with his tribal people. David had been living on the streets for at least 6 months and seemed to have no possessions and no family or friends in the city. Increasingly isolated, his energy seemed to decline, and he lost weight. On admission, speech was of a muttering, incoherent quality, and his gestures suggested that he might be hearing voices. David voluntarily admitted himself to the hospital through the assistance of a social worker from the hot meal site where he had obtained food for the past 6 months. The admitting diagnosis was **schizophrenia**, undifferentiated type, a severe form of mental illness.

As David Deerinwater was being wheeled into the staff meeting, Roberta was startled to see the cold, distant expression in his dark eyes. He stared straight ahead, completely unresponsive to the questions that were asked, yet Roberta sensed that he had some awareness of what was happening around him. After he left, it was confirmed that Roberta would be the social worker for David.

When Roberta went to see David later in the day, she found him in his wheelchair on a sun porch, staring at the trees and park area beyond the window. She was pleased when he motioned her to sit down. Remembering the quiet pride of the Cherokee men she had seen, Roberta sat beside him for a time, not speaking. After a while and without turning to her, he asked, "Well, what do you want?" It was a good sign that he acknowledged her presence, and Roberta was pleased. She explained simply that she wanted to help. He replied, "That is not possible." Roberta then introduced herself slowly and said again that she wanted to help. Several minutes passed before he replied, "Then you will help me to get out of here." Roberta told David that she would need his help for that and that she would work with him to accomplish it. She wasn't sure he heard her. He no longer seemed aware of her as he stared into the distance.

The next morning David Deerinwater greeted Roberta with an almost imperceptible wave of his hand. She again sat quietly beside him. Then, because it was a beautiful, warm day, Roberta asked David if he would like to go outdoors with her for a few minutes. For a moment his expression appeared to be one of startled disbelief. Then a somber, closed expression again came over his face, but he nodded assent. Roberta wheeled his chair outdoors and across the carefully tended lawn to the shade of the ancient catalpa trees. David inhaled deeply. He was silent, perhaps more peaceful than she had seen him previously. Roberta began telling him about the hospital, its location, its purpose (to help people get well and return to their homes), and the staff and how they worked together. Again, Roberta stressed that she would need his help, adding that she needed to understand about his life, his growing up years, and his family. Again David nodded his head, acknowledging that he understood, but he added, "I am very tired now."

The following morning Roberta was surprised to find David Deerinwater waiting for her at the nurse's station. He was no longer using a wheelchair, she noted. She took him to the sun porch. Once there, he spoke: "You said that you could help me to get out of here." She replied that was just what she aimed to do, but that she wanted to be sure that he was feeling better and that he would have a place to go. He replied, haltingly, that he was eating and sleeping much better now, but he was feeling cooped up and didn't think he could stay much longer. Although he was not an easy person to interview, Roberta appreciated the quiet dignity beneath David's cool, distant gaze. She tried not to hurry him as she gently asked about his family and his experiences as a child.

Slowly and somewhat hesitatingly, over the next half hour, David gave Roberta a picture of his youth in the Goingsnake District, including memories of stomp dances (social events centering on spiritual dances), green corn feasts in the fall, and much hard work on the ranch. He spoke, too, of having been sent to boarding school with other Indian children and of the pain he felt when teachers spoke degradingly of Cherokee Indian life and reprimanded the children for speaking in their Cherokee language. He recounted serene times with family as well as hardship and poverty. David's father had been chronically ill with diabetes and had died when David was 16. Joe, 3 years older than David, had taken on major responsibilities for his mother, David, and three younger girls. The family had relied on help from friends and neighbors and had worked their small ranch and summer garden; that was how they had survived. Roberta realized that David was beginning to develop some trust in her when he willingly signed a form giving Roberta permission to share information about him with his family and with the Health and Social Services Department of the Cherokee Nation.

Roberta had not worked with a Cherokee Indian before, and she realized that she would need to acquire a better understanding of this ethnic group before she could adequately assess David Deerinwater's situation and begin to develop a plan with him for life beyond the hospital. She telephoned the Health and Social Services Department of the Cherokee Nation and found that Dorothy White, one of the social workers in the office, knew the Deerinwater family. Dorothy White offered to drive to their small ranch and ask David Deerinwater's mother to telephone Roberta the next day from the Cherokee Nation office because the family had no phone. She also volunteered to send Roberta information about the Cherokee Nation's services. She suggested it might be important to David's potential recovery, both physically and mentally, that he return to his home. She said she suspected that he really needed to be back with his people and in his natural environment where he would be understood and cared for by his family. Through the Cherokee Nation clinic, he could receive medical, rehabilitative, and mental health services that incorporated the beliefs and values of the Cherokees. She explained that the clinic offered group services, for example, that helped people come together to achieve harmony with each other, the community, and the natural world.

Dorothy White proved to be extremely helpful. When she called Roberta the next day, she had both David's mother and Joe (David's brother) in her office. David's mother was very eager for news about her son. She was especially concerned about David's weakness and nutritional state, and she concluded by saying, "We will bring him home. He needs to be with his people." Roberta explained that David was not yet well enough to leave the hospital and that he would have to determine for himself whether he wished to return home or remain in Tulsa. For now, however, he needed to gain strength and to continue taking his medication. David's mother replied that she knew what he would eat; she would cook for him. Then Joe Deerinwater came to the phone and said that he and his wife would drive to the city the next day. They would stay with friends and could visit David daily. They would bring food prepared by his mother. Roberta replied that she would be eager to see them.

In the days that followed, David Deerinwater benefited greatly from the visits of family members, and his nutritional status improved considerably. He also seemed to be responding well to his **psychotropic medication** (drugs prescribed by doctors to improve mental functioning, mood, or behavior). Although increasingly coherent, he remained isolated, interacting minimally with other patients. Roberta explained to the staff that David, like most Native Americans, did not engage readily in frivolous social conversation and would be unlikely to socialize unless he had a reason to do so. He also was probably quite frightened of the institution. Roberta had learned to adjust her own sense of time when speaking with David, and she had learned to respect periods of silence. She helped other staff communicate more effectively with him, too. In the final staffing before discharge, the psychiatric resident described David Deerinwater's response to medication as being very good. The psychologist's summary of the psychological testing he had completed supported the early diagnosis of schizophrenia. The staff was very interested in Roberta's assessment, which included a history of David Deerinwater within the context of his family and his ethnic community and his sense of unity with nature. Roberta was not as convinced as the other team members that David Deerinwater's mental illness was as serious as the diagnostic label, schizophrenia, suggested. He was much more oriented to reality than was usual for schizophrenic patients. She explained the perspective of the Cherokee Nation health center that often behaviors that are appropriate in one culture (such as an Indian's seeing signs in birds or the sky) are considered to be very inappropriate, sometimes even to be indicators of mental illness, in another culture.

Fourteen days after admission, David Deerinwater was released. His discharge diagnosis remained schizophrenia, undifferentiated. David had decided to return home to live with his mother, but he would be receiving follow-up care from the Cherokee Nation health center, which provided a full range of mental health services, including access to tribal medicine men and spiritual healers. He could also see the vocational rehabilitation counselor at the Cherokee Nation about future employment and career options. Roberta was satisfied that David would receive social work services and health care that respected his cultural heritage.

As she said farewell to David, Roberta thought about the Cherokee people and the Deerinwater family. She realized how much she had learned from this person, his family, and community and how much they had enriched her life.[1]

---

[1]Contributions to this case study were made by Dr. Wanda Priddy, former practicum program coordinator, and Dr. Dolores Poole, Northeastern State University Social Work Department, Tahlequah, Oklahoma; Delores Titchywy Sumner, Comanche tribe, assistant professor of library services, special collections librarian, John Vaughn Library/Learning Resources Center, Northeastern State University, Tahlequah, Oklahoma; Linda Ketcher Goodrich, ACSW, deputy director of the Cherokee Nation Health Service, and Beverly Patchell, RN, MS, program director, Jack Brown Center of the Cherokee Nation, Tahlequah, Oklahoma; and Isaac Christie, Malcolm Montgomery, and Jan Mowdy, Behavioral Health Unit, W.W. Hastings Hospital, Tahlequah, Oklahoma.

SOCIAL WORK COMPETENCIES FOR MENTAL HEALTH PRACTICE

Required Practice Behaviors: Knowledge and Skill

Roberta Sholes is a good example of a competent generalist BSW social worker. Take, for instance, the interviewing skills she demonstrated. She spoke quietly, gently, and slowly to David Deerinwater, helping him focus on her words. She reassured him yet confronted him with reality. Roberta's respect for the culture of the Cherokee people and the value of Cherokee family life was clearly present in her interviews with the Deerinwater family and the action she took to involve the Cherokee community in David Deerinwater's mental health care. Would this have been the approach used by David Deerinwater's psychiatrist, nurse, or other mental health professionals? Probably not, but it is uniquely consistent with social work intervention in mental health.

To prepare for a career in mental health, Roberta Sholes might have had a field placement in a mental health setting; even if she did not, there is a good likelihood that any field placement would present opportunities to work with people who are experiencing mental or emotional problems. The courses Roberta completed for her social work major probably didn't have titles such as *therapy* or *counseling,* but, as can be seen from Roberta's competence, the social work courses prepare students well for work in the mental health field. Roberta might also have taken elective courses such as psychopathology if she planned to seek employment in the mental health field.

BSW social workers are not expected to take responsibility for complex psychotherapy. That is the role of MSWs, and if Roberta decided that she would like to become a therapist, she would need to pursue a master's degree. The MSW curriculum, or course, has a generalist practice base, but most MSW programs provide an opportunity to complete a concentration in mental health or clinical social work. With additional experience, MSWs can be licensed to practice psychotherapy. MSWs routinely provide individual, family, and group therapy as well as marriage counseling. They may also be found in administrative positions in mental health hospitals and clinics. In some parts of the United States where MSWs are in short supply, BSWs assist and sometimes even assume major responsibilities for therapeutic work, especially in state hospitals and with persons who have persistent and major mental disorders. BSWs, however, do not claim to be psychotherapists, and they are alert to situations that require assistance from or referral to someone with advanced expertise.

In mental health settings, social workers find that as a professional group, they have certain advantages. Their professional education prepares social workers with competence in practice behaviors and roles such as advocacy, accessing referral resources, brief treatment, and crisis intervention. "The brief, goal-oriented nature of these roles is not new to us in social work. In many respects, this type of treatment mirrors our past practices in task-centered casework and problem-solving focused interventions" (Franklin & Lagana-Riordan, 2009). Social workers' professional demeanor in their communication skills and interdisciplinary teamwork is respectful of clients and colleagues, and often it affords access to leadership positions in mental health organizations.

Professional Identity

Practice Behavior Example: Demonstrate professional demeanor in behavior, appearance, and communication

Critical Thinking Question: What aspects of social workers' conduct could be of special concern in the mental health field?

Mental health crises or emergencies are not uncommon in social work practice across all possible settings; therefore, BSWs as well as MSWs need to have confidence in their ability to work with people with a wide range of problems. BSWs in mental health settings such as hospitals often provide crisis intervention, work with the families of patients, and counsel persons individually and in groups. They serve as the hospital's link to the community, teaching its staff about the population while offering preventive mental health education within the community.

In many community-based programs, BSWs carry important responsibilities for people who are chronically mentally ill. Dorothy White, the social worker in the Cherokee Nation's Health and Social Services Department, was also a BSW who provided advocacy, counseling, and case management services to Cherokee families. After David Deerinwater's discharge from the hospital, Dorothy or another social worker in the department would serve as his case manager. A **case manager** coordinates and ensures that all the services needed by a client (medical, financial, legal, etc.) are, in fact, provided. Case management practice behaviors require that the social worker be skilled both in working within the community and in working individually with lonely, isolated, and sometimes resistant persons. The generalist preparation of BSWs—especially their courses in practice methods and field experience—prepares them with the knowledge and skills they need for the diverse and challenging practice responsibilities they can expect to have in the mental health field.

Psychotherapy is the realm of the MSW. In the past, a social worker who was qualified to engage in psychotherapy was called a psychiatric social worker. Today the term used most often is **clinical social worker**. The National Association of Social Workers (NASW) expects social workers who engage in private practice of psychotherapy to be recognized by the Academy of Certified Social Workers (ACSW) at a minimum. As Chapter 1 noted, the NASW also recognizes with Qualified Clinical Social Worker (QCSW) certification persons who have achieved certain standards, including 3,000 hours of clinical experience. The Diplomat in Clinical Social Work (DCSW) is reserved for advanced clinical social workers with 5 years of post-MSW clinical experience (National Association of Social Workers [NASW], 2010a). Many states also license clinical social workers. All social workers in mental health settings, whether BSWs or MSWs, are responsible for collecting and assessing data that contribute to the mental health team's diagnosis and understanding of individual people in relation to mental health. These social workers are responsible, too, for creating intervention plans in collaboration with people, for implementing the intervention, for monitoring and evaluating the outcomes, and for terminating relationships with clients. Knowledge of the community and its resources is one of social work's unique contributions to the mental health team. The social worker also brings to the team an understanding of social policy and its impact on programs that exist and programs still needed to prevent and treat mental illness. An understanding of and sensitivity to the culture or lifestyle of diverse groups is another contribution made by social workers in mental health settings. When Roberta Sholes provided information about the Cherokee Indian culture and cautioned members of the mental health team not to assume psychosis in David Deerinwater, she was making this kind of contribution.

Engage, Assess, Intervene, Evaluate

Practice Behavior Example: Use empathy and other interpersonal skills

Critical Thinking Question: What would happen to the social work intervention process if the social worker was unable to build rapport with David Deerinwater?

In sharing knowledge about cultural practices, social policy issues, or even community resources, social workers continually educate others.

Values and Integrity

Knowledge and skills alone, however, do not make a good social worker. A third dimension is essential: values. Social workers demonstrate integrity when their personal values and actions are compatible with those of the profession. Professional social work values compel attention to and respect for the uniqueness and intrinsic worth of each person. Social workers empower clients and encourage them to be as self-directing as possible. They are very careful to respect privacy and confidentiality. Their professional values compel social workers to go even further. They urge social workers to work to make social institutions more humane and more responsive to people's needs. In mental health settings, these values take on special meaning. Our society tends not to respect the mentally ill, especially those who are chronically ill. Thus, social workers often have to advocate on behalf of the mentally ill. Within their communities and especially within the health care institutions that employ them, social workers attempt to create an environment that deals humanely with persons who are mentally or emotionally ill.

Ethical Practice

Practice Behavior Example: Conduct oneself ethically and engage in ethical decision making

Critical Thinking Question: In what ways might social work ethics and values be especially challenging in the mental health field?

In this chapter's case study, Roberta Sholes demonstrated much sensitivity for David Deerinwater as a client. Her respect for his uniqueness and worth led her to learn more about Native American ethnicity. Even if she believed that returning to his home community was in David Deerinfield's best interests, she did not force this plan on him. Instead, she engaged him in making decisions about his own posthospital care. Because of Roberta's respect for confidentiality, she obtained written permission before sharing information with his family or other agencies.

Few professions stress values in the way that social work does. This is especially apparent when a social worker practices in a **secondary setting** (one in which social work is not the primary function), such as mental health. Schools and courts are other examples of secondary settings. Not only do social workers in secondary settings need conviction about their values, but they also need to acquire an understanding of the primary function of the setting that they are in. In field practicum courses and on the job, social workers learn about the organizational context in which they work.

Specific Knowledge Base for Mental Health

The settings in which social workers are employed almost always require an additional layer of knowledge and skills. Because social workers are flexible and tend to move from one area to another during their professional careers, this gives them a splendid opportunity to acquire a rich array of specialized knowledge. In mental health, social workers must learn how to work effectively in interdisciplinary teamwork relationships.

Teamwork Relationships

Teamwork skills are key among the credentials sought by employers. The traditional mental health team consists of a psychiatrist, a psychologist, a psychiatric nurse, and one or more social workers. Roles overlap considerably in mental health. All team members provide psychotherapy, often as

> **Box 6.1   Social Work in Mental Health: The Traditional Mental Health Professional Team**
>
> - *Psychiatrists* prescribe medication. They hold the MD (doctor of medicine) degree and have additional training in psychiatry. Some also engage in psychotherapy.
> - *Psychologists* administer and interpret psychological tests. They generally hold the PhD degree in clinical psychology. Clinical psychologists may provide psychotherapy as well as testing.
> - *Psychiatric nurses* have training in nursing, which enables them to administer prescription medications, give injections, and assist in various other medical procedures. They generally hold a master's degree in nursing, however, in some regions of
>
> the country nurses with a baccalaureate degree in nursing (BSN) serve on mental health teams.
> - *Social workers* have specialized knowledge about community resources. They generally obtain the social history of a patient (a chronology of the individual's life events related to a potential mental health problem), which assists the team in arriving at a diagnosis and a treatment plan. Both BSWs and MSWs function as members of the mental health team; MSWs carry primary responsibility for psychotherapy, but both BSWs and MSWs provide counseling, facilitate groups, and provide case management.

co-therapists in family and group therapy. Each team member also performs a unique function (see Box 6.1). The traditional team may be supplemented by speech, recreational, art, and occupational therapists. Teachers are an added component in children's mental health programs.

In addition to direct work with the consumers of mental health services, the roles for social workers in mental health have expanded considerably to include administration of mental health programs; discharge planning; case management; and, of course, therapy for individuals, families, and groups. It is not surprising, then, that mental health teams often comprise several social workers but just one psychiatrist, one psychologist, and one or two nurses.

In our case study, the psychiatric facility's mental health team consisted of:

1. The chief psychiatrist, who served as team leader, conducted staffings, supervised residents, wrote prescriptions, and did some individual therapy.
2. Three psychiatric residents, who were assigned for a 6-month period. (Because they were students, they carried a limited number of cases and were under the supervision of the chief psychiatrist.)
3. Two psychiatric nurses, who administered all nursing and bedside care of patients, participated as co-therapists in group therapy, and supervised student nurses.
4. Three MSWs and one BSW, who provided individual, family, and group therapy; obtained social histories; and linked the hospital with the community.
5. One clinical psychologist, who administered and analyzed psychological tests and engaged in individual, family, and group therapy.

The mental health team in the case study was fairly typical of the teams in teaching hospitals. In hospitals that are not connected with a university medical school and in community practice, the mental health team generally has no medical or nursing students and hence is much smaller. Considerable effort is required to keep a team in any setting functioning smoothly, for friction is inevitable when professional roles overlap. Team members learn quickly that they need to understand the perspectives of other professionals who make up the mental health team.

Classification and Treatment of Mental Disorders

Social workers in mental health settings clearly need an understanding of mental illness. They need to be able to use the terminology of the current psychiatric mental illness classification system. Social work students at the baccalaureate level and in master's programs are generally introduced to the classification system as part of their coursework. Becoming truly adept at its use usually occurs with employment in a mental health setting (or in substance abuse or any other settings that use the same system of classifying mental disorders).

The system widely used in the United States was created by the American Psychiatric Association and is known among mental health professionals as the ***Diagnostic and Statistical Manual of Mental Disorders (DSM)***. The 2000 version of the manual, which is soon to be replaced by *DSM-V*, is known as the *DSM-IV-TR*. It incorporates a numerical coding system that is used on hospital and insurance forms in place of lengthy descriptive terms. More than 200 specific diagnostic categories are listed. Publication of *DSM-V* is expected in 2013. The *International Classification of Diseases,* referred to as *ICD-10* because it is in its 10th edition, is a categorization of mental disorders developed by the World Health Organization that is used by most countries outside the United States. The multinational, research-based thinking that characterizes *DSM-V* will bring it into increased alignment with *ICD-10* (American Psychiatric Association [APA], 2010a).

The *DSM* assumes that while definitions of **mental disorder** are not precise, increased research is needed to support differentiation between categories of mental illness. The new *DSM*'s proposed definition of mental disorder incorporates the following features:

- behavioral or psychological patterns that occur in an individual
- that reflect dysfunction of a psychobiological nature
- that produce suffering, pain, or some level of disability
- that would not be an anticipated response to significant stress or loss or a culturally sanctioned response within, for example, a religious ritual
- and that is not a reflection of socially deviant behaviors or conflicts between individuals. (APA, 2010b)

The *DSM* states clearly that it isn't people who are diagnosed; their disorders are. So it is not correct to speak of a *schizophrenic,* but it is appropriate to refer to a *person with schizophrenia* (APA, 2000).

In the past decade a great deal was learned about how the human brain functions physiologically. Building on this knowledge, researchers of multiple disciplines are now exploring the impact of our biological and genetic makeup, our physical and social environments, and also our emotions and our thinking as these evolve into the human behavior that is seen by others as mental health or mental illness.

In this chapter's case study, David Deerinwater was diagnosed as having a psychosis, schizophrenia: chronic, undifferentiated type. Because cultural factors related to David's behaviors complicated the diagnosis, neither the social worker nor the Cherokee community mental health center staff were convinced that this was the correct diagnosis for David; however, they recognized that he did need treatment, especially treatment that was culturally sensitive in the way it was delivered. Culture, age, socioeconomic status, and intellectual ability are just a few of the factors that may complicate the assessment and diagnostic process. The frequent revisions of *DSM,* too, suggest that even the experts' understanding of psychosis is still evolving. In fact, David's diagnosis of chronic, undifferentiated schizophrenia is slated to be removed from *DSM-V* along with several other current categories of schizophrenia. The concept of **psychosis**, however, will remain; psychosis continues to be considered a serious form of mental illness. Schizophrenia will remain a diagnostic category, but new types of schizophrenia will be defined (APA, 2010c).

Schizophrenia is a form of psychosis that is serious, but that can be successfully treated. Sadly, schizophrenia often makes its appearance in young adulthood, and it may require treatment for the remainder of the person's life. This, however, is not always the case. There are many misconceptions about this mental disorder—most commonly, that it entails one personality that has split into two or that multiple personalities have emerged out of a single personality. Although such symptoms can occur, they are not usual or necessary in order for a diagnosis of schizophrenia to be made. In fact, the characteristic symptoms of schizophrenia include disorganized thinking (sometimes involving strong belief that one is being persecuted) or hallucinations (hearing voices or seeing apparitions).

Anxiety disorders, mood disorders, and personality disorders are also among the more prevalent mental health problems that are likely to remain in *DSM-V*. **Anxiety disorders** include panic attacks and posttraumatic stress conditions, for example.

Mood disorder, as the name implies, is a category that focuses on disturbances of mood. This diagnostic category contains both very serious and more minimal dysfunctions of mood. Depressive (low mood) and manic (abnormally high mood) states are represented, as well as bipolar states in which periods of both depression and mania occur. Among the **personality disorders** there are multiple subcategories as well. Examples would include the paranoid personality (characterized by pervasive suspicion and distrust of others) and the schizoid personality (where inability to form close social relationships occurs, usually coupled with emotional coldness).

It is anticipated that *DSM-V* will introduce even more mental disorders than the 2000 *DSM* edition. Assessment and diagnosis remain an imprecise procedure, and mental health professionals, MSW social workers included, who are responsible for diagnosing mental disorders must exercise great care in their assessments. BSW social workers who are employed in mental health settings, like Roberta Sholes in the case study, learn a great deal about the specific mental disorders in the course of their professional work. BSWs do not diagnose, but they are responsible for gathering data that will be combined with the information obtained by other members of the interdisciplinary mental health teams in their diagnostic work.

Diagnosis, of course, is just the beginning. Treatment of mental disorders is complex. In mental health care today, medication is widely utilized in the treatment of many of the mental disorders. Learning about some of the psychotropic medications used in treating mental illness also became a reality of Roberta's job. She found that all of the mental health team members, including social workers, needed to develop some familiarity with these medications, their uses, and their side effects so that they could be alert to possible complications. Some of the negative side effects could include loss of sense of balance, sexual dysfunction, and even severe emotional reactions. When unpleasant side effects occur, people sometimes discontinue taking their prescribed medication, and this may result in reoccurrence of the mental illness. The medications that have come on the market in recent years have fewer side effects than drugs previously used to treat mental disorders. They have been of significant benefit to large numbers of people. With the newer drugs, though, some people feel so well that they discontinue taking their medications. They are then at high risk of relapse. Other people are unable to afford the extraordinarily high cost of some of the newer psychotropic drugs—costs may be as much as $6,000 per month!

Among the medications used to treat some forms of mental illness are tranquilizers. Tranquilizers can be dangerous, even life threatening, if taken

Box 6.2   A Sample of Major Psychotropic Medications

Drug Type	Examples of Disorder Treated	Generic Name	Brand Name	Usual Daily Dosage (mg)
Antipsychotic	Schizophrenia, bipolar disorders, major depressions, organic mental disorders	Chlorpromazine	Thorazine	75–900
		Chlozapine	Clozaril	200–900
		Fluphenazine	Prolixin	2–20
		Olanzapine	Zyprexa	2–100
		Risperidone	Risperdal	2.5–20
		Aripiprazole	Abilify	0.25–16
		Quetiapine	Seroquel	50–800
		Ziprasidone	Geodon	2–160
Antidepressant	Major depressions, dysthymia (persistent minor depression), adjustment disorders	Fluoxetine	Prozac	5–80
		Sertraline	Zoloft	25–200
		Paroxetine	Paxil	10–60
		Tranylcypromine	Parnate	20–60
		Amitriptyline	Elavil	75–300
		Escitalopram	Lexapro	10–20
		Imipramine	Tofranil	75–300
		Bupropion	Wellbutrin	1.4–6
		Citalopram	Celexa	10–40
Mood stabilizer	Bipolar disorder	Lithium	Eskalith	600–2,400
		Carbamazepine	Tegretol	200–1,600
		Divalproex	Depakote	750–4,000
		Lamotrigine	Lamictal	12.5–700
Antianxiety	Anxiety disorders (including panic disorders, phobias, obsessive–compulsive disorder, posttraumatic stress disorder)	Alprazolam	Xanax	0.5–10
		Clonazepam	Klonopin	1–6
		Diazepan	Valium	4–40
		Lorazepam	Ativan	1–6
		Oxazepam	Serax	30–120
		Chlordiazepoxide	Librium	15–100
		Buspirone	Buspar	5–60
Psychostimulant	Attention deficit hyperactivity disorder	Dextroamphetamine	Dexedrine	20–40
		Methylphenidate	Ritalin	20–60

Source: Adapted from Ronald J. Comer. (2010). *Abnormal psychology* (7th ed.). New York: Worth Publishers. F. F. Oltmanns & R. E. Emery. (2007). *Abnormal psychology* (5th ed.). Upper Saddle River, NJ: Pearson, Prentice Hall. Department of Psychiatry, University of Illinois at Chicago (n.d.). *DCFS psychotropic medication list*. Retrieved from www.psych.uic.edu/csp/DCFS_Psychotropic_Medication.pdf

with alcohol. They can also create lethargy and such overwhelming sleepiness that the person has considerable difficulty holding a job or studying. The opposite effect, hyperactivity, can occur with drugs prescribed for depression. Weight gain is a less-threatening side effect. These are examples of the complexities of psychotropic medication treatment.

Social workers monitor medication use by their clients and often educate clients and family members regarding the use of medications. Ongoing communication with the physician who has written the client's prescriptions is also a part of the social worker's monitoring function. Some of the psychotropic drugs currently used in the medical management of mental disorder are listed in Box 6.2. A list such as this cannot remain up to date for long, because breakthroughs in pharmaceutical research may result in new medications being added and older drugs dropped in just a short time. Some people today, however, are very reluctant to take prescribed medication; recently, there has been renewed interest in the use of vitamins and herbs as an alternative to drug treatment of mental disorders.

Social workers, too, have ethical questions related to the use of psychotropic medications, especially when they are prescribed for children. Concerns relate to the appropriateness of drugs (e.g., use of amphetamines for children), possibility for negative side effects, and the potential development of psychological dependence on drugs. There is concern that children could begin to cope with normal stresses by taking medication rather than learning healthy adaptive behaviors. When children are in foster and institutional care and in the custody of the state, there are times when social workers must make decisions on the child's behalf about medical care. These are not easy decisions, as Box 6.3 suggests. Social workers are often in the unique position of being able to make clear to the physician the preferences and circumstances of the child's parents or the client, if the client is an adult, and to help these people understand the medical situation and available options. The social worker is the professional who "spends more time with the client and family than others

Box 6.3 Up for Debate

Proposed: Medications should be used routinely to help children with Attention-Deficit/ Hyperactivity Disorder (ADHD).

Yes	No
Research has shown that medications such as Ritalin have a quieting effect on hyperactive children.	There are numerous known side-effects of medication, especially Ritalin, including decreased blood flow to the brain, insomnia, and disruption of normal growth in the body, including the brain.
Medication can increase the alertness of hyperactive children at the same time it is decreasing overactivity.	The long-term effects of medicating hyperactive children are not well researched or well known.
With medication, many children with ADHD can function at an acceptable level in the classroom and progress in learning.	Medication does not cure hyperactivity.
The aggressiveness of hyperactive children is lowered through the use of medication, making them less of a threat to their siblings and classmates.	The chemical composition of Ritalin is similar to that of cocaine, and there are instances of recreational use and abuse of Ritalin by college students.

on the treatment team; he or she may be best informed about their perspectives regarding medication and other interventions" (Bentley & Walsh, 2001, p. 131).

Today treatment of mental disorders often consists of a combination of medication, monitoring, various forms of psychotherapy, and patient education. The treatment programs that deliver these services have come to be known as **behavioral health care**. They may be provided during hospitalization or on an outpatient basis. Hospitalization, when needed, tends to be much briefer than it was in the past, in part due to psychotropic medications but also due to curtailed length of stay dictated by insurance or managed-care corporations. Many patients (like David Deerinwater) now remain hospitalized for only a matter of days, followed by outpatient treatment to continue psychotherapy and to monitor the medication.

Hospitalization and, for that matter, even medication are not necessary for all persons who are experiencing mental health problems. Social workers are among the professionals who provide counseling and psychotherapy for individuals, families, and groups with the objective of preventing and treating mental and emotional disorders. The many ways in which social workers, including BSWs, contribute to the prevention and treatment of mental disorders are described in the next section.

GENERALIST PRACTICE WITH GROUPS AND COMMUNITIES

The David Deerinwater case study is an example of generalist social work intervention occurring simultaneously at several different systems levels: the individual client, the family, the mental health team, and the community. The primary focus of Roberta Sholes's social work service, however, was the individual client, David Deerinwater. We now examine social work in other types of mental health settings and in practice situations in which the target for intervention is not an individual but a group or a community.

Working with Groups in Mental Health

In social work, groups are used with people of all ages for providing therapy, counseling, teaching skill development, raising self-esteem, and problem solving of many kinds. In the following example from Gitterman and Shulman's classic social work text, *Mutual Aid Groups* (Vastola, Nierenberg, & Graham, 1994), children were referred to a mental health clinic for emotional problems following the death of a parent or someone of considerable significance to them. Each of five children was first seen in an individual session where the group was described; all the children expressed a desire to participate.

In the first group session, the social worker asked the children to introduce themselves. She asked if anyone knew why the group was meeting; the children readily responded that it was a group for children whose parents had died. She explained in more detail how the group was planned to assist kids in helping each other through this difficult time. She asked the group, "What do you think about being here?" Several children said that the group was a good idea. Then, spontaneously, they began to tell their own stories, identifying who had died and how it had happened. In the next weeks the children continued to work out their grief. There were several episodes of angry outbursts.

In one a child cried out, "I don't want anyone talking about my grandfather.... I just don't want anybody saying that he died!" Other group members agreed: "Nobody really wants to talk about a person's dying, it's too hard" (Vastola et al., 1994, p. 87).

But they did talk. They also shared personal experiences, such as nightmares, that they could not discuss with anyone else. The social worker encouraged group members to bring in pictures or personal mementos. In one touching episode, a boy removed from his jeans pocket a tattered, frayed picture of a beautiful young woman—his mother when she was a teenager. The social worker was able to help this child have the picture laminated so that he could retain this treasured object. The children also had curiosity and many unanswered questions about funeral homes, autopsies, and the decomposition of human bodies. Their questions were respected, and factual information was provided. They needed to be reassured that, if their present caretaker died (one child had lost both parents and was living with an aunt), there would be someone who would care for them.

Although the children found it difficult to terminate the group at the end of 12 weeks, the social worker encouraged the children to verbalize their painful feelings about ending the group. She also helped them review what they had gained from the group and think about how they might be able to apply their newly acquired skills in the future. These children had named their group "The Lost and Found Group."

Community Practice

In addition to practice with individuals and groups, social workers seek to assist communities, at-risk populations, or organizations to promote mental health or to design programs for people with mental health problems. Examples of social work community practice behaviors often appear in *NASW News,* the monthly publication of the NASW.

Sarah Hamil, a social worker who works with child, adolescent, and family therapy, provided community education about the dynamics of bullying in an article in the *Jackson Sun,* a Tennessee newspaper. The newspaper story enabled her to explain that bullying is hazardous both to the bully and to the child who is victimized. She pointed out that bullying is not normal behavior but that this aggressive behavior may occur when children do not have other means of getting their needs met. She explained how parents can better understand and learn to deal with bullying in their child. The parents of children who are victimized by bullies also need to protect their children including providing a safety plan for them ("Social work in the public eye," 2006). Bullying has recently become a major concern for parents and for school systems. It is increasingly an issue confronting social workers in mental health and family and children's services and also school social workers.

When Timothy's Law was passed by the state of New York, it ensured that many people, including children, would receive insurance coverage for mental health care at the same level as that for other forms of health care. This so-called parity law was named after Timothy O'Clair, a 12-year-old child with an emotional disorder who committed suicide. It took an enormous amount of political action before Timothy's Law was successfully passed. Social workers across New York participated in rallies, made multiple telephone calls seeking support for the legislation, and met with their state legislators. Elizabeth Clark, the executive director of NASW and former director of the New York State

Chapter of NASW, wrote to Governor George Pataki urging him to sign the legislation (Pace, 2007). The Timothy's Law example shows how social workers use political processes as they work for change in mental health care in communities and the nation. For years, NASW lobbyists and social workers throughout the United States also energetically advocated for passage of federal law that would guarantee mental health parity. These political advocacy efforts were successful in 2008 with the passage of the Paul Wellstone and Pete Domenici Mental Health Parity and Addiction Equity Act. This law "requires that any group health plan that includes mental health and substance use disorder benefits along with standard medical and surgical coverage must treat them equally …" (U.S. Department of Health and Human Services, 2010, para. 7). The political battle for federal mental health parity legislation had taken 40 years to accomplish, but it was achieved through collaboration among many mental health professional groups, persons who needed mental health care, and concerned citizens.

Policy Practice

Practice Behavior Example: Analyze, formulate, and advocate for policies that advance social well-being

Critical Thinking Question: What can be done to ensure that all people have access to the mental health care that they need?

The growing consumer movement in mental health, composed primarily of persons who have experienced poor treatment by the mental health system, is being assisted by social workers. In some communities, social workers join attorneys in advocacy for patients whose legal rights have been violated by illegal detainment in mental hospitals, by improper use of restraints and medication, or by inappropriate discharge planning.

The NASW, representing all social workers in the United States, seeks to influence government's policies in ways that will benefit vulnerable people, including people at risk of mental health problems. NASW's concern about the quality of mental health care is addressed in the NASW Policy Statement on Mental Health. The NASW statement appears in Box 6.4.

Box 6.4   NASW Policy Statement on Mental Health

To further improvements that have been made in the prevention, diagnosis, assessment, and treatment of mental illness, it is the position of NASW that:

- All people in the United States, including immigrants and refugees, be entitled to a comprehensive system of person-centered mental health care, for both severe and persistent mental illness and for acute and episodic mental health problems that impair the individual's functioning.
- Social workers should advocate for the elimination of stigma associated with mental illness.
- Social workers should recognize outreach services as an important part of mental health services.
- Managed health care and other health care plans should rely on the best judgment of mental health clinicians in conjunction with consumers' judgment about the type and duration of services needed. Mechanisms for the appeal of treatment

decisions are needed to ensure protection of both the consumer and the provider.

- Social workers, in collaboration with the consumer, should involve family members and significant others in assessment and treatment planning. Consumers should be given choices among service options that meet their needs and individual preferences.
- Family members should have access to supportive services to help them cope with the problems posed by the mental illness of a loved one.
- The correctional system should not be used as a de facto mental health system. In addition, incarcerated individuals should have access to mental health services, including assessment, screening, medication, counseling, discharge planning, and referral.
- Services should be fully integrated for consumers with severe mental illness and co-occurring

disorders such as substance abuse and mental retardation.

- People with substance abuse disorders and mental illness should be treated fairly in assessing functional capacity and in rendering social insurance, public assistance, and social services.
- The efforts of people with mental illness to work should be encouraged and should not result in negative sanctions from social insurance, public assistance, or other programs.
- In light of the trend toward involuntary outpatient commitment, careful evaluation must be done to ensure protection of consumers' right to self-determination and safety of family members in the community.
- Culturally responsive treatment in the most therapeutic and least restrictive environment, including use of the consumer's native language, should guide the practice of social work.

- Social workers should take the lead in advocating for viable, comprehensive, community-based mental health services.
- Social workers play a key role in educating the public about mental illness as a means of fostering prevention, encouraging early identification and intervention, promoting treatment, and reducing the stigma associated with mental illness. This responsibility includes efforts to influence public policy in ways that will foster improved prevention and diagnosis and promote comprehensive, continuous treatment of mental illness for all individuals who need these services and not only those who might be considered a threat to society.

Another way in which social workers engage their professional practice behaviors within the community is through case management. Case management focuses more on work with individual people, however, and less on community change. In many mental health community support case management jobs, social workers meet with their clients out in the community: where they live, shop, visit a doctor or dentist, work, or go to school.

GENERALIST PRACTICE IN CASE MANAGEMENT

So, what would social work case management in mental health look like? To begin with, the same generalist practice, multiple-phased change process is used that was described in Chapter 2 of this book. The process begins when the social worker reaches out and seeks to engage the client, establishing a sound working relationship. At the same time, information is gathered about the nature of the mental health problem, other issues in the client's life, and the strengths that the client brings to the situation. Then, with the collaboration of the client, a plan is developed and the case management intervention is implemented. Monitoring is done regularly by the social worker and client to ensure that the client's needs are being met. The case management relationship may be terminated because the client no longer needs this service, because the social worker leaves the agency and a new case manager is assigned, or because the client chooses to end the service.

Case management often, although not always, involves long-term work with people who have multiple and complex problems. In mental health work, these may be persons with severe and persistent mental illness. Some clients may be resistant. Some may have been or currently are homeless and living on the streets. Case managers seek to connect clients with needed services.

At times, strong advocacy is needed to convince an organization or a professional person to provide needed care. Finding a dentist who will see a 45-year-old man who has not had dental care in 25 years may not be easy. Helping the client agree to accept the needed service and keep follow-up appointments may be no easier, but accomplishing these challenges can be very rewarding.

Box 6.5 provides an example of case management involving a 36-year-old Asian woman. The authors of this case study point out that case management is a more comfortable fit with many Asian people than the traditional clinical service model of American outpatient mental health care. Asian people tend to view health and well-being holistically, with mental, physical, emotional, and spiritual elements inseparable. Family relationships are highly valued, and a person's self-concept is intrinsically related to her or his involvement with family. When refugees have endured war, separation from family, and political persecution before coming to the United States, they may transfer their sense of family obligation to others, especially people of their same culture, but they may be very guarded and reluctant to trust professional people or service providers. They may appreciate home visits, however, and may gradually accept help from a social worker who sustains contacts and demonstrates concretely his or her willingness to help (Eng & Balancio, 1997).

Social workers at many different educational levels are involved in case management. Doctoral-level social workers may provide consultation and expert backup for case managers. MSW social workers may supervise case

---

Box 6.5   A Case Management Case Study: Sue Xiong

Sue Xiong (not the client's real last name), a 36-year-old single Cambodian woman, was referred to an outpatient mental health clinic following her third hospitalization within a year. She was unemployed, had no family, and had come to the United States 3 years previously. She was diagnosed with a bipolar disorder and had never kept the previous outpatient appointments given to her on discharge from the hospital. She had also not taken any of the medications previously prescribed. She was said to be in denial about her psychiatric diagnosis but to have complaints about physical disorders.

The social work case manager who was assigned visited Sue Xiong at the hospital before discharge in order to begin the engagement, relationship-building process and to obtain information about her diagnosis and medical recommendations. It quickly became apparent to the social worker that the client believed her three hospitalizations resulted from problems associated with her menstrual cycle. She refused to accept appointments at the outpatient mental health clinic but did agree to regular home visits after the social worker volunteered to take her to a medical clinic to have her concerns about her menstrual irregularities assessed. She was also very relieved when the social worker agreed to help her apply for temporary financial assistance.

In the next 2 months, the social worker met with Sue Xiong regularly and also accompanied her to the women's health clinic and the financial aid office. She often spoke to Sue about mental health and helped her understand more about how mental health services are provided in the United States. The client gradually became more comfortable and open to considering the use of medication to treat the stressful mood-related symptoms she now acknowledged.

After 2 months Sue Xiong decided to come to the mental health clinic to meet with a psychiatrist. She accepted the medication that was prescribed and, with the social worker's encouragement and support, took the medication regularly. Two years after their first visit, Sue Xiong was employed, having also accepted assistance from the vocational rehabilitation service that the social worker connected her with.

management programs or may provide clinical case management themselves. BSW social workers provide extensive case management services. Other professionals—such as nurses, psychologists, and professional counselors—also provide case management services. Some organizations use persons with no academic credentials beyond a high school degree to assist professional staff or to provide case management with special populations.

Case management is just one form of intervention in mental health practice. It incorporates a great deal of counseling, advocacy, and monitoring. These and other well-honed generalist practice skills are truly put to the test when large-scale community disasters strike.

SOCIAL WORKERS RESPOND TO DISASTER: ACUTE AND POSTTRAUMATIC STRESS

When disaster strikes, generalist practice skills enable social workers "to intervene immediately, actively, and directively from a client-centered, problem-focused perspective" (Gelman & Mirabito, 2005, p. 481). According to Ken Lee, social workers may be the best equipped of all mental health professionals to respond to disasters. Lee, a social worker from Hawaii and member of the American Red Cross Air Incident Response Team, is also a mental health trainer for the Red Cross. He was one of countless mental health professionals who assisted at the Ground Zero site following the terrorist attack on the World Trade Center in New York in 2001 (Social work in the public eye, 2002).

Group treatment for survivors of disasters and for volunteers as well is recommended by both the American Red Cross and the Substance Abuse and Mental Health Services Administration (SAMHSA). The focus is present-centered, avoiding vivid details of the actual trauma but listening to the pain of the emotions and helping group members to support and bond with each other. Effort is made to prevent people from retraumatization through exposure to the grim details of their own or others' detailed accounts of the event, but the emotions, pain, and consequences of the experience are thoroughly validated. Energy is directed to "helping locate missing family members, providing food and water, filling out forms" (Johnstone, 2007, p. 40) for federal assistance and helping each other reconnect with family, friends, and spiritual forms of support. Whether disasters are caused by terrorist attack; shootings at a school; or natural events such as hurricanes, earthquakes, tornadoes, floods, or forest fires, social workers respond.

During and immediately following disasters, people may be subjected to overwhelming physical and psychological distress, often known as **acute traumatic stress**. Normal reactions cover a wide spectrum of behaviors. Emotionally, people may experience shock, feeling as though they are in a fog, an unreal world. They may feel numbness and have no physical pain even in the presence of profound injuries. Or they may react with terror, panic, anger and hostility, grief, or a marked sense of isolation. They may be confused and disoriented, have difficulty making decisions, experience racing thoughts, or replay the experience over and over again in their minds. Withdrawal and difficulty communicating is a common behavioral response to traumatic exposure. So is pacing, aimless walking, or an exaggerated startle response. Immediate mental health intervention at the time of the disaster or traumatic experience may prevent or minimize the development of an enduring stress disorder. When the symptoms last beyond a month, however, or depression or intense anxiety persists, the person should be evaluated for possible **posttraumatic stress disorder (PTSD)**. Unless it is treated, PTSD may impair children as well as adults, making it nearly impossible for them to study, work, sustain parenting responsibilities, or even maintain self-care.

People recover from trauma in their own time, using their own strengths and with the support of their family, friends, and community. Life may never be the same again, especially if there has been a death or permanent disability. Many people, however, do survive disasters, and there are even people who actually grow and thrive as a result of their experience. In the weeks that follow the traumatic experience, there is first a period of disorganization with depression and anger and then a period of reorganization when new patterns for functioning evolve and new relationships are built (Lerner & Shelton, 2001).

PTSD, if it occurs, can be treated through individual or family counseling or with group therapy. Some therapeutic models focus on helping the person cognitively, by increasing their intellectual comprehension of the experience and their reaction to it. Behavioral methods seek to change ineffective responses to behaviors that strengthen the person's ability to cope. Medication is sometimes used in conjunction with counseling. Social workers tend to use a holistic approach that identifies strengths in the person and connects people with others who can help: family members, friends, and coworkers. Spiritual beliefs are another source of support that is valued. Referrals are made to community resources if appropriate.

Mental health treatment for PTSD or for any other mental health problem is much like treatment for a physical ailment. It can be taken care of very quickly in some cases, or it may require ongoing care and monitoring. Injustice at several levels, however, can sabotage mental health care.

SOCIAL JUSTICE ISSUES IN THE MENTAL HEALTH FIELD

Social justice concerns abound in the field of mental health. The very diagnostic labels described earlier may cause damage. To label someone as schizophrenic, for example, can be very damaging; a person so labeled is expected to perform (or not to perform) in a specific, predetermined manner. When this label is known to hospital or clinic staff, schools, correctional facilities, employers, or other organizations, other people are likely to assume or to anticipate the expected behaviors. Political careers or administrative promotions have been jeopardized when it is discovered that a person was labeled, correctly or incorrectly, with a psychiatric diagnosis. Diagnostic labels can follow a person for life. Although medical information is supposedly confidential, private, and protected by law, in reality it is remarkably available to a large number of persons the client has never even seen. A child's school record, for example, is passed from one teacher to another, complete with psychological evaluations. Medical records are handled not only by doctors, nurses, and therapists of many kinds but also by clerks, aides, medical records personnel, and insurance staff.

Persons with psychiatric labels may be stereotyped or subjected to bias by others, but something even more devastating may occur when people begin to define themselves by a label. Sometimes, even when people do not know their specific diagnosis, they do understand that they have been labeled with some kind of mental problem. Because of the stereotyping and discriminatory attitudes of society, this knowledge may be devastating! It certainly does not create positive self-regard, nor does it promote motivation to engage in treatment.

Another perspective on social justice and mental health relates to the inadequacy of treatment resources for persons who lack financial resources—possibly as a result of their mental health problem. Reflecting on the presence of high levels of mental illness among people who live on the streets, Ezra Susser, noted psychiatrist and epidemiologist, remarked: "I don't think we would allow people with multiple sclerosis to live in the streets. It wouldn't be morally acceptable. So why is it acceptable for people with disabling mental illnesses to live in such conditions?" (as cited in Wortsman, 2006, para. 11). For most social workers, the inhumane living conditions of homeless persons, especially people with chronic mental illness, are unjust.

Social workers, among others, seek to change social policy and provide programs that will ensure a reasonable standard of living and access to mental health services to homeless persons and all persons in need of care. The NASW Policy Statement on Mental Health, shown earlier in Box 6.4, clearly states the profession's commitment to the development of resources that provide not only treatment in the least restrictive environment but also all of the other services that maximize wellness and encourage resilience (Kelly & Clark, 2010).

Something quite devastating happens when people begin to define themselves according to a diagnostic label.

ENVIRONMENTAL PERSPECTIVES ON MENTAL HEALTH

It is not difficult to imagine how their unsafe and hazardous environments put mentally ill persons living on the streets at great risk of physical health problems, rape, and criminal victimization. While untreated mental health problems may create behaviors that alienate people from their families and leave them homeless, the sometimes toxic environmental context of homelessness can exacerbate existing mental health problems. Not surprisingly, homelessness may precipitate emotional crises as well.

As social workers trained in an environmental perspective, we cannot ignore the physical surroundings of the people we serve. The environmental context is increasingly a focus for mental health practitioners as well as social planners. Environmental degradation affects the physical well-being and also the mental health of people around the globe. Mental health practitioners have learned to respond to the long-term emotional needs of victims of trauma created by industrial accidents, war, and natural disasters as well as toxic physical and social environments.

The World Health Organization report, *Quantifying Environmental Health Impacts* (2007), described mental health and behavioral risks that are linked globally to environment. Suicide, for example, was shown to be linked to work-related stress and stress stemming from degraded environments. Environmental factors varying from country to country were shown to affect access to the means used by people to commit suicide. These ranged from ingestion of pesticides in Trinidad, Sri Lanka, and Malaysia to use of charcoal fumes in China and gunshot in the United States. "Globally, an average of 30% (22–37%) of all suicides were attributable to the environment" (p. 54). The report noted that lives could be saved by improving chemical safety and limiting access to guns. Similarly, interpersonal violence could be reduced globally by reducing access

Hazardous environments
put peope at risk of physical
as well as mental health
problems.

to firearms and improving street lighting. **Epidemiologists**, persons who study occurrence and distribution of a disease within a population, increasingly look at risk factors occurring at multiple levels. Schizophrenia, for example, has been linked to genetic impact on brain development prior to birth. Schizophrenia is also known to lie dormant during childhood, only to appear in late adolescence or early adulthood. Recently, scientists have discovered clues to societal level influences on the development of this disease. The relatively high incidence of schizophrenia among Afro-Caribbeans who immigrated to the United Kingdom and Moroccan immigrants to the Netherlands intrigued epidemiologists, especially when it was found that second-generation persons of these groups born in Europe had an even higher rate of the disease. "Currently, the pattern of results across numerous studies suggests that the social experience of discrimination contributes to this high incidence" (Susser, Schwartz, Morabia, & Bromet, 2006, p. 419).

Can social workers avoid the messages inherent in this research? If social workers are committed to advocating for change, fairness, and an end to discrimination and inequality, then environmental issues must become significant in their work in the mental health field. While we can provide counseling and psychotherapy for individuals, families, and groups, we must also focus our skills on changing the societal factors that affect access to care, quality of care, and nature of the environment in which we live. In other words, we will become much more knowledgeable about and actively involved in the social policies and legislation that affect mental health.

PRACTICE WITH DIVERSE POPULATIONS

Commitment to social justice and increasing appreciation of both the physical and social environment has enriched social workers' valuing of human diversity. Unfortunately, in the past social workers and other mental health professionals have not always been very sensitive to ethnic differences in the people they serve. Today, however, social work education is seeking to prepare students to work with an increasingly wide range of populations in ways that will empower individuals and their communities and will safeguard the integrity of family life, as it is defined by diverse populations.

Cultural competence in social work involves knowledge of the history and patterns of oppression experienced by cultural and ethnic groups and the traditions and values of those groups. It requires appreciation for differences in cultures. Cultural competence includes, first, the "development of academic and professional expertise and skills in the area of working with culturally diverse populations" (Lum, 1999, p. 3) and then putting that knowledge into actions that will generate social change and lead to realization of social justice (Lum, 2007). In this process, social workers need to look carefully at their own ethnic and cultural backgrounds. Because many of us as social workers come from backgrounds with mixtures of culture, race, socioeconomic status, spirituality, and other forms of diversity, looking at our own ethnic identity is definitely not easily done. Yet our appearance, the way we talk, and the way we present ourselves immediately convey messages more powerful than we know to clients of contrasting cultures and backgrounds. If we are to begin to develop skill in utilizing culturally appropriate interventions, we do need to build self-awareness and appreciate our own uniqueness as well as that of each individual client. Social work researchers such as John Red Horse provide guidelines that aid our understanding of the intensity and the differences in our own and our clients' identification with cultural roots.

Social workers need to look carefully at their own ethnic and cultural backgrounds— Sometimes this is not easily done.

Many years ago, John Red Horse (1988) classified Native American families along a spectrum from *traditional* to panrenaissance. Family members in a traditional family, he explained, use their native language at home and in the community, practice the native religion, and sustain tribal beliefs regarding disease. These families rely on traditional rituals and ceremonies to rid them of mental and physical illness and to bring their minds and bodies back into harmony with the spiritual world and the universe. One step from traditional families is *neotraditional* families, in which some members use the English language and have adopted new rituals and spiritual healers; most family members, however, retain traditional beliefs. *Transitional* and *bicultural* families use English in the community but speak the native language at home. They retain some traditional spiritual beliefs and practices, but they are beginning to use contemporary American health care. *Acculturated* families have lost their native language, religion, and often even their extended kinship system; they rely on American contemporary health care systems. Finally, *panrenaissance* families seek to renew their native language fluency and to revitalize some aspects of the traditional religion. Consideration of this continuum can help social workers to be more sensitive to the differences within groups as well as the differences between groups.

Incorporating these understandings into interviews—along with warmth, empathy, and respect—takes time to learn but will become a part of every student's professional preparation for a career in social work. Classroom role-plays of interviews plus actual experience in fieldwork are just the beginning of cultural competence, which is acquired over a professional lifetime.

In the David Deerinwater case at the beginning of this chapter, Roberta Sholes demonstrated sensitivity throughout her work with the client, his family, and the Cherokee community. The result was that Mr. Deerinwater was reunited with his family, and he gained access to a whole set of support networks that would perhaps otherwise not have been available to him. Roberta's newly gained knowledge of Cherokee history, beliefs, traditions, and even food preferences helped other members of the hospital's mental health team to understand this client and others like him. Hopefully it also helped to humanize the institution, resulting in increased respect and social justice for future Native American clients.

NATIVE AMERICAN HISTORY AND THE CHEROKEE EXPERIENCE

Roberta Sholes's respect for the Cherokee people grew as she researched the history of Native American people in the United States and, more specifically, the Cherokee Nation. Aware that Native Americans, also known as **First Nations People**, were the first Americans, Roberta found that scientists now believe that the ancestors of today's Native Americans probably migrated across the Bering Strait from Asia. By the time the first Europeans arrived, there were approximately 1.5 million native peoples thriving in North America, representing a wide variety of tribal groups, customs, and languages (Lum, 1992).

For Native Americans the coming of the Europeans was a catastrophe. Europeans immigrated in massive numbers, dangerously armed with the power of the gun and bringing new diseases that decimated many Indian populations. They drove the Indians from their lands and frequently massacred those who resisted. This genocide is depicted in the story of the Cherokee's Trail of Tears, written by Wilma Mankiller (Mankiller & Wallis, 1993), a social worker and also the first woman to hold the position of principal chief of the Cherokee Nation. According to Mankiller, Cherokee people had long been living in the Great Smoky Mountain region when European settlers arrived on the coast of the United States. The Cherokees developed remarkably advanced communities, attaining wealth through their farms and plantations as well as commercial trading contracts with merchants in European countries. The discovery of gold on Cherokee land in Georgia ultimately led to broken treaties with the U.S. government and to President Andrew Jackson's order for removal of the Cherokee people to western lands. In 1835, 7,000 federal soldiers arrived; they rounded up Cherokee families, held them in stockades, and then forced them westward at gunpoint for the historic Trail of Tears. It is believed that of the 18,000 persons forcibly removed, approximately 4,000 died. According to Wilma Mankiller:

> Old ones and small children were placed in wagons, but many of the Cherokees made that trek by foot or were herded onto boats. Some were in shackles. Thousands perished or were forever scarred in body, mind, and soul. It was not a friendly removal. It was ugly and unwarranted. For too many Cherokees, it was deadly. The worse part of our holocaust was that it also meant the continued loss of tribal knowledge and traditions. (Mankiller & Wallis, 1993, p. 47)

The first winter in Oklahoma resulted in additional deaths from starvation and freezing. By 1839, however, a new constitution was written, and Tahlequah was established as the Cherokee capital. By 1851 the Cherokee Nation had created a comprehensive school system including schools of higher education. The strong work ethic and tribal pride of the Cherokees resulted in the rapid development of commerce, farms, government, and a judicial system. In 1862, during the Civil War, Cherokee land was invaded and taken by the Union Army. War destroyed ranches, homes, and the Cherokee economy. When the Civil War ended in 1865, Congress decreed that all Indians were wards of the government; no prior treaties were honored. Native Americans were then confined to reservations. In the 1870s railroad expansion brought homesteaders from the East. Despite the protest of Indians, the federal government sold previously protected Indian Territory to White settlers.

The General Allotment Act (the Dawes Act) of 1887 dealt a severe blow to Indian territories across the United States. The act provided private ownership of parcels of former reservation land—allotments—to individual Indians, with the remaining lands reverting to the U.S. government for homesteading or other purposes. Many Cherokees unknowingly sold their parcels of land for little or nothing and were left destitute. The Dawes Act dispossessed Indians in Oklahoma and across the country of nearly all their holdings. The next blow to Indian independence and self-rule came in 1898 with passage of the Curtis Act, which ended tribal courts as of that year and tribal government by 1906.

Beginning in the early 1900s additional efforts were made to destroy Native American culture. Children were forced to attend White boarding schools far from their reservations. They were forbidden to speak their own languages or to honor their own religious traditions. It was only in 1924 that Native Americans were finally granted full U.S. citizenship.

In 1934, the Indian Reorganization Act signaled a change in U.S. policy. Providing for the reestablishment of tribal governments, it was strongly supported by John Collier, a social worker and President Franklin D. Roosevelt's appointee as head of the Bureau of Indian Affairs. Collier was a crusader for the welfare of Native Americans. The Cherokee and many other Indian tribes were able to regroup and rebuild their governmental structures and communities under the provisions of the Indian Reorganization Act.

The history of the Cherokee Nation reflects the history of Native American people generally. All shared common experiences of broken treaties and harsh treatment from the U.S. government. All tribes today continue to struggle with poverty; discrimination by the majority society persists. Despite this, there are vast differences among Native American people today. Over 5,200,000 persons identified themselves as American Indian or Alaska Native (single race or in combination with other races) in the 2010 U.S. Census (Humes, Jones, & Ramirez, 2011). Of 500 different Indian nations or tribes, some include fewer than 100 members, while others may have in excess of 100,000 members. Some have very large land holdings, with families often living in isolated rural areas, while others, such as the Cayuga of New York, have no actual land holdings at all. "These nations differ in terms of language, religion, social structure, political structure, and many other aspects of their cultures" (Lum, 2007, p. 256).

While Indian leaders such as Wilma Mankiller have engendered increasing self-respect and pride among native people, the historical tearing of family structures that resulted from the Trail of Tears and all other Indian removal programs is only now beginning to be addressed. Treatment programs—especially in Indian mental health and substance abuse programs—promote

Native American intergenerational healing by focusing on both the strong survival skills and the unhealthy coping behaviors that people used when faced with a hostile environment. Although the history of broken treaties and oppression of Native American people goes back many years, it has links to our time. Maria Yellow Horse Brave Heart, a social work practitioner and educator, is another respected authority on Native American history of trauma. Writing as a Native person herself, she reports that almost all Indian families today include someone who was humiliated and traumatized by Indian boarding schools or who lost family members—generally children—taken by Indian agents or social workers, sometimes even given over by parents for adoption into non-Indian homes to avoid overwhelming poverty (2004). In her work she frequently deals with the unresolved grief and historical trauma of Native people. Clearly, much healing remains to be done. The scars remain deep and painful.

The scars remain deep and painful.

MENTAL HEALTH POLICY AND SOCIAL WORK PRACTICE: HISTORICAL PERSPECTIVES

As social workers today attempt to help people heal from many kinds of traumatic experiences and provide services to diverse populations with complex mental health needs, they do so within the context of governmental policy that creates or limits access to mental health programs. Sometimes it is really difficult to understand government policy and a societal climate that fails to provide care. Unfortunately, attitudes toward mental illness today still reflect the mixture of repulsion, fear, and even amusement with which the mentally ill were regarded for centuries. But progress has been made both in our understanding of and attitudes toward mental illness and in our professional technologies for treating it.

Gradual Enlightenment

To understand the mental health system in the United States today, we must look back to its roots. The colonists who came to the United States from Europe brought attitudes that were harsh and notions about caring for the mentally ill that stressed containment and coercion, whips, and chains. The first state hospital for the mentally ill in the United States was opened in Williamsburg, Virginia, in 1773. Before this, the mentally ill were cared for by their families or in poorhouses that also provided for people with tuberculosis, syphilis, and other contagious diseases and persons with physical or cognitive disabilities.

Social reform began almost simultaneously in the United States and Europe during the late 1700s and early 1800s. Leaders emerged whose reform activities produced a shift in societal attitudes toward mentally ill persons. In Paris, Dr. Philipe Pinel, a physician, attracted public attention in 1779 when he struck off the chains of the mentally ill men at Bicêtre, a "lunatic asylum." A Quaker religious community in York, England, provided funds to William Tuke to develop an institution for the humane treatment of mentally ill persons (no chains were permitted). In the United States, Dr. Benjamin Rush, a physician and one of the signers of the Declaration of Independence, instituted many reforms at Pennsylvania Hospital; he also wrote the first American text on psychiatry.

A Courageous Researcher and Reformer: Dorothea Dix

The most famous reformer, however, was Dorothea Lynde Dix, an activist and reformer whose work in the mid-1800s brought attention to the inhumane treatment of the mentally ill in the United States. A schoolteacher, Dix volunteered to teach a Sunday school class at the East Cambridge women's jail near Boston in 1841. Here she discovered that it had become common practice to place mentally ill poor people in prisons. She was horrified by the inhumane conditions in which they were kept, and she felt compelled to do something about it. Dix's well-trained mind told her that only carefully conducted research to document the conditions of the mentally ill would elicit the attention of public officials. Accordingly, she set about visiting every jail, prison, and almshouse in Massachusetts. The following description of her visit to a Saugus, Massachusetts, poorhouse one Christmas Eve is characteristic of what she uncovered:

> They ascended a low flight of stairs into an entry, entered a room completely unfurnished, no chair, table, bed. It was cold, very cold. Her conductor threw open a window, a measure imperative for the digestive stability of a visitor. On the floor sat a woman, her limbs immovably contracted, knees brought upward to the chin, face concealed, head resting on folded arms, body clothed with what looked like fragments of many discarded garments. They gave little protection, for she was constantly shuddering.
>
> "Can she not change positions?" inquired Dorothea. No, the contraction of her limbs was caused by "neglect and exposure in former years," before, it was inferred, she came under the charge of her present guardians.
>
> "Her bed." As they left the room the man pointed to an object about three feet long and from a half to three-quarters of a yard wide, made of old ticking and containing perhaps a full handful of hay. "We throw some blankets over her at night." (Wilson, 1975, pp. 109–110)

Dix systematically recorded her findings: a woman kept in a cage; another fastened to a stone wall with chains; a man whose feet had been damaged by frostbite who was kept in a box; many mentally ill persons kept in woodsheds without light, heat, or sanitation. The dates, places, and details of her investigations were all documented in a 30-page report that was presented to the Massachusetts legislature in January 1843. According to one biographer, on reading the report, the legislature "exploded like a bombshell. Years later a commentator would refer to it as 'the greatest sensation produced in the Massachusetts legislature since 1775.' Another would call her investigation 'the first piece of social research ever conducted in America' " (Wilson, 1975, p. 124). Legislation authorizing the building of hospitals to treat persons with mental illness was passed in Massachusetts as a result of Dix's investigations, but her work was not done.

Despite ill health, Dix traveled throughout the United States and Canada, continuing her research and reporting on inhumane treatment of people with mental illness. Through her efforts, the Canadian government authorized construction of a new mental hospital for western Canada, and the Kentucky legislature approved construction of a new wing for an existing hospital in Lexington. Illinois, Tennessee, and many other states appropriated funds for hospitals. Because many states were either unwilling or unable to finance hospitals for the mentally ill, Dorothea Dix decided to go to the federal government for help. A bill was passed by Congress that would have permitted funds from the federal government's sale of western lands to be used to care for the mentally ill, but President Franklin Pierce vetoed the bill in 1854.

Unfortunately, the new state hospitals—founded on the principle of humane treatment—soon deteriorated, causing alarm for Dix and her followers. Mental hospitals became dumping grounds for society's problems. For example, hospital wards were filled with immigrants, and antiforeign sentiment defined institutional policy. The foreign-born were housed separately from nonimmigrants and often in inferior quarters. African American people—in those states that even admitted them to state hospitals—were also segregated. By 1900 conditions in state hospitals were investigated and were vividly described in news articles. Across the country, reformers, inspired by the earlier work of Dorothea Dix, demanded strict guidelines for the proper care of the mentally ill.

In 1908 Clifford Beers's book, *A Mind That Found Itself*, captured a more receptive public than might have been the case had it not been for the work of Dorothea Dix, Benjamin Rush, and others. The book told the author's personal story. Beers, a Yale University graduate, suffered a mental breakdown and endured years of inhumane treatment in both private and state facilities. He eloquently described what he saw and heard from attendants and others, even when he was seriously mentally ill. The book aroused the interest of the public as well as professional people. Beers subsequently founded the Connecticut Society for Mental Hygiene and assisted in the development of the national and international mental hygiene movement, which advocated for federal government intervention in the problem of mental illness.

The Past 100 Years

The Social Work Profession Emerges

Even in the earliest days of the profession, the early 1900s, social work pioneers were involved in mental health work. In 1907, Mary Antoinette Cannon was hired by Massachusetts General Hospital to work with mentally ill patients. She was the first social worker to enter this field of practice. Mary Jarrett was employed in 1913 as the first director of social services at the Boston Psychopathic Hospital, where she is said to have coined the term *psychiatric social worker*. Soon social workers began to be routinely hired by hospitals and clinics to provide therapy.

Social casework, emerging from the work of the Charity Organization Society, was the primary social work method in the mental health field. The pivotal work done by Mary Richmond, the founder of social casework, in her seminal texts, *Social Diagnosis* (1917) and *What Is Social Casework?* (1922), demonstrated the strong relationship between poverty and the mental health, personality development, and well-being of social work clients.

World War I, from 1914 to 1918, resulted in battle casualties that were psychological as well as physical. *Shell shock* was the term used to describe psychiatric problems created by war experiences. Mental health staff, including social workers, was needed. Recognizing the need for social workers trained to work with psychiatric disorders, Mary Jarrett initiated a specialized psychiatric social work training program in 1918 at what is now the Smith College School for Social Work.

Sigmund Freud's writings were introduced into the United States in the early 1900s and had become well accepted by the 1920s. Freud's psychoanalytic theory taught that because mental illness derived from unresolved conflicts, patients could best be helped by remembering and discussing early events, even dreams, with a trained person. As Freudian theory was popularized in the 1920s and 1930s, public and private mental clinics began hiring many social workers to provide psychotherapy. These were still the early years of the profession, and the mental health movement gave the profession of social work a real boost. Social workers became valued parts of mental health treatment teams.

The demand for social workers to staff the clinics and hospitals spurred growth of the profession. The American Association of Psychiatric Social Workers, founded in 1926, became a strong force within the profession. In 1955 it merged with other specialized social work organizations to form the NASW.

Bertha Capen Reynolds was one of many social workers who provided leadership in the field of mental health practice. This feisty intellectual, clinical social worker and educator is also remembered for her social activism, strong support for labor unions, and critique of capitalism. In her work and in her writing, Reynolds was committed to fighting against wars, oppression, and human degradation. Her thinking was influenced by Christianity, Marxism, and Freudian theory. Her books, *Between Client and Community* (1934), *Learning and Teaching in the Practice of Social Work* (1942), and *Social Work and Social Living* (1935), helped social workers to build unique skills in meeting psychological and emotional needs of clients and families, at the same time undertaking social change efforts in communities and society. Bertha Capen Reynolds is celebrated as a leader in progressive social work.

The first book on child psychotherapy, *The Dynamics of Therapy in a Controlled Relationship* (1933), written by Jessie Taft, was based on her experiences with a social work agency, the Children's Aid Society in Pennsylvania. Taft, a psychologist, was strongly influenced by the psychoanalytic work of Otto Rank, and she brought his theoretical base to her teaching at the Pennsylvania School of Social Work. Taft and Virginia Robinson, a social worker on the school's faculty, developed what came to be known as the functional school of social work. Use of time and time-limited casework was a major focus of functional theory, thus making the functional school a precursor of modern-day brief, or time-limited, therapy.

When World War II began in 1939, officer-level positions for psychiatric social workers were created by the army, and social workers functioned on military neuropsychiatric teams. During the war, approximately 1 million persons with neuropsychiatric disorders were admitted to U.S. Army hospitals (Callicutt, 1987). This resulted in an expansion of psychiatric social services, especially group work, for the military and their families. By the end of the war, in 1945, the military services and the Veterans Administration hospitals had become the largest employers of professional social workers, and they remain so today.

Evolving Social Policy Affects Service in Mental Health

The first major piece of mental health legislation passed by the U.S. government was the National Mental Health Act of 1946. The act provided federal funding for research, training, and demonstration projects to help the states develop programs for the prevention and treatment of mental illness. The act set the stage for the creation of the National Institute of Mental Health (NIMH) in 1949. The leadership and authority of this federal organization came to be well recognized, and it had a major impact on the development of state mental health programs.

During the 1950s, social work continued its growth in the mental health field. Within the profession itself, social casework dominated practice from the 1940s through the 1960s. Prominent among the theorists and writers were Helen Harris Perlman (*Social Casework: A Problem-Solving Process,* 1957) and Florence Hollis (*Casework: A Psychosocial Therapy,* 1964). Hollis's work has been described as the springboard for the clinical social work movement (Meyer, 1987).

The Community Mental Health Centers Construction Act of 1963 was the next major piece of federal legislation related to mental health policy. With the strong support of President John F. Kennedy, this act gave credibility to the leadership and commitment of the federal government in mental health. It provided grants for the construction of the community mental health facilities to provide care for the persons released from hospitals for the chronically mentally ill. It defined the concept of continuum of care and required that care be provided even to those who could not afford to pay for it. Many historians believe that this legislation revolutionized the mental health system in the United States, because it resulted in large-scale development of community mental health programs as well as the deinstitutionalization of patients.

Over the next decade, as the effectiveness of psychotropic medication grew, the length of inpatient stay declined and the shift to outpatient services dramatically expanded. The plan to provide deinstitutionalized persons with well-integrated, publicly funded community mental health services did not materialize. While some persons received needed care, many others did not. The numbers of homeless, chronically mentally ill persons increased dramatically, calling public attention to the inadequacies of the community mental health centers in meeting the needs of this population. In the 1970s, the NIMH sponsored programs to test new forms of service delivery, many of which incorporated case management.

Decisions in the 1970s by the U.S. Supreme Court *(O'Connor v. Donaldson)* and the U.S. Court of Appeals for the Fifth Circuit (*Wyatt v. Stickney,* an Alabama case) set precedents in the areas of mental health and developmental disability. The rulings directed that mental patients who had been committed to a hospital had a right to release (assuming they were not dangerous to themselves or others) if they were not receiving treatment. Care for mentally ill or retarded persons was to be provided in the least restrictive (i.e., the least confined and most homelike) setting possible. Actions taken in the 1970s resulted in the release of massive numbers of persons from long-term psychiatric institutions where they had been hospitalized for many years. The intent was that they would be cared for in their home communities, but while some were placed in nursing homes or returned to families, large numbers ultimately were homeless and came to live on the streets. Their plight was not well addressed by the health care system nor by legislation.

Private insurance corporations, however, began to cover mental health services for employed persons, although not at the same level as other health care. With insurance money available, private general hospitals expanded their inpatient and outpatient facilities. States began to gradually turn over their mental health programs to private enterprise to administer. A system that had once been largely a governmental operation was slowly transformed to a nonprofit and then, increasingly, to a for-profit economy.

A consumer movement emerged at this time and grew remarkably quickly. The **National Alliance on Mental Illness (NAMI)** was founded in

1979 of consumers (this term is preferred to patients), family members, and concerned professionals. Today NAMI continues to support research, education, and social policy and political activity that will enhance access to community-based services. The organization is supported by members and now has affiliate offices in all 50 states and affiliates in 1,200 local communities (National Alliance on Mental Illness [NAMI], 2010).

The federal Mental Health Systems Act of 1980 finally attempted to address the ramifications of deinstitutionalization. To meet the basic needs of thousands of homeless mentally ill persons and others needing follow-up care, the act authorized the use of case management. Almost immediately, many new programs for homeless persons and others with persistent and serious mental illness were put into place.

The Omnibus Budget Reconciliation Act of 1981 signaled a major shift away from the federal government's willingness to provide leadership for or to finance mental health services. This legislation, supported by President Ronald Reagan but opposed by social workers and many people in the mental health field, effectively repealed the Mental Health Systems Act and shifted responsibility for funding and future development of mental health programs to the individual states in the form of block grants. Most states, however, had already closed or substantially reduced their mental health facilities. Many states responded by developing contractual arrangements with counties and with private organizations to provide community-based services to persons with more serious and chronic forms of mental illness. This led to fragmentation and reduction of services. The election of President Bill Clinton in 1992 signaled a readiness for new approaches to health care financing, and, indeed, many Americans supported some form of national health care. But the Clinton administration's plan met with a great deal of opposition, and eventually it was withdrawn. President Bill Clinton then responded by spearheading a **Mental Health Bill of Rights**, a set of principles to ensure that basic consumer rights would be met. The bill addressed consumers' rights to information about their health plans, their rights to information about the professionals who deliver services, the right to a reasonable choice of providers, the right to have access to emergency services, the right to participate in treatment decisions, the right to receive respectful care, confidentiality, and the right to appeal decisions of the health care plan (KEN Publications/Catalog, n.d.). In an unprecedented move, nine professional organizations, representing more than 500,000 mental health practitioners, collaborated and jointly published a Mental Health Bill of Rights policy statement that was stronger and more inclusive than the set of principles set forth by the Clinton administration. NASW was one of the nine sponsors. This initiative reflected the level of professional practitioner support for patients' rights reform and an end to stigmatization and discrimination for persons who suffer from major or minor mental disorders.

Mental Health Parity Legislation

Years of reduced access to mental health care—from deinstitutionalization of the 1970s, to Reagan's Omnibus Budget Reconciliation Act of 1981, to managed care—led to public outcry in the 1990s. Consumers of mental health services and their watchdog organizations, NAMI and Mental Health America (formerly the National Mental Health Association), along with social work and other mental health professional organizations actively sought public support for meaningful mental health parity legislation. This forced an increasingly conservative U.S. Congress to pass the Mental Health Parity Act of 1996 and many states to pass their own parity acts. *Parity*, here, refers to efforts to equalize benefits for physical and mental health care. The 1996 act was breakthrough legislation and widely acclaimed, but it failed to meet expectations. Its limitations became apparent quite quickly: only employers of 50 or more were mandated to comply and only if they offered provisions for mental health care. The law also allowed insurance plans to limit the number of outpatient visits they would pay for and limit hospital stays; it also permitted charging higher co-payments than people were asked to pay for their physical health care. Social workers, including NASW lobbyists, sought passage of legislation that would rectify the limitations of the 1996 legislation. Momentum continued to build. States as diverse as Connecticut, North Carolina, and Texas passed mental health parity laws. At the federal level, several bills were introduced into the Senate and House of Representatives in 2007.

Finally, in 2008 the Federal Mental Health Parity and Addiction Equity Act was passed. It was hailed as a significant achievement, one that would have "a substantial positive impact on patient access to care" (NASW, 2010b, Analysis section, para. 1). A major change: parity in coverage under the law was extended to care for addiction disorders. The law required that health insurance plans provide equivalence between mental health and physical health coverage. Co-payments, deductibles, out-of-pocket payments, and even limitations on the number or frequency of visits were all addressed in the law. In 2010 the Obama administration wrote additional rules to the 2008 law that exempted self-funded health insurance plans from parity, thus closing a loophole that left employees of some companies without parity in health care coverage.

Parity: efforts to equalize benefits for physical and mental health care.

This occurred at the same time that the Obama administration was successful in passing overall health care reform (to be discussed more fully in Chapter 7) for the United States, thus dramatically increasing access to health care, including mental health care. Nonetheless, issues related to access to mental health care and quality of mental health care remain to be addressed in the near future.

POLICY AND PRACTICE: FUTURE ISSUES

Despite passage of the 2008 mental health parity law and the 2010 health care reform legislation, the primary continuing problem compelling political action by social workers and other health care advocates remains the basic issue of access to good quality health care. Instead of addressing all health insurance coverage, the 2008 Federal Mental Health Parity and Addiction Equity Act exempted small organizations, those with 2 to 50 employees. In addition, parity applied only to plans that included some provision for mental health or substance use disorders. This permitted corporations to discontinue insurance coverage for mental health and substance use disorders with no penalty, and it clearly did not encourage employers to add such insurance to their existing policies.

The 2010 health care reform law, officially the Affordable Health Care for America Act, when fully implemented in 2019, however, is expected to expand health care coverage to millions of U.S. citizens as well as legal immigrants. Rules remain to be written for implementation of the law, but major portions of the law that affect access to mental health care are scheduled for implementation by 2014. Until that time, many people will need to rely on the 2008 mental health parity act to ensure access to mental health care. Of some concern is the considerable political backlash that seeks to dismantle this revolutionary health care reform law either through legislation or through the courts. Social workers and other mental health professionals will surely closely monitor any potential policy changes that could affect the benefits that this law promises.

In addition to access, the quality of mental health care will also continue to be an issue for the future. The system of managed care, used to control the cost of health care, has had a major impact on the persons receiving care and on the practice of social workers. The traditional, open-ended therapies used in the past by social work psychotherapists and the long-term involvement so characteristic of many BSW caseloads have given way to brief, highly focused approaches to practice. In many settings, intermittent services have replaced long-term case contact. Managed care has encouraged the use of groups, often with a psychoeducational focus instead of individualized psychosocial therapy, for inpatient as well as community-based practice. The use of standardized protocols, sometimes referred to by insurance companies as preferred practices, is another response to the demand for short-term, highly focused, cost-conscious intervention. These protocols, or **preferred practices**, are directives that determine the practices to be followed for specific client problems. All these practices may have benefits for some people and for cost containment, but persons with persistent, serious mental health problems often fall between the cracks of this system.

Mental health social and economic policies will continue to influence social work practice in the future, and new forms of practice are likely to evolve. Short-term approaches are already increasingly demanded by managed care. Strategic or solution-oriented approaches are used to help clients focus narrowly on ineffective behaviors and reframe or obtain new perspectives that enable the efficient achievement of goals. Time-limited family and group interventions, even single-session treatment approaches and Internet therapeutic techniques, continue to evolve. Social workers are increasingly using computerized Internet groups and computer-assisted therapy, enabling clients to benefit from cost-effective groups in privacy and without leaving their homes.

Future trends in mental health social work practice will surely continue to be strongly influenced by the evolution of health care policy. Cost containment is likely to remain a pressing issue especially as the new health care reform plan is implemented. "The contemporary challenge is to determine how the social work profession repositions itself to remain current and viable in the transformed mental health field, driven by federal and business sector interests, in controlling costs" (Davis, 2008, p. 255). Social workers of the future will be challenged to design new practice approaches to demonstrate with clear evidence that they are achieving their goals in meeting client needs and to retain leadership in creating and administering mental health programs. Is this a big job? Yes! Clearly it calls for well-educated and prepared professionals who are strongly grounded in compassion for clients and commitment to professional values and who are equipped with advocacy skills to seek the kind of social change that will lead to increased health and well-being for all people.

SUMMARY

Roberta Sholes's work with David Deerinwater demonstrated the unique contribution that social work can make to the mental health team. Her sensitivity to the cultural dimensions of the case enriched her work with the client and enabled her to help other professional staff in their work. Most significantly, this BSW social worker helped David Deerinwater achieve his goal and reintegrate with his family and his people. As a generalist social worker, Roberta had the skills to work within a complex organizational structure, with families as well as individuals, and she was able to understand and use community systems.

Although they are not educated in a medical profession and they have serious concerns about the use of certain diagnostic labels, social workers whose careers are in mental health settings must learn the diagnostic terminology used by members of the mental health team. The chapter, therefore, introduced readers to the *Diagnostic and Statistical Manual of Mental Disorders* of the American Psychiatric Association. An introduction to the more commonly used psychotropic medications was also provided.

Social workers in mental health encounter significant social justice issues. The chapter identified concerns related to the use and abuse of diagnostic labels. Inadequate access to mental health care, especially for persons who are unemployed and homeless and those with persistent, serious mental illness, was also identified as a concern. Environmental causes of mental illness or contributors to mental health problems were also discussed.

The chapter also traced the development of the U.S. response to mental illness from colonial times to the present. Key figures in reforms of the mental health system were Dorothea Lynde Dix, whose research and publications called the nation's attention to the inhumane treatment of the mentally ill, and Clifford Beers, whose book, *A Mind That Found Itself*, furthered public understanding of mental illness and helped promote an emerging mental hygiene movement. Mary Antoinette Cannon, Mary Jarrett, Jessie Taft, and Virginia Robinson were instrumental in the development of professional social services for the mentally ill and of training programs for social workers. Sigmund Freud's works resulted in improved approaches to treatment of mental illness, approaches that were quickly incorporated into the curricula of schools of social work as well as medicine, psychology, and nursing.

Social policy initiatives were described. These included federal legislation that created the NIMH and other laws such as the Community Mental Health Centers Construction Act of 1963 and the Mental Health Systems Act of 1980, all of which promoted programs for the mentally ill. This period of growth, however, ended in the early 1980s as federal budget priorities shifted from mental health to military interests. The Omnibus Budget Reconciliation Act of 1981 shifted primary responsibility for leadership in the development of mental health services to the individual states. Concern about increasing health care costs and growing public reluctance to support health and human services marked the 1990s, signaling shifts in the way that social workers and all mental health professionals would provide care. Policies designed to curtail rising costs nourished the growth of managed care in the field of mental health.

When access to mental health care declined, diverse national organizations, including NAMI, NASW, and other mental health professional groups,

Reinforce what you learned in this chapter by studying videos, cases, documents, and more available at **www.MySearchLab.com**.

Watch and Review

Watch these Videos

* Learning From the Client to Co-create an Action Plan
* Developing an Action Plan that Changes the Internal and External

Read and Review

Read these Cases/Documents

Δ Military Veteran Justice Outreach and the Role of a VA Social Worker

Δ The Leon Family

Explore and Assess

Explore these Assets

Interactive Cases for Practice: Group Work

National Alliance on Mental Illness—http://www.nami.org/

National Center for PTSD, U.S. Department of Veterans Affairs—http://www.ptsd.va.gov/

Substance Abuse and Mental Health Services Administration—http://www.samhsa.gov/

Assess Your Knowledge

Assess your knowledge with a variety of topical and chapter assessment.

Conclude your assessment by completing the chapter exam.

* = CSWE Core Competency Asset
Δ = Case Study

Social Work in Health Care

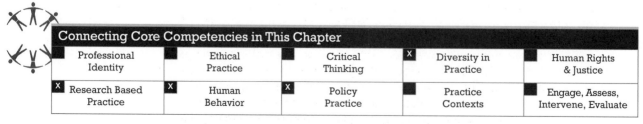

Connecting Core Competencies in This Chapter				
Professional Identity	Ethical Practice	Critical Thinking	X Diversity in Practice	Human Rights & Justice
X Research Based Practice	X Human Behavior	X Policy Practice	Practice Contexts	Engage, Assess, Intervene, Evaluate

Katherine Lewandowski

As Linda Sanders walked down the corridor on the third floor of St. Anne's Hospital, she smiled at some of the nurses she passed. She was just beginning to know the staff, now that she was entering the second month of her senior-year social work field placement at this community general hospital. After all the years of classroom courses, it felt really good to finally be in a program that permitted her to do field work and apply what she had learned.

Linda was thinking now about the patient she was about to visit. Katherine Lewandowski was an 86-year-old widow who had been placed in a nursing home 2 months ago because she had suffered several minor fractures as a result of **osteoporosis**, a bone-thinning disease most commonly found in women over 50. Because of her condition she could no longer live at home. Linda liked the silver-haired, frail woman who spoke both Polish and English. Katherine had a hearty sense of humor, but it was revealed infrequently during her hospitalization, for she was frightened of the medical setting and of staff in white uniforms. Fortunately, she had related well to Linda from the start.

As she approached the patient's room, Linda recalled her two previous visits with Katherine. She had provided emotional support, which the elderly woman badly needed at the time of her arrival at St. Anne's. In the days that followed her admission to the hospital—necessitated by a fall at the nursing home, which had fractured her hip—Linda had tried to help Katherine understand and accept the recommended surgical procedure to repair the break. The surgery, performed 3 days ago, had gone well.

Linda tapped lightly on the door and entered the room. She glanced at Katherine and was startled by her appearance. Katherine's eyes were closed, but there were tears on her cheeks. Her color was poor. From her movements it was clear she was in pain. When Linda spoke a quiet, gentle greeting, Katherine opened her eyes. Linda delivered the message she had come with, that the doctors felt Katherine could return now to her nursing home; an ambulance would take her there in the morning. Linda had spoken with Katherine's daughter, Donna, who had said that she would visit her mother at the nursing home the next evening. Katherine's response to this message was to turn her head toward the wall. Linda asked if Katherine had any questions, if there was anything she could do. Katherine closed her eyes; then, after a silence, she said, "No." Gently, Linda asked, "Katherine, are you okay? You seem to be upset. Can we talk about whatever is troubling you?" Katherine turned her face even more toward the wall. When she said, "I am all right," her tone was one of dismissal.

Linda was troubled as she left the room. She wondered whether Katherine was really ready to be discharged from the hospital. Katherine was in pain, and she was weak and obviously distressed. Linda discussed her concerns with Katherine's nurse, but the nurse said that she had already been in the hospital more than 5 days, and that most patients with hip fractures were able to leave in that period of time. Linda then spoke with her field instructor, who advised her to contact Katherine's doctor. The physician seemed somewhat annoyed with Linda's call and indicated that Katherine had used all the days of hospital care allowed by Medicare. She could recuperate just as readily in the nursing home.

Again Linda sought clarification from her field instructor, an experienced social worker whom Linda admired and respected. Marge O'Brien helped Linda review carefully what she had observed in Katherine's behavior. Then Marge explained that Medicare paid the hospital based on diagnosis, and this determined the length of stay. The Business Office had notified the doctor that Katherine was reaching the end of her predetermined hospital stay. The doctor's discharge plan for Katherine was final unless it was clearly inappropriate or threatened the patient's well-being. Linda had already alerted the doctor to her concerns, which was a very important form of advocacy, because the doctor would continue to be responsible for Katherine in the nursing home. Marge was very sensitive to Linda's concerns about Katherine. Premature hospital discharges were increasing, she said, because of efforts to reduce the high cost of medical care. Hospital social workers were increasingly alarmed about the risk to patients. Marge directed Linda to report her concerns to Katherine's daughter immediately and also to the social worker at the nursing home.

When Linda telephoned Katherine's daughter, Donna said she was concerned, too, but she felt the doctor must surely know what was best. Linda encouraged Donna to remain in close contact with the doctor and to advise him of any change in her mother's condition. Then, as she made ambulance arrangements and gathered medical information for the nursing home, Linda was alert to any additional data that she could use to seek a delay in Katherine's discharge. There were none. Linda faxed the necessary forms and medical records to the nursing home; then she telephoned the social worker there to report her observations and her concerns about Katherine.

Two days later, when Linda returned to the hospital for her next field placement day, she asked about Katherine. The nursing staff reported that Katherine had been discharged and returned to the nursing home without incident. Linda continued to think about Katherine, however, knowing that the discharge to the nursing home— which was still not *home* for her—and the uncomfortable ambulance ride might have been quite difficult.

On Sunday evening Linda picked up the section of the Sunday paper that contained the classified ads and the obituary column. She thought she would check the advertised social work positions. Suddenly the obituary column caught her attention. There was Katherine! She had died 3 days after returning to the nursing home. Linda was stunned. She reviewed her telephone call with Katherine's daughter, her last conversation with Katherine, and her phone call to the doctor. Could Katherine's death have been prevented? Had she given up too quickly? What else could she have done? As she thought about it, Linda realized that it was possible that Katherine might have had additional health complications after returning to the nursing home. She turned back to the newspaper. Then she recognized the name of another patient who had been discharged recently, and then she saw another name she knew. Reading on, she counted five recently discharged elderly patients' obituaries. Feeling very troubled, Linda put the newspaper down. She knew that she would have many more questions to ask her field instructor.

Still troubled by Katherine's death, Linda noted some especially interesting research findings as she worked on a term paper for one of her classes. In a National Association of Social Workers (NASW) publication article by Munch and Shapiro (2007), Linda learned that osteoporosis is frequently undetected in men as well as women (citing the National Osteoporosis Foundation, 2007). Looking further, Linda found articles in several recent medical journals describing the prevalence of osteoporosis among persons with depression (Bab & Yirmiya, 2010; Cizza, Primma, Coyle, Gourgiotis, & Csaka, 2010; & Cizza, Primma, & Csaka, 2009). Several of the articles expressed concern that health care practitioners had not given sufficient attention to the role of depression as a significant risk factor in osteoporosis-related bone fractures. Linda carefully reviewed this research and then reported her findings at the next staff meeting of the hospital social work department.

The staff had not seen this research, but the social workers were very interested, especially when Linda proposed the development of an interdisciplinary study group to determine how best the hospital could assess the existence of depression in the men as well as women who were found to have loss of bone density, which could lead to osteoporosis. Linda suggested that prevention efforts could be initiated, too, through community outreach and education. Dietitians, nurses, physical therapists, and doctors could all participate. Social workers could take leadership roles in creating this change in the way that the hospital as an organization dealt with both inpatient and outpatient osteoporosis prevention and treatment. Linda hoped, too, that older adults with existing osteoporosis like Katherine Lewandowski would no longer be sent off to nursing homes following surgery without careful assessment of their psychological and emotional well-being.

Research Based Practice

Practice Behavior Example: Use research evidence to inform practice

Critical Thinking Question: How might additional research enhance the proposed osteoporosis prevention program?

APPLYING GENERALIST PRACTICE THEORY TO HEALTH CARE

Linda Sanders realized that she and the hospital social workers needed to work on several social systems levels simultaneously. As they assisted individual persons like Katherine Lewandowski and her family, they also needed to create change within the hospital as an organizational system. Ultimately they would need to collaborate with other health care professionals and public citizens to seek the kind of political change that would make health care truly responsive to the needs of people in the local community and elsewhere. In the meantime, however, Linda and the social work staff decided to focus on changing procedures and creating new programs within the hospital.

Starting with the Liberal Arts Base of Social Work Education

Using knowledge acquired in math, sociology, speech and writing courses, statistics, political science, and research courses, Linda could have input into an action research project that would potentially improve the well-being of persons, especially older persons, served by the hospital. Initially, Linda's field instructor, Marge O'Brien, encouraged Linda to deliver her ideas verbally to the social work staff. When Linda's suggestions were well received, Marge asked Linda to write up a proposal for an action plan that would begin with gathering data from each of their perspectives by nurses, dietitians, and other health care staff. As a student in her first field placement, Linda was prepared to participate in but not direct the social work action that lay ahead. The director of the social work department would probably assume the primary leadership role. Linda, however, would have opportunities to experience the research, education, and advocacy that would be primary strategies in changing the hospital's procedures. Linda anticipated learning a lot about the political systems that operated within large organizational systems and was excited about the challenges and the learning she could gain in this field placement!

Meantime, Linda's routine student social work practice experience included seeing patients on a one-to-one basis to counsel, intervene in crises, and help families with discharge plans. Often, too, Linda referred patients and their families to other community resources, such as nutrition or hot meal programs and substance abuse treatment. Generally, Linda and the other hospital social workers did not engage in long-term counseling with individual patients; therefore, patients who needed ongoing, intensive counseling were referred to local social service agencies or to private practitioners in social work, psychology, or psychiatry. Linda might also assist the hospital social workers who provided educational and support groups for persons who were newly diagnosed with cancer or who were dependent on alcohol or drugs. One of the social workers had developed a support group for people who had had stroke and for their friends and families. Linda's field placement gave her a strong sense of growing professional competence.

Births and deaths, accidents and injuries, and acute illnesses and chronic diseases—these are the concerns in health care settings. Social workers must have a solid knowledge base if they are to further other health care team members' understanding of the emotional factors in illness. Coursework in the liberal arts provides a basic understanding of the biological sciences as well as the social, psychological, and cultural sciences. As we saw in Chapter 1, unlike the training of other health care providers, the social worker's professional education stresses the person within his or her environment. The generalist social worker is prepared to intervene with individual persons (like Katherine Lewandowski); with entire families or selected family members (e.g., Katherine's daughter); with small groups; with organizations (like St. Anne's Hospital); and with large groups, neighborhoods, and communities.

Social work students begin their education with liberal arts courses in such areas as literature, writing, biology, sociology, and psychology. By the sophomore and junior years, the curriculum includes professional courses in generalist practice, research, human behavior in the social environment, cultural diversity, and social policy. The liberal arts courses teach students to think critically, to question, and to analyze. They also provide knowledge about human beings, society, and different cultures that professional courses later build upon. This is especially true of the courses in human behavior and social policy. Courses in generalist practice provide the skill base and the knowledge of social work practice theory that lead to competent social work practice in health care or other settings. Beginning in the second semester of the junior year or in the senior year, baccalaureate students spend a minimum of 400 hours in field work. It is in field work that all the theory is applied and that students demonstrate that they have the competence needed to practice social work when they graduate.

Hospitals like St. Anne's generally employ MSW as well as BSW social workers. MSWs generally staff specialized services such as cardiac intensive care and neonatal nurseries because of their complex nature and the immediacy of the services needed by patients and families. Especially fast-paced areas such as the emergency room (ER) also require very skilled, experienced social workers; except in small hospitals and sometimes in rural areas, MSWs are given these responsibilities. The MSW curriculum is also based on liberal arts preparation and a generalist perspective, but advanced, specialized courses are also taken.

Values and Ethics in Health Care Social Work

Hospitals and other health care settings work daily with frightened, hurting, vulnerable people. As organizational systems, hospitals often deliver services in ways that seem cruel and heartless to patients. Social workers in health care, guided by the values of the profession, can help humanize the health care environment for people and teach staff how to individualize patients. Among the values that the profession holds are regard for individual worth and dignity, the right of people to participate in the helping process, and the right of clients to make decisions that will affect them.

Social workers can help humanize the health care environment.

These values and the Code of Ethics of the NASW were introduced in Chapter 1. The Code of Ethics is strongly emphasized in social work courses, and students are required to demonstrate ability to engage in ethical social work practice. Health care, however, is a field of practice that challenges social workers to sustain their commitment to professional values and ethics. The health care environment itself sometimes contradicts social work values. This is especially true when health care organizations make huge profits but deny some people access to health care and when salaries range from hundreds of thousands of dollars for some and barely minimum wage for other health care employees.

Linda Sanders, the student social worker, was shocked by Katherine Lewandowski's death and by the depression that she saw in many other persons who were discharged to nursing homes or back to their families following treatment for fractures caused by osteoporosis. She began to think about the ethical questions related to the care of these people. Was it possible that people were being discharged from the hospital prematurely, without adequate assessment and treatment for depression? If so, was this happening because the professional staff was not aware of the high rate not only of depression but even of death following osteoporosis-related fractures? The National Osteoporosis Foundation reported that in the United States, 24 percent of people who experience a hip fracture will die within a year (2007). Was it instead possible that premature discharge was encouraged by the health insurance companies who sought to expedite discharge to contain costs?

Biomedical ethics is not a concern for physicians alone. Social workers too, especially those in the health care field, encounter ethical and value-laden issues in daily practice. Often social workers assist patients and families with decisions about continued use of life-support systems for terminally ill persons or for profoundly disabled infants. Social workers frequently serve as the conscience of institutions as they challenge policies and procedures that have negative impacts on people. Students preparing for careers in social work develop an understanding of moral and ethical problems through liberal arts courses, such as philosophy and theology, and through content regarding ethics and values in their social work courses.

Focusing on the Community and Populations at Risk

The health care social worker is the essential link between the patient, the health care facility (whether hospital, clinic, health department, or nursing home), and the community and its resources. Knowledge of the community means more than a mere listing of community resources, which would be available to any hospital employee. Truly understanding the community means understanding the diverse racial and ethnic groups that make up that community, their traditional beliefs about illness and health care, and any special healers that people might turn to. The faith and spiritual values of the community must be understood and respected by social workers. Often such values are the one vital, sustaining source of strength for a patient or a family. In health settings, social work has traditionally been the professional discipline that interprets the ethnic, class, or cultural roots of beliefs and behaviors that have influenced patients' responses to illness. Armed with knowledge of cultural diversity and the community, social workers sometimes help families design remarkably creative plans for posthospital care or as an alternative to nursing home placement.

There has been a long history of disparity of health services to lower-class and minority people in the United States. Of serious concern to social workers are the poor (especially members of racial and ethnic minority groups), people with disabilities, and persons who are HIV-infected. These are among the populations that are seriously at risk when some health care professionals avoid or even refuse to treat them. It has become extremely difficult for social workers to locate health services for persons in poverty and those who fall between the cracks of health insurance programs. Sometimes it is even difficult to sustain contact with culturally diverse patients whose needs are not met or whose health care has been delivered in an insensitive, disrespectful manner. As Devore and Schlesinger point out, "advocating for the poor, for those who do not speak English, and for those who have greater faith in the spirits than in modern medicine requires a high degree of self-awareness and comfort with the identity 'social worker'" (1987, p. 260).

For social work students, awareness and appreciation of human diversity and community norms is built gradually. This learning starts with the liberal arts courses taken in the freshman and sophomore years. Courses in literature, history, political science, and sociology help prepare social work students to understand the influences of class, gender, race, and ethnicity. Students begin to understand such concepts as social norms and roles and to appreciate the rich contributions of many cultures to contemporary society. Social work courses taken in the junior and senior years further prepare students for practice within the community and with a variety of populations. The field practice that concludes the baccalaureate-degree program enables students to demonstrate competent social work practice, not in a classroom but out in the community.

Achieving Competence for Practice in Health Care

Accidents, injury, and illness all have impact. Pain, often both psychological and physical, occurs. There may be days lost from work or school. This can mean getting behind on schoolwork or projects on the job. It could even mean loss of a job and loss of income. Competence for practice begins with students understanding the social systems and ecosystems perspectives (as described in Chapter 2). In health care, social workers must anticipate that there will almost always be consequences for persons beyond the patient. There may be impact on the job site, for example, if a person is hurt at work. If a parent is ill or injured, there are consequences for the family. Loss of income could have devastating results for the family, potentially even homelessness. Young children don't understand illness or disability well; they may be very upset emotionally by the events unfolding in their family. In a single-parent family, severe or prolonged illness of the parent may require placement of the children with a relative or even in foster care if relatives are not available. In any event, health care problems of the parents often change the quality of nurturing that is so necessary to the healthy development of young children. In some cases, too, older children must take on greater family responsibility, which may include staying home from school to care for younger brothers and sisters.

The generalist practice theory that social work students acquire, based on social systems theory and the ecosystems perspective, provides a basis for understanding the impact of illness and injury on individuals and families as well as larger social systems. In generalist practice courses, students acquire the interviewing techniques and communication skills that are needed in health care social work practice, and they learn to apply problem-solving process with individuals and families. They also learn how organizations and communities function as systems and how to help organizations, like St. Anne's Hospital in this chapter's case study, change procedures and initiate programs or engage in efforts to prevent illness and injuries.

Whole communities suffer when there are epidemics of flu or much more serious contagious diseases, so social work efforts in prevention are important. Every day social workers help young parents understand the preventive care needed by new babies or young children. Illnesses threaten masses of people in society when the health care system of our country does not ensure that everyone has access to health care. In recent years, vigorous political advocacy for health care reform engaged social workers along with other professions and citizens in an effort to create a national health care policy in the United States. This policy practice gave social work students an opportunity to learn firsthand the skills of political action, and they continue today to use critical thinking to analyze and monitor evolving health care reform as the 2010 Patient Protection and Affordable Health Care Act is gradually implemented. Like Linda Sanders in the case study, students also use fieldwork experiences to apply the theory and skills they have learned in the classroom to achieve competence in health care practice. Because health care is such a large and diverse part of U.S. society, health care field placements may occur within a wide variety of community organizations.

HEALTH CARE SERVICES

Linda Sanders's social work field placement was in a community general hospital, but hospitals are not the only health care settings that employ social workers. The U.S. health care system, fueled by a desire to sustain profitability while controlling rapid increases in health care costs, has created a wide variety of new health care ventures. In metropolitan areas in recent years, many inner-city hospitals were closed and public health services were cut back. Meanwhile, mergers and acquisitions of hospitals, nursing homes, rehabilitation centers, HMOs, pharmacies, and diagnostic testing centers created giant, profitable, in some cases, multinational health care corporations. Users of health care and all of the health care professions have been impacted by these changes. Dramatic change in health care is likely to continue.

The result of ongoing change throughout the system is that social workers may now be found in a very wide variety of health care settings (see Box 7.1 for a sampling of settings). As the list of settings suggests, social work is a viable profession in a growing number of health-related community organizations. Studies reported in Chapter 1 done by NASW and the Association of Baccalaureate Social Work Program Directors showed that many BSW and MSW social workers are employed in the health field. NASW expects that as the 2010 health care reform legislation is implemented, additional social work positions will be created (Malamud, 2010).

Box 7.1   Settings for Health Care Social Work

General hospitals

Children's hospitals and other specialized
    hospitals

Physicians' offices

Public health clinics

Health maintenance organizations (HMOs)

Rehabilitation services

Nursing homes and subacute centers

Home health care organizations

Women's health centers

Health planning boards

Specialized health organizations (American Cancer
    Society, National Kidney Foundation)

Hospice programs

Insurance companies

Private social work practice

Homeless shelter health clinics

Outpatient clinics

Acute Care

The majority of health care social workers today are employed in **acute care** (facilities that provide immediate, short-term care): hospitals, inpatient and outpatient clinics, and rehabilitation centers. Rehabilitation centers provide intensive medical services for people who do not need to remain in the hospital but also may not need, or hopefully can avoid, long-term care. While lengthier and somewhat less expensive than hospitalization, care in a reha-bilitation facility is fast paced. Social workers collaborate with patients and families to plan for the physical therapy and ongoing medical services and appliances that are often needed when patients are discharged home.

The services that are provided by the social worker are short-term but often involve intensive emotional exchanges with patients and family members. Advocacy with staff or with outside community organizations may be involved. Service functions also include social support assessments, discharge planning, psychosocial counseling, case consultation, health education, infor-mation and referral, program interdisciplinary consultation, and community planning.

Hospital social work is changing dramatically, as hospitals themselves are changing. Once there were hospital social work departments administered by MSW social workers. Now social workers are employed by hospitals, but they often work out of designated units such as cardiac intensive care, the spinal cord injury area, or the unit that cares for high-risk newborns (neonatal intensive care). Social work service to hospital emergency rooms is taking on increased importance. Twenty-four-hour social work staffing is now provided in busy metropolitan hospitals. Nonetheless, as Keigher states, "hospitals no longer dominate the field [of health care]. Indeed, they have become remarkably limited, providing mainly specialty treatment and highly techno-logical diagnostics" (2000, p. 7). The shift away from hospitals to outpatient, community-based, and in-home health services means that hospital social work is evolving into a broader concept: health care social work. The NASW has developed a policy statement that addresses some of the political issues related to health care. The statement (see Box 7.2) is based on social work values and principles. It clearly supports the right of all persons to a full range of health care services.

Box 7.2   NASW Policy Statement on Health Care

NASW supports:

- A national health care policy that ensures the right to universal access to a continuum of health and mental health care throughout all stages of the life cycle. The goal of such a policy is to promote wellness, maintain optimal health, prevent illness and disability, treat health conditions, ameliorate the effects of unavoidable incapacities, and provide supportive long-term and end-of-life care. This policy should result in the equitable delivery of services for all people in the United States, regardless of financial status, race, ethnicity, disability, religion, age, gender, sexual orientation, or geographic location.

- An equal right to continuous, high-quality care that is effective, efficient, safe, timely, and patient-centered.

- Efforts to eliminate racial, ethnic, and economic disparities in health service access, provision, utilization, and outcomes.

- The coordination of NASW chapter efforts to influence state and federal health care policy.

- Policies and practices that ensure that patients receive necessary and appropriate care and guarantee patient rights protections.

- Active and organized consumer participation in the planning, implementation, evaluation, and maintenance and governance of health and mental health services.

Box 7.2 represents only a partial listing of the policy statement.

Source: *Social work speaks: National Association of Social Workers policy statements, 2009–2012* by National Association of Social Workers. Copyright 2010. Reproduced with permission of National Association of Social Workers in the formats Textbook and Other Book via Copyright Clearance Center.

Long-Term Care

Although most people think of a nursing home when they think about long-term care, a growing number of services are, in fact, included within the purview of long-term care. In addition to nursing homes, some of the community-based services include home health care, assisted-living facilities, home-delivered meals, and adult day care. **Long-term care** consists of any combination of nursing, personal care, volunteer, and social services provided intermittently or on a sustained basis over a span of time to help persons with chronic illness or disability to maintain maximum quality of life.

Not all users of long-term care are the elderly, but with the population of older persons increasing, a growing segment of long-term care consumers are likely to be older persons. The 1999 U.S. Supreme Court Olmstead decision encouraged states to develop programs to ensure that older adults and persons with disabilities can live in the least restrictive environment possible. With some pressure from the federal government, states are continuing to evolve programs that enable elderly persons to avoid nursing home placement or return to community living if they have been placed in a nursing home. However, **cost containment** concerns—concerns about the need to control rising health care costs—have limited the funding available for home-based care from both Medicare and private insurance. Currently these programs and Medicaid are more likely to provide for nursing home care.

Nursing homes remain one of the most common forms of long-term care. In the United States, a large portion of nursing homes are owned by proprietary (for-profit) corporations. There are also private, nonprofit homes (some operated by religious denominations) plus federal (Veterans Administration), state, and county public facilities. Nursing homes are licensed by the state. Nursing services are provided 24 hours per day, augmented by physical, occupational, and activity therapists; dieticians; and social workers, among others.

Transitional living and assisted living are less restricted and more home-like facilities for older adults who are fairly independent. Both are designed as small apartments, and they are often located on the same property as or attached to existing nursing homes, thus providing for a range of care, depending on need. The residents of these facilities have intellectual, social, political, and spiritual interests and considerable capacity to enjoy them, thus making field trips, even travel, a possibility. Groups and activities of many kinds can be used by creative social workers to meet the social, intellectual, and emotional needs of residents.

Federal law requires that nursing homes provide social services to help residents obtain the highest possible physical and psychological functioning. Homes with 120 or more residents are required to have at least one full-time social worker, but other homes must make social work services available (National Association of Social Workers [NASW], n.d.).

Among the major functions and services that NASW identifies for social workers are:

1. Preadmission services including biopsychosocial assessments, interdisciplinary evaluation of the individual's need for care, and preparation of the incoming resident.

2. Individual, family, and group services focused on maintaining or enhancing the resident's biopsychosocial functioning during inter- or intrafacility transfers; interpersonal relationships; and coping with separation, loss, dying, and death.

3. Advocacy of appropriate care and treatment of residents.

4. Discussion with competent residents and families about advance directives and financial powers of attorney.

5. Facilitation of residents' safe integration into the community or return home through interdisciplinary discharge planning and follow-up services. (2003, pp. 13–15)

In thinking about the ways in which social workers might utilize all available biopsychosocial information to assist nursing home residents, we can recall the case study from the beginning of this chapter. We might ask: what could a nursing home social worker do to help an elderly woman like Katherine Lewandowski? Social history information obtained at the time of admission could tell the social worker that Katherine Lewandowski had a very strong sense of family and that her Polish ethnicity and faith in the Catholic religion were all very important to her. The social worker then would understand the cultural origin of Katherine Lewandowski's sense of abandonment: the highly valued Polish custom of caring for elderly persons within the family, with nursing home placement used only as a final resort. The social worker would also recognize that Katherine's despair was heightened by significant losses: the death of her husband 5 years ago, the death of a son from cancer 18 months ago, and the loss of control over her own body as she became increasingly frail and handicapped by osteoporosis. Human diversity factors are critical dimensions of the uniqueness of each person, and respect for their human differences helps social workers demonstrate caring and compassion as they work with people like Katherine Lewandowski.

Like social workers in all fields of practice, nursing home social workers can advocate for and assist people best when they understand the intersectionality (the coming together) of the client's unique diversity characteristics. A resident like Katherine Lewandowski could benefit from encouragement and reassurance provided by a culturally sensitive social worker during frequent visits to her room and also to the hospital when Katherine had surgery. The social worker could educate and advocate with other nursing home staff so that they could be more sensitive to her needs. The activities staff, for example, could be encouraged to engage Katherine in socialization activities with other Polish women in the nursing home, thereby helping her to reestablish her sense of identity and linkage to a familiar community. The Catholic chaplain or a priest from Katherine's parish might have been a significant resource, helping her find comfort in her faith and thereby engage another source of strength. Too often the spiritual life of clients is ignored in hospitals and nursing homes.

Nursing home social work offers unique opportunities for long-term involvement with people during a phase in their lives when many crises may occur. This area of social work practice also offers opportunities to work with families and with groups, to provide education for resident care staff, and to be one of the decision makers that influence the organization's policies and procedures. Nursing home social workers have remarkable opportunities to become very strong advocates for their clients.

Home Health Care

Home health care is the provision of health care services, including social services, to people in their own homes. The resurgence of home health care in recent years has been generated by economic concerns, by the growing number of terminally ill elderly and AIDS patients, and by humanitarian interests that seek to provide care to loved ones within the comfort and security of their own homes.

Home health services are provided by organizations such as the Visiting Nurse Association, by hospitals, by public health departments, and by proprietary (for-profit) corporations. Social workers are key members of the home care team today. Through counseling, they help family members, especially those in caregiver roles, to work through their feelings of frustration, anger, grief, and pain. Supporting the family and preventing personal and family breakdown during the caregiving time is an objective of the social workers. They also locate needed resources, such as financial aid and bedside nursing equipment. Others routinely on the team are physicians, who provide supervision, and nurses. Ancillary staff often includes homemakers, physical therapists, and dieticians.

With their professional colleagues, home care social workers increasingly deal with ethical dilemmas related to questions about how much autonomy and self-determination to support with elderly persons who have physical or cognitive disabilities or when family caregivers become overburdened. Home health hospice programs—which now serve children and adults of all ages with AIDS, cancer, and heart disease—raise similar ethical questions. Nonetheless, this is a rapidly growing field of service and one that offers considerable satisfaction as well as challenges.

Insurance Companies

Financing of the U.S. health care system today functions primarily through health insurance companies. Because of buyouts and mergers, these are increasingly large, often multinational corporations. Employers and private persons purchase insurance through these companies, which assume responsibility for contracts with and payment to health care providers. In the United States, even the federal Medicare and Medicaid programs use private insurance companies as their carriers. Because the 2010 Affordable Health Care Act was grounded in the use of insurance to guarantee access to health care, insurance corporations will remain central to health care financing in the United States.

A new but fledgling development in health care social work is the establishment of social work services within insurance companies. In recent years, some insurance companies have hired social workers, often BSWs, to provide preventive care to the insurance company's Medicaid subscribers immediately following the birth of a baby. Social workers review educational information with the mothers about risks such as lead poisoning, immunizations, and routine health care the new baby will need. If assessment reveals that other needs exist (such as special assistance for a single mother with cognitive disabilities or if domestic violence is threatened in the home), then referrals are made. Mothers are also assisted with the names and telephone numbers of primary care physicians for their babies, with the paperwork needed to obtain Medicaid care for the new baby, and with information about lead screening. Some insurance companies have added prenatal care coordination and child care programs, too, that enable social workers to do home visits and case management. These services within insurance companies, however, are a recent development, and it is not yet clear if they will prove to be sufficiently feasible economically to be sustained into the future.

Hospice and Palliative Care

Hospice refers to a specialized approach in caring for terminally ill persons, not to any specific place. Hospice care is a program that can be provided at home, in a hospital, or in a facility designed specifically for the purpose of serving persons who are dying. Some nursing homes are now adding hospice care units. The central treatment approach used by hospices is **palliative care.** The World Health Organization (WHO) defines palliative care as the

> active total care of patients whose disease is not responsive to curative treatment. Control of pain, of other symptoms, and of psychological, social, and spiritual problems, is paramount. The goal of palliative care is the achievement of the best quality of life for patients and their families. . . . . Palliative care affirms life and regards dying as a normal process, neither hastens nor postpones death . . . provides relief from pain and other distressing symptoms. (Doyle, Hanks, & MacDonald, 1998, p. 3, as cited in Csikai & Chaitin, 2006, p. 107)

The term *hospice* dates back to medieval times when hospices were way stations, generally run by religious orders or monks or sisters that provided rescue and assistance to travelers. Cicely Saunders, a nurse and social worker, worked at a hospice in Ireland that served dying people. Saunders's commitment to humane care of the dying led her to obtain a medical degree, and, in 1967, she established the famed St. Christopher's Hospice (Richman, 1995). The first hospice programs in the United States emerged around 1970 and were patterned after the model for humane care established by Cicely Saunders.

Hospice care is provided by an interdisciplinary team comprised of doctors, nurses, social workers, and clergy, often supplemented by a core of volunteers. Many insurance programs, including Medicare, cover hospice care because it is less costly than hospital or nursing home care. Insurance policies require a physician's certification that the potential hospice patient is within 6 months of death. The patient must agree to forego curative treatment. Hospice programs provide care to infants and children as well as young and older adults, although older adults comprise the largest cohort of hospice patients.

The NASW policy statement on hospice care notes that "Hospice is a form of compassionate caring for dying people that is fully compatible with the values and ethics of the social work profession" (Kelly & Clark, 2009c, p. 189). The NASW policy statement affirms that "every dying person is of value and deserves individualized care while being served by hospice" and that "client self-determination is inherent in the provision of hospice care so that the dying can choose how they live until their death" (p. 189).

Social workers in hospice programs are an integral part of the health care team. Social workers counsel patients and their families prior to death and offer a great deal of emotional support. They assist dying people to deal with the physical and emotional pain that is so often part of the destruction and end of life. They provide crisis intervention and engage in advocacy to ensure that clients' needs are met. They use the strengths identified in the admissions assessment to help both the dying person and family members and friends with anticipatory grieving (Dziegielewski, 2004). Following death, hospice social workers continue to assist family members and friends with bereavement.

EMERGENCY ROOM: TRAUMA AND CRISIS AMID HUMAN DIVERSITY

Hospitals that operate large, active emergency care facilities employ social workers on all shifts, 7 days a week. In smaller facilities, social workers staff emergency rooms during periods of high demand and they function on an on-call basis during less busy periods. Every television viewer knows well the life-and-death drama of the hospital emergency room. For the social worker, emergency room practice means fast-paced crisis intervention work and brief contact with clients. For example, the 17-year-old who took an overdose of aspirin when her boyfriend threatened to end their relationship needs someone to help her sort out her embarrassment and shame, after the aspirin has been removed from her stomach. The social worker makes a rapid assessment of the young woman's psychosocial situation and determines that referral for counseling is needed both for the young woman and for her family.

Emergency room practice means fast-paced crisis intervention work.

Consider another example: a 5-year-old boy is treated for multiple fractures suffered in a car accident. He will be admitted to the hospital after receiving initial care in the emergency room. Every 15 minutes the social worker provides information to the parents—information obtained from the doctors and nurses who are with the boy. The parents, a young Puerto Rican couple, show their immense concern about their son very openly. The wife, who is pregnant, is extremely nervous and is breathing irregularly, and she appears to be about to have an *ataque* (an episode similar to a seizure; *ataques* are sometimes experienced during periods of severe emotional stress and are recognized in the Puerto Rican culture as a cry for help). The husband's anger with the hit-and-run driver who injured his son takes the form of angry threats, loudly voiced, and of demands that the hospital staff do something to save his son. The social worker provides emotional support to the parents and helps them to a room where they have more privacy and where additional family members can be with them as soon as the social worker is able to contact them.

Before the evening ends, the social worker will also have helped a 55-year-old, White, middle-class woman whose husband's life could not be saved following his third heart attack; an elderly Catholic nun who required admission to the hospital because of pneumonia; and a poor, inner-city African American mother and infant who were hungry and whose heat had been turned off by the landlord for nonpayment of rent. The emergency room social worker interpreted medical information to waiting families, offered psychological strength, demonstrated concern and caring, confronted inappropriate behavior, used crisis counseling techniques, and connected people with needed community resources. In addition, the social worker helped the doctors and caregivers understand and appreciate the cultural dimensions that influenced patients' responses to pain and their families' responses to crisis.

When disaster strikes a community, hospital emergency rooms receive injured and psychologically traumatized patients. All hospitals have disaster plans, so social workers and other staff know their roles in advance. Emergency care of medical needs must take priority, of course. Social workers are important members of the team. They assess and comfort children and adults whose injuries do not appear to require immediate care, if all medical staff are needed for more seriously injured persons. They provide emotional assistance to persons whose trauma is threatening their mental health status. All of this is done with appreciation for the diversity of the people involved and for the community environment.

Social workers' well-developed interdisciplinary teamwork relationships are extremely valuable when serious emergencies strike. The experience and expertise hospital social workers develop in their day-to-day work with persons who are ill, injured, dying, or recovering from surgery and facing a bright new future—all of this serves the social worker, the health care team, and traumatized persons who are helped during times of disaster.

HEALTH CARE IN RURAL AREAS

Health care facilities in rural areas often require considerable community involvement from the social worker. In rural settings, social workers call on all their generalist practice skills as they work with families and communities to help people obtain health care and to provide care following hospitalization. Long distances between health centers, isolated dwellings, poverty, and lack of transportation make it difficult for many rural people to obtain high-quality health care. Pregnant rural women, for example, are at increased risk because they often have inadequate access to prenatal care. The Rural Assistance Center (2010) explains the specific nature of health disparities in rural areas:

> Geographic isolation, socio-economic status, health risk behaviors, and limited job opportunities contribute to health disparities in rural communities. While 20% of the United States population lives in rural areas, higher rates of chronic illness and poor overall health are found in those communities when compared to urban populations. Rural residents are older, poorer,

and have fewer physicians to care for them. This inequality is intensified as rural residents are less likely to have employer-provided health care coverage; and if they are poor, often not covered by Medicaid (para 2).

Hospitals in rural areas or small towns generally have no more than 50 to 100 beds. Complex and expensive medical services such as **hemodialysis** (a procedure to cleanse the blood of persons with chronic kidney disease) are often not provided. Severe financial pressure is often experienced by small hospitals, and many have closed in the past 15 years.

Usually a small hospital employs only one or two social workers. Generalist practice skills are vital. Social workers in small health care facilities have to be very knowledgeable about the local community and its resources. In rural areas when needed resources such as home health care are not available, the social worker helps to create them or calls on clergy, police, or neighbors for assistance. In small towns, friends, neighbors, and coworkers sometimes provide exceptional help, as this single mother of a son with AIDS explains:

> And then when he was deteriorating so bad in December, I just decided that I needed to be at home with him. I was given an open-ended leave, and when my accumulated hours of pay were used up, they let people donate hours to me, and I never lost a paycheck. I work with a really super group of people . . . very caring, very giving. (McGinn, 1996, p. 276)

Rural communities sometimes lack information about medical conditions such as AIDS. This may exacerbate existing lack of tolerance for diversity. Sometimes negative responses to people who are HIV-positive stem from concerns about contagion or from moral judgments that derive from very strongly held religious values. Social work support for the patient and for her or his partner and family may be needed to deal with the emotional burden and with social isolation. Social workers also advocate for needed community resources, and, if necessary, they advocate with other staff to ensure that health care is delivered compassionately.

The rural health care facility—a rehabilitation center, hospital, or nursing home—often serves people from a very large geographical area. The social worker must have a good understanding of several counties' welfare and human service resources. One county may have a Meals on Wheels program, for example, while another does not or can provide only general nutrition but no special diets (such as a diabetic diet). A large geographical area may also mean long-distance travel for the social worker when a home visit is needed.

THE ENVIRONMENTAL CONTEXT OF PRACTICE

Rural communities were once assumed to be free of the environmental conditions in cities that create hazards to health and well-being. As increasing understanding is developed about the forces causing destruction of the biosphere, however, it is increasingly apparent that environmental degradation and disease are created in rural areas by agricultural practices such as the use of chemical fertilizers and pesticides, permitting polluted water to flow into crop irrigation systems, and deforestation practices. Of course, the industrial smokestacks and vehicle emissions of metropolitan areas are responsible for major environmental impacts that may have consequences for health and well-being.

Concern about threats to public health actually goes back to the mid- to late 1900s, when social reformers in England came to believe that overcrowding in urban areas was toxic to the physical and mental health of the population (Susser & Morabia, 2006, p. 16). The social reformers perceived that the rapid urbanization, poor sanitation, overcrowding, and stark inequalities of the Industrial Revolution were responsible for the concurrent spread of disease. Awareness that environmental toxins such as mercury and lead could contribute to specific physical and mental illnesses, however, has evolved steadily over the years until today; a great deal is known about the relationship between environmental issues and health.

In the United States, social work as a profession has been slow to embrace environmental concerns. Carol Germain and Alex Gitterman were two of the early social work contributors to the ecological systems theory that underpins practice today. Their 1980 text, *The Life Model of Social Work Practice,* incorporated a great deal of content related to the natural environment. In the mid-1990s, Berger, in a series of articles in the journal *Social Work,* challenged social workers to stop ignoring the perilous reality that all of humanity faced as a result of ongoing environmental degradation. In 1995 Berger pointed to accumulating evidence that human immune systems were increasingly compromised; asthma and allergies were more prevalent; and diseases such as lupus, multiple sclerosis, Graves disease, and rheumatoid arthritis had also begun to increase. In 1994 Hoff and McNutt published *The Global Environmental Crisis: Implications for Social Welfare and Social Work,* clearly demonstrating how all areas of social work practice are affected by and respond to environmental issues.

Gradually, the profession began to respond. Besthorn, for example, wrote about a shift he believed was occurring in the way that Western society was beginning to evolve a new "sense of self" characterized by increased appreciation for the natural environment and for nonhuman beings that share that environment. In social work practice, he saw potential in exposing clients to wilderness experiences and other activities involving therapeutic contact with natural environments (2002). One entire issue of the journal *Health and Social Work* was devoted to the social work research, practice, and community initiatives that were being implemented to secure healthier community environments (Galambos, 2003).

Meantime, Saleebey (pioneer developer of the "strengths perspective") began to urge social workers to pay more attention to the spaces in which social work clients live their daily lives. He pointed to many small but meaningful changes that could be made within clients' homes (e.g., repairing a broken window), in neighborhoods (community garden projects or creating a children's play area in a neglected lot), in local school buildings, or to school playgrounds (2004). Social workers and even social work student organizations could readily take on such initiatives. These small projects hold power to transform otherwise forbidding and nonnutritive environments. The most recent NASW policy statement on the environment (see Box 7.3) envisions social work practice and social welfare policy that incorporates ecological and human rights concepts. Perhaps it will take today's students and a whole new generation of social workers, who are enlivened by an appreciation of the natural environment, to truly implement the actions that the NASW policy statement envisioned. Clearly there is much work to be done if social workers are to assume the kind of leadership on environment that the profession is capable of.

Box 7.3 2008 NASW Policy Statement on the Environment

Social workers need an environmentally responsible credo to which we can subscribe and that will influence our individual and collective actions. Social workers must become dedicated protectors of the environment. Together, we can model environmental awareness for those who come in contact with us in our personal and professional lives.

NASW supports and advocates for:

- Policies that reduce environmental risks to poor, minority, and disadvantaged communities who have been disproportionately affected
- Secure and affordable food systems that are free of toxic chemicals and pesticides
- The reduction of children's exposure to pesticides and other chemicals through approaches such as the precautionary principle and integrated pest management
- The protection of individuals who work in hazardous jobs by strict national and international environmental standards, including effective enforcement mechanisms
- Social work education at all levels, incorporating discussions of the natural environment, ideas

of habitat destruction, chemical contamination, environmental racism, environmental justice, and sustainability

- The inclusion of the natural environment as a routine part of the assessment and treatment planning activities of social workers in all settings with all clients, especially those clients who are most likely to be victimized by unsound and unsafe environmental practices

In addition, NASW advocates against:

- Policies that allow toxic waste to be relocated or exported from wealthy industrialized areas and nations to less economically favored areas and nations
- Government and corporate policies that further environmental injustice

Box 7.3 represents only a partial listing of the policy statement.

Source: *Social work speaks: National Association of Social Workers policy statements, 2009–2012,* by National Association of Social Workers. Copyright 2010. Reproduced with permission of National Association of Social Workers in the formats Textbook and Other Book via Copyright Clearance Center.

HUMAN RIGHTS AND HEALTH: GLOBAL PERSPECTIVES

The 2006 NASW policy on the environment, in part, states: "Global justice cannot exist unless all people of the world share the Earth's resources. Global justice cannot exist when a minority of people in technologically developed countries consume a disproportionate share of the available resources" (NASW, Environmental Policy, 2006, p. 140). Health and well-being, too, are amazingly dependent on the state of the environment and on equitable sharing of resources. The World Health Organization (WHO) noted that "A girl born today can expect to live for more than 80 years if she is born in some countries—but less than 45 years if she is born in others." The report concluded: "Within countries there are dramatic differences in health that are closely linked with degrees of social disadvantage. Differences of this magnitude, within and between countries, simply should never happen" (Commission on Social Determinants, 2008). The WHO's data demonstrate serious inequities in health care resources between developing countries and industrialized nations and inequities in access to care even within some of the wealthiest nations.

HIV/AIDS remains a factor in child deaths worldwide, but 1.4 million of the world's 2 million AIDS-related deaths in 2008 were of children in sub-Saharan Africa. In this southern region of Africa, more than 14 million children have

216   *Chapter 7*

LINKAGES BETWEEN HEALTH AND HUMAN RIGHTS

Promoting and protecting health and respecting, protecting and fulfilling human rights are inextricably linked:

- Violations or lack of attention to human rights can have serious health consequences (e.g. harmful traditional practices, slavery, torture and inhuman and degrading treatment, violence against women and children).

- Health policies and programmes can promote or violate human rights in their design or implementation (e.g. freedom from discrimination, individual autonomy, rights to participation, privacy and information).

- Vulnerability to ill-health can be reduced by taking steps to respect, protect and fulfil human rights (e.g. freedom from discrimination on account of race, sex and gender roles, rights to health, food and nutrition, education, housing).

Examples of the linkages between health and human rights:

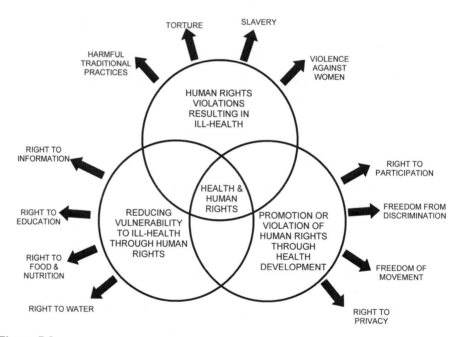

Figure 7.1

Linkage between Health and Human Rights

Source: Reprinted by permission of the World Health Organization.

been orphaned by AIDS (UNAIDS, 2009). In rich nations as well as poor nations, children are at much higher risk of dying if they live in poverty and are malnourished. In the world's poorest nations, social, political, and economic instability contributes to deteriorating rates of adult survival, too. The essential interdependence between health and social justice is well illustrated in Figure 7.1. Violations of human rights that potently threaten the health and well-being of people include such current practices as trafficking in women and children. **Trafficking** refers to the use of physical or psychological coercion in transporting persons, often for financial gain; women may be trafficked for commercial sex or domestic labor purposes, while children may be transported for sexual purposes, to provide low cost labor, or for illicit adoption. The U.S. Department of State 2010 Trafficking in Persons Report begins with a powerful statement:

> The victims of modern slavery have many faces. They are men and women, adults and children. Yet, all are denied basic human dignity and freedom. . . . All too often suffering from horrible physical and sexual abuse, it is hard for them to imagine that there might be a place of refuge.—President Barack Obama

The report estimates that 12.3 million persons, adults and children, are currently victims of this modern form of human slavery, a 59 percent increase over the previous 2008 report.

The U.S. Department of State notes that there is a worldwide $32 billion business in trafficking, and it is actually growing. Some countries, 104 in 2009, as yet have no laws against this form of human slavery. Asian and Pacific countries have the highest incidence. Trafficking implies more than abduction for purposes of sexual exploitation. Among the forms of human trafficking are:

- *Forced labor.* Persons, primarily women and children, are utilized for domestic servitude; they are often exploited sexually as well.
- *Sex trafficking.* Women and children, primarily, are either forced into prostitution or forcefully sustained beyond their wishes in prostitution.
- *Bonded labor.* Often persons, especially migrants, are forced to continue as a laborer with or without wages for inability to pay off a real or assumed debt.
- *Child soldiers.* Children who are captured from their homes are forced to become combatants, spies, cooks, messengers, etc.
- *Child sex trafficking.* Currently an estimated 2 million children have been forced into prostitution in the global commercial sex industry with devastating consequences including disease, trauma, unwanted pregnancy, malnutrition, and even death. (U.S. Department of State, 2010)

Human rights violations of the kind described put both children and adults at great risk of ill health, injury, and sexually transmitted disease (including HIV/AIDS), regardless of the country in which the exploitation occurs. When people are transported from one country to another, diseases of many kinds travel with them, thus placing other populations at risk. War, famine, and poverty—all facets of social injustice—carry negative implications for health and human rights.

HISTORICAL PERSPECTIVES

The chapter content now shifts to history. We begin with a quick look at the origin of hospitals and then trace the history of social work within the broader field of health care. Of special interest here is the proud history of medical social work as one of the earliest pioneers in the social work profession. This is also a field of practice that has become quite agile in adapting to changing times.

Early History: Caring for the Poor and Sick

It is not clear when health care institutions were developed, but archaeologists have uncovered ruins of what may have been such facilities dating from the 6th century B.C. The tithing of the early Christians produced funds that churches could use for the care of the poor and the sick. Around the 3rd century A.D., monks of the Roman Catholic Church began to provide rescue service and health care to avalanche victims in shelters known as hospices. The victims were mostly southern Europeans who were fleeing from famine and economic hardship and were trying to reach northern regions in search of a better life. They were unfamiliar with and unprepared for the harsh weather of the mountains. Gradually the term *hospice* came to be used for institutions that cared for ill persons. In Western Europe hospices housed not only the sick but, until almshouses were organized, the poor as well. Gradually hospices developed into larger institutions that were run primarily by religious orders of priests or sisters. (Even today, in most of Europe, a nurse is called *sister.*) In England during the mid-1500s, monasteries were confiscated by the Crown in the historic dispute between Henry VIII and the Roman Catholic Church. With the seizure of religious holdings, the settings that cared for the sick were gradually converted into publicly held institutions.

Origins of Health Care Social Work

The English forerunners of today's health care social workers were the **lady almoners,** persons who provided food and donations to the poor. In 1895 a lady almoner was stationed at the Royal Free Hospital with the understanding that she was to interview patients to determine who would receive free, or partly free, medical service "and to exclude those unsuitable for free care. But in serving this restricted purpose the worker was soon aware that many patients accepted for medical treatment were in sore social difficulties as well" (Cannon, 1952, p. 8). This early social worker, like many today, preferred to define the nature of her professional practice herself, rather than permitting hospital authorities, physicians, or others to govern how she understood and carried out her professional responsibilities. In fact, she became an advocate for patients, fighting for the rights and needs of the poor and underserved, whom the Royal Free Hospital saw as unsuitable. The use of social workers spread throughout British Commonwealth hospitals, and their role soon broadened to include advocacy, referral to other community resources, patient education, and counseling.

The Emergence of Health Care Social Work in the United States

The person who is generally considered the originator of medical social work in the United States is Ida Cannon. As a young woman, Ida Cannon had worked as a visiting nurse in the slum areas along the Mississippi River in St. Paul, Minnesota. Inspired by Jane Addams, the great settlement house worker, Cannon became interested in social work and went to Boston to pursue her studies at the Boston School of Social Work. In 1905 Dr. Richard Cabot, whose concerns about poverty and its impact on illness paralleled her own, asked Ida Cannon to join the staff of Massachusetts General Hospital.

In her professional practice, Cannon was not only a competent social worker but also a dynamic leader, a teacher of medical and social work students, and an articulate author. Health care social workers were the first among the various social work specialty groups to organize professionally. Ida Cannon was among the founders of the American Association of Hospital Social Workers in 1918. This organization, later known as the American Association of Medical Social Workers (AAMSW), published its own journal, *Medical Social Work.* The AAMSW eventually merged with other independent social work organizations to become the NASW in 1955. Cannon's 1952 text, *On the Social Frontier of Medicine: Pioneering in Medical Social Service,* describes the early years of hospital social work.

Soon after Ida Cannon developed the social service department at Massachusetts General Hospital, Bellevue Hospital in New York hired a social worker. Slowly hospitals across the country began hiring social workers. Soon public health concerns about patients with tuberculosis and venereal disease resulted in the employment of social workers by state health departments and tuberculosis sanatoriums. The passage of the Social Security Act in 1935 resulted in entitlements that further encouraged the expansion of social work in health care settings. Both the American Hospital Association (AHA) and the American Public Health Association developed standards and requirements for social workers in the facilities they regulated.

One of the most influential persons in shaping health care social work over ensuing years was Helen Rehr. For more than 30 years she provided leadership, creating many innovative programs within the social work department at Mount Sinai Medical Center in New York. A prolific author, she published many works related to health care social work, among them: *Medicine and Social Work: An Exploration in Interprofessionalism* (1994) and *Advancing Social Work Practice in the Health Care Field* (1982). Although now retired, this health care social work pioneer continues to consult, to contribute to her community, and to publish; her most recent book is *The Social Work–Medicine Relationship: 100 Years at Mount Sinai* (2006).

SOCIAL POLICY: POLITICS AND ECONOMICS IN HEALTH CARE

By 1905 when Ida Cannon initiated the first hospital social work department, the U.S. health care system had evolved from one delivered by women within their own households, relying primarily on homemade medical preparations, to an industry dominated by specialized professionals, pharmaceutical corporations, and institutions. Massive hospitals, first built during the Civil War, utilized new techniques of hygiene and by the early 1900s vastly increased the number of surgical procedures performed, thanks to the development of diagnostic X-rays and anesthesia.

By the early 1900s many European countries (England, Germany, Austria, and others) and Russia had initiated compulsory health insurance programs, thereby ensuring access to health care for all citizens. (Compulsory health insurance is a key feature of the United States' 2010 Affordable Health Care Act.) Interest in such programs was emerging in the United States. In 1912 Jane Addams and social workers in the settlement house movement, well aware of unmet health needs—especially of women and children—threw their support behind presidential candidate Theodore Roosevelt when he advocated compulsory health insurance for the United States. With the advent of World War I (1914–1918) and the Bolshevik Revolution in Russia, however, the U.S. public began to perceive anything that appeared German (e.g., compulsory health insurance) as negative and threatening or anything Russian as Communistic. Jane Addams and other proponents of compulsory health insurance were branded as traitors. Even the Federation for Social Service of the Methodist Church faced extremely adverse publicity. The American Medical Association (AMA) changed course and began what was to become a lengthy history of opposition to any form of what they called "socialized medicine" (Moniz & Gorin, 2010).

Social workers and other health care policy reformers did not give up, however. Julia Lathrop and Grace Abbott, both former colleagues of Jane Addams and former residents of Chicago's Hull House, disseminated research findings showing that the exceptionally high rate of infant mortality in the United States was related to inadequate prenatal care and poverty (Trattner, 1999, as cited in Moniz & Gorin, 2010). Another social worker, Jeanette Rankin, serving as the first woman elected to the U.S. Congress, introduced and achieved the passage of the Sheppard–Towner Infancy and Maternity Act of 1921. This legislation provided funding to states for numerous public health programs aimed at improving the health of women and children. With the advent of the Great Depression and concerted opposition from the AMA, which saw public health services as interfering with its right to free enterprise, the Sheppard–Towner Act was terminated in 1929. The establishment of Blue Cross and Blue Shield insurance programs in the 1930s "laid the foundation for a third-party payment system, completely changed health care financing, and led the way for employment-based insurance" (Moniz & Gorin, 2010, p. 23).

Policy Practice

Practice Behavior Example: Know the history and current structures of social policies and services, the role of policy in service delivery, and the role of practice in policy development

Critical Thinking Question: What lessons on social reform advocacy can we learn from the profession's pioneers?

In the 1930s, social workers again provided courageous leadership in health care reform efforts. Harry L. Hopkins, a social worker who had worked with Franklin D. Roosevelt in New York when Roosevelt was governor, became a trusted adviser of Roosevelt when he was elected U.S. president. Hopkins and Frances Perkins, another social worker and Roosevelt's secretary of labor (the first woman to occupy a cabinet position), both supported compulsory health care and hoped to have it included in the Social Security Act of 1935. As a result of a flood of opposition orchestrated by the AMA, compulsory national health insurance was removed from the final version of the Social Security Act.

By the 1940s, "former charity hospitals transformed themselves into profit-making, or surplus-generating (among the nonprofit institutions) businesses, increasingly dependent on cash-paying customers and third-party payers (for example, insurers)" (Weiss, 1997, p. 13). Hospitals and physicians controlled the Blue Cross and Blue Shield insurances, thereby ensuring payment for medical services that were delivered by the private sector. Public health services, which had served the nation through several waves of infectious diseases and provided health care to low-income populations, were politically crushed by the increasingly powerful entrepreneurial, for-profit, health care industry.

> By the 1960s, however, it was clear that private health insurance was not capable of providing benefits to large numbers of people and that it was not capable of containing costs. At the same time, nationwide pressure was building for national health insurance. (Weiss, 1997, p. 86)

Medicare

The federal government's involvement in health care financing became a reality in the 1960s with the enactment of the programs known as Medicare and Medicaid. **Medicare** was created in 1965 with an amendment, Title XVIII, to the Social Security Act. Labor unions strongly supported this legislation while the AMA, the AHA, "and the insurance industry engaged in a bitter, vitriolic battle to keep government out of health care. These interests perceived government involvement as a threat to the realization of maximum profit and to professional autonomy" (Weiss, 1997, p. 153). It may be that the compromises made to secure passage of Medicare are partially responsible for some of the program's current problems with skyrocketing costs, fraudulent charges by health care providers, and mismanagement. Some of the compromises won by the AMA and the AHA included limiting government control over reimbursements for services and, a major victory, allowing for Blue Cross and Blue Shield (and other insurance companies) to be the conduit for payments made to providers.

Medicare currently covers 45 million Americans who are:

- People who are 65 years old
- People who are disabled
- People with permanent kidney failure (U.S. Department of Health and Human Services, 2009)

Although Medicare has been dramatically changed by the 2010 Affordable Health Care Act, it continues to have four parts. Part A provides insurance for hospital care and 100 days in a nursing home. Medicare comes from payroll taxes paid while people are working; however, it is definitely not free. It requires substantial co-payments. Hospice care is provided for terminally ill

Social workers assist poor pregnant women to obtain health care for themselves and their children.

persons, but only if they are expected to die in 6 months. Many qualifications must be met before a person may receive home health care under Medicare.

Part B is different from Part A. It closely resembles a private health insurance program. It is entirely voluntary, but it is vital to most people because it pays for some of the health care expenses not covered by Part A. Like private insurance, there are monthly payments (approximately $96 monthly in 2011). The payment amount is almost always increased when there is a raise in Social Security. Part B is often thought of as outpatient insurance since it provides payment for physicians, laboratory services, medical equipment such as wheelchairs or walkers, and outpatient surgeries.

To the surprise of some people, Medicare does not cover all medical expenses of the elderly. Often social workers must explain the limitations of Medicare to disbelieving elderly persons who have trusted that the money they paid into Social Security would take care of all of their medical needs in old age. (Could concern about the cost of her medical care have caused some of Katherine Lewandowski's depression in the case study at the beginning of this chapter?) Services not provided by Parts A or B include:

- Long-term nursing or custodial care
- Dentures and dental care
- Eyeglasses
- Most prescription drugs

It should be noted, however, that Medicare provides an option in the form of managed-care plans that sometimes do cover some of the services listed earlier. These are **capitated plans,** prepaid by Medicare, in which comprehensive health care is provided and services are coordinated by the plan. Clients may not receive any health care services outside the plan.

Several options to Medicare were initiated in 1997 as Part C. Also known as the Medicare Advantage Plan, it includes a variety of managed-care plans plus Medical Savings Accounts. The Medical Savings Accounts require a very high deductible payment plus monthly premiums. If illness occurs, the deductible has to be paid before the plan takes over, but when it does, it pays all remaining medical expenses.

An advantage of the Medicare Part C programs was that many included prescription drug coverage. The failure of Medicare Parts A and B to provide coverage for prescriptions became so volatile that in 2003, as part of the Medicare Modernization Act, a prescription drug benefit plan, Part D, was created. This very complex plan became effective in 2006. This plan is administered by private health insurance companies, is sold to individuals on a competitive basis, and requires a monthly premium. While there are numerous plans for persons to choose from, each of the plans must adhere to some degree to the basic elements of a "standard plan." In the standard plan, after a $310 deductible, most subscribers pay a monthly premium (possibly $35 per month) and a percentage of their prescription costs (possibly 25 percent) up to approximately $2,830 in total drug costs per year. If the person has very expensive medications and reaches the magical $2,830 amount, most plans offer absolutely no coverage until the person has paid $4,550. This coverage gap when the subscriber receives no prescription drug coverage at all is referred to as *the doughnut hole.* After the subscriber has spent $4,550 coverage resumes; subscribers then pay only a small co-payment until the year ends, and then the cycle starts all over again.

NASW, among other organizations, expressed grave concern about the devastating impact Part D had on persons who were unable to obtain needed medications. In a hearing before the U.S. Senate Committee on Finance, an attorney from the Center for Medicare Advocacy testified regarding some of the problems with Part D. Foremost was the complexity of the program, which makes it extraordinarily difficult for subscribers to understand, but which also makes it ripe for marketing scams and unscrupulous practices by sales agents. Also of significant concern was the large number of persons with minimal incomes who experience devastating financial circumstances when they reach the "doughnut hole," despite the supposed availability of emergency subsidies. The primary concern, however, for the Center for Medicare Advocacy was that with each of the Medicare reform efforts, the "private plans have shown that they are unable to provide the same services as the traditional Medicare program at reduced costs without drastic subsidies from the federal government" (Center for Medicare Advocacy, 2007).

Medicare, despite its failings, is a remarkable program. It provides health care to millions of people, many of whom could otherwise not afford it. It is expensive, and it has problems, one of which is the millions of dollars lost each year in fraud that is perpetrated by laboratories, managed-care plans, physicians, hospitals, nursing homes, and others, sometimes including patients.

Medicaid

Social work as a profession has a special commitment to people who are poor or vulnerable. Of course, this includes people who are at risk of or who have existing physical and mental health problems. Because **Medicaid** is the largest U.S. financial aid program for poor people, it is obvious that social workers need to know something about Medicaid. Most social workers, however, will not need to know all of the intricate details; they do need to know where they can find information about Medicaid. One of the best sources is the Medicaid website, currently at http://www.cms.hhs.gov/home/medicaid.asp. Some very basic information about the Medicaid program follows.

Medicaid, also known as Medical Assistance, was enacted in 1965 as Title XIX of the Social Security Act. It is jointly funded by the federal government and states, but the states administer the program. It now covers approximately 54.6 million people, including people who receive Supplemental Security Income because they are blind, aged, or have disabilities. Pregnant women and children with a family income below 133 percent of the poverty line, in general, are also eligible. Medicaid is a lifeline for poor people because it pays for prescriptions, laboratory tests and X-rays, inpatient and outpatient hospital care, skilled nursing home care, and home health care.

Medicaid is a means-tested program, which means that applicants must provide proof of poverty according to their state's definition. Many people find the application procedure humiliating. Medicare, by contrast, is automatically available to people who are 65 or older, who are disabled, or who have permanent kidney failure.

In recent years, the states' power over Medicaid has increased considerably. Now each state:

- Establishes its own eligibility standards
- Determines the type, amount, duration, and scope of services
- Sets the rate of payment for services
- Administers its own program

With mounting political pressure to cut the costs of Medicaid, states have been given special authority to design their own programs. Some have trimmed Medicaid to its bare bones while others have provided more generous benefits. Cost-cutting methods have included eliminating some health care benefits, moving people out of nursing homes, putting all persons into managed-care programs, and cutting mental health services.

Health Care Reform and the 2010 Patient Protection and Affordable Care Act

Health care reform has been pushing its way to the top of the political agenda since the 1990s. The first proposed large-scale health care reform proposal was the Clinton Health Security Act of 1993, which would have created a national health insurance plan for the United States if it had become law. **National health insurance** plans are those systems of a given country that ensure participation in comprehensive, generally compulsory health care insurance, thus giving all citizens access to health care services.

In the 1990s when Hillary Rodham Clinton campaigned across the country seeking support for the Clinton Health Security Act, her message was not well received. According to one magazine, she "invokes the rhetoric of rights and morality. Health care is the 'right' of all Americans, she says, and assuring that they get it is a matter of 'social justice' " (Barnes, 1994, p. 15). Opponents argued that national health care was so expensive that it would destroy the country's economy. Liberals failed to support the Clinton proposal because it retained private insurance corporations as program administrators (hence ensuring huge administrative costs and built-in profitability) and it failed to require a single-payer system. A **single-payer system** exists when either the government or a single selected corporation administers the insurance program. The Clinton Health Security Act would have given states control over the system, including the right to select and use a private enterprise single-payer system, but the federal government would have had oversight. What happened to defeat this major piece of health care reform legislation? Gorin's analysis provides insight:

> Although the Health Security Act would have preserved the employer-based system of coverage and the private insurance industry, it also would have transformed our health care and political systems. Establishing a right to health care would have dealt conservatives a severe blow and strengthened efforts to expand the social safety net. Interestingly, conservatives had a clearer understanding of this relationship than many progressives did. William Kristol, a key Republican strategist, warned that the Health Security Act posed "a serious *political* threat to the Republican Party" (Skocpol, 1997, p. 145). He warned that the plan's enactment would revive faith in government and enable the Democrats to pose as the "protector of middle-class interests." Conversely, the act's defeat would be a "watershed in the resurgence of a newly bold and principled Republican politics." (Skocpol, p. 146; Gorin, 2000, p. 141)

So the Health Security Act went down in defeat. Even before the act was voted down, managed care was expanding rapidly and moving with dizzying speed into all segments of the health industry. Once the Clinton national health care reform was clearly dead, "vast sums of federal money (Medicare and Medicaid) were already flowing through private, for-profit MCOs [managed-care organizations]" (Davidson, Davidson, & Keigher, 1999, p. 164). The resounding failure of the Health Security Act meant that a **national health insurance** plan would not be politically acceptable again in the very near future.

Change

Change, however, was inevitable. Massive numbers of persons were uninsured. As health care costs skyrocketed, employers began to shift more of their health insurance costs to their employees through increased deductibles or co-pays. Doctors' authority over hospital admission and discharge was increasingly taken over by insurance corporations' managed-care policies. The political winds began to shift as dissatisfaction with the health care financing system grew.

Between 2006 and 2007 Massachusetts and Vermont passed health care reform laws, and additional states had similar legislation pending. Lack of action on the part of the federal government resulted in state action to deal with growing numbers of uninsured persons, mostly young adults and children. Some of the states' bills required all citizens to purchase health care insurance through their employers or a variety of other programs, and they incorporated disincentives for employers who failed to provide insurance coverage. Other states moved more slowly and incrementally, with plans focusing on only portions of their uninsured citizens. Interestingly, some of the leadership in health care reform came from Republican state governors such as Arnold Schwarzenegger of California and Mitt Romney, the former governor of Massachusetts. Citizen action groups emerged ranging from diverse citizens' groups such as Health Care for All to physicians' groups dedicated to health care policy reform.

But, others asked, how could health care financing be changed for the entire country? What options existed? It became apparent that health care reform could be initiated with small, incremental steps, or through a major overhaul of the existing health care system. Would the United States create a **national health service** system similar to that of England and Germany, where citizens receive health care through government-owned and operated hospitals? That option was not likely to garner much support in the United States. Reform could also mean federal funding to states to develop programs that would ensure quality health insurance for all citizens, with most existing systems remaining in place. Or it could require a **single-payer program** such as the Canadian system, where each state negotiates with a single insurance corporation to handle all claims, thereby dramatically reducing bureaucracy as well as billing, marketing, and other health care administrative costs. Some public citizen health advocacy groups were convinced that the single-payer approach was the only option that would make universal coverage affordable (Wolfe, 2006). Elimination of the profit motive currently driving the U.S. health care industry, they believed, "arrests the growth of health care costs and, in the end, will prove less expensive than the current privatized system" (Karger & Stoez, 2010, p. 325). It was clear, though, that the private enterprise health care industry in the United States would vigorously oppose government-administered health care, preferring that individual citizens be required by law to purchase insurance from private insurance providers whose plans met prescribed requirements. With skyrocketing costs in health care, change became inevitable.

With skyrocketing costs in health care, change became inevitable.

The Patient Protection and Affordable Care Act

There was no landslide majority that won passage of this 2010 federal legislation; indeed it was passed by a narrow majority. It was, however, a political victory for the president, Barack Obama, who made health care finance reform a central priority of his administration. The Affordable Care Act, as it came to be known, was revolutionary for it created the first nearly universal health care system for the United States. It was breakthrough legislation in that it ensured access to health insurance, thus to health care, for the 32 million Americans who had no health insurance. It was not a major overhaul of the system but, instead, sustained current providers; employment-based insurance programs; and a familiar system of hospitals, doctors, and government as well as private providers. Built into the law was a plan for incremental implementation over several years. The plan sought to bring health care costs under control by introducing and supporting new therapies that promised to promote health and focus on disease prevention.

The Affordable Care Act did not reform health care directly but, instead, sought to enhance the quality of health care through new thinking about preventive care and through health insurance reform. Portions of the law were implemented immediately, but much of the law remained to be gradually implemented through 2018. An Internet site, www.healthcare .gov, was designed to provide information updates and track implementation. Some of the major provisions of the law and their scheduled implementation dates are shown in Box 7.4.

Box 7.4   The Patient Protection and Affordable Care Act of 2010

This law, commonly referred to as the Affordable Health Care Act, sought to reform health care through incremental changes to the health insurance system in the United States. Some of the major provisions of this law are listed here according to the timeline for their implementation.

2010

- Provides immediate access to insurance for uninsured persons with preexisting conditions
- Eliminates lifetime limits on coverage and restricts annual limits
- Includes preventive health services insurance coverage in all new plans
- Extends dependent coverage up to age 26 for young people not covered by their own employer-provided coverage
- Provides rebates of $250 for all Medicare Part D enrollees during the donut hole period
- Gives states the option of covering parents and childless couples up to 133 percent of the federal poverty level through Medicaid
- Strengthens the health care workforce (including social workers) by improving low-interest student loan programs, scholarships, and loan repayments

- Holds insurance companies accountable for unreasonable rate hikes

2011

- Provides funds to build new and expand existing community health centers and further expands scholarships and loan repayments for health care practitioners working in underserved areas
- Increases Medicare reimbursement to primary care physicians and general surgeons by 10 percent
- Provides Medicare beneficiaries with a free annual wellness visit and personalized prevention plan
- Establishes the Community Care Transitions Program to provide transition (e.g., at discharge from hospital) services to high-risk Medicare beneficiaries
- Gives states the option of offering home and community-based care to disabled persons through Medicaid rather than through institutional care
- Initiates a 50 percent discount on all brand-name drugs during the donut hole for Medicare Part D enrollees prior to completely closing the donut hole by 2020

- Establishes a new Center for Medicare and Medicaid Innovation to test models to reduce health care costs and enhance quality of care; also introduces reductions to Medicare Advantage payments and a variety of other efforts to reduce health care costs

2012

- Initiates tracking of hospital readmissions for high-cost conditions and implements incentives to encourage hospitals to undertake reforms to reduce preventable readmissions
- Provides enhanced payments for primary care services; physicians are encouraged to form cooperative centers to achieve efficiencies
- Introduces value-based payment systems to provide incentives to hospitals to achieve higher-quality outcomes

2013

- Requires health plans to implement uniform standards to reduce paperwork and administrative costs
- Increases the hospital insurance tax rate for high-wage workers
- Implements an annual fee on insured and self-insured plans to fund a patient-centered outcomes research trust fund

2014

- Requires most individuals to obtain health insurance coverage or pay a penalty, which increases annually; if affordable coverage is not available, there is no penalty
- Health plans can no longer exclude coverage for treatments based on preexisting conditions

nor impose annual limits on coverage; limits the charging of higher rates due to health status, gender, and other conditions

- Establishes health insurance exchanges where individuals and small employers can comparison shop for insurance, and persons with minimal income exceeding Medicaid levels can obtain tax credits in order to prevent bankruptcy due to medical expenses
- Requires employers of 50 or more employees to pay considerable penalties for not offering health care coverage to their employees; small business tax credits are available for qualified small employers
- Imposes an annual fee on the health insurance sector
- Increases access to Medicaid for nonelderly individuals to enable them to obtain affordable health care

2015

- Establishes an independent advisory board to submit proposals to Congress aimed at extending the solvency of Medicare and lowering health care costs
- Creates a value-based, as opposed to volume-based, physician payment program for Medicare patients

2018

- Implements an excise tax on high-cost employer-provided health plans

Source: Adapted from Affordable Health Care for America: Health insurance reform at a glance, Implementation timeline (Publication No. 8082), *HealthCare.gov.* (2010). Retrieved from www.healthcare.gov/law/introduction/index.html.

Although the law was passed by a narrow majority, the Henry J. Kaiser Family Foundation reported that its poll taken several months following enactment of the bill showed general support for certain significant provisions. These included support for implementation of a Health Insurance Exchange, provision of tax credits to assist small businesses, help with the Medicare doughnut hole, and subsidies to help individuals obtain insurance. The least favored provision of the law was the requirement that individuals must obtain health insurance (The Henry H. & Kaiser Foundation, 2010). This mandate to purchase insurance became a rallying point for opposition. In general, conservatives opposed the law, even calling for total repeal of the Affordable Care

Act, while political liberals tended to support the law. Because so much of the law remains still to be implemented, it will be especially interesting to see if inevitable political and economic changes in the country will modify, sustain, or destroy this effort at health care reform. The conservatives that were voted into office in 2010 sought to repeal the entire Affordable Health Care Act by declaring it unconstitutional. Nevertheless, change seems inevitable in American health care financing.

Cost–Benefit Analysis

The cost of health care is of concern not only in the United States but globally, so it is instructive to see what benefits we achieve from our health care dollars. As Figure 7.2 shows, the United States expends a much greater percentage of its gross national product on health care than other countries. But what has this investment purchased?

For many years health-index statistics have been tracked by country, so it is now possible to compare critical indicators of health across many nations. Two prominent measures traditionally used to evaluate health systems' performance are infant mortality rates and life expectancy. Compare the health-index data in Figure 7.2 with the per person health care expenditures in Table 7.1. It is quickly apparent that in the United States the cost per citizen is not achieving the results on these important indicators that national

Human Behavior

Practice Behavior Example: Understand human behavior across the life course, the range of social systems in which people live, and the ways social systems promote or deter people in maintaining or achieving health and well-being

Critical Thinking Question: How will the 2010 Affordable Health Care Act impact infant mortality and life expectancy rates for the United States?

health care systems attain in the other industrialized countries. Note that the lowest rates of infant mortality came from countries like Iceland and Japan (only one death) and tiny San Marino, located within Italy (with 0 deaths). Table 7.1 also provides data for life expectancy of selected other countries. If one considers that the United States spends nearly twice the amount on health care of other industrialized countries, would it not seem likely that the United States could achieve better life expectancy and infant mortality rates than it currently does?

As U.S. citizens seek answers to the health care dilemmas in the United States, some look to the Canadian system. Enacted in 1971 and known as Medicare, it is of considerable interest, because Canadians share many of the values and beliefs of Americans. An overview of the basic

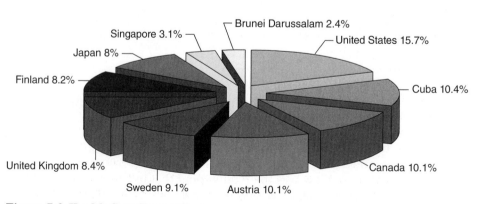

Figure 7.2 Health Care Expenditures

Source: Reprinted by permission of the World Health Organization.

Table 7.1	**Measures of Health Systems' Performance**	
Country	Infant Mortality (Deaths per 1,000 Live Births)	Life Expectance at Birth (Years)
Afghanistan	50	40
Austria	3	78
Brunei Darussalam	3	75
Canada	4	79
Cuba	3	76
Finland	2	76
Iceland	1	80
Japan	1	79
San Marino	0	81
Sierra Leon	45	48
Singapore	1	79
Sweden	2	79
Switzerland	3	80
United Kingdom	3	78
United States	4	76
Global averages	26	66
Range	0–50	40–81

Source: Reprinted by permission of the World Health Organization.

Box 7.5   Basic Principles of the Canadian Health Care System

1. *Universality.* Everyone is covered and has the same benefits.
2. *Portability.* Benefits are not linked to employment and can be used in any province and even in the United States, if necessary.
3. *Comprehensiveness.* Benefits include full coverage of medical and hospital care, long-term care (covered separately and differently, depending on the province), mental health services, and prescription drugs for people over 65 and for people with catastrophic illnesses, and other services.
4. *Public, nonprofit administration.* The system is publicly run and publicly accountable, with provincial governments as the single payers of physicians and hospitals.
5. *Freedom of choice of provider and accessibility.* Patients are free to choose their own health care provider. Care can be provided in hospitals, the home, or community. Specialist care is provided through referral of a primary care physician.

Source: Adapted from *Health care system, Health Canada (2005).* Canadian and American health care: Myths and realities. *Health & Social Work, 18*(1): 7–8. Retrieved from http://www.ch-sc.gc.ca/hcs-ss/delivery-prestation/index-eng.php.

---

principles of the Canadian system is provided in Box 7.5. Because Canada has a single-payer system, there are minimal expenses for billing. It is estimated that approximately half of the difference in cost between Canadian and U.S health care relates to administrative expenses. Canadian officials also expend only minimal time and cost in determining who is eligible for care and what the extent of their insurance coverage is; Canadians merely present their provincial health identification card. Hospitalization is immediately covered, so they are not billed.

Access

Although no Canadian is denied health care based on financial ability, what happens for the many uninsured or underinsured Americans is that they postpone preventive or diagnostic care. The result for many years has been more expensive care, debilitation, and even premature death. The 2010 Affordable Care Act focused on ensuring access to health care, but it kept in place an array of public and private insurance programs with varying levels of coverage and with bloated administrative costs.

It does seem likely that at present the United States has more technology for organ transplants, diagnostic imaging, and other complex procedures, but the Canadian system is not far behind and routinely performs open heart surgeries and other major operations. Access to high-tech medical procedures is more uniformly available to Canadian citizens than to U.S. citizens. In terms of pioneering new technology, Canadian doctors, too, have made important contributions: the discovery of insulin for the treatment of diabetes, the pioneering of lung and bone marrow transplants, and the development of very lightweight batteries to supply power for artificial hearts.

Bureaucracy

Americans are highly suspicious of bureaucracy. This suspicion then generates fear about government regulation and centralized authority. It is a mistake, though, for Americans to think that the U.S. health care system is not bureaucratized and regulated: it is increasingly regulated by thousands of insurance and managed care corporations. The U.S. system isn't centralized. Sometimes that is an advantage, but when it leads to fragmentation and lack of access to needed care, it can be a serious limitation. The Canadian system is also not managed by a single government bureaucracy; instead the 10 Canadian provinces (similar to U.S. states) administer their own services. The Canadian federal government partially funds the system and requires that each province meet the system's principles (see Box 7.5).The inequity and huge administrative costs of the present system made change inevitable, but it is unclear whether the 2010 Affordable Care Act will be sustained as designed. Box 7.6, the Up for Debate box, offers arguments for and against a national health plan for the United States that would be based on the Canadian single-payer system. In this plan private as well as public hospitals would continue to exist and doctors could be employed in public health or could operate private practices. Their health care system is generally well liked by Canadians. As one doctor stated: "Today a politician in Canada is more likely to get away with canceling Christmas than canceling Canada's health insurance program" (New Rules Project, n.d.).

"Today a politician in Canada is more likely to get away with canceling Christmas than canceling Canada's health insurance program." (New Rules Project)

A single-payer system (where one insurance plan selected by the state or federal government pays hospitals and providers directly) would eliminate the multiplicity of insurance carriers and administrative overhead that inflate health care costs. This design was not acceptable to Congress when the Affordable Care Act was passed, but it remains an option for the future. Health care financing remains a volatile political topic of discussion in the United States. Hopefully, the outcome will be a system that provides excellent quality, dignified health care to all Americans. If we have the political will to do so, we can accomplish this social justice goal.

Box 7.6 **Up for Debate**	

Proposition: The United States should implement a single-payer system of health care financing.

Yes	No
Use of a single, public system to process claims based on standardized forms would be cost-efficient, saving billions of dollars.	If desired, it would be possible for the U.S. insurance industry to standardize billing forms; there has been no call for this.
The health insurance industry should not be where the U.S. health care dollar is invested.	The nation's economy would be adversely affected by the demise of the health insurance industry.
A single-payer system would eliminate duplication of information and reduce the frequency of misinformation.	A single-payer system with standardized billing forms would tend to stagnate the development of technological advances in billing procedures.
Co-payment by patients is nonexistent in most Canadian provinces.	Even in the Canadian system, co-pays are used in some provinces, so billing to patients still takes place.
Equal access and the same level of care, which is inherent within a single-payer health financing program, is a moral right of all citizens.	There is no constitutionally defined right of citizens to health care.

FUTURE TRENDS FOR SOCIAL WORKERS

The Bureau of Labor Statistics' publication *Career Information* predicts that between now and 2018, "jobs for social workers are expected to grow faster than the average for all occupations through 2018" (2010, section 5, para. 1). Their experts anticipate rapid growth of medical and public health social work positions resulting from the increase in the elderly population. Home health care, assisted-living centers, hospices, rehabilitation centers, health clinics, and nursing homes are among the health care settings where social work assistance will be needed. It is also expected that within hospitals, social work responsibilities will continue to shift toward emergency and trauma centers, cardiac and intensive care units, oncology and hospice programs, and perinatal centers. The growth of community-based centers, including outpatient surgeries and diagnostic centers, is predicted to provide additional employment opportunities, too.

SUMMARY

Linda Sanders, a senior social work student in field placement, introduces the reader to the field of health care. Because her courses are preparing her for generalist social work practice, Linda is able to use her critical thinking skills to assess the tragedy of Katherine Lewandowski's death within the context of a whole population of frail elderly persons who might be at risk because of premature discharge from the hospital. The case study is designed to illustrate why it is necessary for social work students to acquire knowledge and skill not only in counseling and one-on-one work but also in advocacy and larger systems change. These practice skills are needed in health care as much as—perhaps even more than—in any other field of social work practice.

Social workers frequently serve as members of health teams that grapple with ethical dilemmas. Ethics and values content pervade the social work curriculum and are also derived from philosophy, theology, and literature courses, giving social work students in health care settings a basis from which to examine ethical issues. In addition, the Code of Ethics of the NASW provides guidelines for ethical practice.

The health care field encompasses much more than hospitals. Indeed, social workers are employed in rehabilitation centers, nursing homes, hospices, hemodialysis units, home health care services, insurance companies, and other specialized care centers—in large cities, in small towns, and in rural areas. The community itself, including its economic well-being, its potential environmental risks, and its racial and ethnic characteristics, must be understood by the health care social worker to provide a bridge between the community and the health care facility. Human rights and social justice issues related to health must also be understood from a global perspective.

The history of social work in health care is a proud one. Not only have social workers in this field helped patients and their families, but for 100 years they have worked to make health care organizations and social policy more responsive and more sensitive to the needs of people.

Today the impact of public policy is immense. The entire health field seems to be in crisis. At the center of the debate is health care financing. As health care costs keep rising, business corporations and nonprofit organizations are less willing to pay for employees' health insurance. The cost containment procedures that have been implemented have the potential result of leading to inadequate medical care or premature discharge of hospital patients. Reform of the U.S. health care system is under way with the enactment of the 2010 Patient Protection and Affordable Care Act, but public support for a comprehensive national health care finance program remains uncertain. Social workers, who witness daily the tragedy of unequal access to health care, will undoubtedly continue to advocate for a U.S. health care system that ensures excellent quality health care for all.

To meet the challenges of this exciting and rapidly evolving field of practice, social workers will need to sustain commitment to their professional values just as social workers have since the days of the lady almoners at the Royal Free Hospital in London.

PRACTICE TEST The following questions will test your knowledge of the content found within this chapter. For additional assessment, including licensing-exam type questions on applying chapter content to practice behaviors, visit **MySearchLab.**

1. Acute care services include _____.
   a. physician/medical call-in radio programs
   b. physical therapy
   c. hospitals, clinics, and rehabilitation centers
   d. retirement villages

2. Hospital social workers date back to _____.
   a. Jane Addams in 1905, Chicago
   b. an 1895 lady almoner in Great Britain
   c. a visiting nurse in Massachusetts
   d. Dr. Richard Cabot's work in Minneapolis

3. The Patient Protection and Affordable Care Act provides _____.
   a. a single-payer health care system
   b. strategies for health care cost containment
   c. a centralized system of health care services
   d. additional health care coverage for all Americans beginning in 2018

4. Long-term care _____.
   a. is designed to help individuals with chronic illness or disability maintain the best possible quality of life
   b. is limited to home health care and adult day care
   c. does not include home-maker and assisted-living services
   d. focuses on emergency health care and nursing home care

5. Hospice care is _____.
   a. provided by a team that includes doctors, nurses, social workers, clergy, and volunteers
   b. available for those who are 65 years or older
   c. only provided to those who are dying at home
   d. not usually covered by health care insurance

6. The social worker's role in home health care services is _____.
   a. housekeeping
   b. mental health therapy
   c. transportation
   d. supporting the family and preventing personal and family breakdown during the caregiving time

7. Effective social work practice in health care requires a range of competencies. The chapter identifies practice behaviors from all 10 of the expected CSWE competencies. Identify at least three specific practice behaviors, and provide an example of how a health care social worker would demonstrate effective practice behaviors.

Reinforce what you learned in this chapter by studying videos, cases, documents, and more available at **www.MySearchLab.com**.

Watch and Review

Watch these Videos

* Advocating for the Client
* Developing an Action Plan that Changes the Internal and External

Read and Review

Read these Cases/Documents

Δ Annie

Δ Bob and Phil

Δ Mrs. Smith and Her Family

Explore and Assess

Explore these Assets

Henry J. Kaiser Family Foundation—http://www.kff.org/

National Institutes of Health—http://www.nih.gov/

The Century Foundation Health Care—http://tcf.org:8080/Plone/healthcare

The Urban Institute—http://www.urban.org

Centers for Medicare and Medicaid Services—http://www.cms.gov/

Assess Your Knowledge

Assess your knowledge with a variety of topical and chapter assessment.

Conclude your assessment by completing the chapter exam.

* = CSWE Core Competency Asset
Δ = Case Study

Social Work in the Schools

Connecting Core Competencies in This Chapter				
X Professional Identity	Ethical Practice	Critical Thinking	Diversity in Practice	Human Rights & Justice
X Research Based Practice	X Human Behavior	Policy Practice	Practice Contexts	X Engage, Assess, Intervene, Evaluate

Lisa and Loretta Santiago, Children at Risk

Frank Haines, social worker for the Valdez Middle School, checked the memos in his mailbox as he did every weekday morning. Sure enough, there was a new referral concerning **truancy.** Two sisters, Lisa and Loretta Santiago, had been absent for nearly 2 weeks.

Children whose primary language was Spanish, such as Lisa and Loretta, could learn basic subjects like math and reading in their native language at this school, enrolling at the same time in English as a Second Language (ESL). Other Spanish-speaking children who had a better grasp of English could take most classes in English, and a bilingual teacher would assist them in Spanish as needed. Frank Haines, the social worker, was not Latino, but he spoke a fair amount of Spanish. In his former training to be a Catholic priest, Frank had traveled to two Latin American countries and had also served as a street worker among Latino youth. He recognized that there were great differences as well as similarities among Latino families and that linguistic dialects and cultural norms differed significantly among Spanish speakers from Mexico, Puerto Rico, Cuba, South America, and the southwestern United States.

Frank had eventually changed his career goals to social work because he wanted to have a family of his own. He then earned the MSW, the degree most commonly required for this type of employment in the public schools. He also took courses in education to obtain certification in school social work, as required by his state's department of public instruction.

To begin his work with the Santiago sisters' case, Frank examined the girls' school files for records of attendance, conduct, and grades. He found that the two sisters had transferred from a school in Texas 3 years before. Their attendance had been regular until recently. The younger girl, Loretta, a seventh-grader, had good grades up to the most recent report. Lisa, an eighth-grader, had only fair grades the previous year, but her grades for the first quarter of this year were absolutely terrible. Frank wondered if something might have happened recently to upset the children, especially Lisa.

Frank then checked with the children's teachers. Loretta's teachers expressed concern for the girl and worried about her absence, but otherwise reported that she was a good student. Her homeroom teacher had sent the parents a note about attendance, but there had been no response.

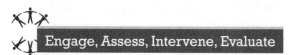

Engage, Assess, Intervene, Evaluate

Practice Behavior Example: Social workers collect, organize, and interpret client data

Critical Thinking Question: Social workers utilize a systematic assessment process. How does Frank Haines demonstrate this practice competence?

Lisa's teachers reported that ever since summer vacation, the girl had seemed "different." The mathematics teacher and the ESL teacher said that Lisa stared at the classroom walls for long periods of time. Sometimes she would cry or chew on her knuckles. Teachers had sent notes home, asking for a conference with the parents, but so far, no one had responded.

Frank's next step in his investigation was to try to talk with the parents. No one answered his first several telephone calls. Finally, a young woman answered who said that she was the children's stepmother. She told Frank that the girls had run away 2 weeks before. Frank made an appointment for a home visit late the next day, when Mr. Santiago would be home from work. He mentally crossed his fingers, hoping he would get his work done in time to have supper with his family. All too frequently, Frank's work hours conflicted with his precious time at home.

Fortunately, both Mr. and Mrs. Santiago were present when Frank arrived for his appointment. In the Latino culture it is often considered improper for an unrelated man to visit alone with a woman, even on official school business. Frank greeted the couple in Spanish, which warmed the atmosphere immediately. Mrs. Santiago served the two men coffee and then withdrew to manage several small children. Frank began the interview with Mr. Santiago in his best halting Spanish, but the latter, with a broad smile, responded in imperfect but much better English. "Spanish is a beautiful language," he said, "but I think perhaps it will be easier for you to speak in English. I understand you are here because of my two older daughters, Lisa and Loretta. You see," he said, "they come from my first wife, who still lives in Texas, and sometimes they cause me a great deal of trouble."

Frank soon learned that Mr. Santiago had been battling with his former wife over custody of Lisa and Loretta for years. The court had awarded him custody because his second marriage was intact, whereas the biological mother was not legally married to her live-in boyfriend in Texas. Mr. Santiago loved Lisa and Loretta as well as his five younger children by his second marriage, but, like many urban men of Mexican descent, he translated his love for his daughters into powerful protectiveness and control.

The girls had run away, he said, because Lisa broke his rule against dating. Lisa had taken Loretta with her on the date as a family chaperone, but that was not enough to satisfy the father. When he learned what had happened, he became very angry, gave them both a severe lecture, and grounded them for 2 weeks. Then he locked them in their bedroom, but they broke out and ran away. Mr. Santiago knew where they were, he said: with his current wife's sister. They were afraid to come home, he said, because they knew he was so angry he "might be tempted to use the belt."

"How will the girls learn that you are ready to let them come home without that kind of punishment?" Frank said. "You know that's not a good way to discipline your children."

"Oh," Mr. Santiago replied breezily, "if I tell my wife it's OK, they'll be home soon enough."

Frank suspected that the father might be ready for an excuse to let his daughters come home, as he cared enough about them to let them stay in a safe place until he calmed down. The social worker seized the moment to tell Mr. Santiago that he was very worried; the father was breaking the law by allowing his daughters to remain truant. If they stayed out of school much longer, a parental conference would have to be set up with the principal. That would mean Mr. Santiago would miss work and could lose hours of pay.

After a few minutes, Mr. Santiago said he had decided it was time. He would speak to his wife, and she would bring the children home. Two days later, Lisa and Loretta were back in school. Frank called them into his office for a conference. Both girls moaned to Frank that they would never be able to lead a normal life. All their friends were allowed to go out with boys when they were in junior high, they said.

"All of them?" asked Frank. "You know, I've heard that girls from Latino families are often not allowed to date, at least without a brother or sister along."

"But I took my little sister," Lisa wailed, "even though I know lots of girls who don't have to. None of the Anglo kids have to do that."

Frank empathized with the girls, but he pointed out that because they lived with their parents, they would have to obey their parents' rules.

"But we don't live with our parents," Lisa wailed again, "and these aren't our parents' rules. We live with our father, and they are our father's rules. And I hate him," Lisa said suddenly in a much different tone, intense and furious. "He was mean to my mother, very mean. Last summer I was visiting her in Texas, and he was staying with my grandparents there. I was walking with my mother when my father saw us on the street. He came up and stood in her way and wouldn't let her by. He called her horrible names and shoved her until she nearly fell. I thought he was going to hit her. My mother was shaking all over. He made her cry, and I heard every terrible word he said. I hate him."

Now Frank understood why Lisa was acting so troubled and defiant. She had been through an emotionally traumatic experience. He let both girls talk at length. He wondered out loud if they might want to see a counselor either by themselves or with their father and stepmother. But they insisted a counselor wouldn't help.

A few weeks later, Lisa and Loretta violated their father's curfew again. When they returned home, Mr. Santiago lost his temper and began shouting at his daughters, yelling that they were no good and would be grounded for a month. They would not be allowed to go on a school trip they had been counting on. The girls retaliated by calling their father every nasty name they could think of, in both English and Spanish. Mr. Santiago locked them in their room, but they left through the window.

Soon afterward, the girls showed up at Frank's office door at school, sobbing angrily. Fortunately, no one else was there, so he invited them in right away. Before Frank could find out what was wrong, however, Mr. Santiago himself arrived, clearly in a rage. Lisa immediately began to scream and curse. Mr. Santiago shouted for her to be quiet and then yelled at Frank that he had had all the disrespect and disobedience from his daughters that he could take. "Listen to that!" Mr. Santiago shouted, jabbing at Lisa and Loretta with a powerful forefinger. "Listen to how my daughters defy me! Listen to the kind of language they use with their own father! These girls are runaways, Mr. Haines! I want you to call the police! They are no longer welcome in my home!"

Lisa and Loretta continued to cry and yell. The more they carried on, the angrier Mr. Santiago became. Suddenly, he turned abruptly and began to stalk out of the office.

Frank stopped him. "Obviously, Mr. Santiago," he said quietly, "you have had a very difficult time. But I think we need to talk a little longer to decide what to do now."

"I will not talk any more!" Mr. Santiago shouted. "I have had all the disrespect I can take from these children! They must be punished! I want you to call the police. I will not allow these girls to darken my door again." He stormed out of the office and was gone.

After calming Lisa and Loretta as best he could and finding out what had happened at home, Frank determined that it would not be safe for the girls to return there. He called the protective services unit of the county social services department. No one was free to come to the school. Underfunding and understaffing are perennial problems of protective services programs. Frank therefore took the girls to protective services in his own car, a personal risk for him, beyond his professional obligation. If he had had an accident, his automobile insurance company might not cover him because he was doing work-related driving.

The social worker on duty tried to place Lisa and Loretta temporarily with their step-aunt, the person they requested. But the woman declined a formal arrangement, saying it might ruin her relationship with her brother-in-law. So the girls were placed with strangers. And unfortunately, soon afterward, their foster father was charged with sexually molesting a former ward. The girls could not be left in that home. The protective services worker consulted with Frank. Should Lisa and Loretta be transferred to a different foster home, enduring another major adjustment, or should Mr. Santiago be approached about taking the girls back again? The worker said she had already looked into sending the girls to their mother in Texas, but lengthy court action would be required because of the prior custody battle and interstate regulations. Additional time in foster care would be required during that process.

Frank felt compassion for the children. They had been through a great deal. But he thought that Mr. Santiago and his second wife basically meant well. The problem was that Mr. Santiago set rigid rules that drove his daughters to disobey. The rules were within the bounds of his cultural norms but different from those of many of the girls' Anglo friends. The father verbally assaulted Lisa and Loretta when they disobeyed and gave them lengthy punishments, but the girls provoked him further with their own harsh words. If the cycle of provocation could be stopped, Frank believed that this family could learn to live together more peacefully and happily. As the discovery of sexual abuse in the foster home illustrated, life elsewhere was no bed of roses either.

Frank felt the best plan for the girls would be to go back home, with family counseling to help improve communication and understanding among the generations. He knew, however, that the girls should be consulted first and that the father would need some persuading. The protective services worker was more than willing to let Frank take on those tasks.

Frank talked with the girls the following day and learned they were ready to return to their father and stepmother. They were lonely and afraid in the foster home. Frank made an appointment with Mr. Santiago through the stepmother. When he arrived, he was not surprised to hear Mr. Santiago announce that the girls were no longer welcome in his home. Frank called on his former training for the priesthood to help accomplish his goal of having the children return. Given Mr. Santiago's cultural heritage, he expected that the man would be a devout Catholic. So he told the story of the Prodigal Son in somber, measured tones, inviting this father to forgive like the father in the Bible. Eventually, Mr. Santiago was persuaded to take his daughters back and to participate in family counseling if a Latino counselor could be found. Mr. Santiago's job provided very limited insurance benefits, so a very low cost provider would have to be found. Frank took on the challenge. He soon found a Latino social worker with expertise in family counseling, Ramon Garcia, who was willing to see the family free of charge providing that he could use the opportunity to train two graduate students in field placement. Mr. Santiago agreed, and Frank arranged the first session personally.

A week passed, and then another. Lisa and Loretta both attended school regularly. There were no more incidents of truancy. At a meeting with Frank, they explained that Ramon had helped family members talk to each other without fighting so much. At a follow-up home visit, Frank learned that the parents were also pleased with the counseling experience. They believed they understood the girls better. They had become a little more flexible with their rules, and the children no longer tested them so severely. Life for the family was much happier.

PEOPLE OF LATINO OR HISPANIC HERITAGE: A BRIEF HISTORY

Lisa and Loretta Santiago and their parents were members of the largest minority group represented in the United States today—Latinos. Latinos are classified as Hispanics by the U.S. Bureau of the Census, but *Latino* is the term more commonly used. Including people from 26 countries, Latinos form a rapidly growing, diverse minority group that constitutes approximately 16.3 percent of the U.S. population, overtaking African Americans in 2003 to become the nation's largest minority group. They comprise more than 50 million people.

Approximately 63 percent are of Mexican origin, 9.2 percent are Puerto Rican, 3.5 percent are Cuban, 3.3 percent are Salvadorian, 2.8 percent are from the Dominican Republic, and 2.1 percent are from Guatemala. Of the remaining Latino population, no other single country of origin accounts for more than 2 percent. Today, half of the Latino population resides in two states, California and Texas. Arizona, Colorado, Florida, Illinois, New Mexico, and New York also have prominent Latino communities, and this population is growing rapidly in many other states such as Arkansas, Kentucky, Mississippi, North and South Carolina, and Tennessee (Bernstein, 2007; Keck, 2011; "USA Quick-Facts," 2011).

Texas, California, Arizona, and New Mexico originally belonged to Mexico. There were border disputes in Texas and California between White settlers and Mexicans, however. Texas declared its independence from Mexico in 1836, and the United States admitted it as a state in 1845. President Polk accepted the boundary claimed by Texas rather than that claimed by Mexico and ordered General Zachary Taylor to enter the eastern bank of the Rio Grande to defend the disputed territories, thus precipitating the Mexican–American War. Mexico City was captured in 1848, resulting in the Treaty of Guadalupe Hidalgo. Under this treaty, the United States took ownership of the disputed territories.

Mexicans who lived in the formerly disputed territories (lands that became Texas, California, Arizona, and New Mexico) were allowed to stay, with American citizenship, or to leave for what remained of Mexico. Those who chose to stay in the United States were supposed to keep ownership of the lands they held before the war. However, the burden of proof of ownership was placed on the Mexicans, and many legal records were deliberately destroyed during and after the war. Gradually, people of Mexican heritage who stayed lost their land, becoming second-class citizens (Lum, 1992).

After losing their land, Mexican Americans resorted to work as laborers, primarily in agriculture. And because economic conditions in Mexico were poor, other Mexicans crossed the border to seek work in the United States. These immigrants, legal and illegal, formed the backbone of the migrant laborers who traveled the nation to harvest crops according to the season. Low wages, poor housing, and lack of sanitation and health care greeted them in many places. As a result, strong efforts were made to win the right for farm workers to form unions and engage in collective bargaining. In the late 1980s, the work of self-advocacy organizations such as La Raza resulted in amnesty being offered to many illegal aliens who had lived in the United States for a significant period of time.

Today, the challenge continues as desperately poor people from Mexico continue to enter the United States illegally, looking for work (although due to the recession that began in 2008, many also return to Mexico). Mexican immigrants, legal and illegal, are viewed by many industries as a good source of cheap labor, so they are often hired—angering many American workers who view them as competitors. The status of illegal laborers continues to be debated across the nation today. Arizona's 2010 law, allowing any person to be stopped, interrogated, and jailed or deported if lacking proof of citizenship or legal immigration status indicates the level of tension surrounding this issue.

Puerto Ricans form another major group of Hispanic or Latino people in the United States. Puerto Rico became part of a commonwealth of the United States in 1917. Many Puerto Ricans later migrated to the mainland to pursue economic opportunity, usually settling in New York City. Today most still live in the northeastern region of the country. Unfortunately, many subsist in inner-city neighborhoods and suffer high rates of unemployment.

Cubans migrated to the United States in large numbers in the early 1960s to escape Fidel Castro's government. They settled primarily in Florida. Early immigrants from Cuba were usually professionals and businesspeople who were economically advantaged. Later, however, many of the immigrants arrived destitute and required numerous services for basic survival. Latino immigrants from Central America have also come primarily as refugees. In particular, wars in Nicaragua and El Salvador forced many to seek asylum in the 1970s and 1980s. Numerous people were denied entry and returned forcibly to dangerous situations. The needs of those who were allowed to stay strained the resources of agencies and programs designed to assist them (Lum, 1992). In recent years, there has been widespread pressure in the United States to modify immigration policy.

Given such multiple origins, it is easy to understand that Hispanic peoples are racially as well as ethnically diverse. When asked to describe their cultural heritage, most Latinos refer to their national identity (e.g., Mexican or Puerto Rican). Not all speak Spanish, and not all have surnames that appear Spanish in origin.

Like other minority groups, Latino Americans face discrimination and limited economic opportunity in the United States. A sad result is that a large percentage live below the poverty line: 26.6 percent in 2010 ("About Poverty," 2011).

HISTORY OF SOCIAL WORK IN THE SCHOOLS

School social workers do what they can to assist all students, including Latinos, to succeed in school. Frank Haines, the social worker who assisted Lisa and Loretta Santiago, came from the proud but relatively short tradition of school social work. The history of this field is described in this section. It is important to realize, however, that even today many schools lack social workers. In many other schools, these hard-working professionals may have to educate administrators and teachers as to their potential roles.

Early Years

As with many of the fields of professional social work today, social work in American public schools began with the far-sighted efforts of voluntary organizations (see Box 8.1). In 1906 two New York City settlement houses, Hartley House and Greenwich House, assigned "visitors" to do liaison work with three school districts. One of these visitors, Mary Marot, was a teacher and a resident of Hartley House. A natural leader, she formed a visiting teacher committee at the settlement house. The Public Education Association of New York became interested in her work and asked her if she would make her committee part of its organization. She agreed, and the association publicized the concept of "visiting teacher." At about the same time, the Women's Education Association in Boston established a "home and school visitor" to improve communication between the home and school settings. In Connecticut, the director of the Psychological Clinic of Hartford hired a "special teacher" to assist him in making home visits and to act as a liaison between the clinic and the school (Hancock, 1982).

Box 8.1	Timeline: History of School Social Work
1906–1907	School social work services begin independently in New York City, Boston, and Hartford.
1913	Rochester, New York, becomes the first school system to finance school social work services.
1921	National Association of Visiting Teachers is established.
1923	Commonwealth fund of New York increases the visibility of school social workers by providing financial support for a program to prevent juvenile delinquency that includes the hiring of 30 school social workers in 20 rural and urban communities across the United States.
1943	The U.S. Office of Education recommends that a professional school social work certificate be a master's degree in social work (MSW).
1955	NASW by-laws provide for the establishment of a school social work specialty.
1959	Specialist position in school social work is established by the U.S. Office of Education.
1969	"Social Change and School Social Work" is the national workshop held at the University of Pennsylvania, and its proceedings resulted in the publication of the book entitled *The School in the Community* (1972).
1973	NASW Council on Social Work in the Schools meets for the first time.
1975	Costin's school–community–pupil relations model of a school social work practice is published.
1976	The first set of standards for school social work services are developed by NASW. These standards emphasize prevention as an important theme.
1985	NASW National School Social Work Conference "Educational Excellence in Transitional Times" is held in New Orleans, Louisiana, and results in the publication of *Achieving Educational Excellence for Children at Risk*, which contains papers from this conference.
1992	The school social work credentialing exam, developed by NASW, the Educational Testing Service, and Allen-Meares is administered for the first time.
1994	NASW launches school social work as its first practice section.
1994	The School Social Work Association of America (SSWAA) is formed, independent of NASW.

The fact that the concept of visiting teacher took hold at about the same time in three separate cities indicates that this was an idea whose time had come. Initially, visiting teachers were financed by settlement houses or other private associations or agencies. But from about 1913 to 1921, various school boards began hiring them, beginning with Rochester, New York, in 1913 (Dupper, 2003). The movement gradually expanded from the eastern to the midwestern states. The early focus of these workers was community based; settlement houses in particular lent an orientation toward finding ways to alter the environment to improve individual lives. Visiting teachers tried to find ways to intervene in the school and community settings to help prevent delinquency, improve attendance, and develop scholarship.

The passage of compulsory attendance laws during this time reflected growing societal awareness of the importance of education and that every child had not only a right but an obligation to go to school. Compulsory education laws increased the employment of visiting teachers (Costin, 1987). Increasing numbers of visiting teachers led to the establishment of the National Committee of Visiting Teachers in 1921 (Freeman, 1995).

During the 1920s, the initial emphasis on community liaison and change gradually shifted toward concentration on adjustment of the individual child. Attention was focused on reducing delinquency and improving mental health, not so much through improving school and community conditions as through helping the child personally to adjust. This shift in emphasis paralleled the growth in popularity of Freudian psychology, which strongly focused on individual treatment rather than social change.

The Great Depression of the 1930s drastically reduced employment for social workers in the schools. Early in this period, those who retained their jobs tended to become heavily involved in locating and distributing food, shelter, and clothing. When the federal government began to provide these necessities, social workers gradually resumed their trend toward becoming caseworkers with individual students and their families. This orientation was well in place by the 1940s.

Middle Period

Throughout the 1940s and 1950s, with the federal government providing many basic financial and material needs to American families, social workers tended to maintain a clinical orientation, which increased their prestige in the school setting. Refinement of practice techniques to help individual students adjust to their environments then became the primary goal. Florence Poole, however, helped shift the focus from the "problem pupil" alone to a perspective that pupils and schools need to mutually adapt to each other, using the rationale that children had a right to an education. As early as 1949, Poole wrote that it was the responsibility of the school to offer its students something that would help them benefit from an education (Constable, 2006).

The 1960s brought a number of social protest movements, and with them came a shift in emphasis to changing the school environment to help better meet the needs of diverse students. Social workers were to pursue this goal in collaboration with other school personnel. In the 1970s, development of systems theory and the ecological perspective helped focus social workers' attention on the complex problems of schools and communities, including racism and students' rights. Not all workers made the transition, however (Freeman, 1995). During this time, the term *visiting teacher* gradually changed to *school social worker.*

Employment of school social workers expanded in the 1960s and continued to expand in the 1970s. One reason was that legislation provided a variety of new employment settings. For example, the Economic Opportunity Act of 1964 created Head Start programs, which often employed social workers full or part time. Moneys appropriated under the Elementary and Secondary Education Act of 1965, an act that sought to improve educational opportunities for disadvantaged children, sometimes were used to employ social workers. In 1975 the Education for All Handicapped Children Act created new roles for social workers as part of a special education team. This act later evolved to become the Individuals with Disabilities Education Act (IDEA) (Dupper, 2003).

In the mid-1970s the National Association of Social Workers (NASW) developed standards for school social work. This project was initiated by the NASW Task Force on Social Work Services in the Schools and completed by its successor, the Committee on Social Work Services in the Schools. The basic purpose of these standards was "to provide a model or measurement that school social workers can use to assess their scope of practice and their practice skills" (Hancock, 1982). The standards identify three major targets of service: pupils and parents, school personnel, and the community. Clearly, the intent of the standards is that school social work services maintain a strong preventive, ecological perspective.

Recent Times

In the 1980s, school social workers began to pay more attention to students' rights, cultural diversity, parental involvement in the schools, and school–community–family partnerships. The impact of IDEA legislation in particular encouraged active parental involvement in educational planning for their children. The 1997 IDEA amendments established the Individualized Education Program (IEP) as the major tool in assisting every student to progress; every IEP requires parental input. Social workers have assumed much of the responsibility to make the goals of the act a reality. They frequently provide information to parents about programs and services, serve as mediators in conflicts regarding educational decisions, and provide mental health services in the classroom (Freeman, 1995; Dupper, 2003).

The growth of child poverty and homelessness over the past several decades has presented school social workers with increasing challenges, given the associated negative impact on attendance, achievement, and graduation rates. The impact of poverty on school performance will be discussed in more detail in a later section. Sadly, the recession beginning in 2008 accelerated these problems, at the same time that social work positions were being cut in many schools due to budget shortfalls.

SOCIAL WORK ROLES IN THE SCHOOLS

Roles of school social workers vary from community to community and are constantly changing to meet shifting school, community, and societal needs. Social workers must be creative, innovative, and proactive in developing, implementing, and interpreting potential new roles in this challenging setting. Nevertheless, like all social workers, they utilize a variety of levels of intervention, as discussed in the rest of this section.

Working with Individuals

Social workers perform a variety of roles in the schools. First of all, as illustrated in the Santiago case, social workers frequently counsel with individual students. Students may be referred for a variety of reasons, among them truancy, undesirable behavior, and pregnancy. In schools where there is a guidance counselor, such cases may be assigned either to the counselor or to the social worker, depending on who has more time available.

School social workers today work with individual school personnel in a variety of ways as well: consulting with teachers about the needs of particular children, sharing with teachers and each other knowledge about cultural factors in the educational process, informing staff about important community resources, consulting with teachers about classroom relationships, and so on.

Some school social workers become involved in screening individual students for material aid, such as free or reduced-fee lunch programs. Some schools also distribute donated books, clothing, writing materials, and the like, to needy children. Often it is the social worker who identifies the children who need this material help.

Family Work

Another type of social work service in the school setting involves working with parents and families. The social worker is the main link between the family and the school; the worker is often the *only* person from the school who can make home visits. Parents are contacted to gain information that may help teachers work more effectively with particular children. The worker may also make suggestions about parenting techniques in the home.

When a student is referred to **special education** for evaluation, especially for suspected **emotional or behavioral disturbance,** the school social worker usually interviews the parents to learn more about that child's early development and about how he or she currently behaves in the home and community settings. This responsibility will be discussed in more detail in a later section of this chapter. When appropriate, school social workers refer families to community agencies for material assistance, counseling, or other services.

Group Work

School social workers also often develop and lead groups of students. Group work utilizes peer processes and other motivational techniques to help resolve attendance, academic, and social difficulties (Pawlak, Wozniak, & McGowen, 2006; Rose, 1998). Topics are sometimes controversial, such as pregnancy prevention, sexual orientation, preventing sexually transmitted diseases, and coping with parents who are drug abusers. Groups can become the focus of heated community debate because some parents want these topics to be discussed only at home.

School social workers may also become involved in leading groups of parents and/or teachers, with topics depending on circumstance and need. Some school social workers become involved in leading groups to promote change in the school system or the wider community.

Working with Organizations and Communities

In accord with the generalist approach, educating and organizing school personnel and the wider community is an important part of school social work. The social worker is often the major link between the school and the wider community. This role is increasingly important today as children's problems grow and school resources shrink. For example, more and more children today find themselves without a parent to go home to after school, because in most families both parents must work outside the home to support their families. Social workers increasingly find themselves doing community assessments to find resources for after-school programs, only to end up organizing these programs themselves within the school setting using laboriously recruited volunteer staff.

Involvement with school-linked, integrated services (discussed later) is another undertaking that requires skill in working with organizations and communities.

Teamwork

Perhaps the most important thing to note about teamwork in the schools is that the school presents the social worker with a **secondary social work setting,** or host setting, for employment (see Box 8.2). The primary purpose of the school system is educational. The position of the social worker within the school setting is to support the educational function of the institution. In contrast, a family service agency is an example of a **primary social work setting** for a social worker. The primary purpose of the family service agency is to enhance social functioning, which is also the primary purpose of the social work profession; thus, the majority of the staff are social workers.

Professional Identity

Practice Behavior Example: Social workers serve as representatives of the profession, its mission, and its core values

Critical Thinking Question: How can school social workers help their non-social work colleagues understand its mission and role in the school setting?

Social workers almost always function as part of a team in school social work. That team might consist only of the social worker and a referring teacher, working together to meet the educational needs of a particular child. It might be a multidisciplinary team assessing a student referred for special education evaluation. In the latter situation, the team might include the regular classroom teacher; a special education teacher; the school principal, guidance counselor, and school nurse; a county social worker; and one or more parents. Teams are constructed by their members according to the need at hand; decision making is collaborative, implying shared ownership of problems and solutions. Teamwork is an important element in planning and carrying out change in the wider school environment as well. Because social workers value cooperation and are trained to communicate well across disciplinary boundaries, they are often assigned to work as team coordinators and leaders (Constable & Thomas, 2006).

School-Linked, Integrated Services

Many American children enter school with so many needs that they are unable to learn—they are poor, undernourished, and come from deprived environments. Many have health care needs that have not been met, and many suffer from mental health problems as well. For these reasons, a movement toward school-linked, integrated services has been under way in many communities across the United States. The intent is to make schools "hubs" for the delivery of a full range of services, involving various health, mental health, and social

Box 8.2   The Secondary Social Work Setting

The social work job function is affected in major ways when it is performed in a secondary, or host, setting. For example, most of the employees in a school are teachers; if there is a social worker, usually there is only one employed in that setting. This can be a lonely position because nobody else is likely to have the same knowledge, values, and skills. In addition, many social workers are assigned to several schools. They may not have private offices but instead must share space with other staff, holding interviews in temporarily empty classrooms or even utility closets. Private telephones may be unavailable, so scheduling home visits or discussing family problems by phone is difficult if not impossible. Organizing the political support required to secure needed changes is not easy in a secondary setting where the social worker may be the sole representative of his or her profession.

service agencies from the wider community (Franklin, 2000; Kronick, 2005). Sometimes these services are provided at the schools themselves, and sometimes they are simply coordinated by school personnel.

Schools where coordinated community services are actually delivered on site are sometimes called "full-service" schools. They have been developed in several states to help children at risk: those who arrive unprepared for the educational process and are unable to concentrate on school work due to abuse, neglect, homelessness, poverty, and poor health. Services such as counseling, family intervention, and group work may be targeted toward children displaying specific at-risk behaviors. Some full-service schools also offer comprehensive health and mental health services. Other, more broadly based services may also be available, such as case management, advocacy, child care, and transportation.

Only a few schools have achieved full-service status today. One interesting example is a middle school in the Washington Heights section of New York City, which has teamed with the Children's Aid Society to create a settlement house right in the school facility. Other New York City schools are less comprehensive but are working toward the full-service model. Located in low-income areas, they describe themselves as "community schools" and seek to serve as nerve centers for comprehensive neighborhood revitalization (Constable & Kordesh, 2006).

THE IMPACT OF CULTURAL DIVERSITY IN THE SCHOOLS

Cultural diversity has been increasing rapidly in the United States over the past few decades. The impact of cultural diversity on the city school system where Lisa and Loretta Santiago attended was considerable. When Latino children first began attending the public schools, they were a small minority and were placed in classrooms where only English was spoken; some of these children swam, but many of them sank. No help was offered to those who could not handle the experience. This is still the situation in many schools in the United States today. Rural school systems are particularly devoid of resources for children whose native language is other than English. Yet the need continues to grow as the Latino population increases; the Latino birth rate is more than double the national average (Martin et al., 2009).

Rural school systems are particularly devoid of resources for children whose native language is other than English.

The American cultural myth of the melting pot has lulled many people into assuming that children who are not native speakers of English can assimilate the language effortlessly. Yet many children struggle and cannot keep up in basic subjects like math and history. Crucial early learning time, the foundation for more advanced study, is lost (see Box 8.3).

Many schools have devised innovative programs to meet the needs of children from diverse backgrounds. The primary thrust came from educators, but social workers provided strong support. Two models for teaching children whose native language is not English have emerged. The **bilingual** model allows students to take courses like math and history in their native languages, while studying English in specialized **English as a Second Language (ESL)** courses. The other model plunges students immediately into intensive **Sheltered English Immersion (SEI)** to get them up to grade level in English and into regular classrooms as quickly as possible (Llana & Paulson, 2006).

An astonishing number of children in the United States live in homes where a language other than English is spoken—over 20% and growing. They often begin their educational experience bewildered by the school environment because they do not understand the language in which they are being taught. Their parents may not be able to help them because the parents themselves do not speak English very well, if at all. The cultural background of these homes may be worlds away from that of the school, so that communication gaps between children, parents, and teachers go well beyond language. Another confounding condition concerns economic deprivation—children who come from non-English speaking homes are much more likely to be poor, so they lack the family resources that otherwise might help them overcome language barriers. Tutors, for example, may be economically out of reach. Thus the likelihood of successful achievement in school for these children is limited.

The model used at the Valdez Middle School that Lisa and Loretta Santiago attended was bilingual. Hispanic children could take all their classes in Spanish, if desired, enrolling concurrently in ESL courses. Students with more understanding of the English language were **mainstreamed,** or educated in English in as normal a fashion for an American child as possible, while still having bilingual teachers available who could assist them in Spanish when needed (see Box 8.4).

California passed a law in 1998 eliminating bilingual education from its public schools, followed by Arizona and Massachusetts. The rationale was that students would learn English faster in an "immersion" type program and that they would be able to join their English-speaking peers in less than a year. However, a recent study in Massachusetts found that 83 percent of its SEI students were unable to join regular classrooms after a year, and more than half had not achieved fluency in English after 3 years in an SEI classroom. No study has actually shown that students learn faster in an English immersion classroom; many educators today believe that the most effective programs are "dual language" or programs where children learn in their native language for part of the day and study in English for part of the day. These educators also argue that in today's shrinking world, it is important for at least some

Box 8.4   Up for Debate

Proposition: Bilingual education should be provided in the public schools.

Yes	No
Children learn more easily in their native language, especially complex concepts.	Children need to learn the language of the majority culture as quickly as possible.
Children feel more comfortable in an environment where their native language is spoken.	Children need to learn to feel comfortable in an English-speaking environment in the United States.
Teaching in one's own language affirms children's cultural identity and thus enhances self-esteem.	Pride in one's cultural heritage should be taught outside of the school.
Some children simply fail when they must learn in a language that is not their own.	Some children will fail regardless of the language in which they are taught.
The United States needs bilingual citizens to maintain an enlightened place in the world.	All Americans should speak English as their primary language.

Americans to be fluent in more than one language and knowledgeable about more than one culture, so that maintaining bilingual education is good for the nation as a whole (Llana & Paulson, 2006).

Bilingual teachers, social workers, and other staff are needed in schools where a large proportion of children speak languages other than English; however, these professionals need to know about the cultural backgrounds of their students as well. Frank Haines, for example, secured his job at the Valdez Middle School partly because he spoke basic Spanish but also because he had direct experience working with various Hispanic peoples in his prior training for the priesthood. To work effectively at the Valdez school, for example, Frank needed to know about dating customs constraining young Hispanic girls and to understand normal disciplinary practices among Hispanic families living near the school. He needed to understand sex-role behaviors and authority patterns (see Box 8.5).

Social workers can learn what behavior is appropriate in a given culture or **subculture** by talking with other workers who are knowledgeable, by observing behavior directly, by talking with members of the subculture in question, by taking classes, and by reading. Many sources of information are available, but they must be conscientiously pursued.

Another important impact of cultural diversity in the schools involves the fact that the children learn from each other. **Norms** that might go unquestioned within a single culture may be questioned as the children learn that there are other ways of doing things. On the positive side, this can lead to flexible, informed, tolerant citizens later on in life. On the negative side (as in the case of the Santiago sisters), it may lead to rebellion against family norms and expectations because other alternatives are readily in evidence.

Particularly during the teenage years, most children enter a period of rebellion as they attempt to define who they are. A major developmental task of adolescence is to differentiate the emerging self from parents and other family

Human Behavior

Practice Behavior Example: Social workers know about human behavior across the life course; the range of social systems in which people live; and the ways social systems promote or deter people in maintaining or achieving health and well-being

Critical Thinking Question: What conditions in the social environment particularly affected the behavior of Lisa and Loretta Santiago?

Box 8.5   Exploring Cultural Diversity in Today's Schools

Cultural assessment of the child and family requires that the school social worker be open and willing to learn from the client, and to use that knowledge on the client's behalf. In every culture, there exist some expectations and codes of behavior around areas of discipline, time, health, and religious beliefs. A worker's understanding of what these values are, where they fall on a value continuum of traditional to modern, and how they interface with behavioral expectations of the education system regarding children's learning is a key element of cross-cultural practice in school settings.

People from diverse racial and ethnic groups have experienced different forms of oppression and racism in their interactions with the majority culture. Placing these concerns into a cross-cultural perspective involves exploring the client's historical experiences with the majority culture and, if applicable, with migration and immigration. This history may include movement both within the United States and across foreign borders. In this connection, there may be historical conflicts among or between certain cultural groups that will need to be explored.

Source: F. S. Caple & R. M. Salcido. (2006). A framework for cross-cultural practice in school settings. In R. Constable, C. Massat, S. McDonald, & J. Flynn (Eds.), *School social work, practice, policy, and research* (6th ed., pp. 299–320). Chicago: Lyceum Books.

members. Cross-cultural issues complicate this normal process. Social workers may need to reach out to contact children who are experiencing difficulty because some cultural norms do not promote a tendency to seek professional help. On the whole, the value of exposure to differences and the learning that children must undertake to deal with conflicting information probably far outweigh the discomfort of temporary confusion or rebellious behavior.

Alternative Schools and Charter Schools

Another impact of cultural diversity in the schools is a proliferation of what are known as **alternative schools,** schools that operate outside the regular public system. Although these schools are usually privately run, at least two cities, Milwaukee and Cleveland, provide taxpayer money to poor parents to help finance tuition. Alternative schools may develop formal agreements with public schools and even share staff. Alternative schools are not limited to children of ethnic minority background, but in many places minority parents have become strong advocates.

Probably a reason many minority parents have become advocates for alternative schools involves the fact that cultural or religious teachings may be incorporated into the regular curriculum. Also, these schools often have much smaller classes than regular public schools, providing students with more personal attention. A problem, however, is that most lack the resources to provide special education services.

Baccalaureate-level social workers (BSWs) usually have a better chance to be hired in alternative schools than in regular public schools, since most regular schools require the MSW. Even more attractive to the BSW, many alternative schools hire full-time social workers on staff, sometimes more than one. By contrast, a single social worker is often shared among several schools in the regular school system.

Charter schools are a type of alternative school growing rapidly in states that permit them. They are public schools (financed through tax revenues like regular public schools) that are operated independently. They are regulated at the state level and deal with complex financial and management challenges. Most emphasize the particular academic philosophy that motivated their creation (Hare, Rome, & Massat, 2006).

President Obama made charter schools a primary ingredient of his educational reform policies, probably due to the success of the charter school movement in Chicago, where he lived for many years. As part of a $4.35 billion initiative, President Obama encouraged states to make it easier to start these schools. As a result, several states have lifted their restrictions on charter schools.

The first charter school was opened in Minnesota in 1991 to meet the needs of children from families mired in poverty. Today there are approximately 4,600 charter schools serving about 1.5 million of the nation's 50 million public school students. These schools have grown in number due to taxpayer frustration over the slow pace of improvement in traditional public schools. Many of the children charter schools serve are members of ethnic minorities and come from families challenged by poverty.

Results have been mixed—according to a recent study involving 2,403 charter schools, student achievement has been no better than that in regular public schools. However, this study has been criticized as being "slanted" (in other words, the questions asked may not have been appropriate for charter schools).

A study of New York City charter schools found that students randomly assigned to charter schools performed better on state exams than regular public school students (Gardner, 2009; "Respect for Charter Schools," 2009).

INVOLVEMENT IN SPECIAL EDUCATION

Since 1975 many social workers have been hired by schools to work with special education programs. Before that time, many students with special needs were simply refused admission to public school. In 1975, however, landmark federal legislation—Public Law 94-142, the Education for All Handicapped Children Act—changed public education forever. This law is now known as the Individuals with Disabilities Education Act, or IDEA, promising free and appropriate public education to all children with disabilities (Dupper, 2003). Amended in 1997, it was reauthorized as the Individuals with Disabilities Education Improvement Act of 2004, aligning many of the principles of IDEA with the No Child Left Behind Law (NCLB) to be discussed later in this chapter (Constable & Kordesh, 2006).

While a great boon for the students and families it helps, the law has placed a strain on state and local community financing. That is because educating a child with disabilities costs approximately twice as much as educating the average child. IDEA law requires the federal government to pay up to 40 percent of the "excess cost" of serving special needs children, but Congress has never authorized sufficient funding. In fact, the federal government has never provided even half the funding promised when Public Law 94-142 was passed in 1981 ("Idea Funding Gap," 2010).

IDEA requires that social workers be part of a **multidisciplinary team** (sometimes called an **M-team, pupil planning team,** etc.) that evaluates referrals. Students are referred to special education services for a variety of reasons: speech or language impairment, physical disability (including visual or hearing impairment), learning disability, cognitive or other developmental disability, emotional or behavioral disturbance, pregnancy or health impairment, autism, and traumatic brain injury. Many children who never would have received an education, or completed one, now have a much better chance.

Part C of IDEA 2004 reinforces federal legislation originally passed in 1986, extending the right of special education services to infants and toddlers with disabilities. Part C has a strong focus on family; it signals a change in philosophy for early childhood intervention from child-centered to family-centered services. The family-centered model guides social workers toward family–professional collaboration whether they are working directly with families or developing policy, programs, or evaluation strategies (Bishop, 2006).

Social workers in special education programs assume many roles, but a prominent one involves evaluating children who are referred because of suspected "emotional disturbance" (sometimes labeled "behavioral disturbance"). Essentially, these are the children who are identified by teachers as behaving in harmful or inappropriate ways. School social workers often need to become involved before evaluation of a referral can take place, because under special education law all parents must consent in writing. Usually a child's referring teacher contacts the parents about a referral and the reasons it was made. Then a permission slip is sent for the parents to sign. If the parents do not return the form, the social worker usually makes a home visit to explain the situation further and try to obtain permission.

Once permission to do an evaluation has been obtained, the social worker's next responsibility is to interview the parents to determine whether a referred child exhibits disturbance in the home or community environment. If a referred child misbehaves at school but gets along well in the home and community settings, then perhaps the problem lies with the school and not with the child.

A multidisciplinary team (M-team) will meet to determine whether a referred child qualifies for special education services. Social workers serve on many of these teams, particularly if a child is referred for emotional disturbance. The M-team will comprise a variety of professionals depending on the nature of the referral (e.g., regular education teacher, special education teacher, psychologist, nurse, guidance counselor, social worker, school principal, etc.). The referred child's parents are also invited to be part of the team.

Once a child has been accepted into special education, the law requires that the educational program be in the least restrictive environment and in an environment tailored to each child's special needs; an Individualized Education Program (IEP) must be developed for each child. An important role for social workers is to mobilize a variety of services to help attain IEP goals. Social workers may provide direct services themselves to assist these children, such as individual or group counseling, and they may assist teachers and parents in developing behavior management programs (Dupper, 2003).

Educational Evaluations as Applied Research

What the evaluation team does when activated by a school special education referral is an example of applied research. Each member of the multidisciplinary team seeks information about the referred child in his or her area of expertise. Results of these research efforts are used in joint decision making. Within 90 days, the M-team must meet together to determine whether the child is indeed qualified to receive special services and, if so, what kind. This type of applied research has serious, immediate consequences for a given child.

The social worker researches the child's developmental history and also investigates his or her current behavior at home and in the community. When researching the child's developmental history, the social worker gathers information that will help determine if the child has developed "normally" or not. How did the parents feel about the child's birth? Did the child walk and talk at about the same age as most children? How has the child related to the parents? How does he or she behave at home? Has the child been in any sort of trouble in the community? If so, what kind? What concerns do the parents have about the child today? About the school? These are only a few of the questions a social worker might ask. Assurances of confidentiality can help concerned parents to provide detailed information.

Research Based Practice

Practice Behavior Example: Social workers use research evidence to inform practice

Critical Thinking Question: What types of research do school social workers undertake as part of their professional responsibilities?

While the social worker is conducting his or her part of the investigation, other members of the evaluation team will also be at work. The psychologist may be conducting a battery of psychological tests designed to indicate evidence of emotional disturbance and may also administer an IQ test. The teacher for the emotionally disturbed will observe the child in the regular classroom, taking detailed notes to document the percentage of the time the

School social worker interviews parents at home regarding truancy of their child.

child is doing assigned work ("on task"), as opposed to how much time the child spends misbehaving, wandering around, daydreaming, and the like.

After the various members of the multidisciplinary team have gathered their data, an M-team meeting will be held to which the parents are invited. At this meeting, the team will determine whether the child demonstrates needs that qualify him or her for special education services. Parents must then agree in writing for their child to receive these services. They may also refuse services, or they may appeal an M-team decision that has determined that the child does not need special services.

The social worker's role on the school's special education team then often involves securing cooperation and information from the family. Both BSWs and MSWs perform this type of work, although BSWs will usually find greater opportunities in rural areas, where the professional labor supply is limited. Additional training in child development and education is desirable for both BSWs and MSWs. Appropriate expertise is especially important in school social work because the lives of children with special needs are affected so directly.

Unfortunately, the beliefs and actions of people in the wider society sometimes create clients for social workers in special education.

Unfortunately, the beliefs and actions of people in the wider society sometimes *create* clients for social workers in special education. In an ideal society, special education evaluation would be a waste of time for these children because, given acceptance by others, they would have no problems to evaluate. The following is an example of such a circumstance, sadly still common today.

School Social Work with Other Special-Needs Children: The Ordeal of Two Gay Brothers

Todd Larkin was about 11 years old when he began to sense he was different. As early as the sixth grade he sometimes felt very alone. His buddies made cracks and catcalls at the girls, and the girls flirted in return. Everyone seemed to share some sort of secret. Todd, who had many friends who were girls, couldn't grasp what it was all about. He liked girls as people, but the flirting and catcalls left him bewildered. However, he didn't talk to anyone about his confusion because he was afraid there might be something wrong with him. Since he was handsome, athletic, and gregarious, nobody noticed his pain.

When Todd was in his early teens, he noticed a strong attraction to his male friends. No other boy mentioned such an attraction, so he felt confused and scared. Other boys were starting to date, but they dated only girls. Todd felt a desire to date boys. Increasingly, he wondered if something was wrong with him. He was afraid to talk with anyone about his fears, however. He didn't even have the words in his vocabulary to help him name his difference from other children.

Then, by chance, Todd saw a movie on television one evening at home. The movie was called *The Truth about Alex.* The movie's hero, Alex, was handsome, athletic, and outgoing, just like Todd. And also like Todd, he was physically attracted to boys, not girls. Alex kept his difference a secret for a long time, but eventually he told a close friend in high school. As a result, Alex was labeled **homosexual** and ostracized by all his former friends.

Todd began to believe that he was homosexual too; but, given Alex's experience in the movie, he determined to remain absolutely silent. He even began to date girls to make sure no one would ever suspect. He "passed" very successfully. He was popular among the young ladies. But he graduated from high school with the whole burden of worry about his sexuality on his own shoulders. He didn't even talk with his parents about it.

Because Todd felt so lonely and misunderstood in high school in his small, rural town, he decided to go away to college in a large city. He hoped he might be able to talk with someone there about his concerns. Being extremely bright and an academic achiever, he was admitted to a prestigious private urban university. But his first days at college were disappointing. Right across the hall from his dorm room, for example, a large poster was displayed making fun of gay and lesbian people. And in theology class, Old Testament scriptures were quoted that rebuked gay people. Again, the boy felt lonely and afraid.

One day a hall director found Todd staring at the poster on the door across from his room. The director, a sensitive young woman who also served on the Campus Ministry staff, asked Todd if the poster offended him. Todd admitted that it did. The director agreed and suggested that Todd talk with a certain priest at the university, who felt the same way.

For several weeks, Todd tried to find the courage to call the priest. He was afraid, however, of being overheard in the dorm. Finally, he decided to call from a pay phone. Slumping down in the booth, Todd dialed the priest's number six times in a row. Each time his call was answered, he hung up in embarrassment and confusion. At last, on the seventh call, a warm, gentle voice spoke before the boy could hang up. "Come to my office today at 3 p.m.," Father Healy said.

Todd arrived at the priest's office door feeling sick to his stomach and not sure what to say. However, Father Healy's gentle sense of humor broke the ice. "Hello, son," the man began with a smile as he saw the boy's tense face. "I hate hang-ups. Come on in, and let's talk." Todd did just that. By the time he left Father Healy's office, he had been invited to attend a group of **gay** students run by Campus Ministry, co-led by the priest and Todd's own hall director.

When the boy didn't appear after a couple of weeks, Father Healy called to tell Todd he was sending a student to fetch him. In this way the priest gave Todd a chance to refuse and yet actively expedited his appearance. The hall director met Todd at the door of the meeting and eased his way into the group by finding a place for him to sit. It took several weeks for the boy to tell his story. But in the nurturing environment provided by the Campus Ministry gathering, Todd began to understand that his worth and dignity as a spiritual being were not diminished by his sexual orientation. He began to open up. Six months into the school year, Todd decided that he was, indeed, gay and that it was time to come out of the closet.

Encouraged by his support group, Todd began by telling his mother about his sexuality. To his shock, Todd's mother told him that she had suspected he was gay for some time and that she was glad he was finally able to tell her. Todd's mother eased the boy's way toward acceptance in the family by telling his father and stepfather for him. Todd's stepfather accepted the news fairly well; his biological father was more ambivalent. Neither man, however, totally rejected Todd, as he had feared they would.

The one person Todd pledged his mother not to tell, however, was his younger brother Tim. Todd felt that Tim, having weathered his mother's divorce and remarriage, needed a stable male role model in his life. Todd believed he was that role model and feared Tim would be upset at a critical time in his life if he learned that Todd was gay. The mother consented.

Ironically, Tim was struggling with questions about his own sexuality. Like his brother before him, he was afraid to talk to anyone. At age 11 the boy began to abuse drugs, perhaps to mask his worries and confusion about his sexuality. At age 13 Tim took a major overdose and had to be hospitalized to save his life. It was there, by Tim's bedside at the hospital, that Todd learned what his brother had been going through. As Todd sat in the visitor's chair and asked Tim what was wrong and why he had tried to kill himself, he heard the younger boy say things like "I'm all alone" and "No one understands me."

For a while, Todd could not understand what his younger brother was trying to tell him. But suddenly, he recognized his own feelings and experiences in high school. Was it possible that Tim too had doubts about his sexuality? Finally, Todd asked. Tim began to cry, and then Todd cried, and the two brothers shared as they never had before.

It would be nice if the story ended happily here, but life had more trials in store. Two weeks after the suicide attempt, Tim decided to confide in a close friend in junior high. He chose the friend carefully, hoping to be accepted.

But Tim was not accepted. A terrible replay of *The Truth about Alex* began to take place in his small, rural town. Within a week, everyone seemed to be pointing at him. The boy felt betrayed, angry, confused, ashamed, and scared. His family's house was pelted with eggs, and his mother's car tires were slashed. When the family appealed for help from the police, the police did nothing.

A couple of weeks after that, a boy in Tim's eighth-grade class pointed at him rudely and jeered loudly, "You're a fag, Tim Larkin! You're a fag!"

Tim's teacher should have protected him. But, instead, the man pointed a long finger at the boy. "Well, Tim," the man said, looking down his considerable nose, "is it true?"

Tim couldn't speak at first. Then he took a deep, slow breath. "I don't know, Mr. Humphrey," he replied bravely. "I'm not sure yet."

The class roared with laughter. The teacher glared and said, "I thought so; I thought so."

Mr. Humphrey's tone was so harsh, and the laughter in the classroom so derisive, that Tim couldn't bear to stay in his seat. He leaped up and ran home, shut the window shades, and locked the door. He refused to go back to school.

When his mother and stepfather were able to persuade him to go back a few days later, Tim found himself thrown against lockers, spat upon, and beaten up. The school principal refused to help. "We aren't in the business of protecting queer kids from discrimination here," he said, when Tim's parents went to the school to complain.

When Tim continued to refuse to go to school, the school administration threatened to prosecute for truancy. At this point Tim's mother appealed for help at the state level, wanting to know her and her son's rights. She also took Tim to a social worker in private practice, an MSW who specialized in family counseling.

The social worker helped Tim and his mother understand that confusion about sexual orientation was a normal part of adolescence. She helped the mother provide Tim with much-needed understanding and support so that despite the harsh daily reality of rejection from the outside world, Tim did not attempt suicide again. Instead, he brought his troubles and frustrations to the safe haven of home or a counseling session. On the suggestion of the state office of public instruction, Tim's mother also referred the boy for special education services at the school. The social worker who was counseling privately with the family wrote a powerful letter to the evaluation team describing the school as an environment hazardous to Tim's physical and mental health. The team then determined that Tim was a student at risk and authorized homebound instruction.

Tim continued to face difficulties, however. He was harassed when he went to school to pick up his assignments for homebound instruction. So the family enrolled him in a homeschooling organization. However, trapped in the house, afraid to go out even to the grocery store, Tim couldn't concentrate on his studies by correspondence. He then decided to work for his general equivalency diploma (GED) at a technical school in a neighboring town. Again, however, the boy suffered ridicule by students who had heard of his situation.

Discouraged, Tim dropped out of the GED program. About this time, hoping to help create positive social change, Tim's mother courageously agreed to take part in a public radio program discussing challenges for parents with homosexual children. When she returned to her job (she had been a caretaker for an elderly woman for more than 15 years), she found her belongings piled on the front porch, the door of the house locked, and a note telling her she was fired. She was never allowed to speak with her former client, a shut-in, again.

With such truly depressing experiences, one could hardly blame this family for becoming bitter and giving up. But instead, they maintained hope and overcame the odds with help from people who cared. For example, a dedicated GED teacher tutored Tim outside the regular GED program; he passed the exam! Tim's family, excited and relieved, gave him a formal graduation ceremony along with Todd's new partner, who completed his GED at approximately the same time. Many celebrating friends and family members attended. Tim was accepted into college. Todd now has his MSW and counsels gay and **lesbian** youth.

Tim's mother explains that she maintains a safe haven for her two sons at home. It is still dangerous for them to walk alone in the neighborhood. She declares that antigay people, even long-term family friends, are not allowed in the house when her sons are present. This impressive woman has also paid attention to her own needs. Not only has she survived being fired from her job, but she has updated her nursing credentials and developed entrepreneurial skills as well. Today she runs her own bridal shop.

SOCIAL WORK VALUES IN THE SCHOOL SETTING: POLICY IMPLICATIONS

Social work professional values strongly affect the policies social workers promote in the school setting. The Santiago and Larkin cases will be used as illustrations followed by a discussion of other serious school issues that tend to be addressed in very different ways depending on value orientation.

The Santiago Sisters

Let us begin with the Santiago sisters. Years ago, truancy would have been viewed simply as bad behavior, and the response of the school system would have been punitive. However, over the years more enlightened values in the fields of education and social work together have led to the development of a more individualized approach to truancy. Today, many schools have a policy of assigning a social worker to approach the investigation not as an effort at social control but as a fact-finding task. The uniqueness of each child's personal circumstance is recognized, and the worth and dignity of each child is respected. Usually the truant child needs assistance with some underlying problem.

The very existence of bilingual education illustrates how values have affected policy in the schools. The primary thrust for the development of bilingual education came from the profession of education, of course, but social work values such as self-determination strongly support it if that is what minority people request. Recognition of minority languages and cultures in public schools not only helps children learn but also shows respect for the worth and dignity of all persons. Such attention helps children gain self-esteem and pride in their own heritage.

Values also were the fuel for the development of special education programs in the public schools. Certainly it is easier for a school system simply to refuse admission or to expel children who bring with them special problems and needs. But over time, the values of fairness and individual worth and dignity have led to the recognition that children don't have much of a chance to make it in this society without an education. Even children with special problems should thus have a right to public education. Committed organizing and political strength were required to translate these values into public law, however.

The Larkin Case

The Larkin case is an example of what happens when conformity rather than diversity is valued by a school administration. Social work values, by contrast, honor the worth and dignity of all persons, and they teach respect for diversity. If social work values had been activated in Tim's school during his ordeal, new school policy would have been proposed, at the very least, to protect the rights of minorities. However, no one on the staff stepped forward to organize for change. Ideally, such a task would have been taken on by a school social worker (see Box 8.6). Unfortunately, even today, some social workers may be **homophobic,** or at least **heterosexist,** themselves.

While conditions for gay and lesbian students are somewhat improved in many schools today, challenges remain. Gay and lesbian students are frequently bullied, and it is important that school policies against such bullying are in place and enforced. Positive role models, such as respected gay and lesbian teachers, should be part of the school staff. Sex education curriculum should include accurate information regarding sexual orientation. Social workers should challenge negative stereotypes and discrimination against gay and lesbian youth, and serve as positive role models for respect and appreciation of diversity in all its many forms. They should provide in-service training for teachers and other staff to help improve the school's climate for gays and lesbians.

How different life for gay and lesbian students would be if school personnel, including social workers, took a serious interest in this issue and worked hard to solve it! Schools can be ideal settings to provide education about sexual orientation because almost all children and families become involved in them. School programs can help teach understanding and acceptance of diversity to students and parents alike, given the commitment to do so.

To assist school social workers to better serve lesbian, gay, bisexual, and questioning (LGBQ) students, the NASW sponsored a professional development workshop in June 2006. It addressed several issues of concern for school social workers, in particular the role of the social worker in addressing health and mental health issues of LGBQ students. The workshop also offered information on prevention of HIV and other sexually transmitted diseases and unintended pregnancy. NASW today considers working effectively with LGBQ youth a "core competency" required of all school social workers (Stoessen, 2006).

Beyond the school setting, social work values support protective laws for people with same-sex orientation and their families. Without such laws, people like the Larkins may find it difficult to obtain police protection when harassed, and they may be without recourse when fired from their jobs.

Bullying and Violence in the Schools

Almost everyone today is aware of violence in the schools. The mass shooting at Columbine High School in Littleton, Colorado, in April 1999 awakened everyone to its frightening reality. The massacre at Virginia Tech in April 2007 reawakened such fear in a manner horribly reminiscent of the Columbine killings. The student who murdered 30 of his peers at Virginia Tech and then killed himself imitated the clothing and stance of the Columbine killers and called them martyrs in videotapes that he left behind (O'Driscoll, 2007).

How can such horrors be prevented? As far back as 1994, the federal government mandated **zero-tolerance** policies in the public schools under President Bill Clinton's Gun-Free Schools Act. Zero tolerance means that a student *must* be expelled from school for a calendar year if caught carrying a weapon (although administrators are given slight latitude according to the circumstance). After the mass shootings at Columbine, many schools began bringing in police, posting hall monitors, installing metal detectors and surveillance cameras, requiring student ID badges, and the like. Students began being disciplined for very minor infractions. The major response to safety concerns in many schools has thus been one of increased security and punitive measures.

Box 8.7   Surveillance: The Best Answer to Violence?

A collaborative study between the DOE (U.S. Department of Education) and the U.S. Secret Service of 37 acts of violence in American schools found that the incidents were rarely impulsive. It showed that someone almost always knew of the plot. The perpetrators had often been bullied, experienced a significant personal loss, and exhibited striking changes in behavior. . . .

Mr. Modzeleski (a security specialist at the DOE) and others are convinced that the answer lies not in more metal detectors or school guards, but in a shift in culture. "It's easy to focus in on shootings, but we also need to look at what we're doing about harassment, teasing, bullying," he says. The real key is "putting adults in there that kids can talk to when they have a problem, making sure they can listen, that they have the willingness to listen, and can provide them with guidance."

Source: © By Amanda Paulson. Reprinted with permission from the March 25, 2005 issue of *The Christian Science Monitor.* © 2005 *The Christian Science Monitor* (www.CSMonitor.com).

Is zero tolerance and strict disciplinary action the best way to prevent violence? Many social workers disagree. Our professional values stress the worth and dignity of every person and the provision of options and choices, not repression. Perhaps surprisingly, many other professionals also advise that preventing attacks involves far more than punitive measures. The school shootings over the past several years have not been carried out by the bullies, but rather by the victims of bullying (Openshaw, 2008). Surveillance measures may only make already victimized students feel even more afraid (see Box 8.7).

Bullying can take many forms: physical threats (such as pushing, kicking, unwanted sexual contact) and/or verbal intimidation such as ridicule, rumor-spreading, name-calling, insults attacking race or sexual orientation, and so on. Today the Internet can spread bullying rumors to hundreds of students at the click of a mouse, greatly exacerbating the bullying problem.

Twemlow and Sacco (2008) assert that in order to successfully address bullying, the entire school *system* and the climate surrounding the school system must be addressed. For example, they note that in many high-achieving schools, there is such strong emphasis on achievement that the environment is extremely coercive, encouraging competition to the point that students are dehumanized. These authors point out that school systems must also address the "undiscussables" if they are to reduce bullying and other forms of violence: teachers who bully students, nonteaching staff who bully students, administrators who bully teachers and staff, coaches who bully athletes by pressuring them too hard to succeed, parents who bully teachers, and prejudice (usually denied but exhibited through bullying) against various minorities. When authorities model bullying, students follow suit.

Professionals, including police, stress the importance of good relationships between staff and students in the school setting, listening, spotting warning signs, and persuading students to report threats (Paulson, 2005). Preventive efforts such as conflict resolution and peer mediation programs, after-school programs, and family intervention programs have significant, positive effects. Research indicates that even preschool programs have significant long-term effects, reducing the frequency and severity of juvenile delinquency by the age of 18 (Mann & Reynolds, 2006). Disciplinary action may be necessary to help create pro-social behavior. However, environmental analysis, programs to address issues identified in such analysis (including the undiscussables identified earlier), social skills training and counseling are far more lasting,

Today the Internet can spread bullying rumors to hundreds of students at the click of a mouse, greatly exacerbating the bullying problem.

transformative experiences and help create a much more positive, trusting wider environment. School social workers can provide the expertise needed to create and carry out such programs.

Sexuality and Teen Pregnancy: Environmental Factors

Sexuality and teen pregnancy are issues for schools because sexual behavior often begins while children are still students in school. Early sexual activity is particularly risky among children today because girls are physically maturing earlier and thus at greater risk of pregnancy.

No one is certain why girls are maturing physically so much earlier than in previous times, but many scientists believe that environmental pollution is a major culprit. Dr. Joseph Mercola (2001) warns that certain synthetic chemicals in the environment mimic estrogens (female hormones). These are derived in many cases from plastics, ingested through food (commonly wrapped in plastic), water, and mother's milk. Mercola cites evidence from the *Journal of Epidemiology* that contamination of foods by the chemical polybrominated biphenyl (PBB) is associated with early puberty; and plasticizer chemicals called phthalates are also associated with early puberty in a major study published by the *Journal of Pediatrics*. Dr. William Hobbins (2007) cautions that in addition, hormones ingested for purposes of birth control or to cope with hot flashes in menopausal women often end up in the sewage system. These are not removed by normal sewage plant treatments and can end up in the water supply.

Regardless of the reasons young girls are maturing sexually so early, whether schools should get involved in sex education has been a controversial issue for decades. Many people insist that sex education should take place in the home only. However, sadly, comprehensive sex education is rather uncommon in the home. For this reason, school social workers frequently advocate for sex education in the schools. They may work in teams with school nurses, guidance counselors, physical education teachers, and others. Social workers are likely to take on the difficult but important task of developing parental support for these programs (see Box 8.8).

From 1990 until a few years after the turn of the century, teen pregnancy and birth rates declined by about one-third. However, beginning in 2006 statistically significant increases began to occur in the majority of states. Increases occurred among teens 15–17 and 18–19, and among Whites, Blacks, and Hispanics. Why such a major change? A likely reason is that funding for abstinence-only sex education tripled during the Bush administration, while funding for comprehensive sex education languished. Teens were taught that

---

Box 8.8   Sex Education in the Schools?

One of the most difficult subjects schools teach is sex education. Pressure from parents and community members often results in sexual education ending up on the "evaded" curriculum—never discussed, and its side effects ignored and relegated to the area of "personal problems." Even if sex education is taught as part of the formal curriculum in health class, *meaningful* school-based support systems for teen mothers are still relatively rare.

Teen mothers rarely have good options for child care and alternative scheduling that will allow them to work toward, and complete, their high school degree. "Sex education school initiatives tend to place primary responsibility for adolescent pregnancy on girls."

Source: Quoted from A. Ginorio & M. Huston. (2001). *Si, se puede! Yes, we can, Latinas in school.* Washington, DC: AAUW Educational Foundation, p. 26.

the only acceptable approach to sex was to abstain. Virginity pledges were promoted. Yet several studies found that frequency of sexual activity was no different among participants of these programs than among nonparticipants. A longitudinal study by the Johns Hopkins School of Public Health found that teens who had taken the virginity pledge were not only as likely to have intercourse as other teens, they were *less* likely to protect themselves when they did. Experts concluded that abstinence-only education provided a negative or faulty view of contraception (Jayson 2009; Thomas, 2009).

Not all teens become pregnant by accident, of course. While statistics often correlate early pregnancy with dropping out of school, and many social scientists assume that pregnancy *causes* the dropping out, evidence sometimes indicates that the relationship may be the other way around. Discouragement at school can lead to pregnancy as a means of escape. What can social workers do to help make schools more hospitable places for their students so that they want to stay and learn? When the question is posed in this way, many creative ideas can be generated. For example, cultural events that help members of ethnic minority groups feel more comfortable can be organized. Family outreach and family life education programs can be developed, along with after-school tutorial and recreational programs, sex education and self-defense programs, support groups for pregnant teens and young mothers, day care for their children, and the like. Myriad possible programs may help prevent early pregnancy or at least help young parents complete high school.

No Child Left Behind?

In another effort designed to help children succeed in school, the No Child Left Behind Law (NCLB), was signed into law by President George W. Bush in January of 2002. The NCLB involved a sweeping reform of Title I of the Elementary and Secondary Education Act that was originally passed in 1965. Title I was intended to assist states to provide additional resources for educationally disadvantaged children (Hare et al., 2006).

The NCLB has impressive goals: to set high standards for achievement and to establish strong accountability measures via ongoing standardized testing. Students are to be tested in grades three through eight to assess their progress in reading and mathematics; results are to be tabulated for multiple subgroups including minority, low-income, special education, and limited-English students. By 2014, every American child is supposed to meet specified achievement standards in reading and math (Paulson, 2007).

Many problems became evident as the law was implemented, however. For example, while states can set their own achievement standards, the NCLB requires that every school in a given state, including every subgroup in every school, achieve the same standards. The underlying NCLB assumption is that schools by themselves can achieve major leaps in educational achievement for all students in a very short time, and that if this does not happen, the fault lies entirely with the school and its teachers (Sunderman, Kim, & Orfield, 2005). Not taken into account is what some people have described as "America's dirty little secret": a substantial proportion of American children live in dire poverty. A shamefully large number are homeless. Children whose lives are scarred by poverty and homelessness can rarely concentrate long enough to complete a standardized test, much less achieve a desirable score. Schools and teachers alone simply cannot solve the issue of educational achievement in American schools (see Box 8.9).

Box 8.9 Costs of Child Poverty and Homelessness

To children whose basic needs are met, *misery* means their parents can't afford to provide the latest designer jeans. To children in poverty, *misery* means not knowing where they will sleep at night because their parents can't afford to provide a home.

In the United States today hundreds of thousands of children—according to some studies well over a million—are homeless. They live in cars, or under bridges, or with luck in temporary shelters but with no assurance that they will be able to stay. They are often unable to attend school because they lack an address as proof of residency. If a school with a compassionate policy should allow them to enroll, they have no place to do their home work. They lack decent clothing and shoes that fit. They often go to bed hungry, and hungry children cannot concentrate in a classroom even in the best of schools. If these children should get sick, health care is inadequate or lacking entirely.

Poor and/or homeless children lose out on the education required for economic success in the future. If they have been severely malnourished, their brains may not fully develop. In addition, severe stress triples the blood flow to the muscles of their arms and legs, a "fight or flight" coping strategy intended by Mother Nature to allow people to deal with enemies in the wild by *temporarily* increasing muscle strength. Today the stress response has become chronic for many poor children, depriving their developing brains of essential nutrients because their bodies remain in "fight-or-flight" mode. Thus their ability to learn in school is impaired. It is sobering to realize that these children represent a large part of America's future.

A further problem with the NCLB is that the promised increase in federal funding enacted into the law to assist with the cost of testing did not materialize after the first year. Schools find implementation a heavy burden in terms of both financial cost and the time required to administer the tests. Additionally, schools whose students do not achieve at the required rate for 2 years in a row are sanctioned—they may lose funding, and their students are allowed to transfer. This means in practice that schools with the greatest majority of poor and minority students, the very schools that need assistance the most, are the ones most likely to lose funding under the NCLB (Paulson, 2007; Sunderman et al., 2005).

The NCLB was to be reauthorized by Congress in 2007, but due to its controversial nature, debate was postponed. A coalition of 100 groups, including the National Association for the Advancement of Colored People (NAACP) and the National Education Association, signed a list of 14 requested changes to the law, including a lowering of proficiency targets; giving schools credit for making strides toward meeting standards, even if they fall short of proficiency; encouraging testing designed to measure higher thinking skills and performance throughout the year; providing more assistance to failing schools; and getting rid of sanctions altogether (Paulson, 2007).

In September 2011, because of Congressional inaction, President Obama issued an executive order permitting states to apply for waivers to the NCLB. To qualify, states must provide evidence that they have developed their own plans to boost student and teacher performance, as well as their own means for measuring student growth, including readiness for college or a career (Abramson, 2011).

Teen Dropout Rates

The problem of teens dropping out of school is a serious one, because teen dropouts are far more likely than other teens to land in prison, on public assistance, or unemployed (Paulson, 2006). According to the National Center on Educational Statistics, the percentage of public high school students who graduated in 2008 with a regular diploma 4 years after starting ninth grade was only 74.9 percent. Students from low-income families dropped out of high school approximately four and one-half times more often than students from high-income families between 2007 and 2008. Moreover, the dropout rate for Black and Hispanic students was far higher than that for White students. In 2009, 5 percent of White youth ages 16 to 24 were not enrolled in school and had not completed high school, compared with 10 percent of Black youth and a dismaying 18 percent of Hispanic youth (Chapman, Laird, & KewalRamani, 2010; "High School Dropout Rates," 2011).

Unfortunately, the NCLB does not provide incentives to keep students in school. NCLB may even be a factor promoting dropping out, as schools needing to raise overall achievement scores to avoid sanctions may quietly ignore the exit of underachieving students. Hopefully, the 2011 executive order by President Obama allowing schools to obtain waivers to the NCLB will help prevent this problem.

Social work values promote the goal of assisting all students to succeed at school, to help them achieve better opportunities in life, and to maximize their potential. Such goals clearly involve access to good schools so that students are motivated to stay, but they involve much more: a decent standard of living for all students, a safe environment, and parents (or parent-figures) who have the means to participate in their children's education (e.g., parents who are not forced by low wages to work multiple jobs so that it is impossible for them to attend parent–teacher conferences; fluency in the English language, etc.). That is why school social workers must advocate for students and their families not only in the school setting but in the wider political arena.

Spiritual Development and Empowerment

Helping empower students to develop the inner strength to remain in school, a challenging environment under the best of circumstances, can involve some unusual and creative strategies. For example, biofeedback techniques can dramatically reveal to students the connection between the inner workings of the mind and the mind's effect on the physical body. Students can actually *see* on biofeedback monitors how their angry thoughts lead to increased muscle tension and decreased hand temperature. Students can teach themselves how to calm their own minds and reduce their own physiological stress. A calm mind and reduced physiological stress permit much greater impulse control. Biofeedback can be an excellent tool not only in learning anger management, for example, but also in developing self-understanding and thus personal empowerment.

While merely a technique for physiological monitoring if viewed narrowly, biofeedback also provides a view into the workings of the inner self. It provides new self-awareness and the ability to modify, intentionally, one's own emotional and physiological stress responses. Many professionals believe that increasing understanding of the mind–body connection, along with the ability to bring about desired emotional and physiological changes, can lead to enhanced personal and spiritual growth (Matuszek & Rycraft, 2003).

Helping assist in the development of students' spiritual growth in the school setting must be done with care, as spirituality and religion are often confused. Because of the legally required and very important separation of church and state, religion must not be taught in the public schools. But there

While merely a technique for physiological monitoring if viewed narrowly, biofeedback also provides a view into the workings of the inner self.

Box 8.10   Social-Emotional Learning

Arthur Zajonc, physicist and director of the Center for Contemplative Mind in Society, says that he sees education "as the sole means for interior harmony, which in the end is the capacity for *freedom and love*." Yet in modern secular educational systems, directly providing the tools that lead to this harmony have been problematic because many practices stem directly from spiritual and religious traditions, potentially breaching the separation of church and state. Patricia Jennings, director of the Garrison Institute's Initiative on Contemplation and Education (ICE), cautions, "We need to be sure that the language we use is scientific and secular, and that the techniques do not require any kind of belief system to work." Despite this challenge, a dedicated corps of educators has been bringing "social-emotional learning" (known by its acronym, SEL) and contemplative practices into public schools.

Though solid definitions are sometimes hard to come by in this emerging educational field, SEL usually includes recognizing emotions in oneself and others; regulating responses to conflict and stress through breathing exercises, meditation, or yoga; and intentional moments of silence and reflection, among other practices.

Source: Quoted from The 2007 Shift Report, *Evidence of a World Transforming*. (2007). Petaluma, CA: The Institute of Noetic Sciences, pp. 57–58.

are effective ways to assist in the development of spiritual growth and personal empowerment that are compatible with any religion. One contemporary approach is known as **social–emotional learning (SEL).** SEL involves recognizing emotions and using a variety of methods to regulate responses to stress such as contemplative practice or meditation and breathing exercises (see Box 8.10).

According to Dr. Maurice Elias, research has shown that social–emotional skills can be taught in the classroom and that they improve students' ability to remember and use what they are taught. Not only do they enhance academic learning, they help students develop a sense of responsibility and concern for the well-being of others as well as themselves. These skills involve both head and heart. The result is that students are more willing and able to learn and classrooms run more smoothly (Elias, 2003).

Social–emotional skills have been taught in classrooms around the world for many years. Social workers can be effective SEL promoters and practitioners in American schools. They can be instrumental in organizing such programs.

AN INTERNATIONAL COMPARISON: SCHOOL SOCIAL WORK IN GHANA

A brief discussion of social work in Ghana, a nation on the west coast of Africa just north of the equator, demonstrates both the similarities and differences in social work services offered in the United States and in this former British Colony.

Ghana was the first African nation colonized by the British to win its independence. It did so in 1957, only to fall into a dictatorship. This dictatorship was eventually overthrown, and various governments, mostly military, ruled until 1992. At that time a fourth republic headed by an elected president was established, and the nation remains a republic today.

Ghana is ethnically diverse, home to more than 100 distinct ethnic groups. More than 50 languages and dialects are spoken. Thus it should be no surprise that English, the language introduced by the British, is used as a lingua franca (a language used for communication between different peoples). The government and the public schools use English as their official language.

More than half of Ghana's population is under the age of 18. Since 1996, education has been free, compulsory, and universal. With so many children to educate, many Ghanaian schools have instituted "shift" systems: one group of children attends school in the morning and another in the afternoon. No special school programs are available for physically disabled children. These children are integrated into regular classrooms; some may receive treatment at state rehabilitation centers. There are no special provisions for children with learning disabilities. Each teacher does the best she or he can to assist as needed.

The British government initiated social work services in Ghana in the 1950s under its Department of Social Welfare, but in 1967 the Ghana Education Service established its own social work service, the School Welfare Service. Truancy and delinquency had increased by that time to alarming proportions. Due to a need for more trained professionals, the Ghana Education Service contracted with the University of Ghana in 1975 to provide professional training for social workers. A 2-year graduate program was developed, leading to a diploma in social administration, recognized by the International Council for Social Work Education. In 1990, the University of Ghana initiated a 3-year undergraduate program in social work.

School social workers in Ghana serve multiple roles. Families in this nation are matrilineal, which means that children are supported by their mothers' extended families, primarily their mothers' brothers—not their fathers. While Ghana's extended family system was strong prior to colonialism, today the family structure is in disarray due to colonialism's after-effects. Men are frequently missing, searching for work far away. Poverty is widespread, so many children are mired in child labor or abandoned on the streets. School social workers (known as welfare officers) do their best to assist children who are hungry, homeless, neglected, abandoned, abused, exhausted, and frequently truant. They assist children who are engaged in prostitution; addicted to alcohol, drugs, and gambling; bullied; and/or challenged with various physical and other disabilities.

Recognizing the widespread problem of hunger, school social workers were the professionals who organized Ghana's school meal program, helping provide at least one balanced meal to each student every day. School social workers currently serve as nutrition officers, making sure that school meals are nutritional and properly prepared. In addition, they serve not only as consultants to teachers regarding the learning needs of particular students, but they directly assist new teachers in finding accommodations for themselves and their children. They arrange school placements for teachers' children, and make sure that teachers' salaries are paid on time. They ensure that each teacher understands his or her duties, obligations, and rights. They organize seminars for teachers on the latest teaching techniques and methods designed to meet the psychological needs of their students.

Ghanaian school social workers serve as the primary link between the school and the family. They make home visits to assist families to become more active in their children's education and to help resolve any problems between the school and the home. They assist parents to develop positive parenting techniques and provide family life education programs. They assist parents with special needs children to keep their children in school and to find additional resources such as state rehabilitation centers. They refer parents to appropriate community resources to help resolve other issues such as marital problems and child support disputes.

School social workers in Ghana also help develop and run parent–teacher associations. The main purpose is to bring parents together to identify common interests and to provide forums for joint parent–teacher discussion and collaboration.

Overall, school social work services offered in Ghana are designed to be preventive—the parent–teacher associations, home and school collaborative activities, nutritional programs, and family life education programs are all designed to help parents, teachers, and school children prevent school-related problems or to alleviate them before they become serious (Sossou & Daniels, 2002).

CURRENT TRENDS

As this chapter is being revised, headlines in many local newspapers document crises in the schools. That is because the recession that began in 2008 involved massive job losses. Job losses led to major losses in tax revenues at both the state and local levels. Local school budgets therefore faced major shortfalls. Rather than increasing support to make up for these shortfalls, states began cutting aid to the schools because of budget shortfalls of their own. The result: teachers losing their jobs, more children in every class, loss of art and music programs, loss of kindergarten programs, loss of school librarians, and yes, loss of school social workers.

This news is particularly unfortunate because the real needs are in the opposite direction: Robert Balfanz of the Johns Hopkins "Everyone Graduates Center" states that schools need to reorganize so that teachers can work with a manageable number of students and students can receive ongoing counseling and tutoring. Sadly, at the current time only about half of American high school students who are *both* minority *and* poor graduate, and those who do are unprepared for college (Paulson, 2010). Clearly, larger classrooms and fewer social workers and librarians are only going to make things worse (see Figure 8.1).

Dealing constructively with violence remains an important issue for the schools, and a major concern today is that tight budgets may lead to more reliance on technology and physical security measures rather than the development of a more supportive culture (Khadaroo, 2009, April 19). Social workers, of course, can serve as expert members of an educational team to develop a more supportive culture.

Schools serve almost all children in the United States today and can thus be primary sites for preventive efforts and early intervention. What better locus for social work leadership? Not surprisingly, whenever possible social workers today are involved in macrolevel intervention to stretch scarce resources and prevent problems from arising. Efforts are myriad in scope, including organizing after-school programs, child care programs, weekend recreational programs, parenting classes, substance abuse prevention programs, and the like. Service learning programs, in which students volunteer in the community as part of their learning experience, have been shown to improve graduation rates, and developing them is a productive effort for school social workers ("Students Who Serve, Graduate," 2009). Increasingly, social workers must secure outside funding to support the programs they develop, which necessitates sophisticated grant-writing skills.

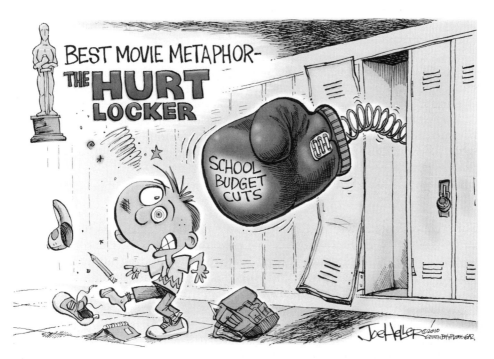

Figure 8.1

Ironically, as discussed earlier, schools in poverty-stricken areas that need help the most are the ones most likely to find themselves losing funding under the NCLB. That is because disadvantaged students are among those most likely to score poorly on standardized tests, resulting in sanctions being taken against their schools. The NCLB does not take into account factors external to the schools, including other government policies (e.g., the very low minimum wage and TANF program requirements) that tend to increase poverty, hunger, and homelessness among children, directly obstructing their school performance.

The trend toward increased numbers of alternative and charter schools has also been discussed earlier. In addition to charter schools, President Obama and Education Secretary Arne Duncan support a longer school year and longer hours in the school day for all public schools. Studies show that low-income students lose over 2 months of reading skills over the summer. Several schools in Massachusetts have added more than 300 hours to their school year through the Expanded Learning Time Program. Stronger test scores and a narrowing of the achievement gap are already being measured (Paulson, 2009). Another approach, aimed at expanding the school year at lower cost, has been to offer online summer school classes (Khadaroo, 2009, August 23).

Special-needs populations today include children with developmental disabilities, emotional and behavioral disorders, cognitive disabilities, physical disabilities, and the like. Budgetary issues are very important as the cost of educating special-needs children is high, and, as discussed earlier, the federal government has never met its funding obligations. Still, early assessment and planning for services in the least restrictive environment remain important tasks for the school social worker. Assessing how home and community environments affect student development is another important focus of the school social worker (Dupper, 2003).

School social work has been a strong and growing field for many years, although the recent recession has resulted in setbacks due to school budget cuts. School social workers developed the first specialty practice section within the NASW in 1994, the School Social Work Section. The School Social Work Association of America was also founded in 1994. These associations are important because they provide forums for development and discussion of important issues in the field and for dissemination of current research findings. They can also, ideally, lead to the development of political action groups to lobby for needed legislation and funding.

SUMMARY

This chapter begins with a case study of two Latino sisters who were referred to the school social worker because of attendance problems. The social worker approaches the referral from a generalist perspective, finding out what the girls' past history of attendance has been and consulting with the parents, teachers, and the girls themselves to determine the nature of the problem. The social worker does not assume that the problem lies with the girls, but explores the possibility that family, school, or other environmental factors might be contributing to their truancy. After gathering and assessing data concerning the problem and determining appropriate goals (reducing conflicts at home, increasing school attendance), the social worker develops a plan of action, referring the children and their family to appropriate resources. The social worker thus mobilizes the resources of family, school, and community.

The impact of cultural diversity on the schools is clearly illustrated in this case study by the organization and planning invested in making a bilingual, bicultural program available for Latino children. Social work values such as self-determination support the development of such programs. Not only can the children learn better and faster in their own language, but self-esteem is enhanced in circumstances where the children's heritage is recognized and honored. The nation itself benefits from bilingual, bicultural citizens.

The public school is a gathering place for most of the children of America. For that reason, representatives of almost every minority will be found there. This chapter's second case study concerns two brothers with a homosexual orientation. It is offered to illustrate the serious challenge the social work profession faces in helping to expand tolerance for diversity in the school setting. Social work values affirming the worth and dignity of every person serve as a beacon to help guide the worker through circumstances involving ignorance and intolerance.

The school is a secondary, or host, setting for the social worker, so the social work role is often as a member of a team. The social worker serves as the major link between the school and the home. On the special education team, the social worker is the designated liaison between school and family; she or he gathers information about children's developmental histories and behavior patterns in the home and community settings. Special education evaluations can be viewed as applied research with important consequences pertaining to multidisciplinary team decision making.

Social work values help orient social workers in influencing and implementing policies in the schools that deal with issues such as violence, sexuality, and teen pregnancy, and accountability. How policies may differ according to value orientation (e.g., the orientation toward educating, developing new social skills, and maximizing potential, rather than controlling or punishing) is discussed. Developing a positive culture in the schools is reported as more effective than using technology for control, but budget cuts may cost the jobs of the professionals such as social workers who could help develop such a culture. Student spiritual development and empowerment are discussed as means of assisting these young people to deal with challenging school environments.

School social work services in Ghana are described as a means of comparison and contrast with services offered in the United States. Many services are the same, including those involving assisting poor, hungry, homeless, neglected, and abused children and their families. In both nations, social workers are the primary link between the school and the home.

Social work roles in the schools are generalist in nature, ranging from working with individuals and families to working with small groups, organizations, and communities. Problems such as violence in the schools have their roots in the community as a whole, so that intervention on a single level will not suffice.

PRACTICE TEST   The following questions will test your knowledge of the content found within this chapter. For additional assessment, including licensing-exam type questions on applying chapter content to practice behaviors, visit **MySearchLab.**

1. Which of the following statements is FALSE?
   a. The term *Latino* refers to people with backgrounds from 26 different countries.
   b. The Latino population is growing in many southern states.
   c. Forty-two percent of the population in New Mexico has a Latino background.
   d. People with a Latino background make up over 16% of the US population.

2. What two federal laws were adopted in the 1960s that increased employment opportunities for school social workers?
   a. No Child Left Behind and Individuals with Disabilities Act
   b. Charter Schools funding and the Education for All Handicapped Children Act
   c. IDEA—Part C and TANF
   d. Economic Opportunity Act and the Elementary and Secondary Education Act

3. Which of the following statements is CORRECT?
   a. School social work was first initiated and funded by the Public Education Association of New York.
   b. The National Committee of Visiting Teachers was established in 1913.
   c. The School Social Work Association of America was founded in 1994.
   d. In 1965 NASW developed standards for school social work.

4. Which factors led to the development of roles for social workers in the public school?
   a. Requirement for compulsory school attendance and recognition that the home environment impacted a child's educational performance
   b. Changes in child labor laws and the impact of the Great Depression
   c. The popularity of Freudian Psychology and the need to reduce juvenile delinquency
   d. Regular standardized testing of students and bilingual education needs

5. How do school social worker roles in the United States differ from those of school social workers in Ghana?
   a. School social workers in Ghana serve as nutrition officers facilitating the school meal program, while this is not typically a role for school social workers in the United States.
   b. School social workers in the United States regularly conduct positive parenting workshops, whereas school social workers in Ghana usually organize other parents to provide these services.
   c. School social workers in Ghana have so few resources that they rarely refer families to community support resources, whereas this is common practice in the United States.
   d. School social workers in Ghana organize seminars for teachers on how to meet student psychological needs, however, U.S. school social workers rarely conduct such seminars.

6. What levels of intervention did the school social worker, Frank Hains NOT employ in his work with the Santiago family?
   a. Work with parents to resolve educational problems
   b. Work with agencies outside of the school
   c. Counseling with individual students
   d. Group work with students

7. What social work values was the school social worker, Frank Hains, demonstrating in his work with the Santiago family? Provide three specific examples of diferent social work values he demonstrated.

Reinforce what you learned in this chapter by studying videos, cases, documents, and more available at **www.MySearchLab.com**.

Watch and Review

Watch these Videos

* Advocating for the Client
* Providing Leadership to Promote Change to Improve Quality of Social Services

Read and Review

Read these Cases/Documents

Δ Lost in a Foreign Land

Explore and Assess

Explore these Assets

Interactive Cases for Practice: School Social Work

National Association of Social Workers—http://www.socialworkers.org

Gay, Lesbian, and Straight Education Network—http://www.glsen.org/cgi-bin/iowa/all/home/index.html

Collaborative for Academic, Social and Emotional Learning—http://casel.org/

School Social Work Association of America—https://www.sswaa.org/

Assess Your Knowledge

Assess your knowledge with a variety of topical and chapter assessment.

Conclude your assessment by completing the chapter exam.

* = CSWE Core Competency Asset
Δ = Case Study

Substance Abuse Services

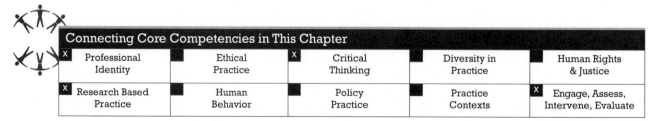

Connecting Core Competencies in This Chapter				
X Professional Identity	Ethical Practice	X Critical Thinking	Diversity in Practice	Human Rights & Justice
X Research Based Practice	Human Behavior	Policy Practice	Practice Contexts	X Engage, Assess, Intervene, Evaluate

Dan Graves

Dan was so cold that he knew he might freeze. He looked down at his feet and remembered that he had given his boots to an old man by the train station. Now his broken shoes did little to protect his feet from the snow on the streets. If he could just keep walking, he would not freeze. If he could get a drink, he would feel warm. Dan saw a familiar figure, stooped and hacking with a cough, turn into the alley behind the library, his hand in his pocket. Dan followed, and soon both men were sitting in George's cardboard-box shelter, sharing a bottle of brandy. It warmed them as they talked about better times. George had been a preacher in Mississippi until he came north in search of a secure job. That was around 2000, and the secure job had never materialized. Alcohol had eased his disappointment, but it never erased the memories of the family he had left behind.

Dan, at 23, was much younger and was not ready to give up hope. True, he had left his wife... well, not really. Angela had told him to leave because of his drinking. He wouldn't believe that he had a drinking problem. He thought it was her imagination. But thinking about Angela hurt too much; he'd better have another drink of that brandy. George had fallen asleep, Dan noticed. Dan looked around for some newspapers to cover George, to keep the cold out, but he saw none. He was feeling sleepy himself, his body exhausted from walking all day on the cold city streets.

When the police found George and Dan, both men were unconscious. For the paramedics who were called, this was the third conveyance of street people to hospitals that evening. The first call had led them to a White woman with a baby, both with frostbite; the baby was listed in serious condition. The second call involved an African American man, but he had not been drinking, and—although suffering from malnutrition and exposure—he had been admitted in stable condition. George and Dan, also African Americans, were in more serious condition. George had no heartbeat; Dan's was very weak.

St. Francis Hospital was very busy with emergencies that night, but when Dan and George were brought in, the staff rallied. Dan had **hypothermia** (extreme loss of body temperature) and frostbite; one foot looked very damaged. He was admitted to the hospital for further care. After 10 minutes of effort by the emergency room medical staff, George was pronounced dead. It was a bitter cold night in Chicago.

Two weeks later, Dan was talking with the social worker at the Salvation Army Emergency Lodge. Dan had arrived at the shelter the previous afternoon, having been referred there by the alcoholism counselor at the hospital. Madeleine Johnson, the shelter's social worker, knew about the treatment program he had begun at the hospital, but she questioned him again to gather more information about his drinking history. Dan instinctively liked this African American social worker, but he found himself somewhat irritated by the persistence of her questions. He found he could talk fairly easily about his days drinking with high school friends when he was 17. It was much more difficult to talk about what happened later. Admitting that he had lost two good jobs as a computer programmer because of his drinking was definitely not pleasant. But it was true. Having to talk about all this was so hard!

But most difficult and painful to admit was what his drinking had done to his marriage. Angie was so beautiful, and their love had been so deep, so incredible. His pain was unbearable when he thought about Angie. The social worker probed this painful area too, and she made him talk about Angie and the last time he had spoken with her. For 3 months after Angie had asked Dan to leave and he had begun living on the streets, he would phone her from time to time. He tried to make her believe that he was managing just fine. But he had not telephoned her from the hospital, and he had not given anyone her name, even when he was in critical condition and needed surgery to remove the frostbitten toes of his left foot. Following surgery, he entered the AA program at the hospital. Here he realized and admitted out loud for the first time that he had let alcohol ruin him and that he was an alcoholic. Now, at the Salvation Army Emergency Lodge, he was determined to continue attending AA meetings. The program made sense to him even if it was humbling to have to admit, in front of a group, what alcohol had done to his life.

Madeleine Johnson, the Salvation Army social worker, described the AA meetings held every evening at the Emergency Lodge. Dan said that he was serious about ending his drinking. He planned to attend the meetings daily. They also discussed how they would work together to locate employment opportunities for Dan as soon as the doctors said he was well enough to work. When Dan missed an AA meeting on the third day of his stay at the Emergency Lodge, the social worker asked to see him. Dan knew that Madeleine was disappointed that he had missed the meeting; that was a goal he had set for himself. But he was angry too. He claimed that the meetings were not intended for Black men and that he was not—and probably never would be—comfortable with the group. He told her about the comments several of the men made. It was clear they did not want minority members, especially Blacks, in their group. Stan, an older man, had been especially outspoken; most of the others, even the two Puerto Ricans, had sided with Stan.

Then Madeleine revealed that she herself was a recovering alcoholic. She too attended meetings and needed the support of others to prevent a return to active drinking. Some AA groups did not meet her needs as an African American woman and a professional person, so she had searched out and found a group that was right for her. Dan was stunned by her admission and her honesty. After further discussion Dan resolved to return to AA meetings, but he planned to explore other groups as soon as he was able to walk better on his healing foot.

In the weeks that followed, Dan did attend meetings faithfully. Through meetings and through his interviews with the social worker, Dan grew to better understand himself and his reaction to alcohol. Madeleine Johnson was a BSW with 4 years' experience at the Emergency Lodge. She was able to help Dan acknowledge his anger about the misunderstandings and prejudices against African American people that he encountered in the AA group and among other residents of the shelter. Dan's trust in Madeleine grew as he discovered that she shared his deep concern about the people like George, even families with children, who were living on the streets.

Dan learned from another Emergency Lodge resident that Madeleine and the other social workers had written a grant proposal that just last week had been approved for funding to begin a health care program for homeless people. They would need volunteers, Dan thought. Perhaps there was something he could do to help. He would silently dedicate his volunteer work to his friend George.

After Dan had lived at the shelter for 3 weeks, his doctor at St. Francis Hospital said that he could return to work soon. Madeleine and Dan had been talking about Dan's future plans. Now they developed a strategy that involved temporary employment in a service-industry job and evening classes to enable Dan to get back into the computer field. Dan was encouraged to find that the social worker did not want him to settle for a service-industry job for good. But he did need to start somewhere, and he would need income immediately to pay rent for a single room. Dan began searching the classified ads in the newspaper for a job that was near public transportation. Within a week he was hired at a fast-food restaurant. Dan knew that it was only temporary; he had other plans.

Dan registered for classes at the community college immediately. On the day that he began his computer class, he telephoned Angie. He had found a single room that he could afford with his minimum-wage job; he was leaving the shelter the next day.

Angie was clearly reluctant to believe that Dan was really no longer drinking. She had heard that story before. Still, she was relieved to hear from him and to know that he was OK. She seemed excited about his computer class. Later, as he was leaving the shelter, Dan thanked Madeleine Johnson. She encouraged him to stay in touch with her when he returned for AA meetings and the volunteer work that he would soon begin. Dan sensed her sincerity when she wished him well in the new life he was beginning. In his heart Dan wished her well too, for now he understood the special lifelong demands imposed by addiction to alcohol.

THE PROFESSION'S HISTORY IN THE SUBSTANCE ABUSE FIELD

Social workers need to value their clients as unique human beings and to believe in the potential growth and contribution of each client. Dan Graves's social worker did this well. Madeleine Johnson was not burned out by the broken promises of numerous alcoholic clients. Unfortunately, however, social workers and other human service professionals in the past often held very negative attitudes toward this client population. As a result, potential clients and their families sometimes were refused treatment or were shunted to the least experienced staff. One reason for professionals' avoidance of substance abuse clients was the frustration of working with persons who regularly denied drinking to excess or who denied abusing other substances. Today this attitude is giving way, somewhat, to a better understanding of why and how people (and not just substance abusers) use resistance and denial. To gain a perspective on the change that is taking place, let us review the history of social work in the field of substance abuse.

Mary Richmond: An Early Leader

The history of the social work profession in the substance abuse field began with the early social work pioneer, Mary Richmond. She proposed the use of the term *inebriety* to replace *drunkenness* and the term *patient* to replace *culprit* in social work practice. She incorporated the new terminology in an interview guide that she devised for the assessment of clients. This instrument has much to recommend it even today. Sections of Richmond's interview guide focused on heredity of the inebriate, duration of the drinking behavior, causal factors, drinking habits (when, where, etc.), the physical condition of and any current medical treatments needed by the person, and a description of the social conditions in which the person lived. Richmond's insights into the human condition enabled her to elicit information about the client's employment, home and family life, use of drugs in combination with alcohol, and even the potential use of alcohol by women to help them nurse their babies (Richmond, 1917).

As the director of the Russell Sage Foundation's Charity Organization Department in New York City, Mary Richmond was a highly respected and influential social worker. She was also noted for her work as a writer and teacher and is said to have contributed substantially to the acceptance of social work as a profession. Her sensitive discussion of social work practice with "the inebriate" may have helped to move social workers away from the extremely rigid, moralistic view of the early 1900s.

Social Work Contributions and Leadership Evolve

The social work literature from 1920 to 1950 contains little reference to intervention with alcoholic or drug-dependent persons. Instead, it appears that social workers tended to work with the spouses or families of such persons. In 1956 Catherine M. Peltenberg wrote in *Social Casework* that the few psychiatrists, psychologists, and social workers who did work in alcoholism treatment programs had to deal with their own as well as societal attitudes that alcoholism was a moral weakness and that these patients were morally depraved and lacked character. The year 1956, however, was a turning point. In that year the American Medical Association proclaimed alcoholism as a disease, making it a treatable illness. Jean Sapir's 1957 *Social Casework* article urging social workers to help change public attitudes toward alcoholism is a classic in the field of social work and substance abuse; it was also one of the first articles to describe an effective working relationship between social work and AA and an attempt to differentiate those clients who could benefit from referral to AA from those who would not be appropriate candidates for this form of intervention.

In 1970, important legislation was passed that was to affect the delivery of services, including social work services, to alcoholic clients. The Comprehensive Alcohol Abuse and Alcoholism Prevention, Treatment, and Rehabilitation Law was the first piece of legislation that recognized alcohol dependence as an illness in need of treatment. The law established the National Institute on Alcohol Abuse and Alcoholism at the federal level, and it authorized grants to help the states develop alcoholism prevention and treatment programs. With such strong leadership from the federal government, many programs were initiated across the country.

Responding to the new federal initiative, the Council on Social Work Education commissioned a text to assist social work educators; the book, *Alcoholism: Challenge for Social Work Education*, was published by Krimmel (1971). This innovative work was useful to the schools that soon began offering courses on alcoholism. With the 1981 election of Ronald Reagan as president, a new era of diminished federal funding for substance abuse prevention and treatment began. Funding was increasingly shifted to military and police crackdowns on the import and sale of illegal substances and also to imprisoning immense numbers of people whose sentences were drug related. Insurance companies' decisions to pay only for substance abuse care delivered in general hospitals led to the closure of many residential treatment centers. In the 1990s, however, new, short-term, community-based programs began to be developed. Social workers designed, implemented, and staffed many of these organizations.

Social workers made their mark on substance abuse services by the beginning of the 21st century. These included Charles Currie, the first social worker appointed to head up the federal Substance Abuse and Mental Health Services Administration (SAMHSA) and Mary Ann Amodeo who became the administrator of the Association for Medical Educators and Researchers in Substance Abuse (Steiker & MacMaster, 2008).

In recent years, social workers have used the person-in-environment perspective in many ways in their work with addictions and substance abuse–related problems. This chapter will describe some of the prevention and treatment currently being done with culturally diverse populations, with youths as well as older adults, with persons whose substance abuse results in sentencing for criminal acts, and with some interventions that are still not generally well accepted in society. Today's social workers encounter substance abuse across all fields of practice because addiction is often present in relation to other health problems, such as various cardiac diagnoses, or because addictions are contributing to family problems that bring people into counseling, into the child welfare system, or into contact with an employee assistance program (EAP) related to their employment.

The prevalence of addictions across social work practice is seen in research conducted by National Association of Social Workers, where it was found that 70 percent of social workers in their study group had worked in some way with substance abuse in the previous 12 months (Smith, Whitaker, & Weismiller, 2006). The Dan Graves case study at the beginning of this chapter provides one example of a social worker intervening with a substance abuse problem that was clearly a factor in this client's homelessness.

CRITICAL COMPONENTS OF PROFESSIONAL PRACTICE

Case studies, like that of Dan Graves, are interesting, but they also pose some problems. In reading this case study, for example, one might conclude that all street people are alcoholics, which, of course, is not true. Another incorrect conclusion based on this case study would be that a history of substance abuse is a necessary background for a social worker. Madeleine Johnson, after all, was able to use her own alcoholism effectively in working with client Dan Graves. In reality, however, a social worker's effectiveness is based on the application of skill and knowledge. Case studies can teach a lot about social work practice, but critical thinking skills must guide this learning.

The problem-solving or planned change process that has been a part of case studies in many chapters of this book also applies to social work practice in the substance abuse field. You may recall that this process includes four phases: engagement, assessment, intervention, and evaluation. Applying those phases to the substance abuse field sometimes requires special skills and learned practice behaviors.

Engagement

It would be hard to overestimate the significance of the beginning, engagement, phase of practice with persons who experience addiction. Whether we refer to this as rapport or a therapeutic alliance, the essential ingredient is relationship building. Persons with substance abuse problems may be frightened, suspicious, angry, defensive, and possibly in physical pain.

Achieving engagement actually begins with preparation. As students, social workers learn a set of practice behaviors that starts with accessing and thoughtfully reading all available information on the client to prepare themselves cognitively and emotionally to begin work with this person, family, or group. In the initial meeting, even in the greeting, interpersonal skills are used. The social worker invests energy, empathy, and genuine interest in interaction with the client. Listening skills are critical to convince the client that the social worker cares and is eager to assist. Interruptions from other staff and

Engage, Assess, Intervene, Evaluate

Practice Behavior Example: Use empathy and other Interpersonal skills

Critical Thinking Question: Is it possible to develop a trust relationship with a person who is addicted to alcohol?

telephone calls are avoided so that focus can be given to the client and family. Engagement does not end with the initial interview. Instead, it continues to thread its way through the work that occurs, whether this is short or long term. Engagement is, in essence, the cornerstone of a constructive, ethical, and professional relationship.

Assessment

In substance abuse work, assessment is complicated by the variety of substances used and abused. It is further complicated by the need to determine whether a pattern of addiction is involved or whether the use/abuse might be related to other causes such as a person's response to experiencing disaster or trauma. An understanding of the causes of addiction continues to evolve. Although alcoholism was initially thought to be sinful and a sign of weak character development, it is increasingly understood to be a constellation of many types of problems that have genetic, neurochemical, psychological, and environmental contributing mechanisms. A growing body of research points to the importance of genetic factors in substance abuse disorders, especially alcoholism. Genetic factors are a powerful force, but "it is not likely that genetics alone will account for the full range of alcohol and drug problems" (Butcher, Mineka, & Hooley, 2008, p. 309). Psychosocial and environmental factors are also known to be powerful contributors, especially in relation to the drug availability and motivation for drug use. Additionally, biological and biochemical changes in the brain of addicted persons can now be detected through sophisticated diagnostic tools.

Assessment focuses on gathering information. It builds upon and is a continuation of the engagement phase. In assessment, the social worker encourages the client to share her or his story. A screening instrument may be used to identify harmful levels of substance use or abuse. Multiple screening instruments have been developed, some for use with adolescents and others for adults, older adults, or pregnant women.

The World Health Organization's Alcohol Use Disorders Identification Test (AUDIT; see Box 9.1) is currently the only assessment instrument that has been validated across six countries: the United States, Kenya, Norway, Bulgaria, Mexico, and Australia. It is used internationally with women as well as men, for college students as well as older adults, and it has been translated into many languages. The first three questions of AUDIT provide data that may point to the existence of hazardous alcohol use, questions 4–6 evaluate the risk of dependence, and questions 7–10 evaluate harmful alcohol use. Hazardous, dependent, and harmful alcohol use are the categories used internationally instead of the dependence and abuse categories used in the United States. Hazardous is the least serious and dependence the most serious of the three levels. How is the AUDIT scored? A quick assessment might look only at the total score. A total score of 8 or above suggests the presence of alcohol use at least at the hazardous and possibly at the harmful level. A more careful look at scores for individual instrument items provides a more sensitive analysis. For example, a score of 1 or more on question 2 or 3 is a pretty good indication of alcohol consumption at a hazardous level. Any points scored on questions 7 to 10 are strong indicators that a harmful level has been reached (Babor, Higgins-Biddle, Saunders, & Monteiro, 2001).

Screening instruments such as the AUDIT are intended to be only a part of a more comprehensive effort to understand the person who presents with a potential drinking problem. If alcohol is the substance of concern, an effort

Box 9.1   The World Health Organization's Alcohol Use Disorders Identification Test (AUDIT)

Patient: Because alcohol use can affect your health and can interfere with certain medications and treatments, it is important that we ask some questions about your use of alcohol. Your answers will remain confidential, so please be honest.

Place an X in one box that best describes your answer to each question.

Questions	0	1	2	3	4
1. How often do you have a drink containing alcohol?	Never	Monthly or less	2–4 times a month	2–3 times a week	4 or more times a week
2. How many drinks containing alcohol do you have on a typical day when you are drinking?	1 or 2	3 or 4	5 or 6	7 to 9	10 or more
3. How often do you have six or more drinks on one occasion?	Never	Less than monthly	Monthly	Weekly	Daily or almost daily
4. How often during the last year have you found that you were not able to stop drinking once you had started?	Never	Less than monthly	Monthly	Weekly	Daily or almost daily
5. How often during the last year have you failed to do what was normally expected of you because of drinking?	Never	Less than monthly	Monthly	Weekly	Daily or almost daily
6. How often during the last year have you needed a first drink in the morning to get yourself going after a heavy drinking session?	Never	Less than monthly	Monthly	Weekly	Daily or almost daily
7. How often during the last year have you had a feeling of guilt or remorse after drinking?	Never	Less than monthly	Monthly	Weekly	Daily or almost daily
8. How often during the last year have you been unable to remember what happened the night before because of your drinking?	Never	Less than monthly	Monthly	Weekly	Daily or almost daily
9. Have you or someone else been injured because of your drinking?	No		Yes, but not in the last year		Yes, during the last year
10. Has a relative, friend, doctor, or other health care worker been concerned about your drinking or suggested you cut down?	No		Yes, but not in the last year		Yes, during the last year
					Total

Box 9.2   Criteria for Substance Dependence

A maladaptive pattern of substance abuse, leading to clinically significant impairment or distress, as manifested by three (or more) of the following, occurring at any time in the same 12-month period:

1. Tolerance, as defined by either of the following:

   a. A need for markedly increased amounts of the substance to achieve intoxication or desired effect.

   b. Markedly diminished effect with continued use of the same amount of the substance.

2. Withdrawal, as manifested by either of the following:

   a. The characteristic withdrawal syndrome for the substance. [Each substance has two criteria for withdrawal: (1) cessation or reduction of use that has been heavy and prolonged and (2) specified mood and physiological changes.]

   b. The same (or closely related) substance is taken to relieve or avoid withdrawal symptoms.

3. The substance is often taken in larger amounts or over a longer period than was intended.

4. There is a persistent desire or unsuccessful efforts to cut down or control substance use.

5. A great deal of time is spent in activities necessary to obtain the substance (e.g., visiting multiple doctors or driving long distances), use the substance (e.g., chain-smoking), or recover from its effects.

6. Important social, occupational, or recreational activities are given up or reduced because of substance abuse.

7. The substance use is continued despite knowledge of having a persistent or recurrent physical or psychological problem that is likely to have been caused or exacerbated by the substance (e.g., current cocaine use despite recognition of cocaine-induced depression, or continued drinking despite recognition that an ulcer was made worse by alcohol consumption).

is generally also made, following screening, to determine whether alcohol dependence or alcohol abuse is occurring. The American Psychiatric Association's *Diagnostic and Statistical Manual of Mental Disorders* describes criteria that differentiate abuse of these substances from dependence (a more serious condition). These criteria are explained in Boxes 9.2 and 9.3. **Alcohol dependence,** using the criteria, is characterized by compulsive drinking

Box 9.3   Criteria for Substance Abuse

1. A maladaptive pattern of substance use leading to clinically significant impairment or distress, as manifested by one (or more) of the following, occurring at any time in the same 12-month period:

   a. Recurrent substance use resulting in a failure to fulfill major role obligations at work, school, or home (e.g., repeated absences or poor work performance related to substance use; substance-related absences, suspensions, or expulsions from school; neglect of children or household).

   b. Recurrent substance use in situations in which it is physically hazardous (e.g., driving an automobile or operating a machine when impaired by substance use.

   c. Recurrent substance-related legal problems (e.g., arrests for substance-related disorderly conduct).

   d. Continued substance use despite having persistent or recurrent social or interpersonal problems caused or exacerbated by the effects of the substance (e.g., arguments with spouse about consequences of intoxication, physical fights).

2. The symptoms have never met the criteria for substance dependence for this class of substance.

that produces such symptoms as tolerance for alcohol, withdrawal from it, ineffective efforts to cut back on its use, and failure to change the drinking behavior despite evidence that it is causing serious difficulty. **Alcohol abuse** is the recurrent use of alcohol to the extent that repeated use results in an inability to fulfill normal role functions, presents legal or social/interpersonal problems, or creates a hazard to self or others (American Psychiatric Association, 2000). Note that alcohol abuse does not produce the physiological ramifications that occur with alcohol dependence. **Alcoholism,** then, can be understood as the compulsive use of alcohol characterized by evidence of abuse or dependence, as defined by the American Psychiatric Association, and resulting in some level of personal and social malfunctioning.

Finally biological, psychological, and social dimensions are assessed. The biological dimension is assessed by reviewing the person's medical history and current health and nutrition. (Nutritional needs may be neglected during heavy and prolonged bouts of drinking.) A drinking history is obtained that incorporates responses to the following questions: "What does the client drink, how much, how often, when, where, and in conjunction with which other substances? What are the eating, sleeping, and drug-taking patterns? When did the drinking begin? Is the pattern daily or binge drinking? How about blackouts, tolerance, delirium tremors (DTs), and hallucinations?" (van Wormer, 1995, p. 312). The biological assessment provides clues to medical treatment needs.

The psychological dimension reviews the client's mental health history to determine the possible presence of underlying mental disorder. Questions are asked about current level of anxiety, depression, and suicidal thinking as well as unresolved trauma or grief. The connection between alcohol and psychological functioning emerges when questions about psychological functioning shift to "reasons for starting, stopping, and resuming drinking" (van Wormer, 1995, p. 312).

The social dimension of assessment engages the client in a review of family, friends, coworkers, and other social network relationships. Who has or currently provides friendship and support? Where do stresses and tensions exist? Which relationships have been impacted by the person's drinking? Are there religious or other organizations or community memberships or involvements that serve to protect against drinking? What about spiritual beliefs and practices? Who and what matters to the client? A careful, thorough multidimensional assessment provides insight for the client as well as the professional staff (van Wormer, 1995).

Assessment that explores strengths in addition to the negative, problem-focused facts provides better balance and is respectful. For this reason, engaging people in their own assessment and possibly including close family members or friends can provide an understanding that leads to motivation for change and to an effective and realistic intervention plan. A strengths-based, person-centered assessment process focuses on what clients want in their lives. The client's priority may be to salvage the relationship with his girlfriend, not to work on his drinking or substance abuse. This client's motivation to stop or control his substance use may be triggered by the social worker's agreement to work with him to achieve that objective. Questions like "What would you stand to gain if you decide to stop using?" shift away from a blame orientation toward energizing and giving control to the client (Kisthardt, 2009, p. 61).

Once an assessment of the situation has been made and shared with the client, the next step is to develop an intervention plan. Because the problem, the person, and the situation are all unique, the intervention must be creative.

An early decision that must be made is: where should the action be targeted? What does the client want, and what is he or she willing and able to do? Is the person who is actively drinking or abusing another substance the appropriate client? Perhaps the entire family should be seen as a unit. Perhaps an organization, possibly a worksite, inherently promotes substance abuse (e.g., a brewery that encourages its employees to drink on the job); if so, quite a different intervention plan would be needed. Are new programs needed in the community? Perhaps vulnerable populations can best be reached through community outreach work. Together, the social worker and client develop at least the beginnings of an intervention plan.

Intervention

Many different and sometimes overlapping interventions are available. The social worker and client select one or more strategies based on compatibility with client needs, culture, and goals. Some possible intervention approaches include:

- Inpatient detoxification during withdrawal
- Behavioral approaches
- Family intervention
- Group therapy or self-help groups
- Chemical treatment (prescribed medications)
- Therapeutic communities
- Program development
- Community outreach

Medically monitored intensive inpatient treatment may be needed initially to deal with withdrawal and to identify and treat existing medical problems. Dan Graves, in this chapter's case study, for example, needed hospitalization. While still an inpatient, assessment was initiated and he became involved with AA. Brief inpatient treatment or partial hospitalization, if necessary, is generally followed by less restrictive forms of intervention.

Behavioral approaches to intervention seek to change behaviors that are harmful through the use of positive and negative reinforcement. Self-help approaches generally involve groups of persons with similar problems who use what they have learned to help each other. Social workers may initiate and lead such groups, or they may refer people to existing groups. These forms of treatment can be initiated during inpatient care, or they may be implemented with no prior hospitalization.

Interventions that include work with the family can confront patterns of interpersonal relationships and family communications that subtly encourage or excuse excessive alcohol consumption or drug use and abuse. Securing the family as an ally in treatment and support for the client can be highly beneficial. Group therapy conducted by social workers, psychologists, or other professionals focuses on the whys of drinking and chemical addiction. Feelings are also explored and worked within a group environment that is at once supportive and confrontational.

Prescription medications are sometimes used alone or in conjunction with one of the other intervention approaches; they may produce unpleasant effects such as nausea if alcohol is used (Antabuse), or they may block the pleasurable sensation of opiates (Methadone). Therapeutic communities are live-in programs where the resident is intensely and repeatedly confronted by staff and other residents when his or her thinking or behavior is inappropriate. Always alert to the needs of the community, generalist social workers may focus their intervention on building bridges between vulnerable persons, such as people living in isolation or on the streets, and the services that can help them with substance abuse problems. Sometimes it is first necessary to create new services or to put established treatment programs into entirely new areas; suburban communities and rural areas are examples. Social work interventions typically do focus on work at several different systems levels, as Chapter 1 explained.

Individuals and Families

Work with individuals who have alcohol or other addictions occurs across a wide range of health and social service organizations, not just within substance abuse treatment programs. Of course it also involves a wide array of interventions. The **stages of change model** of Prochaska, Norcross, and DiClemente has been adapted by practitioners across multiple settings to assess, plan, implement, and evaluate interventions with individuals. Their approach helps practitioners to monitor and support the change process:

1. Precontemplation (individual is unaware a problem exists)
2. Contemplation (individual develops an awareness of the problem and starts to think about making changes)
3. Preparation (individual intends to make changes soon)
4. Action (individual successfully changes his or her situation)
5. Maintenance (individual makes continued changes to avoid relapse) (Prochaska et al., as cited in DiNitto & McNeece, 2009, p. 694)

Awareness of this change process enables practitioners to appreciate and encourage clients' efforts. This should not detract from the knowledge that there can be regression or that some stages may be missed as the change process unfolds.

Case management has been found to be a useful approach in practice with chemically dependent persons. Rapp (1997) describes his experience using a strengths-based model of case management with persons whose substance abuse had primarily been with crack cocaine. This approach was so different from and contrary to the medical models previously used with these clients that initially they were confused. It was very difficult for some of them to identify any personal strengths, any competence, or even any good decisions that they had made. Nonetheless, Rapp found that they responded well to this approach—case managers met with them in their own environments, developed relationships with them, and helped them obtain needed resources. Recent empirical research also has demonstrated the effectiveness of brief strengths-based case management in improving linkage with medical and social services that meet clients' needs (Rapp & Lane, 2009).

Much of the family therapy that has been done in conjunction with addictions has kept the person with the addiction at the center of the action, with family members learning behaviors that will confront, control, and support the addicted person. A newer approach, based on the strengths perspective, gives credit to families that have endured and survived the stress and misery that accompanies addiction. Instead of viewing the family system as dysfunctional and family members as codependents, this approach helps family members identify the strategies they used to survive and manage the chaos that exists when there is substance abuse within a family. Reframing is used to relate behaviors. The simple mechanism of replacing the term *relapse* with *lapse* recharges family energy to assist rather than punish and blame a family member. A lapse, after all, is a setback, quite possibly one that might be predicted when battling addictions, yet one that is only temporary and can be managed. Family members are encouraged in their caring and support for each other. As healing occurs for the entire family, it is increasingly possible for the family to reclaim what was once lost through addiction: "the fun in life, one's sense of peace and safety, one's spirituality, one's wholeness" (van Wormer & Davis, 2008, p. 411).

Groups

Although empirical research has not yet demonstrated the superiority of group treatment over other forms of intervention, practical experience has shown that groups offer many advantages. Among the potential advantages of group intervention are the facts that they "alleviate the social stigma associated with addiction by providing social acceptance from peers and they facilitate identification with peers who are further along in recovery" (Smyth, 1995, pp. 2329–2330). Groups can also be confrontational, making denial of drug dependence less possible, and can help members achieve a level of self-awareness that is essential to the development of self-control. Citing a National Institute on Drug Abuse study and other recent research, Shulman reported that "retention in residential drug treatment" was influenced by "alliance to supportive-expressive group therapy" (2011, p. 396).

Social workers use a variety of intervention approaches in their work with groups. Psychoeducational groups, often cofacilitated by a social worker and a physician, frequently use a lecture format to teach members about addiction, including the body's reaction to alcohol and other chemical substances, the signs and symptoms of addiction, and the stress reduction and other coping techniques that can be used in recovery. Therapy groups, on the other hand, use member involvement to provide feedback, confrontation, and support. Role-playing is sometimes used to help members learn new behaviors (Smyth, 1995).

Social workers help group members to confront each other and also offer each other support and encouragement.

Despite the advantages of group intervention, groups are not the best choice for all chemically dependent persons. Clients must be able to function well enough to tolerate the emotional intensity of group encounters. Chronically mentally ill persons, for example, might find some groups devastating. Usually, however, social workers can structure their groups to meet the needs of specific populations or persons.

Self-help groups such as AA and Narcotics Anonymous (NA), which will be discussed in further detail later in this chapter, typically involve persons who share the same problem and meet together for mutual assistance. Until recently, most self-help groups avoided involvement with professional people. After many years of antipathy between professional groups and such organizations as AA, social workers and other professionals now recognize the value of self-help groups for specific clients, and they frequently refer people to them or combine another form of therapy with self-help group participation. Sometimes, too, social workers will initiate a group for this purpose and then guide the group in developing its own leadership and group processes.

Organizations and Communities

Effective organizational change can potentially benefit a far larger population than one-on-one counseling or group work. Social workers practicing from a generalist perspective often target an organization for change rather than an individual or a group. Social workers on the faculty of colleges and universities, for example, sometimes help to initiate support groups for students, faculty, and staff with chemical dependencies. Organizational change can result in new or improved prevention or treatment programs. Serving as consultants, social workers help businesses, industrial corporations, and unions to implement EAPs that offer help to people involved in chemical abuse. Within alcoholism and drug rehabilitation centers, social work staff attempt to effect policies and procedures to ensure that service will be provided in a humane manner. Educational programs are also offered by the social work staff to help other staff of the rehabilitation center better understand and serve the patients, their families, and the community.

Another role for social workers is community education. Seminars and workshops are offered by social workers in community centers, churches, or schools. In this manner, substance abuse prevention programs can target specific populations such as a youth group or older adults, religious groups, and ethnic or cultural populations. Educational programs may be offered in the language spoken by the group members, or a person from the group may serve as a cultural interpreter, ensuring that the content and communication are truly relevant. This kind of outreach work enables social workers to reach youth gangs, immigrants, and other populations that would be less likely to attend seminars at, for example, a hospital or university. Other social workers staff local and state alcoholism councils or mental health associations that distribute informational materials or develop media messages designed to prevent problem drinking and drug use.

Community outreach can also be used to try to engage people in substance abuse treatment. "Street workers," social workers who visit sites where homeless people live or gather, can make contact with homeless persons who are abusing alcohol or chemical substances. Coffee and hot food are a good entrée, especially in cold weather. If community outreach had been available, Dan Graves's friend, George (from the case study), might not have died. Community outreach social workers do save lives through early detection and strong

Community outreach social workers do save lives through early detection and emotional support.

emotional support that brings people who are at risk into treatment centers. Ability to form trust relationships and engage even hard-to-reach people is critical to successful outreach work with homeless people and also with teen gangs. Recognizing that a considerable portion of health crises are related to (even generated by) substance abuse, social workers have also begun initiating assessment procedures in hospital emergency rooms in suburbs as well as central city areas. A physician's forceful recommendation for treatment can be a strong motivator.

Evaluation

Throughout the intervention process, social workers monitor their work for effectiveness. Progress notes routinely recorded allow the social worker to critically appraise the impact of intervention. Videotaping groups or sessions can be an asset to evaluation, both for the practitioner and for the clients. Some common elements of practice evaluation include:

- **Assessment of baseline functioning:** strengths as well as problems targeted for change, if identified at the onset, provide the basis for goal setting, contracting, and evaluation.
- **Progress measurement is used throughout the intervention:** some kind of systematic measurement is utilized. This can be informal discussion of the intervention work and its results, a problem checklist, or other formal assessment instrument.
- **Measurements are conducted both at specified intervals and at termination:** these, again, may range from informal evaluative discussion to use of outcome measurement instruments, possibly in the form of questionnaires.
- **Follow-up evaluations can be conducted:** ideally follow-up contacts are planned from the beginning of service. (Murphy & Dillon, 2011)

Much research has been undertaken to explore the effectiveness of different interventions. Walsh et al.'s 1991 research with clients who were given a choice in treatment programs demonstrated the effectiveness of inpatient treatment followed by mandatory AA attendance. The Gibbs and Hollister study of 1993 made an important contribution to the scientific literature by isolating four distinct types of alcoholic clients based on measures of social stability and intellectual functioning. Their findings suggested that clients with strong social stability and intellectual functioning were 25 percent more likely to achieve sobriety at 6 months through outpatient as opposed to inpatient treatment.

The largest clinical research trial ever to be implemented regarding alcoholism, Project MATCH, attempted to match clients with the most effective treatment. This 8-year, rigorous, multidisciplinary research effort sought to determine which of its three treatment approaches was most effective with specific configurations of characteristics. The surprising result was that each of the three forms of treatment—cognitive-behavioral therapy, motivational enhancement therapy, and therapy aimed at facilitating clients' involvement in a 12-step program—"appeared to do quite well and, perhaps more importantly, patients' gains were well sustained throughout 39 months' follow-up" (Allen, 1998, p. 43).

Another contribution that research can make to the study of addictions is to provide clear, factual evidence of the impact produced. Social workers in child welfare, family services, the corrections system, schools, and domestic violence centers know so well the tragedy and pain caused by substance abuse and addictions. A growing body of data now documents the harm that is done. Here is just a sampling of this evidence as reported by Butcher, Mineka, and Hooley (2008):

> Heavy drinking is associated with vulnerability to injury (Shepherd & Brickley, 1996) and becoming involved in intimate partner violence (O'Leary & Schumacher, 2003)....Depression ranks high among the mental disorders often comorbid with alcoholism. It is no surprise that many alcoholics commit suicide (Hufford, 2001; McCloud, Barnaby, et al., 2004)....Alcohol abuse is associated with over half the deaths and major injuries suffered in automobile accidents each year (Brewer, Morris, et al., 1994) and about 40 to 50 percent of all murders (Bennett & Lehman, 1996), 40 percent of all assaults, and over 50 percent of all rapes (Abbey, Zawacki, et al., 2001). (p. 302)

This kind of data draws attention to the compelling need to create treatment programs and social environments that effectively reduce the terrible damage and broken lives that lurk behind the numbers and percentages. That, in fact, is the essence of the harm reduction approach that exists in other countries and that is beginning to gain some attention in the United States. The harm reduction approach does not focus on what the very best outcome might be; it focuses on doing whatever works to reduce harm, harm to the person who is addicted and harm to everyone who will be affected by the addiction. The role of research, though, is to carefully evaluate not only the effectiveness of treatment in terms of the individual receiving care but also the effectiveness of prevention and treatment programs for families, communities, and society.

A EUROPEAN PREVENTION AND TREATMENT APPROACH: THE HARM REDUCTION MODEL

The two models of substance abuse prevention and treatment used most commonly in the United States are the abstinence model and the 12-step recovery program. Both seek a complete and total end to substance use. An alternative but controversial program that is used far more frequently in Europe, Canada, and Australia than in the United States is known as the **harm reduction model**. The intent of harm reduction is to reduce the harm or damage that can occur when people are using chemical substances, including alcohol. The intent is to gradually reduce substance use, but with the recognition that addiction is a powerful force that takes time to change and that people who are using substances can seriously harm themselves and others.

European children grow up in a culture that incorporates alcoholic beverages in everyday life. "There is no negative stereotype attached to the act of drinking" (Loebig, 2000, p. 1). Some of these European countries have a more open attitude toward the rights of people to use other substances, and many, but not all, have been prescribing Methadone for the treatment of addiction for a long time. Needle exchange programs, in which used needles are exchanged for sterile ones, are much more common in Europe than in the United States. This is the primary treatment for drug addiction in Switzerland, for example. Interestingly, it was the threat of an AIDS epidemic in Europe in the 1980s that generated a groundswell of support for harm reduction programs and policies. Instead of criminalizing drug use, many European countries began to view it as a medical or public health issue, not just to protect the health of the users but to protect the well-being of the public. Programs were set up in the community that provided a safe supply to drug users and also to health care professionals for monitoring the use of drugs. Some cities in the United States have created similar programs (van Wormer & Davis, 2008).

From a social work practice perspective, the harm reduction approach is strongly grounded in the strengths perspective. Persons using or abusing drugs or alcohol are not labeled "alcoholic," "substance abuser," or with other negative terms. Instead, respect and collaborative relationships are essential. Spiritual as well as social, psychological, and medical needs are met, but the client is in control and is afforded the opportunity of making decisions for himself or herself (van Wormer & Davis, 2008).

Does the harm reduction model work? The World Health Organization (WHO) has found harm reduction strategies to be effective in diverse regions of the world and across multiple public health problems. HIV is one of the most serious health problems that WHO addresses. Exchange of dirty needles among drug users compounds the spread of this virus. "WHO strongly supports harm reduction as an evidence-based approach to HIV prevention, treatment and care for drug users. WHO advocates for Universal access to a comprehensive harm reduction package of interventions for drug injectors..." (World Health Organization, 2010, para. 3). A 2010 research report from a Michigan study also demonstrated the effectiveness of a harm reduction needle exchange program in a non-urban U.S. environment (Knittel, Wren, & Gore, 2010). Earlier international research showed that countries with liberal harm reduction programs tended to have fewer drug addicts. The Netherlands, for example, had 1.66 drug addicts per 1,000 persons in its population, Belgium had 1.75, Germany had 1.38, compared with the United States' 6.36 (Loebig, 2000). Much more empirical research is needed to evaluate the harm reduction model, but it does pose another alternative to the present prevention and treatment approaches favored in the United States.

Critical Thinking

Practice Behavior Example: Use critical thinking augmented by creativity and curiosity

Critical Thinking Question: How might expansion of harm reduction–based substance abuse programs benefit communities in the United States?

A U.S. MODEL: ALCOHOLICS ANONYMOUS

Although it began in the United States, Alcoholics Anonymous (AA) has spread throughout the world so realistically it can no longer be considered strictly a "U.S. model." In fact, there are 116,000 AA groups in 150 countries (Alcoholics Anonymous [AA], 2009). Also known as the "12-step program," this organization has spawned mutual aid groups for friends and relatives of alcoholics (Al-Anon) and groups for the adolescent children of people with alcoholism (Al-Ateen). In addition, the Adult Children of Alcoholics organization assists people struggling with past childhood experiences that continue to damage their present adult relationships.

Narcotics Anonymous (NA) is structured like AA and uses the same principles and philosophy as AA, including the 12 steps. Cocaine Anonymous functions similarly but is probably not as well known as NA. Alternative self-help groups have borrowed some of the AA philosophy but use other strategies. Rational Recovery, for example, is based on cognitive-behavioral theory that seeks to change self-defeating thinking patterns. Women for

---

Box 9.4   The Legacy of "Bill W."

The history of the founding of Alcoholics Anonymous (AA) is an interesting one. Bill Wilson was a stockbroker with a string of failed business ventures and years of alcohol abuse when he met Dr. Robert Holbrock Smith, a proctologist and surgeon, who was a graduate of Dartmouth College and Rush Medical College in Chicago. Dr. Bob's alcohol abuse was beginning to interfere with his medical practice. Talking together, they discovered, helped Bill Wilson deal with his compelling desire for a drink, and it helped Dr. Bob face and begin to deal with his own alcoholism. Bill W.—his "anonymous" name to others in the organization that came to be known as AA—was gregarious, impulsive, and an inspirational speaker. Dr. Bob, a man of few words, avoided public speaking and left that function to Bill W. Dr. Bob's authority, however, molded the new AA organization in many ways. Women were not admitted to AA for years because Dr. Bob opposed their inclusion, preferring to keep AA an exclusively male organization (Robertson, 1988).

Without media publicity, the notion of a person-to-person supportive network spread only gradually, and yet its appeal touched the lives of many people. By 1939 about 100 persons belonged to AA. They pooled what they had learned from their own experiences and created the book *Alcoholics Anonymous,* a classic that is still known as "The Big Book." It describes the 12 steps, which is the basic process by which members had learned to keep themselves sober. After the publication of The Big Book, AA grew rapidly. Five thousand people attended the 20th anniversary convention in St. Louis in 1955; by 1957 AA had grown to 200,000, with groups meeting in 70 countries. Today AA has more than 2 million members throughout the world.

Sobriety emphasizes self-respect for women who abuse alcohol. Some groups have emerged that avoid the spirituality of AA and instead focus on personal responsibility. A brief history of AA is provided in Box 9.4.

AA describes itself as a "fellowship of men and women who share their experience, strength, and hope with each other that they may solve their common problem and help others to recover from alcoholism" (AA Grapevine, n.d., para. 1). AA is well known in the United States and generally believed to be very effective in changing alcohol abuse and dependence. Because of the nature of AA, though, empirical evidence of its effectiveness has been difficult to document. Part of the difficulty is that there are no records, no therapies, and no paid professional leaders for group sessions.

Evidence, however, has begun to emerge that some of the helping behaviors that are intrinsic to the AA 12-step program are, themselves, related to improved outcomes (Emrick, 1987). In research conducted in 2002, an important role in AA, that of being a sponsor, was demonstrated to increase the likelihood of abstinence (Crape, Latkin, Laris, & Knowlton, 2002). In 2010 an assessment instrument was developed called the Service to Others in Sobriety, which holds promise for future, more rigorous scientific research on the effectiveness of AA members' helping behaviors as predictors of change in problem drinking (Pagano et al., 2010). But the helping role is only one component of the AA program. Much additional research is needed to provide clear scientific evidence to support the pronounced belief in this program among the many people it appears to have helped.

AT-RISK POPULATIONS

Generalist practice theory directs social workers to develop intervention plans based on a careful assessment of the individual client within the totality of her or his life situation. Logan, McRoy, and Freeman (1987) underscore the need for social workers to take into consideration the client's "age, ethnicity, gender, availability of other supports, and other factors such as the particular client's orientation to change and principal mode of learning" (pp. 183–184) when developing intervention plans for chemically dependent clients.

When people abuse alcohol or other substances as a reaction to grief or the overwhelming trauma of disaster or war, this seems understandable to society. Less well understood are the socioeconomic stressors that also exist. Of the various professionals who work in the substance abuse arena, social workers probably have the best understanding of these stressors. As Roffman states, "Regardless of their negative consequences, psychoactive drugs [and alcohol] are used excessively precisely because they are effective, if only temporarily, in reducing pain—including the pain of being poor" (1987, p. 482). Social work in the substance abuse field today operates from a holistic perspective that incorporates biopsychosocial as well as spiritual dimensions (Steiker & MacMaster, 2008).

Women and Children

Among the most vulnerable populations in the United States are addicted women and their children. The 2010 National Center for Health Statistics data demonstrate that a smaller percentage of women than men use alcohol or consume alcohol heavily (see Table 9.1), yet women and their children are at risk. It is estimated that only a small portion of addicted women receive services. The reasons for this vary but include an outmoded societal attitude that it is acceptable for men to drink to excess but for women, especially mothers, to drink excessively is immoral.

Downs and Miller, who have studied the effects of trauma, propose that a lifetime of traumatic abuse, which is the experience of many addicted women, "causes low self-esteem and self-disgust that presses these women into further abuse" (2002, as cited in van Wormer & Davis, 2008, p. 464). Earlier research demonstrated that women who are depressed often self-medicate with alcohol (Turnbull, 1988). Because alcohol itself is a central nervous system depressant, the result for these women is that they become further depressed. Research data from the 2005 National Survey on Drug Use and Health showed that persons who experienced major depressive episodes were statistically more likely to be dependent on alcohol or drugs than those persons who did not have this serious form of depression (Substance Abuse and Mental Health Services Administration [SAMHSA], 2006, p. 8). Often suicide ideation and serious marital and family disruption occur before depressed women seek treatment. When depression occurs, too, relapse is likely. Clearly there is a need for careful assessment and early treatment of women who would be likely to turn or return to alcohol or other drugs.

Some women need counseling, probably with a female social worker, that focuses on childhood or current experiences with violence and victimization. Family and couple's therapies are helpful to many women, as is parent training, given the guilt that addicted women experience because of their failures in this area. As early as 1994, Rhodes and Johnson reported that teaching women to accept that alcohol has taken power over their lives—which is a tenet of AA and may be more useful with men—is potentially devastating to some women. Instead, they encourage the use of empowerment approaches, helping women to acquire competence and self-esteem. Then, because addicted women are

Table 9.1   **National Center for Health Statistics 2010: Alcohol Consumption by Adults 18 Years and Over (%)**

Characteristic	Both Sexes			Male			Female		
	1997	2000	2009	1997	2000	2009	1997	2000	2009
Drinking Status									
All	100	100	100	100	100	100	100	100	100
Lifetime abstainer	21.2	24.2	20.0	14.0	17.5	13.6	27.6	30.0	25.8
Former drinker	15.7	14.4	14.6	16.2	14.8	14.8	15.3	14.2	14.6
Current drinker	63.1	61.4	65.3	69.8	67.6	71.6	57.0	55.8	59.6
Consumed Five or More Drinks on At Least 1 Day in Past Year									
Age (years):									
18–44	29.2	26.9	32.3	40.6	37.8	43.4	18.3	16.5	21.6
45–64	15.9	14.4	18.7	25.3	23.5	27.9	7.2	6.0	10.2
65 and over	4.9	3.8	5.2	9.3	7.4	9.8	1.6	1.2	1.6
Race/culture:									
White only	22.9	20.8	26.0	32.8	29.9	35.9	13.5	12.1	16.5
Black or African American only	11.7	11.6	14.2	18.4	19.8	21.5	6.5	5.2	8.4
American Indian or Alaska Native only	29.2	23.7	24.5	45.7	29.2	33.5	18.1	19.0[a]	14.9[a]
Asian only	11.4	8.8	10.8	17.8	14.1	16.7	5.2[a]	3.7[a]	5.4
Hispanic origin and race:									
Hispanic or Latino	20.4	17.3	19.9	30.9	27.9	30.4	9.7	6.8	9.2
Mexican	21.2	19.9	21.0	34.2	32.2	32.1	8.2	7.1	8.6
Not Hispanic or Latino:									
White only	23.5	21.5	27.5	33.3	30.6	37.3	14.2	13.0	18.2
Black or African American only	11.6	11.5	14.2	18.4	19.7	21.6	6.2	5.2	8.4

[a]Denotes an estimate that is not considered reliable.

Source: Adapted from the National Center for Health Statistics. (2011). Table 64 Lifetime alcohol drinking status among adults 18 years of age and over, by selected characteristics: United States, selected years 1997–2009. Table 65 Heavier drinking and drinking five or more drinks in a day among adults 18 years of age and over, by selected characteristics: United States, selected years 1997–2009. *Health, United States, 2010: With special feature on death and dying* (pp. 242–247). Hyatsville, MD.

less likely than men to have health insurance, substance abuse intervention is needed in the places such women frequent: shelters, public health departments, and even jails.

Health care systems tend to be particularly punitive toward homeless women because they lack health insurance. If inpatient addiction care can be obtained, women's guilt may be compounded by the need to place their children temporarily in foster care. Much support is needed, and social workers can help the mothers understand that they are making painful but good decisions.

Children who were neglected or abused are especially confused and vulnerable. The needs of these children must be addressed, and the children must be provided a safe environment, too. Group homes or community centers can sometimes be found that will offer nurturing posthospital care for recovering mothers and their children.

Fetal alcohol syndrome (FAS), the name given to the abnormalities in children that can result from heavy alcohol consumption during pregnancy, also places both women and children at risk. Among the abnormalities that accompany FAS are growth deficiencies, mental retardation, characteristic facial features, cleft palate, small brain, and behavioral problems. These children require special care—sometimes institutional care—for many years. Physicians who have studied FAS persons into adolescence and adulthood have found that they sustained significant attention deficit and diminished intellectual ability and had problems with judgment. Sadly, as adults these persons are also very likely to abuse and become dependent on alcohol.

According to the National Women's Health Information Center, "Prenatal alcohol exposure is one of the leading known causes of mental retardation in the Western world" (2000, p. 2). At one time, FAS was thought to affect only the children of very heavy alcohol abusers, but currently physicians are urging caution in the use of alcohol in any amounts during pregnancy. The U.S. surgeon general has revised previous recommendations and now suggests nonuse of alcohol during pregnancy and even when trying to conceive. The governments of France and Canada also advise abstinence (Brown, 2006).

The increased media visibility given to the danger of alcohol consumption during pregnancy has had beneficial effects. While decline in consumption is clear, there remain at-risk groups such as young pregnant women in the age range of 15 to 17 whose alcohol consumption in a recent study averaged 24 drinks a month (SAMHSA, 2008), placing them and their babies at high risk. Brief counseling with low-income pregnant women at Women, Infants, and Children community nutrition sites was found to be successful in improving the outlook for newborns in a study reported by O'Connor and Whaley (2007). Following counseling, the pregnant women in their study were five times more likely to abstain from alcohol than those who did not receive counseling. Babies born to the women who had participated in counseling had higher birth weights, and the newborn mortality rates were actually three times lower than those for the women who received no counseling.

Adolescent and young adult drug and alcohol use that occurs as a part of their developmental process is also of concern to parents and the community. While this use may not necessarily result in adult dependency, it may be associated with unsafe sexual activity leading to sexually transmitted diseases (such as HIV infection) and/or pregnancy as well as car accidents, drowning, and illegal activities. Government reports showed marked increase in the use of illicit drugs by 12- to 17-year-olds, from 5.3 percent in 1992 to 11.6 percent in 2002, followed by a decline to 9.3 percent in 2008, but then an increase to 10.1 percent in 2010. The most recent National Survey of Drug Use and Health also reports a slight increase in the use of marijuana and the nonmedical psychotherapeutic prescription drugs, and a slight increase in the use of hallucinogens since 2008. Among 18- to 25-year-olds, hallucinogen and marijuana use increased, while cocaine and nonmedical prescription drug use remained essentially unchanged (SAMHSA, 2011). The 18- to 25-year-old group consistently comprises—by far—the heaviest users of illicit drugs, so prevention and treatment efforts focused on these youths remain a priority.

Older Adults

Shifts take place frequently in the drugs that teens and young adults use. The frequency and amount of their alcohol and drug use, too, has changed over time. A new phenomenon is emerging, not in adolescent drug use but in the use of illicit drugs by older adults. **Baby boomers** (generally defined as persons born between 1946 and 1964) are just beginning to reach age 65, and they bring with them high lifetime usage of illicit drugs.

The 2009 National Survey on Drug Use and Health reported that among persons age 50 or older who used illicit drugs in the past year, 44.9 percent used marijuana, 33.4 percent used prescription drugs (painkillers, sedatives, etc.) for nonmedical purposes, and 6.1 percent used other illicit drugs. Interestingly, marijuana was more commonly used by the younger group, the 50- to 59 year-olds, while prescription drugs were more frequently used nonmedically by those 65 years and older. *Nonmedical use* refers to drugs obtained either without a doctor's prescription or by prescription but used only for the sensation or experience they provide. The 2011 survey noted that the illicit drug use of adults aged 50 to 59 increased from 2.7 percent in 2002 to 5.8 percent in 2010 (SAMHSA, 2011).

These findings are a bit startling because substance abuse is not usually thought of as a problem for people who are reaching retirement age. However, there is increasing concern because the physical and social changes that inevitably occur with aging will make this cohort of older adults more vulnerable to debilitating effects of current and past drug use. Compounding this is older adults' frequent use of over-the-counter medications and some inadvertent misuse of appropriately prescribed pharmaceuticals to treat existing health conditions such as arthritis, diabetes, and heart disease. The potential magnitude of the situation calls for a new focus on prevention and care planning for this emerging at-risk population.

Older adults as a group tend to respond well to treatment efforts, whether they receive individual counseling or a form of group intervention. Clients often enjoyed the mix of ages in the substance abuse groups in her social work practice, according to van Wormer. She found that: "Older clients seemed to benefit from giving advice and sharing their stories with younger group members. They also seemed to like getting personally involved in hearing of the intrigues and relationship crises of others in the group" (van Wormer & Davis, 2008, p. 264). Groups that are supportive rather than confrontational may be beneficial for some older adults. Focusing on coping with the grief and loneliness that might have precipitated drinking or drug abuse in the older adult, too, can be very helpful. Social workers' skill in rebuilding social support networks can greatly benefit lonely older adults (van Wormer).

Focusing on coping with the grief and loneliness that might have precipitated drinking or drug abuse can be very helpful.

Native Americans

The case study at the beginning of this chapter suggests that racism and poverty can be factors in substance abuse. Native American women clearly belong to several at-risk groups and, perhaps not surprisingly, they have a high rate of children born with FAS. A *Journal of General Psychology* research report indicated that Native Americans had the highest rate of alcohol use and the highest rate of FAS of all other ethnic groups studied. Note that this report is consistent with Table 9.1 in this chapter. This report cautions, however, that it is important to understand Native Americans' misuse of alcohol within the context of their history of trauma, poverty, and numerous other factors (Szlemko, Wood, & Thurman, 2006).

Figure 9.1

Source: A. P. Streissguth, R. A. LaDue, & S. P. Randels. (1988). *A manual on adolescents and adults with fetal alcohol syndrome with special reference to American Indians* (2nd ed.). Washington, DC: U.S. Department of Health and Human Services, Indian Health Service.

A hospital-based program at the Tuba City Indian Medical Center in Arizona was successful in achieving abstinence from alcohol in 19 of 21 pregnant Navajo women who were at risk of delivering alcohol-affected infants. Statistically, more Navajo women abstain from alcohol than women in the general U.S. population, but heavy alcohol consumption exists among those women and families where poverty and social problems abound. Even though it was described many years ago, the Tuba City program remains noteworthy because of its intentional incorporation of cultural sensitivity and respect, as reflected in the hiring of Navajo staff and use of the Navajo language (Masis & May, 1991). This comprehensive ethnic- and gender-sensitive program had a remarkable level of acceptance among the women it served.

FAS, associated with excessive alcohol consumption, is not the only risk factor for American Indian or Alaska Native peoples. They also have one of the highest rates of all illicit drug use. The result is exceptionally high rates of suicide, homicide, car accidents, and deaths associated with cirrhosis.

Hispanic Americans

The Hispanic population in the United States, according to the last census, is increasing more rapidly than most other population cohorts. The higher birthrate of this population results in a large youth cohort, which is an at-risk population especially among low-income families. Hispanic people have lower rates of illicit drug use (8.1 percent past-month use in 2010) than Native Americans, African Americans, or Caucasians, according to the 2010 National Survey on Drug Use and Health (SAMHSA, 2011).

Despite lower rates of illicit drug use, there is a strong relationship between drug use and HIV/AIDS among Hispanic people. The Center for Disease Control and Prevention's 2007 research suggested that Hispanic people born or living in Puerto Rico had a greater likelihood than other Hispanic persons of contracting HIV through injected drug use or through unprotected sex with persons with HIV infection or at risk of infection. New AIDS diagnosis data in this report were startling: for Hispanic/Latino men in general (not necessarily Puerto Rican), the rate was three times higher than that for White men, and for Hispanic women the rate was five times higher than that for White women.

Cultural differences between Hispanic groups are very great, yet cultural factors greatly impact behaviors as well as readiness to seek treatment. Family and a close circle of friends are strongly valued among Hispanic people but within families, cultural norms differ. Mother–son relationships, for example, tend to be central for Cubans and Mexicans. Among Puerto Ricans, mother and sibling relationships are very strong. The strongest familial relationship for Bolivians and Peruvians tends to be to their families of origin rather than to spouses or siblings (Comas-Diaz, 1986; Melus, 1980, as cited in Steiker & MacMaster, 2008). Families can serve as a protective mechanism, thus reducing the need to turn to drugs during times of crisis. That powerful sense of family pride, however, can produce overwhelming shame in persons who do engage in illicit drug use or contract HIV. It may isolate people from their families. Because of the traditional sanctions against drinking or drug use by women, this is especially relevant to those women who are minimally acculturated to the majority U.S. culture. Social workers in substance abuse practice need to be sensitive to cultural differences but also need to help support the cultural facets that sustain identity, integrity, and support that are important to Hispanic people.

African Americans

Significant efforts of African American churches and schools resulted in a marked decline in the use and abuse of alcohol by African Americans. The 2010 National Center for Health Statistics report, however, does not show the very steep decline of the African American alcohol consumption rate from nearly 60 percent in 1979 to 47.8 percent in 1997, but it does show a gradual increase to 53.2 percent in 2009 (Table 64). This decline, however, should be acknowledged because it is evidence of the success that can come from strong commitment and concerted community action. In the current report, African Americans still show a lower rate of alcohol use than White, Hispanic, or Asian American people (2010, Table 64). Despite this, African Americans continue to experience barriers to treatment facilities associated with lack of funds or health insurance. In addition, White and other ethnic professional staff often lack the cultural understanding needed to work successfully with African Americans with substance abuse disorders.

Table 9.2 provides data from the National Survey on Drug Use and Health demonstrating variations in illicit drug use according to age and ethnicity. Nearly all ethnic and age cohorts showed at least a small increase in illicit drug use in the past few years. The Native American cohort represented the only decrease in illicit drug usage. It was encouraging to note decline in illicit drug use among persons aged 12 to 17 between 2004 and 2010. In the past, significant declines in illicit drug usage seemed most evident in the years of strong economic growth in America. The current data demonstrate some increases in illicit drug use that may represent a consequence of economic recession.

Table 9.2   **National Survey on Drug Use and Health: Illicit Drug Use[a] by Persons Aged 12 or Older by Demographic Characteristics: 2004 and 2010 (%)**

| | *Time Period* | | | | | |
| | Lifetime | | Past Year | | Past Month | |
Demographic Characteristic	2004	2010	2004	2010	2004	2010
Total age	45.8	47.1	14.5	15.3	7.9	8.9
12–17	30.0[b]	25.7	21.0[c]	19.4	10.6	10.1
18–25	59.2	57.8	33.9	35.0	19.4	21.5
26 or older	45.6	48.1	10.2	11.3	5.5	6.6
Gender						
Male	50.7	52.2	16.9	18.2	9.9	11.2
Female	41.1	42.3	12.2	12.5	6.1	6.8
Hispanic origin and race						
Not Hispanic or Latino	47.3	48.8	14.7	15.3	8.0	9.1
White	49.1	50.9	15.0	15.3	8.1	8.1
Black or African American	43.3	45.1	14.6	16.8	8.7	10.7
American Indian or Alaska Native	58.4	58.4	26.2	22.6	12.3	12.1
Native Hawaiian or Other Pacific Islander	—[d]	—[d]	—[d]	10.4	—[d]	5.4
Asian	24.3	25.2	6.9	8.7	3.1	3.5
Two or more races	54.9[b]	57.4	21.0	22.4	13.3	12.5
Hispanic or Latino	35.4	37.2	12.9	15.3	7.2	8.1

[a]Illicit drugs include marijuana/hashish, cocaine (including crack), heroin, hallucinogens, inhalants, or prescription-type psychotherapeutics used nonmedically.

[b]Difference between estimate and 2005 estimate is statistically significant at the 0.01 level.

[c]Difference between estimate and 2005 estimate is statistically significant at the 0.05 level.

[d]Low precision: no estimate reported.

Source: Adapted from the Substance Abuse and Mental Health Services Administration. (2006). Table G.11 Illicit drug use in lifetime, past year, and past month among persons aged 12 or older, by demographic characteristics: Percentages, 2004, p. 234. Substance Abuse and Mental Health Services Administration. (2011). *Results from the 2010 national survey on drug use and health: Detailed tables.* NSDUH Series H-41, HHS Publication No. (SMA) 11-4658. Rockville, MD.

Research Based Practice

Practice Behavior Example: Use research evidence to inform practice

Critical Thinking Question: What questions for social work practice are prompted by the recent research findings showing some increases in illicit drug use?

Drug abuse has had a devastating impact on African American families. Drug-related family violence and crime have resulted in the need for shelter care for women and children, imprisonment, and foster care for children. Cocaine abuse has led to addictions to other drugs and also to very high rates of HIV/AIDS and other infections and diseases. Families struggle to remain intact under the pressure of drug abuse. Grandparents and even elderly great-grandparents carry heavy burdens as they take on the care of children whose parent or parents are absent from the home.

Let us now turn to some other populations who are at risk for substance abuse but for whom data on use and abuse are less readily available.

Lesbian Women and Gay Men

The government statistical reports cited for other groups record no data regarding alcohol or drug use or abuse by gay men and lesbian women. Some recent comparative data, however, are provided by Gillespie and Blackwell who found generally lower frequencies of alcohol and drug use in their 2009 study of gay, lesbian, and bisexual persons than a similar previous study conducted in 1996 by Skinner and Otis. Alcohol use in the past month by lesbian women in the 2009 study, for example, was found to be a surprising 54.2 percent compared with 72.7 percent in the 1996 study. Similarly, past-month use of cocaine by lesbian women was 2.4 percent in 1996 and only 1.2 percent in 2009. In 1996, gay men reported 80 percent past-month use of alcohol and 1.8 percent use of cocaine while only 48 percent of gay men reported past-month use of alcohol in 2009 but 5 percent use of cocaine. These studies do not represent the same level of reliability as the annual government studies; however, they offer some insight into patterns of drug and alcohol use among persons who are gay, lesbian, and bisexual.

The possibility that "oppression of gay men and lesbian women and subculture support of drinking could produce higher rates of alcoholism among them" has been proposed by Anderson, who further suggests the possibility that, "internalized homophobia results in tremendous anxiety and self-hatred, sometimes assuaged by alcohol" (1995, p. 209). Gay bars have served as places to socialize and, until the recent development of substance-free establishments, this may have hampered the efforts of gays and lesbians who are in treatment.

Among the homosexual community, Black male alcoholics are at special risk of encountering misunderstanding and negative attitudes that can interfere with treatment. Not only do some substance abuse programs and professional staff display negativity, but the African American community is sometimes not accepting of homosexuality, and some members of the gay community are racially biased. Social work intervention must help these clients deal with their substance abuse and also help them locate and link with a positive support system and integrate their sexual identity with their racial identity (Icard & Traunstein, 1987).

Persons with Disabilities

Persons with disabilities—physical, cognitive, or psychiatric—may use or abuse drugs (sometimes their own prescriptions) and alcohol just to make their lives more bearable. If they become dependent on chemical substances, treatment is complicated because it must be adapted to the situation of the specific client. Coexistence of mental illnesses and chemical dependence, known as **dual diagnosis,** requires well-coordinated treatment from both mental health and substance abuse programs. When these are not available within the same facility, careful attention must be given to ensure responsible integration of treatment.

Among the homeless or people living on the streets, it is estimated that roughly 10 to 20 percent are persons with dual diagnosis, which is actually a lower percentage than is generally believed. It is unclear whether these people became homeless because of substance abuse or whether homelessness led to substance abuse. Some are chemically dependent and have health problems and disabilities other than mental illness. It is extremely difficult for them to comply with treatment regimes or to keep scheduled appointments. Outreach work by social workers, other professionals, and volunteers is undertaken to try to bring some forms of health care to the streets. Concern about transmission of HIV infection through sharing of dirty needles has prompted needle exchange programs in some communities. Although politically controversial, these programs exist globally but are most developed in Western Europe and Australia. A 2004 WHO study involving many countries "produced convincing evidence that needle exchange programmes significantly reduce HIV infection, and no evidence that they encourage drug use" (World Health Organization, 2004, as cited in AVERT.org, 2010, Evidence section, para. 4).

BUILDING A KNOWLEDGE BASE

Social workers in virtually every setting and across all population groups encounter substance abuse. Students entering any of the social service or human service fields must prepare themselves to work with people who abuse chemical substances and with others who have been victimized or hurt by parents, spouses, friends, or employers who are dependent on drugs or alcohol.

Where do students find curriculum content on substance abuse? The response is that it permeates many of the courses in the liberal arts (courses such as sociology and psychology) and the courses taken in the social work major. Field placements may also expose students to practice with or on behalf of persons with chemical dependence and alcoholism. Some field placements will be in substance abuse treatment programs in which the entire client population has abused alcohol and/or drugs. Elective courses on alcoholism or substance abuse may also be available.

Their generalist professional education prepares BSWs to enter practice in a variety of settings with the expectation that they will continue to develop and refine their knowledge, especially in reference to the client population they serve. MSW candidates, on the other hand, add a specialization—possibly in substance abuse treatment—to their generalist practice base. An MSW with this area of specialization is more likely to take courses entirely devoted to substance abuse than is a BSW student or an MSW student who has chosen another specialization. Social workers meet their responsibility for career-long learning by continuing their education through their own research, reading, seminars, and workshops.

Professional Identity

Practice Behavior Example: Engage in career-long learning

Critical Thinking Question: Why should social workers continually build their knowledge related to substance abuse?

SUBSTANCES OF ABUSE

Because substance abuse is encountered by social workers throughout social work practice, social workers need to have an understanding of the substances that are most frequently misused and abused. Box 9.5, which provides basic information about drugs that are commonly abused, is a modified version of the classification created by the National Institute of Drug Abuse (NIDA). Box 9.5 does not include all of the substances in the NIDA classification, but, instead, it focuses on those most frequently misused. Box 9.5 is organized under two major headings: the commonly used substances and the prescription drugs that are abused.

Box 9.5   National Institute on Drug Abuse Commonly Abused Substances

Drug	Method of Administration	Potential Consequences
Cannabinoids		
Marijuana	Swallowed, smoked	Euphoria, slowed thinking, confusion, impaired balance, cough; impaired memory and learning; increased heart rate, anxiety; panic attacks; tolerance, addiction
Hashish	Swallowed, smoked	As above
Opioids and Morphine Derivatives		
Heroin	Injected, smoked, snorted	Euphoria, drowsiness, impaired coordination, dizziness, confusion, nausea, sedation, slowed or arrested breathing, endocarditis, hepatitis, HIV, addiction, fatal overdose
Opium	Swallowed, smoked	As above
Stimulants		
Cocaine	Injected, smoked, snorted	Increased heart rate, blood pressure, metabolism; feelings of exhilaration, energy, alertness; tremors; reduced appetite; irritability; anxiety, panic; paranoia; violent behavior; psychosis; insomnia; heart attack or stroke; seizures; addiction
Amphetamine	Swallowed, snorted, smoked, injected	As above
Methamphetamine	As above	
Club Drugs		
MDMA (Ecstasy, Adam, clarity, Eve, lover's speed, peace, uppers)	Swallowed, snorted, injected	Mild hallucinogenic effects; increased tactile sensitivity; empathic feelings; lowered inhibition; anxiety; chills; sweating; teeth clenching; muscle cramping; sleep disturbances; depression; impaired memory; hyperthermia; addiction
Flunitrazepam (Rohypnol; forget-me-pill, R-2, Roche)	Swallowed, snorted	Sedation; muscle relaxation; confusion; memory loss; dizziness; impaired coordination; associated with sexual assaults; addiction
Dissociative Drugs		
Ketamine (cat Valium, Special K)	Injected, snorted, smoked	Feeling of being separate from one's body and environment; impaired motor function/anxiety; tremors; numbness; memory loss; impaired memory; nausea; analgesia; delirium; respiratory depression and arrest; death

(Continued)

Box 9.5   (Continued)

Drug	Method of Administration	Potential Consequences
PCP and analogs (angel dust, boat, hog, love boat, peace pill)	Swallowed, snorted	Feeling of being separate from one's body and environment; impaired motor function/anxiety; tremors; numbness; memory loss; impaired memory; nausea; analgesia; psychosis; aggression; violence; slurred speech; loss of coordination; hallucinations
Dextromethorphan (DXM)	Swallowed	Feeling of being separate from one's body and environment; impaired motor function/anxiety; tremors; numbness; memory loss; impaired memory; nausea; euphoria; slurred speech; confusion; dizziness; distorted visual perceptions

Hallucinogens

Drug	Method of Administration	Potential Consequences
LSD (acid, blotter, cubes, microdot, yellow sunshine, blue heaven)	Swallowed, absorbed through mouth tissues	Altered states of perception and feeling; hallucinations; nausea; increased body temperature, heart rate, blood pressure; loss of appetite, sleeplessness, numbness, weakness, tremors; impulsive behavior; rapid shifts in emotion (plus, unique to LSD: flashbacks; Hallucinogen Persisting Perception Disorder)
Mescaline (buttons, cactus, mesc, peyote)	Swallowed, smoked	As above
Psilocybin (magic mushrooms, purple passion)	Swallowed	As above plus nervousness, paranoia; panic

Other Compounds

Drug	Method of Administration	Potential Consequences
Anabolic steroids (Anadrol, Oxandrin, Durabolin, Depo-Testosterone, Equipoise: roids, juice, gym candy, pumpers)	Injected, swallowed, applied to skin	Blood clotting and cholesterol changes; liver cysts; hostility and aggression; acne; adolescents: premature stoppage of growth; males: prostate cancer, reduced sperm production, shrunken testicles, breast enlargement; females: menstrual irregularities, development of beard and masculine characteristics
Inhalants (solvents: paint thinners, gasoline; glues; gases: butane, propane, aerosol propellants, nitrous oxide; laughing gas)	Inhaled through nose or mouth	Stimulation, loss of inhibition; headache; nausea; slurred speech; loss of motor coordination; muscle weakness; depression; memory impairment; damage to cardiovascular and nervous systems; unconsciousness; sudden death

Drug	Method of Administration	Potential Consequences
Prescription Drugs of Abuse:		
Depressants		
Barbiturates (Amytal, Nembutal, Seconal, Phenobarbital)	Injected, swallowed	Reduced pain and anxiety; feeling of well-being; lowered inhibitions; slowed pulse and breathing; lowered blood pressure; poor concentration/confusion; fatigue; impaired coordination, memory, judgment; respiratory depression and arrest, addiction
Benzodiazepines (other than flunitrazepam)	Swallowed	Also, for barbiturates—sedation, drowsiness/depression, unusual excitement, fever, irritability, poor judgment, slurred speech, dizziness
Fluitrazepam (Rohypnol; forget-me-pill, R-2, Roche)	Swallowed, snorted	Visual and gastrointestinal disturbances, urinary retention, memory loss of the time under the drug's effects
Dissociative Anesthetics		
Ketamine (Ketalar SV, cat Valium, Special K, vitamin K)	Injected, snorted, smoked	At high doses, delirium, depression, respiratory depression and arrest
Opioids and Morphine Derivatives		
Codeine (Empirin with Codeine, Fiorinal with Codeine, Robitussin A-C, Tylenol with Codeine)	Injected, swallowed	Pain relief; euphoria; drowsiness; respiratory depression and arrest; nausea; confusion; constipation; sedation; unconsciousness; coma; tolerance; addiction. Note: codeine has less analgesia, sedation, and respiratory depression than morphine
Fentanyl (Actiq, Duragesic, Sublimaze)	Injected, smoked, snorted	As above except for the note regarding codeine
Morphine (Roxanol, Duramorph)	Injected, swallowed, smoked	As above
Opium (laudanum, paregoric)	Swallowed, smoked	As above
Other opioid pain relievers: oxycodone, meperidine, hydromorphone, hyrocodone, propoxphene (Percodan, Percocet, Demerol, Dilaudid, Vicodin, Lortab, Lorcet, Darvon, Darvocet)	Swallowed, smoked Swallowed, injected, suppositories, chewed, crushed, snorted	As above
Stimulants		
Amphetamine (Biphetamine, Dexedrine, bennies, speed, uppers, truck drivers, black beauties, crosses, hearts)	Injected, swallowed, smoked, snorted	Increased heart rate, blood pressure, metabolism; feelings of exhilaration, energy, alertness; weight loss; rapid or irregular heart beat; heart failure; rapid breathing; hallucinations; tremor; loss of coordination; irritability; anxiousness; delirium; panic, paranoia; impulsive behavior; aggressiveness, tolerance, addiction

(Continued)

Box 9.5   (Continued)

Drug	Method of Administration	Potential Consequences
Cocaine (blow, crack, rock,snow, rock, bump; C, candy, coke, toot, Charlie)	Injected, smoked, snorted	Same as for amphetamines plus increased temperature; chest pain; respiratory failure; nausea; headaches; abdominal pain; strokes; seizures; malnutrition
Methamphetamine (Desoxyn,crystal, chalk, crystal, fire, glass, go fast, ice, meth, speed)	Injected, swallowed, smoked, snorted	Aggression, violence, psychotic behavior, memory loss, cardiac and neurological damage, impaired memory and learning, tolerance, addiction
Methylphenidate (Ritalin, JIF, MPH, R-ball, Skippy, the smart drug, vitamin R)	Injected, swallowed, snorted	Increase or decrease in blood pressure, psychotic episodes/digestive problems, loss of appetite, weight loss
Other Compounds		
Anabolic steroids (Anadrol, Oxandrin, Durabolin, Depo-Testosterone, Equipoise, roids, juice)	Injected, swallowed, applied to skin	Hypertension, blood clotting and cholesterol changes, liver cysts and cancer, kidney cancer, hostility and aggression, acne; adolescents: premature stoppage of growth; in males: prostate cancer, reduces sperm production, shrunken testicles, breast enlargement; in females: menstrual irregularities, development of beard and other masculine characteristics
		No intoxication effects. Potential health consequences: hypertension; blood clotting and cholesterol changes; liver cysts; hostility and aggression; acne; adolescents: premature stoppage of growth; males: prostate cancer, reduced sperm production, shrunken testicles, breast enlargement; females: menstrual irregularities, development of beard and masculine characteristics

Source: Adapted from U.S. Department of Health and Human Services. National Institute on Drug Abuse. (n.d.) Commonly abused drugs. Retrieved from http://www.drugabuse.gov/ DrugPages/DrugsofAbuse.html.

Alcohol is the most abused substance, but it is not a drug and therefore is not included in Box 9.5. Alcohol, often mistakenly believed to be an "up" drug, is, in reality, a depressant. It has potentially serious side effects. Withdrawal from alcohol can actually result in death. It continues to be used excessively, and it is, in fact, the major substance that is abused in the United States and many other countries today.

The cannabinoids comprise the first category in Box 9.5. Marijuana, the most frequently used drug in this category and the most commonly used of all of the illicit drugs, was used by 17.4 million people in the United States in 2010 (SAMHSA, 2011). Marijuana may produce a sense of well-being and relaxation, but it also may result in social withdrawal, anxiety, and even paranoia. It has been found to be useful in the treatment of diseases such as glaucoma and for persons suffering from cancer. Its advocates seek legalization, especially for medical use of the substance. Its opponents seek stiffer penalties for its illegal use. Hashish, made from the leaves of the hemp plant, is also a mild narcotic.

The next major category of substances that social workers should be familiar with are the opioids and morphine derivatives. They are used medicinally to deaden pain. Vicodin and oxycodone HCL, heroin, morphine, and codeine are among the more commonly used drugs in this category. Because many of these drugs are injected, they present a significant danger for the spread of AIDS and other diseases. This class of drugs can also result in physical dependence and addiction. Serious consequences such as coma and death may result from overdose.

New production methods have resulted in increased purity and potency of heroin, raising the possibility of overdose. Sometimes heroin, like cocaine, is diluted with other substances to lower its cost to users and to increase profits for drug dealers; the user cannot immediately tell if the drug has been diluted. Morphine is illegal (when not prescribed by a physician), addictive, and hazardous because of the frequent use of unsterile needles for injection. Malnutrition often occurs because of the depressant nature of the drug and because people can become so dependent on it that they are unable to take care of their own basic needs.

Stimulants are drugs that produce energy, increase alertness, and provide a sense of strength and well-being. They are sometimes taken for weight loss. Illegally obtained methamphetamines are used by students and truck drivers, among others, to avoid sleep to complete work. The resulting errors in judgment range from a poor exam grade to highway fatalities. Ice is a form of methamphetamine that can be administered by injection, swallowed, inhaled, or smoked. An overdose can cause coma and death. Addiction occurs very rapidly, sometimes after only a single use.

Cocaine, once considered a narcotic, is now classified as a stimulant. Cocaine is implicated as a cause of child abuse and neglect, family violence, suicide, and unprovoked shootings. Repeated or prolonged use of cocaine can produce physical and psychological intoxication and withdrawal symptoms, including suicide. Use of contaminated needles is of great concern. Cocaine combined with alcohol results in a dangerous level of toxicity. Crack is a less expensive pellet form of the more expensive and relatively pure powder forms of cocaine hydrochloride. "Designer drugs" are a form of stimulants. They are chemically produced drugs that differ slightly from the illegal drugs that they were formulated to replicate. Often they are many times stronger than the drugs they imitate. Their potential danger is often underestimated. In some cases a single use can cause irreversible brain damage. Ecstasy is the designer drug used—sometimes in combination with marijuana, heroin, and cocaine—in rave parties that have spread across Europe and America.

"Club drugs" comprise a wide combination of drugs used at college parties, bars, and dance clubs. Some are used to enhance the highs produced by cocaine or to reduce the negative effects of crack. One of these is rohypnol, the "date rape" drug, a tablet that can be easily crushed and put into a drink. Its immediate effect is a sense of intoxication, relaxation, and drowsiness that can last for many hours. It can be fatal when used in combination with alcohol or another depressant.

Dissociative anesthetics were actually developed to be anesthetics. They act on the brain to change the perception of pain, and they also produce a sense of detachment from reality. Some were formerly included in the hallucinogens category. Probably the most used of the dissociative anesthetics is PCP. The consequences of dissociative drug use vary from mildly pleasurable experiences to nausea, dizziness, and hallucinations.

Hallucinogens are drugs that produce sensory distortions (dreamlike experiences, visual and/or auditory effects). Heavy users of hallucinogens report flashback experiences months after the drug use. LSD, the well-publicized drug of the 1960s, is being used again today. More frequently, however, people are using a variety of other hallucinogenic chemicals that are synthesized in black-market and home laboratories and are sold on the streets.

The final major category in the classification of commonly abused drugs is called "other compounds." This includes steroids, which are sometimes used by college and professional athletes to rapidly build muscle and physical strength. Of special concern with steroids are the aggressive behaviors and the physical changes that may occur. Inhalants form the other substance in this category. People inhale (huff) such products as gasoline, ether, paint thinner, propane, and glue with mixed results. They may hope for a high or improved sexual performance, but they may experience blindness, conjunctivitis (eye infection), or simple disappointment. Youths aged 10 to 17 are especially vulnerable.

The second half of Box 9.5 depicts the prescription drugs that are among the most frequently abused. The 2010 National Survey on Drug Use and Health reported that 7.0 million persons had used psychotherapeutic drugs nonmedically in the previous month, data which were unchanged from the two previous years (SAMHSA, 2011). Notice that there is considerable crossover between the substances of abuse and the prescription drug abuse sections of Box 9.5. Prescription drug abuse is of increasing concern in the United States.

Depressants, which were not included in the substances of abuse list, are drugs that depress the central nervous system. Physicians rely on these drugs to treat various conditions such as epilepsy and anxiety, and for their anesthetic properties. Barbiturates (downers) are generally obtained through a physician's prescription. Most frequently, barbiturates are taken in pill form. Their danger is greatest if injected because of their immediate and powerful effect. Withdrawal has the potential for mental disorder, seizures, and even death. Barbiturates are often the drugs used in suicides and in mercy killings of animals as well as humans.

Tranquilizers and sleeping medications are milder depressants that are among the most frequently prescribed substances in the United States. While they can create psychological dependence, they are most hazardous when combined with alcohol or other drugs, causing a condition referred to as **potentiation**. This term denotes the dramatically increased potential for serious consequences to the health and well-being of the user. Social workers have learned to inquire about prescription drug use when obtaining a drinking history. When central nervous system depressants are combined or taken with alcohol, they can be truly lethal. Women—perhaps because they see physicians more frequently than men do—are more likely than men to have prescriptions for the minor tranquilizers. They are more likely to become involved in **cross-addiction**, that is, addiction to two or more substances at the same time.

The remaining pharmaceuticals on the prescription drugs of abuse list also appeared earlier on the Box 9.5 substances of abuse list, and they have already been described. As this section of the chapter concludes, we should recall that chemical substances are not the only form of addiction. Worldwide, compulsive gambling has led to bankruptcy for millions of persons. Sexual addictions have wreaked havoc in many families. Computer addiction is on the rise.

ENVIRONMENTAL PERSPECTIVES

The previous section of this chapter identified some of the major substances that are abused and explained the concerns and hazards of those substances. Earlier in the chapter, we identified populations that are at risk for substance abuse. Building on this groundwork, we now consider the role environment plays in substance abuse. In social work, it is important to think about the interactions between persons and their environment. Sometimes environments—neighborhoods and communities—have profoundly negative and harmful impacts on people, but the environment also has the potential for being nurturing and supportive of human well-being.

Neighborhoods were the focus of a New York City ecological study that linked environmental conditions to deaths resulting from substance abuse. The study found that a low level of homeownership in certain city census tracts was correlated with exceptionally high rates of drug abuse and with what the study referred to as "drug dependence mortality." In census tracts with the very lowest levels of homeownership, deaths from substance abuse were exceptionally high. The researchers' explanation for this finding was that in the absence of homeownership, levels of social control and social stability fell dramatically, leaving whole neighborhoods without needed human support and connectivity. The researchers also looked at land use and housing structures that created environmental conditions inviting drug usage. The study demonstrated that the presence of boarded-up, vacant homes (which intensified drug activity) was also significantly related to the high level of substance abuse deaths within these census tracts (Hannon & Cuddy, 2006).

In census tracts with the very lowest levels of homeownership, deaths from substance abuse were exceptionally high.

Studies such as this one of specific New York City neighborhoods teach us something important about the toxic effect of neighborhood and community land usage, but they also hold clues to how these environments can become stronger and healthier for people. The drug dependence mortality study concludes by recommending policy initiatives that would increase homeownership. "Policies geared toward increasing homeownership in economically disadvantaged areas may contribute to decreases in drug dependence by encouraging community pride and decreasing levels of neighborhood social disorganization" (Hannon & Cuddy, 2006, p. 461). Creating policies or programs that reduce the number of boarded-up, abandoned buildings that facilitate drug activity was also recommended. The report authors concluded wisely: "While most policies addressing drug dependence focus exclusively on the rehabilitation of the individual, the revitalization and rebuilding of neighborhoods may also be a worthwhile approach" (p. 461).

The economic recession that the United States has experienced over the past several years has resulted in unprecedented bank foreclosure of millions of homes. As foreclosed homes are abandoned and boarded up, they become an environmental hazard for entire neighborhoods. They are broken into, fires occur, and they become a location for illicit drug activity. Community action groups, often organized by churches or social service organizations, have taken initiative in several cities to protect the environment through volunteer neighborhood cleanup efforts, block watches, and community policing. In Milwaukee, Wisconsin, an organization known as Common Ground is challenging the banks that now own these properties to exercise social responsibility in caring for the homes and providing security. With churches, college and university faculty and students, and neighbors of foreclosed homes vigorously united in demanding action, the banks have begun to respond, thus decreasing the environmental threat to entire neighborhoods.

This brief introduction of the ecology of substance abuse is now broadened through a cross-national review of several countries' efforts to deal with substance abuse issues.

GLOBAL DIFFERENCES IN PREVENTION AND TREATMENT

Globally, the supply and demand of illicit drugs is dealt with very differently. Singapore, for example, has achieved remarkable success through drug laws that are considered among the strictest in the world. The ironfisted policies of Singapore are unique in the Asian region. Anyone found guilty of trafficking in large amounts of dangerous drugs is subject to the death penalty. Drug abusers identified through urine tests or medical exams are subjected to mandatory treatment including "cold turkey detoxification" in a drug rehabilitation center for up to 36 months. The community-based portion of the rehabilitation program uses minimal counseling or social work intervention; instead, worship and religious education are emphasized, with Islam, Buddhism, and Christianity as the major religions utilized. There is also a well-organized school-based prevention program in which thousands of designated students are responsible for spreading an antidrug message to friends, schoolmates, and family members (Osman, 2002; SANA, 2008; Teo, 2010).

Germany stands in contrast to Singapore. Germany has a longtime history of alcohol and drug tolerance and has used social workers in drug prevention and treatment programs since the early 1900s. In schools, social workers are a part of the prevention effort. Teams of social work experts assist teachers in preparing educational programs for children. Outpatient treatment programs are said to be dominated by social workers, but they also provide case management and individual and group treatment in inpatient facilities, although social workers are only about 30 percent of inpatient staff. Social workers developed harm reduction techniques and helped establish "low-threshold" facilities that are easily accessible and that offer both day and night programs. Germany has an extensive network of treatment facilities. Alcohol treatment is handled in a rather traditional, counseling-focused manner, with detoxification, if necessary, completed in a general hospital. Drug treatment in cities generally includes "the distribution of condoms and sterile needles; day and night shelters; injecting rooms; individual counseling and case management; medical services, including emergency treatment; methadone dispensaries; and treatment of HIV-infections and other chronic illnesses" (Vogt, 2002, p. 76). Persons may be sentenced for drug law violations including the use or sale of marijuana.

Germany and the Netherlands as well, utilize an environmental approach to a greater degree than a clinical approach to the treatment of substance abuse. Social workers are vitally involved in urban regeneration and the development of antipoverty programs. A great deal of emphasis is placed on community work (Harrison & Straussner, 2002). The Netherlands has historically had one of the most open and liberal substance use/abuse environments, with a generous harm reduction program that documented positive effects on the health and the mortality rates of persons addicted to hard drugs. The environmental approach is aimed at rehabilitating deteriorating city neighborhoods, reducing the poverty of inhabitants, improving safety, and lowering the crime rates in larger cities. Tolerance is also apparent in the continued growth of user-friendly places where people can take drugs in a safe environment in Rotterdam; some provide outreach and case management services. Rotterdam also has a facility designed for elderly drug addicts to receive their drugs in a secure location that meets their special needs as older adults. Social workers are involved across the broad range of Dutch substance abuse programs (de Koning & de Kwant, 2002).

The social welfare policies of each country govern the availability and nature of substance abuse programs. These policies reflect the values of people within the country. In the Netherlands, we see increasing concern about public safety, resulting in a small shift toward legally mandating treatment. Ireland appears to be shifting away from a clinical approach to treatment (a U.S. model) toward increased focus on changing the environment. There also appears to be less support for use of law enforcement and prison sentences to treat addiction in a number of countries, including Australia and the United Kingdom (Harrison & Straussner, 2002).

Dealing with the supply of illicit drugs remains a challenge globally and is understood differently across cultures and nations. Many European countries use prevention and harm reduction programs to decrease demand for drugs. The United States favors incarceration for the use of or dealing in illicit drugs. Singapore uses capital punishment. Today small, poor African countries like Guinea-Bissau are being used as distribution locations by powerful drug suppliers to move cocaine and other drugs from dealers in South America into the hands of international traffickers. A 2010 *New York Times* article described the way in which "Guinea-Bissau has emerged as a nodal point in three-way cocaine-trafficking operations linking producers in South America with users in Europe" (Traub, 2010, para 1). Sometimes the cargo brought in by the planes carries guns as well as cocaine and other drugs. Extreme poverty and the corruption of local officials complicate the efforts of United Nations, Interpol, the European Union, and the United States to resolve the problem.

Dealing with the supply of illicit drugs remains a challenge globally and is understood differently across cultures and nations.

U.S. SOCIAL WELFARE POLICY RELATED TO SUBSTANCE ABUSE

A brief review of history may help us understand how the United States arrived at its current social welfare policy concerning substance abuse and addiction. If we begin with the early colonists of the United States, we find that their ship's log appears to provide evidence that it was the Pilgrims' diminished supply of food and beer that resulted in their decision to land at Plymouth in 1620 (Kinney & Leaton, 1995).

During the late 19th century, the Industrial Revolution brought social turbulence and imposed strains on normal family life in the United States. Morphine, cocaine, and alcohol became more available through new means of production, distribution, and marketing. In the view of many who joined the social reform movement that had begun in the mid-1800s, domestic violence was incited by alcohol abuse. Women in those years were almost totally dependent on their husbands as providers for themselves and their children. Letters and diaries from the 1870s provide ample evidence of the wife and child abuse that brought thousands of women into the temperance movement (Lacerte & Harris, 1986).

The Woman's Christian Temperance Union (WCTU) was founded in Cleveland in 1874 to pursue social reform, education, and legislation regarding alcohol abuse, which came increasingly to be seen as the root of all evil. Together with another powerful prohibitionist organization, the Anti-Saloon League, the WCTU rallied the vote and was largely responsible in 1919 for the passage of the Eighteenth Amendment (commonly referred to as the Volstead Act), which prohibited the manufacture and sale of alcoholic beverages in the United States. However, Prohibition of the 1920s proved to be neither enforceable by the authorities nor fully acceptable to American society. It was repealed in 1933 by the Twenty-First Amendment. With the repeal of Prohibition, alcohol use increased steadily until the 1970s, then leveled off, and began to decline by the 1980s.

Drug regulation in the United States was also influenced by the social reform movement that brought the WCTU into existence and that resulted in Prohibition. Opium was widely used in many parts of the world by the 1850s, and U.S. merchants joined in the lucrative opium trade. Drug use in general was so common that before 1900 narcotics were available from grocery stores and over the counter in pharmacies. Women used them to relieve discomfort related to menstruation and gave their children cough syrup containing opium. In fact, Coca-Cola's original formula contained cocaine.

It was not until the Harrison Narcotics Act of 1914 that the use of narcotics for nonmedical purposes was prohibited. The public, which never completely supported the banning of alcohol, did support the suppression of narcotics. Federal laws resulted in increasing control of narcotics, with the 1956 Narcotic Drug Control Act providing the stiffest of penalties, including the death sentence for anyone convicted of selling heroin to a minor.

The 1960s saw a massive increase in the use of drugs. Social reform efforts by the end of the decade resulted in the Comprehensive Drug Abuse Prevention and Control Act of 1970. Recodification of the substances separated alcohol and tobacco from drugs with a high potential for abuse; this left heroin, LSD, and marijuana in a category that brought penalties, including imprisonment, for their sale (1988 legislation added penalties for possession). Prevention and treatment funding was appropriated by the 1970 act, although alcoholism treatment centers had actually been developed shortly after the founding of AA in 1935.

When the introduction of psychoactive drugs made methadone and antabuse available to treat heroin and alcohol abuse, new treatment programs emerged. The public became increasingly convinced that substance abuse was treatable. Then, with the advent of the Reagan administration in the 1980s, the role of the federal government shifted away from funding prevention and treatment and toward use of law enforcement and prison sentences to curtail the use and sale of drugs. Already overcrowded correctional facilities could not accommodate a rush of new offenders, and new facilities soon filled to capacity. In election after election, the public supported prison sentences as an answer to the perceived drug problem. The prison industry grew markedly, and it remains a growth industry today.

Despite the perception of the public, use of illicit drugs in the United States has actually declined markedly over time. The National Survey on Drug Use and Health changed its research design in 2001, making comparisons with previous years' data somewhat less accurate; however, some trends remain evident. Back in 1979, when the highest illicit drug usage was reported, 14.1 percent of the population of the United States used illicit drugs in the previous month (SAMHSA, 1998). By 2010 that figure was 8.9 percent of the U.S. population over 12 years of age (SAMHSA, 2011).

The most constructive handling of alcohol and drug concerns remains a potent issue in politics, especially in the current politically conservative environment. Substance abuse is often linked in the media with crime and has been used to promote lengthy prison sentences. But political support for the

---

Box 9.6   Up for Debate

Proposition: Use of marijuana should be legalized for medical purposes.

Yes	No
Legalization would allow doctors to practice medicine more humanely, relieving pain and reducing nausea and vomiting caused by anticancer drugs.	There is no empirical evidence that affirms the medicinal value of marijuana to humans.
Hundreds of patients and their doctors have filed applications seeking compassionate use of marijuana.	If the use of marijuana for medical purposes were legalized, there would immediately be a demand to legalize it for recreational purposes.
A synthetic form of marijuana, Marinol, is available, but patients have found it to be less effective than marijuana in relieving pain.	Tax dollars should be spent on research to find new alternatives to marijuana.
Marijuana isn't nearly as potentially harmful as numerous other prescription medications in current use.	The Drug Enforcement Administration is firmly opposed to making this illicit, potentially addictive drug available.

War on Drugs continues, with billions of taxpayer dollars funding that war with Coast Guard vessels, assault helicopters, and NASA satellites in addition to all of the local law enforcement resources (McNeece & DiNitto, 2005). Meantime, of course, billions of dollars are paid in federal excise taxes by people who use and abuse legal substances of addiction, primarily alcohol. The government has become dependent itself—on income from alcohol—and Native American tribes as well as state governments rely on income from legal, although potentially addictive, gambling. Legalizing the use of marijuana remains an unresolved issue. Struggle over the legalization of marijuana for medical purposes (see Box 9.6) is a reflection of the interconnectedness of health and drug policies.

SOCIAL JUSTICE, HUMAN RIGHTS, AND THE WAR ON DRUGS

Sometimes it is difficult to know why Americans are attracted to the notion of war or believe that war is the best approach to problem resolution. We've had a war on poverty, a war on terrorism, a war on drugs, and assorted other wars. The War on Drugs was initiated by President Richard Nixon in 1971 to fight the use and trafficking of illegal drugs. With the support of Congress, Nixon increased the criminal penalty for drug dealing. Subsequent presidents and Congresses have supported that war by stiffening penalties for use as well as selling drugs and by massively funding legal enforcement for the interdiction of drugs coming into the country and imprisonment for drug abusers and drug traffickers within the United States (McNeece & DiNitto, 2005).

The War on Drugs has been popular with Congress to the extent that even the U.S. Sentencing Commission began to question some of the legislation that had been passed. According to van Wormer and Davis (2008), the War on Drugs includes several dimensions. The first relates to the mandatory minimum prison sentences for possession as well as sale of drugs. Incorporated in this dimension is the criminalization of drugs. This focuses the efforts of that war on use of the courts and prisons instead of the approach taken by some other countries that focus efforts on prevention and treatment (criminalization versus medicalization). The final dimension is the legislative as well as financial support for international interdiction with billions of dollars spent to intercept drugs in South American countries and in border surveillance.

The social justice issue relates to the lives of people who have been affected by the criminalization of drug use in the United States. Even though the War on Drugs has been popular, people in the United States are less and less supportive of incarceration for minor drug offenses. As long ago as 2001, it was reported that "the number of people entering prison for drug offenses had increased by more than *1,000 percent*" in the preceding 2 decades (Justice Policy Institute, as cited by McNeece & DiNitto, 2005, p. 241, emphasis added).

A huge increase in sentencing and phenomenal growth of the U.S. prison industry was fueled by the Anti-Drug Abuse Act of 1986, which established a framework of mandatory minimum prison sentences for offenses related to specific drugs. This law reserved the harshest sentences for crack cocaine offenses. In 2007 the U.S. Sentencing Commission requested that Congress enact a remedy for the "100-to-1" law that differentiated between crack cocaine and powder cocaine, providing a minimum 5-year mandatory sentence for a first-time offense (possession or trafficking) involving 5 grams or more of crack cocaine compared with the same minimum sentence for 500 grams or more of the powder form of cocaine. Crack cocaine is most used by poorer, often inner-city, African American people, while the powder form of cocaine is more frequently associated with White, higher-income, and often rural populations. The African American prison population grew significantly as a result of the War on Drugs.

The Obama administration, which vigorously advocated for change, succeeded in passing the Fair Sentencing Act of 2010. Subsequently the U.S. Sentencing Commission issued guidelines for mandatory sentencing, which dramatically revised the previous "100 to 1" to the equivalent of "18 to 1," or 18 grams of crack cocaine to 1 gram of powder cocaine. The guidelines eliminated the mandatory minimum sentence for simple possession of crack cocaine. The new mandatory sentence of 5 years requires a minimum of 28 grams of crack cocaine related to a conviction for manufacture or trafficking, compared with only 5 grams of crack in the previous law. The amount of crack cocaine for a 10-year sentence was changed from 50 to 280 grams of crack cocaine. The change in the levels of crack cocaine needed to trigger imprisonment sentencing, it was noted, would impact approximately 3,000 people each year, 80 percent of whom were African Americans ("Major Victory," 2010; U.S. Sentencing Commission, 2010).

The social justice impact of the new sentencing guidelines would have been more dramatic if the guidelines had directed that persons currently serving prison sentences for low-level crack cocaine offenses were also covered by the 2010 Fair Sentencing Law. The Sentencing Project, a Washington-based research and reform organization, estimated that reduced prison sentences could affect approximately 19,500 persons and potentially save up to $1 billion in federal prison costs, and the early release of significant numbers of African American prisoners could actually reduce racial disparity in federal prisons (The Sentencing Project, 2007). (More discussion of the impact of drug offenses on prison populations can be found in Chapter 11 of this book.)

Other human rights and social justice issues emerge from the field of child welfare. Recent research has demonstrated that addiction is a disease of the brain, and new technologies can now demonstrate the physical healing of the human brain during recovery (NIDA, 2010a). Despite these new scientific findings, juvenile courts that have jurisdiction in cases of child abuse or neglect still utilize guidelines from the 1997 Adoption and Safe Families Act that provide very limited time for parents to demonstrate recovery in order to have their children returned from foster care or to avoid permanent termination of their parental rights. Social workers in child welfare are often challenged as they try to ensure safe, secure homes for children with their own families while helping parents to obtain and utilize needed substance abuse treatment and still meet the time frame required by the law (Center for Substance Abuse Treatment, 2010).

SUMMARY

The setting for the chapter's case study is an emergency shelter, and the social worker is a BSW who is herself a recovering alcoholic. Madeleine Johnson's disclosure that she, too, is a recovering alcoholic helps Dan Graves to trust her and decide to continue AA attendance while at the shelter. The client's housing, social, medical, financial, and educational needs are addressed, and the social worker then extends her concern to Dan's relationship with his wife, Angie.

The context for social work in this field of practice is explained through a brief discussion of history that acknowledges the contributions of Mary Richmond and other pioneers in substance abuse practice. In today's practice, substance abuse and addiction problems are found across all fields of practice. The roles and responsibilities of social workers are identified. The populations that are most at risk because of substance abuse, such as women and children, are introduced.

As prevention and treatment programs evolve and change in the United States, it is often helpful to look at the goals and philosophy of services being offered in other countries, including services that emphasize the harm reduction model. This chapter introduces AA, a program that has become global in scope. The substances most frequently abused in the United States are identified. In addition to alcohol, the most commonly abused substances are described. Environmental perspectives are explored.

Social welfare policy and the provision of funding for prevention and treatment programs are described in relation to the political context of U.S. society. Changes being made to the sentencing for crack cocaine offenses are discussed, along with the complex issues of parents whose addiction results in the potential loss of their children if they are unable to satisfy court requirements. These circumstances represent social justice and human rights concerns of social workers today. Today there is a resurgence of interest in substance abuse among social work students. This is hopeful because the profession will look to them in the future to create humane programs that will be sensitive to the needs of women and children, minority groups, gay and lesbian clients, persons with disabilities, and other at-risk persons. They will have opportunities to educate the public and to advocate for laws and policies that advance social justice. It will be important for them to understand addiction and to sustain the "never-give-up" attitude of a skilled professional in this field of practice.

PRACTICE TEST The following questions will test your knowledge of the content found within this chapter. For additional assessment, including licensing-exam type questions on applying chapter content to practice behaviors, visit **MySearchLab.**

1. What event precipitated a major shift in the way alcohol dependence was treated by helping professionals?

   a. In 1970 the Comprehensive Alcohol Abuse and Alcoholism Prevention, Treatment, and Rehabilitation law was passed by the U.S. Congress.

   b. In 1981 Ronald Regan was elected president, and he significantly reduced federal funding for substance abuse prevention and treatment.

   c. In a 1956 article in *Social Casework*, Catherine Peltenburg encouraged helping professionals to examine their own attitudes regarding the moral implications of alcoholism.

   d. In 1956 the American Medical Association proclaimed alcoholism as a disease.

2. The WHO Alcohol Use Disorders Identification Test is NOT _____.

   a. an assessment tool that has been validated across six different countries

   b. a complete and comprehensive method for understanding clients who present with a potential alcohol use problem

   c. an assessment tool comprised of 10 questions, which assesses hazardous drinking behavior, dependent drinking behavior, and harmful drinking behavior

   d. often used in combination with other substance abuse and mental health assessment methods

3. The Harm Reduction Model _____.

   a. aims to reduce the damage associated with using chemical substances

   b. aims to encourage clients to completely abstain from using drugs or alcohol

   c. exclusively prescribes Methadone and collects used needles from clients

   d. is widely employed in the United States

4. Which of the following statements is TRUE?

   a. Nearly all people who live on the streets in metropolitan cities abuse drugs and/or alcohol.

   b. In order to be effective in working with substance abusers the social worker should be in recovery from addiction to alcohol and/or drugs.

   c. A social worker's effectiveness with clients who abuse drugs and/or alcohol is based on his or her application of skill and knowledge.

   d. According to a 2006 NASW study, only about 30% of social workers work with substance abuse–related issues in their practice, regardless of the agency setting.

5. Project MATCH found that _____.

   a. cognitive-behavioral therapy is the most effective substance abuse treatment approach

   b. 12-step programs are the most effective approach to resolve substance abuse problems

   c. cognitive-behavioral therapy, motivational enhancement therapy, and 12-step programs are relatively equally effective in sustaining substance abuse recovery

   d. motivational enhancement therapy is the most effective substance abuse treatment approach

6. A social worker in an inpatient substance abuse treatment center would likely employ the following intervention strategies with a client experiencing similar circumstances to Dan Graves.

   a. Methadone, needle exchange, and program development.

   b. Therapeutic community living, psychoeducational group, and mental health treatment.

   c. Confrontational group treatment, Narcotics Anonymous, and attendance at community education seminars.

   d. Detoxification, group therapy, and family counseling.

7. Consider your role as a generalist social worker in an inpatient substance abuse treatment center exclusively designed for women. Identify specific assessment, intervention, and evaluation issues the social worker should consider that are unique to women.

Reinforce what you learned in this chapter by studying videos, cases, documents, and more available at **www.MySearchLab.com.**

Watch and Review

Watch these Videos

* Tolerating Ambiguity in Resolving Conflicts
* Contracting with the Client to Select an Evidence-Based Therapy
* Assessment

Read and Review

Read these Cases/Documents

Δ Carrie

Δ Frank

Δ Oliver

Explore and Assess

Explore these Assets

World Health Organization—http://www.who.int/en/

Office of National Drug Control Policy—http://www.whitehousedrugpolicy.gov/

National Institute on Drug Abuse—http://www.nida.nih.gov/nidahome.html

National Institute on Alcohol Abuse and Alcoholism—http://www.niaaa.nih.gov/Pages/default.aspx

Substance Abuse and Mental Health Services Administration—http://www.samhsa.gov/

Assess Your Knowledge

Assess your knowledge with a variety of topical and chapter assessment.

Conclude your assessment by completing the chapter exam.

* = CSWE Core Competency Asset
Δ = Case Study

Social Work with Older Adults

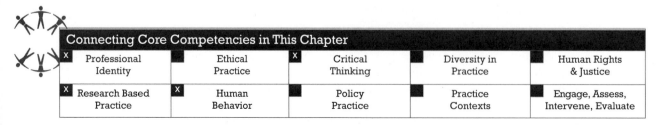

Connecting Core Competencies in This Chapter				
X Professional Identity	■ Ethical Practice	X Critical Thinking	■ Diversity in Practice	■ Human Rights & Justice
X Research Based Practice	X Human Behavior	■ Policy Practice	■ Practice Contexts	■ Engage, Assess, Intervene, Evaluate

Abbie Heinrich

A loud voice wailed persistently. Pat Smythe, BSW, who was toiling over some complicated paperwork at Oak Haven Nursing Home, tried to ignore it at first. He suspected the voice belonged to Abbie Heinrich. Abbie frequently turned on her call light and then yelled if help didn't come quickly. The care staff, occupied with other patients, took time to respond. To make matters worse, Abbie sometimes hit her call light button by accident. Rheumatoid arthritis had left her arms and legs severely contracted so that her movements were clumsy. Aides who responded to Abbie's light sometimes found they weren't needed. So they might ignore the light, muttering, "There she goes again."

Abbie's voice began to take on a hoarse, desperate tone. Pat decided to check on her himself. He put his paperwork aside and headed down the long hallway. He found a frail old woman lying flat on her back with her eyes closed but mouth wide open, emitting insistent cries.

"Abbie!" Pat called loudly, as she was hard of hearing. "What's going on?"

Abbie's eyes flew open, a startlingly clear blue beneath her crown of silver hair, direct and challenging. "Nobody comes when I turn on my call light," she accused, as articulate as any member of the staff. "I turned my light on over half an hour ago."

"I'm really sorry, Abbie," Pat said sincerely. "The aides must be very busy today. What do you need?"

"A pain pill," Abbie responded. "My back is hurting something terrible today." "I'll stop at the nursing station and let them know, Abbie," Pat said soothingly. After a few gentle assurances, he left to find assistance.

Pat found the charge nurse for Abbie's floor, Cindy Murphy, RN, down the hall and told her about the request for a pain pill. Cindy said thoughtfully, "You know, Pat, Abbie has been asking for a lot more pain medication lately. Maybe we should reevaluate her level of need."

"She is due for a staffing soon," Pat replied. "Let's talk about her pain medication at the next meeting."

Pat was responsible for organizing quarterly meetings for all 80 of his clients, so he sent notices to Abbie's county social worker, Helen Haines, and to Abbie's only "family," a community volunteer named Harriet Locke who served as her **power of attorney** for health care. He checked back with Cindy, the nurse, and was able to schedule a meeting time that would work for everyone.

Organizing meetings took a lot of Pat's time, but his work responsibilities comprised a great deal more. He held conferences with families to help them understand issues such as living wills and powers of attorney. He mediated roommate disputes; counseled patients with personal problems; made referrals to other departments of the nursing home and to external resources, such as clinical social workers or psychiatrists; filled out numerous forms required by private **insurance** plans, Medicaid, and Medicare; and even, on occasion, used his handyman skills. For example, Pat had become proficient at cleaning filters in hearing aids and changing batteries, tasks too small to refer to the maintenance department. Needless to say, there was no such thing as a typical day for Pat Smythe at the nursing home.

Helen Haines, BSW, worked for the Department of Human Services in the rural county where Abbie Heinrich was born and raised. Helen was assigned to the unit serving people with developmental disabilities. Many of her 60 clients lived in family care homes out in the community. Helen was responsible for monitoring the care they received. Besides consulting with her individual clients, Helen needed to cultivate professional relationships with biological families, family care home staff, group home managers and staff, sheltered workshop managers and staff, state Developmental Disability Services Office personnel, social workers in nursing homes such as Oak Haven, and the like. Her work was complex and required facilitating cooperation among many different community agencies and staff to secure the best possible care for her clients. Helen's job title was **case manager**, but in addition to "managing cases," she frequently was involved in community organization work. For example, she often testified at county and state budgetary hearings, describing the need for additional services. She sometimes took clients with her to tell their stories. It distressed her that so many local residents attending the hearings opposed additional services for their vulnerable fellow citizens because of the fear of higher taxes.

A growing proportion of Helen's clients with disabilities were older adults. She found it necessary to consult regularly with social workers in nursing homes where many of her older clients resided. Once every year, for example, all nursing home clients had to be reassessed according to Medicaid regulations to make sure their placements and levels of care were appropriate.

Helen met with Pat Smythe at Oak Haven Nursing Home more frequently than she met with most nursing home workers. That was because Helen served as Abbie's power of attorney for financial matters, and also because Abbie Heinrich was an unusual case. She had absolutely no family left, and while totally bedridden, she was mentally sharp and needed to socialize. Only social workers were available to check that Abbie had sufficient clothing, to purchase personal toiletries, or to buy the occasional box of chocolates Abbie loved. Helen took more time helping Abbie than she actually had, meaning that she sometimes visited the old woman on her own time. The county discouraged case managers from visiting "unfunded clients" by assigning large case loads. Abbie was classified as an "unfunded client" because the county could not receive partial reimbursement from the state for the cost of supervisory visits by one of its case managers. Only clients participating in special programs providing "community care" were eligible for state funding (this will be explained in more detail later).

Professional Identity

Practice Behavior Example: Social workers attend to professional roles and boundaries

Critical Thinking Question: Given the NASW Code of Ethics' concern about professional "boundaries," do you think that Helen's relationship and services to Abbie Heinrich were professionally ethical? Why or why not?

Helen knew that she was going beyond the requirements of her job description by visiting Abbie regularly. She also knew that in some ways she had a dual relationship with the elderly woman, a genuine closeness as well as a worker–client relationship, and that the social work Code of Ethics counseled caution with respect to dual relationships. But Helen had learned from experience that Abbie was much less depressed about her dependent condition when she received regular visits, and practically speaking, Abbie needed someone to buy clothing and other personal items for her. The National Association of Social Workers (NASW) Code of Ethics states that the social worker's primary ethical responsibility is to promote the well-being of clients. Helen was doing just that.

Helen knew her attention and **advocacy** were crucial for Abbie. In the recent past she had advocated on Abbie's behalf with a psychiatrist, as the psychiatrist had prescribed medication for anxiety that gave Abbie terrible nightmares. Abbie had asked the psychiatrist to stop prescribing this medication, but instead he had prescribed an additional medication that was supposed to quell the nightmares. It didn't, and Helen feared from her extensive experience with older clients that two strong medications would be too much for Abbie's frail body. She discussed this problem with the psychiatrist, but he was unwilling to heed either her or Abbie's concerns. Finally, Helen persuaded Abbie's regular physician to take over all medication; this physician listened to Helen's suggestions, and at last, Abbie could sleep again.

Helen knew Abbie needed her services, but still, given her ever-increasing work load, she had recently told the frail old woman that she might have to cut back on visits in the future. Abbie had been a client of Helen's county Department of Human Services for nearly 25 years. An only child, she had been crippled with polio when she was 3 years old. Her parents had cared for her at home for nearly 50 years, but then her mother had died and her father became too frail to carry on alone. County social workers placed Abbie in a group home where she had thrived. Abbie even participated in a sheltered workshop for a time and became a favorite because of her active mind and strong sense of humor. But, cruelly, disease struck again, this time in the form of rheumatoid arthritis. The group home could no longer meet Abbie's physical needs. At that time, Helen had hoped to place Abbie in a skilled family care home, but Abbie now required 24-hour care. She needed to be turned regularly throughout the night to prevent bed sores, as she could no longer turn herself. If Abbie were to be placed in a skilled family care home and participate in a community day care program, the state would pay 60 percent of the cost, but the county would have to fund 40 percent. The county's portion would run more than $60,000 annually. The county, unfortunately, was having budgetary problems because more and more **frail elderly** and disabled people were requiring assistance. So Helen was told to place Abbie in a nursing home where Medicaid, funded by the federal government and the state, would pay the whole bill.

Helen had recently asked Pat Smythe if he could help her find a volunteer for Abbie, as Abbie's former power of attorney for health care, a retired social worker, was moving away. A new power of attorney was needed. Although Helen served as Abbie's power of attorney for financial matters, county policy would not allow her to take on both roles due to potential conflict of interest. Pat turned to the Volunteer Department, but there was no one available. He then tried the Department of Pastoral Care, and found Harriet Locke.

When the date for Abbie's staffing meeting arrived, Pat Smythe, Cindy Murphy, Helen Haines, and Harriet Locke all met at the old woman's bedside. Because Abbie was alert and capable, she was an integral part of her own staffing meeting. Pat initiated the discussion.

"Hello, Abbie," he began conversationally. "How are you today?"

"Not so good," Abbie replied. "The pain is bad again today."

"Where does it hurt, Abbie?" Pat asked.

"My back, mostly," she replied.

"On a level of 1 to 10, where '1' means no pain and '10' means such strong pain you can't bear it, where would you say your pain is today?" Pat inquired.

"It's about a 7," Abbie replied.

At this point Cindy, the nurse, joined the conversation. "Is your pain worse today than it was yesterday, Abbie?" she asked.

"It was about the same yesterday," Abbie replied. "My back hurts all the time."

The high pain level concerned everyone present, and it was decided that Cindy would consult with Abbie's doctor. Perhaps the pain medication needed to be changed or provided on a regular, scheduled basis.

Pat then asked Abbie if she had any other issues she wanted to discuss. Abbie complained that the nursing home staff were slow in responding to her call light. Cindy apologized, explaining that staff were busy but promising to ask the aides to respond to the light more quickly. Next, Abbie requested a different roommate, one that she could talk with, as her current roommate was deaf. She then remarked that her own hearing aid wasn't working properly and that she was almost out of her favorite hand lotion. Two of her best blouses hadn't returned from the laundry, and she was afraid they were lost.

Pat promised to investigate the whereabouts of the blouses and to check the hearing aid himself. He promised to have the hearing aid representative who came to Oak Haven every week take a look at the device if he himself couldn't fix it. Pat explained to Abbie that he couldn't provide a different roommate, however—there was no one else available. Softly, as an aside that Abbie couldn't hear, Pat explained to the others that Abbie needed a deaf roommate as she yelled so often that her two former roommates had requested different rooms.

Helen promised to purchase hand lotion and new hearing aid batteries using Abbie's tiny Medicaid allotment, which she managed as financial power of attorney.

Cindy offered another idea—she said she would ask the nurses' aides to greet Abbie and make a little fuss over her even when they were coming in to assist the roommate. That might help Abbie feel less lonely.

Helen had a sudden thought. "It's such a shame," she remarked, "that Abbie can't occupy her mind with reading. She used to love to read, but now she can't even hold a book."

"What about getting her recorded books?" Harriet, the new volunteer, suggested.

"That's not a bad idea," Pat replied. "The local library brings recorded books to the nursing home every 2 weeks. But we have a very limited supply of tape recorders and CD players to loan out here." He turned to Helen. "Does Abbie have enough money in her account to purchase a CD player of her own? CDs wouldn't need to be changed as often as tapes, and Abbie can't change anything by herself."

"I wish it were so," Helen replied. "I think Abbie would enjoy listening to books very much—but unfortunately, there is nowhere near enough money in her account."

Everyone looked sad as they remembered that Abbie was completely dependent on Medicaid and that Medicaid's personal allowance barely covered the cost of a haircut every couple of months.

"Tell you what," said Harriet, "if Abbie says she is interested in listening to recorded books, I'll ask her if she would accept a CD player as an early birthday present. I'd be glad to buy one for her."

"That's good news," Helen said quickly. "Listening to stories might help distract Abbie from her pain as well as provide her with something she could enjoy."

"I agree, I think listening to recorded books would be very good for Abbie," said Cindy, the nurse.

"If Abbie is interested," Pat said, "I can have the Activities Department put her name on its list for the library's outreach program right away. We could probably get some books for her next week."

"Abbie," Pat continued more loudly, turning to the older woman who was straining to hear, "I know it looks like we are plotting in whispers. I apologize. We're talking about books—do you think you might enjoy listening to recorded books, books you could listen to where you wouldn't need to use your hands to turn any pages?"

Abbie's blue eyes gleamed. Her mouth opened in a wide smile, showing every one of her false teeth. "Oh yes!" she said. "I used to love to read, especially mystery stories. Can you bring me mystery books? Lots of them?"

Then she paused, and her face fell. "But how could I listen to them?"

Pat explained about the CD player.

And so it was decided. In Pat's next quarterly report, he recorded that Cindy would have Abbie's pain medication reevaluated, that Helen would bring needed personal supplies, and that Harriet would provide a CD player. Pat would search for the missing clothes, check Abbie's hearing aid, and make a referral to the Activities Department so that she could receive recorded books from the public library. Now, he reflected, all he had to do was meet the needs of his other 79 clients.

SOCIAL WORK WITH OLDER ADULTS: A BRIEF HISTORY

Older adults have served as role models and mentors to younger generations throughout human history, providing care and guidance instrumental to the survival of the human species. In the United States, the contributions of older adults were recognized, and older people were viewed in a positive light as survivors who had mastered the secrets of long life well into the 19th century. But by the turn of the 20th century, this perception had changed. The focus turned to the problems of older persons, rather than their wisdom and strengths.

Social workers in the early years of the profession worked with older adults in institutions and in their own homes where possible, but such work was not emphasized as a special field until the number of older people began to increase significantly. Nathanson and Tirrito (1998) note that social work with older adults shifted its focus over time. In the early 1900s, the profession focused on alleviation of social ills through pursuit of social programs. Then, during the 1920s, the focus shifted to developing practice methods for work with individuals. One school, using Sigmund Freud's psychoanalytic theories, concentrated on treating individual psychopathology among older adults. A second school, the functional, emphasized utilizing health, growth, and self-determination along with social programs to help alleviate problems of older persons. Then, after the onset of the great depression in the 1930s, the emphasis shifted to alleviation of poverty.

Social workers have been instrumental in improving conditions for older adults. For example, Harry Hopkins, a social worker, led the nation's relief efforts during the great depression. Hopkins worked hard to achieve passage of the Social Security Act, crucial for the survival of many older Americans ("Hopkins Led Nation's Relief Effort," 1998). Another social worker, Bernard E. Nash, organized the first White House Conference on Aging in 1961. This significant conference, which reconvenes every 10 years, led to such important legislation as Medicare and the Older Americans Act. Nash later became executive director of the American Association of Retired Persons (AARP) ("About Bernard Nash," 2006). Rose Dobroff, also a social worker, founded Hunter College's Brookdale Center on Aging in 1975 and served as its director until 1994. In 1995 Dobroff was appointed by President Clinton to the policy committee of the White House Conference on Aging and to membership on the Federal Council on Aging. She cochaired the U.S. Committee for the Celebration of the United Nations Year of Older Persons in 1999 ("Rose Dobroff, DSW," 2001).

Soon after the Great Depression, social work practice tended to focus once more on addressing the problems of individual older adults. In the 1960s, however, the War on Poverty inspired a shift back toward developing programs to alleviate the widespread social disadvantages they experienced. Legislation such as Medicare and the Older Americans Act (to be discussed later in this chapter) improved the lot of older people as a whole. Today the profession recognizes the need for multi-faceted approaches: addressing social ills and developing improved practice methods with individuals and families.

The National Association of Social Workers (NASW) has developed several continuing education courses to help social workers understand the most important issues surrounding working with older adults (Nadelhaft, 2005) and new aging credentials for social workers (Nadelhaft, 2006). The credentials include:

- Certified Social Worker in Gerontology (CSWG) at the BSW level
- Certified Advanced Social Worker in Gerontology (CASWG) at the MSW level
- Certified Advanced Clinical Social Worker in Gerontology (CACSWG) at the advanced clinical level

The Council on Social Work Education (CSWE), recognizing a need for more social workers prepared to work with older adults, recently developed the National Center for Gerontological Social Work, also known as the CSWE Gero-Ed Center. The Center provides many resources for social work programs across the nation to encourage and assist in the development of curriculum dealing with issues of later life.

THE IMPORTANCE OF GENERALIST SOCIAL WORK

Work with older adults requires practitioners who can operate from a generalist framework; every level of intervention is required, from individual to community. The generalist approach is illustrated well by the work of both of the social workers in this chapter's case study, Pat Smythe and Helen Haines.

Pat Smythe, for example, worked with all 80 of his clients on an individual basis. He frequently met with Abbie individually because she was so alert and yet so frustrated due to her pain and physical limitations. Pat met regularly with family members of most of his clients, answering questions and including them in care conferences. Abbie didn't have any family members left, so Pat took care to consult with Abbie's county social worker, Helen, and the new volunteer, Harriet. Pat used his group work skills effectively in leading quarterly staffing meetings and his organizational skills in arranging and coordinating those meetings. He also helped organize and coordinate a residents' council within the nursing home. In the wider community he, like Helen, lobbied at county and state levels for better funding for services for his indigent clients.

Helen Haines also took care to utilize every level of social work intervention. She met regularly on an individual basis with her clients with disabilities, their biological families, their foster families, their group home care staff, and the like. She organized or participated in care conferences for her clients on a regular basis, wherever they happened to live. She frequently intervened in various organizational settings where her clients were placed to improve the quality of their care—for example, when Abbie complained about the quality of the food she was provided at Oakwood Manor, Helen consulted with Pat Smythe, who called in the home's dietitian. At the community level, Helen frequently lobbied to increase funding to improve services for her clients. Where funding was not available, Helen was creative, sometimes calling on volunteers (see Box 10.1).

Box 10.1   Abbie and the Volunteer

"Abbie," murmurs the volunteer, Harriet, peering down into the old woman's face, noting the closed eyes and moving lips, "Today I've brought your DVD player." The CD player Harriet had brought previously had been a big success.

The blue eyes fly open, clear and bright as the Utah desert sky. Recognition dawns, and the eyes smile as wide as the mouth full of false teeth. "Oh, they're beautiful," Abbie says. She means the flowers the volunteer holds in her hands.

"For you, Abbie," Harriet says, lowering the flowers so the old woman can see them, her head still upon the pillow. "A bit of spring. Shall I put them in a vase for you?"

"Yes, yes," Abbie says, and when the flowers are in their vase and the conversation resumes, the volunteer says, again, "and today I've brought you your new DVD player, Abbie."

The blue eyes narrow. "I'm not so sure about that machine," she says. "I have my Bible channel on the TV, and I get the news, and the Gospel, and that's what I want to hear."

"But Abbie," says Harriet, who has spent a weekend finding just the right DVD and a table stand for it small enough to fit in her half of the little nursing home room, "wouldn't you like to see movies? They'd show right on your TV screen. Like the movie *The Sound of Music*. Wouldn't you like to see that?"

"Saw it when I was younger," says Abbie. "Didn't like it. I like my Channel 30, where they teach every chapter of the Gospel. I think you should watch Channel 30. You know, only those who are saved are going to go to heaven. I've been praying for you, but it would help if you would watch Channel 30."

"But Abbie," says the volunteer, "we could get Gospel movies—maybe like *The Ten Commandments*. You'd have more choice of things you'd be able to watch."

"Saw it," she said. The blue eyes closed.

"But Abbie, remember your care conference last week, when the nurse and the social worker asked you about a DVD player and you said you might like one?"

"Well, I wasn't sure that day, and there was a lot else we were talking about, like fixing my hearing aid."

"Wouldn't you give the DVD a try, just once? Try something new?"

"Well, I suppose I might—but you know, I couldn't see it anyway."

"But Abbie, you watch TV all day!"

—And then the volunteer stops. Stares down at the ancient figure, tiny in the bed below her. Legs contacted into a frog-like heap beneath the blankets. Arthritic hands contracted into flannel-covered braces. Head propped carefully on a pillow on a hospital bed that has cranked lower year by year, year by year, easing pressure on a painful back.

Harriet suddenly sees Abbie's eyes in her own mind's eye—closed—always—when she comes to visit—the TV always on. She lowers herself by the bed, tips her head back where Abbie's is tipped and sees—only the ceiling, only the ceiling.

"Oh Abbie," Harriet sighs. "You don't watch TV at all, do you?"

"Not any more," Abbie replies. "But I hear it. I hear my Gospel every day. And last week I saw an angel. Right in my room. She had the most beautiful smile."

"Tell you what, Abbie," says the volunteer. "I'll return the DVD."

GERONTOLOGICAL OR GERIATRIC SOCIAL WORK

Pat Smythe and Helen Haines can be described as gerontological or geriatric social workers. In this context the terms *gerontological* and *geriatric* are virtually interchangeable, although *geriatric social worker* is the term usually used in settings involving health care. The work requires creativity, flexibility, and dedication of purpose. In return, it is rewarding and often exciting. Results

Box 10.2   Gerontological Social Work

Gerontological social work is practiced in a wide range of community-based and institutional settings with active healthy elders as well as with the oldest old who face chronic illness and disability. Increasingly, leadership roles for geriatric social workers are emerging within the context of new initiatives such as civic engagement, health enhancement, and the creation of elder-friendly communities and new models of "aging in place." Because of the central role of informal caregivers to the care of elders, the body of evidence on the effectiveness of social work interventions with older adults and their family or other informal caregivers is growing.

Source: From the National Center for Gerontological Social Work Education (CSWE Gero-Ed Center). Reprinted with permission.

may be tangible and immediate or take considerable time, but older adults can be stimulating and appreciative clients.

Most gerontological or geriatric social workers have MSWs, and most education for work with older persons takes place at the master's level, but increasing numbers of BSWs are being hired today in a variety of settings serving this population. Hence the need for educational resources for undergraduate social work programs to better prepare BSWs to work in this field. The CSWE Gero-Ed center was developed to promote social work education at the BSW as well as the MSW level (see Box 10.2).

Case management, or coordination of care, is a major task for social workers who work with frail or ill older adults. Rosengarten (2000, p. 100) describes the goals of this kind of case management as:

1. Helping older adults remain safely, independently, and happily within their own homes and communities for as long as possible.

2. Helping older adults and their families to cope with transitions to more dependent status when needed (such as living with a family member or aide on a part-time or full-time basis; accepting nutritional and health care interventions; assisting with finances, transportation, and so on).

3. Helping those older adults and their families who need to consider a move to a more protected living environment, such as senior housing, enriched housing, a continuing care facility, or a nursing home.

Case managers also need to monitor client services to make sure they actually meet the needs of each particular client, and assist clients and their families to navigate the increasingly complex systems of services, programs, and agencies that serve older adults (Austin & McClelland, 2003).

WHO ARE OUR OLDER ADULTS?

In terms of both total number and percentage of the population, more and more Americans are reaching the age of 65. In 1900, approximately 3.1 million Americans were over 65, or about 4.1 percent of the population. By 2009, however, the percentage of Americans over 65 had more than tripled, comprising 12.9 percent of the population, about one person in eight, or 38.9 million. The population is expected to reach 55 million by 2020 (Greenberg, 2011; "USA QuickFacts," 2011).

Should a person over 65 be considered "old"? Traditionally, age 65 has been considered old indeed—time to retire. That is because life expectancy at the turn of the twentieth century was only 47 years. Today, however, life expectancy in the United States is almost 78 years. The population of Americans over 65 is expected to exceed 70 million by 2030. People over 85 are expected to increase from 4.2 million in 2000 to 6.6 million in 2020. There are nearly 100,000 older adults in America who are over 100 today! Thus, 65 doesn't seem as old as it once did (Greenberg, 2011).

Perhaps surprising to some, the average life span of Americans is not the highest in the world. Americans do not even fall among the top 10 nations for longevity. Those are, respectively, Japan, Sweden, Hong Kong, Iceland, Canada, Spain, Australia, Israel, Switzerland, and France (Lamb, 2004).

Geographical Distribution

Contrary to popular belief, most older adults do not move to warmer climates immediately upon retirement. In fact, older people are far less likely to move than adults of other age groups. Only about a fifth of those who do move go out of state. In only 13 states do older adults comprise 14 percent or higher of the total population: Florida, West Virginia, Pennsylvania, Maine, Iowa, Hawaii, North Dakota, South Dakota, Arkansas, Montana, Delaware, and Rhode Island. Over 80 percent of persons over 65 live in metropolitan areas today (Greenberg, 2011).

Older people are far less likely to move than adults of other age groups.

Marital Status

Marital status is an important factor for older adults because at this stage of life a spouse is a significant resource for independent living. Older men are far more likely to be married than women: 72 percent of men vs. 42 percent of women. An older widow's chance of remarriage is low because there are nearly four times as many widows as widowers among older adults. Half of the women over 75 live alone (Greenberg, 2011). Women generally take care of their husbands until they die, and then the women often have to cope on their own.

Employment

Many older Americans seek work, primarily for economic reasons. In 2009, 6.5 million (17.2 percent) of Americans age 65 and over were working or seeking work, including 3.6 million men (21.9 percent) and 2.9 million women (13.6 percent). They comprised approximately 4.2 percent of the paid labor force.

Patterns of participation in the paid labor force in the United States have changed over time, of course. Labor force participation of men over 65 decreased steadily from two of three in 1900 to 15.8 percent in 1985; it stayed at 16 to 18 percent until 2002 but has been increasing since then to over 20 percent today. The participation rate for women over 65 rose slightly from 1 of 12 in 1900 to 10.8 percent in 1956. It fell to 7.3 percent in 1985 and was 7 to 9 percent from 1986 to 2002. Beginning in 2000, however, labor force participation of older women has been steadily rising to over 13 percent today. This increase is especially noticeable among those between 65 and 69 (Greenberg, 2011).

Because the oldest of the huge baby boom generation reached the age of 65 in 2010, it is likely that more and more older adults will need to remain in the paid workforce, at least part-time. Traditional pension plans providing adequate income for retirement are becoming increasingly rare. Most private pension plans have been replaced by 401(k) plans, which leave all risks to the individual employees. Public pension and health insurance funds for public employees were underfunded by over $1 trillion in 2008, according to the Pew Center on the States (that was *before* the collapse of Wall Street and the real estate market) (Toedtman, 2010).

Economic Status

While economic conditions among older persons are a concern today, circumstances are better than they were in the mid-20th century. In 1960 fully a third of older Americans were poor. Their economic situation improved in large part due to federal government initiatives such as indexing Social Security benefits to inflation, Medicare, and Supplementary Security Income (see Chapters 4 and 7). The greater financial stability of older adults today has been widely publicized and unfortunately tends to pit elders against other groups competing for resources. However, many retired people experience great difficulty making ends meet and thus have to seek paying work. Today the senior unemployment rate (those seeking work who cannot find it) is close to a historic high—6.2 percent. Many more have become discouraged and stopped looking, and thus do not show up in the unemployment statistics (Schwartz, 2010).

In 2010, 9 percent of older Americans had incomes below the official U.S. poverty line ("About Poverty – Highlights," 2011). The U.S. poverty line formula, however, assumes that people over 65 eat less than younger people. This may or may not be true for any given older adult. Furthermore, the poverty line is determined simply by multiplying the cost of the U.S. Department of Agriculture's emergency food basket by 3. It was formulated according to 1955 consumption patterns, when food did comprise about a third of the average household budget (although the emergency budget comprised less, designed for crises only).

But housing and health care costs have risen much faster than food prices since 1955. Yeoman (2010) points out that the poverty line determination method is thus obsolete; it doesn't even take into account the geographical area in which a person lives. The cost of living is much higher in northern metropolitan areas, for example, than southern rural areas.

Yeoman discusses an alternative poverty measure developed by the National Academy of Sciences in 1995, which assesses the costs of food, clothing, and shelter and also factors in regional differences, government benefits, and expenses such as medical costs. By this formula, 18.7 percent of older persons live in poverty.

Members of ethnic minority groups and women are especially likely to be poor among older adults. The percentage of elderly African Americans and Hispanics with incomes below the poverty level in 2009 (19.5 and 18.3 percent, respectively) was well over twice as high as that for older Whites (6.6 percent). Poverty increases with age and is highest among women who are members of ethnic minorities and who live alone. Fully 33 percent of Black and 44.6 percent of Hispanic older women living alone had incomes below the poverty line in 2009 (Greenberg, 2011).

Social Security is a major source of income for more than 90 percent of older adults today, lifting many out of poverty. Nearly 14 percent of people 65 and older rely on Social Security for 100 percent of their family income.

The program provides benefits to 52.5 million Americans; about 50 percent of older persons count on benefits for 50 percent of their income. In December 2009, the average monthly Social Security benefit for a retired worker was $1,168. For a worker retiring in 2010 at the full retirement age of 66, the highest monthly amount was $2,346 (Miller, 2010).

When the Social Security Act of 1935 was passed, it was not intended to be a sole source of income but rather to supplement people's pensions and savings. However, for many older adults, pensions and savings are nonexistent. The poorest elderly can receive Supplemental Security Income (SSI, see Chapter 4) in addition to any Social Security income for which they may be entitled, but SSI even in combination with Social Security does not raise its recipients' total income above the poverty line.

Housing

Despite the popular belief that most older adults live in nursing homes, in fact, only 4.1 percent resided in one of these institutions in 2008. That percentage goes up to more than 15 percent for those over 85, however, and the cost of such care is very high. The average nursing home stay lasts 2.5 years and costs about $175,000. A large percentage of institutionalized elderly suffer from Alzheimer's disease or other dementia (Fischer, 2010). Older heads of household usually own their own homes (80 percent) rather than renting (20 percent); nearly 65 percent of these homeowners own their homes free and clear. Not surprisingly, their houses are older on average than those of younger people (median year of construction is 1970); 4.3 percent of the houses have physical problems such as rotting window frames or leaky roofs. Nearly half of older homeowners spend more than a quarter of their income on housing; 70 percent of older renters spend more than a quarter of their income on housing. A disturbing trend is that increasing numbers of older American homeowners have mortgages on their houses. While only one in five had mortgages in 1989, with a median debt of $15,000, one in three had mortgages in 2007, with a median debt of $60,000 ("A Mortgage in Retirement?," 2010; Greenberg, 2011).

Although many of the poorest older Americans need safe, low-cost housing, the federal government has not invested in constructing additional units for many decades.

Physical and Mental Health

The health of older adults is better than younger people may believe: in 2009, for example, 41.6 percent of all noninstitutionalized older adults rated their health as excellent or very good (compared with 64.5 percent of younger adults). But only about a quarter of older Blacks, Hispanics, and Native Americans reported their health as very good or excellent, as compared with nearly 42 percent of Whites (Greenberg, 2011).

Most older people experience at least one chronic health condition. Of these, the most frequently reported are hypertension, arthritis, heart disease, cancer, diabetes, and sinusitis. Approximately 25 percent of older adults who reside in the community have difficulty performing their **activities of daily living (ADLs),** such as cooking, eating, dressing, bathing, toileting, and moving around the house; the percentage increases dramatically as these adults grow older. Of older people receiving Medicare who reside in nursing homes,

83 percent have difficulty with one or more ADLs, and many have severe cognitive impairments. Approximately half of the institutionalized elderly today are over 85 years old.

Nearly 37 percent of older adults reported some type of disability in 2009 (difficulty in hearing, seeing, thinking, walking, or self-care). Nearly 11 percent needed some kind of personal assistance as a result. Disability increases with age; 56 percent of those over 80 reported a disability and 29% of these elders needed some form of assistance (Greenberg, 2011).

Despite the great improvement in the availability of medical care for older adults through the Medicare and Medicaid **insurance** programs, which cover virtually all older people, elders today face substantial health costs that are not covered. Medicare premiums and **co-insurance** make appropriate medical care out of reach for many; approximately half of health spending must come from other sources. Some older adults (approximately 58 percent) purchase additional private health insurance, and over 8 percent have military-based health insurance. The most impoverished of the older people still living out in the community (9 percent) receive assistance from Medicaid, and nearly 62% of Medicare beneficiaries living in nursing homes receive assistance from Medicaid (Greenberg, 2011).

Still, millions of older persons have inadequate health insurance coverage. This is an important problem because chronic health conditions such as those listed earlier are persistent and afflict a large percentage. Such conditions can become long term, if not permanent, requiring adjustments in lifestyle and continuing care and attention.

Another problem for older people dependent on Medicare is the issue of prescription drugs. Until 2006, persons enrolled in Medicare received no assistance in purchasing prescribed medications. Finally, 40 years after Medicare was first enacted, a bill authorizing a drug benefit (known as Medicare Part D) was passed in 2005, taking effect in 2006. Indigent persons receiving Medicaid were enrolled automatically by the government; some older persons participating in Medicare **health maintenance organizations** (HMOs, discussed in Chapter 7) were also automatically enrolled. But of the older adults allowed freedom of choice, only about 1 million, or 4 percent, of the 25 million eligible signed on by the starting date, largely because Medicare Part D as originally designed was very confusing. It contained a provision whereby after a small amount of money was spent by the older person on prescription drugs, a "doughnut hole" was encountered where the person had to pay full cost again. The doughnut hole was invented by Congress in large part because drug companies hired more than 800 lobbyists (spending more than $100 million) to pressure Congress to forbid the government to negotiate prices or price controls. This made drug coverage so expensive for the government that the doughnut hole was required to make the new program financially feasible ("The New Medicare (Part D) Drug 'Benefit,'" 2006).

A major focus of President Obama was to pass health care legislation. The Affordable Health Care Act, which not only provided health insurance to most Americans but included provisions to fill the doughnut hole over the ensuing 10 years, was passed in 2010. However, Republicans immediately began trying to dismantle the bill; its future remains uncertain as this chapter is being revised.

Alzheimer's Disease

Alzheimer's disease is one of the most serious chronic conditions afflicting older adults today. It affects both physical and mental functioning. First described by Alois Alzheimer in 1907, the disease produces tiny lesions in the brain. It causes irreversible dementia, or loss of one's mental faculties. Symptoms of Alzheimer's disease are progressive; eventually, the afflicted person loses use of both body and mind. People with this condition generally live 4 to 6 years after diagnosis, but some live as long as 20.

Today more than 5.3 million people in the United States are affected. African Americans are nearly twice as likely to have Alzheimer's as Whites, and Hispanics are about 1.5 times more likely than Whites to develop the disease. The reasons are unclear. There appears to be no known genetic factor for these differences, but high blood pressure and diabetes increase Alzheimer's risk, and these conditions are prevalent in the African American and Hispanic communities.

Societal costs of Alzheimer's disease are enormous. It is the seventh leading cause of death and incurs $172 billion in annual costs. It takes the time and energy of 10.9 million unpaid caregivers ("Alzheimer's Facts and Figures," 2010).

Alzheimer's can be difficult to diagnose. There is no specific lab test that can confirm a diagnosis, and symptoms can be confused with depression, stroke, and many other debilitating conditions. Symptoms progress at different rates for different people and vary with the individual; one person may have difficulty with speech, for example, while another has difficulty with spatial relations and gets lost easily. Some people become severely depressed or agitated. Unfortunately, over time, every patient gets worse and eventually dies.

Despite the dismal long-term prognosis for Alzheimer's patients, new treatments are being developed that can help slow the progression of symptoms. These include medications for depression, psychosis, and agitation. While Medicare, Medicaid, and private insurance pay for much of the medical care, families assume most of the cost and provide most of the personal care. Families of these patients need attention: at least half of primary caregivers develop significant psychological distress. Prolonged stress is likely to develop into physical illness (Small et al., 1997).

Providing supportive care to families of Alzheimer's patients can be an important role for social workers; social workers can also help maximize the functioning of afflicted elderly people by helping them exercise whatever faculties they have left. Structured small-group activities are excellent for this purpose and are comparatively easy to organize in nursing home settings (Naleppa & Reid, 2003).

Mental Health Challenges

The aging process is inevitably accompanied by personal losses. Body strength declines, for example, and one tends to suffer more chronic illness. Spouses, family members, and friends may die. Retirement brings loss of income and loss of the worker role; age discrimination limits one's ability to secure paying employment. The older adult gradually loses the necessary resources to remain independent. Independence, of course, is a major cultural measure of personal worth, and its loss undermines self-esteem. Without understanding, support, and care from loved ones, chronic depression can result even for those who have led successful, full lives.

Of the older adults who become institutionalized in nursing homes, well over half suffer from cognitive deficit, or loss of mental acuity; only about 5 percent of community-based elderly people suffer from this condition. As discussed earlier, Alzheimer's disease is an increasing cause of mental confusion in older adults. In earlier stages of the disease, patients can be aware of their diagnosis; depression and anxiety are likely to follow. Support from social workers, along with medication (which social workers may monitor), can help ease the resultant emotional pain.

Ethnicity

The population of older Americans is becoming increasingly diverse. In 2009, for example, 19.9 percent of persons over 65 (nearly one in five) were of ethnic minority heritage. But by 2020, older adults of minority heritage are projected to comprise nearly 24 percent of the population of elders. In 2009, African Americans constituted 8.3 percent of older persons. Hispanics (of any race) constituted 7 percent; Asian or Pacific Islanders, 3.4 percent; and Native Americans, less than 1 percent. Persons who identified themselves as belonging to more than one race constituted about 0.6 percent (Greenberg, 2011).

Life expectancy differs according to race and presents what researchers describe as a "Hispanic paradox:" Hispanics, despite less education on average than Whites and greater poverty rates, outlive Whites. This surprising finding was reported by the Center for Disease Control (CDC) in 2010. The CDC projects that a Hispanic person born in 2006 can expect to live for 80 years and 7 months, compared to about 78 years for Whites and 73 years for African Americans. No one knows why, but diet, exercise and close extended family ties are thought to be important factors (Wright & Blackburn, 2010).

OLDER ADULTS AND THEIR FAMILIES

Daily Life in Later Years

Young people often believe that older adults have plenty of time to do whatever they want because they are no longer required to earn a living and their children have left home. These young adults may fantasize that older persons spend most of their time resting (perhaps as young people themselves often need more rest!). Perhaps surprisingly, however, the daily life of most older adults is filled with activity, even those "empty nesters" who have fully retired from paid employment. Their lives are full, and they have as many (or more) interests, goals, and aspirations as younger people (Hodge, 2008).

Given freedom to spend their time more as they like, elders soon fill it with activities such as volunteer work, hobbies, travel, visiting friends and relatives, attending classes, engaging in exercise programs—so that a common wail among the newly retired is "I can't believe it—I don't have any more time now than I ever did!" Older adults are valuable and productive members of society. For example, they have taken over a good deal of the volunteer work that formerly was done by married women in the days when married women were unlikely to have paid employment. Older volunteers tutor children; supervise playgrounds; visit sick people in homes, hospitals, and hospices; participate in political campaigns; care for animals in shelters; work to preserve the environment; serve on foundation boards; and provide a number of other important services.

Senior center activities promote social interaction among older adults.

Research on Family Strengths

There is a myth in our times that Americans abandon their elders, callously storing them away in nursing homes, never to see them again except perhaps at funerals. Although such tragedies undoubtedly do occur, research consistently refutes this myth with respect to most families. For one thing, older adults in need of long-term care have been relatively rare until recent times. Stories about families caring for parents until death in the early days of the United States may have been true, but that death would probably have occurred rather quickly. The average life expectancy in 1900 was more than 25 years less than it is today. More families are caring for elderly members today than ever before, and for many more years. The monetary value of unpaid care for family members, friends, and neighbors is estimated at $375 billion annually (Malamud, 2010). Many older adults are living so long today that a four-generation family is common; some families have five. Conner (2000) even offers a term for this type of structure: the "beanpole family."

Greene (2000) points out that family developmental tasks have traditionally centered on the nuclear family and child rearing. Families today, however, increasingly encounter developmental tasks in later life. Establishing a mutually satisfying parent–child relationship in later years involves the issue of dependency, a normal and important family process. Dealing with issues of dependency constructively involves both a realistic acceptance by the older adult of strengths and limitations and the ability of the adult child to accept a caregiving role. The adult child must also recognize his or her own strengths and limitations.

Unpaid informal support from family and friends is by far the most prevalent form of long-term care today. About two-thirds of all caregiving (for all in need, not only older adults) is provided by women, and many women put careers on hold as they juggle part-time caregiving with full-time jobs. Approximately 75 percent of caregivers work outside the home. A 2009 study found that 29 percent of Americans (65.7 million people) are caregivers, serving 31 percent of all households. They provide an average of 20 hours of unpaid care per week. The average age of today's caregiver is 49, and the average age of today's care recipient is 69 ("Caregiving in the US," 2009).

Caregiving is hard work and takes a toll on the caregivers. A recent report by the Association of Retired Persons (AARP) states that 40 to 70 percent of family caregivers demonstrate symptoms of clinical depression. A major reason is that these compassionate people are often devalued and stigmatized in the workplace due to the amount of time required to provide adequate caregiving (Abrahms, 2011).

Older Adults as Caregivers

Family members do not just assist their older adult relatives. Older adults are often the primary caregivers themselves. First of all, many care for each other. Married elderly, for example, particularly women, frequently take care of a spouse through long-term illness, including dementia, right up until death brings release. Many others also care for relatives and friends.

Older people also frequently care for children. Sometimes they provide child care for grandchildren while the children's parents work. But more than that, today many families are headed by older adults who are assuming increasing responsibility for raising grandchildren. In 2009, 475,000 grandparents over 65 had primary responsibility for the care of grandchildren who lived with them. Fully 716,000 grandparents over 65, along with 262,000 of their spouses, had grandchildren living in their homes (Greenberg, 2011).

The primary reasons compelling many children to be cared for by their grandparents are substance abuse, incarceration of the parents, and child maltreatment. Custodial grandparents often suffer increased health problems because of their additional responsibilities. Others experience increased psychological distress and social isolation. Innovative programs have been developed in a few places to help support their caretaking efforts, such as case management, support groups, parenting skills groups, respite care, assistance with legal concerns such as adoption, and welfare benefits; informational audiotapes regarding health, caregiving, and well-being have been developed to assist grandparents (Kropf & Wilks, 2003).

Many older adults adopt children. For example, elders who were serving as foster parents in 1997, the year of the Adoption and Safe Families Act, frequently decided to adopt their wards. This act encouraged states to speed up adoptions of children unlikely to have the opportunity to return to their biological families. Rather than risk losing the children in their care, many foster parents over the age of 60 decided to adopt. Because children older than 5 are considered hard to place, many of the older adults who applied were allowed to do so. Even an 80-year-old received permission to adopt (Stevens, 2001).

Beyond caring for members of their immediate families, many older adults today are caregivers for their communities, their states, and even the nation. An inspiring example is Senator Barbara Mikulski (see Box 10.3).

Caregiver Stress and the "Sandwich" Generation

While millions of families provide care to their older members with goodwill and grace, providing help to older adults can be stressful. Activities of daily living (ADLs) such as shopping, cooking, cleaning, helping with laundry, and

Box 10.3 Senator Barbara Mikulski

From a young age, Barbara Mikulski planned to make a difference in her community. She grew up in East Baltimore and worked at her family's grocery store, often delivering groceries to homebound neighbors including many older adults. She saw that her father frequently opened the store early so that steel workers in the neighborhood could buy lunch before their morning shift.

Barbara decided to become a social worker. She earned her MSW at the University of Maryland School of Social Work, and then worked for Catholic Charities and the Baltimore Department of Social Services. In these positions she served at-risk children and educated older adults about Medicare. Later, she learned that planning was under way to run a 16 lane highway right through Baltimore's Fells Point neighborhood. She became active in community efforts to stop it. Her efforts helped to prevent the road from being built, and today Fells Point and Baltimore's inner harbor remain thriving residential and commercial areas.

Spurred on by her experience with social activism, Barbara Mikulski decided to run for political office and was elected to the Baltimore City Council in 1971. She was defeated in a run for the U.S. Senate in 1974 but was elected in 1976 to the U.S. House of Representatives, representing Maryland's 3rd congressional district. She served in the House for 10 years until elected to the U.S. Senate in 1986. At this time she was 50 years old. She has served continually in the Senate since 1986 and is currently the second longest-serving female senator. She was re-elected in 2010 at the age of 74.

Barbara Mikulski is a true "elder" in the time-honored sense of the word—a person of experience, wisdom, and dedication to service. She is an effective leader in the Senate, serving as a mentor to other women when they first take office. She successfully builds coalitions among the Senators to accomplish joint objectives.

Senator Mikulski puts her values into action—she works to make quality education accessible to all students; works to improve programs for seniors, including Medicare; supports Alzheimers and stem cell research; pursues women's health issues; works toward competent health care for veterans; and supports volunteerism and national service programs such as AmeriCorps.

Source: Adapted from Senator Barbara Mikulkski's website: http://mikulski.senate.gov/About/Biography/index.cfm.

---

bathing all take time and money. Even more time is required when caring for an older person who is ill. Since, as mentioned earlier, some three-quarters of caregivers work outside the home in addition, it is clear that caregiving takes a toll on the giver. As also mentioned earlier, a serious toll today is depression (Abrahms, 2011).

In addition, many caregivers have children as well as older family members for whom to care: caregivers with responsibilities to the generation both above and below are known as the **sandwich generation.** Their conflicting duties create additional stress (see Box 10.4). A survey conducted by the NASW with the New York Academy of Medicine in 2006 found that women of the sandwich generation have a higher level of stress than the rest of the population and are not as happy. Four in ten have sought professional help to assist in coping with their heavy responsibilities; two in ten have consulted a social worker. The survey indicated that only a little more than a third of respondents were aware that social workers provide assistance to aging adults and their caregivers, prompting the NASW to consider new ways to reach a wider percentage of this population (Stoessen, 2006).

Elder Abuse

Most families do their best to provide for their older members. But given the pressures of caregiving, it may not be surprising that reports of elder abuse are

---

Box 10.4 The "Sandwich" Generation

Caregiving is a time-consuming and expensive endeavor, although it is provided patiently and with love by many families. While women provide about two-thirds of the caregiving in the United States today, many men provide it too. For those who also work outside the home, the strain can be heavy. In earlier times most families had a woman caregiver toiling at home full-time and free of charge, who could take over elder care in addition to her other responsibilities when needed. That is not the case today, when the majority of women, married and single, are out in the paid work force.

What happens when a family has minor children at home to care for plus older family members in need? This is the family that belongs to the "sandwich" generation, the generation with responsibilities to care for members of both older and younger generations.

Let us consider the example of a person we shall call Dora Kline (not her real name). Dora was married with two young sons when her mother had a stroke and needed help with dressing, bathing, shopping, and housecleaning. Both Dora and her husband worked full time, Dora as a hospital receptionist and her husband as a mechanic. Dora could not go to live with her mother, who had her own apartment a few miles away, because of her responsibilities to her husband and children, and there was not enough room in Dora's home for her mother to move in. So with great difficulty, Dora arranged for part-time help for her mother to assist with daily needs such as bathing and eating lunch, but the ongoing chores of shopping and housecleaning fell to Dora. She drove to her mother's apartment every morning before work to help her dress and eat breakfast. She stopped by the apartment every evening to make sure her mother was safe and to make dinner before going home to make dinner for the rest of her family. The work was exhausting, until finally, thankfully, Dora's mother recovered enough from the stroke to manage her own affairs again.

The cost of the part-time help was borne by Dora and her husband, since Dora's mother's primary source of income was Social Security, which barely covered rent and food. Dora's husband and children paid a price in terms of Dora's time and attention as well.

---

rising nationwide. While the prevalence of this problem is not fully known, a recent report indicates that about 11 percent of the older adults surveyed had experienced abuse or neglect during the previous year (Acierno et al., 2010). This survey did not include elders with dementia, or those living in nursing homes, both populations believed to be at greater risk for mistreatment.

Abuse may occur in several ways (Kosberg & Nahmiash, 1996; Naleppa & Reid, 2003):

- Physical maltreatment, in which pain or injury is inflicted
- Sexual abuse
- Verbal or emotional abuse, in which a person is insulted, humiliated, or threatened
- Material or financial abuse, in which money or property is misused
- Passive or active neglect, or not providing adequate food, shelter, and other necessities for daily living
- Violation of civil rights, or forcing someone to do something against his or her wishes
- Self-neglect, in which a person retains responsibility for his or her own care but manages poorly in areas such as nutrition and hygiene.

Self-neglect, which is especially common among the elderly, can raise ethical dilemmas for social workers who serve this population. Many elderly people choose, for example, to live in their own homes, but they may grow too frail to cope well alone. Some suffer injuries that temporarily prevent them from being able to provide adequate self-care. Some older people in need refuse assistance even when it is offered. Social workers can face difficult dilemmas involving client self-determination versus physical safety.

Increased social services to older adults, including day care for frail elderly and **respite care** or temporary relief for their caregivers, could help prevent a large proportion of the elder abuse occurring today.

WORKING WITH OLDER ADULTS OF DIVERSE BACKGROUNDS

Ethnic and Cultural Minorities

The number of older adults who are members of ethnic minority groups is growing faster than average. Because of discrimination and other factors, minority elders are especially vulnerable to poverty and are likely to have an increased need for social services.

Such services should be carefully designed to meet the needs of particular clients in light of their cultural backgrounds.

Cox (2005) points out that work with ethnic and cultural minorities requires the recognition that social workers must be knowledgeable about the values, beliefs, and traditions of their clients. Such knowledge requires ongoing, sensitive communication, necessitating at least some fluency in the language and dialects of the persons being served. In addition, sensitivity to nonverbal cues is important, including gestures, posture, and eye contact. These can have very different meanings to members of diverse groups.

Recognizing one's own biases is essential for the social worker who serves older adults of diverse cultural backgrounds. Older persons may cling to traditional values to an extent not experienced with younger clients, so that acceptance of difference is especially important in working with this population.

Services should reflect appropriate roles for the life cycles of diverse individuals, and they must be accessible to elders who may cope with mobility and other disabilities. Family circumstances should be assessed, and presenting problems should be defined in terms of family and community mores.

Gay and Lesbian Older Adults

Another minority that has had to learn to live in at least two different cultural systems simultaneously comprises gay and lesbian older adults. If they are female, persons of color, or poor, they have had to survive multiple barriers. Many have chosen not to reveal their sexual orientation in fear of rejection by family and friends. Yet many serve as caregivers for parents, spouses, or partners.

Gay and lesbian older adults have the same concerns as all older adults: health care, housing, employment, transportation, and so forth. They need support, both formal and informal, to help cope with the ongoing concerns of old age. This represents a challenge for social workers because many gays and lesbians choose to remain invisible due to fear of social stigma and prejudice. Many remain isolated and alone, although the situation has improved in the past decade due to several states permitting gay marriage or civil unions. The recent acceptance of gays and lesbians into the military should help increase societal acceptance of gays and lesbians as well.

Schope (2005) has found that gay men and lesbian women differ in their perceptions of the aging process. Gay men tend to have more negative views of

---

Box 10.5   The R-E-S-P-E-C-T Model for Serving Older Gays and Lesbians

R—Review existing policies and practices at one's agency. How are lesbian/gay consumers treated at the present time?

E—Educate administration, staff, and residents about a range of taboo topics such as human sexualities and gender differences.

S—Share ideas and experiences for the unlearning of homophobia and heterosexism.

P—Promote diversity and prevention of homophobic practices. Illustrate the comparison between heterosexism and other "isms" such as racism, sexism, and classism.

E—Explore and evaluate areas for continued learning and teaching.

C—Change belief systems and taboos that devaluate diversity, including sexual diversity.

T—Transition to a diversity-friendly facility that offers support and attention to older gays and lesbians.

Source: From *Staff development for working with lesbian and gay elders,* by P. Metz. In Jean K. Quam (Ed.), *Social Services for Senior Gay Men and Lesbians,* (pp. 35–45). Reprinted by permission of the editor, Jean K. Quam.

---

aging and to consider themselves old as early as age 39. Lesbians, on the other hand, reject what they view as male bias regarding age. Some even form social organizations with names such as *CRONES* or *OWLS,* terms honoring old age. Schope concluded that gay males in particular face a difficult future, especially as AIDS has devastated their support networks.

Metz (1997), given his perception of the needs of this vulnerable population, recommends a model called R-E-S-P-E-C-T in meeting their special needs (see Box 10.5).

EMPOWERMENT PRACTICE

Social workers are encouraged to use an **empowerment** model when working with older adults, to help them enhance coping skills through consciousness raising, education, and support. Healy (2003) suggests that empowerment with older adults should include three basic strategies: assisting older adults, individually and collectively, to define their own needs; promoting conscious awareness of social and economic injustice; and encouraging political action.

Empowerment practice can assist older adults to advocate for government policies to improve the conditions of their lives.

Senior centers can be effective settings to assist older adults, providing supportive environments to engage in consciousness raising and promoting political action about issues of importance to older adults. Encouraging older persons to join advocacy groups such as the AARP or the Gray Panthers can also aid in the process of empowerment. Empowerment practice can assist older adults to advocate for government policies to improve the conditions of their lives.

SOCIAL POLICY AND OLDER ADULTS: PAST TO PRESENT

Family Care

Historically, before governmental social policies dealing with older adults were developed, services to the elderly were provided almost entirely by their families. This was workable because of the short life span that was the norm at that time and because there were many tasks an elderly parent or relative could perform as a way of reciprocating.

By the late 1800s, however, industrialization had changed family patterns. Grown children tended to move to the cities. Individual achievement as a value took precedence over loyalty to one's extended family. The nuclear family supplanted the extended family as the primary locus of responsibility. Changes such as these undermined family support systems for older adults. The need for new forms of support began to appear. In early times, the only alternatives were the church or almshouse. Later, **pension plans** were established in some countries.

Early Pension Plans

Germany initiated a compulsory pension program in 1889 that provided a regular source of income for older, retired workers. Employers, workers, and the state each contributed equal amounts to the financing. Britain introduced a pension program in 1908, which permitted general tax revenue to be transferred to elderly poor persons (Huttman, 1985). By comparison, the United States has been slow in developing universal pension plans for the elderly. Some states had pension plans by the 1920s, but they all required a means test (only people with very low incomes could qualify).

Not until the Great Depression beginning in 1929 did this country enact a nearly universal pension plan for the elderly, via the Social Security Act of 1935. The intent of Title II of this act was to stabilize income for older Americans without the appearance of the dole, or a government handout. People were required to contribute to Social Security through a special tax during their working life. Thus, they could perceive the program as a contributory insurance plan, not charity. Workers who were required to pay Social Security taxes were eligible to receive benefits after retirement, whether rich or poor. In 1939, coverage expanded to include widows and children. Eventually, many other categories such as self-employed people, farm and domestic workers, government workers, the military, and religious personnel were included (Huttman, 1985).

Trends in American Private Pensions

In recent generations, American workers have grown accustomed to receiving not only government Social Security benefits but substantial retirement benefits from the companies for which they worked most of their lives. This situation is changing rapidly, however. Not only do workers tend to change jobs frequently today, due to both personal choice and involuntary layoffs, but companies have seriously underfunded the private **pensions** they have promised. About 44 million Americans are covered by company pension plans, but these plans are underfunded by many billions of dollars. The federal government guarantees benefits through the Pension Benefit Guarantee Corporation, but this entity also faces a gap of billions of dollars between obligations and income ("Smoothing the way to retirement pay," 2006).

In late 2006 the federal government passed the Pension Protection Act, requiring employers to fund pension plans fully (up from 90 percent). While this legislation should help protect American taxpayers from having to subsidize underfunded company pension plans, an expected side effect will be that fewer companies will offer such plans (Trumbull, 2006). Many Americans today need to finance their own retirement.

Social Security Today

Social Security is a federal **entitlement program,** a program in which a legal right to receive benefits has been bestowed by law on people who meet certain eligibility criteria. (These criteria vary with the law and the program.) Because of the increasing financial insecurity many older people are experiencing due to loss of traditional pension plans, Social Security benefits are more important today than ever before. They are indexed to inflation, which can help keep poverty at bay. Indexing, however, has become a political football in recent years as conservative politicians attempt to chip away at the program.

Almost all retired persons receive Social Security benefits today. The program, however, was designed only as a supplement to private pensions and personal savings. Americans have a hard time saving, however, and while more than 80 percent of employees in 1980 worked for companies that provided pensions, only slightly more than 20 percent do so today. Most employees must now save for their own retirement, usually through **tax-sheltered annuities** such as 401(k) plans. Employers often offer to match employee contributions to such plans, but the investment risk lies entirely with the employee (Magnusson, 2006). Thus more and more people are likely to reach retirement age with insufficient funds.

Social Security taxes have generated a substantial surplus every year to date. In 2009 the surplus was invested in government Treasury bonds and held in a trust fund comprising $2.5 trillion, earning 4.9 percent interest, allowing payment of all benefits until 2037. At that time tax revenue alone would allow payment of 78 percent of benefits (Hinden, 2010). However, a disturbing compromise with Republicans in late 2010 will reduce Social Security revenue, to be discussed in more detail later in this chapter. Work needs to be done to ensure that the trust fund remains solvent and that future benefits will not be cut.

Decisions regarding Social Security are extremely important, because the program helps support more than retired workers. More than a third of beneficiaries are disabled workers, spouses of retired or disabled workers, and survivors of deceased workers (including their minor children and the widowed parent).

Conservatives, including the commission appointed by the George W. Bush administration, argue that the program should be privatized to allow maximum returns to investors (those who happen to be lucky). However, Jeanne C. Marsh (2005), in an editorial in *Social Work* has pointed out the dangers of such a plan. Because retiree benefits would continue to be paid in full for a time, while a percentage of worker payments would be diverted to private accounts, the cost to taxpayers to fill the gap would be massive. At the same time, retirement security for the average worker would be greatly reduced due to the substantial and ongoing risks of the stock market.

Most people of progressive political persuasion argue that the Social Security program could be financially sound well into the future with very minor modifications. The danger it faces today comes from political conservatives. From the liberal or progressive perspective, the program has had no part in creating the federal budget deficit and thus should not be cut as a way to fill that deficit. Social Security has created a surplus every year to date; but unfortunately the surplus has been borrowed by the government to finance other outlays such as military spending. The program holds Treasury bonds securing the debt, however, that are as sound as any other government Treasury bonds.

As this chapter is being revised, Social Security revenues continue to create a surplus, but the entry of the baby boomers into the system threatens that surplus. Also alarming is the fact that under a compromise with the Republicans to secure their agreement to extend unemployment benefits in late 2010, the Democratic Obama administration agreed to lower Social Security taxes for a year. Then, after Republicans gained a substantial majority in Congress in 2011, President Obama, attempting to gain Republican support for his jobs bill, proposed extending the Social Security tax cut for individuals and to offer it to businesses as well. The issue has not been resolved as this chapter is being revised; however, any Social Security tax cut destabilizes the program. The Treasury bonds held by the Social Security program will have to be redeemed in the very near future to continue paying promised benefits, and income tax revenues will need to be used to redeem them. This situation will probably increase the national debt, and if such a scenario takes place, conservatives are likely to demand that Social Security benefits be cut.

Currently, the portion of a wealthy person's income exceeding $106,800 is not subject to the Social Security tax. Including higher incomes in the tax levy would go a long way toward financing the program well into the future. Raising the retirement age has also been suggested, but this move would put a heavy burden on older Americans.

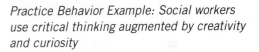
Critical Thinking

Practice Behavior Example: Social workers use critical thinking augmented by creativity and curiosity

Critical Thinking Question: The Social Security tax was temporarily lowered in 2010 as a compromise to finance extending unemployment benefits. Using your critical thinking, do you conclude that this was a worth-while bargain?

Supplemental Security Income

Supplemental Security Income (SSI), another federal entitlement program, was initiated in 1972 as an amendment to the Social Security Act of 1935. As explained in Chapter 3, this program was developed to reduce the stigma of public assistance for poor people falling into three categories: the elderly, the blind, and the disabled. It established uniform national eligibility requirements and benefits. Stigma was reduced by allowing people to apply for SSI benefits through federal Social Security offices rather than local "welfare" offices. Benefits, however, although federally established and administered, remain very low.

Housing Assistance

As noted earlier in this chapter, the vast majority of older adults own their own homes. But many struggle to make ends meet and cannot afford such a luxury. To assist with this problem, the Federal Housing Assistance Program, through the U.S. Department of Housing and Urban Development (HUD), subsidized nearly 2 million apartments for poor people, about half of them for the elderly, for many years (Salamon, 1986). However, the Reagan administration slashed HUD funding after the 1980 election; the funding losses have never been restored. In addition, many units of public housing have been demolished as unsafe.

Thus, affordable housing has been increasingly out of reach for all of the nation's poor, including older adults. A Republican Congress tried to cut HUD funding entirely during Clinton's tenure as President; to save the department, the Democratic Clinton administration converted HUD programs into a system of block grants to the states in 1996 (Popple & Leighninger, 1999). Then, in 1998 Clinton signed the Quality Housing and Work Responsibility Act, which transferred primary responsibility for publicly assisted housing to local Public Housing Authorities (PHAs), making them semiautonomous. In line with the 1996 Personal Responsibility and Work Opportunity Act (see Chapter 4), under the 1998 Quality Housing and Work Responsibility Act, PHAs can consider prospective tenants' employment histories in admissions decisions, and tenants in TANF programs who do not fulfill their work requirements can be evicted (Karger & Stoesz, 2010).

The Republican G. W. Bush administration continued to reduce funding for low-income housing throughout his years as President, but fortunately HUD survived. Today it includes several grant, subsidy, and loan programs. Probably the most important HUD programs for older adults are the Section 8 Housing Choice Voucher Program and Public Housing. The Housing Choice Voucher Program provides rent vouchers to low-income applicants and also provides some funding for new construction and rehabilitation of old buildings. In 2007 more than 324,000 seniors relied on Housing Choice vouchers, comprising about 16 percent of all Section 8 households. Median annual income for these elders (of whom nearly one quarter were 80 years old or older) was $8,550, and 90 percent relied on Social Security as their primary source of income (Karger & Stoesz, 2010).

In addition, more than 400,000 older adults relied on public housing in 2007. These elders comprised approximately 31 percent of all residents in public housing. More than one quarter of them were 80 years old or over, and their median annual household income was $8,250, with Social Security as their primary source (Karger & Stoesz, 2010).

Clearly, the income levels of these older adults reveal their substantial need, despite their many decades of hard work.

Medicare and Medicaid

Before 1965, most health care costs for older adults were paid by the elderly themselves, with the result that many lacked any care at all. This situation greatly improved after the 1965 passage of Medicare, Title XVIII of the Social Security Act. As noted elsewhere in this book, all persons over 65 qualify for Medicare benefits whether they have paid into the Social Security system or not and whether they are poor or not. Part A of Medicare pays for hospital care and some follow-up care. Part B pays for some outpatient hospital care and some physicians' services (elders must pay a special premium to receive Part B coverage). Neither Part A nor Part B of Medicare pays for prescription drugs, however, nor is nursing home care covered unless licensed nursing services (such as drawing blood) are required. Even then, the number of days covered for nursing home care is limited to 100, and a very small percentage of the actual cost is paid.

Medicare Advantage programs were introduced after the original Medicare A and B with the idea that these HMOs, privately administered, would reduce costs. Unfortunately, however, they did not, but rather increased costs by about $1,000 per person. The result was increased premiums for all, including the 77 percent of seniors not enrolled in these plans. Among the provisions of President Obama's new health care law, the "playing field" is to be leveled by gradually eliminating the increased payments to insurance companies offering Medicare Advantage plans and by requiring a minimum of 85 percent of revenues to be paid out in benefits rather than going to administration and profits (Sebelius, 2010).

Medicare Part D was enacted in 2005, effective in January 2006. As described previously, it introduced a new concept in insurance, the doughnut hole. The average enrollee, after paying a relatively small out-of-pocket co-pay, enters the doughnut hole and has to pay the full cost of prescription drugs until paying out $3,600. Coverage then resumes with a 5 percent co-pay (Barry, 2006). Under Obama's health care law, however, the doughnut hole is to be phased out over the next 10 years (Sebelius, 2010).

With the exception of some Medicare Advantage plans, Medicare leaves substantial health care costs unmet so that people who can afford to do so purchase private supplementary health insurance policies to cover some of the gaps.

Medicaid came into being in 1965 through an amendment to the Social Security Act, Title XIX. Title XIX was passed at the same time as Medicare, Title XVIII. Medicaid was designed and added specifically to aid older adults with low incomes. This is the program that paid for nursing home care for Abbie Heinrich of our chapter's case study. Medicaid is administered under each state's public welfare system, and benefits differ from state to state. Costs are shared between state and federal governments.

Since 1993, a federal law has required that states recover the money spent on long-term care of a Medicaid beneficiary after the beneficiary dies. In many cases, the only asset to seize is the deceased recipient's former home. This requirement is exempted if a surviving spouse or child under 21 lives in the home, but in many cases the person living there is an adult child who cared for the deceased for many years. He or she may have given up a former home and a paying job to serve as caregiver. If the adult child cannot buy the deceased parent's property, he or she will have to leave. Often the families involved are pitifully poor—the average monetary recovery per state is only about $5,000. Thus, to fatten state coffers, an indigent family loses its only asset (Green, 2006).

Medicaid pays for certain hospital expenses, physicians' expenses, prescription drugs, nursing home fees, and other health-related services. Benefits have been changing in recent years, and in general poor people are being required to pay more of their own fees as part of cost containment legislation.

Food Stamps/Supplemental Nutrition Assistance Program

Food stamps, also discussed in Chapter 4, are a federal entitlement program available to poor older adults. The program is also known today as the Supplemental Nutrition Assistance Program (SNAP). Eligibility requirements involve both income and the number of persons in a given household who presumably share income.

Older Americans who are eligible for SNAP/food stamps are significantly less likely to participate in the program than younger people. While 7 million seniors over 60 are eligible today, only one-third (about 2.4 million) receive assistance from the program. Reasons for not applying for food stamps include lack of information, the stigma of **charity,** mobility barriers, complexity of application processes (including technology), and low benefits. In fact, the average benefit for a single older adult over 60 in 2009 was only $74 per month. However, even this amount could be very helpful for an extremely poor older person, the situation for the average applicant whose average gross monthly income at that time was only $694.00 ("Poverty and Aging," 2010).

Food insecurity (lack of a reliable source of adequate nutrition) is a serious problem for all, but especially elders. About 11 percent of older adults are marginally food insecure, 6 percent are food insecure, and 2 percent are very low food insecure. Thus about 2.5 million seniors are at risk for hunger (Kamp et al., 2010). Food insecure older adults are more than twice as likely to report fair or poor health status as other elders. The condition increases the risk of disability, decreases resistance to infection, and extends hospital stays. Ironically, many seniors skip meals in order to have the means to purchase medication, only to see the "Take with Food" label on the prescription bottle ("SNAP/ Food Stamps," 2010).

In a wealthy country such as the United States, there is no excuse for citizens to be allowed to go hungry, especially older persons.

In a wealthy country such as the United States, there is no excuse for citizens to be allowed to go hungry, especially older persons. The food stamp/ SNAP program is designed to alleviate hunger, but assists only the most destitute, and the application process can be formidable for older persons.

Current Innovative Programs and Alternative Lifestyles

A major challenge faced by older people is the prospect of living alone when family members have scattered or died. Cohousing is a concept developed in the United States by architect Charles Durant of Berkeley, California, who imported the idea from Denmark in the 1980s. Cohousing helps meet many needs of thousands of older Americans. People work together for 2 years, designing their housing together with the assistance of architects skilled in creating shared-living spaces (Brown, 2004). There is now a National Shared Housing Resource Center that helps people (not only older adults) locate shared-living opportunities (Cox, 2005; National Shared Housing Resource Center, 2006).

Many communities are developing volunteer "friendly visiting" programs such as Little Brothers–Friends of the Elderly in Jamaica Plain, Massachusetts. Volunteers are matched with older adults living alone who otherwise would rarely have opportunity for social interaction (Gardner, 2006).

Loneliness among older people is not just an American, but a worldwide problem. For example, a 79-year-old man put himself up for adoption in Italy. Although this man owned several pets and a treasured book collection, he felt so desperate for human contact after his wife's death that he advertised in a newspaper, offering to pay a healthy monthly fee to live with a family and teach their children. Fortunately, the man received a new home where his talents were wanted and appreciated, and the issue of the plight of the elderly gained new attention in Italy (Aire, 2004).

A recent study found that 35 percent of Americans ages 45 and up are chronically lonely, but somewhat surprisingly, loneliness *decreases* for the very old. The survey, which used the UCLA Loneliness Scale (a standard chronic-loneliness measurement tool), found that 43 percent of people 45 through 49 are lonely, and 41 percent of those 50 through 59 are lonely. But "only" 32 percent of older adults 60 through 69 were rated as lonely, and the percent went down to 25 percent for elders over 70. These results are not well-understood, but one suspicion is that working Americans are laboring harder and longer than in prior years, and don't have much time to socialize.

In addition, e-mail, Twitter, texting, and so on, swallows up what used to be face-to-face socializing time (Edmonson, 2010).

MORE FEDERAL LEGISLATION RELATING TO OLDER ADULTS

The Older Americans Act

The mid-1960s were important years for the elderly. The Older Americans Act of 1965 focused on coordinating comprehensive services for all people over 60, not just the poor. It established the Administration on Aging at the federal level and authorized state units and local area agencies on aging. These units assess the needs of the older adults and try to develop programs to meet them. State and local autonomy is permitted within federal guidelines. In 1993, President Clinton raised the position of commissioner of the Administration on Aging to an assistant secretary level (Torres-Gil & Puccinelli, 1995).

Amendments to the act in 1981 established priorities: information and referral services (including those for non-English-speaking elderly); transportation; in-home assistance (homemakers, health aides, visiting and telephone reassurance efforts); and legal services. Nursing home ombudsman programs (programs to investigate complaints) were required, as were nutrition programs.

Funding under the Older Americans Act has always been low. Still, it supports nutrition programs, senior centers (which often house the nutrition programs, consisting of low-cost congregate meals for all persons over 60), and information and referral services. In 1999 the National Family Caregiver Support Program was authorized under the act, calling for coordination between state and other community service programs to provide support services for caregivers ("Older Americans Act," 2006). The act was last reauthorized in 2006 and included a provision allowing the Assistant Secretary for Aging to have the authority to establish Aging and Disability Resource Centers in all states (Administration on Aging, 2010).

In these times of social service cutbacks, many argue that services should be provided only for older adults who are also poor or disabled. However, others point out that two-tiered services separate people according to economic status, place a stigma on services, and result in competition for scarce resources instead of cooperative self-help efforts. National organizations such as the AARP and the Gray Panthers support offering services to all elderly people (see Box 10.6).

The Social Services Block Grant

Before the 1970s, people who applied for financial assistance received services from social workers in public welfare departments, who routinely assessed social service needs while determining eligibility for financial aid. However, beginning in the early 1970s, eligibility for financial aid was determined by clerical staff who made no further assessment of need (Cox & Parsons, 1994).

Social services for older adults began to be funded by the Social Services Block Grant in the mid-1970s. It is a limited source of financing for homemaker services and adult day care. Originally known as Title XX of the Social Security Act, implemented in 1975, this program was renamed and modified under

---

Box 10.6   Up for Debate

Proposition: Services under the Older Americans Act should be means-tested

Yes	No
Funding under this act is low, so that services should be limited to the most needy.	All older Americans benefit from balanced meals and an opportunity for social interaction.
Taxpayers are unwilling to subsidize services for all elderly.	All taxpayers will one day be elderly. Services for all can help make old age a rewarding experience for everyone.
Poor elderly need help the most.	Services limited only to the poor separate people according to economic status and place a stigma on services.
Because money is scarce, it should be targeted to poor people.	Limiting services to the poorest people pits the non-poor against the poor, rather than encouraging all older adults to develop cooperative self-help efforts.
Taxpayers may resist using tax dollars to provide universal services for all older adults.	If most taxpayers know they will be denied services when they get old because they are not poor enough, no wonder they protest using tax money to provide these services for others.

the Omnibus Budget Reconciliation Act of 1981 (Eustis, Greenberg, & Patton, 1984). Funding is very limited, and states are allowed freedom in determining how to use it (Karger & Stoesz, 1998).

Today the Social Services Block Grant continues to help fund community-based services for elderly and disabled adults such as in-home aide services, preparation of meals, and adult day care ("The Social Services Block Grant Plan," 2009–2010).

VALUES AND PUBLIC POLICY

Funding for programs for older adults involves national policy choices; such policy choices translate into dollar terms the values of those who determine the policy. Should all American older adults be offered tax-supported services such as congregate meals, for example, or only the poorest, frailest elderly? Is it important for all older adults to have access to balanced meals along with a social group experience, or should these services be limited to the poor? Research can provide helpful data, but even the selection of questions for research is guided by values. The debate around privatizing Social Security relates much more to values than to real financial concerns. Conservatives who want to privatize the program are primarily interested in promoting the free enterprise system so that the stock market gets the money contributed for retirement rather than the government. Under their plan, people who invest the most successfully will benefit the most. Liberals are more concerned about providing a reasonable standard of living for all older adults, their survivors, and people disadvantaged due to disabilities.

The "Continuum of Care": Prolonging Independence

Most older adults want to maintain independence as long as possible. Recognition of this preference has led to the concept of the **continuum of care.** Highly relevant is the principle of "least restriction: the least that will get you the most is the appropriate intervention" (Huttman, 1985). Generally, whatever can be done to enable the elderly person to remain in his or her own home setting (the **least restrictive environment**) is appropriate.

Figure 10.1 illustrates the major components of a long-term continuum of care for older adults. The diagram illustrates how many services for the elderly can fit into more than one category; for example, nutrition programs can be offered either in the home or in the community, perhaps at a senior center. The following sections briefly describe each major category of care.

Human Behavior

Practice Behavior Example: Social workers apply theories and knowledge from the liberal arts to understand biological, social, cultural, psychological, and spiritual development

Critical Thinking Question: Keeping in mind perspectives from the liberal arts regarding human behavior in the social environment, do you agree with the author that all older adults should be eligible for tax-supported services such as congregate meals, not only the poor? Why or why not?

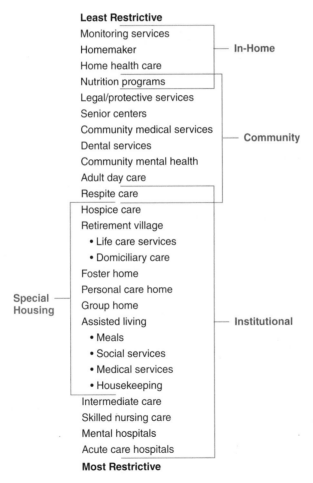

Figure 10.1

Components of Long-Term Care for the Elderly

Source: Adapted from R.R. Greene (1986). *Social work with the aged and their families* (p. 177). New York: Aldine de Gruyter.

In-Home Services

Monitoring services usually involve telephone calls to make sure that an older person is alive and well and to provide support and reassurance. Today, electronic devices are available where the push of a button alerts special services to investigate potential emergencies.

Homemaker services involve housecleaning, laundry, shopping, minor home repairs, yard work, and other routine chores. A more intensive kind of homemaker service may involve personal care, such as help with bathing and dressing. Home health aides provide medically oriented care, under the supervision of a skilled nurse. Home health aides may change bandages, give injections, and take a client's blood pressure.

Medicare and Medicaid pay for some of these services, but eligibility requirements are complicated and restrictive. Sometimes elders can receive homemaker services at low cost by applying to an agency partly funded by the Older Americans Act or the Social Services Block Grant. Most need to purchase these services privately.

Community Services

Nutrition programs can help older adults remain in their own homes. Meals on Wheels is a well-known example. In some communities, programs funded under the Older Americans Act provide congregate meals at senior centers or other sites 5 days a week.

Occasionally, family or other caretakers abuse or neglect older people. Protective services for the elderly are a fairly new phenomenon; in 1968 fewer than 20 communities had such programs (Dunkel, 1987). Today, however, almost every state requires helping professionals to report suspected abuse or neglect of older adults.

Senior centers are important means for older adults to maintain social interaction. Many are privately funded and administered by organizations such as churches or by local cities or counties. Some centers receive funding through the Older Americans Act or Social Service Block Grants.

Community medical and dental services include private-pay arrangements that older adults finance themselves as well as public services financed partly by Medicaid and Medicare. An important public policy issue involves how much of their own medical costs older adults should have to finance themselves.

Community mental health services can help older adults cope with various stresses of living, including the stress of caring for a spouse who is ill. Mental health services also can assist other family caregivers. For example, a daughter or a daughter-in-law may have to give up a paying job and most personal freedom to provide round-the-clock care for an elderly relative. Mental health services may assist the caretaker (see Box 10.7).

Adult day care services provide regular programming outside the home to supervise and maintain elderly persons who cannot get through the day alone. Many older adults who spend their days in adult day care programs live with relatives who regularly assist them but must work during the day.

Institutional Services

Some institutions, including nursing homes, offer a service called respite care, whereby an older person resides in the institution for a few days, a week, or even a month. This temporary arrangement allows family caretakers to take a break, go on vacation, or otherwise "recharge their batteries" physically and emotionally. After the respite, the elder returns home to their care. Many institutions also offer day care services as described earlier.

Box 10.7 Common Community Settings for Working with Frail Older Adults	

- Home bound services such as Meals on Wheels
- Outreach/case-finding programs
- Elder abuse programs
- Financial management programs
- Legal services programs such as legal aid andeviction prevention programs
- Mental health programs
- Adult protective services
- Guardianship programs

Source: Karen Bassuk & Janet Lessem. (2001). Collaboration of social workers and attorneys in geriatric community based organizations.*Journal of Gerontological Social Work, 34*(3), 103–104. Copyright © 2001 by Routledge. Reprinted by permission of the publisher (Taylor & Francis Group, http://www.informaworld.com).

The next several categories in Greene's continuum of care (Figure 10.1) are institutional, in that they involve long-term care outside the older person's home in an institution such as a hospital or nursing home. Greene also places them in the subcategory of special housing, however, because the service is sometimes offered in a person's home or in a small home-like setting. The first of these services is hospice care, or care for the dying. The purpose of hospice care is to help the patient die with dignity, with as little pain as possible. Medicare will pay for hospice care for persons whose prognosis indicates that they have 6 months or less to live. (Medicare covers the medical charges, but not room and board.)

The next item with both institutional and special housing aspects is the retirement village. Many retirement villages offer lifetime care with a continuum of services; many are private, nonprofit arrangements established by religious denominations. Older adults who are economically advantaged may purchase lifetime rights to an apartment or other housing unit. Some such programs offer the option of purchasing congregate meals. Many include a domiciliary option, or a large housing unit where a number of older people live and are offered personal assistance and meal services. The most advanced retirement villages include skilled nursing home care as needed.

Some older adults reside in foster homes or in small group homes, where they can receive individual attention and protection if needed, as long as on-going medical attention is not required. Others live in larger **personal care homes,** which usually provide meals and are sometimes called nursing homes because the services of nurse's aides are available to help with bathing, eating, dressing, and the like. Technically speaking, however, a personal care home is not a nursing home because very limited nursing care is available.

An increasing demand for community living options for older people who need some level of assistance, but do not need an environment dominated by nursing requirements, has led to the recent development of an option known as **assisted living.** Assisted living is a step between independent living and living in a nursing home. The term became recognized nationally after the Assisted Living Federation of America was incorporated in 1992 ("About ALFA," 2007). Older adults who reside in assisted-living settings have their own small apartments including kitchens, bedrooms, and bathrooms. The environment is much more attractive than a room (usually shared) in a personal care home. Yet the same services are available: assistance with cooking, shared meals when desired, assistance with **ADLs** (dressing, bathing, laundry, housekeeping, etc.), and occasional nursing care as needed. Unfortunately, assisted living is usually available today only to people with significant financial means.

The institutional settings that provide the most restrictive environments for care of older adults are nursing homes and hospitals. Most elderly people do whatever they can to avoid them. However, as living into one's 80s and 90s is becoming common, an increasing number of older adults do face an eventual move to a nursing home. These facilities provide the only reasonable alternative to 24-hour family or hospital care when an older person is very ill or very frail. This is the setting that provided life-giving care to Abbie Heinrich of our chapter's case study.

Fortunately, nursing homes now are professionally organized and staffed. Many, especially the nonprofits, provide responsible services along with opportunities for older adults to enjoy the companionship of peers. "Intermediate care" and "skilled nursing care" are categories that reflect the level of nursing care provided. The former is less intensive than the latter, and monthly fees are lower. Abbie Heinrich, with her extensive physical challenges, required the highest level of skilled nursing care (see Box 10.8).

Unfortunately, because many nursing homes are administered by for-profit private organizations today, staffing levels are low to increase profits. Non-profit homes provide nearly an hour more care per resident per day and nearly twice as much care from registered nurses. Federal rules require only 8 hours of registered nursing and 24 hours of licensed nursing care per day in any given facility, so large homes can have the same size staff as small ones. Many states have their own regulations, but state inspectors underreport deficiencies due to staff shortages of their own. Cuts in Medicaid reimbursements have also contributed to nursing home understaffing. These institutions should be utilized only when less restrictive alternatives have been exhausted ("Nursing Homes," 2006).

Hopeful news is that the Affordable Care Act passed by Congress in 2010 and signed by President Obama includes a provision titled the Elder Justice Act, designed to help improved nursing home quality (Sebelius, 2010).

Box 10.8   Making Nursing Homes Livable

For many older persons, having to move to a nursing home is experienced as the "kiss of death." The belief is that they are going there to die, and quite naturally they become despondent, depressed, and lonely. Sadly, two frail older persons can live in adjoining rooms, sometimes even in the same room, yet crave company and never think it worthwhile to get to know each other as they are "only going to die." To alleviate this unfortunate state of affairs, progressive nursing homes encourage their residents to engage in activities ranging from reminiscence groups to exercise groups to music and arts and crafts. Many homes bring in volunteers as "friendly visitors," including young children. Children can be especially effective as visitors to frail older adults; their very presence seems to transfer a sort of vibrant energy.

In the best nursing homes today it is not uncommon to see bird cages full of active parakeets chattering away in day rooms, surrounded by smiling residents enjoying the sounds and the vibrant colors. Therapy programs bring in dogs and cats; the response of older residents to these feline and canine visitors is overwhelmingly positive. Plants are brought in to add color and a sense of purpose to the lives of residents who often "adopt" them and lavish time and attention upon them. Such stimulating sights, sounds, and activities can dramatically decrease depression and loneliness among older adults residing in nursing homes.

Rural versus Urban Issues

Services to assist older adults to live independently in the community are scarce almost everywhere, but gaps in the continuum of care are far more likely to occur in rural areas (see Box 10.5). Even where important programs such as congregate meals and adult day care exist within a given rural county, transportation over long distances may be required to obtain them; thus, many seniors and their families are effectively blocked from participating in their benefits. Many rural areas are lacking in crucial services such as senior centers with congregate meals, Meals on Wheels, affordable housekeeping help, medical screening services, adult day care programs, and the like. In 2009, 19 percent of older adults lived in rural areas, and while 80% of all older adults lived in metropolitan areas, more than a quarter of them lived outside the principal cities (Greenberg, 2011). The result is that many seniors lack the services they need to remain living in the community when they become frail and ill and find that their only option is to enter a nursing home.

Coming to Terms with Long-Term Care

We usually do whatever we can, both personally and collectively as a society, to live longer lives—and we are succeeding. That is the good news. Ironically, however, it is also bad news in some ways. Longer lives present new problems. Long-term care is a major one. It requires considerable financial outlay for which most of us are unprepared and raises important issues regarding quality of life.

About 1.3 million older adults reside in nursing homes today. Elders who live to 65 have a 40 percent chance of requiring nursing home care in their lifetimes; risk increases with age. Today more than half of nursing home residents are over 85 years old (Fischer, 2010, Greenberg, 2011). Yet despite questionable care, the cost of nursing home living is very high, over $70,000 per year in 2010 and increasing almost daily. Most elderly adults cannot afford to pay, so a majority receive help from Medicaid. To qualify for Medicaid older adults must spend virtually all of their savings first; it is not uncommon for an older couple to have to divorce in order for the ill spouse to qualify for Medicaid so that the healthy spouse does not land in the street (Fischer, 2010).

A few elders have purchased private long-term care insurance to assist with nursing home care. Medicare is not a serious resource because it covers only short periods of skilled nursing home care after a hospital stay (see Box 10.8). The Affordable Care Act passed under President Obama includes a new voluntary insurance program called CLASS to help pay for long-term nursing home care as well as support at home (Sebelius, 2010). A major problem with long-term care insurance policies is cost—they are expensive and most people cannot afford them.

Medicaid payments to nursing homes are lower than the fees charged to private clients, and they do not usually cover the full cost of care. Most nursing homes, therefore, accept private-paying clients first. When private-paying clients' money runs out, they turn to Medicaid. Most nursing homes will allow these people to stay, but had they originally applied as Medicaid clients, their chances of admission would have been minimal. Frail older adults who have experienced lifelong poverty find nursing home care very difficult to obtain. Abbie Heinrich was lucky in a way—she was admitted to Oak Haven many years ago when Medicaid payments still met the true cost of care.

When an older adult needs round-the-clock care, care at home can be more costly than nursing home living. Hence many seniors who desperately want to avoid the nursing home end up there anyway. The Affordable Care Act passed under the Obama administration, including the voluntary long-term care insurance program called CLASS, hopefully can make a difference for those who are able to purchase it.

END-OF-LIFE ISSUES, RELIGION, AND SPIRITUALITY

Death and Dying

Coping with such loss often awakens spiritual concerns—not only for the older adult but for the social worker.

Older adulthood involves many life changes, as noted previously. The possibility of death begins to feel very real. By this time the older person has lost members of his or her family and probably friends. Coping with such loss often awakens spiritual concerns—not only for the older adult but for the social worker. Questions may arise such as "Does life have meaning?" "Does *my* life have meaning?" "Will death be the end?" "What, if anything, comes next?" Even if clients do not ask these questions aloud, both they and their social workers may wonder.

Spirituality and Religion

Naleppa and Reid (2003) suggest that spirituality and religion are important to older adults since they address questions such as those just listed. However, social workers have tended to avoid discussions of these issues, referring them instead to the clergy. It is, of course, important to involve clergy where available. Still, many clients do not belong to a church and feel embarrassed about asking to see a clergyperson who is unknown. The social worker, on the other hand, may be a person with whom they already feel comfortable, so workers are encouraged to discuss spiritual issues if requested.

Of concern, of course, is that social workers and clients may have very different religious orientations. **Religion** involves a formal belief system as taught by a particular church or theological tradition, whereas **spirituality** refers to a process involving a universal search for meaning. It is important for social workers not to impose religious beliefs on clients. However, in many instances workers and clients share similar beliefs. For example, a comparative study by Hodge (2003/2004) found that social workers in the United States share similar concepts of human nature with nonsocial workers (more good than corrupt) and God (more like father than mother, more like judge than lover). Social workers, on the other hand, are less likely to view the Bible as the literal word of God.

Regardless of a social worker's religious orientation, it is entirely possible to assist clients—even of very different traditions—to cope with spiritual issues. Encouraging clients to reminisce about their lives can help them work through meaning-related questions, for example. Allowing clients to talk about their beliefs, whatever they may be, can help them clarify these beliefs in a manner that may comfort them.

Social workers may find it helpful to clarify their own religious and/or spiritual beliefs. A spiritual grounding can help a worker cope with the fact that clients die, for example. Many other professionals grapple with religious and spiritual issues, of course. For example, Herbert Benson, a prominent physician who became famous for his scientific studies of the relaxation response, spent many years studying comparative religion. That is because he found that the relaxation response enhanced healing, and he recognized that there were many parallels between the relaxation response and the affects of prayer. He wrote in *Timeless Healing* (1996) that:

> Every culture had religious or secular practices that consisted of two basic steps—a repetitive focus and a passive attitude toward intrusive thoughts. There was a transforming power in prayer, no matter what the words, from a Hindu prayer to the Catholic "Hail Mary, full of grace," from Judaism to Buddhism, Christianity, and Islam. There were multitudes of descriptions of the peaceful state these religious practices elicited (p. 199).

Benson hypothesized that human beings are physically "wired for God" and that the transcendent experience shared by various religious traditions and spiritual practices may be part of our genetic inheritance. Evidence of such a possibility is presented by Newberg, D'Aquili, and Rause (2001) in their book *Why God Won't Go Away*. These scientists found that the hypothalamus in the brain can produce transcendent experiences. Under a shutdown of neural input, as can occur during contemplative practice, silent prayer, or meditation, the "left orientation area" of the hypothalamus is unable to find the boundaries of the body so that the person feels a sense of unity with the universe. The result can be a profound spiritual experience and a lessened fear of death.

Western science and religious traditions may argue the meaning or even the existence of a "biology of belief," but at the very least, learning to use the relaxation response in any form can be an effective self-care tool for the social worker.

End-of-life decisions can be particularly challenging. Some clients, usually when suffering extreme pain, ask for assistance in ending their lives. How is a social worker to respond? The NASW, in its *Standards for Social Work Practice in Palliative and End of Life Care,* "does not take a position concerning the morality of end of life decisions, but affirms the right of the individual to determine the level of his or her care" (Mackelprang & Mackelprang, 2005). One state, Oregon, permits people who are suffering and who have a life expectancy of less than 6 months to ask their doctors for medication to end their lives. Oregon's Death with Dignity Act was upheld by the U.S. Supreme Court in the *Gonzales v. Oregon* case (Stoessen, 2006). While it is important for social workers to assist their clients to identify all options available to them, advocacy regarding pain management is especially important. People in terminal situations who are not in pain are much more likely to choose to live as long as possible.

There is an interesting literature on near-death experiences (NDEs), which seem to help reduce the fear of dying for both social worker and client. The NDE, in which all vital signs have ceased but the person is later revived, was first studied by sociologist Raymond Moody (1976). The phenomenon has been investigated since by many others. It is described by scientist and author Dean Radin (2006) as follows:

> NDEs involve a sequence of distinctive experiences: finding oneself floating above the body, moving down a tunnel, being immersed in an intense beautiful light, interacting with deceased relatives or loved ones, and sometimes having to decide whether to return to the body or to continue on the disembodied journey. Those who come back to report the NDE often express deep regret at finding themselves embodied again because the out-of-body state is usually experienced as exceedingly blissful. (pp. 40–41)

Radin reports that in three studies of 496 patients with cardiac arrest (Dutch, British, and American), between 11 and 18 percent of patients had an NDE. Profound, positive personality changes were present in these people at follow-up studies 2 and 8 years later.

Does this mean that some part of the personality survives death? Not necessarily, as oxygen deprivation can trigger similar results. Yet patients who have registered as clinically brain dead on electronic monitors have later reported these experiences. How can a dead brain experience anything at all? Arguments are ongoing, and the studies that they instigate are intriguing.

Hospice Services and Complementary Therapies

Hospice services are designed to assist people to cope with the dying process in a more humane and personal way than can be provided in traditional hospitals. The catalyst for the hospice movement in the United States was Dr. Elisabeth Kubler-Ross, who published her famous book, *On Death and Dying*, in 1969. In it she lamented the mechanized treatments provided by traditional hospitals and advocated for care of the whole person, including psychological and spiritual needs. The first hospice in the United States was opened in 1974 (Seeber, 1995). Today hospices exist in almost every state. In 2009, 1,020,000 dying patients received hospice care, comprising 41 percent of all who died that year ("NHPCO Facts and Figures," 2009).

Hospice services include medical care and psychological and spiritual counseling for patient and family and bereavement services for the family after the patient has died. Pain management is a primary concern. Patients can be accepted by hospice programs when life expectancy is 6 months or less and comfort rather than cure is the goal. Hospice care may be offered in one's own home or in homelike residential facilities; many services are covered under Medicare.

An important complementary therapy offered in many hospices today has been developed by Therese Shroeder-Sheker. Shroeder-Sheker worked in a nursing home during her college career and was saddened to see people die alone and afraid. She began to sing to her patients as they lay dying. Eventually she founded the Chalice of Repose project, teaching others how to use music to ease the transition of the dying. Many scientific studies have demonstrated that music can help ease pain—physical, psychological, and spiritual. The instrument primarily suggested for this purpose is the harp, given its particular vibrational effect on the human body, but other instruments including the human voice are also used (Shroeder-Sheker, 2001). Chalice of Repose served as a catalyst for the development of several related projects such as the Music for Healing and Transition Program developed by Melinda Gardner in New York.

AN INTERNATIONAL PERSPECTIVE: THE NETHERLANDS

Provisions for older adults in the United States today could clearly be improved, and research regarding services provided by other nations may provide ideas. The AARP surveyed 16 industrialized nations (including the United States), weighing 17 criteria, and concluded that the country that provides the best care for its older citizens in the early years of the 21st century is the Netherlands (Edwards, 2004).

Social policy in the Netherlands is designed specifically to prevent social exclusion of older persons. The central government provides a policy framework that specifies the various responsibilities of finance agencies and service providers. Older people are encouraged to make their own decisions regarding the services they need and where and how they want to live. "Custom-made care," or care designed to meet the needs of each unique individual, is a central concept in the Netherlands' social policy. Another concept is that care should be "demand driven": the supply of care should meet the demand or need (Ex, Gorter, & Janssen, 2004) rather than being limited by a set budget allocation.

All older adults in the Netherlands receive a full old-age pension at age 65 whether or not they have worked outside the home (approximately $1,000 for a single person, $1,400 for a couple, married or not), but they must have lived in the country continuously between the ages of 15 and 64. Every older adult also receives a $700 "holiday allowance" in May, in time for a spring celebration. Free travel is provided for 7 days in a given year on the nation's efficient railway system, and museums, movies, concerts, and holiday motels offer discounts. Government health insurance covers not only medical care, including prescription drugs, with tiny co-payments but also hospital care and coverage for nursing care if needed, both short and long term.

Such comprehensive services can be provided to older people in the Netherlands because the government controls almost all health care costs (drugs, physicians' services, hospital care, etc.). Taxes are higher than those in the United States, but public attitudes support this trade-off. In general, younger people support generous treatment of older adults because older people are viewed as having earned assistance; they also recognize that the time will come when they themselves will need help (Edwards, 2004).

Interestingly enough, the Netherlands, like the U.S. state of Oregon, allows older people who are in extreme pain to request medication from their physicians to enable a peaceful death by choice. The Netherlands' law is broader than Oregon's, in that the excruciating pain justifying such a request may be psychological, not just physical. Two independent physicians, one of whom is a psychiatrist, must review and accept the request in order for it to be carried out (Mackelprang & Mackelprang, 2005).

SOCIAL WORK WITH OLDER ADULTS: A GROWING FUTURE

Older adults in the United States and around the world are growing in number and proportion every day. Even with the predictable waxing and waning of public financing for social services for older persons, reflecting shifts in the values of the politicians in power and the people who elect them, older adults are developing growing political sophistication. As a group, they are making themselves heard at all levels of government. Their needs are many. Thus, employment for social workers in the field of aging will continue to grow well into the foreseeable future (see Box 10.9).

Social workers who work with older adults encounter a varied and challenging client population. These are people who have led full lives and have developed the wisdom and perspective that come with many years on this

| Box 10.9   **Employment of Gerontological Social Workers** |

Employment of social workers is expected to increase by 16 percent during the 2008–2018 decade, which is faster than the average for all occupations. The growing elderly population and the aging baby boom generation will create greater demand for health and social services, resulting in rapid job growth among gerontological social workers.

Source: Bureau of Labor Statistics, U.S. Department of Labor. *Occupational outlook handbook, 2010–11 Edition.* Social Workers, on the Internet at http://www.bls.gov/oco/ocos060.htm

planet. Older people are fascinating, enriching clients who can enlighten social workers as well as command their skills.

On the other hand, probably no other field of social work requires so much soul-searching on the part of the practitioner. Older adults are manifestly nearing the end of their journey on earth, and this certainty makes many thoughtful workers ponder the "meaning of it all."

SUMMARY

The case study of Abbie Heinrich, a severely disabled older adult, illustrates some of the challenges faced by older people today—health problems, poverty, and lack of living family members, to name a few—as well as the challenges faced by the social workers who serve them.

Currently, 12.9 percent of the population of the United States is over 65, over 38 million persons or about one person in eight. The number of people over 65 is expected to increase to 55 million by 2020. This growing group of older persons, while resilient and self-sufficient in many cases, challenges the nation's social service system. The risk of poverty increases with age and is especially serious for members of ethnic minority groups and women. Those with lower incomes suffer the greatest problems in terms of health and adequate housing.

Many families are active in helping their older members cope with their special needs. Because people are living longer, more families are contributing to the care of older relatives than ever before, and for many more years. Middle-aged children, especially middle-aged women, often find themselves part of the sandwich generation, those who have children to care for in addition to elderly relatives. Social workers can help many families cope with the stresses involved in intergenerational care.

Social workers are encouraged to use an empowerment model when working with older adults, assisting them to advocate for themselves and to utilize whatever resources are available. Pension plans and federal entitlement programs such as Social Security, Supplemental Security Income, housing assistance, health insurance, and food stamps help elders meet financial and material needs to some extent. Limited services such as information and referral, congregate meal programs, low-cost homemaker aids, and protective services are provided under the Older Americans Act and the Social Services Block Grant. However, need for services far outstrips supply, and a large burden of care today falls upon families, creating intergenerational stress.

The concept of the continuum of care, designed to help older adults maintain independence for as long as possible, includes in-home services, community services, special housing, assisted living, and institutional services. Whenever possible, older adults should be helped to remain in the least restrictive environment.

Given increasing longevity, the need for careful attention to long-term care is growing in importance, not only for individuals but for families and society as a whole. While an impressive continuum of care has been developed, we have not yet managed to come to terms with the financing of care or with quality-of-life issues. Fortunately, the Affordable Health Care Act passed by the Obama administration may be of help, offering a voluntary insurance program to help pay for long-term care.

Another challenge is recognition of the spiritual needs of older adults, a responsibility no longer assigned to clergy alone. Social workers themselves may find themselves spiritually challenged as they work closely with clients who are facing a final transition.

The chapter concludes with a description of services to older adults provided in the Netherlands, considered the best place to grow old today according to a comparative study by the AARP. While services to older persons are not nearly so comprehensive in the United States, social work practice with elders here is still likely to grow rapidly because of the increasing number of people who are reaching retirement age. Members of the baby boom generation began to reach 65 in 2010.

PRACTICE TEST The following questions will test your knowledge of the content found within this chapter. For additional assessment, including licensing-exam type questions on applying chapter content to practice behaviors, visit **MySearchLab.**

1. Which of the following statements is FALSE about older Americans today?
   a. Americans 65 and older comprise nearly 13 percent of the population.
   b. Eighty percent or more of those 65 and older live in metropolitan communities.
   c. The United States ranks among the top 10 nations for longevity of age.
   d. Americans 65 years and older comprise 4 percent of paid employees.

2. What percentage of older Americans who have reached retirement age rely on Social Security benefits for 100 percent of their family income?
   a. 14 percent
   b. 25 percent
   c. 50 percent
   d. 68 percent

3. Common attributes of primary caregivers (those who assist with activities of daily living) of ill or frail elders do NOT include _____.
   a. spouses of elders
   b. professional registered nurses
   c. middle-aged, employed, adult children who are also caring for their own children
   d. close friends who seek professional help to cope with their heavy responsibilities

4. Hospice services are _____.
   a. only authorized by a state government approval board
   b. designed to help dying patients decide if they want to take charge of ending their own life with prescription drugs
   c. provided to patients who have had a near-death experience
   d. designed to offer medical, psychological, and spiritual care, which provides comfort during the dying process for people with a life expectancy of 6 months or less

5. Which of the following is a current concern regarding the future of Social Security?
   a. Social Security payments will be privatized in 2020 and be subject to the investment skills of individual investors and the risks of the stock market.
   b. The Social Security contribution to the federal debt places the program at risk for continuation.
   c. If Social Security taxes continue to be lowered, as in 2010, the current surplus will be eliminated and available benefits to baby boomers will be at great risk.
   d. Social Security taxes on incomes over $200,000 are scheduled to be eliminated in 2015.

6. The continuum of care for Abbie Heinrich likely included _____.
   a. in-home services to support her parents, special housing, and long-term nursing home care
   b. Meals on Wheels, protective services, and adult day care services
   c. an electronic monitoring system in her home, mental health services, and hospice care
   d. homemaker services, shared housing, and free public transportation

7. Describe how daily life might be different for Abbie Heinrich if the U.S. policies and practices toward elders were like those in the Netherlands.

Reinforce what you learned in this chapter by studying videos, cases, documents, and more available at **www.MySearchLab.com**.

Watch and Review

Watch these Videos

*Professional Demeanor

Read and Review

Read these Cases/Documents

Δ A Qualitative Inquiriy to Adult Child–Parent Relationships and Their Effects on Caregiving Roles

Δ End-of-Life Decisions in an Intensive Care Unit

Δ Resident's Rights to Intimacy in an Assisted Living Residence

Explore and Assess

Explore these Assets

National Institute on Aging—http://www.nia.nih.gov/

AARP—http://www.aarp.org/

Healthy Aging, Centers for Disease Control and Prevention—http://www.cdc.gov/aging/

Assess Your Knowledge

Assess your knowledge with a variety of topical and chapter assessment.

Conclude your assessment by completing the chapter exam.

* = CSWE Core Competency Asset

Δ = Case Study

Social Work and Criminal Justice

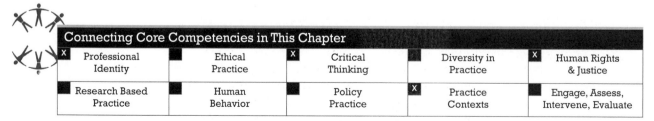

Connecting Core Competencies in This Chapter				
X Professional Identity	Ethical Practice	X Critical Thinking	Diversity in Practice	X Human Rights & Justice
Research Based Practice	Human Behavior	Policy Practice	X Practice Contexts	Engage, Assess, Intervene, Evaluate

Alan Martin

Alan Martin slumped in his chair and sighed. Then he picked up the file again. Another new case had just been added to his already overloaded caseload. You're letting yourself burn out, he thought. Then, reminding himself that he was just tired but he could go home soon, he picked up the telephone and dialed the number he had found in Brian Cook's folder. He talked briefly with Brian's mother, Laura Cook, scheduling an office appointment with Brian for Friday. The file showed that Brian had been released on parole from the state juvenile corrections center just 5 days ago. He had served 2 years of a 5-year sentence for selling illicit drugs. He had apparently been a model prisoner.

The telephone rang, and Alan reached for his notepad—an emergency; the police had just arrested another of his clients, a 13-year-old, for selling cocaine at the bus stop across the street from a school. There had been a scuffle; weapons were involved. One officer and the 13-year-old were badly injured and being transported to the hospital by ambulance. A picture of 13-year-old Ramon flashed through his mind: a bright, defiant, angry kid whose father died 6 months ago. Without hesitation Alan replied to the voice on the phone: "I'll be at the hospital in 10 minutes." It was very late when Alan finally got home that night.

Alan Martin was an experienced BSW social worker who had worked in the criminal justice field for 6 years now, initially in adult probation and parole and, for the past 6 months, in Youth Correctional Services. Alan was respected by his colleagues, police, and the judges. Among his clients he was viewed as tough, demanding, and fair. Once actively involved with the National Association of Social Workers (NASW) and careful to sustain continued professional learning activities, Alan had gradually drifted away from identification with his profession and, in fact, had forgotten to renew his NASW professional membership. Alan felt vaguely unsettled with his life and his work.

On Friday, minutes before Brian Cook's scheduled appointment, Alan pulled out his file. Brian's 14-year-old face stared back from the photo taken at the time of his arrest 2 years ago. This image was quite a contrast to the older-looking, broad-shouldered, passive but mistrustful person he had met at the correctional facility 2 weeks ago. Kids who weren't criminals before they arrived at that place were quite likely to be so by the time they were released, Alan thought as he snapped the file closed and went out to get Brian from the drab, vaguely filthy waiting room.

Their first session in Alan's office included a review of the parole contract. Brian's cool, almost sullen expression was annoying. Alan found himself talking loudly, lecturing Brian about the consequences of failure to abide by the terms of the contract. He told Brian about the procedure for providing a urinalysis to check for drugs each time he came in. He was angered by Brian's comment: "So, you don't trust me. I told you I don't do drugs." "No, I don't trust you," he responded, using the very words he didn't like but often heard other parole officers use. Further annoyed with himself for having said this, Alan changed the subject to school. Brian said that he had enrolled in and started attending classes this week but hated the school. Alan ignored this, instead warning Brian about associating with anyone related to his conviction, especially Shari, the girl for whom he had purchased drugs.

After Brian left the office Alan returned the telephone call that had come in from Ramon's mother. She was at the hospital; Ramon was not doing well, but she couldn't understand the doctor's explanation about what was happening to him. Alan decided to stop by the hospital during his lunch break. The expression of the policeman guarding the room told Alan that all was not well. One look at Ramon's face, contorted with pain and discolored by jaundice, confirmed that Ramon was in serious condition. Alan beckoned Ramon's mother to follow him. Tearfully she told him that in her heart she did not think that Ramon was going to live. She didn't know what was wrong; she was terrified. Alan searched frantically for a nurse, finally finding one who would talk with them. The nurse was dignified but cold. Ramon had developed an infection related to the gunshot wound in his abdomen. He was not responding to antibiotics. His lab reports this morning were very bad. She certainly didn't know why these teenage criminals thought they could get away with fooling around with guns. As she turned to leave, Alan heard her say, "Sometimes they have to pay the price." Struck to the core by her remark and instantly, painfully aware of the negative attitudes he had been developing, he turned to Ramon's mother, hugging her to defend her from the added pain of the nurse's remark. He took her to a quiet corner, explained what the nurse had said about the seriousness of the infection, and sat with her for a time while she cried. Alan left when Mrs. Perez's sister arrived. That night Ramon died.

Thoughts about Ramon's tragic death and the judgmental attitude of the nurse remained with Alan for weeks. Attending Ramon's funeral service both refreshed him spiritually and strengthened his determination to fight for real justice, a justice built on dignity and respect for people, not on retribution and various prejudices. Alan made time at night to do a bit of reading—some light short stories that were delightful and refreshing and some professional articles from social work journals. Rereading the NASW Code of Ethics renewed Alan's awareness that as a professional person he was responsible for the quality of his own practice. In his work with his clients, Alan consciously struggled to become more self-aware and more attuned to the reality of their lives.

On the day that Brian Cook was scheduled to see him again, Alan received a report from the school indicating that Brian was not attending classes. This was a violation of his parole contract, and it also raised questions about what he was doing with his time. Was he back into the drug scene again? Alan confronted Brian with all of this. To his annoyance, Brian insisted that he was attending school. Brian added: "I know you won't believe me about this. You don't believe anything that I say." Alan showed him the report, but Brian still insisted that he was attending school even though he hated it. Then, despite the report, Alan decided to suspend his disbelief until he and Brian could check out the report together. Brian was quite surprised when Alan proposed this but readily agreed to wait while Alan met with his next client. Then they drove to the school in Alan's car.

On the drive Alan encouraged Brian to talk about his classes. By the time they reached the school it seemed more and more likely that Brian really had attended at least some of his classes. They were fortunate in being able to meet briefly with two of Brian's teachers, who affirmed that Brian had indeed been in class. Both gave Brian suggestions about how to improve his work. When Alan presented their case to the school attendance clerk, she reviewed her records and found that a mistake had been made.

Back in the car, Brian smiled for the first time. He said, "This time truth was on my side." Alan agreed. Suddenly Brian's expression changed. He said, "I can understand better now about truth…. I was lied to and I actually did lie to you, too." He explained that Shari had promised him when he was convicted that she would be true to him while he was away. He counted on that. Since getting out he had been trying to contact her, but she wasn't returning his phone calls. Today he found out that she was pregnant and due to have a baby shortly. So he had been lied to. And he had lied to Alan, too, when he agreed not to contact Shari. When Brian looked up at Alan, there was pain in his eyes. It was quiet in the car for several minutes; Alan let the silence hang in the air unbroken, feeling Brian's pain. Then he said, "OK, Brian let's start over now … and we'll begin by trusting each other."

HISTORY OF SOCIAL WORK IN CRIMINAL JUSTICE

The history of the profession in the very interesting field of criminal justice is one that has slowly evolved out of a distant past when punishment for misdeeds was instantaneous and severe. Archaeological findings have provided evidence of the use of beatings and slavery for those who violated societal norms in ancient times. In the enlightened period of Greek civilization, around 400 BC, new ways of looking at criminal behavior emerged. Hippocrates insisted that natural causes, rooted in the environment and in the family, shaped behavior more significantly than did evil spirits.

Evidently such enlightenment failed to continue, for by the Middle Ages in Europe severe punishments were being used: branding, cutting out an offender's tongue, public hanging, beheading, or burning at the stake. In the 1600s many of these punishments were brought to America by the colonists. Following the Revolutionary War in America, the Pennsylvania Quakers became alarmed about the harshness of punishments being used. "They argued that offenders might be reformed through segregation from the evil influences of other persons and the opportunity to become penitent (thus the term *penitentiary*)" (Galaway, 1981, p. 259). This, then, was the precursor of the present prison system.

In France the Napoleonic Code of 1807 created a new and more humane approach to Western society's thinking about criminal justice for children. The Napoleonic Code established a minimum age at which children could be charged and punished for offenses. Thus was born the principle of differentiating juvenile from adult crime. Separate correctional facilities for children—facilities then known as refuges—began to be provided in the United States in the early 1820s. These privately funded, supposedly charitable organizations unfortunately grew into large institutions characterized by severe discipline.

John Augustus, a Boston shoemaker, is credited with the establishment of probation. In 1841 Augustus requested permission of the courts to serve as surety—to accept personal responsibility and provide supervision—for a man charged with drunkenness. That first successful experience led Augustus to continue his work with other offenders. In 1869 the first formal position for probation work was created by the Commonwealth of Massachusetts; the agent was required to appear at criminal trials of juveniles, to locate suitable homes for them, and to supervise them. In 1878 Boston began to provide probationary supervision for adult offenders.

During the mid-1800s, people in England began to realize that the concept of transporting convicts to other lands was not an effective approach to the problem. Captain Alexander Maconochie, who was responsible for the British penal colony on Norfolk Island in the South Pacific, devised and promoted a concept of conditional release for prisoners. The first correctional system in the United States to experiment with the concept was the Elmira Reformatory in New York State in 1877. The use of parole soon became an accepted principle in corrections in the United States.

By the early 1900s, juvenile courts began to be established across the United States. A special concern of juvenile courts was provision of competent, professional service for children. These courts looked to the new profession of social work for staff to assist juvenile court judges. In contrast, the adult probation and parole agents of the time represented a variety of disciplines but tended to use sheriffs and people with police experience. Gradually this area too was professionalized, but even today probation and parole agents come from a variety of disciplines with quite different philosophical approaches to criminal justice.

Women such as Jane Addams of Hull House and Edith Abbott, dean of the School of Social Service Administration at the University of Chicago, provided much of the leadership, teaching, and research in correctional social work in its early days. Abbott, for example, studied crime and incarceration of women during the Civil War and World War I. Florence Kelley, another of the Hull House residents, was an attorney who advanced the social work profession through the creation of the U.S. Children's Bureau and by developing training programs for the Children's Bureau staff. She also worked to develop child labor laws (Edwards, 1991, as cited in Barker & Branson, 2000). The social work profession, in its infancy, was also assisted by another attorney, Sophonisba Breckinridge, who helped bring training of social workers into universities and, in fact, became the dean of one of the earliest schools of social work, the University of Chicago's School of Social Service Administration (Quam, 1995, as cited in Barker & Branson, 2000). The early schools of social work taught courses on law and social work, and, indeed, much of early social work practice was within courts, child welfare agencies that involved court investigations, and probation and parole systems.

Social casework was introduced within the U.S. Bureau of Prisons in the 1930s. By that time society had begun to accept Freudian concepts of causation of behavior. Increasingly, counseling for prisoners incorporated some of this theory. The federal prisons were fraught with riots resulting from overcrowding, understaffing, and overall poor prison conditions. Reform efforts introduced social casework as part of a rehabilitation effort. Kenneth Pray (1945), a community organizer and educator, helped to clarify the role of social casework in the prisons with his writings in the 1940s.

Police social work programs grew out of demonstration projects initially funded by the federal government, generally by the Law Enforcement Assistance Administration in the 1970s. Harvey Treger, of the Jane Addams School of Social Work at the University of Illinois, is probably the most significant figure in the development of this field. Victim/witness programs were also initially created through governmental funding.

Innovations that occurred in probation and parole in more recent years include the use of home confinement, electronic monitoring, intensive supervision as a substitute for incarceration, and restitution. Victim/witness programs, police social work, alternatives to incarceration, and forensic social work have also continued to evolve. All of these programs brought opportunities for new approaches to practice for social workers in the corrections field. The expansion of prison privatization resulted in custodial care with minimal attention to prisoner rehabilitation. Many of the private prison facilities were located in southern states but were frequently used to house prisoners from northern states. The frail linkages between prisoners and their families became even more tenuous.

Today the criminal justice system is reacting to public sentiment through harsh sentencing and long prison terms, but there are calls for reform. Today, too, social workers and social work students are renewing their interest in police social work, probation and parole, victim/witness assistance programs, domestic violence services within district attorney's offices, and alternative-to-incarceration and prevention programs. Within this context, **forensic social** work is developing and evolving. Forensic social work is viewed by many as a highly specialized area of practice related to the law, while for others forensic social work encompasses practice across broad areas including all of criminal justice as well as areas of child welfare and mental health (Ashford, 2009). The broader definition acknowledges BSWs as well as MSWs as engaged in forensic practice (van Wormer, Roberts, Springer, & Brownell, 2008). Forensic social workers utilize expertise in legal matters related to child welfare, juvenile offenses, divorce issues such as custody determination, and various areas of dispute negotiation (Barker, 2003; O'Neil, 2003). Forensic social work will be further described later in this chapter, but the chapter as a whole will address social work and social policy as they have evolved within the field of criminal justice.

The social work perspective, one that looks at poverty, prejudice, housing, education, and family support, needs to become a part of public policy debate. Hopefully the social work profession will join with other professions such as law, psychiatry, and criminal justice to challenge the punitive and ultimately destructive direction criminal justice policy has taken. The field of criminal justice could be a very exciting arena for new social justice activism and reform!

COMPONENTS OF THE CRIMINAL JUSTICE SYSTEM

Alan Martin, the social worker in the chapter case study, was experienced in the adult as well as juvenile corrections systems. In his practice Alan Martin worked with all of the subsystems of the criminal justice system. Sometimes referred to as the three Cs (cops, courts, and corrections), the criminal justice system in the United States grew out of the system brought to this country by colonists from England. Over time it developed into a complex and somewhat fragmented system, with separate subunits that did not always interact effectively. It acquired a strange and somewhat inconsistent combination of goals: to punish, to deter crime, to rehabilitate, and to remove criminals from society.

Specific laws and regulations pertain to each of the three criminal justice system areas. Social workers will need to learn the laws and regulations that guide the area of the criminal justice system in which they work. A police social worker, for example, will develop an understanding of arrest procedures, statutory rape laws, and laws pertaining to child and spouse abuse. A social worker serving as a parole agent, such as Alan Martin in the case study, will become familiar with the administrative law that defines the responsibilities of probation and parole agents, with parole contracts, and with revocation procedures.

Two terms that will be used in the remainder of this chapter, and that should be understood by all informed citizens, need further definition: *misdemeanor* and *felony*. A **misdemeanor** is a relatively minor offense but certainly more serious than a misdeed; it is punishable by fines, probation, or a relatively brief jail or prison sentence unless taken to extreme or done repeatedly. A **felony** is a serious crime. Murder, rape, and armed burglary are felonies, while defacing public property is a misdemeanor. Assault could be a misdemeanor, while aggravated assault (involving deadly force or intent to rob, kill, or rape) would be considered a felony. Under federal law and also in many states, the consequence of a felony is a prison sentence of 1 or more years; the most extreme penalty for a felony is the death penalty. Professional people, such as social workers, may be prohibited from being licensed or certified to practice in their state if they have a criminal record.

Two additional terms, *probation* and *parole,* were encountered in the Alan Martin case study, and these terms will be used frequently in this chapter. It is important to understand the differences between the two. **Probation** is a sentence, following conviction for a crime, in which the offender is ordered to undergo supervision for a prescribed period of time instead of serving that time in prison. Brief sentencing to jail may precede release under probation, but the majority of the sentence may be served in the community if the terms of the probation contract are met. The community supervision is provided by a court-designated probation officer who may be a social worker. In **parole**, a person has served a portion of his or her sentence in prison and then receives an early release to complete the sentence in the community under supervision. In probation, the prison sentence is said to be suspended in that the person does not normally go to prison unless revoked (sent to prison) because of behavior that violates the probation contract. Persons on parole, too, can be revoked, returned to prison for the remainder of the sentence.

Let us now examine the three major components of the criminal justice system in the United States and the interesting ways in which social work as a profession has found a niche in each of these areas.

Law Enforcement

When we speak of law enforcement, we are essentially referring to the police. The police, as law enforcement officers, comprise the first of the three areas of the criminal justice system. What exactly is the role of the police? It is much broader than most citizens realize.

Police are responsible for responding to citizens' complaints and for questioning and apprehending persons. Before charging a person with a crime, however, police have considerable decision-making responsibility. Figure 11.1, for example, illustrates the decisions made by police in 2009 for the juvenile offenders they took into custody. Note that more than two-thirds of these youths were turned over to the juvenile courts, 22.3 percent were handled within the police department and released, and 8.8 percent were referred to criminal or adult courts. This compares with 50.8 percent of juveniles referred to juvenile courts, 45 percent handled within the police department and released, and 1.3 percent referred to criminal or adult courts in 1972 (Pastore & Maguire, 2005, Table 4.26.2005; U.S. Department of Justice, 2010). Police decide whether a charge is warranted or another alternative might be considered. Current law determines the officer's decision. Prevailing public sentiment or the political climate might also be influential and might, in part, account for the tougher sentencing of youths in recent years. Often it is a matter of chance, visibility (as in a high-crime neighborhood that is under greater scrutiny than other areas), or past behavior that determines whether a violation of the law even results in contact with the police. Shopkeepers, school authorities, and neighbors may be more prone to call the police in some parts of the city or community than in others.

In addition to responding to criminal complaints, police are also responsible for keeping the peace. In this role they encounter families in crisis, domestic violence, suicidal behavior, and substance abuse. One of the frustrations of police officers is that they receive little recognition by the community or even by the police system itself for the human services they routinely provide.

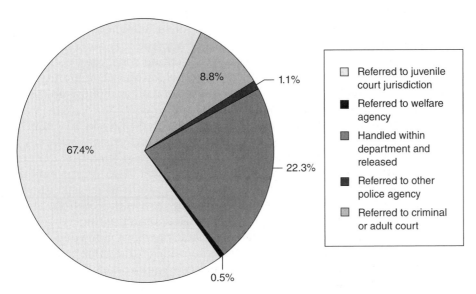

Figure 11.1

Police Dispositions of Juvenile Offenders Taken into Custody, 2009

Source: Adapted from Table 4.25.2009, Juveniles taken into police custody, *Sourcebook of Criminal Justice Statistics Online* (2009). Washington, DC: U.S. Department of Justice, Bureau of Justice Statistics. Retrieved from http://www.albany.edu/sourcebook/pdf/t4252009.pdf

Police social work is the practice of social work within police departments, within courthouses, or in jails. Police social work is still a relatively underdeveloped area of social work practice, but it appears to be an expanding area of the profession. Police and social workers share a common concern about personal and family crisis situations. A considerable portion of police calls are of a social service nature, because people are most likely to call the police when they don't know where else to turn for help. In communities where police social workers are available, dispositions of cases frequently result in redirection from the criminal justice to the social service system.

When social workers were first employed by police departments, they were assigned to youth services. Their tasks included resolution of parent–child conflicts; referral of children to child guidance or child psychiatric clinics; assessment of child abuse, neglect, and abandonment situations; and a variety of crisis roles. Police social workers have proven their value in domestic dispute situations. Because these are some of the most dangerous cases for police, police social workers' ability to ease the tension in such situations, as well as to assess and intervene, has impressed police departments.

Cases handled by police social workers may include traffic accidents and fatalities, child abuse, suicide, alcohol and substance abuse, mental health emergencies, and family disputes. Social workers provide crisis intervention, brief individual or family counseling, referrals, victim assistance and sexual assault intervention, as well as community crime prevention efforts. The same problem-solving process used in other areas of generalist social work practice applies to police social work. Skill in engaging clients and quickly forming effective, empathic, respectful working relationships is an essential asset in volatile situations. Psychosocial assessment requires collecting and organizing information, but in police work, risk factors must be especially carefully determined. This

Psychosocial assessment requires collecting and organizing information, but in police work, risk factors must be especially carefully determined.

is true in domestic disputes and child abuse, and even lethality potential must be considered in cases involving potential suicide or homicide. Intervention often involves negotiation, mediation, and advocacy, and it is generally handled collaboratively with police officers. As an intervention concludes, police social workers often engage the clients, police personnel, or other community representatives in evaluating the results of the intervention effort. Follow-up contacts may be considered at this time, too (Knox & Roberts, 2009).

Police social workers are obviously not confined to desks in police departments. In addition to home visits and crime scene crisis work, they are increasingly involved in crime prevention work in the community. Often, a team consisting of a social worker and a police officer seeks to prevent crime through educational programs provided to youth groups, in the schools, or to civic associations. Today, suburban police systems are in the forefront of community organization work, with police personnel participating in and often leading community action efforts related to crime prevention, the development of youth services, drug courts, and even the reform of mental commitment laws. Their professional education makes police social workers especially well suited for such responsibilities.

The Courts

Courts exist at the federal, state, and local levels, and they range from municipal courts to the highest court in the land, the U.S. Supreme Court. Courts have two primary functions: civil and criminal. Civil functions deal with the rights of private citizens and may result in fines or monetary damages. Criminal functions involve determination of guilt or innocence; punishment such as a prison sentence may result. In the criminal court system, a case begins with an arrest.

Some persons may have charges against them dropped, and therefore they discontinue their involvement in the criminal justice system. In fact, at each step along the way—from the point of police questioning through arrest, charging, and sentencing—a certain percentage of persons exit the system. Only a fraction of those initially detained for questioning are actually found guilty and incarcerated. In this "criminal justice funnel," the top of the funnel represents all the crimes that have been committed. The people who exit the system along the way are found in the slanting sides of the funnel. At the bottom of the funnel are those persons actually prosecuted and sent to prison—approximately 3 percent. As research studies described later in this chapter suggest, racial biases may be among the factors that influence decisions at each step from questioning through incarceration.

Social workers are increasingly found in the courts of the United States, where they serve in several interesting ways. One role for social workers is work with and on behalf of victims of crime. Social workers were among the pioneers of victim/witness programs. These programs, often housed in the local district attorney's office, assist people who are intimidated by the legal process. Programs to help battered women through the court system were among the first to emerge. Today social workers assist victims of domestic abuse to obtain restraining or harassment no-contact orders, and they serve as client advocates in the courts. Persons who are injured in crimes are also provided services that emphasize compassion, affirmation, and emotional support.

Testifying in court is a responsibility for social workers in child and family services; across all areas of criminal justice and forensic social work, this is a primary area of expertise. NASW has a variety of resources that help to prepare social workers, beginning with how to deal with receipt of a **subpoena** (an order to appear in court on a specified date). Another role for social workers in the court system is that of work on behalf of the court in conducting a **presentence investigation**. If a case goes to court and the offender is convicted, a presentence investigation may be requested by the judge. Presentence investigations are conducted by probation officers, many of whom are social workers; the investigations typically involve both office and home visits with family members, the client, and other collaborative sources. The report is likely to be very detailed and comprehensive, including a social history and descriptions of the offender's home and work environment, education and employment, and physical or mental health problems, as well as an identification of existing social supports. The concluding recommendation often evaluates "the merits and risks of keeping an offender in the community," which can be especially "important in cases involving the physical and sexual abuse of children, where the needs of the victim constitute a major factor in the presentence investigation" (Isenstadt, 1995, p. 71).

When the court decides to sentence a convicted person, the result may be a jail term, probation, or imprisonment. Note that there are significant differences between jail and prison. A **jail** is a correctional facility used for short sentences or for detaining persons while they await a court hearing. A **prison** is used for lengthier sentences, generally for a number of years. In passing sentence, judges are required to abide by the legal code, which provides parameters for the length of imprisonment; therefore, judges' options are somewhat limited.

Alternatives to prison are less costly than prison, and they are a good deal more humane than a prison sentence. Any alternative program mandated by the court is usually attached to a sentence of probation. **Community-service sentencing** usually requires the offender to work without pay in a private or governmental human service organization for a specified period of time. **Restitution** programs require that offenders, adult as well as juvenile offenders, compensate their victims (usually monetarily) for the losses suffered as a result of the criminal offense. Restitution is most frequently used in conjunction with property crimes, which are the most prevalent of all crimes committed. Social workers often find that a monetary payment made by the offender has less long-range meaning than the experience of facing the victim, explaining the offense, and seeking to restore the loss.

Forensic Social Work

While forensic social work can be broadly defined to include almost all areas of social work practice in criminal justice, the more narrow definition views it as a specialized area of practice built on in-depth knowledge of the law and litigation in civil and criminal justice. "It is the assessment and evaluation expertise of the social worker, as an unbiased party in the legal system, that forms the foundation for this type of social work practice" (Ritter, Vakalahi, & Kiernan-Stern, 2009, p. 154). Courts, for example, may request an evaluation and recommendation for the purpose of determining child custody in a divorce situation or following the death of a sole parent. After a careful psychosocial study including interviewing the child, the social worker will provide testimony as an unbiased expert to assist the judge in determining what is in the best interests of a child or children. Similarly, social workers may assist in mental competency hearings when defendants' criminal behaviors appear to be related to mental illness or developmental disability (Ritter et al., 2009).

Forensic social workers may also be requested by the court to conduct a presentence investigation, or they may be asked to obtain information from the family of, for example, a child who has been physically or sexually abused. The forensic social worker may be asked by the court to recommend "ways to resolve, punish, or rehabilitate those found guilty of crimes or negligence in civil actions" (Barker & Branson, 2000, p. 16). If the forensic social worker recommends community service, for example, the court may further ask that social worker to facilitate and monitor the sentence.

Forensic social workers are employed by court systems on a full- or part-time basis, or they may function as private practitioners. They are highly specialized and function only within their areas of expertise. The National Organization of Forensic Social Work has been in existence for approximately 30 years. In 2011 it initiated the *Journal of Forensic Social Work;* it also offers annual conferences. (See http://www.nofsw.org for additional information on this organization.)

The Correctional System

The **correctional system** is that part of the criminal justice system that uses imprisonment, probation, parole, and various alternatives to change the behaviors of persons convicted of crime. The two major components of the correctional system in the United States are prisons and community-based programs. Each of the 50 states has its own correctional system with varying structures, sanctions, and administrative laws. The federal government has the Bureau of Prisons, which operates the federal prison system and is a component of the U.S. Department of Justice, and a federal probation system operated by the courts. In addition, the Department of Defense maintains military prisons. States have their own correctional systems; at the local level, some counties and cities also operate correctional facilities and probation departments. There is considerable variety of organizational structures as well as weak linkages among these many systems.

Prisons
Across jurisdictional systems, prisons are classified as minimum-, medium-, and maximum-security facilities. Until recently, all prisons were owned and administered by governmental bodies, but private enterprise has created a very profitable prison industry in some parts of the country. There has been considerable construction of new prisons, yet they tend to be extremely overcrowded, housing populations in excess of their capacity day in and day out. Juvenile facilities are separate from prisons for adults. They too are seriously overcrowded, presenting the same health, safety, and security problems found in adult facilities. Smaller, community-based correctional programs serve as prerelease centers, halfway houses, and group homes.

The various jurisdictions have different procedures for assigning persons to correctional facilities. Often newly sentenced persons are observed in specially designated reception facilities for several weeks while vocational and psychological testing is done to help select the most appropriate prison facility. Social workers participate in the evaluation procedure, gathering social history data or supplementing information already available if a presentence investigation was done.

An amazing increase is now occurring in the rate of imprisonment of women (see Figure 11.2). As van Wormer points out, women "are receiving

Female Prisoners

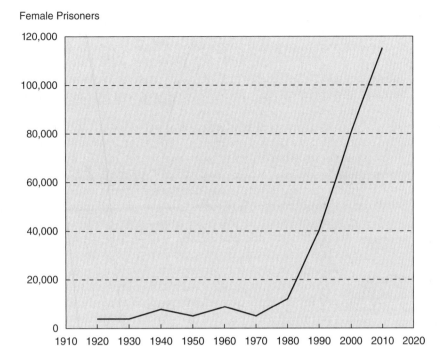

Figure 11.2

Sentenced Female Prisoners under Jurisdiction of State and Federal Correctional Authorities, 1925–2009

Source: Washington, DC: U.S. Department of Justice, Bureau of Justice Statistics; Table 6.41.2009, Number and rate (per 100,000 U.S. resident female population) of female prisoners under jurisdiction of State and Federal correctional authorities, *Sourcebook of Criminal Justice Statistics Online* (2009). Washington, DC: U.S. Department of Justice, Bureau of Justice Statistics. Retrieved from http://www. albany.edu/sourcebook/pdf/t6412009.pdf. K. Maguire & A. L. Pastore. (Eds.). (2001). Figure 6.2. Sentenced female prisoners under jurisdiction of state and federal correctional authorities on December 31. *Sourcebook of Criminal Justice Statistics* (2000) (p. 505).

treatment in a system run by and designed for men" (2010, p. 3). The same classification system tends to be used for both male and female prisoners, yet research demonstrates that women prisoners are significantly less of a threat to other inmates or to the outside community, should they escape. Instead of basing the system on risk, Farr (2000) calls for a prison classification system for women based on need in treatment areas such as substance abuse counseling; obstetric and gynecological health care; improving the connections between women and their children; instituting parenting skills training; and treatment for the mental disorders, such as depression, that appear to be more prevalent among women prisoners. Strengths-based approaches are gradually emerging, too, in group work with women inmates and in preparation programs as women, especially older women with lengthy sentences, plan their return to the "free world" (van Wormer, 2010).

Prison social workers are prisoners' links to their home community. In women's prisons, for example, it is often the prison social worker who communicates with the foster care agency when children have been placed in care pending the mother's release from prison. Family members often have great difficulty accepting the imprisonment. Feelings of anger, abandonment, fear, and denial have to be worked with. Just as families need to make very difficult adjustments when a member is imprisoned, other social, emotional, and economic adjustments are required when release from prison is anticipated. It would be wonderful if all prisons had social workers with sufficient time to provide these services. The reality is that some prisons have no social work staff at all, and other prisons have so few social workers that staff must carefully prioritize their tasks.

Although social workers are members of the prison staff, they do serve as communication facilitators between inmates and other prison staff. As advocates for prisoners, social workers attempt to secure resources, such as access to scarce educational, social service, or vocational programs. Social workers advocate with prison administrators for changes in policies or procedures affecting the inmate population. They also promote an exchange of information between families of inmates (especially children in foster care) and the prisoners. During medical emergencies, prison social workers provide updated medical information between family members and prisoners and, if appropriate, with other segments of the prison community.

Prison riots have demonstrated the role of social workers in negotiation. Social workers have been selected by prisoners to present their issues to administrators and to the outside world. Given the serious overcrowding of prisons today, most prison facilities experience tension and violence almost daily. Fighting between prisoners is a common occurrence. Violence in prisons is not limited to inmate-inflicted abuse, nor is it only a function of modern times. Inmates of some of the early prison facilities were forced to work as servants in the homes of wardens, where many abuses were suffered, including beatings and death for disobedience. Female prisoners have always been subject to sexual abuse. Lawsuits filed on their behalf and public investigations into such abuses have resulted in the implementation of procedures that require a formal hearing and response to the complaints of inmates in correctional facilities, but this has not eliminated exploitation or violence.

The absence of heterosexual outlets encourages same-sex relationships in prisons and jails. These relationships may provide some level of comfort and closeness, but they may also produce jealousies, heated altercations, and acts of reprisal for unfaithfulness. Especially in prisons that are overcrowded, rape also occurs, sometimes with extensive physical injuries.

In prison and jail facilities social workers seek to reduce violence by building bridges between inmates and staff, by helping prisoners develop or enhance their sense of self-worth, and by reducing the inmates' sense of powerlessness. Behavior rehearsal and role-playing are used to teach new behaviors or to modify existing actions. Educational and skill-building programs are implemented. Techniques including reality therapy, behavior modification, transactional analysis, and educational programs are used, depending on the social worker's level of skill and on inmates' needs.

Professional Identity

Practice Behavior Example: Social workers practice personal reflection and self-correction to assure continual professional development

Critical Thinking Question: How can social workers sustain their professional identity and values when working within the criminal justice system?

Community-Based Corrections

Community-based corrections are programs that provide an alternative to incarceration. Probation and parole, the major community-based programs, require ongoing supervision until the original sentence is concluded. The person providing that supervision is generally referred to as a parole (or probation) agent or officer. Preferences regarding the use of *agent* or *officer* vary among the many federal, state, county, and city jurisdictions; we will use *agent*. Most state probation and parole positions require a bachelor's degree in social work or criminal justice. Federal positions require 1 year of graduate courses in addition to the bachelor's degree. Sometimes a related degree is acceptable.

While parole provides for the early release of a prisoner from a penal institution, probation permits the offender to avoid imprisonment, remaining in the community to serve her or his sentence. Both parole and probation are conditional; that is, if the terms of the probation or parole agreement are violated, the offender may be subject to **revocation** (may be returned to prison for the remainder of the sentence). The terms of the agreement are identified in a contract signed by the client and the agent. A typical contract is shown in Box 11.1. Note that space is provided for specific terms for the individual client. Box 11.2 illustrates a set of specific terms that might be used with someone convicted of a sex offense.

Helping people to meet the terms of the probation or parole agreement is a key function of the social worker. In truth, the client's life is subject to almost continuous scrutiny by the social worker. Developing a relationship of trust with a corrections client is not always easy. It requires skill and commitment from the social worker.

Alan Martin, the social worker in the case study, carried many of the responsibilities of both parole agent and probation agent. As a professional social worker in the role of parole agent, Alan Martin sought to apply the knowledge, values, and skills of generalist practice that he had learned while in college. He used the same problem-solving steps cited in Chapter 1, a process that underpins all generalist social work practice. If Brian Cook had been sentenced by the judge to probation instead of prison, Alan Martin might have been assigned as his probation agent. The role of the probation agent is very similar to that of the parole agent, so Alan would have engaged Brian in the same problem-solving work that was done during Brian's parole.

The correctional system requires the agent, in this case Alan Martin, to assist the client in meeting the terms of the probation agreement. The same contract form, citing the very same terms, may be used for both probation and parole, as is the case with the contract shown in Box 11.1. Some correctional systems, however, use separate forms. The probation client generally has not left his or her home community as a result of the conviction and sentence; therefore, the agent has the advantage of working with a person who is still connected to family, neighborhood, and job or school. The pressing need to find housing or employment—so often the case with parole clients—is not usually present, nor is reintegration into the community an issue to be worked through.

Probation and parole agents often have extremely large caseloads. They range widely, from 20 to 100 clients. This makes it difficult for some agents to know their clients well. Often they use much of their time managing crises and barely spend more than 15 minutes with the client who reports for scheduled monthly meetings. Technology—computers, cell phones, fax machines—helps probation and parole agents handle heavy workloads. Some agents may use technology to work, in part, from their homes.

Probation and parole departments have analyzed the workload and have found that there are identifiable corrections populations that need more time and greater expertise than others. Accordingly, some jurisdictions have created

Box 11.1   Probation/Parole Rules

DEPARTMENT OF CORRECTIONS
Division of Community Corrections
DOC-10 (Rev. 12/2006)

RULES OF COMMUNITY SUPERVISION

WISCONSIN
Administrative Code
Chapter DOC 328 & 332
Federal Law
42 U.S.C. ss 290DD-3, 290ee-3
Federal Regulation
42 C.F.R. Part 2

OFFENDER NAME _____

DOC NUMBER _____

Notice: If you are on parole and sentenced for crimes committed on or after June 1, 1984, or have chosen to have the new Good Time Law apply to your case and you violate these rules, the highest possible parole violator sentence will be the total sentence less time already served in prison or jail in connection with the offense.

As established by Administrative Rule DOC 328.11, you have an opportunity for administrative review of certain types of decision through the offender complaint process.

The following rules are in addition to any court-ordered conditions. Your probation, parole, or extended supervision may be revoked if you do not comply with any of your court-ordered conditions or if you violate any of the following rules.

1. You shall avoid all conduct which is in violation of federal or state statute, municipal or county ordinances, tribal law or which is not in the best interest of the public welfare or your rehabilitation. Some rules listed below are covered under this rule as conduct contrary to law and are listed for particular attention.

2. You shall report all arrests or police contact to your agent within 72 hours.

3. You shall make every effort to accept the opportunities and counseling offered by supervision.

    The confidentiality of drug, mental health, and alcohol treatment records is protected by Federal and/or state laws and regulations. Generally programs you are involved in may not say to a person outside the Department of Corrections that an offender is attending the program, or disclose any information identifying him/her as a drug/alcohol abuser unless: 1) You consent in writing; or 2) The disclosure is allowed by a court order; or 3) The disclosure is made to medical personnel in a medical emergency or to a qualified personnel for research, audit, or program evaluation; or 4) You commit or threaten to commit a crime either at the program or against any person who works for the program. Programs that contract with the Wisconsin Department of Corrections can release information to Wisconsin Department of Corrections staff.

    Violation of the Federal law and regulations by a program is a crime. These regulations do not protect any information about suspected child abuse or neglect from being reported under state law to appropriate authorities.

    Refusal to sign the consent for releasing information, including placement for treatment, shall be considered a refusal of the program.

4. You shall inform your agent of your whereabouts and activities as he/she directs.

5. You shall submit a written report monthly and any other such relevant information as directed by your agent.

6. You shall make yourself available for searches or tests ordered by your agent including but not limited to urinalysis, breathalyzer, DNA collection and blood samples or search of residence or any property under your control.

7. You shall not change residence or employment unless you get approval in advance from your agent, or in the case of emergency, notify your agent of the change within 72 hours.

8. You shall not leave the State of Wisconsin unless you get approval and a travel permit in advance from your agent.

9. You shall not purchase, trade, sell or operate a motor vehicle unless you get approval in advance from your agent.

10. You shall not borrow money or purchase on credit unless you get approval in advance from your agent.

11. You shall pay monthly supervision fees as directed by your agent in accordance with Wis. Stats. s.304.073 or s.304.074, DOC Administrative Rule Chapter 328.043 to 328.046 and shall comply with any department and/or vendor procedures regarding payment of fees.

12. You shall not purchase, possess, own or carry any firearm or any weapon unless you get approval in advance from your agent. Your agent may not grant permission to carry a firearm if you are prohibited from possessing a firearm under Wis. Stat. s. 941.29, Wisconsin Act 71, the Federal Gun Control Act (GCA), or any other state or federal law.

13. You shall not, as a convicted felon, and until you have successfully completed the terms and conditions of your sentence, vote in any federal, state or local election as outlined in Wisconsin Statutes s.6.03(1)(b).

14. You shall abide by all rules of any detention or correctional facility in which you may be confined.

15. You shall provide true and correct information verbally and in writing, in response to inquiries by the agent.

16. You shall report to your agent as directed for scheduled and unscheduled appointments.

17. You shall submit to the polygraph (lie detector) examination process as directed by your agent in accordance with Wisconsin Administrative Code 332.15.

18. You shall pay fees for the polygraph (lie detector) examination process as directed by your agent in accordance with Wisconsin Administrative Code 332.17(5) and 332.18 and shall comply with any required Wisconsin Department of Corrections procedures regarding payment of fees.

19. You shall follow any specific rules that may be issued by an agent to achieve the goals and objectives of your supervision. The rules may be modified at any time, as appropriate. The specific rules imposed at this time are stated below. You shall place your initials at the end of each specific rule to show you have read the rule.

I have reviewed and explained these rules to the offender.		I have received a copy of these rules.	
AGENT SIGNATURE	AREA NUMBER	OFFENDER SIGNATURE	DATE SIGNED

Source: Provided by Peggy Kendrigan, State of Wisconsin Department of Corrections, Division of Community Corrections. (2007). Madison, WI: Wisconsin Administrative Code.

separate units to work with mentally ill offenders, for example, or those whose crime involves substance abuse or sex offenses. Social workers in specialized units usually have a smaller caseload; frequently they have MSW degrees plus experience.

Box 11.2 Standard Sex Offender Rules

DEPARTMENT OF CORRECTIONS
Division of Community Corrections
DOC-10SO (Rev. 12/2006)

STANDARD SEX OFFENDER RULES

WISCONSIN
Administrative Code
Chapter DOC 301, 328, 332
Federal Law
42 U.S.C. ss 290DD-3, 290ee-3
Federal Regulation
42 C.F.R. Part 2

OFFENDER NAME _____ DOC NUMBER _____

Notice: If you are on parole and sentenced for crimes committed on or after June 1, 1984, or have chosen to have the new Good Time Law apply to your case and you violate these rules, the highest possible parole violator sentence will be the total sentence less time already served in prison or jail in connection with the offense.

As established by Administrative Rule DOC 328.11, you have an opportunity for administrative review of certain types of decision through the offender complaint process.

The following rules are in addition to any court-ordered conditions. Your probation, parole or extended supervision may be revoked if you do not comply with any of your court-ordered conditions or if you violate any of the following rules.

1. You shall have no contact with _____ nor any prior victims of your offenses nor their family members without prior agent approval. This includes face-to-face, telephone, mail, electronic, third party, or "drive by" contact.

2. You shall have no contact with anyone under the age of 18 without prior agent approval and unless accompanied by an adult sober chaperone approved by your agent. This includes face-to-face, telephone, mail, electronic, third party, or "drive by" contact.

3. You shall not establish, pursue, nor maintain any dating and/or romantic and/or sexual relationship without prior agent approval.

4. You shall fully cooperate with, participate in, and successfully complete all evaluations, counseling, and treatment as required by your agent, including but not limited to sex offender programming. "Successful completion" shall be determined by your agent and treatment provider(s). If sex offender treatment is required, you must attend and account for the details of the behavior committed in your conviction offense(s). Failure to admit the offense(s) or provide a detailed description will be considered a violation of your supervision and may result in disciplinary action including the recommendation for revocation of your supervision. Information revealed in treatment concerning your conviction offense(s) cannot be used against you in criminal proceedings.

5. You shall not reside nor "stay" overnight in any place other than a pre-approved residence without prior agent approval. "Overnight" is defined as the daily period of time between the hours of _____ p.m. and _____ a.m. unless redefined by your agent in advance.

6. You shall permit no person to reside nor stay in your designated residence between the hours of _____ p.m. and _____ a.m. without prior agent approval.

7. You shall not possess, consume, nor use any controlled substance nor possess any drug paraphernalia without a current prescription from a physician from whom you are receiving medical treatment. Verification must be provided to your agent as directed.

8. You shall not possess nor view any sexually explicit material-visual, auditory, nor computer-generated-without prior agent approval.

9. You shall seek, obtain, and maintain employment as directed by your agent. You shall obtain agent approval before accepting any offer of employment and prior to beginning any volunteer work.

10. You shall not purchase, own, nor manage any residential rental properties without prior agent approval.

11. You shall fully comply with all sex offender registry requirements as applicable and directed by your agent and/or required by statute. You shall immediately respond to all correspondence from the Sex Offender Registry Program.

12. You shall fully comply with Wisconsin Statute 165.76 requiring a biological specimen to be submitted to the State Crime Lab for DNA testing as applicable and as directed by your agent.

13. You shall pay all court ordered financial obligations and treatment co-payments as directed by your agent in accordance with your established payment plan.

14. You shall not purchase, possess, nor use a computer, software, hardware, nor modem without prior agent approval.

I have reviewed and explained these rules to the offender.		I have received a copy of these rules.	
AGENT SIGNATURE	AREA NUMBER	OFFENDER SIGNATURE	DATE SIGNED

Source: Provided by Peggy Kendrigan, State of Wisconsin Department of Corrections, Division of Community Corrections. (2007). Milwaukee, WI.

One approach to minimizing **recidivism** (the repetition of criminal behavior resulting in return to prison or reinstatement of a prison sentence) is **risk rating** in which clients with higher risks of recidivism are placed under closer and more frequent supervision. A risk-rating assessment similar to the one shown in Box 11.3 is now used in most state and county probation and parole departments as well as in Canada and Australia. Considerable work by the National Center for Crime and Delinquency and other corrections agencies has been done to validate the risk assessment instruments that are used. A score of

Box 11.3   Admission to Adult Field Caseload

DEPARTMENT OF CORRECTIONS
Division of Community Corrections
DOC-502 (Rev. 7/96)

ADMISSION TO ADULT FIELD CASELOAD
ASSESSMENT OF OFFENDER RISK

WISCONSIN

A

OFFENDER NAME	Last	First	MI	DOC NUMBER
DATE PLACED ON PROBATION OR RELEASED ON PAROLE IN WISCONSIN (MM/DD/YY)		AGENT LAST NAME		AREA NUMBER
FACILITY OF RELEASE			CODE	DATE COMPLETED (MM/DD/YY)

(Select the appropriate answer and enter the associated weight in the score column.)   **SCORE**

Number of Address Changes in last 12 Months:
(Prior to incarceration for parolees)
- 0 None
- 2 One
- 3 Two or more

Percentage of Time Employed in Last 12 Months:
(Prior to incarceration for parolees)
- 0 60% or more
- 1 40% - 59%
- 2 Under 40%
- 0 Not applicable

Alcohol Usage Problems:
(Prior to incarceration for parolees)
- 0 No interference with functioning
- 2 Occasional abuse; some disruption of functioning
- 4 Frequent abuse; serious disruption; needs treatment

Other Drug Problems:
(Prior to incarceration for parolees)
- 0 No interference with functioning
- 1 Occasional abuse; some disruption of functioning
- 2 Frequent abuse; serious disruption; needs treatment

Attitude:
- 0 Motivated to change; receptive to assistance
- 3 Dependent or unwilling to accept responsibility
- 5 Rationalizes behavior; negative; not motivated to change

Age at First Conviction:
(or Juvenile Adjudications)
- 0 24 or older
- 2 20 - 23
- 4 19 or younger

Number of Prior Periods of Probation/Parole Supervision:
(Adult or Juvenile)
- 0 None
- 4 One or more

Number of Prior Probation/Parole Revocations:
(Adult or Juvenile)
- 0 None
- 4 One or more

Number of Prior Felony Convictions:
(or Juvenile Adjudications)
- 0 None
- 2 One
- 4 Two or more

Convictions or Juvenile Adjudications for:
(Include current offense, Score must be either 0,2,3, or 5.)
- 0 None of the Offense(s) stated below
- 2 Burglary, theft, auto theft, or robbery
- 3 Worthless checks or forgery
- 5 One or more from the above categories

Convictions or Juvenile Adjudication for Assaultive Offense within Last Five Years:
(An offense which involves the use of a weapon, physical force or the threat of force)
- 15 Yes
- 0 No

TOTAL _____   Total all scores to arrive at the risk assessment score

CASE FILE

Source: Provided by Peggy Kendrigan, State of Wisconsin Department of Corrections, Division of Community Corrections. (2007). Milwaukee, WI.

15 or higher on the form in Box 11.3 would suggest the need for a maximum level of supervision; scores of 7 to 14 support a median level, and a score of 6 or below would normally result in a minimal level of probation or parole supervision. Generally, a minimum level of supervision or monitoring would involve contacts only once every 3 months, although more frequent telephone

or mail-in reports might be required. By contrast, a maximum level of supervision could involve office visits every 2 weeks and possibly a home visit every month (Kendrigan, personal communication, January 2, 2008).

Interestingly, 2010 data from the Bureau of Justice Statistics demonstrate that for the first time since 1980, the number of persons in state and federal probation and parole programs has declined. A decline of 0.9 percent (from 5,064,975 to 5,018,855) in 2009 resulted from an increase in the number of persons who successfully completed the terms of their probation or parole. There was also a decline in the recidivism rate: the number of persons who were reincarcerated for violating their parole contracts. It will be interesting to see if this downward trend continues.

Intensive probation is a specialized category of probation for persons who have committed violent crimes or who have displayed violence or hostility and are considered to be of high risk. This form of probation utilizes frequent client contacts—daily or at least several contacts per week. Electronic monitoring using wrist or ankle bracelets (increasingly with GPS) also provides a means of controlling clients' movements. Intensive probation is more cost efficient than imprisonment and provides a relatively high level of community protection. It is also useful with special client populations such as those who chronically abuse alcohol or drugs.

No other area of social work practice gives the social worker as much police authority as probation and parole. "In most jurisdictions the probation and parole officer not only performs supervision, surveillance, and counseling roles, but also has the authority to handcuff, search, arrest, and seize property and otherwise restrict clients' freedom" (Netherland, 1987, pp. 356–357). The agent also has the right to recommend a client's return to prison if terms of parole are not met. Agents may require clients to participate in treatment such as substance abuse counseling or batterers' group therapy. This power cannot be taken lightly.

Several other forms of community-based corrections programs exist. Some, such as victim–offender mediation and restitution, have already been described. Informal diversion and community service requirements are consistent with the principles of restorative justice, which values healing over punishment and retribution. Informal diversion is used with first offenders or for minor offenses and is most common in juvenile justice systems. With informal diversion, an authorized intake worker (sometimes a social worker) or officer obtains agreement from the offender to abide by the law and, possibly, to make restitution, in lieu of being prosecuted for the offense. This is both humane and cost effective. Community service may be a component of diversion, or it may be the sentence following conviction. It requires unpaid labor that is useful to the community and that, when possible, utilizes the client's knowledge or skills. With house arrest, people are confined to their homes with electronic or computer surveillance ensuring that they do not leave.

There is a growing body of empirical research demonstrating that community-based programs do work and that lengthy prison sentences are not effective deterrents to crime. Recidivism rates are often higher for persons spending, for example, 30 months in prison than for those in prison for 12 to 13 months. "Policies such as California's three strikes law or mandatory minimums that increase imprisonment not only burden state budgets, but also fail to enhance public safety" (Wright, 2010, p. 9). Programs provided in prison, such as sex offender treatment, appear to be less effective in reducing further offenses than cognitive-behavioral programs provided while offenders are living in the community. Shock probation and Scared Straight (programs that incite fear to prevent crime) and correctional boot camps have also been found to be ineffective with youths or adults (MacKenzie, 2000).

The Juvenile Justice System

The juvenile court system evolved from quite a different philosophy than the adult court system and came out of the pioneering and social reform work of Jane Addams and Hull House workers, among others. Established in 1899 in Chicago, it was born of the belief that children were not fully developed human beings capable of making judgments about their behavior or controlling their lives in the same way adults were expected to do. Juvenile courts were designed to intervene when children misbehaved or were in need of protection. There was a strong belief that children could be rehabilitated. Treatment was stressed, as well as separation of the child from adult court systems. Juvenile court proceedings were conducted informally, often without legal representation.

While Jane Addams and her Hull House colleagues in Chicago spearheaded social reform including the founding of the first juvenile court in 1899, Margaret Murray Washington (wife of Booker T. Washington) was actively pursuing similar goals in the South. The pioneers of this movement were later referred to as the "child savers," because their efforts led to the establishment of child labor laws, kindergartens, compulsory school attendance, and, perhaps their most ambitious project, the development of a juvenile justice system (Moon, Sundt, Cullen, & Wright, 2000). Removing children from the adult court and prison system was a major breakthrough. It required the skills of noted civic leaders like Margaret Murray Washington, whose personal involvement led to the development of Mt. Meigs Reformatory for Juvenile Law-Breakers in Alabama and the Mt. Meigs Rescue Home for Girls (Dickerson, 2001).

From the beginning, social workers were a major presence in the day-to-day operation of the children's courts and juvenile justice programs. By the 1960s, a major philosophical shift occurred. After two landmark Supreme Court decisions, primarily the 1967 case, *In re: Gault,* formal legal processes were instituted within juvenile courts, affording children increased legal protections. No longer could the courts imprison or detain children without due process. An **adversarial court** evolved in which attorneys representing the prosecution and attorneys representing the defense were permitted to engage in cross-examination. Children's courts quickly lost their former informal environment in which parents, children, judges, and social workers talked across a table. Constitutional rights and legal processes increasingly became paramount. Legal issues emerged relating to detention, search and seizure, and questions about transfer of children to adult courts.

Today, youth encounters with the juvenile justice system proceed through several phases: arrest, intake, detention, adjudication, and disposition. Behaviors in violation of the law bring youths into contact with the police. The officer determines whether to file charges. While there is considerable variability across states in the United States, most youths who come in contact with police are not arrested but are instead given a warning, or the problem is resolved in some other way. The Juvenile Justice and Delinquency Prevention Act of 1974 discontinued the earlier practice of jailing youths for offenses such as curfew violations and truancy and required that arrested youths be separated from adults in jails or prisons. As a result, juvenile detention centers were constructed. They are now the locations that receive arrested youths. In rural areas, where juvenile facilities do not exist, youths may be held in jails, but they are kept in cells separate from adults.

Following arrest an intake process is begun. The intake process will conclude with a decision to detain, dismiss, or make some other disposition of the case. The risk-and-needs assessments that are increasingly part of the intake process may affect the disposition decision. Juvenile court or probation officers (often social workers) generally conduct the intake-and-assessment process. The data collected include any history of past offenses, violent or aggressive behavior, mental health or substance abuse needs, family or peer problems, educational deficits, medical problems, and sexual abuse history. In addition, information is gathered from parents, police, schools, and other health and social service organizations (Mears & Kelly, 1999).

It is increasingly apparent that youths' entry into the juvenile justice system is influenced by a pattern of social and medical needs and by individual characteristics such as poverty, race/ethnicity, and gender that place some youth at increased risk. Researchers Maschi, Hatcher, Schwalbe, and Rosato (2008) have concluded that children's rights to services should be promoted. They suggest that schools, among other human service agencies, accept increased responsibility for identifying needs and for coordinating referrals for appropriate services in order to prevent vulnerable children from becoming involved with the juvenile court system. They also suggest increased diversity training for police, judges, and the professionals involved in the juvenile justice system.

Social workers in juvenile detention centers regularly provide individual and group counseling, often with a behavior change focus. Juvenile court work ideally includes service to families as well, but significant staff shortages often preclude the provision of significant family service.

Adjudication, the next phase, refers to the decisions made by the juvenile court judge when the charge against the youth is reviewed. The court may decide to drop all charges, but if instead the youth is found guilty, sentencing follows. The **disposition** of a case entails the carrying out of the court order. Probation is the most common sentence in juvenile courts. It is similar to adult probation and may require regular monthly contacts or more intensive and frequent meetings with a probation agent, who is often a BSW social worker. Restitution and/or community service may be a component of probation or may be court ordered as an alternative to probation. If the assessment done at intake identified the need for mental health or substance abuse treatment, placement in a community-based residential treatment program or group home may be court ordered. Serious crimes or frequent offenses may result in sentencing to a secure juvenile prison, commonly referred to as a training school. Sentencing is for a specified number of years. Training schools are typically designed as a series of cottages, a school, and administrative facilities, all enclosed by walls topped with razor wire. Parole, which resembles probation, typically follows incarceration. Another possible disposition of a juvenile justice case is waiver to adult court for sentencing. This action, which is used with increasing frequency, is generally reserved for serious or violent criminal behavior. Serious and violent crimes, however, have actually declined.

VALUE DILEMMAS FOR SOCIAL WORKERS

Opportunities abound for social workers in the field of criminal justice. There are also employment opportunities at all levels of federal, state, and local government as well as with private organizations. Salaries tend to be good, and there are additional opportunities for advancement to administrative positions.

While only a small percentage of social workers enter this field, a larger percentage of BSWs than MSWs do so. Increasingly, too, student social workers are regaining an interest in humanizing the criminal justice system. They will need an understanding of the value dilemmas that confront practitioners.

The use and abuse of authority represent one of the most consistent value dilemmas for social workers in criminal justice settings. For one thing, the legal system gives the probation or parole agent substantial policing authority and responsibilities, and this may well conflict with—or at least appear to conflict with—the professional obligations to a client that are defined in the NASW Code of Ethics.

The Code of Ethics's strong emphasis on confidentiality presents a dilemma since social workers in criminal justice settings are required to testify, as requested by the courts, regarding their contacts with offenders and to report any new or suspected offenses. This requirement may place special strain on the relationship between social worker and client. Hard decisions sometimes have to be made by the social worker. If a teenaged girl, on probation for running away, admitted to a probation officer that she had been running away because of her father's sexual abuse, the social worker would feel sad about having to violate the confidence so painfully shared by the teenaged girl, but there would be no doubt that this situation would have to be reported and assessed further.

The profession of social work has long struggled with the issue of coercion in help-seeking. No other field of practice presents social workers with the dilemma with having 100 percent of their clients as mandated—forced to see them by the law. This potentially sets up a negative working relationship from the start and promotes conning, where clients tell social workers just what they want to hear and nothing more. The correctional system, which has a history of negative attitudes and disrespectful treatment of clients, who are referred to as offenders and inmates, often promotes violence rather than changing violent behavior.

In correctional settings, too, social workers become agents of social control, enforcing specified behaviors from unwilling clients. Social workers ask: Is this a professional, even an ethical role? Hutchison responds that "social workers in mandated settings must acknowledge that they represent society's need, as well as desire, for a functional level of social stability" (1987, p. 587). She further suggests that there are always limits to individual self-determination, since human beings live in societal systems that are defined by their attempt to meet the greater good of the entire community. Sometimes societal systems are repressive, abusive, and unjust. Social workers do not wish to become agents of repression. Provided this is not the case, Hutchison believes that the social control role is legitimate if it is practiced with care and critically analyzed and if the social worker also seeks changes within the organization needed to humanize it and make it responsive to the needs of its clients as well as the larger society.

SOCIAL WORK WITH GROUPS AND ORGANIZATIONS

Although the case study and most of the discussion to this point have focused on correctional social work practice with individuals and families, there is a growing trend toward work with groups and entire organizations.

Social work practice with sexual abuse and domestic violence victims as well as perpetrators is often most effective when groups are used. Mothers of sexually abused children, for example, can be helped through the use of mutual aid groups where the strong support and empathy of group members enable many to heal.

Similarly, groups for women sexual abuse survivors help them share intimate, painful experiences of devastation they had never revealed before. They, too, learn to deal with their anger and grief as they acquire self-forgiveness and ability to empathize deeply with others (Schiller & Zimmer, 2005). As they regain self-respect, they are significantly better able to nurture their children.

Group work with men who have abused others in intimate relationships, interestingly, works with some similar themes. Trimble described such groups, noting that though the men were typically court-mandated, their fear of intimacy, angry feelings, and lack of self-respect emerged in group sessions. The detailed and painful sharing of ugly past experiences of their own abuse of others was made possible by the emotional environment of the group. These men were able to regain self-respect as they learned to control their behaviors. The social worker's use of strengths perspective helped them learn about and use the gentle, nurturing part of themselves whether or not they were ever able to return to the relationships that they had abused (Trimble, 2005).

Group work has been shown to be especially useful in prisons. Historically, women's prisons have provided even fewer social services than have prisons that house men. As a result, opportunities for individual counseling in prison facilities are limited. Group work has been found to be a useful alternative, and some believe that it is the treatment of choice in institutional settings. In women's prisons groups can provide much needed educational experiences related to "HIV/AIDS, substance abuse, and high-risk behaviors including sharing of dirty needles." As a result of prior exposure to physical and sexual abuse, many women prisoners benefit from groups that deal with

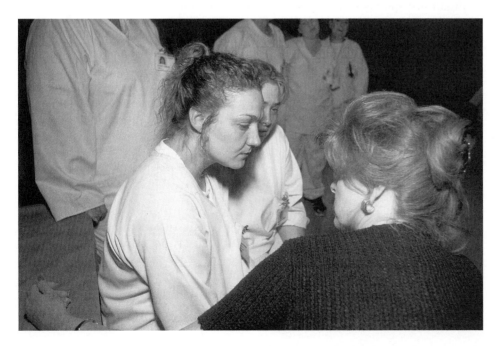

Preparing prisoners for parole and return to their home communities is just one of many uses for group work in prisons.

*Well-designed groups
can be educational,
emotionally supportive,
empowering, and
nurturing, as well
as fun-loving and
entertaining.*

the aftermath of abuse. Well-designed groups can be educational, emotionally supportive, empowering, and nurturing, as well as fun-loving and entertaining. "Within the confines of the stark prison setting," such groups "can be individually transformative, the more so among women who have been removed from and punished by society, estranged from loved ones," and confronted with the daily disrespect, control, and authority of the prison system (van Wormer, 2010, p. 159).

Problems with anger management may also be a complication of daily life in prison. In prison, for example, it is not uncommon for guards to demand that a work task, such as scrubbing a floor, be repeated several times even though it was satisfactorily completed initially. Personal possessions may be taken by other inmates or even by guards when similar prison materials (e.g., a radio) are missing. An inmate may have to share a small cell with a mentally ill or disabled person who is verbally or physically abusive, or someone who urinates in bed. Anger, frustration, depression, and mental deterioration are common in prisoners. Groups can help prisoners verbalize their upset and dissatisfaction.

Group work can also be the primary problem-solving approach used in community-based homes for adolescents just released from correctional institutions. Because peer influence is so significant during adolescence, group work can sometimes be more beneficial than individual work with this age cohort. Establishing communication and relationships with withdrawn, socially immature teenagers is often an important goal for social workers in group homes.

Group home placement can be a desirable intervention plan, but a limitation is the high rate of staff turnover. To keep the group home or community-based correctional facility functioning, the social worker must tackle organizational tasks such as training the youth care staff, helping them understand and work more effectively with the residents. Youthful residents of group homes are often violent, impulsive, and very difficult for staff to work with; therefore, group sessions, in which problems of the home or the unit are discussed by staff and residents, are beneficial. The ability of the staff and the group home as an organization to meet the needs of this complex resident population depends heavily on the effectiveness of the social worker.

When social workers are the administrators of community-based correctional facilities and group homes, they are responsible for the budget, for recruitment and supervision of staff, and for the quality of care provided. A BSW holding the middle-management position of house manager is responsible for the day-to-day operation of the home, for direct supervision of staff, and for program planning for the residents. Whether serving as a house manager, an administrator, or a parole agent, the social worker has a professional responsibility to help make her or his organization as humane, just, and responsive to clients as possible.

ENVIRONMENTAL PERSPECTIVES

Criminal justice is a field of social work practice that brings police, police social workers, and probation and parole agents into communities that are known to people of those communities as high-crime areas. Prison staff, including social workers, psychologists, and nurses also work in institutional environments where there is risk of violence and where imprisoned people are often housed in degrading, even unclean conditions. The social work person-in-environment perspective implies that we need to consider the impact on our clients of the physical space in which they live and work.

Crime and Communities at Risk

Too often in social work we tend to ignore the immediate environments where, in Dennis Saleebey's words, "people live out the rhythms and tempos of their daily lives—rooms, apartments, office cubicles, cars, atria, restaurants, bars, gardens, city blocks, hallways, neighborhood stores, waiting rooms, malls, cells, and the like" (2006, p. 242). We could argue about whether crime causes deterioration in neighborhoods or whether neglected neighborhoods cause crime, but it is pretty clear that dilapidated, poorly cared-for properties and crime generally coexist.

In probation work, social workers' responsibility to their employing organization (usually the county, state, or federal government) is to try to prevent additional criminal activity in the persons they are supervising. When the social worker probation agent visits the client, however, many problems emerge in addition to the crime that resulted in a sentence of probation. Often the client's environment is filled with guns, drugs, and violence. Family, school, and even employment (if the client is lucky enough to still have employment) may actually promote rather than deter criminal activity.

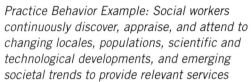

Practice Contexts

Practice Behavior Example: Social workers continuously discover, appraise, and attend to changing locales, populations, scientific and technological developments, and emerging societal trends to provide relevant services

Critical Thinking Question: What facets of social and physical environment would skilled, competent, criminal justice social workers be alert to? Why?

Why are these communities and the families that live within them at risk? There are probably many factors involved, but now special concern is being voiced about the steep increases in imprisonment of youth and young adults as a result of drug-related arrests. These arrests have had serious consequences for the fabric of community health and well-being: Travis' research demonstrated that specific blocks in urban neighborhoods predictably send "disproportionately high numbers of individuals (mostly men) to be housed in America's far-flung network of prisons and jails ... the sheer magnitude of these local effects is staggering" (2004, p. 188). In Brooklyn, New York, for example, one out of every eight parenting-age man was sentenced to jail or prison every year.

The impact on families and neighborhoods is dramatic. Older adults, for example, can anticipate raising grandchildren and even great-grandchildren. Children grow up not knowing their fathers and, increasingly, their mothers. The economy of many already impoverished communities suffers. Pinard's 2010 study of the collateral consequences of incarceration identified several ways in which possession of a criminal record threatened the likelihood of successful reintegration into society. He found that access to public housing was restricted for individuals with certain offenses. Numerous employment restrictions existed for persons with felony convictions. Criminal background checks, which quickly identify misdemeanors and felonies, are required by large numbers of employers who might otherwise be likely to hire persons following release from prison. Pinard noted that since 1996, cash assistance and even food stamps have been denied to persons convicted of felony offenses, and the majority of states also ban voting by persons serving time on probation or parole for felony offenses.

Research is also demonstrating a potential link between environment and factors that may decrease crime. Economist Jessica Reyes, for example, systematically tracked the surprisingly low criminal activity in the teen population born after leaded gasoline was phased out and the United States switched to unleaded gasoline in the early 1990s. This unexpected benefit that environmental protection appears to have provided should also become apparent soon in countries like the United Kingdom and Australia, which switched to unleaded gas more recently than the United States while Indonesia and Venezuela, which only recently discontinued the use of leaded gasoline, should experience a decline in crime among teens in another 20 years (Hoffman, 2007). The teen crime rate was studied because this tends to be the age group with the highest level of violent crime. Studying crime statistics cross-nationally should provide intriguing data for environmentalists and criminal justice experts alike in the years ahead.

Community Strengths, Restoration, Spirituality, and Resilience

Dennis Saleebey, whose strengths perspective enriches social work practice today, is a firm believer that small changes in environment can bring big changes in the behavior of people. Citing what he refers to as the "Broken Windows" theory, he suggests that creating small changes, such as repairing or replacing broken windows, in areas where crimes occur reap dividends in crime reduction. "If a neighborhood or space looks like no one cares for or about it, then criminals are less likely to be restrained in their activities there" (2006, p. 242).

The strengths perspective tells social workers that all social systems (individuals, families, groups, organizations, and communities) have strengths. We sometimes have to look hard to find them. Supposedly bad or high-crime neighborhoods have strengths, too. They have churches, schools, hard-working people, and children full of energy and spirit. Often they contain large, old, ornamented, beautifully designed housing stock. Sometimes small changes, such as fixing a sagging porch or painting a picket fence, can mobilize other improvements in a community and contribute to an overall change in the neighborhood environment. Green space can be created out of abandoned parking lots. Flower or vegetable gardens add color and beauty. They present an alternative to bars as places for people, old and young alike, to congregate, coming out of the fearful isolation of their homes to chat, share stories, and nurture helping neighborly networks.

Some of these exciting changes are already under way because churches, youth, and neighborhoods have begun to rally "their internal resources to save their neighborhoods from the onslaught of violence" (Travis, 2004, p. 177). In addition to green spaces, block watches, tenant organizations, and local business improvement organizations have sprung into being through the efforts of local community residents.

Churches have been a wellspring of energy and creativity in promoting community health and healing in many areas. While many American religious denominations support restorative justice, the American Baptist Church provides resources to enable churches to mediate community conflicts, especially those involving cultural differences. To sustain or rebuild family relationships, some churches have developed programs that enable children to visit parents in prison. Others offer social services and mentoring programs and provide church space for free health clinics, child care centers, and food pantries and as meeting places for women's alcohol and drug support groups, youth groups, and even for probation and parole agents to meet with their clients. The Catholic bishops' statement, *Responsibility, Rehabilitation and Restoration: A Catholic Perspective on Crime and Criminal Justice* (2000, cited in Misleh & Hanneman, 2004), resulted in funds being allocated to local community efforts toward prisoner rehabilitation and restoration of safe, viable neighborhoods.

Volunteers from many Christian and other denominational groups are increasingly working with local residents to build the capacities of neighborhoods and to change American social welfare policies that exacerbate poverty (Misleh & Hanneman, 2004).

The emerging resiliency of neighborhoods affected by crime and the resurgence of faith community resources could not have come at a better time. The extraordinarily high rates of incarceration are just now beginning to pose new challenges: prisoners are now reaching the end of their sentences and are being released to the community, some on parole but many with no mandated ongoing supervision because their sentences have been served in full.

PROMOTING HUMAN RIGHTS AND SOCIAL JUSTICE

As communities undertake the challenge of reintegrating large numbers of persons coming out of prison, it will be important to understand the injustices that people experience within prison systems. The environment of prisons in the United States and in many other countries as well makes them breeding grounds for abuses of many kinds.

Amnesty International (AI) is the primary organization that works on these issues internationally. This organization has exposed inhumane treatment in prisoners of war camps, the detention of political prisoners of conscience, and executions without trial by the Taliban in Afghanistan. In 2000 AI filed a briefing with the United Nations, alleging that the treatment of prisoners in the United States was in violation of the United Nations Convention against Torture and Other Cruel, Inhuman or Degrading Treatment or Punishment. When the United States ratified this UN convention in 1994, it had agreed to abide by the principles of the convention.

AI's listing of concerns included the following:

- Beatings, excessive force, and unjustified shootings by police officers
- Physical and mental abuse of prisoners and detainees by prison guards, including use of electroshock equipment to inflict torture or ill-treatment, and cruel use of restraints
- Sexual abuse of female prisoners by male guards
- Prisoners held in cruel conditions in isolation units
- Ill-treatment of children in custody
- Failure to protect prisoners from abuses by staff or other inmates
- Inadequate medical or mental health care and overcrowded and dangerous conditions in some facilities
- Racist ill-treatment of ethnic or racial minorities by police or prison guards
- Ill-treatment of asylum seekers held in detention, including in adult jails
- Cruel conditions on death row and violations of human rights standards in the application of the death penalty (Amnesty International, 2000, p. 1)

Progress has occurred in some areas. All 50 states now have legislation intended to protect women from sexual abuse by guards and corrections staff. The Federal Bureau of Prisons barred shackling of pregnant prisoners in 2008. Nevertheless, the majority of state and local prisons have minimal or no legislation banning the use of restraints such as shackling during labor and delivery. "And the U.S. Immigrant and Customs Enforcement (ICE), which increasingly detains immigrant women who have never committed a crime, has refused to specifically end the use of restraints on pregnant women" (Leveille, 2008, para. 7). In 2011 the State of Virginia was considering a ban on shackling of incarcerated pregnant women. So it remains clear that improvements based on internationally accepted human rights standards are still needed in U.S. correctional facilities. AI has also consistently recommended that children be incarcerated only as a last resort, that solitary confinement of children be used only as a last resort, and that the death penalty be discontinued for children and the mentally retarded (2000).

Social workers can promote social justice for prisoners by supporting the efforts of AI and other organizations seeking reform. Indeed, social work students on many college and university campuses are actively working with AI campus chapters to secure humane treatment of prisoners in the United States and internationally. Action is often targeted at specific areas of injustice. One of the most dramatic examples of social work student human rights activism on behalf of women prisoners occurred in Michigan where a group of Michigan social workers and students engaged a Detroit city council member, a coalition of community leaders, and the state Department of Corrections in the development of the Women and Infants at Risk (WIAR) program. Social work students did much of the research and organizing work for this project. Especially alarming to them was their finding that in Michigan "women in labor were secured in 'belly chains' while being transferred to the hospital, and a corrections officer—male or female, depending on who was on duty—remained with the client through the birth and the entire hospital stay" (Siefert & Pimlott, 2001, p. 130). The mothers were separated from their babies after a brief hospitalization and returned to the prison. The WIAR project was housed in a residential facility in a Detroit neighborhood. The women who qualified for the program were moved to the WIAR home, provided with maternity clothes (not normally available to prisoners), engaged in prenatal classes, linked with prenatal health care in the community, and given nutritional supplements. When the women went into labor, they were admitted to the local hospital where they delivered their babies.

Human Rights and Justice

Practice Behavior Example: Social workers engage in practices that advance social and economic justice

Critical Thinking Question: How can social workers creatively address compelling social justice issues in the criminal justice system?

They were not chained or shackled during transport, during labor, or following delivery. They returned to the WIAR facility and were able to care for their babies for a full month before returning to a reduced level of work responsibilities.

The students and social workers who created the WIAR program clearly understood the forms of injustice within the prison system. They used their knowledge and skills to advance social justice for mothers and their infants. But this is barely a beginning. In the criminal justice system, numerous social justice issues remain to be addressed by social workers in collaboration with other human rights advocates.

SOCIAL WELFARE POLICY IN CRIMINAL JUSTICE

Punitive programs or rehabilitative programs—what do we want for our country? What type and location of prisons do we want: community-based or massive prisons far from population centers? Decisions about these social policies are made by the people we elect to office. The way we vote and how we interact with our elected representatives determine the nature of our criminal justice system.

The liberal and conservative political ideologies concerning incarceration are summarized by McNeece (1995):

> *Liberals* assume that most of the defects of human behavior have their origins in the social environment.... Liberals assume that incarceration should provide treatment to rehabilitate, reeducate, and reintegrate offenders into the community. *Conservatives* support the notion of retribution or just deserts, not necessarily as vengeance, but because it serves utilitarian purposes as well. Punishment is not only proper, but necessary, because it reinforces the social order. Deterrence is an expected outcome of incarceration, because punishing offenders for their misdeeds will reduce both the probability of their repeating the act (specific deterrence) and the likelihood of others committing criminal acts (general deterrence). (p. 61)

The strength of political conservatives in recent years has resulted in more use of imprisonment, longer sentences, and less concern about rehabilitation. This approach, however, ignores the simple fact that after a severe prison sentence and with minimal rehabilitation or preparation, most prisoners will someday be released back into the community. What kind of security or protection does this provide our communities? Is this true social or criminal justice?

The Prison Population

"New BJS report shows first decline in correctional populations in decades." This was the headline at the December 2010 Sentencing Project website ("Sentencing Report," 2010) . After decades of ever-increasing incarceration in the United States, this was a major shift. Figure 11.3 clearly demonstrates the astounding increase in incarceration over the past nearly 90 years. Comparing the 1970 data, for example, with those of 2008 shows a rise in the prison population from a rate of 96 per 100,000 persons in the population to 756. By 2009 that rate had dropped to 748 ("Sourcebook of Criminal Justice Statistics," 2009a, Table 6.13.2009). While this is a small decline, it may represent welcome new trends in the way the criminal justice system functions in the United States.

It is also useful to look at the rate of imprisonment from state to state within the country. Typically it varies dramatically. In 2009, for example, Maine had an imprisonment rate of only 150, while Louisiana had a rate of 816 ("Sourcebook of Criminal Justice Statistics," 2009a, Table 6.29.2009). Three states, New York, Michigan, and New Jersey, led with declining prison populations in recent past years: New York experienced a 20 percent decline from 1999 to 2009, and New Jersey had a 19 percent decline in the period; from 2003 to 2009 Michigan had a 12 percent reduction in prison population. Several factors appear to account for this shift. Legislators have initiated sentencing reforms in several states. New York, for example, reduced mandatory sentences, while several other states changed sentencing guidelines to divert persons convicted of drug possession into mandatory treatment instead of prison or created new drug treatment programs that could accept prison-bound defendants. New Jersey used risk assessment testing results plus electronic monitoring in the community to encourage parole boards to grant early release from prison. Michigan was among several other states that provide re-entry services such as assistance with housing and employment to reduce the number of parole revocations. Reinvesting in services to persons returning to the community is increasingly found to impact the rather considerable flow of persons back into prison following release (Greene & Mauer, 2010).

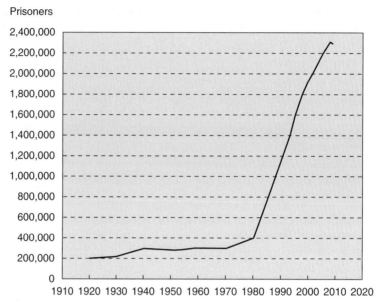

Prisoners

Figure 11.3

Number of State and Federal Prisoners in Custody, 1920–2009

Source: U.S. Department of Justice, Bureau of Justice Statistics, *Prison and jail inmates at midyear 1998*, Bulletin NCJ 173414, p. 2, Table 1; *2005*, Bulletin NCJ 213133, p. 2 Table 1. Washington, DC: U.S. Department of Justice; U.S. Department of Justice, Bureau of Justice Statistics, *Prisoners in 2002*, Bulletin NCJ 200248, p. 2; *2005*, Bulletin NCJ 215092, p. 2, Table 1; *2007*, Bulletin NCJ 224280, p. 6; *2008*, Bulletin NCJ 228417, p. 8; Prison inmates at midyear 2009—statistical tables, NCJ230113, p. 18. Washington, DC: U.S. Department of Justice. Table adapted by SOUCEBOOK staff. Retrieved from http:www.albany.edu/sourcebook/pdf/t6132009.pdf

Many years of staunch taxpayer support for prison construction, staffing, and maintenance resulted in decreasing portions of governmental budgets available for allocation to universities, social service programs, health care, and other needs An entire new industry evolved: private, for-profit prisons. Corrections Corporation of America, the founder of the private prison system, became one of the largest corrections systems in the country, nearly as large as the federal government system. With growing state budget deficits, however, several states including California began implementing early prison release programs in 2011 and 2012. Today, with huge state and federal budget deficits, it appears likely that legislators will find prison reform a much more interesting subject than was the case just a few years ago.

Despite an apparent trend toward decreasing use of incarceration, the rate of imprisonment in the United States remains close to an all time high, and the United States sustains its position at the top of the list of international incarceration data (Walmsley, 2009). In the 1990s, Russia's rate of imprisonment was higher than that of the United States and, before apartheid ended in South Africa, that country had the highest incarceration rate in the world (Mauer, 1994).

Since the early 2000s, the world prison rate (the average of all countries) has remained at approximately 140 incarcerations per 100,000 persons in the population. The most recent data place Russia at 629, second to the United States at 756, but South Africa's rate fell to 335 incarcerations per 100,000 persons. By contrast, England and Wales at 153 was slightly above the mid-point, while the rate for Canada was 116. Switzerland's rate was 76, Japan's was 67, India had 33, Nigeria 28, and Liechtenstein's rate was 20. The United States, China, and Russia combined hold just about half of the total number of persons held in prison in the world (Walmsley, 2009). It will be very interesting to observe changes in world prison population data in the next few years as pressure to reduce federal and state budgets and growing questions about the effectiveness of incarceration increasingly influence social policy.

The Death Penalty

Another social policy issue relates to **capital punishment**, the death penalty. Since its founding, the ultimate penalty for criminal conduct in the United States has been death. It remains a hotly debated issue. Comments in favor of the death penalty and in opposition to it include:

> Justice is better served. The most fundamental principle of justice is that the punishment should fit the crime. When someone plans and brutally murders another person, doesn't it make sense that the punishment for the perpetrator also be death? (Messerli, 2010, p. 4)
>
> I like it the way it is. (Comment by then Governor George W. Bush of Texas at the time that a law prohibiting execution of the mentally disadvantaged was defeated)
>
> We oppose the death penalty not just for what it does to those guilty of heinous crimes, but for what it does to all of us: It offers the tragic illusion that we can defend life by taking life. (Most Rev. Joseph A. Fiorenza, President, National Conference of Catholic Bishops/U.S. Catholic Conference, 1999)
>
> . . . in Canada, the death penalty has been rejected as an acceptable element of criminal justice. Capital punishment engages the underlying values of the prohibition against cruel and unusual punishment. It is final and irreversible. Its imposition has been described as arbitrary and its deterrent value has been doubted. (Supreme Court of Canada, as quoted in Robinson, 2001, p. 2)

As the final quote suggests, Canada does not have capital punishment. Nor do most of the other industrialized nations of the world. The European Union even bans the use of executions by member nations. Some nations refuse to extradite prisoners to the United States because of the U.S. death penalty. Many U.S. organizations—including the NASW, the American Bar Association, the American Civil Liberties Union (ACLU), and various religious organizations—are now calling for the suspension or discontinuation of the death penalty. Inadequate legal representation for poor persons, racial bias, execution of child criminals, execution of mentally impaired persons, and execution of innocent persons are among the concerns of opponents to the death penalty. In recent years, DNA testing has confirmed the innocence of a number of persons sentenced to death. The ACLU has called for a moratorium on capital punishment in the United States. In signing the most recent law abolishing the death penalty in Illinois, Governor Pat Quinn said: "If the system can't be guaranteed, 100-percent error-free, then we shouldn't have the system" (Wills, 2011, para. 3). He also commuted to "life without parole" the sentences of the remaining 15 persons on the Illinois prison system's death row.

From a human rights perspective, progress is being made in the United States. New Mexico eliminated its death penalty in 2009, New Jersey did so in

"MAYBE THIS WILL TEACH YOU THAT IT'S MORALLY WRONG TO KILL PEOPLE!"

Figure 11.4

2007, and New York in 2004. In 2005, the U.S. Supreme Court struck down the juvenile death penalty by a narrow 5–4 decision, citing the state laws authorizing capital punishment for 16- and 17-year-old offenders as unconstitutional. At that time, "the United States was one of only six countries in the world in which the juvenile death penalty was lawful. The United States has been responsible for two-thirds of the juvenile executions worldwide since 2002" (Human Rights Watch, n.d., p. 4).

Public sentiment, as measured by the Gallup poll, still supports the death sentence by 64 percent (Newport, 2010), and 35 states and the federal government have capital punishment statutes. The number of prisoners on death row in the United States has begun to decline, with 3,173 persons on death row at the beginning of 2011, 81 fewer than the past 5 years. Forty-six persons were executed in 2010 compared with 53 persons in 2006. Texas executed the largest number of persons in both 2010 and 2006 (24 each year) (U.S. Department of Justice, 2010a). Arguments for and against capital punishment are shown in Box 11.4.

Capital punishment for mentally ill persons has become a current social policy issue. This is clearly a thorny issue; mental illness ranges widely, from forms of illness that can be well managed to circumstances of truly severe impairment. Decisions would have to be made, too, about those persons who became mentally ill while in prison versus those who, like Kelsey Patterson, clearly demonstrated profound mental illness at the time of the offense. Kelsey Patterson, a 50-year-old man diagnosed with paranoid schizophrenia, was apprehended as he walked naked down a street near his home on a warm fall afternoon, mumbling incoherently. He was found to have committed a double murder for which no clear motive was established. Kelsey Patterson was executed by the state of Texas in 2004. Complicating the death penalty issue related to mental illness is the fact that "mental health experts believe that many

---

Box 11.4   Up for Debate

Proposal: The death penalty should be abolished in the United States.

Yes	No
The death penalty is cruel and inhumane, a fact that is acknowledged by almost all other industrialized countries in the world.	The death penalty is "just rewards" for the crime of murder.
Governments have no more right to take a life than does a person.	Each government has a right and an obligation to determine appropriate sentences. In the United States, the Supreme Court has ultimate authority to determine the constitutionality of laws enacted by state courts.
Capital punishment is not a deterrent, and it does nothing to protect citizens against crime.	As a result of capital punishment, thousands of people have been executed over the years, all of whom represented a threat to society.
As recent DNA evidence in the state of Illinois has demonstrated, there is always the potential for execution of an innocent man or woman.	With technology such as DNA laboratory findings, there will be very little future likelihood of state execution of innocent persons.
There is clear racial, socioeconomic, and even geographic discrimination in the way in which offenders reach death row and are subject to execution.	The majority of persons subject to the death penalty and executed by the United States are White males.
Capital punishment is a failed, morally wrong social policy.	The death penalty should be expanded to include accomplices and others indirectly involved in committing a murder.

---

mentally ill prisoners would never have ended up on death row in the first place if they had been able to find treatment when they were free" (Malone, 2005, p. 21).

Social Policy and Juvenile Justice

Since 1996, juvenile crime has declined steadily and has fallen to a level last seen in the 1970s. Interestingly, juvenile arrests between 1999 and 2008 scored a more pronounced decline than arrests for adults. In the area of violent crime, the U.S. Department of Justice reported that arrests in 2008 (most recent data available) were markedly decreased. The juvenile murder arrest rate rose from 5.7 in 1983 to a peak in 1993 of 14 per 100,000 juveniles age 10 to 17, but it has fallen fairly consistently to a rate of 4 per 100,000 in 2008. Forced rape followed a similar pattern. After increasing from 1980 to 1991, it reached its lowest level in 2008, having declined since 1991 by 57 percent. Robbery was 46 percent less in 2008 than in 1995; however it showed some increase since 2004. Aggravated assault data for 2008 were at its lowest point since the 1980s (Puzzanchera, 2009).

Despite the decline in juvenile offenses, public attitudes continue to support punitive policy for youths. Many professional persons involved with juvenile justice, however, hold a different perspective.

Jensen and Howard (both social workers) propose looking at the social context that places youths at risk for delinquency, including such factors as poverty, family instability, and substance abuse. They suggest developing prevention programs targeted at youths known to be at high risk for antisocial behavior and investing in community economic development aimed at providing opportunities for young people (1998).

Scott and Grisso, an attorney and a psychiatrist, urge the incorporation of understandings from developmental psychology in social policymaking. They point to statistics that show that delinquent behavior is both fairly common in adolescence and likely to conclude as youths become young adults. Adolescents' knowledge base and decision-making abilities are sufficiently immature, they state, that it impairs their ability to make sound judgments when they are read their rights, at arrest, and in their ability to stand trial. Sometimes immature judgment is also involved in the behavior that leads to arrest. They conclude that severe sanctions (transfer to adult courts, imprisonment in adult jails, severe sentences) on youths for first offenses, even for serious crimes, are not in the best interests of the youths or of society. Not surprisingly, they are opposed to the termination of separate juvenile and adult justice systems in the United States, which has been proposed (1998).

Since 2005, the federal government has encouraged the use of community-based programs with small correctional facilities for violent or chronic offenders. Federal funding has become available to states that replace large juvenile training schools/prisons with smaller, community-based facilities (Bartollas & Schmalleger, 2011). The result is that gradually many old, large state juvenile facilities are transferring youths from their facilities into adult prisons or returning them to the communities they came from. Closing their old state juvenile facilities is also economically beneficial to states that have large budget deficits.

Differences between juvenile and adult prisons account for some of the risks that await juvenile offenders who are sentenced to adult correctional facilities. Inmates in adult prisons tend to be much older, while juvenile offenders are usually between 15 and 17 years old. According to Myers, "Older offender ages are correlated with greater size and physical strength, longer and more violent criminal histories, and more experience with incarceration, meaning transferred and incarcerated youths are exposed to a different type of criminal than typically exists in juvenile institutions" (2005, p. 100). The sheer size of adult facilities, often holding upward of 1,000 prisoners, further complicated by overcrowding, creates an environment that, at best, fails to nurture rehabilitation and at worse puts youths at risk of theft, battery, and sexual assault by older prisoners and sometimes by guards. A Florida study several years ago found that youths who had been transferred from juvenile to adult correctional facilities were 49 percent more likely to reoffend when returned to the community compared with 35 percent of youths who did not experience transfer (Lanza-Kaduce, Lane, Bishop, & Frazier, 2005, as cited in Bartollas & Schmalleger, 2011).

At least today juveniles are no longer subject to the death penalty. It was terminated by the U.S. Supreme Court in 2005. Of concern, however, is the remaining policy that permits youths as young as 13 or 14 years old to be sentenced to life without parole, a sentence that ensures that they will die in prison. This policy, however, may be reviewed by the Supreme Court relatively soon.

Populations at Risk

Which populations in the United States are most at risk of being victims of crime? Data from the 2009 Bureau of Justice Statistics' *Criminal Victimization Report* demonstrated racial disparity among victims of violent crime; 27 out of 1,000 Black persons experienced violent crime compared with a rate of 16 for Whites, but 42 for persons of two or more races. One encouraging finding from this report was that there has been a steady overall decline in violent crime victimization. In 2003, 24,212,800 violent crimes were reported compared with 20,057,180 in 2009, a decline of 40,003,960 over just 6 years.

Racial disparity is found among victims of violent crime.

Poor people were more likely to be victims of property crime (including theft, household burglary, and motor vehicle theft) than those who were not poor. Those households with incomes of less than $7,500 in 2009 experienced 201.1 property crimes per 1,000 persons compared with 124.9 for households with an annual income of $75,000 or more. This disparity is significant because it demonstrates how much more likely extremely low-income families are to experience victimization related to their meager belongings than households of greater means. The *Crime Victimization Report* does demonstrate declining overall property crime rates in the United States from 2004 to 2009 (U.S. Department of Justice, 2009a).

Imprisonment rates provide another perspective on the demographics of crime and victimization. In the United States, the rate of incarceration of African American males is shocking: 563,500 African American men were in a state prison or jail compared with 479,000 White men and 303,500 Hispanic men in 2009; one of every eight Black men in their 20s was incarcerated (U.S. Department of Justice, 2009c). Black women, too, were imprisoned at exceptionally high rates: approximately three times the rate of White women and almost twice the rate of Hispanic women (U.S. Department of Justice, 2009c). To date social welfare policy has not addressed well the unique needs of African Americans as they are released from prison. Having obtained little education, substance abuse treatment, or preparation for reentry, they immediately face reluctance of employers to hire them and few resources in terms of housing. The communities most return to are already experiencing economic disadvantages. High rates of incarceration and reentry tend to further destabilize communities as well as families (Brown, 2010).

Does this mean that African American men and women actually commit more crime? What does all of this mean to social workers? Social workers are committed to working with poor people. Given the huge overrepresentation of minority groups among the poor and the fact that crime is one way of surviving poverty, then perhaps the data may represent reality. If this is the case, then social workers must be aware of this reality. On the other hand, racially discriminatory behavior from the time an arrest decision is made through sentencing may also profoundly affect the data.

Critical Thinking

Practice Behavior Example: Social workers distinguish, appraise, and integrate multiple sources of knowledge, including research-based knowledge, and practice wisdom

Critical Thinking Question: What sources of information and knowledge could be used to explain elevated African American incarceration rates?

Paralleling the increase of older persons in the general population is an increase of the elderly in prisons. In 2009, 16,700 persons aged 65 or older were incarcerated, 300 more than the previous year. Only approximately 4 percent were women. Unlike younger prison populations, African Americans comprised only 23 percent, while White, non-Hispanic persons made up 60 percent of the older adult prison population. Prison systems, however, define *older adult* as younger than 65, possibly even as young as age 50. The harsh reality is that prison life ages people quite rapidly for a variety of reasons including lack of physical and mental health care prior to and following incarceration, victimization (which disproportionately impacts aging prisoners), stressors such as isolation from family members, and the prospect of living the remainder of life in prison (Chiu, 2010).

Health care problems included incontinence (the inability to control bowel movements or urination), high blood pressure, hearing and vision loss, diabetes, cardiac disease, cancer, and dementia. Most prisons are not adequately staffed to deal with problems of advancing age and disability, nor with needs for wheelchairs, walkers, hospital beds, and large amounts of medications. Today, however, states are developing geriatric units, assisted-living areas, and even hospice programs for dying inmates. A *Fox News* reporter who visited a prison ward for the elderly noted that some of the prisoners were totally bedridden and the place "looked like a nursing home with razor wire" ("Aging Inmates," 2010, para. 17). In general, it costs two to three times more to incarcerate prisoners of advanced age than younger persons, but the public has supported three strikes laws and life without parole. As a result aging prison populations are likely to persist until overburdened state budgets compel new social policy for the population of infirm, elderly inmates who no longer pose a safety risk.

GLOBAL PERSPECTIVES

The world we live in has become increasingly small. Events that take place in one country are now communicated instantly around the globe. The United States has gained a very negative reputation in other parts of the world for its prisons, its sentencing, and its entire criminal justice system. The United Nations considered the United States to be in violation of the International Covenant on Civil and Political Rights, which bans the execution of juveniles until 2005 when the U.S. Supreme Court finally banned execution of children. Today the international community remains concerned about treatment of people in U.S. prisons, overcrowding, shackling of women prisoners during labor and childbirth, and the death penalty (van Wormer, 2004). The international community has also expressed alarm with the U.S. detention of noncitizens suspected of terrorist acts and the use of military commissions to try cases of noncitizens.

The United Nations' Universal Declaration of Human Rights of 1948, and its more recently developed sections related to the rights of women, children, and trafficked persons, provides a basis for agreed-upon international guidelines to human rights. While the United Nations does not have strict enforcement powers, it does set goals for nations and requests progress reports on identified needs. Member states of the United Nations also seek to hold other nations to the principles affirmed in this document. The United States signed the Universal Declaration of Human Rights; however, the U.S. Senate has never ratified it. The Universal Declaration of Human Rights, however, remains a respected legal instrument that is used to effect change globally.

In many respects, the NASW Code of Ethics parallels the Universal Declaration of Human Rights as it asserts the rights and dignity of all persons and calls social workers to culturally competent practice. The entire final section of the Code of Ethics, which deals with social workers' ethical responsibilities to the broader society, appears to have been written from a global social justice perspective. The social justice issues that this chapter has identified within the criminal justice area are clearly addressed, whether from a national or an international perspective. The code requires that social workers "improve social conditions in order to meet basic human needs and promote social justice," that social workers "promote policies that safeguard the rights of and confirm equity and social justice for all people" and also that social workers must seek to prevent as well as end the "exploitation of, and discrimination against any person, group, or class on the basis of race, ethnicity, national origin, color, sex, sexual orientation, gender identity or expression, age, marital status, political belief, religion, immigration status, or mental or physical disability" (NASW, 2008).

The human rights perspective of the NASW Code of Ethics invites social workers to think globally and to appreciate the interdependence of all people and all nations. Increasingly, social workers in all parts of the world are expressing concern about illicit criminal child labor that operates on an international level. This includes drug trafficking, smuggling goods of various kinds across borders, as well as petty theft. According to Lyons, Manion, and Carlsen (2006), authors of *International Perspectives on Social Work: Global Conditions and Local Practice,* the commercial trafficking and exploitation of children has become a multi-billion-dollar international industry that involves traveling businessmen, military personnel, and the tourism industry.

Distinctions among international child adoptions, fostering, smuggling, and even trafficking are sometimes less than clear in today's world. UNICEF has special concern about the 1,000 or more young children that are annually trafficked from Guatemala to North America for questionably legal adoption. The trafficking of children as young as 13 from primarily Eastern Europe and Asia as "mail-order" brides is another of UNICEF's concerns along with the thousands of young African children being trafficked as domestic laborers or for sexual exploitation (UNICEF, 2009). For women, distinctions among voluntary migration; forced migration; smuggling; and trafficking for sexual, entertainment, or housework purposes are also sometimes unclear. The United Nations Office on Drugs organization works with nongovernmental agencies and religious denominations to educate communities about this issue.

AI is one of several international organizations seeking to ensure human rights for persons who are members of the lesbian, gay, bisexual, and transgender (LGBT) community and to achieve the decriminalization of homosexuality. Globally, gender identity and sexual orientation are often punished by local criminal justice systems through torture, imprisonment, and even execution. AI has identified recent threats of violence, arrests, and torture of LGBT human rights activists in Uganda, Latvia, and Malawa (Amnesty International, 2010). It should be noted that the 2008 revision of the NASW Code of Ethics added language to the code that called upon social workers to work to achieve social policies that ensure justice and human rights for all people including persons who are LGBT, or distinguished by gender identity or expression.

Today, international social work is literally coming to the doorstep of social workers everywhere; increasingly, we need to anticipate and be prepared to assist persons whose human rights have been denied anywhere in our global society.

The NASW Code of Ethics calls upon social workers to work to achieve social policies that ensure justice and human rights for all people.

SUMMARY

Alan Martin, the social worker in the case study, was experienced in the field of criminal justice. He had worked in the adult justice system before taking his current position with juvenile justice. In fields of social work practice such as criminal justice, where social work is not necessarily the primary profession, it takes special effort to sustain professional self-awareness; Alan Martin had begun to lose his professional identification and was becoming tired and unmotivated. Fortunately for Brian Cook and for Alan's future clients, he was able to confront and not to become lost in the pain of one client's tragic death. Instead, Alan Martin forced himself to reconnect with his professional knowledge base, including a strengths perspective that did not devalue his clients.

The complexities of the criminal justice system are introduced with an examination of its three major components: law enforcement, the courts, and the correctional system. The juvenile system, including its own courts and correctional programs, is also presented. While both BSWs and MSWs are employed in police departments and the courts, it is correctional systems that offer most of the social work employment opportunities today. In fact, many more social workers are employed in probation and parole than in prison facilities.

This chapter offers readers not only an introduction to the population served but also the value dilemmas and role conflicts that social workers in the correctional field experience. Generalist social work practice with individual clients as well as with groups, organizations, and within the community is described. Special attention is given to the juvenile justice system and work with youthful offenders because this is an area that often appeals to social workers and that has historically held more career opportunities for social workers.

The environments in which criminal justice programs operate are described, because this is a field of social work practice that challenges social workers with risks as well as rewards. These environments include jails, prisons, and local communities; they sometimes present danger. Communities known as high-risk neighborhoods are also shown to possess strengths in their people, in their churches, and in sometimes untapped resources. Many of these communities have shown amazing resilience in the face of significant loss of young, parenting-age adults to incarceration. But challenges lie ahead as potentially large numbers of people will soon be released from prison and will need assistance in successfully reintegrating into the community. The experiences these people have had in the prison system are described, and it is apparent that many will be reentering society with little by way of rehabilitation. Punitive juvenile justice policies are also discussed.

A brief historical overview of criminal justice efforts was provided as a context for the evolution of social work within this field of practice. The perspective of social work, rooted in its knowledge of community and social as well as psychological systems, is somewhat unique within criminal justice. It is, nonetheless, a perspective that is needed—one that could challenge the system to seek new approaches and the kind of reform that would ensure true social as well as criminal justice. This field of practice offers career opportunities and exciting challenges for social workers.

The social policy context of corrections is frustrating and challenging for social workers with the current emphasis on punishment (even execution) of offenders rather than prevention and rehabilitation. Issues of poverty and racism that affect both the victims and the perpetrators of crime call out for social justice. Populations that were shown to be at special risk were people who are poor or elderly, African American males, and the youths, especially young women who are now increasingly housed in adult prisons.

The chapter concludes with a consideration of the interdependence of the global community in which we live and practice our profession of social work. It is pointed out that the injustices of the U.S. criminal justice system are not unknown to the rest of the world. The United Nations' Universal Declaration of Human Rights was introduced, and linkages to the NASW Code of Ethics were noted. The Code of Ethics calls social workers and students alike to act to prevent social injustice globally as well as locally. Several areas of international social injustice related to crime are described, including the trafficking of children and discrimination and oppression on the basis of sexual orientation or sexual identity. Social workers are urged to internationalize their thinking as they practice their profession.

PRACTICE TEST The following questions will test your knowledge of the content found within this chapter. For additional assessment, including licensing-exam type questions on applying chapter content to practice behaviors, visit **MySearchLab.**

1. The narrow view of forensic social work practice includes _____.

   a. requiring social workers to hold an MSW and 2 years of practice experience working in prisons in order to be a forensic social worker

   b. limiting practice to child custody investigations in divorce situations

   c. specialized expert assessment and evaluation in both criminal and civil litigation situations

   d. conducting cognitive-behavioral groups in prison with inmates in order to change their thinking processes to be more effective in mainstream society

2. Which of the following is FALSE regarding the Women and Infants at Risk (WIAR) program in Michigan?

   a. Women in this program are handcuffed and shackled during transport to the hospital for delivery of their babies.

   b. WIAR participants engage in prenatal classes and health care from the local community.

   c. WIAR participants are able to care for their newborn babies following delivery.

   d. Social work students were actively engaged in promoting and advocating for the funding and implementation of WIAR.

3. Offenders who are under the supervision of probation _____.

   a. have served at least 1 year in prison and have returned to the community to live, work, and engage in rehabilitative services

   b. are limited to those who have committed nonviolent drug offenses

   c. must have family available who are willing to help monitor their activities in the community

   d. live and work in the community to serve their sentence and are regularly supervised by an agent who has the power to send them to jail or prison

4. Which of the following is NOT an ethical dilemma for social workers working in corrections?

   a. Testifying in court regarding information about sexual victimization that was disclosed during a presentence assessment by a convicted offender.

   b. Working within the department of corrections to change policies and practices that are repressive toward inmates.

   c. Holding clients accountable for their illicit drug use behavior, which may involve sending them to prison, when this behavior is restricted to personal use.

   d. Working with clients who are mandated by law to work with the social worker.

5. What is the primary difference between the juvenile justice system and the adult corrections system?

   a. The adult corrections system prohibits children under 18 from being prosecuted as adults.

   b. Adults can be sentenced to life in prison where juveniles can only be sentenced to incarceration up to age 18.

   c. Juvenile justice is focused on protecting and rehabilitating children.

   d. Juvenile justice programs employ a cognitive-behavioral approach to behavior change.

6. What do Jensen and Howard (1998) suggest may have helped keep Ramon from being shot and killed?

   a. More restrictive gun ownership laws.

   b. Making sure youth know that they can face the death penalty when they commit violent crimes.

   c. Increase government funding for juvenile training schools and prisons.

   d. Community-based antisocial behavior prevention programs for youth.

7. Consider that Alan Martin's client, Brian Cook, was only 14 when he was incarcerated. Review the information on alternative and community-based sentencing, and devise an alternate sentence for Brian Cook that would keep him living at home with his mother and attending school in his community.

Reinforce what you learned in this chapter by studying videos, cases, documents, and more available at **www.MySearchLab.com.**

Watch and Review

Watch these Videos

*Engaging the Client to Share Their
  Experiences of Alienation, Marginalization,
  and/or Oppression

*Engaging in Research Informed Practice

*Building Alliances

Read and Review

Read these Cases/Documents

Δ Faith Harper

Δ Military Veteran Justice Outreach and the
  Role of VA Social Worker

Explore and Assess

Explore these Assets

National Criminal Justice Reference Service—http://www.ncjrs.gov/

Office for Victims of Crime—http://www.ojp.usdoj.gov/ovc/

Cognitive Interview—http://www.umsl.edu/~sauterv/analysis/interview/cognitive_int.html

National Alliance on Mental Illness—http://www.nami.org/

Assess Your Knowledge

Assess your knowledge with a variety of topical and chapter assessment.

Conclude your assessment by completing the chapter exam.

* = CSWE Core Competency Asset
Δ = Case Study

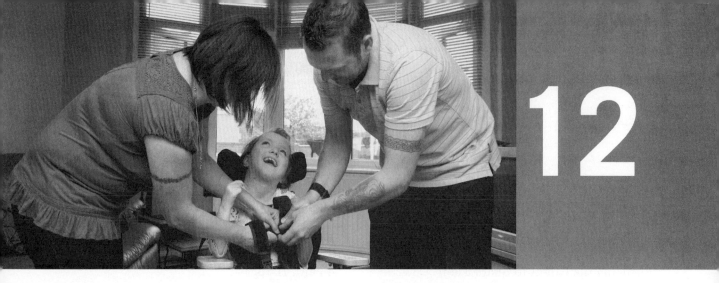

Developmental Disabilities and Social Work

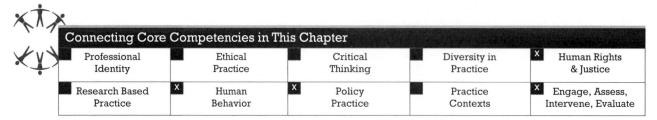

Connecting Core Competencies in This Chapter				
■ Professional Identity	■ Ethical Practice	■ Critical Thinking	■ Diversity in Practice	X Human Rights & Justice
■ Research Based Practice	X Human Behavior	X Policy Practice	■ Practice Contexts	X Engage, Assess, Intervene, Evaluate

Mary and Lea Perkins

Mary Perkins called the Department of Social Services (DSS) early one morning. Her teenage daughter, Lea, had been sexually assaulted by an unknown person during the night. The attack had taken place on the front steps of the family apartment. Mary had already called the police, but then she decided to call the DSS as well, because she believed that Lea was out of control and needed help. The girl had disobeyed Mary's curfew rules again, contributing to her traumatic experience. Moreover, she had skipped school almost daily for months. Mary asked the DSS for help in supervision. She knew the department offered these services because her older daughter, Lorraine, already received them. Lorraine had been arrested for drug possession the year before, and DSS supervision had been ordered by the court under a CHIPS petition (child in need of protection).

Shortly after Mary's call for help, a neighbor called to report Mary herself for neglect, complaining that the mother was rarely home and allowed her children to "run wild all day." The case was scheduled for investigation. The social worker making the initial contact regarding Lea found a mother who was overwhelmed by the demands of parenting three children, Lorraine, 16; Lea, 14; and Jeff, 11. Mary was openly seeking assistance. The children's father was not a resource for her. Alcoholic and unemployed, he had abused the mother physically and emotionally for years. Mary had recently secured a divorce; social workers at a local women's shelter had assisted her. With three children to support on her own, Mary worked long hours every day to try to make ends meet.

Because of Mary's admitted lack of control, Lea was at risk for foster placement. The case was contracted out to a private agency according to a service agreement reflecting the current trend toward privatization. The agency assigned the case to its Home Base program, which provided intensive in-home intervention designed to prevent foster placement. According to the agency's contract with DSS, services could be provided in the home setting for up to 3 months, for 4 hours per week. If in-home intervention failed, foster care would follow. The Home Base program assigned the case to one of its social work student interns, Jenny Chambers.

New to her internship, Jenny felt understandably anxious when she read the referral information. She tried to make an appointment right away, but the Perkins's telephone had been disconnected. Jenny sent a note to schedule a late-afternoon appointment, when she hoped Mary would be home from work. Thankfully, she was. Mary met Jenny at the door and invited her in graciously. With an embarrassed smile, she raised her arms upward in a helpless gesture, motioning at the room around her. It was in total disarray. Clothes lay scattered all over the floor, and dishes overflowed the sink. "I'm so sorry," Mary said softly. "I tried to clean up last night for your visit, but the children wouldn't help, and they messed everything up again today. I might as well not have bothered."

Jenny took a deep breath and smiled at the mother warmly, complimenting her on the one item she could see giving her an opportunity to do so, an appealing family picture hanging on the wall.

Mary began to talk about her troubles. Jenny soon learned that the family not only lacked a telephone but heat as well. In addition, the rent was 3 months overdue, and the landlord was threatening eviction. Mary cried as she told Jenny that as her bills piled up, she simply did not know what to do, so she threw them in a grocery bag and tossed the bag in her bedroom closet. That way she could pretend they were gone. But the children made her so nervous she withdrew into the bedroom early in the evening and shut the door. Part of this problem was that two teenage boys, Lorraine's boyfriend and one of his buddies, stayed in the apartment most of the time.

They had been rejected by their families, and Mary felt sorry for them. To add to the confusion, Lea had recently thrown a frying pan at a friend's mother during an argument and had been arrested for assault. The neighbor had taken out a restraining order, and there would be a court appearance for Lea soon.

Jenny's social work courses at school had prepared her to look for strengths and resilience. She was grateful, as otherwise she suspected she would feel overwhelmed listening to Mary's situation. She began consciously searching for strengths. She already knew of one: Mary had read Jenny's note and kept her appointment. There were several others. Mary had tried to clean her apartment for Jenny's visit. Two of her three children were attending school. She wanted to hold her family together. Prior to the neglect charge, Mary had had the strength to request assistance for Lea. Now that the DSS was considering foster placement, Mary was willing to do whatever she could to prevent that from happening. She worked long hours due to economic necessity, not because she wanted to neglect her children. She was managing a full-time job responsibly. Like many poor people, she was generous, sharing her meager resources with two needy teens who were not even related to her.

Jenny next talked with Mary about Lea. Mary felt sorry for her daughter about the sexual assault but was also angry with her, as Lea had disobeyed Mary's curfew rules. Jenny asked how Lea usually behaved. Mary described Lea as "out of control, disrespectful, and nasty." Mary frankly stated that she felt exhausted from trying to function as a parent. But she did not want to lose her daughter, as so many of her neighbors had lost their children. Lea could be killed or injured on the street, for example. She could end up in foster care due to the neglect charge or to repeated truancy. Mary said that Lea probably refused to go to school because she was a very poor student.

On a hunch, Jenny asked Mary about her own experience as a student. To her surprise, she learned that this mother had an intellectual disability. School had been a desperate struggle for her, but a special education program had been opened when she was in her early teens. A teacher had referred her for evaluation, and she was placed in a class for children with mental retardation. While ashamed at first, Mary began to blossom with the new attention she was receiving. During her senior year, she participated in a school-to-work program, where she learned to assist in a physician's office. That education had served her well: Mary worked in a physician's office still.

Was it possible that Lea too had an intellectual disability, Jenny wondered? Could a special education placement make a positive difference for her? Certainly a referral for assessment was in order. And what about Mary's unusual coping style? Could her disability help explain the bag of unopened bills? Jenny also learned that Mary was taking prescribed medication for anxiety. Anxiety, too, could affect Mary's coping skills.

Before Jenny left her appointment with Mary, she made another to talk with Lea. When she returned 2 days later, Lea was waiting for her. A slim, appealing young girl with auburn hair and expressive blue eyes, she was dressed in baggy jeans, an old sweatshirt, and torn sneakers. Lea told Jenny straight away that she was tired of being poor and wanted to move out of the "ghetto," as she described her neighborhood. People who lived there were looked down upon as "criminals or bums." Lea admitted that she used alcohol to feel better and had been drunk the night of the sexual assault. She was having difficulty sleeping now because of flashbacks and nightmares. She admitted that she was fighting a lot at home and had recently been arrested for attacking a friend's mother.

Jenny recognized the emotional turmoil Lea was experiencing and the associated behavioral problems. However, she also recognized many strengths. Lea had kept

her appointment with Jenny and talked to her with surprising candor for a first interview. She could express her feelings verbally. She was aware that some of her behavior was inappropriate. She was aware of her external environment and its dangers,
even though she was careless about protecting herself. Lea also expressed a strong
interest in sports. Jenny thought this might help lure the young girl back to school.

Jenny met next with Mary and Lea jointly. Together an intervention plan was developed, including a contract that was
signed by all parties. The contract called for (1) school attendance and educational testing for Lea; (2) house rules for Lea;
(3) consequences for Lea if she did not follow the rules, which
Mary must enforce; (4) therapy for both mother and daughter;
and (5) convincing DSS not to place Lea in foster care (this
was the component that motivated Lea to agree to the other
conditions).

To make the contract feasible, Jenny assisted the family in dealing with some very practical matters: the rent, the
telephone, and the heat. She reviewed with Mary every bill in
the grocery bag. She role-played talking with the landlord and encouraged Mary to
approach the man in person. A payment plan for the back rent was successfully
negotiated. Next, Jenny encouraged Mary to talk with the telephone company. A
payment plan was worked out, and service was restored. Jenny found a state energy
assistance program and encouraged Mary to call for more information. Mary did so,
and her heating bill was substantially reduced with funds from the energy assistance
program. Another payment plan was worked out. Heat was restored.

But if Mary were to meet the conditions of the payment plans for rent, telephone,
and heat, something would have to be done to balance her income and expenses.
So Jenny helped Mary develop a budget. That involved a great deal of effort. While
many single mothers are unable to make ends meet due to inadequate wages, Jenny
suspected that Mary might have an especially difficult time due to her intellectual
disability. So she showed Mary how to write her income and expenses on paper and
how to record her payments. To help cut expenses, she shopped for groceries with
Mary and showed her how to compare prices and use coupons. She even helped
Mary plan simple meals, demonstrating how she could save money by avoiding fast-
food takeouts.

Through these efforts, Jenny and Mary together realized that feeding two extra
teenagers was impossible on Mary's income. Moreover, Mary recognized that their
presence had a lot to do with her withdrawing to her bedroom every evening. With
Jenny's coaching, she found the courage to tell the boys that they would have to find
another place to stay. Jenny offered to help them approach their parents or to refer
them for foster care. The boys opted for help in talking to their parents and soon
went home.

Now Jenny decided it was time to clean up the Perkins apartment, if Mary was interested. She was. Jenny moderated a family meeting, where Mary assigned regular
chores to herself and the children. Together, they drew up a chart to record their accomplishments, displayed conspicuously on the refrigerator. While Jenny did much
of the initial cleanup work with the family, gradually they took over.

Getting Lea to go to school or to attend therapy was not easy. The girl finally
agreed to attend school only after her probation officer threatened to put her in
juvenile detention if she didn't. (Lea had been put on probation for the frying pan
incident shortly after Jenny began working with the family.) She then agreed to attend if Jenny would accompany her. Jenny agreed and then referred Lea for a special
education evaluation. Only after several meetings with Jenny, the special education

Engage, Assess, Intervene, Evaluate

*Practice Behavior Example: Social workers
assess client strengths and limitations*

Critical Thinking Question: Why do you suppose
that Jenny took the time to talk with Mary and
Lea Perkins separately, and then together, in
her assessment process?

staff, and Lea would Lea attend school on her own. Jenny also found she had to accompany Lea to her first few therapy sessions.

Assessment by the special education program determined that Lea did not have an intellectual disability. Her intelligence tested above average, in fact. However, she did have another disability, emotional disturbance (ED). Lea demonstrated disturbance in three environments: school (truancy), home (disobedience), and community (fighting behavior). Moreover, Lea's therapist submitted a diagnosis of posttraumatic stress disorder (PTSD). The PTSD related not only to the recent sexual assault but to prior physical and sexual abuse by her father, which the therapist reported to DSS for further investigation. Lea soon began receiving special services at the school and became a much happier person. She joined the girls' basketball team, making new friends. Her grades improved dramatically. Lea's lively blue eyes flashed with pride as she told Jenny about her new accomplishments.

To Jenny's dismay, however, Mary Perkins initially did not follow through with parts of her contract, either. She did not attend therapy, nor did she often enforce consequences when Lea broke house rules. Lea continued to roam the streets at night, and because the rapist remained at large, danger was real. Jenny sometimes wondered if foster placement might not be appropriate after all. Mary seemed to say one thing and do another. However, after much deliberation, Jenny decided to trust in the underlying love between mother and daughter.

Believing in the power of a strengths-based approach, Jenny continued to meet and talk with Mary regularly. She learned that Mary had suffered physical and sexual abuse from her own father. Jenny was then able to help the mother understand Lea's trauma (and need for firm parental protection) in terms of her own. Jenny helped Mary understand that she needed to serve as a role model for her daughter and to maintain consistent discipline to help Lea gain a sense of security and importance. Finally, Mary began to attend therapy, which helped her deal with long-term anxiety and develop the strength to enforce her own house rules.

As the initial 3-month contract with DSS came to a close, Jenny did not believe that either Mary or Lea was ready to carry on without assistance. She applied for, and received, a 6-week extension. By the end of that time, the situation had stabilized. Lea was attending school every day on time, participating in the ED program, and actually earning A's. Mother and daughter were attending therapy regularly, reporting that it was useful. Mary was writing down on paper her behavioral expectations and consequences for Lea and enforcing them. She was discussing possible alternative living situations for Lea if her expectations were not met. Lea was following the house rules.

Termination wasn't easy for anyone. Lea, in fact, said she felt "sad and out of control" when Jenny reminded her that their time was coming to a close. Jenny helped Lea recognize that she had many other caring people in her life now, such as her therapist and the special education staff. She reminded Mary and Lea that they could call the agency for services again if needed, but that she herself would no longer be an intern there. Jenny was sad at the end of her allotted time with the family, as she had grown fond of every member.

A few weeks later, Jenny's supervisor visited the family to evaluate Jenny's work. In response to her questions, Mary replied, with tears in her eyes, that Jenny had been "an awful nag, but we miss her terribly."

Policy Practice

Practice Behavior Example: Social workers distinguish, appraise, and integrate multiple sources of knowledge, including research-based knowledge, and practice wisdom

Critical Thinking Question: In what ways did Jenny integrate multiple sources of knowledge in her work with Mary and Lea Perkins in this case study?

DEVELOPMENTAL DISABILITIES: WHAT ARE THEY?

Some developmental disabilities are so obvious that everyone agrees the person so affected is, indeed, "disabled." A clear example of such a disability might be a bone deformity such as a club foot that makes it difficult for the afflicted individual to walk. On the other hand, some disabilities, while just as real, are much less visible. This was the case with Mary and Lea Perkins, who coped with developmental disabilities which could not be seen. In addition, many children today are diagnosed with "learning disabilities," which require painstaking assessment of problems in reading, spelling, and writing to be detected.

Difference between *Disability* and *Developmental Disability*

Many disabilities are truly disabling but are not "developmental." For example, President Franklin Delano Roosevelt became confined to a wheelchair in midlife because of polio; he was disabled, but not developmentally disabled. According to the federal definition of **developmental disability**, the condition must occur before the affected individual has reached the age of 22.

How developmental disability is defined is not just an academic exercise. The definition affects real people in very real ways. For example, funds reserved for special education services for people with developmental disabilities may be spent only for those who qualify for that funding under the legal definition. A person who may need reeducation in midlife due a disease like polio or some kind of serious accident will not qualify for the services in the public schools that assisted Mary and Lea Perkins in this chapter's case study.

Categorical versus Functional Definitions of Developmental Disability

Some states define developmental disabilities according to category—for example, intellectual disability or cerebral palsy. Persons who fall into these categories are eligible for whatever financial aid is provided by state law for such classifications.

The federal definition of disability, on the other hand, is functional. For a given person to qualify for federal funds, his or her disability must be severe in function and the functional impairment must be chronic (of extended duration). The disability must significantly limit the person's ability to live independently and be self-supporting. Therefore, a person who might qualify categorically for state aid because of a mild disability might not qualify for federal aid.

SERVICES FOR PEOPLE WITH DISABILITIES: A BRIEF HISTORY

Throughout most of history, very little has been done for persons with disabilities. At one extreme (ancient Sparta), individuals unfortunate enough to have an obvious disability were left outside to die of exposure. Native Americans, on the other hand, allowed people with disabilities to live unharmed as children of the Great Spirit.

There are a few early recorded efforts to make special provisions for persons with disabilities. In the 1300s, a colony of persons with mental retardation (persons with intellectual disabilities, to use today's terminology) was established in Belgium, and in 1325 King Edward II of England issued a statute distinguishing between people with intellectual disabilities and those afflicted with temporary mental illness. He established guidelines to protect the rights of "idiots" and to provide for their daily care (Dickerson, 1981). Later on, the Elizabethan Poor Law of 1601 provided limited food and shelter for people with disabilities (along with the elderly, the mentally ill, and the sick). Apparently, no thought was given to providing services or education to improve the lives and opportunities of such individuals.

France provided the pioneers who first educated persons with disabilities. Jacob Rodriguez Pereira demonstrated that people with speech and hearing problems could be taught to read words and to add simple numbers. By the late 1700s, Pereira had become so famous for his work that he was honored at the court of King Louis XV. Later, in the early 1800s, Jean Marc Gaspard Itard took on the education of a young boy, about 12 years old, whom he named Victor. The boy had been discovered living in a forest in France in 1799, and Itard hoped to help him learn how to function as a normal human person. Itard worked intensively on this goal for about 5 years. The extent of Victor's intellectual disability was too great, however, and Itard initially considered the project a failure. However, he was able to teach Victor basic self-care skills such as feeding and dressing. The boy remained mute but learned to read and write a few words. The French Academy of Science, impressed by Itard's accomplishments, recognized him and asked him to write a report. The result became a classic, *The Wild Boy of Aveyron* (Patton, Blackbourn, & Fad, 1996).

Another Frenchman, Itard's student Edouard Seguin (who was also influenced by Pereira), worked with small groups of children with intellectual disabilities in a hospital in Paris in the mid-1800s. Seguin demonstrated that these children could be taught to speak, read, obey instructions, and accomplish simple tasks.

Training Schools

At the same time Seguin was working with children with intellectual disabilities in Paris, a Swiss physician named Johann Guggenbuhl started a residential facility for people afflicted with cretinism. Cretinism is common in mountainous regions of Europe. Caused by a thyroid deficiency, it results in severe intellectual disability and physical crippling. Guggenbuhl was inspired by a religious vision; he was determined to prove that these people could be taught. Guggenbuhl succeeded in his long-term goal, stimulating further work with people with disabilities all over the world, including the development of training schools in the United States. In the short run he ran into trouble, however, partly because he misunderstood the causes of cretinism. Like others of his time, Guggenbuhl thought the condition was caused by poor diet, unclean air and water, and lack of sunlight. He corrected these problems in his training school but promised too much in too short a time. His facility was closed in 1858.

In 1848, Dr. Samuel Gridley Howe, an American reformer, traveled to Europe and visited Guggenbuhl's training school and Seguin's hospital program. Back in the United States, he lobbied for funds to begin similar work. He established training schools for children with disabilities in Massachusetts, New York, and Pennsylvania during the late 1840s and early 1850s. These schools were small and usually served fewer than 20 children each; their goal was to prepare children with disabilities (such as vision impairment or mild intellectual disability) for productive adult lives in the community. Admission was limited to those children who were considered to have the most potential for **rehabilitation** and eventual discharge.

Seguin emigrated to the United States in 1848 after the rise of Napoleon III, a dictator with whom he had political and religious differences. As Seguin became active in the early movement establishing training schools for children with disabilities in America, he advocated for small facilities, each ideally serving no more than 200 children, so that each child could receive individual attention and planning. He suggested that these institutions be built near cities and towns so that younger children could receive instruction by parents, who, in turn, could be coached by the training staff of the school. Seguin's intent was that children should be returned to the community when they gained sufficient skills (Switzky, Dudzinski, Van Acker, & Gambro, 1988).

Protective Asylums

Because of the lack of other resources for people with developmental disabilities in the community, the vision of the training school as a small institution to educate a few disabled children for community living was soon overwhelmed by the demand for protective shelter for disabled people of all kinds. By the 1870s, parents and relatives were begging the schools to take on the daily care of their family members with disabilities. The training schools quickly turned into huge impersonal institutions. They tended to be built in rural areas, which isolated the residents from the rest of society. To reduce costs, higher-functioning residents were set to work the land, so their education was abandoned in favor of using their abilities as a means of producing income for the asylums. Other talented residents were required to cook, clean, and provide personal care for the less able. Thus, tax input to support the institutions could be kept low, reducing taxpayers' complaints.

Custodial care, rather than education or rehabilitation, became the purpose of these large asylums. By the late 1860s, Samuel Gridley Howe was advocating that the institutions be closed. He urged that their residents be reintegrated into society rather than being segregated into the cheaply built, warehouse-style, oppressive facilities designed to provide mass management rather than individualized care.

The Eugenics Movement

The institutions were not closed, however. The next period of history was one that demeaned people with developmental disabilities and tended to keep them not only socially isolated but also despised. By the 1880s, social Darwinism was in full swing. Its advocates took Charles Darwin's fascinating discoveries regarding evolutionary trends in whole physical species and inappropriately applied them to single individuals within the species called *Homo sapiens* in a way Darwin never intended. Social Darwinists preached that because persons with disabilities were "inferior," they were second-class citizens, and taxpayers should not be required to assist them. In fact, it was better that they be allowed to die off according to "natural law."

Members of the eugenics movement whipped up a hysteria of fear regarding people with disabilities. A book in 1883 by the English scientist Francis

Social Darwinists preached that because persons with disabilities were "inferior," they were second-class citizens, and taxpayers should not be required to assist them.

Galton, a cousin of Darwin, asserted that people with intellectual disabilities committed terrible crimes and that "morons" were multiplying like rabbits compared with the rest of the population. Galton insisted that cognitively disabled people were spreading venereal diseases and sexual immorality. Frightened by such assertions, eugenicists (people who believed that human perfection could be achieved if those they regarded as defective were eliminated) clamored successfully for massive sterilization of people with intellectual disabilities (Patton et al., 1996). They called for confinement of people with all types of disabilities in segregated, jail-like institutions from which there could be no escape without sterilization. Obviously, social Darwinists and eugenicists found natural allies in one another.

The eugenics movement took strong hold in both the United States and Europe in the late 19th and early 20th centuries, and many people today are still in the sway of its viewpoint. Perhaps its most horrific manifestation was Hitler's "final solution" in the 1930s and 1940s. It is estimated that Hitler slaughtered 250,000 people with disabilities in pursuit of his idea of perfection (Rothman, 2003).

A third social influence tending to demean people with disabilities was the development of the standardized intelligence test. The most famous IQ test of the time was devised by the French psychologists Alfred Binet and Théodore Simon. It was in widespread use by the early 1900s. The intelligence tests placed powerful labels such as "moron" on individuals with intellectual disabilities and tended to set in stone other people's ideas of the potential of a person with disabilities. "Once feebleminded, always feebleminded" became a belief of the times. With such an outlook, why establish educational or rehabilitative programs for people with handicapping conditions?

Between 1880 and 1925, institutions for people with disabilities grew into huge facilities designed for subhuman "animals"; the model was that of the hospital, where everyone residing therein was viewed as "sick"; where living units were called "wards"; and where the residents were prevented from "hurting themselves" by being confined to locked wards with barred windows, little or no furniture, and nothing in the way of comfort or hope. Dehumanizing routines removed almost all opportunity for persons with disabilities to learn to live like people without disabilities; the "inmates" or "patients" truly seemed subhuman by the time the institution was through with them (Switzky et al., 1988).

New Research, New Attitudes

In 1919, W. E. Fernald published a study of what happened to 1,537 residents with disabilities who were released from institutions between 1890 and 1914. He delayed publication of his results because they astonished him; he had previously supported the "social menace" theory. Fernald found that most of the men and women released exhibited socially acceptable behavior. Few married or bore children; many became self-supporting. Fernald conducted another study in 1924 of 5,000 children with intellectual disabilities in Massachusetts schools and found that fewer than 8 percent exhibited any kind of antisocial behavior (Switzky et al., 1988).

Other studies of the time demonstrated similar results. For example, Z. P. Hoakley investigated people discharged from public institutions in 1922 to determine how many had to be readmitted within 1 year; his results demonstrated that only 6 percent of males and 13 percent of females had to be readmitted. H. C. Storrs investigated 616 adults discharged from an institution in New York State in 1929 and found that only 4 percent had to be readmitted (Willer & Intagliata, 1984).

Attitudes toward people with disabilities began to improve in the 1920s, partly as a result of research but mostly because of the passage of time and the gradual dying down of the eugenics hysteria. Institutions made attempts to "parole" their highest-functioning residents into the community, at first to relatives' homes and later, by the 1930s, to family care homes. Some institutions developed "colony" plans that relocated residents to smaller institutions intended to provide more nearly normal, but still supervised, living arrangements. Some of the colonies were farms, where residents could be nearly self-supporting; some were located in towns, where residents could work in factories.

Economic factors interfered with the process of **deinstitutionalization**. The Great Depression of the 1930s made it impossible to find community-based jobs for all who could perform them. World War II improved public attitudes toward the disabled because so many war veterans came home with disabilities, but the war effort itself drained money away from other pressing social needs. Although the rate of institutional growth slowed during the 1940s, admissions to institutions continued to exceed discharges during this entire period, despite attempts at community placement (Willer & Intagliata, 1984).

Normalization and the Deinstitutionalization Movement

Normalization is a concept that was first developed in the Scandinavian countries in the 1950s. The principle can be summarized as "making available to persons with mental retardation, as well as to persons with other handicapping conditions, patterns and conditions of everyday life that are as close as possible to the norms and patterns of mainstream society" (Switzky et al., 1988, p. 32). The idea took shape in the 1950s and continues to evolve today.

Normalization involves the recognition that people with disabilities are people first, people who simply happen to have physical or mental disabilities with which they must cope. They deserve caring, humane assistance. Parent groups such as the National Association for Retarded Citizens (organized in 1950, known today as the American Association on Intellectual and Developmental Disabilities, (AAIDD), as well as professional organizations such as the National Association of Social Workers (NASW), have provided leadership in this direction. The goal has not yet been achieved, but steps are being taken in the right direction, as illustrated in the case of Sandra McLean in Chapter 2 and Mary and Lea Perkins in this chapter's case example.

Normalization for a person with disabilities requires a plan of care providing for education, training in daily living skills, community-based rather than institutional care, and an opportunity for employment or some other occupation designed to maximize one's potential for independent living. Deinstitutionalization of persons with disabilities came to be perceived as part of the overall thrust of the 1960s toward upholding the rights of minority groups. Funding has been a continual problem in achieving this goal, however, as also is illustrated in the McLean case in Chapter 2. Zoning is another barrier keeping group homes for people with disabilities out of residential neighborhoods. Both problems illustrate that people without disabilities still discriminate against those who are less fortunate.

Deinstitutionalization as a Goal

An important piece of legislation, the Developmental Disabilities Act of 1969, called for establishing planning councils and advocacy agencies in every state. The act helped create a service structure that could help make deinstitutionalization a realistic goal (Parkinson & Howard, 1996). Also very important was the Rehabilitation Act of 1973, which established the first community-based Centers for Independent Living (CILs). Where available, CILs today provide information and referral services, peer support, and independent living and self-advocacy training for people with disabilities (Putnam, 2007).

The deinstitutionalization movement accelerated during the 1970s and 1980s. This acceleration was spurred in part by court decisions. For example, in 1971 a class action lawsuit was initiated on behalf of patients with mental illness at Bryce State Hospital and residents with cognitive disabilities at the Partlow State School, both in Alabama. The decision of the U.S. Supreme Court in *Wyatt v. Stickney* (1972, cited in Willer & Intagliata, 1984) affirmed not only that institutionalized people have a constitutional right to **habilitation** services (services designed to help one achieve and maintain one's maximum level of functioning) but also that mildly or moderately intellectually disabled persons should be admitted to institutions only if this is the least restrictive environment available (Willer & Intagliata, 1984).

The economic climate of the early 1970s also helped the deinstitutionalization movement. The economy was strong, helping provide funding for staff to organize community placement and permitting employment for the more independent of those discharged. That deinstitutionalization occurred at a dramatic rate has been well documented by research. Between 1967 and 1988, for example, the percentage of people with developmental disabilities residing in institutions dropped from 85 to 34 percent (Wolfe, 1992).

Many people simply were shifted from large state institutions to private custodial settings such as nursing homes because nursing homes were cheaper.

Figures such as these probably overstate the reality experienced by people with disabilities, however. As inflation became a severe problem in the late 1970s, the coalition fueling community placement (political conservatives who desired reduced government spending and liberals who wanted more humane care) fell apart (Segal, 1995). Many people simply were shifted from large state institutions to private custodial settings such as nursing homes because they were cheaper. Many of the new settings provided inadequate services for the population they absorbed. It has been suggested that, sadly, *reinstitutionalization* better describes what actually happened to many people (Johnson & Surles, 1994).

TYPES OF DEVELOPMENTAL DISABILITIES

Developmental disabilities appear in many forms. Let us describe 10 diagnostic categories (see Box 12.1). In addition, we will discuss fetal alcohol syndrome (FAS) and cocaine- and other drug-affected babies.

Intellectual Disability

Intellectual disability has previously been known as mental retardation, but President Obama signed "Rosa's Law" in 2010, requiring that references to mental retardation in federal law be changed to "intellectual disability." Intellectual disability is caused by a wide variety of factors. Sometimes it results from injury at birth, as in the case of Sandra McLean in the Chapter 2 case study.

Box 12.1	**Major Categories of Developmental Disabilities**
Intellectual disability	Epilepsy
Cerebral palsy	Traumatic brain injury
Autism	Learning disabilities
Orthopedic problems	Emotional disturbance
Hearing problems	Co-occurrence of disabilities

Sometimes the mother has had a serious illness during pregnancy (measles is a well-known example). Sometimes, as in Down syndrome, the cause is genetic and involves chromosomal abnormalities. Sometimes the problem involves inadequate nutrition for the pregnant mother, a terrible potential side-effect of poverty. Early infant nutrition has an effect as well, as does early sensory stimulation. A mother's drinking, smoking, or drug use may result in intellectual disability of her child. Some conditions are reversible with early intervention. Myriad factors—some identifiable, some not—may affect a young child's mental development.

A child who has an intellectual disability is unable to learn at the rate most children do or cannot apply what is learned in the normal way to requirements of daily living. Preschoolers with this diagnosis tend to learn more slowly than other children to crawl, sit, walk, and talk. Such school-aged children have difficulty developing academic skills and often social skills as well. Such adults have trouble living and working independently in the community, although they may do well with supervision and other assistance.

The AAIDD (previously the American Association for the Mentally Retarded, or AAMR), defines intellectual disability as follows:

> *Intellectual disability* is characterized by significant limitations both in intellectual functioning (reasoning, learning, problem solving) and in adaptive behavior, which covers a range of everyday social and practical skills. This disability originates before age 18.

While the criteria for diagnosing intellectual disability is generally a score of 70 or less on an IQ test, the AAIDD cautions that the IQ score is only one aspect of determining the presence or absence of an intellectual disability. Other tests determine the extent of any limitations in adaptive behavior: conceptual skills, social skills, and practical skills such as feeding and dressing ("FAQ on Intellectual Disability," 2010).

Limitations in adaptive behavior skills and evidence that the disability occurred at a young age are also significant. Both Sandra McLean of the Chapter 2 case study and Mary Perkins of this chapter's case study suffered from intellectual disabilities. Sandra's disability was profound, but Mary's was mild, and with appropriate support she could live a normal life.

Cerebral Palsy

Cerebral palsy results from damage to the brain, usually before or during birth. It takes three major forms: spastic, athetoid or dyskinetic, and ataxic. Some children manifest elements of all three types. Cerebral palsy may affect the entire body or only parts, such as various limbs. Spastic cerebral palsy is the most common form; about 70 to 80 percent of affected individuals have this type. Movement is difficult, slow, stiff, and sometimes jerky. Intellectual disability frequently, but not always, accompanies this condition. Children with spasticity in both arms and legs (spastic quadriplegia) usually cannot walk.

The athetoid or dyskinetic type is manifested in 10 to 20 percent of individuals with cerebral palsy. Movement may be continuous but random and uncontrolled, especially under stress. Facial features may also move in an uncontrolled manner. The walking gait is lurching.

Ataxic cerebral palsy is the least common form, manifested by 5 to 10 percent of affected individuals. It is primarily a balance disorder; children with this disability may walk with feet spread wide apart for stability. Movements that require precise coordination, such as writing, present special difficulties for these children.

According to the Centers for Disease Control and Prevention (CDC), about 1 in 303 children have cerebral palsy, and the condition is more prevalent in boys than in girls. It is generally diagnosed by 3 years of age. About 800,000 children and adults are affected in the United States. Causes include infections to the mother during pregnancy, insufficient oxygen reaching the fetus, premature birth, lack of oxygen to the baby during birth, blood diseases, and other birth defects. Risk is particularly great with premature and low-birthweight

A child with a physical disability enjoys the company of other children.

children. For those who develop cerebral palsy after birth, head trauma and brain infection are the most frequent causes ("Cerebral Palsy," 2007; "Cerebral Palsy: Signs and Causes," 2011).

Autism

Autistic children are often described as being in a "world of their own." At birth these children may appear perfectly normal, and they may continue to appear perfectly normal for the first year or 2. Then the parents will become disturbed by the child's repetitive motions and apparent inability to hear. Hearing tests will reveal, however, that the child does hear but pays attention to random sounds rather than to meaningful words. Language development is delayed, and the child may only repeat back exactly what is said, without apparent comprehension of meaning (such repetition is called *echolalic speech*). Intellectual disability often accompanies autism, although intellectual functioning is difficult to test because of the child's language delays and behavior abnormalities. Autistic children do not respond positively to attention; instead, they withdraw and often behave violently or fearfully when approached. Such behavior, of course, can be heartbreaking to the parents (McDonald-Wikler, 1987).

The prevalence of this pervasive developmental disorder has increased dramatically over the past 20 years. Autism affected around 1 in 2,000 children 20 years ago; today, it affects 1 in 110 children overall, and 1 in 70 boys. In an effort to understand why, Autism Speaks, an advocacy organization, and the CDC cosponsored a national workshop in 2011. The statistical analyses generated by the workshop did not produce reasons for the huge increase, but they did determine that the increase is real, not just an artifact of better reporting or better recognition of symptoms (Halladay & Rosanoff, 2011).

Symptoms of autism include:

1. Difficulties interacting with others and making friends
2. Communication problems, both with spoken language and with non-verbal gestures
3. Insistence on sameness
4. Repetitive movements, such as hand flapping or frequent tantrums
5. Some degree of mental retardation or learning disabilities in most (but by no means all) affected children ("Autism," 2007).

Children with Asperger syndrome share some of the features of autism but have normal intelligence and learn to speak at the expected age.

The causes of autism are not understood. At one time, parents were blamed for being aloof and unresponsive, but this theory has been proved false. There are other theories today, some held with great passion. Three of the most controversial link vaccines and autism: the first theory suggests that the mumps-measles-rubella vaccine may cause intestinal problems that lead to development of autism. The second suggests that a mercury-based preservative used in some vaccines could be connected. A third suggests that children are given too many vaccines at once for their bodies to assimilate and that multiple interactions among vaccines may be damaging. Other theories suggest a genetic link, atypical brain development, immune deficiency problems, food allergies, poor nutrition, and environmental toxins. It is likely that several factors combine to cause autism ("What Causes Autism," 2009).

Orthopedic Problems

Orthopedic problems include a wide variety of physical disabilities, such as problems with physical functioning of bones, joints, and muscles. Spina bifida is a well-known example. A child with this condition is born with an incomplete spinal column so that nerve impulses cannot reach the legs and the child cannot walk. Other examples of orthopedic problems include bone deformities, missing limbs, club feet, or extra fingers and toes. Some such problems can be corrected at birth by surgery or more gradually by corrective appliances such as braces.

Children with minor orthopedic problems may not be classified as developmentally disabled because functional impairment is not severe enough to meet the definition. Other children with severe orthopedic problems may receive services under a different classification (e.g., cerebral palsy). For this reason, the exact prevalence of orthopedic problems in the United States is difficult to determine.

It should be kept in mind that children with physical impairments may experience rejection, embarrassment, feelings of insecurity, stigma, and so forth. Today such challenges may be compounded with insensitive messages transmitted by thoughtless peers via computer or cell phone text messaging. Social workers need to be sensitive to the emotional challenges that these children face in addition to the physical ones.

Hearing Problems

Hearing problems can cause massive developmental disabilities, and they are one of the most common birth defects. About 3 in 1,000 babies in the United States are born with some degree of hearing impairment, or about 12,000 each year. Children who are hearing impaired are often diagnosed incorrectly as having a cognitive disability because their language development is so grossly delayed that they cannot be tested accurately. Without language development, the thinking process may be hampered, and social development is drastically impacted.

Hearing loss may range from mild to profound. Conductive hearing loss occurs when something interferes with sound passing through the outer or middle ear so that sound does not reach the inner ear. Such conditions may include wax, infections, or ruptures of the eardrum, and they are usually treatable. Sensorineural hearing loss usually occurs when the hair cells in the inner ear cannot detect incoming vibrations or when neural impulses are not transmitted to the brain. Some children suffer from both conditions, called mixed hearing loss.

Hearing loss may be present at birth (congenital hearing loss) or developed later in life. About half the cases present at birth are caused by genetic factors. Other causes include the mother's illness during pregnancy (e.g., German measles, herpes, syphilis) and premature birth. Causes of hearing impairment after birth include head injuries, childhood infections, certain medications, and ear infections ("Hearing Impairment," 2010; "Hearing Loss," 2004).

Epilepsy

According to the Epilepsy Foundation ("About Epilepsy," 2010; "Understanding Epilepsy," 2007), epilepsy is the most common neurological disorder in children. It is the third most common disorder in adults, after Alzheimer's disease and stroke. More than 3 million people suffer from epilepsy in the

United States today, and nearly a third are children. Many other people have epilepsy that is undetected and untreated; at least 25 million Americans will have a seizure at some point in their lives. There is no known cause for about 70 percent of epilepsy cases; the rest seem to be caused by tumor or stroke, head trauma, poisoning, infection, or maternal injury.

The Epilepsy Foundation defines the disorder as follows:

> Epilepsy is a medical condition that produces seizures affecting a variety of mental and physical functions. It is also called a seizure disorder. When a person has two or more unprovoked seizures, they are considered to have epilepsy. Seizures happen when clusters of nerve cells in the brain signal abnormally, which may briefly alter a person's consciousness, movements or actions. Seizures can last from a few seconds to a few minutes. They can have many symptoms, from convulsions and loss of consciousness to some that are not always recognized as seizures by the person experiencing them *or* by health care professionals: blank staring, lip smacking, or jerking movements of the arms and legs.

Two types of seizures are particularly well known: tonic clonic, formerly known as grand mal, and absence seizures, formerly known as petit mal. A tonic-clonic seizure is also called a convulsion. The afflicted person thrashes around on the ground for a few minutes and may be unconscious for a period of time afterward. This is the type of seizure experienced by Sandra McLean of Chapter 2. An absence seizure is less dramatic. There is a lapse of consciousness for a few seconds, during which the person appears to be staring or daydreaming. Absence seizures may occur several times a day. They disturb the afflicted person because they interrupt ongoing activities and thinking and tend to result in memory loss.

In another type of seizure, called a drop attack, the legs simply give way and the afflicted person drops to the ground. The attack lasts only a minute or two. Children with this disorder usually wear protective helmets.

There is no central registry of cases of epilepsy in the United States. Prevalence is estimated via surveys of physicians and patients, self-reporting, and studies in matched populations overseas. Approximately 200,000 new cases of epilepsy are diagnosed in the United States each year; 45,000 of new cases are children under the age of 15 ("Epilepsy and Seizure Statistics," n.d.). Sadly, returning veterans today demonstrate a high incidence of epilepsy, relating to brain injury in combat zones ("About Epilepsy," 2010).

Traumatic Brain Injury

Traumatic brain injury includes any trauma to the head that causes brain damage. Brain injuries generally occur in three ways: through blunt injuries, as when the head is hit by a fixed or moving object (such as a windshield or a baseball bat); penetrating injuries, as when the head is penetrated by an object such as a bullet; and compression injuries, as when the head is crushed.

Head injuries may result in fractures or broken or dented skull bones. Loose bone fragments may place pressure on the brain. Concussion, or temporary loss of consciousness, may occur. Severe blows may cause contusions, or bruising of the brain tissue. Lacerations of the head may tear brain tissue.

Symptoms of mild traumatic brain injury include headache, confusion, dizziness, blurred vision, ringing in the ears, memory loss, agitation, confusion, lack of inhibition, and loss of concentration. Persons with moderate to severe traumatic brain injury may experience a serious headache that continues to worsen, repeated vomiting, convulsions or seizures, dilation of one or both pupils of the eyes, slurred speech, loss of coordination, and increased confusion. Approximately half of severely head-injured patients will require surgery to remove ruptured blood vessels or contusions ("NINDS Traumatic Brain Injury Information Page," 2010).

Learning Disabilities

Some children have disabilities that interfere with their ability to read, write, or do mathematical calculations. They may also have trouble listening, speaking, or thinking. Often these children appear perfectly normal until they go to school, where they encounter a whole new set of demands. They score normally on IQ tests, but somehow they do not seem to perceive written language in the same way that other children do. While they may be able to read written words, many cannot translate their meaning. No matter how hard they try, these children seem unable to learn in the usual way. Although there is much about learning disabilities that we do not understand, a number of techniques have been devised to help children so afflicted.

The Individuals with Disability Education Act (IDEA) defines "learning disability" as:

> a disorder in one or more of the basic psychological processes involved in understanding or in using language, spoken or written, that may manifest itself in an imperfect ability to listen, think, speak, read, write, spell, or do mathematical calculations, including conditions such as perceptual disabilities, brain injury, minimal brain dysfunction, dyslexia, and developmental aphasia.

In general, for regulatory purposes, the inability to learn cannot be the result of low intelligence, socioeconomic circumstances, or poor sensory skills. The most frequent method of identifying learning disabilities involves measuring and comparing ability and achievement in the school setting. Thus, the disabilities are rarely identified before a child goes to school ("Learning Disabilities," 2010).

Learning disability is an umbrella term encompassing a number of more specific disabilities such as dyslexia, a language and reading disability; dyscalculia, a disability involving math skills; and dysgraphia, a disorder resulting in illegible handwriting. This disability varies widely from person to person.

Emotional Disturbance

Many terms have been used to describe emotional or behavioral disorders, but the term currently used in the Individuals with Disabilities Education Act (IDEA) is *emotional disturbance.* IDEA defines this disability as follows ("Emotional Disturbance, Fact Sheet 5," 2010):

> a condition exhibiting one or more of the following characteristics over a long period of time and to a marked degree that adversely affects a child's educational performance—

> 1. An inability to learn that cannot be explained by intellectual, sensory or other health factors.

> 2. An inability to build or maintain satisfactory interpersonal relationships with peers and teachers.

   3. Inappropriate types of behavior or feelings under normal
      circumstances.

   4. A general pervasive mood of unhappiness or depression.

   5. A tendency to develop physical symptoms or fears associated with
      personal or school problems.

Emotional disturbance is an umbrella term including (but not limited to)
anxiety disorders, bipolar disorder (sometimes called manic depression), conduct disorders, eating disorders, obsessive-compulsive disorder (OCD), and
psychotic disorders.

   Families who have children with emotional disturbance often need help in
understanding their children's condition and in learning how to cope effectively.
This chapter's case study, Mary and Lea Perkins, illustrates such a situation.

   According to the CDC, approximately 8.3 million children (14.5 percent)
aged 4 to 17 years have parents who have sought help from a health care provider or a school staff member about their child's emotional or behavioral difficulties. Nearly 2.9 million children have been prescribed medication for these
difficulties ("Emotional Disturbance, Fact Sheet 5," 2010).

Fetal Alcohol Syndrome; Cocaine- and Other Drug-Exposed Babies

Babies who are born affected by alcohol, cocaine, and other drugs are a growing concern in the United States. Each year, it is estimated that 1 in 750 to 1
in 1,000 infants are born with physical, developmental and functional problems manifested in a pattern known as fetal alcohol syndrome (FAS), and an
additional 40,000 newborns show some degree of alcohol-related damage, a
condition known as fetal alcohol effects (FAE) ("Alcohol or Drug Abuse During
Pregnancy," 2010; "Fetal Alcohol Syndrome," 2008).

   Many women are aware that heavy drinking can cause harm, but far fewer
realize that light to moderate drinking can be harmful depending on the developmental stage of the fetus. In addition, many thousands of women use
cocaine and/or other drugs such as marijuana, heroin, or Ecstasy during pregnancy, also placing their unborn children at serious risk of birth defects.

   FAS involves both physical and mental birth defects. Babies born with FAS
are abnormally small at birth and remain below normal in size. They usually have
flat cheeks; small eyes; and short, upturned noses. Most have small brains and a
degree of mental retardation. Poor coordination, a short attention span, and
behavioral problems are characteristic of FAS. Babies born with FAE have some,
but not all, of these difficulties. The effects of FAS and FAE are lifelong.

   Mothers who drink heavily (four to five drinks daily or more) have a very
high risk of giving birth to an infant with FAS, but even a single drink at a
critical time during pregnancy can cause problems. Alcohol passes through
the mother's placenta into the developing fetus, whose immature organs cannot break the substance down as fast as the mother's can. Hence, the alcohol
level in the baby's blood may exceed that of the mother's and may result in
irreversible damage. Unfortunately, cocaine and other drugs also pass through
the mother's placenta into the fetus.

   Drugs can trigger labor so that many cocaine- or other drug-exposed babies
are born prematurely. Those who survive are likely to have brain damage causing intellectual disabilities, cerebral palsy, and visual and hearing impairments.
Cocaine babies tend to have small heads, which possibly indicate small brains.
Many appear to experience drug withdrawal; the babies are irritable and jittery,

making it difficult to bond with parents or other caretakers ("Alcohol or Drug Abuse During Pregnancy," 2010; "Illicit Drug Use during Pregnancy," 2006).

While substance abuse during pregnancy clearly places a mother's infant at risk, there is increasing evidence today that substance abuse by fathers also increases the risk. More research is needed.

Overall Prevalence and Co-Occurrence of Disabilities

In 2010, the U.S. Census Bureau conducted the American Community Survey in which families were asked about the incidence of disabilities in their members who were *not* institutionalized. In that year over 36 million people (11.9 percent) were reported to have a disability as defined by the study, including hearing, vision, cognitive, ambulatory, and self-care difficulties. Nearly 3 million of the people with disabilities were under 18 (4 percent). Nearly 37 percent of persons over 65 reported that they had a disability, clearly demonstrating that this condition increases with age ("Selected Social Characteristics," 2010).

People who suffer from more than one disability at a time have a condition known as co-occurrence of disability. Sandra McLean, introduced in Chapter 2, suffered from both epilepsy and intellectual disability. Persons with cerebral palsy and autism frequently also have intellectual disabilities. Children with FAS and those who are exposed to cocaine characteristically suffer multiple disabilities. It is important to remember that all disabilities involve psychological and social dimensions. Professional intervention must involve attending to the whole person.

SOCIAL WORK ROLES WITH PEOPLE WHO HAVE DISABILITIES

Social workers have worked with people with disabilities in a variety of roles for many years. Early in the history of the profession, the Charity Organization Society (COS) workers investigated the needs of disabled people. Their work was described by Mary Richmond in her classic text, *Social Diagnosis* (1917). Richmond, a leader in the COS, devoted an entire chapter to "The Insane—The Feebleminded."

Institutional Settings

Traditionally social workers have tended to work with people with disabilities in institutional settings such as hospitals and nursing homes. That is because disabled persons have routinely been institutionalized in the past, given the attitudes of the wider society. Severely disabled persons tend to reside in institutions even today, and social workers are employed in these settings. Their roles with the disabled are multifaceted, including providing direct services to clients, program development, administration, and evaluation. As direct service providers, social workers usually function as members of rehabilitation teams, engaging in assessment and referral, education, and advocacy. Usually they are the only members of the team with knowledge and responsibility to focus on the social needs of their clients (Beaulaurier & Taylor, 2001).

Community Settings

Today, more and more social workers are working with people with disabilities who are living out in the community, as illustrated in this chapter's case study. As the service system continues to shift from an institution-based model toward a community-based one, social work roles have evolved to encompass increasing amounts of "boundary work," or intervention between and among social systems. Such work includes educating people with disabilities and their families about their civil rights and appropriate programs and services in the community that may be of assistance. Important social work roles involve information and referral services, social brokerage between families and larger systems, and advocacy (Freedman, 1995). Assisting in the development of new or additional services and programs that are widely needed is another important role.

Human Rights and Justice

Practice Behavior Example: Social workers analyze, formulate, and advocate for policies that advance social well-being

Critical Thinking Question: How is the development of new services for people with disabilities an example of policy practice as well as a means of promoting human rights?

Beaulaurier and Taylor (2001) offer a useful framework for services intended to assist people with disabilities:

1. Expand their range of options and choices.

2. Prepare them to be more effective in dealing with professionals, bureaucrats, and agencies that often do not understand or appreciate their heightened need for self-determination.

3. Mobilize and help groups of people with disabilities to consider policy and program alternatives that can improve their situation. (p. 81)

Within the community, then, social workers need to assist clients with disabilities to advocate for programs and services that will allow them to maintain their sense of personal dignity and maximize their independence. Within the family, social workers can be helpful in assisting parents to develop positive expectations toward their children with disabilities and to cope with the ongoing stresses of daily living. Individual, group, and family counseling may be helpful, as can parent training groups and parent-to-parent programs. Respite care opportunities and other supportive services such as day care may be crucial in ensuring the success of family care. A systems-based, empowerment approach that recognizes and builds on family strengths is recommended (Freedman, 1995). Martha Raske (2005) offers an important perspective regarding how various theories of intervention can be blended to best serve clients with disabilities (see Box 12.2).

A fairly new role for the social worker in the area of disabilities is that of **job coach**, or employment specialist, in a supported employment setting. **Supported employment** is a vocational option that provides individualized supports to people with disabilities, so they can achieve their goals in the workplace, especially integrated settings where people with disabilities work alongside those without disabilities. The role of job coach helps ensure the success of supported employment. This specialist provides direct services to the consumer such as skill assessment, locating jobs, contacting employers, making job placement arrangements, providing onsite training, assisting with work-related issues, and providing other types of support as needed (Wehman, Inge, Revell, & Brooke, 2007).

Box 12.2   Blended Theories in Disability Practice

Model	Key Concepts	Basic Principles	Practice Strategies
Strengths perspective	Hope Transformation	1. People/communities have capacities, talents, and resources. 2. Trauma/impairment viewed as potential opportunities/challenges.	1. Strengths first in assessment. 2. Client dreams documented.
Empowerment	Oppression Power	1. People are experts regarding their own conditions. 2. Problems are located in the structure of society/organizations. 3. Focus of attention on oppression and marginalized groups.	1. Collaborative problem solving. 2. Consciousness raising. 3. Targets of change = individuals and society. 4. Group work.
Resiliency	Survival	1. People with disabilities have found ways to master their own life experiences. 2. Focus on client survival techniques.	1. Make resiliency part of client's self-concept. 2. Reframe negative into pride of survival.
Disability discrimination model	Discrimination Impairment	1. Disability is socially constructed. 2. Disability is a diverse experience.	1. Develop receptive environments. 2. End discrimination. 3. Focus on pride/ accomplishment.
Medical model	Diagnosis Scientific method	1. Medical care is part of holistic services. 2. Systematic review of signs and symptoms shape diagnosis and treatment.	1. Assess and treat for acute care needs. 2. Differential diagnosis and prescribed treatment protocols.

Source: Gary May and Martha Raske, *Ending Disability Discrimination: Strategies for Social Workers,* 1st Edition, © 2005, pp. 106, 107, 82–83. Reprinted by permission of Pearson Education, Inc., Upper Saddle River, NJ.

Genetic Counseling

Genetic counseling is another important role for social workers in this field. Scientific knowledge of genetics and its impact on birth defects is expanding exponentially. Genetic counseling translates scientific knowledge into practical information. Genetic counselors work with people who may be at high risk for inherited disease or abnormal pregnancy, assessing their chances of having children who are affected ("Genetic Counseling," 2007; see Box 12.3).

Spirituality Dimensions

People with disabilities confront special challenges, and spiritual sustenance can help them meet these challenges. Morrison-Orton (2005) conducted an important study to find out what, if any, strategies involving spirituality and/or religion were utilized by social work practitioners in assisting disabled clients. She conducted in-depth interviews with 15 rehabilitation specialists. Sadly, she found that not a single one was aware of the many empirical studies showing a positive relationship among spirituality, religion, belief, and healing (Dossey, 2003; Schlitz & Amorok, 2005).

Box 12.3 Up for Debate	
Proposition: Genetic testing should be encouraged for people planning to have children.	
Yes	No
Genetic testing can help reduce the overall incidence of developmental disabilities.	Any life is worthwhile, even one with a disability.
A life with a disability may bring much struggle and little satisfaction.	Many people with disabilities express strong satisfaction with their lives.
Family members, especially caregivers of people with disabilities, experience heavy burdens.	Many families find special rewards in providing care to members with disabilities.
Society as a whole is burdened by the special needs of people with disabilities.	People with disabilities are citizens who have the right to full participation in society like all other citizens.

However, Morrison-Orton did find that 11 of the 15 participants believed that the helping relationship itself was spiritual and that the relationship was the catalyst for positive change. She writes:

> Overall it can be said that the participants went through three stages during the interview. In sequence all but one person went through the same process. The first step in the sequence was the initial denial of any and all use of spiritual or religious strategies. Second was awareness that they could not separate themselves from their spiritual or religious beliefs. Therefore, they did engage in spiritual or religious ways of behaving that enhanced their skills as rehabilitation professionals and were used in their own personal coping with this sometimes-difficult work. Third was the insight that they directly used the strategies in practice with clients. Related to this was the dawning belief that there should be more training (in these areas) while they were in school and on-going professional education once they left school. (2005, p. 32)

EDUCATION FOR WORK WITH PEOPLE WHO HAVE DISABILITIES: COUNCIL ON SOCIAL WORK EDUCATION STANDARDS

Social work education can offer an excellent background for working with people with disabilities because of its person-in-environment perspective. But the profession has been slow in recognizing the opportunities and need for work in this area. Educational Policy and Accreditation Standards of the Council on Social Work Education included disability as a category for which programs are required to provide learning contexts to promote understanding and non-discrimination only as recently as 2001 (Council on Social Work Education, 2001; May & Raske, 2005).

Social work education can offer an excellent background for working with people with disabilities because of its person-in-environment perspective.

According to May and Raske (2005, p. 148), content on disability has tended to be confined to diversity content courses, "already chock full of mandates and advocacy for including numerous discreet populations thought to be 'at risk' as a consequence of their membership in identified out groups. A sad consequence of this reality is that disability content is irregularly included and education is frequently superficial."

As Morrison-Orton (2005) notes in the study discussed earlier, education in the role of spirituality would be very beneficial for social workers who work with people with disabilities. But in this area and others, social work education has a long way to go to provide students with a satisfactory understanding of the strengths and needs of disabled clients. Students who aspire to work in the field of disabilities are encouraged to augment their formal education through outside reading, discussion with experienced professionals, attending workshops, and the like.

NASW STANDARDS FOR SERVICE

The National Association of Social Work's standards for professional service reflect the need for social workers who are involved with disabled people to have generalist knowledge and skills. In 1982 the NASW collaborated with the American Association on Mental Deficiency to develop specific standards. These are summarized in Box 12.4.

The NASW provides extensive interpretations of these standards. Services described include outreach, identification of individuals at risk, community liaison work, coordination of services, advocacy, and discharge planning. Services also include policy development, program planning and administration, research, and program evaluation.

HUMAN DIVERSITY AND POPULATIONS AT RISK

Persons with disabilities can be viewed as members of diverse populations, in particular as members of diverse populations that are at risk because of discrimination by the wider society. As discussed previously, discrimination has led to disabled people being warehoused for years in prisonlike facilities. People with severe disabilities are frequently still institutionalized today, often in private nursing homes that have few facilities for this population. Social workers are

---

Box 12.4   NASW Standards for Service

1. All social workers working with developmentally disabled clients shall possess or acquire and develop knowledge about developmental disabilities.

2. All social workers shall subscribe to a set of principles regarding developmental disabilities which should underlie their practice.

3. Social work practice and research shall seek to prevent or reduce the incidence of developmental disabilities.

4. All social workers shall participate in an interdisciplinary approach to serving the needs of developmentally disabled people.

5. The functions of the social work program shall include specific services to the client population and the community.

Box 12.5 Strengths of Autistics

People with autism demonstrate diverse strengths and abilities, not only disabilities. For example, Temple Grandin, PhD, a woman with autism, has become prominent in two professional fields. First, she is the author of at least seven books and a DVD dealing with various aspects of autism. She has labored tirelessly to teach parents and professionals how to help children who have the disorder to build on their special talents and achieve their highest possible functioning. Dr. Grandin has become famous for her insightful writings about what it is like to grow up autistic. She hosts frequent conferences on autism around the nation.

In addition, Dr. Grandin is famous for her work helping people to understand how animals think and feel. For her, the experience of autism has provided important insights into this usually hidden realm. To date, Dr. Grandin has written two influential books on the topic. One well-known result is more humane treatment of cattle on their way to the market.

Dr. Grandin maintains a website where people can send questions and request advice. She responds openly over the Internet so that all interested parents and professionals can be assisted.

Source: Based on Temple Grandin Books. Retrieved from http://www.templegrandin.com/templegrandinbooks.html

---

urged to advocate for all persons with disabilities and to prevent institutionalization wherever possible. Today many people with disabilities are actively advocating for themselves and others like them, working toward achieving the most normal lives possible and maximizing their potential (see Box 12.5).

Preventing institutionalization requires a continuum of care available in the community. Fortunately, the service system moved from the primarily institution-based model in place prior to the late 1960s to a community-based model in the 1970s and 1980s (Freedman, 1995). The positive change was advanced by the Developmental Disabilities Act of 1969 and the Americans with Disabilities Act (ADA) of 1990, which will be discussed later in this chapter. It was further advanced in 1999 by the Supreme Court's Olmstead decision. This decision, *Olmstead v. L.C.,* interpreted Title II of the ADA to require states to provide services in the "most integrated setting" appropriate for a given person (Rothman, 2003).

The Continuum of Care

The **continuum of care** begins at home, the least restrictive, most normal environment in which children can be raised. **Respite care** to help prevent burnout of family caregivers can be crucial to the success of care in the home. Adults with disabilities may be able to live independently in homes or apartments of their own with appropriate assistance. Other reasonably independent adults may do well in boardinghouse-type arrangements, with room, board, and a minimum of supervision. Days may be spent in activity centers, regular employment, or **sheltered workshops** (places of employment that provide special training and services for people with disabilities) or supported employment in integrated work settings, as discussed earlier.

Foster homes, or **family care homes**, are the next step along the continuum of care. They provide family-like settings with foster parents. Lea Perkins would have been placed in one had her own mother not been able to improve her parenting skills. Next, somewhere near the middle of the continuum of care, are small group homes. These facilities are staffed by aides and skilled professionals who provide care, supervision, and training for up to eight people.

L'Arche USA, a pioneering organization, provides family-like group homes in small communities where people both with and without disabilities can share their lives. L'Arche communities began in France in 1964; the first L'Arche community in the United States began in Erie, Pennsylvania, in 1972. Today there are 17 L'Arche communities across the United States ("Welcome to L'Arche USA," 2011).

Nearing the institutional end of the continuum of care are nursing homes. Nursing homes range from those providing only room, board, and minor personal assistance to those offering skilled nursing care for persons with extensive physical needs. When large numbers of people with disabilities were moved to nursing homes in the 1970s, many of these facilities developed special programs for them. Unfortunately, however, many did not, and almost 20 years passed before federal Medicaid regulations required special certification and appropriate programming.

At the far end of the continuum of care are the large state institutions, where people with disabilities reside in highly restrictive, regulated environments. Today, most people who live in these facilities have severe and multiple disabilities.

Research Suggests Direction for Service Improvement

For family care to have the best chance for success, specialized services are often needed. However, a study by Christopher Petr and David Barney (1993) found that parents received limited help from professionals and may have even experienced adversarial treatment. For example, some professionals recommended institutional placement when the family desired additional home-based services. Sometimes, however, home-based services were recommended but simply did not exist or were financially out of reach because private insurance refused to pay.

The situation has not improved much, if at all, since the time of Petr and Barney's study. For example, Doris Mitnick, a social worker who has worked with children with chronic illness for more than 15 years, finds (Stoessen, 2005):

> The biggest lack is not in the strengths of the family. It's the strengths of community resources. Things just keep getting tighter and tighter. (The lack of) resources in the community and state is the biggest challenge families face . . . . That's where our development needs to be—in community resources and the creative application of those resources.

In the years since Mitnick made her observation regarding community resources, they have continued to grow tighter. And unfortunately families find that working with professionals, including social workers, can be difficult as well. Even a social worker suddenly thrust into the role of client finds the transition from professional to "parent of disabled child" a daunting experience (see Box 12.6).

Providing Supportive Services to Diverse Families: A Chinese Illustration

Barnwell and Day (1996) point out that to intervene successfully, social workers and other professionals must understand that the values and experiences of the families they deal with may be very different from their own. Moreover, family needs change over time. Services required to cope successfully with infants with disabilities, for example, are very different from those required to meet the needs of adolescents, adults, or the elderly.

Box 12.6 How Parents View Professionals

Janice Fialka, a social worker, gave birth to a son with disabilities. She writes: "I had been a practicing social worker—what I was struck by was that I was in a waiting room where I had taken teen moms, and there I was, sitting as a client. I was quite humbled and very aware that I did not choose to be there. When I was the social worker, I made a conscious choice.

However, when you're the parent, especially in the early years during the transition—when it's not your choice—you're not so eager to join into this dance."

One night Fialka wrote a poem, "Advice to Professionals who Must 'Conference Cases,'" as a way to get her feelings onto paper. The poem reads, in part,

Please give me back my son
undamaged and untouched by your labels, test results
descriptions and categories
If you can't, if you truly cannot give us back our son
then just be with us quietly
gently and compassionately as we feel.

Source: NASW news by National Association of Social Workers. Copyright 2005. Reproduced with permission of National Association of Social Workers in the formats Textbook and Other Book via Copyright Clearance Center.

These authors note that different ethnic and cultural groups utilize professional services at different rates and provide professionals with different amounts and types of information. They point out that service systems tend to be designed according to White, middle-class values, yet the values of other groups may differ. Cultural sensitivity is required to help develop service systems that are responsive to the needs of diverse families with members who have disabilities. Cultural perspectives differ as to the meaning of disability, the causes of disability, and the appropriate roles of families with respect to disability. What may be experienced as a terrible tragedy in one culture may in another be experienced as God's will and an opportunity to serve. Professional intervention must take account of these cultural differences.

Liu (2005) offers an interesting illustration of differing cultural perceptions of disability from a Chinese point of view. In many areas of China, Liu writes, disability is viewed as a punishment for sins committed in past lives—sins committed either by the disabled person or by that person's parents. Thus, a stigma is attached to disability, and families experience a sense of shame, guilt, and fear of social disgrace. A Taoist priest may be sought to perform rituals to try to seek a cause or a solution.

Because the family is the most fundamental unit of society among the Chinese—three generations living in one household is still common—it is important for the professional to do whatever possible to establish a strong working relationship with extended family members. Liu points out, however, that the family in China today is diverse given the 10-year cultural revolution that separated many families and undermined respect for the elderly. The one-child-per-family policy has also undermined the traditional family system. Hence, the social worker must carefully assess family structure as part of the intervention process. Competence in the Chinese language is also helpful to achieve best outcomes (see Box 12.7). Social workers need, with great sensitivity, to help the family understand the cause of disability from a more neutral (less blaming) point of view and to discuss possible treatment options.

Box 12.7   Cross-Cultural Competence from a Chinese Perspective: Sun

I worked as a case manager for a 25-year-old woman, Sun, a Chinese American who was legally blind, nonverbal, and diagnosed with moderate mental retardation. Sun was able to understand Cantonese, which was the only language that her parents spoke, and a few words in English. She responded to questions by nodding, shaking her head, or making certain sounds. When I started working with her, she had been attending, for a few years, a traditional day treatment program for people with mental retardation. She seemed to be comfortable there, but on the occasion of a home visit to see her and her parents in their Chinatown apartment, it became apparent that Sun's parents really preferred that she attend a special school for the blind. They said that even though they had this wish for a long time, they were not able to make their needs known because of language barriers.

Sun's past case managers spoke only English. They would periodically check as to whether Sun's parents were satisfied with the day treatment program, and the parents would always say "yes," unable to express their wish for a more appropriate setting for their daughter. I worked with Sun's parents and located an excellent program for adults and children with visual impairment. Sun was transferred to this program and appeared to be happier because she was more comfortable with the environment and was able to engage in activities designed for the blind. Sun has been attending the special program ever since.

Asian Americans: A Brief History

People of Chinese descent comprise the largest subgroup of Asian Americans in the United States today. Asian Americans as a whole comprise approximately 5 percent of the population. Their number totals approximately 15.5 million persons, of whom 3.62 million are Chinese ("Asian/Pacific American Heritage Month," 2010). Other Asian Americans originate from Japan, India, and the Pacific Islands.

The Chinese were the first Asian people to come to America in large numbers. They arrived in relatively recent times, toward the middle of the 19th century, attracted by economic opportunity. In Hawaii the Chinese worked as sugar plantation laborers, and in California they took part in the Gold Rush of 1849. Many became construction workers for the Southern Pacific Railroad. Their success led to fear of competition, which culminated in the Chinese Exclusion Act of 1882, barring further immigration. People of Chinese descent were denied citizenship and the right to intermarry (Lum, 1992).

Large numbers of Japanese emigrated during the early 20th century, in response to the need for farm workers in California. The Immigration Act of 1924 closed the door to immigration of Asians after that time, however. This law set low immigration quotas for dark-skinned people of all nationalities and excluded Asians entirely. Then, after the bombing of Pearl Harbor in 1941, Japanese Americans were forcibly interned in camps for the duration of World War II. Their property was liquidated and never returned. Although the U.S. Supreme Court in 1944 declared this treatment unconstitutional, not until 1988 were petitions for redress of grievance accepted by Congress. The settlement even then was token, $20,000 for each living survivor.

The 1965 Immigration Act changed U.S. policy to make it more equitable to people of diverse racial and ethnic heritages. Political refugees from the Philippines and Korea included many educated Asian professionals at that time.

Then the Vietnamese War brought waves of refugees from Vietnam, Laos, and Cambodia, particularly after the fall of Saigon in 1975. The early refugees were highly educated people who had been allies of the Americans, but later refugees included less privileged people who have experienced much more difficulty adjusting to life in the United States.

Traditional values strongly affect Asian family life today. These values include deference to parental authority and the expectation that children will sacrifice personal ambition to meet family needs. Families may experience stress when children encounter other values and begin to question differences. This type of stress, of course, is experienced across generations by all immigrant groups.

SOCIAL JUSTICE ISSUES

In an accommodating environment, a person with a disability can often function independently and at a high level of performance. Such a situation is ideal, but sadly too uncommon.

Mismatch between Person and Environment

Putnam (2007) points out that disability may be viewed as a "mismatch" between a person's abilities and his or her environment. In other words, where there is a problem related to disability, that problem is a result of the interaction between person and environment and not the individual's issue alone. For a person with a disability to function at a high level, the environment must be modified to accommodate the person's needs. Along these same lines, May (2005) asserts that *disability* and *impairment* are not inherently linked. These observations are important. Mary Perkins, for example, with her intellectual disability, could have functioned without assistance in a less complex environment and would not have been viewed as impaired. Lea Perkins would not have developed her disability of emotional disturbance at all had she been fortunate enough to live in a safe environment. Once Lea received supportive services, she could function as well as any other teenager; she was not impaired despite her emotional disability.

Discrimination

Instead of understanding and accommodation, however, persons with disabilities frequently experience discrimination. It is important, therefore, for social workers to recognize that social justice issues are inherently involved in working with this significant minority, a population at risk. Advocacy is a very important role for the social work professional, and it is important for the worker to assess a disabled client's environment for strengths, resources, and limitations as well as the client's own strengths, resources, and limitations.

Smart (2001) reminds us that there are four important resources professionals can bring to their work with clients who have disabilities: hope, ideas, understanding of the prejudices and discrimination they face, and a willingness to stand by them. Jenny Chambers, in our chapter's case study, brought these very resources to Mary and Lea Perkins, and the result was that their quality of life was clearly improved.

Empowerment, Self-Determination, and Self-Advocacy

In addition to advocating for their clients, standing by them and offering hope, ideas, and understanding, the effective social worker will assist people with disabilities in strengthening important personal qualities and skills. Assistance should include education in empowerment, self-determination, and self-advocacy.

Human Behavior

Practice Behavior Example: Social workers engage in practices that advance social and economic justice

Critical Thinking Question: How can empowerment help people with disabilities achieve more rights and a greater degree of social justice?

Empowerment is an attitude, a process, and a set of skills involving the ability to gain some control over valued events, outcomes, and resources. Empowerment requires genuine choices and the power to make one's own decisions (Gilson, 1998) and is strongly in accord with social work's professional value of self-determination.

People with disabilities, like other people, want to have as much control over their own lives as possible. Even people with severe disabilities can make decisions for themselves if they have access to support services, barrier-free environments, and appropriate information and skills. The desired outcome is independent living wherever possible.

The empowerment model strongly encourages self-advocacy among people with disabilities, both as individuals and in groups. Self-advocacy in fact has become a national movement, modeled after the civil rights movement. The AAIDD describes some of the goals ("Fact Sheet: Self Advocacy," 2005):

> When we speak of "the civil rights movement," "the parents' movement," or "the independent living movement," we are referring to something like a crusade, powered by people who have been directly affected by unfair attitudes and practices, which has fostered change in our society. Similarly, the self-advocacy movement has redefined the "disability problem" as being less about rehabilitation and more about equality. People involved in the movement are very clear about not wanting to be called retarded, handicapped, or disabled or to be treated like children. They are clear that self advocacy represents "rights" not "dependence"—the right to speak out, the right to be a person with dignity, and the right to make decisions for themselves and others.

The concepts of empowerment, self-determination, and self-advocacy do not mean that society (or social workers) should abandon people with disabilities to struggle alone.

The concepts of empowerment, self-determination, and self-advocacy do not mean that society (or social workers) should abandon people with disabilities to struggle alone. It means, instead, that society must recognize that the individual with a disability is not the problem; the problem is an environment that discriminates, does not provide viable choices, and does not meet the special needs of all its citizens.

Self-advocacy goes beyond individuals advocating for themselves alone. It also involves groups of people with disabilities working together to fight discrimination, gain more control over their lives, and work together toward greater justice in society. Toward this end a national organization called Self Advocates Becoming Empowered (SABE) was founded in 1990. SABE is a major self-advocacy organization in the United States. It has been working toward the full inclusion of people with developmental disabilities in the community throughout all 50 states for many years. It is a nonprofit advocacy organization run by a board of self-advocates representing nine regions of the country ("Self Advocates Becoming Empowered," 2010).

Collective efforts such as SABE hopefully can lead to new legislation bringing important advances in social policy affecting people with disabilities.

THE DISABILITY RIGHTS MOVEMENT, SOCIAL POLICY, AND APPROPRIATE TERMINOLOGY

Disabilities have been viewed historically as medical problems or personal tragedies. This prevailing view began to be challenged in the 1960s, when, along with other minority groups, people with disabilities sought to redefine their identities and to change popular perceptions of the sources of their problems (Christensen, 1996). By the late 1960s, first in Scandinavia and then in the United States, a disability rights movement developed, advocating that people with disabilities should be seen as "subjects in their own lives rather than simply as objects of medical and social regimes of control" (Meekosha & Jakubowicz, 1996, p. 80). Community prejudice and discrimination were overtly identified as major barriers preventing people with disabilities from taking control of their own lives, as were stereotypes portrayed in the popular media (see Box 12.8).

The crux of the new thinking, as noted by Beaulaurier and Taylor (2001), was that an individual's disability in itself was not so much the problem as the lack of accommodation provided by the wider society. Lack of accommodation was not so much a result of hostility as from simple failure to consider everyone's needs. So those who became involved in the disability rights movement determined to get the requirements of people with disabilities onto the national agenda.

In the United States, the disability rights movement promoted deinstitutionalization and independent living and helped secure the passage of the Developmental Disabilities Act of 1969. The movement was strengthened in the 1960s by the civil rights movement. Then, in the late 1960s and early 1970s, thousands of veterans returned from the Vietnam War with extensive disabling conditions, both physical and emotional. Their added influence helped achieve passage of the federal Rehabilitation Act of 1973. Title V of this act prohibits recipients of federal funds from discriminating against people with disabilities in employment, education, or services.

Box 12.8 A Disability Paradigm

The disability paradigm states that the study of the experience of people with disabilities focuses on the following variables which impinge on the phenomenon of disability and interact with each other and other human characteristics: (1) the process in which the performance of social roles and tasks produced discrimination; (2) the discriminatory treatment of people with disabilities produced by the organization of society; (3) the recognition that an impairment does not imply tragedy and a low quality of life; (4) the stark reality that people with disabilities are an oppressed minority which experiences discrimination; (5) the need of all people, including people with disabilities, for various services in order to live independently; (6) the realization that all people have agendas so that the unstated assumptions of disability policy must be revealed; (7) the knowledge that people over time move on a continuum from non-disabled to disabled so that eventually everyone experiences disability; (8) the rejection that there is "normal" human behavior on which social policy can be based; and (9) the all pervasiveness of discrimination against persons with disabilities.

Source: Gary May and Martha Raske, *Ending Disability Discrimination: Strategies for Social Workers,* 1st Edition, © 2005, pp. 106, 107, 82–83. Reprinted by permission of Pearson Education, Inc., Upper Saddle River, NJ.

The Rehabilitation Act of 1973 was followed in 1975 by the Developmentally Disabled Assistance and Bill of Rights Act and the Education for All Handicapped Children Act, which later became IDEA (Meekosha & Jakubowicz, 1996; Asch & Mudrick, 1995; Pardeck, 1998; Rothman, 2003).

As publicly signaled by appropriate terminology in the IDEA, sensitivity is needed with respect to terminology. Certain commonly used phrases and adjectives can be experienced as demeaning and inappropriate. For example, in IDEA, the term *handicap* is replaced by the more neutral term *disability*. And as noted previously, the more recent Rosa's Law replaces the term *mental retardation* in federal law with *intellectual disability* ("Self Advocates Becoming Empowered," 2010).

Another major piece of legislation promoting disability rights, the Americans with Disabilities Act (ADA), was passed in 1990; it was greatly strengthened by the Civil Rights Act of 1991. These acts are described next.

THE AMERICANS WITH DISABILITIES ACT OF 1990 AND THE CIVIL RIGHTS ACT OF 1991

The Americans with Disabilities Act (ADA) was designed to assist all people with disabilities, not just those with developmental disabilities. Its purposes are identified in its Section 2 as providing a mandate for ending discrimination, providing enforceable standards of treatment for disabled people, and creating a central role for the federal government in enforcing these standards (see Box 12.9).

Title I of the act makes special requirements of employers. One is that employers with 15 or more employees may not discriminate against people with disabilities who are otherwise qualified. Another is that employers must make accommodations for people with disabilities. The law intends that the accommodations should be "reasonable." Existing physical barriers, for example, need to be remedied only if this can be done without much difficulty or expense.

Other titles of the ADA call for reasonable access to public services (e.g., special accommodations as needed to allow usage of buildings, buses, and trains) and accessibility to public accommodations such as restaurants, hotels, theaters, schools, day care centers, colleges, and universities. Telephone companies must provide telecommunications services for hearing-impaired and speech-impaired persons.

Box 12.9   The Americans with Disabilities Act Recognizes Discrimination

Section 2 of the Americans with Disabilities Act states, among other things, that:

. . . historically, society has tended to isolate and segregate individuals with disabilities, and, despite some improvements, such forms of discrimination against individuals with disabilities continue to be a serious and pervasive social problem; discrimination against individuals with disabilities persists in such critical areas as employment, housing, public accommodations, education, transportation, communication, recreation, institutionalization, health services, voting, and access to public services.

Unlike individuals who have experienced discrimination on the basis of race, color, sex, national origin, religion, or age, individuals who have experienced discrimination on the basis of disability have often had no legal recourse to redress such discrimination. . . .

Source: Quoted from Section 2, "Findings and Purposes," Public Law 101–336, Americans with Disabilities Act of 1990.

The Civil Rights Act of 1991 strengthened the ADA by allowing jury trials and compensatory and punitive damages in accord with those available to minorities under the Civil Rights Act of 1964. Complaints are handled by the Equal Employment Opportunity Commission (EEOC). It is interesting that a large number of job discrimination suits were filed with the EEOC by people with disabilities that no one anticipated because they were invisible. The first plaintiff to win a monetary award, for example, experienced job discrimination related to a diagnosis of cancer (Pardeck, 1998).

Pardeck (2005) notes that over the years, the Supreme Court has had a profound effect on the ADA. Some rulings have limited the scope of the law. For example, in 2002 a plaintiff with carpal tunnel syndrome lost her case as the Court did not consider the condition serious enough to be covered under the ADA. In 2004, however, the law was strengthened when the Court upheld the right of disabled individuals to sue the states for equal access to public services and facilities (Richey, 2004). Interpretations of the ADA continue to change regarding what is considered a disability and what must be done to accommodate the disability. Supreme Court decisions have fluctuated over time, with only some meeting the needs of the plaintiff with a disability (Bagenstos, 2009).

GLOBAL EFFORTS ON BEHALF OF PEOPLE WITH DISABILITIES

Discrimination against people with disabilities is not confined to the United States. Rather, it is a worldwide phenomenon. For this reason, the United Nations, an international organization often more visionary than its individual member states, determined to address the matter in 2006. The outcome was the Convention on the Rights of Persons with Disabilities in 2007. According to the AAIDD ("Convention on the Rights of Persons with Disabilities," 2007):

> The Convention on the Rights of Persons with Disabilities and its Optional Protocol was adopted on 13 December, 2006, at UN Headquarters in New York, and was opened for signature on 30 March, 2007. There were 82 signatories to the Convention, 22 signatories to the Optional Protocol, and 1 ratification to the Convention. This is the highest number of signatories in history to a UN opening day. It is the first comprehensive human rights treaty of the 21st century—it marks a "paradigm shift" in attitudes and approaches to persons with disabilities.
>
> The Convention is intended as a human rights instrument with an explicit, social development dimension. It adopts a broad categorization of persons with disabilities and reaffirms that all persons with all types of disabilities must enjoy all human rights and fundamental freedoms. It clarifies and qualifies how all categories of rights apply to persons with disabilities and identifies areas where adaptations have been made by persons with disabilities to effectively exercise their rights and areas where their rights have been violated, and which must be reinforced.

Through the convention, the United Nations has initiated international acknowledgment of issues and rights of persons with disabilities. A major purpose is to encourage the development of progressive new policies and programs in member nations.

VALUE DILEMMAS AND ETHICAL IMPLICATIONS

Both personal and professional values come into focus in social work with people with developmental disabilities. Today, because of new knowledge of genetics and new medical procedures, value issues in this field are more complex than ever. Some of these issues are identified next.

Complex Issues

Today genetic counseling is available to those who request it. This type of counseling makes it possible for a couple to know beforehand if they run a substantial risk of abnormality in a pregnancy. Should a concerned couple seek this type of information? What should they do if a substantial risk is identified?

A procedure called amniocentesis can identify many types of fetal abnormalities during a pregnancy. Corrective measures sometimes can be taken in utero, but sometimes nothing can be done. Should such a pregnancy be continued? Does this question involve absolute principles? Or can it involve consideration of probable quality of life for the fetus? For the family?

Social workers advocate self-determination. But who is the client in cases such as the previous example? The fetus? The family members who will need to provide special care? Individual and family systems are both legitimate focuses for intervention, and the different systems might make different choices. Whose choices should be honored? But how can one even know the choices a fetus might make?

Perhaps if society provided sufficient supports to family caregivers, sufficient options such as universal access to respite care and day care services, choices could be made that would satisfy every member of a family. But increasing available family supports requires advocacy and political action in a larger arena. The NASW Code of Ethics provides a guide to expanding choice (see Box 12.10).

The Americans with Disabilities Act of 1990 and the Civil Rights Act of 1991 discussed earlier are important examples of legislation aimed at improving social conditions and promoting social justice for people with developmental

---

Box 12.10   Social and Political Action

The NASW Code of Ethics, provision 6.04, as quoted in part here, strongly advocates expansion of choice to make self-determination a more realistic opportunity for client systems.

(a) Social workers should engage in social and political action that seeks to ensure that all people have equal access to the resources, employment, services, and opportunities they require to meet their basic human needs and to develop fully. Social workers should be aware of the impact of the political arena on practice and should advocate for changes in policy and legislation to improve social conditions in order to meet basic human needs and promote social justice.

(b) Social workers should act to expand choice and opportunity for all people, with special regard for vulnerable, disadvantaged, oppressed, and exploited people and groups.

Source: 6.04 Social and Political Action, *NASW Code of Ethics 1996*, National Association of Social Workers. Copyrighted material reprinted with permission from the National Association of Social Workers, Inc.

disabilities. People with disabilities themselves, their families, social workers, and many, many others participated in the effort that resulted in these new laws.

Social workers may be able to affect social policy directly through their work if they should have an administrative position. Even with direct-service positions, however, social workers may help create change by doing such things as writing informed letters to their agency administrators or to influential legislators. They may serve as expert witnesses at legislative hearings. Social workers may be even more active in creating policy by running for and holding public office. There is a great deal of work that still needs to be done with, and on behalf of, people with disabilities.

Current Trends

Because community care today so often means ongoing care by the family, a continuing trend is collaboration between families and professionals. The strengths, or empowerment, model has helped encourage a paradigm in which families are viewed as competent, full partners in professional service, as illustrated in this chapter's case study with Mary and Lea Perkins. The role of social workers is primarily to assist families and consumers of services to meet their own goals. Mutual respect, trust, and open communication are imperative, as well as an atmosphere in which cultural traditions, values, and diversity are acknowledged and honored (Liu, 2005; Rothman, 2003).

Although community care, especially care in one's own family, may be the option of choice for the individual with disabilities, caregiver stress among family members is an ongoing concern. For example, a recent study of parents of children with autism found that while their divorce rate is about the same as the divorce rate for parents of children without disabilities until the child reaches the age of 8, after that their divorce rate remains high, while it goes down significantly for parents of children without disabilities (Devitt, 2010). Such a study indicates the toll a disability can wreak on families.

As children with disabilities grow up, they see their age-mates leaving home, and they also frequently desire to live independent of their families. Independent living benefits not only them but their families, as it provides relief from caregiver stress. Special housing is often required, however. Today there is nowhere near enough special housing to meet the need. Part of the issue is that people with different disabilities require different supports. For example, people with impaired mobility have very different housing requirements than people with intellectual disabilities. Another part of the issue is budget cuts—special housing is put on the chopping block during hard economic times. Sadly, existing group homes for people with disabilities have long waiting lists—years long in many places (Wehman, 2006). Given the economic recession of recent times, the shortage of special housing is likely to get worse.

The increasing lifespan of people with disabilities is another major trend, made possible by advances in medicine. The 2010 American Community Survey identified over 14 million *noninstitutionalized* people over 65, nearly 37 percent of citizens of that age group, who indicated that they had a disability ("Selected Social Characteristics," 2010). While increasing lifespan should be something to celebrate, the problem is that there is not enough special housing to meet the needs of the older population with disabilities. In many cases assistance from their parents is no longer available; parents have died or become disabled themselves. A horrifying result is that huge numbers of people with disabilities have become homeless. The 2010 Annual Homeless Assessment Report, commissioned by the U.S. Department of Housing and Urban Development, found that 37 percent of homeless people seeking help in shelters had a disability (Sullivan, 2011).

Fortunately, hope is beginning to be offered to people with disabilities who are chronically homeless. An Obama administration initiative, *Opening Doors,* is an unprecedented federal strategy designed to end veteran and chronic homelessness by 2015 and to end homelessness among children, families, and youth by 2020. Of those who are chronically homeless today (homeless for at least a full year), the majority have a disability (Sullivan, 2011). High unemployment is another concern for people with disabilities. Despite legislation designed to assist (e.g., the ADA), about 63 percent of Americans with disabilities are unemployed according to a recent study (Hall & Parker, 2010). Thus most are unable to improve their circumstances through paid work. They are dependent on their families or on public programs, which all too often are insufficient. Social workers, therefore, need to work alongside people with disabilities (and their families) to find available resources and to develop new ones if possible.

SUMMARY

This chapter begins with a case study that illustrates contemporary, community-based social work with people with disabilities. Mary Perkins has an intellectual disability. She has been served in the past by a special education program that prepared her for gainful employment, and she is doing well at her paying job. Mary's daughter Lea, however, has suffered traumatic abuse resulting in emotional disturbance and ongoing truancy. The family is experiencing myriad other difficulties as well. Through intensive family-based intervention, a young social work intern, Jenny Chambers, assists Mary to develop the skills required to keep her family together and to remain in their own apartment. She engages Lea in a special education program at school where the girl begins to excel.

While social workers traditionally have worked with people with disabilities primarily in institutional settings, today their services are becoming increasingly community based. Social workers assist families to expand their options so that far more often today, children with disabilities are raised at home. Social workers assist individuals with disabilities and their families to advocate for their own ideas and choices, deal constructively with bureaucratic agencies, and join with others in promoting new policies and programs that can maximize their options.

By examining the differences between categorical and functional definitions of disability, we see why such differences are important in terms of funding resources and eligibility for service. Ten major categories of developmental disability are discussed: intellectual disability, cerebral palsy, autism, orthopedic problems, hearing problems, epilepsy, traumatic brain injury, learning disabilities, emotional disturbance, and co-occurrence of disabilities. Fetal alcohol syndrome and cocaine- and other drug-affected babies are also discussed.

Until comparatively recently, little has been done for persons with disabilities. For centuries, people with mental retardation and other disabilities were cruelly incarcerated. Reformers such as the Frenchmen Pereira, Itard, and Seguin worked to demonstrate that people with disabilities can be taught. Huge institutions replaced training schools, however, and not until the 1920s did research contribute to a change in public opinion. In recent years, the concept of normalization has spurred efforts toward removing people with disabilities from large institutions and placing them back in the community, ideally in homelike settings with special provisions to meet their needs.

Efforts toward home care have been hampered by lack of resources in the community. The Education for All Handicapped Children Act of 1975 (currently known as the Individuals with Disabilities Education Act), its 1986 amendment extending service to infants and toddlers, the Americans with Disabilities Act of 1990, and the Civil Rights Act of 1991 were discussed as examples of enabling legislation providing legal bases for equal opportunity and empowerment for people with disabilities. However, competition for scarce resources makes implementing the full intent of these laws difficult. The Convention on the Rights of Persons with Disabilities, adopted by the United Nations in 2007, lends hope that this population at risk will receive increasing social justice efforts around the world in the coming years.

The NASW has developed standards for service for working with people with disabilities and their families. The chapter presents these standards and also discusses how professional values and ethics guide contemporary practice efforts in this field.

Opportunities for social workers to work with people with disabilities are growing. More community-based services are needed, not only for younger people with disabilities but for ever-increasing numbers who survive into old age. A continuing problem is underfunding for community-based services.

PRACTICE TEST
The following questions will test your knowledge of the content found within this chapter. For additional assessment, including licensing-exam type questions on applying chapter content to practice behaviors, visit **MySearchLab.**

1. Which of the following beliefs is NOT related to the eugenics movement?
   a. A person with a disability would be better off if left to die according to "natural law."
   b. Human perfection is attainable if those who are defective are eliminated.
   c. A person with a disability should live unharmed as a child of the Great Spirit.
   d. A person with a disability is an inferior tax burden.

2. The continuum of care begins with the least restrictive services for adults with disabilities and likely includes _____.
   a. independent living support, supported employment, and easy access to public transportation
   b. foster care or group care and center-based activities
   c. respite care for overstressed caregivers, case management, and parent training
   d. L'Arche community living, assisted living in a nursing home, and financial assistance

3. Which of the following characteristics is NOT common in children with autism?
   a. They usually walk with their feet spread wide apart.
   b. They have difficulty communicating both verbally and nonverbally.
   c. They frequently engage in repetitive movement.
   d. They often withdraw in social situations.

4. The functional definition of a disability was established by _____.
   a. state regulations to specify eligibility for state social service support
   b. the federal government for the purpose of qualifying for federal aid
   c. Jacob Rodriguez Pereira in France in 1799
   d. the U.S. Census Bureau in 2009

5. Which of the following goals is NOT consistent with the framework developed by Beaulaurier and Taylor for effective services developed by social workers to assist people with disabilities?
   a. Services should expand the range of options for people with a disability.
   b. Services should encourage and facilitate people with a disability to be self-determined.
   c. Services should assist people with a disability to become mobilized to change policies to improve their situation.
   d. Services should not be concerned about the social and spiritual needs of potential clients.

6. In the case study of Mary and Lea Perkins, which federal law provided assessment and supportive services for Lea at her school?
   a. The Civil Rights Act of 1991
   b. Individuals with Disabilities Education Act
   c. The Americans with Disabilities Act of 1990
   d. Rehabilitation Act of 1973

7. Consider the case study of Mary and Lea Perkins. Identify at least three strategies that Jenny, the social work intern, employed to empower Mary and Lea to improve their circumstances and achieve their identified goals.

432

MySearchLab CONNECTIONS

Reinforce what you learned in this chapter by studying videos, cases, documents, and more available at **www.MySearchLab.com.**

Watch and Review

Watch these Videos

* Demonstrating Effective Oral and Written Communication

* Attending to Changes and Relevant Services

Read and Review

Read these Cases/Documents

△ Sarah and Robert

△ Stephanie and Rose Doer

Explore and Assess

Explore these Assets

Downs Syndrome, Kids Health—http://kidshealth.org/parent/medical/genetic/down_syndrome.html

Administration on Developmental Disabilities, U.S. Department of Health and Mental Health—
http://www.acf.hhs.gov/programs/add/states/ucedds.html

Individuals with Disabilities Act, National Early Childhood Technical Assistance Center—
http://www.nectac.org/idea/idea.asp

Assess Your Knowledge

Assess your knowledge with a variety of topical and chapter assessment.

Conclude your assessment by completing the chapter exam.

* = CSWE Core Competency Asset
△ = Case Study

13

Future Challenges and Closing Notes

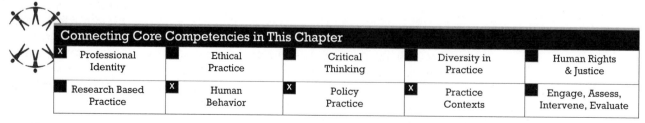

Connecting Core Competencies in This Chapter				
X Professional Identity	■ Ethical Practice	■ Critical Thinking	■ Diversity in Practice	■ Human Rights & Justice
■ Research Based Practice	X Human Behavior	X Policy Practice	X Practice Contexts	■ Engage, Assess, Intervene, Evaluate

Rachel Fox: Student Social Worker In An International Field Placement[1]

At first time had moved slowly, but near the end of the internship the time to leave had come quickly. Rachel reflected on her internship in South Africa during the 21-hour flight back to the States, remembering that day 2 years ago, when a South African social worker who was an internship supervisor spoke to her policy class on campus. It was then that she decided to apply for the internship in South Africa. A year later she was required to interview with social work internship faculty and a different South African supervisor. She described to them her experiences in other countries, including summers spent in France with family, and her interest in South Africa. She was very pleased to learn that she had been accepted for an internship in a child welfare agency in the Western Cape of South Africa for that fall. She would be accompanied by another intern from the program, her friend Emma.

The next 6 months were spent finishing her social work classes and preparing for the internship. She met with the three other interns and a coordinator and spent many hours reading about the history of South Africa, about social work and social services, about South African social welfare policy (especially the new Children's Bill), and about cultures, customs, and languages. She even began to learn the basics of Xhosa, the local native language. She applied for her passport, a student visa, and registration as a student social worker.

The actual trip to South Africa seemed to take forever, but finally Rachel was at King William's Town Child and Youth Care Center in a small city in the Eastern Cape Province. It took a few days for both interns to overcome the jet lag and to go through the agency orientation. At first it was difficult to come to know the staff, especially the Black staff, who were primarily Xhosa-speaking. As Rachel entered into her work, she discovered that there was a divide between White staff and Black staff which was partly cultural and partly a result of the past apartheid policies, and so she made a concerted effort to work with the Black staff. She also had to deal with the language divide, as she struggled to learn Xhosa, with its clicks and other unusual sounds. She did learn enough to be polite and to know what was being said, but not enough to be fluent with her clients and their families. She had to rely on interpretation for part of her work.

Rachel and her student friend, Emma, entered the work gradually, first learning all of the services of the agency and then developing a working knowledge of the social work processes of the agency and of the provincial department of social welfare. They had had to reframe their understanding of social welfare policy and of social work itself because they were in a different policy environment, in a country with a unique recent history and a parliamentary polity. Rachel learned that the basic policy principle is *Ubuntu*, from the Xhosa saying: "A person becomes a person through other persons."

Rachel and Emma had already become familiar with the Children's Bill, the first major revision of child welfare policy since 1983. Both interns quickly discovered that they actually knew more about the policy than most of the social workers with whom they were working because although the law had been passed 2 years previously, the implementation was slow; the regulations were still being drawn up. That was definitely a challenge in the child welfare environment. However, the agency social workers would gather for case discussions and to learn more about the Children's Bill and its implementation. Rachel also observed what seemed to her to

[1]The Rachel Fox case study was contributed by Nicholas P. Smiar, PhD, ACSW, Professor Emeritus, University of Wisconsin-Eau Claire, with input from his student, Rachel. Nick Smiar has extensive experience with international field placement of social work students.

be ethical lapses when case files were not secured or confidential information was discussed openly, without safeguards; but she learned that a code of ethics had just been drawn up by the South African Council for Social Service Professions (SAC-SSP) and had not yet been integrated into social work education. The other major challenge was working with the social workers in the public department of social welfare, who had very large caseloads and were generally nonresponsive when it came to permission to return a child to his or her family.

The saddest part of Rachel's experience was working with very young children who were HIV-positive or had AIDS. The agency had a residential unit for infants, many of whom were infected or were orphans of AIDS. Many of the parents had died of the disease. HIV and AIDS, Rachel learned, are everyday realities in South Africa, which has the highest HIV-AIDS rate per capita in the world, and the country has only recently begun to address the problem with clinical treatment and prevention. This was not Rachel's only experience with the health care system. One day, while driving to an appointment, Rachel was injured in an auto accident. She learned firsthand about the two health care systems, one for the poor and one for those who had private insurance. In her work at the agency, she had already seen the system for the poor, when the young children with HIV or AIDS were sent to the local public clinic, where care was not the finest. When a White boy became sick, he was taken to the private clinic and received good quality care; when a Black girl became sick, she was taken to one of the inadequate public clinics. Now Rachel saw for herself a very different system from the public clinics where she had to take children for care. She experienced the other private system, where she received far better care. Unfortunately, however, for some time following the accident she could no longer pick up the infants, who wanted so much to be held.

As a primary part of her fieldwork, Rachel helped three families to reunite. This involved navigating the social welfare system, advocating for her clients, squeezing permissions out of public social workers, and helping to make placement arrangements in very poor communities with few resources. She saw people with very few material possessions who struggled every day to survive but would help neighbors in need. She saw *ubuntu* in action and came to understand the strong communal ties and traditional values among the Xhosa people. She experienced the bedrock faith of the people when she attended a local Baptist church, when she heard a prayer before every social work or community meeting, and when she heard the workers sing hymns whenever the start of a meeting was delayed.

One of the first children Rachel heard about when she arrived at the Children's Center was James. James had spent most of his life in residential care. When she arrived at the Child and Youth Care Center, everybody talked about James because he was the most challenging case that the Center was dealing with at the time. Although there was uncertainty about how to proceed with James, it was decided that Rachel could work with him. James was 11 years old; he had been removed from his home when he was 5 years old. He lived in a single-parent household and had experienced a difficult childhood. His mother tried to kill him twice, and it was suspected that she had also prostituted him out for extra income. James had lived at several different child care centers before he ended up at Rachel's field placement agency. By the time Rachel arrived he had been there 6 months and he was not attending school. He had initially attended school but was removed when he stabbed a classmate with a pencil and threatened a teacher. There were no public schools in the area that would accept him as a student.

Once Rachel became familiar with the case, she set up a team that would meet on a weekly basis and focus on James. This team consisted of the director of the facility, who had worked closely with James, the social work supervisor, and the child care workers from James's unit. This team worked together so that everybody had the same information and provided consistency in James's life. James was given incentives for good behavior. When the team discovered that money was an important motivator for James, they set up an allowance that James could earn by doing his chores and following rules. This system did not seem to work well at first, so Rachel reevaluated it and talked with James. Fortunately James, like most other teens, had learned English in school, so communicating with him was not a problem. James was actually multicultural; his mother was White and his father was from India. Although he identified as White, he spoke Xhosa fluently, was well accepted by Xhosa people, and participated in Xhosa cultural songs and dances, which was a real strength in an environment where there was still separation between White and Black people, even among the staff of the Child Care Center. James stated forcibly that he did not think he was being evaluated fairly. So Rachel and James together designed a checklist for the staff to evaluate James's chores and behavior. As the staff began to work with this checklist, they found that James was actually doing better than they first thought he was. Having decided on his own goals and helped in creating the checklist, James became increasingly motivated to do well.

The next hurdle was transitioning James back into school. After many phone calls a private school was finally found that was willing to take James as long as he followed strict rules. James was a likeable child and the teachers enjoyed having him right away. James was easy to get along with, but Rachel understood that he could push the limits. Early on, Rachel talked with the principal to ensure that there would be open communication about James's progress. The principal and the teachers found it difficult to believe that such a likeable kid would cause any problems. After the school encountered some behavior problems, however, the communication between the school and the Child Care Center became better. Improved communication between the school and the Child Care Center made it easier for the Center staff to encourage James with his homework and extracurricular activities at school. James's overall behavior and attitude changed gradually. James was able to establish friendships with roommates, and he began to take pride in the change that he was making in his life.

Then James began to express a desire to live with his mom again. His mother had given up her parental rights, but she was still allowed to continue to be part of his life through visits. It was decided that it might be best for James if he was moved to a child care center that was closer to where his mother lived so that she could visit James more often. Because of the progress that James made, Rachel and the staff were able to find a child care center that was in the same city where his mother lived and that was willing to accept him.

Rachel had developed a close relationship with James, and she missed him. Just before it was time to return to the United States, Rachel was gladdened when information was received from his new Child Care Center that James had made a good adjustment and was doing well.

Although Rachel and her friend, Emma, had told the children and families of their agency at the very beginning that they would be leaving in early December, when that time came the separation was very difficult. It seemed that they had just arrived and now they would be leaving. It seemed that they were doing everything with much greater intensity. They were in a countdown to the very last day, and everything seemed more dramatic. The day had come, however, and they did say their good-byes, tearfully, of course.

Now, on her return flight to the United States, Rachel looked out the window of the airplane over the Atlantic Ocean and thought back over her amazing experience. How could she ever explain this experience to anyone else? Only one word came to mind: life-changing!

SOCIAL WORK: PROFESSION
AT THE EDGE OF CHANGE

Rachel Fox is a compassionate, ethical, student social worker. She is also attuned to change, adventuresome, willing to take risks, and ready to use promising opportunities when they emerge. She cares deeply about the children of the world and their families. As a student social worker, Rachel is building confidence in her social work knowledge and skills. The profession's values are her values. She is also very committed to a lifetime of learning and humble in her awareness that she has much to learn. She is fully aware that her efforts to help people will not always work; when they don't, she is ready to look for new interventions. As a generalist social worker, Rachel may begin her work with individuals and their families. As a result of her experience in a South African child care center, she discovered that in her future practice, she may need to seek change within organizations, sometimes the very organization that may be her employer. She realized that in the United States, just as in South Africa, organizations too have problems that need to be overcome in order to best serve the needs of families and children. Because she was a generalist, Rachel recognized that in her career, she may need to work not at the individual or family level but also within her own field placement agency as that organization experienced change and possibly at the community or governmental level as well. This would probably be true whether she held a social work position in South Africa, the United States, or anywhere else in the world. Change that will truly help people, she came to realize, often needed to be made at the larger social system level. Today, as she begins her career as a social worker, Rachel is committed to helping people, and she is ready to work where change is needed, even if this is not within her own familiar local environment or her own country. Social work is, at its core, a change profession wherever it exists.

Author Ann Fadiman (1997) describes her position as the storyteller, a perspective very much like that of the social worker:

> I have always felt that the action most worth watching is not at the center of things but where edges meet. I like shorelines, weather fronts, international borders. There are interesting frictions and incongruities in those places, and often, if you stand at the point of tangency, you can see both sides better than if you were in the middle of either one. (p. viii)

Indeed, a stream of exciting, sometimes frightening, highly energized forces is rapidly reshaping our world. Perhaps Rachel Fox, the student social worker, represents the social work profession at this confluence of change. Like Rachel, social workers live with change every day. Social workers also create change. Key to much of the change taking place in the world today is cultural transformation and globalization.

In the next 10 years, the United States will become far more culturally diverse than it is today, and social work practice will be at that confluence of change. This is not an easy or comfortable place to be. The profession of social work will be challenged by a society that still does not understand it or its clients well. The old stereotype of the welfare worker (social worker) dispensing "the dole" to lazy, fraudulent recipients (clients) truly needs to change. This book attempts to destroy such stereotypes by providing extensive case studies that illustrate the true nature of social work practice and the people social workers work with. The people in the case studies—the clients as well as the social workers—were drawn from real-life situations. These are people of dignity. They do not fit into stereotypes. Instead, the varying circumstances of their lives lead naturally into an exploration of the values, social policy issues, research findings, practice, and history of the profession of social work.

Just as the clients do not fit into any preconceived stereotype, neither do the case study social workers. Certainly they do not fit old stereotypes such as the welfare worker or the lady bountiful. Neither, however, does social work fit the image of a glamorous, high-status profession. In reality, social work is not the right profession for everyone. At the heart of the social work profession lie a set of values that ultimately guide practice. Concern for the poor, the oppressed, those discriminated against, and those in pain and most at risk is central to the mission of social work. Belief in the dignity and worth of every human being is not merely a philosophical stance; it is—and must be—inherent in all social work practice. Social workers of the future will need to fight to make social institutions more humane and more responsive to human needs. Their commitment to social and economic justice will need to be carried out in action, not just in silent intent.

Many persons considering a career in social work will find that the value base of the profession is inconsistent with their own values, and they will need to look for another career. Those who enter social work will find that the profession is strongly influenced by various outside forces: demographic trends, political trends, economic conditions, technological advances in science and health care, and environmental concerns, just to name a few. These forces contain energy that drives change. When these forces overlap and intermingle, they sometimes build momentum that speeds change. Increasingly, they are not contained within national borders but, instead, operate globally. They are among the forces that futurists analyze when they seek to forecast change that will take place in the next 5 to 25 years on this planet.

This chapter, then, is about change. It cites the work of social workers, of other researchers, and of **futurists.** Futurists are people who study global trends to predict the nature of life in the future. They do not predict specific future events but instead provide alternative scenarios. True futurists are exceptionally well educated, often holding several PhD degrees; they are fluent in multiple languages; and they often live and work in several countries. This chapter uses the work of futurists as well as other writers and researchers to examine trends in the United States and other parts of the world and to generate thinking about the implications of these trends for the profession of social work.

Futurists' Perspectives on Globalization

The term *globalization* has come to have different meanings within different contexts. One futurist, James Canton, believes that this concept is evolving over time. He sees globalization currently as "a new synthesis of ideas, trade, communications, and collaboration that should promote future global prosperity, freedom, and opportunity" (2006, p. 183). For Canton, the interconnectedness of all regions and people of the world emerges from continuing advances in communication and transportation; he views this evolution as having a positive outcome for the world. Canton's concept is far broader than the usual way that the media tends to depict globalization, which primarily emphasizes international commerce.

John Naisbitt, another futurist, considers the question: does globalization imply Americanization? In many parts of the world there is concern that globalization will result in the adoption of American culture everywhere. According to Naisbitt, "America itself is changing more dramatically than America is changing the world. It is the world that is changing the world" (2006, p. 179). He argues that the United States itself is undergoing rapid and profound change primarily as a result of immigration, which we will discuss in more detail shortly. Naisbitt also points out that everywhere in the world, people are actually working hard to strengthen or regain their cultural connections and identities. They are seeking to retain their native language, even while learning another or several other languages. They are actively ensuring that their children learn the history and traditions of their culture and heritage. Cultural and ethnic communities are celebrating festivals with traditional music, dance, food, drink, and spiritual practices. Communities are safeguarding historical central city areas and architectural treasures through protective legislation.

But futurists, other researchers, and the media have not yet agreed on a definition of globalization. The absence of a precise definition could, perhaps, be attributed to the multiplicity of forces driving global change as well as the fact that globalization is itself a process that is ever evolving. So, where did globalization actually begin? Two sociologists, Hewa and Stapleton, note that from early human history forward, people have changed locations, often crossing geographic as well as tribal or national borders. Human movement, communication, and development of social relations, however, increased markedly during the 20th century. Hewa and Stapleton define globalization as "a growing 'sense of interconnectedness of humankind' around the globe" (2006, p. 4). Critical to their definition is the concept of an exchange of ideas and values that crosses national borders and creates global communities.

Instead of letting ourselves think of globalization as merely a form of modernization or just from the perspective of commerce and trade, a more informed understanding of globalization considers four central themes:

1. Globalization is, in fact, a sustained process that has been under way across human history.

2. Globalization includes economics but, perhaps more importantly, it includes the communication of culture, values, technological advances in communication and transportation, and urbanization.

3. Globalization as a process does not move in a single direction (e.g., top-down) but instead is multidirectional.

4. This process has an impact on local and global dimensions alike, not as a clash with one victor, "but in the reconstitution of both." (Grew, 2006, p. 17)

Yet another perspective of globalization comes from the corners of the world where "there is a growing sense of exclusion from a rapidly interconnected and modernizing world" (Brown, 2008, p. 43). In some areas of Asia, Africa, and the Near East, globalization may even breed alienation and discontent with the Western world (Olzak, 2011).

National and International Strategic Planning

Each country, the United States included, engages in strategic planning to anticipate and guide the direction the future will take. In the United States, the U.S. Government Accountability Office (GAO) is responsible for helping

Congress to engage in planning within a global context. The GAO's 2010–2015 Strategic Plan was developed around several key themes considered likely to shape the future of the nation and of the world. These include threats to national security, fiscal sustainability, economic recovery and growth, global interdependence, science and technology, networks and virtualization, shifting role of government, and demographic and societal change (U.S. Government Accountability Office [GAO], 2010). Goals and objectives establish priorities for Congress as it oversees federal programs and engages in planning. You will encounter additional references to the GAO Strategic Plan in the next several sections of this chapter.

Internationally, the strategic plans of other countries often emphasize similar concerns to those of the United States. On a global scale, the United Nations in 2000 articulated a set of millennium development goals (MDGs) with 2015 as the target date for accomplishment. This goal statement was adopted by all member nations. In the years that followed, the world experienced terrorism, wars, earthquakes, and other natural and manmade disasters that could have totally defeated efforts to attain the goals. By 2010, the United Nations was able to report that progress had been made but in some areas, goals were unlikely to be met.

Goal 1 of the UN development plan was to eradicate extreme poverty and hunger. Figure 13.1 depicts areas in the world where people experience critical lack of food. Goal 1 was an area in which some progress was made despite the global financial crisis that began in 2008. Extreme poverty declined from

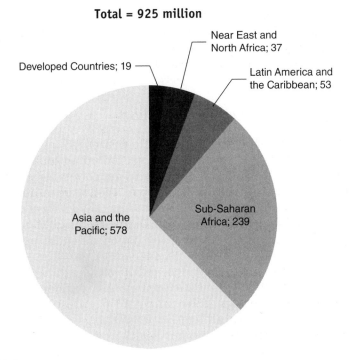

Figure 13.1

United Nations Global Hunger Report: **925 Million Hungry People in 2010**

Source: Adapted from Food and Agriculture Organization of the United Nations. (2010, September). *Global hunger declining, but still unacceptably high: International hunger targets difficult to reach* Retrieved from http://www.fao.org/docrep/012/a1390e/a1390e00.pdf

nearly one-third of the world's population to less than one-fifth and the overall poverty rate was still on target to fall to less than 15 percent by 2015 although this could be impacted by the sluggish rate of world economic recovery. Goal 2, to achieve universal primary school education, demonstrated remarkable improvement even in the poorest regions: by 2007, 88 percent of the children in southern Asia and sub-Saharan Africa (the world's poorest regions) were enrolled in primary schools (United Nations Development Programme, 2010). The promotion of gender equality and empowerment of women, Goal 3, also demonstrated improvement in the number of women who are participating in political activity; in some countries, where in the past only men were permitted to run for political office, women have now achieved seats in the parliament. Goal 4, the reduction in child mortality, has also shown positive results: child mortality has declined globally with deaths due to child killers such as measles declining most dramatically (Ki-Moon, 2007, United Nations, 2010).

The improvement of maternal health, Goal 5, demonstrated the least progress of all of the goals. According to a UN report: "over half a million women still die each year from treatable and preventable complications of pregnancy and childbirth" (Ki-Moon, 2007, p. 5). Women in sub-Saharan Africa are most at risk. While the number of people receiving antiretroviral HIV treatment increased from 400,000 to 4 million, reversing the spread of HIV/AIDS by 2015, Goal 6, has been extremely slow and disappointing. Goal 7, the final goal, also had negative results. Ensuring environmental sustainability, as reflected in deforestation, and providing access to safe drinking water and basic sanitation were slightly improved but not on target for achievement by 2015. The United Nations Development Programme reported that "at current trends, most developing countries are projected not to meet most of the MDGs" by 2015 (UNDP, 2010, p. 12). The armed conflicts and civil unrest of recent past years have threatened human security and, along with it, the MDGs.

Globalization: Relevance to Social Work

The 2001 terrorist attacks on the World Trade Center in New York and the Pentagon in Washington, DC, awakened people, including social workers, in the United States to globalization in a new and dangerous form. Americans came to realize that even as a world superpower, they were vulnerable to international terrorism even within their own borders. The military campaign to end terrorism that has stretched out for years following the 2001 attacks in the United States has not satisfactorily answered important questions about why terrorism exists. What nourishes, supports, and sustains it? While social workers don't have answers to these questions, social workers do understand that frustrations related to poverty, economic exploitation, differences in religion and in worldview, among others, drive much of the unrest and strife in the global environment in which we all live.

Social workers, in concert with other health and human service professionals, play a key role in the healing and transformation of the world. This has been true since the days of Jane Addams and the pioneers of the social work profession. Social workers from the United States act internationally as well as at home. The cross-national practice experience of Lyons, Manion, and Carlsen, authors of *International Perspectives on Social Work*, lead them to believe that "social work across the globe is now operating under different conditions, which produce new social problems—or exacerbate old ones. Social [work] professionals therefore need to review services and practices in the light of international events and perspectives. For some, this entails working in international settings, but for others it means incorporating internationalized perspectives into local practice" (2006, p. 1). They view globalization as a form of interdependence in which "global events and processes now impact on individuals, communities, and societies everywhere" (pp. 1–2).

Social work is, indeed, a profession at the edge of change. As the world around us changes, so must our profession. As we prepare for the future, the values of the social work profession—service, social justice, dignity and worth of all persons, and the importance of human relationships—remain as beacons, guiding our actions and our practice. Standard 6 of the NASW Code of Ethics reminds us that social workers have ethical responsibilities, not just to our individual clients, but to the broader society on local as well as global levels (NASW, 2008).

The Rachel Fox case study initiated an international perspective at the start of this chapter and globalization will remain a theme throughout the remainder of this chapter. It is inherent in the five major forces that are energizing, shaping, and transforming the world. We begin with what is arguably the most significant transforming force: demographic change. Following this, this chapter will consider other forces of change: political trends, economic conditions, biomedical and scientific advances, and environmental sustainability.

DEMOGRAPHIC TRENDS

The cross-national practice of the student social worker in this chapter's case study reflected the social work profession's shift from a "casework" approach that focused on individual people to emphasis on practice that is able to move comfortably across social systems. This more nimble generation of practitioners works with individuals, families, groups, organizations, communities, or even larger societal systems, often with several systems at once, depending on what is needed to prevent or resolve problems. Adapting to the needs of changing client populations is essential to effective practice in an increasingly diverse society.

Demographics, the study of population characteristics and trends, is an area of considerable interest to researchers and futurists who monitor patterns of change from which they develop forecasts of the future. Demographics is one of the most significant forces creating change in the United States today, change that will carry into the next 40 or 50 years. The U.S. Census Bureau, which charts population shifts, predicts that by the year 2050, the nation will be 54 percent minority. As early as 2023, more than half of the children in the United States will be minority (2008). In reality, the "new" multicultural world that is predicted may be new for some people, but not for all. Already, in some parts of the country, there is so much diversity that there is no single majority population. With rapidly changing demographics in the next few decades the social work profession, with a value system that respects diversity, should be well positioned to take on the challenges that lie ahead. Other demographic trends that will influence social work practice are the increase in our elderly population, evolutions in American family structures, and the changing immigrant and refugee population.

Adapting to the needs of changing client populations is essential to effective practice in an increasingly diverse society.

A Multicultural America

Although White Americans made up 85 percent of the U.S. population in 1950 (U.S. Bureau of the Census, 1950), White, non-Hispanic persons are expected to decline in population during the 2030s and 2040s and comprise only 46 percent of the 2050 U.S. population (U.S. Census Bureau, 2008). In anticipation of this rapid shift, Farai Chideya (1999) observed:

> This is uncharted territory for this country, and this demographic change will affect everything. Alliances between the races are bound to shift. Political and social power will be reapportioned. Our neighborhoods, our schools and workplaces, even racial categories themselves will be altered. Any massive social change is bound to bring uncertainty, even fear. But the worst crisis we face today is not in our cities or neighborhoods, but in our minds. (p. 5)

Chideya's vision is that the new generation, the millennium generation of 15- to 25-year-olds that is already far more culturally diverse than any previous generation, will create a future that is less negatively biased on issues of race. In the year 2000, the Census Bureau permitted people to check more than one box under "race." As a result, the 2010 census and future censuses will more accurately report on the multifaceted racial composition of the United States.

Americans have typically thought about race in terms of Black and White. This tends to be how race continues to be covered in the media. The reality, though, is that America is really very diverse. The 2010 census data showed that 13 percent of the population was Black, 16 percent was Hispanic, 5 percent was Asian, 0.9 percent was American Indian and Alaska Native, with only 0.2 percent identified as Native Hawaiian and Other Pacific Islander. An additional 3 percent included persons who identified as more than one race. Hispanic and Asian populations were the fastest growing in the United States at the time of the 2010 census (U.S. Census Bureau, 2011).

The social work profession was birthed in a spirit of reform and celebration of multiculturalism, as revealed in the history sections of past chapters of this book. The Council on Social Work Education has written curriculum standards that ensure inclusion of human diversity content in all baccalaureate and master's degree programs. **Ethnic-sensitive approaches** to social work practice are now taught in schools of social work that link knowledge of culture and ethnicity with understandings of social class differences (Devore & Schlesinger, 1999). In many ways, social work as a profession has meant being an advocate and a supporter of human diversity.

But there is much more for social work to do to create a just society, and the predicted transformation of our nation's ethnic and cultural makeup will challenge the profession to become much more proactive. An **ethnoconscious approach** incorporates ethnic sensitivity with empowerment tactics that build upon appreciation for the strengths already existing in ethnically diverse communities. An ethnoconscious approach would seek to create antiracism organizations that reflect the ethnic makeup of the community served by the agency from agency board members to executives, and all levels of staff. "Organizations can make antiracism commitments in their mission statements; hire, retain, and empower more staff of color" (Miller & Garran, 2009, p. 932) and be "dually focused on bringing about social change and providing empowering programs and services to its clientele" (Gutierrez & Nagda, 1996, p. 206).

Linked not only to its service community, but also to the region, nation, and other countries, the organization and its social workers could take on human problems in the lives of people as they live in families and function in groups, organizations, and entire communities.

The Graying of America

As indicated in Chapter 10, "Social Work with Older Adults," a significant shift in the age of the population is taking place in the United States. During the colonial period of American history, approximately half the population was under the age of 16, and relatively few persons lived to age 65. By 1900 about 4 percent of the population was 65 years of age or older. In 1970 the proportion of persons 65 or older had grown to 9 percent. By 2000 this had increased to 12.4 percent (34,991,733 persons), and estimates for the year 2050 indicate that the population aged 65 and older is expected to reach 88.5 million (Vincent & Velkoff, 2010; U.S. Census Bureau, 2004).

Despite a long history of age discrimination in the United States (unlike most Asian countries, where age is revered), the new and rapidly growing cohort of older adults may produce shifts in ageism attitudes. Today's older adults are quite different from previous generations. They have achieved higher levels of education than their predecessors, they generally have a higher level of income and buying power, and they are politically active. They have fewer disabilities, and if disabilities do occur, they have better designed equipment (e.g., motorized wheelchairs) to enable them to sustain an active lifestyle. The baby boomers, who started reaching their 65th birthdays in 2011, are expected to redefine what aging means in America.

Today social workers provide financial counseling, recreation and wellness programs, housing assistance, advocacy (especially in relation to health care), adult protective services, counseling, and case management. People who compose the oldest cohort of the elderly, those 85 years and older, require the greatest number of services. As Table 13.1 indicates, this segment of the elderly population is growing most rapidly. Because of advanced age, these people are more likely to have cognitive disorders such as dementia as well as physical disabilities, so they require care that is physically and psychologically demanding for caregivers. Intervention, then, would seek to strengthen bonds of intergenerational caregiving as well as economic and social service policies to ensure good quality of life.

A demographic characteristic that influences the planning and delivery of social services to the elderly is the lifespan of women. Women tend to outlive men by several years and they also tend to marry men who are several years older, so it is common for women to outlive their husbands by 10 years or more. Women are more likely than men to have to deal with the complex health, economic, and housing problems of old age, first as caregivers of others and later as receivers of care.

The complex problems of aging require social workers to have both a sound understanding of the aging process and a broad generalist practice background that enables them to work simultaneously with individual clients, families, and community systems. Fortunately, the number of students interested in social work with older adults has increased in recent years. Encouraged by the financial support of organizations like the Hartford Foundation, schools of social work have increased the aging content in required courses, and some have also added elective courses on social work with older adults. More field

Table 13.1   **Projected Population 85 Years and Older (in millions)[a]**

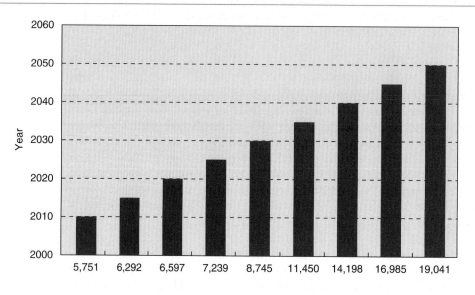

Source: Vincent, G. K. & Velkoff, V. A. (2010, May). Appendix Table A-1. Projections and distribution of the total population by age for the United States: 2010 to 2050, *The Next Four Decades: The Older Population in the United States: 2010 to 2050,* p. 10. U.S. Census Bureau. Retrieved from http: //www.census.gov/prod/2010pubs/p25-1138pdf

[a]Table used 2008 National Projections based on 2000 census.

Human Behavior

Practice Behavior Example: Social workers know about human behavior across the life course

Critical Thinking Question: What do social workers need to understand about aging in order to assess and intervene with persons aged 85 years and older?

placements in aging, too, are now available. As a result, it appears that the new generation of social workers will be better prepared for work with older adults, especially when the older adult population is increasing and the number of social work positions in this field is growing substantially.

The Evolving American Family

The American family, too, has undergone considerable change, and it continues to evolve. In the 1980s, some writers predicted the imminent collapse of the traditional American family. Such gloomy reports, however, were replaced in the 1990s by a renewed valuing of family life, including increased interest in issues such as early childhood education, long-term health care, and enriched marriage. Families were valued once again by society. Society has continued to place value on families. This trend is expected to continue. The World Future Society predicted that as the 21st century continues to unfold, workers will continue to make sacrifices, sometimes of higher salaries, to spend more time with their families (World Future Society, 2007).

Interesting patterns have been developing in families. According to the American Community Survey conducted by the Census Bureau in 2005–2009 there were 113 million households in the United States, up from 105 million in 2000 (U.S. Census Bureau, 2010a). The percentage of family households with children living at home stood at 52 percent in 1950 and decreased to

46 percent by 2008 (U.S. Census Bureau, 2009). This demonstrated a continuing, although relatively small, decline. Also, since the early 1990s, nonfamily households have remained a bit over 30 percent of all households.

So, as the population increases, the trend has been for families to exist, with relative stability in the percentage of family households since the 1990s. What is changing, however, is the size of family households. The average household is shrinking in size. There are an increasing number of households consisting of one person living alone: from 17 percent of all households in 1970 to 27.3 percent in 2008 (U.S. Census Bureau, 2010a).

As other chapters in this book have reported, there are many grandparents raising children today because drugs and AIDS have left parents unable to care for their children. Approximately 6.6 million children under age 18—9 percent of all children in the United States—lived in a household that included a grandparent in 2008. More than half of these children actually lived in the grandparent's home, and most had a parent living there, too (U.S. Census Bureau, 2008). This is increasingly the face of poverty. Many sacrifices are made by parents and grandparents to try to keep their families intact or to try to help young parents to continue their education.

Since its beginnings, the profession of social work has provided service to the American family. As families and societal conditions changed over time, the profession found that it needed to rethink how it worked with families. In the past two or three decades, for example, the profession switched from strongly encouraging unmarried mothers to place their babies for adoption to helping families to remain together. Federal legislation, much of which was promoted by social workers, also resulted in renewed efforts to keep families together. The 1978 Indian Child Welfare Act, for example, discouraged adoption of Indian children into non-Indian families and gave tribes limited funds for family support services. The 1980 Adoption Assistance and Child Welfare Act was considered benchmark legislation for its attempt to ensure permanent families for children. The 1997 Adoption and Safe Families Act furthered commitment to adoption rather than long-term foster care by shortening the time limits of foster care and speeding up the adoption process.

This sounds quite wonderful, but there is another perspective on adoption that social workers must consider. Some cultures define family differently from the nuclear family concept that is valued by people of White, European descent. African Americans, for example, have traditionally valued the extended family. The Association for Black Social Workers has articulated clear preference for **kinship care** over adoption. Kinship is a broad concept, incorporating persons related by blood or legal ties, plus persons related by strong affectional ties. Bonding with family members, permanency of care, and uninterrupted cultural identity are all potentially available through kinship care, which often evolves into long-term foster care (Holody, 1999). Social work as a profession has learned to appreciate the strengths of kinship care.

Families clearly are changing. The family of the future is likely to be diverse in culture and ethnicity, in age, and in structure (single-parent, two-parent, gay- or lesbian-parented, blended families, kinship units, or nonmarital parenting by either biological parents or nonrelated couples). Poverty tends to increase the numbers of related and nonrelated persons occupying the family household as persons attempt to share resources especially on a temporary basis. Nevertheless, "what matters more than family form are family *processes* involving the quality of caring, committed relationships" (Walsh, 2009, p. 425).

Social work research and practice over the past 10 years has provided considerable insight into the remarkable strengths of families. This has led to a new paradigm in which social workers are shifting away from focusing on problems and dysfunction to an acknowledgment of the assets and resilience of families. Out of this new way of thinking has evolved ways of working with families in which collaboration and partnership are emphasized. Caring professional relationships with children and families are paired with high expectations. Social workers today appreciate "the rich, ongoing possibilities of complex kin relationships, which are sources of connection and life support" (McGoldrick, 2009, p. 421). Similarly, social workers have learned that it is critical to support not only family members but also the people outside the family (teachers, caregivers, mentors, etc.) who nurture, educate, socialize, and often transform the lives of children. Finally, helping families requires lobbying for and even creating programs that ensure the existence of basic social and economic resources to all families (Benard, 2006).

The Changing Immigrant and Refugee Population

The demographic trends that we have looked at so far include multicultural diversity, aging, and evolving patterns in families. Immigration, the final process affecting change, is contributing dramatically to the increasing multiculturalism of the United States. Immigration, however, is not happening in America alone. This is a worldwide phenomenon, and it is yet another way in which regions of the world are increasingly interconnected. Actually, throughout history patterns of human migration have evolved, often reflecting events such as war, famine, natural disasters, and religious or political persecutions. The early history of the United States is replete with descriptions of waves of immigrations. People arrived on U.S. shores to seek a fortune; for adventure; or as indentured servants, slaves, or promised brides. Precipitated by war, financial crisis, civil unrest, and natural disasters, thousands of people around the globe have become displaced in recent years. The United States has admitted some of these refugees. Canada and several European countries have also done so, and they have provided the newcomers with quite generous welfare programs. The startling fact, reported by the United Nations Development Programme, is that currently approximately 1 billion people, nearly one out of seven, are migrating either within their own countries or beyond (as cited in U.S. Government Accountability Office, 2010).

People, in general, enter another country through three legal means: immigration, asylum, or as a refugee. An **immigrant** is someone who moves to another country for the purpose of settling there permanently. **Asylum** is a protected status that is granted only on a case-by-case basis to persons who can substantiate serious, possibly life-threatening political persecution. **Refugees** are people who leave their country "because of persecution or a well-founded fear of persecution on account of race, religion, nationality, membership in a particular social group, or political opinion" (Bruno, 2006, p. 1).

Applications for refugee status in the United States are processed by the State Department before entry to the United States. Persons seeking asylum, on the other hand, may already have arrived in the United States, or they may be physically present at a border. Persons who persecuted others are not accepted for either asylum or as refugees. Once they have been admitted and lived in the country for 1 year, both refugees and persons accepted for asylum may

Social workers assist newly arrived refugees with the complexities of resettlement.

apply for permanent resident status (Bruno, 2006). If granted, they then have a "green card"; after 5 years, they may apply for full (naturalized) citizenship.

The U.S. Congress sets the refugee admission ceiling each year, traditionally at approximately 70,000, and that policy has remained fairly constant; approximately 10,000 persons are admitted under asylum status each year. In the aftermath of the terrorist attacks on the United States in 2001, refugee admissions were temporarily suspended, new security procedures were implemented, and applications were much more cautiously screened. The number of persons accepted as refugees plunged from 73,000 in 2000 to 27,000 in 2002 (Bruno, 2006). It resumed previous levels within a few years. In 2011 the ceiling was increased to its highest level: 80,000 (U.S. Department of Homeland Security, 2011).

In addition to these legal forms of entry, there is, of course, illegal immigration. The United States has implemented border patrols, specialized policing, and considerable legislation to stop illegal immigration. While many people do enter the United States over guarded land or water routes, which is the way illegal immigration is often portrayed in the media, others arrive quite legally. They simply overstay the expiration of their employment, student, or other legal visa. The disparity between countries' standards of living and economic well-being will remain the catalyst for continued immigration, legal and illegal, into the United States and other industrialized countries for years to come.

Concern about the significant numbers of persons and goods illegally entering the United States has resulted in the GAO identifying this as a targeted area in its 2010–2015 Strategic Plan. Performance Goal 2.1.4 requires an assessment of efforts to "strengthen border security and address immigration enforcement and services issues" (GAO, 2010, p. 118). The Department of Homeland Security's success in preventing illegal migration across U.S. borders will now be reviewed along with its ability to effectively and fairly process applications for immigration benefits. Immigration reform initiatives and proposals will be monitored and evaluated by the GAO as they emerge over the next several years. This attention to illegal as well as legal immigration in the GAO Strategic Plan reflects the level of concern immigration has become relative to the Strategic Plan's Goal 2: "Respond to changing security threats and the challenges of global interdependence" (2010, p. 109).

Until the 1970s, persons who became U.S. citizens came primarily from European countries. The 1970s saw a considerable increase in the number of Asian immigrants, and Asian immigrants continue to make up a significant portion of new U.S. citizens. In 2010, 41 percent of new citizens came from Asia; 26 percent from North America; 13 percent from Europe; with smaller portions coming from Africa, South America, and other regions. According to the U.S. Department of Homeland Security, the leading countries from which new citizens came in 2010 were Mexico, India, the Philippines, China, and Vietnam (Lee, 2011).

The sharp increase in citizenship and naturalization beginning in 1907 and its uneven pattern are depicted in Figure 13.2. Changes in law, crackdowns on illegal immigration, and worldwide migration pressures account for the volatile shifts that are reflected in citizenship patterns in recent years. Immigration has become a huge political issue, not just in the United States, but worldwide. According to the International Organization for Migration (IOM), "migration is a catalyst for change and development, and in a world that is changing at a lightning pace, not harnessing the power of migration is shortsighted" (McKinley, n.d.).

The IOM is a nongovernmental organization that works at the global level to resolve the deep social and political rifts occurring in many countries where migrants, often without legal documentation or work permits, compete for extremely low-paying jobs with higher paid, more educated, native laborers. The failure of many countries to provide legal options for immigration has resulted in migrants' use of expensive and potentially life-threatening smuggling networks to seek employment. Often, however, they find themselves

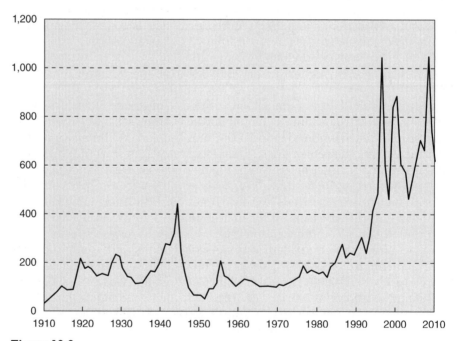

Figure 13.2

Naturalized United States Citizens: Fiscal Years 1910 to 2010 (in thousands)

Source: Lee, J. (2011, April) *Annual Flow Report: U.S. Naturalizations: 2010*. U.S. Department of Homeland Security, N-400 naturalization data, Fiscal years 1907 to 2010. Retrieved from http:dhs. gov/http://www.dhs.gov/assets/statistics/publications/natz_fr_2010.pdf

at the margins of society and open to exploitation of many kinds. The IOM visualizes a possible solution in the development of an international circulatory migration program that uses technology to determine where the mismatch exists between labor shortages on the one hand and eager laborers on the other. The IOM is seeking assistance from the World Bank and the United Nations to move this plan forward (McKinley, n.d.). IOM's proposal is, indeed, a creative, fresh approach to the volatile international migration issue.

In the United States, the foreign-born population tends to be young, be employed in service industries, have less education than the native population and, not surprisingly, be at increased risk of poverty (Larsen, 2004). The increasing number of immigrant persons in U.S. cities has resulted in need for more bilingual employees and for culturally sensitive programs that provide high-quality services to a diverse population. Bilingual social workers are in even greater demand now than in the recent past. The profession needs to be able to recruit people who reflect the culture of the immigrant newcomers. It is anticipated that East and West Coast port cities will see an influx of immigrant groups in coming years. Existing ethnic communities will likely expand, and new ethnic communities may emerge. Throughout the United States—in schools, health care centers, shelters, and advocacy programs—social workers are among the first professional persons to assist new residents with resettlement.

As advocates for at-risk and vulnerable populations, social workers may be called on increasingly in the future to assist immigrants, refugees, and asylum-seekers. Social workers will be involved in resettlement work and may also help organizations such as church groups to sponsor new immigrants or asylum-seekers. In international social service agencies such as the Red Cross, social workers will communicate across borders to keep relatives linked, especially during disasters or in the event that a person becomes a prisoner of war. Program planning will be undertaken, too, to assist communities in providing for the child care, health, and other needs of new immigrants.

POLITICAL TRENDS

Politics is the basis for the second major force that will generate change in the future. Political trends and political balance of power shift over time, and these shifts have enormous impacts on the health, welfare, criminal justice, and educational services that are available to people. Of course, these same shifts also determine social work employment opportunities. Looking back over the past several decades, it is apparent that politically conservative forces were gaining power in many countries, including the United States. In America, the election of Obama in 2008 was somewhat surprising given the strength of political conservatives, including the self-proclaimed Tea Party movement. Legislation favored by liberals was passed in the early years of the Obama administration but soon national and global economic crises shifted voter support toward more conservative policies that threatened newly enacted programs such as health care reform as well as stable, well institutionalized programs such as Social Security.

Welfare Reform and Poverty

Welfare reform was a popular political movement that swept the United States in the 1990s and brought about the TANF (Temporary Assistance for Needy Families) program. The TANF program has been referred to frequently in this book. A feature of TANF that did not exist in AFDC was a lifetime limit of 60 months on benefits. Under TANF, too, parents may be required to work after 24 months of assistance, and TANF assistance could be cut off for a variety of reasons—if a family failed to cooperate with the work requirement, for example, or if a teen mother stopped attending school. Discontinuation of benefits for failure to comply with TANF requirements became known as **sanctioning.** If another child was born while a family was receiving TANF, the state was not obliged to provide any additional assistance for the newborn. With a significant level of funding provided to states to design and administer their own TANF programs (which most states renamed to reflect their state's philosophy), some states provided child care funding and other services to encourage rapid transition to work from welfare.

The TANF program is widely regarded as very successful. As Figure 13.3 illustrates, there was indeed a dramatic decline in welfare caseloads and TANF payments to recipients beginning in 2003 until 2008 when the nation plunged into economic recession. It is true that many persons have become employed and have left the TANF program, but other persons left the program because they gave up, were sanctioned for failure to comply with requirements, or they had reached the 5-year lifetime limitation.

There is also a growing concern that a portion of people receiving assistance have serious, persistent barriers to employment and self-sufficiency. A 2007 Urban Institute analysis (Acs & Loprest, 2007) of TANF data found increasing TANF cases of persons with health conditions that limited employability of recipients who failed to complete high school (a factor that reduces likelihood of employment). Numerous other circumstances affect ability to work: mental health or substance abuse problems, a history of imprisonment, recent exposure to domestic violence, and learning disabilities. TANF is a social program that is affected by changes in the economic cycle of the country. When the economy is "soft," or slowing down, jobs are lost or harder to find and TANF cases increase. Even the educational attainment of recipients increases during difficult economic conditions. In the years 2008 and 2009 when the nation suffered severe economic crisis, the number of people below the poverty line increased by 42.9 million (an increase of 14.2 percent), and not a single state in the United States had a statistically significant decrease in the number of people in poverty or in the state poverty rate (U.S. Census Bureau, 2010b).

So, despite apparent success, the TANF program also has critics who are increasingly concerned about issues such as work requirements that probably cannot be met, the program's ability to sanction recipients who fail to comply with regulations, and the 5-year lifetime limit. States, having enjoyed power and control in administering the program, are also increasingly concerned about their ability to deal with potentially large numbers of "hard-core poor" families who will not be able to transition from TANF to employment. Issues of social welfare tend to polarize Americans, but it is very likely that the political process will soon need to take on some difficult issues regarding poverty, welfare reform, and TANF. Although his data are now a bit old, Wolff offers a broader economic analysis:

> If social welfare programs work, then countries with more extensive programs should report a smaller percent of their population living in poverty. And that is exactly what we find. According to UNICEF, the percentage of children living in poverty in 2005 was: Denmark, 2.4%; France, 7.5%, Norway, 13.4%; Canada, 14.9%; United Kingdom, 15.4%; United States, 21.9%. (2010, p. 2)

TANF Cases - Fiscal Year Averages

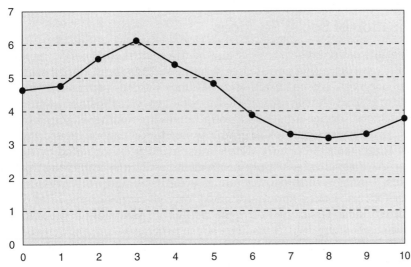

TANF Fiscal Year Paymets

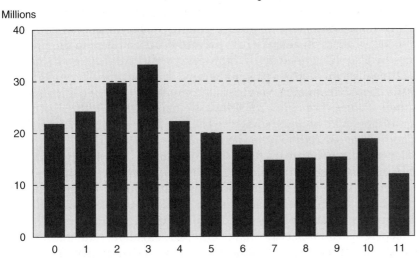

Figure 13.3

Temporary Assistance for Needy Families (TANF): **February 2011**

Source: Adapted from U.S. Department of Public Health and Human Services Office of Budget and
Finance Division. (2011, February). *Temporary Assistance for Needy Families*, p. 1. Retrieved from
http://ww.dphhs.mt.gov/statisticalinformation/tanfstats/tanf022011/tanf022011fullreport.pdf

Policy Practice

*Practice Behavior Example: Social workers
collaborate with colleagues and clients for
effective policy action*

Critical Thinking Question: How could students
join with social workers to pursue legislation
that supports more humane welfare reform?

Social workers need to become more involved in the
political arena, because political forces, of course, will
continue to determine the availability of human services
in our country and in the nations of the world. If social
workers truly care about people and about social change,
they will not sit idly by, merely providing psychotherapy for the emotional and physical pain suffered by the
victims of politics and poor public policy; instead,
they will assume responsibility for their own political

behavior and will also empower their colleagues and clients to engage in the democratic process.

Privatization of Social Services

Privatization of social services is one of the results of the shift toward an increasingly conservative political environment. This trend can be seen in the advent of corporate prison systems, child abuse services provided by for-profit organizations, and states contracting for social services instead of sustaining their own social service programs. Group homes are another example of privatization. Twenty years ago, foster group homes for teenagers, developmentally disabled adults, and the elderly were almost exclusively operated by state and county welfare departments or nonprofit agencies. In most communities today, only a small portion of the group homes are run by nonprofit organizations. Instead, most are owned and operated by private corporations, often headed by social workers. The same is true of residential treatment centers for emotionally disturbed children. Substance abuse programs—once provided almost exclusively by tax-supported hospitals or denominational facilities—have become big business and are being marketed aggressively.

The entrepreneurial practice of social work has also expanded significantly, especially for MSWs. Social workers in private practice offer their services for a fee in much the same way that physicians or attorneys in private practice do. Often health insurance policies cover the cost of counseling through social workers. In social work, **private practice** refers to the provision of services by a social worker with appropriate credentials (e.g., a license to practice clinical social work or psychotherapy) with payment provided by the client or the client's insurance. Service is terminated when the contract is completed, often with no provision for follow-up care, although social work private practitioners who are guided by the Code of Ethics typically refer clients needing additional services to other organizations, if needed.

On the surface, this may look like economic efficiency, but when vulnerable populations such as the frail elderly or emotionally disturbed children are involved, such apparent efficiency may actually be detrimental to clients. Neither economic nor human justice interests are served when clients' well-being suffers because of disrupted or prematurely discontinued service. What is needed instead is service that is efficient, effective, humane, and readily available—whether it is delivered through a public or private agency or through a professional person in private practice.

The trend toward privatization in human services, whether prisons or family therapy, breaks with a long tradition of tax-supported public services delivered without the cost and the potential conflicts of interest of the for-profit, entrepreneurial enterprise. This trend raises concerns about the inherent values of human service organizations. Is monetary profit the primary goal, or are the best interests of the client the real goal? While moving more and more into for-profit practice, the profession of social work nevertheless maintains a somewhat skeptical stance about it. Of concern is the potential that social workers might lose their traditional commitment to advocacy, to social change, to social and economic justice, and to service to vulnerable populations.

The political drive to shift public health and social services to the private sector remains very strong. Yes, it can save money for taxpayers by reducing personnel costs and fragmenting services, but at a substantial cost of the quality of services. Although professional people may be accused of being self-serving, they will need to become proactive to ensure that the quality of professional services provided in the private sector is not further jeopardized and that public social services continue to exist.

Women's Issues

The profession of social work, because it serves many poor and vulnerable women and is comprised of significant numbers of women, is especially attuned to the needs of women and their struggle for equality. Even in the past, social work pioneers such as Jane Addams and Florence Kelley of Chicago's Hull House were leaders in the struggle for the right to vote and for equality for women. Despite public ridicule and imprisonment in the early days of the women's movement, these women and the men who supported them succeeded in 1920 in obtaining passage of the Nineteenth Amendment to the U.S. Constitution—the right to vote for women.

The next effort of women, to pass the **Equal Rights Amendment (ERA)** prohibiting discrimination on the basis of gender, was not as successful. The effort to achieve the ERA was immense, with huge political rallies, statewide and regional conventions, parades, and much demonstration of public support. In 1972 Congress did pass the ERA, but it was defeated when the necessary number of states failed to ratify this proposed amendment to the U.S. Constitution.

Another gain for women, although a painfully slow one, has been the narrowing of the wage gap between men and women. Table 13.2 documents the progress that has taken place in narrowing the wage gap between American women and men. Between 1963 and 2010, the wage gap for women working full time began to close, but only at the rate of less than half a cent each year (National Committee on Pay Equity, 2010). It is also very important to note that real annual wages have actually fallen for both men and women who have lost

Table 13.2 **Wage Gap by Gender**

Median Annual Earnings of Full-Time Workers by Sex: 1960–2010

Year	Women's Earnings as a % of Men's	Earnings in Real Dollars	
		Women	Men
1960	60.7%	$11,003	$18,175
1970	59.4	13,719	23,105
1980	60.2	13,589	22,587
1990	71.6	15,166	21,177
1995	71.4	14,762	20,667
2000	73.0	27,355	37,339
2005	77.0	31,858	41,386
2010	77.4	36,931	47,715

Source: Adapted from National Committee on Pay Equity. (2006). The wage gap over time: In real dollars, women see a continuing gap. Retrieved August 17, 2007, from http://www.pay-equity.org/info-time.html; National Committee on Pay Equity. (2011). Wage gap statistically unchanged. Retrieved from http://www.pay-equity.org

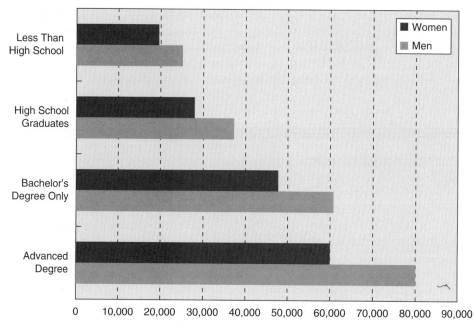

Figure 13.4

Weekly Earnings by Sex and Education Achievement: Second Quarter, 2010 (dollars)

Source: Adapted from U.S. Bureau of Labor Statistics (2010, July 26). *TED: The Editor's Desk: Usual weekly earnings in second quarter 2010 by education.* Retrieved from http://data.bls.gov/cgi-bin/print.pl/opub/ted_20100726.htm

jobs because dramatically increased international trade has expanded the supply of low-skill, low-wage workers producing goods for the American market.

Figure 13.4 is a clear demonstration of the considerable income differences between women and men associated with further education. The shocking differences in the wages at each level is heightened by a close examination of the growing differentials as women and men complete high school, then among college graduates, with the most significant difference by far demonstrated among women and men who have earned graduate or professional degrees. Annual wages based on the Figure 13.4 data are quite revealing:

- No high school diploma: males earn $25,220 and women $19,604
- High school graduates: males earn $37,128 and women $28,184
- College graduates: males earn $60,892 and women $47,840
- Advanced degrees: males earn $80,392 and women $60,216
  (U.S. Bureau of Labor Statistics, 2010, July 26)

The assumption that additional education and credentials narrow the gender wage gap is simply not true. This is quite a shocking realization for many women college students.

As pronounced as the wage differences are for upper income women, poor women are actually most at risk of being economically exploited. With low-wage competition from lesser developed nations, the U.S. economy attempts to locate potential low-wage employees wherever possible. This may mean recruiting migrant workers, or it may mean employing persons who are TANF recipients. As the TANF program tightens work requirements, many recipients are pushed into low-wage jobs.

Not surprisingly, inequality in wages became a political issue that women's organizations in particular targeted for change. As women's professional groups such as the 70,000-member Business and Professional Women/USA (BPW/USA) joined with labor unions and other politically active women's groups, the pragmatic concept of **pay equity** emerged. Pay equity is defined by the National Committee on Pay Equity as:

> a means of eliminating sex and race discrimination in the wage-setting system. Most women and people of color are still segregated into a small number of jobs—such as clericals, service workers, nurses and teachers. These jobs have historically been undervalued and continue to be under-paid because of the gender and race of the people who hold them. Pay equity means that the criteria employers use to set wages must be sex and race neutral. (*Questions and answers on pay equity*, 1998, p. 1)

With more women than ever in the workplace, pay equity is one political issue that will be on the agenda of women in the future.

Historically and currently, men far outnumber women in legislative offices in the United States, but women are becoming a political force in state legislatures, and they are now challenging men in races for the highest political offices in this country. The next decade seems poised to produce many exciting political races with high-powered women running effective campaigns for key offices. The 112th Congress (2011) included 76 women, with 17 in the U.S. Senate. Notable among them is a social worker and the longest serving of current women senators, Barbara Mikulski of Maryland. Senator Debbie Stabenow, from Michigan, is another social worker. Of the five social workers in the U.S. House of Representatives in the 112th Congress, three are women (NASW, 2011).

Meanwhile, in developing countries as well as industrialized parts of the world, women have been elected as presidents and prime ministers. Countries such as Switzerland, Pakistan, Ireland, Norway, and Great Britain have had women presidents and prime ministers.

ECONOMIC TRENDS

The people served by social workers, especially generalist baccalaureate social workers, are often poor people. Of course, social workers work with all sectors of society and all people are affected by the economy, but poor people and near-poor persons are likely to be most dramatically impacted by economic conditions. Not surprisingly, political forces and economic conditions are strongly interrelated. And now more than ever, events and conditions in other parts of the world affect our lives. In the past decade there has been an expansion of industrialization around the globe, especially in third world countries, in Eastern Europe, and in the former Soviet Union. Some of the industrialization exploited the masses of poor people in emerging countries, luring them into urban areas and leaving their villages and farms bereft of able-bodied workers. In the United States, economic development has increasingly moved from central-city areas to suburbs and from northern to southern states.

During the late 1980s in the United States, **underemployment**—which is employment at or near minimum wage, often part time and without health insurance or other benefits—had begun to replace unemployment. The numbers of employed persons receiving financial and medical assistance and food stamps increased, while the unemployment rate decreased dramatically.

Food pantries provided groceries, and community feeding programs served meals to the families of employed persons whose income was inadequate to meet their daily needs.

Meanwhile, a very small portion of the U.S. population had doubled its income in a single decade, ending in the late 1980s; the poorest 20 percent of the population, however, saw their share of the national income fall from 5.1 percent in 1980 to 4.5 percent by 1991.

For many Americans the 1990s brought increased prosperity and a surge in consumer products. The number of households with telephones, televisions, cars, computers, and air-conditioning increased. When the federal welfare reform law, Temporary Assistance for Needy Families, was passed in 1996, it was heralded as an end to poverty in the United States. TANF caseloads did continue to decrease, unevenly and at an increasingly slower pace, for years.

Shocks to the U.S. economy began in 2007 and a global economic downturn was underway by 2008 resulting in a recession for the United States that was the most severe since World War II. From December 2007 to December 2009, 8.8 million jobs were lost, bank failures emerged, and record-high home foreclosures and bankruptcies occurred (U.S. Government Accountability Office, 2010). By 2011 some meager signs of stabilization were apparent. Much of Europe, too, appeared to be slowly coming out of the global recession but Portugal, Ireland, Spain, and Greece remained in serious economic straits. The United States 2010 to 2015 Strategic Plan recognized the need for Congress and the federal government to clearly identify the greatest needs of the country and then strategically ensure resources that meet those needs. Goal 1 of the Government Accountability Office's strategic plan is to "address current and emerging challenges to the well-being and financial security of the American people" (2010, p. 59). The severe economic deterioration in the U.S. economy, with a full recovery of the labor market not expected until 2016, however, will require cautious and wise fiscal policy to prevent loss of momentum for the gradual economic recovery that appears underway. Competing needs and desires of the American people will shape this country's response to the economic dilemma facing the nation.

In recent years, Americans have also become increasingly aware that income inequality exists in the United States. In this country, we are much less comfortable talking about income disparity or social class differences than people in other countries, where social class differences much more overtly shape politics. Rich or poor, most people in America like to consider themselves part of the middle class. An examination of the data, however, tells a different story.

In 2010 it was reported that the United States had "the greatest income disparity among the advanced capitalist countries" (Walsh, 2010, para 6). The gap between rich and poor has become the largest on record. Persons with income of $100,000 or more accounted for nearly 50 percent of the income of the United States, while persons living below the poverty line, 44 million of them, earned only 3.4 percent of the total U.S. income. The U.S. Census Bureau reported increasing income inequality even in a single-year period, 2008 to 2009, with a per capita decrease in income of 1.3 percent for Whites but a 3.5 percent decline for Blacks in just that one-year period (Wall, Proctor & Smith, 2010). Other indicators of wealth and income disparity (wages, stock ownership, personal savings) tell the same story. Clearly, income disparity has been quietly but steadily increasing and the majority of Americans are no longer "middle class."

In the United States, the gap between rich and poor has become the largest on record.

"Sorry, Perliss, I can't give you a raise. I'm suffering from compassion fatigue."

Figure 13.5

What does this mean for the future? Obviously, the persons with the lowest income will be most vulnerable. These are often the people social workers serve. They are the people social workers seek to empower. Perhaps middle-income people, with growing awareness of their own potential vulnerability, will increase their support for the pro-poor, poverty reduction programs and other social programs that are so necessary for the well-being, not just of the poor, but of all people.

TECHNOLOGICAL AND BIOMEDICAL ADVANCES

The fourth major trend or force influencing and shaping the future is that of technological and biomedical advancement. The evolution in these areas in the past decade has generated energy and knowledge that will continue to produce new products, software, and biomedical options in the near future. The ongoing change in these areas will influence social work practice and challenge the profession in many ways.

Information and Communication Technology

Today's social work students are more computer literate than any cohort of students that preceded them. Their college class assignments anticipate that they will have a higher level of technology competency than previous classes of students. Increasingly, they will be asked to run statistical analyses for their research projects and work with spreadsheet and database programs. Text messaging and Internet access have come into use in the home visits made by students in their field placements. Before they graduate from college, they will become proficient with library electronic databases such as *Social Work*

Abstracts, which is available in many college and university libraries. Social work education increasingly incorporates emerging technologies including podcasting lectures and the use of webcams in distance education programs. Social media sites and youtube.com's videos are potential assets, too, in social work education.

As a profession, however, social work was slow to adopt computerization, and some small agencies are still, only now, beginning to use databases, spreadsheets, and word-processing software to manage their administrative work and case records. A legitimate concern of some agency directors was that storage of clients' records in computer databases might be very efficient, but it could also present risks to confidentiality. On the other hand, computerized databases, e-mail, chat rooms, and other technology resources actually help social workers keep connected and may remedy one of the most serious problems in social work: fragmentation of services.

Access to information about social work agencies, services, and social work employment opportunities is readily available on the Internet to students and social workers, and social workers increasingly refer clients to these same sources. (One such source is http://www.fosterclub.com, a youth-driven Internet source that provides support and advice to young people aging out of foster care.) While it is true that computer access is still not available to all of the people social workers see, this is less and less true as libraries and other public services make computers available. Social work practice has been enriched through the use of computerized client self-assessments that screen for anxiety, depression, and chemical dependency. Several years ago, a survey of the clients of an employee assistance agency found that some had initially turned to websites for help "because they had issues too embarrassing to share face to face" (O'Neil, 2002, p. 14). This poignant description of vulnerability, added to the fact that Internet counseling is rapidly increasing, underscores the importance of social workers adhering to strict ethical guidelines when using electronic technology.

Today's office technology—including computers, fax machines, cell phones, telephone answering machines or answering services, voice mail, and all other electronic equipment—is a potential source of ethical problems. The NASW Code of Ethics holds social workers responsible for protecting confidentiality for clients, which includes accepting responsibility for the careful use of current technology in handling client records. Security systems are available within computer software or agency computer network systems. Social workers need to ensure that they have access to security systems that protect confidential documents.

Increasingly sophisticated software is being developed that can assist social workers in assessing client problems, developing intervention plans based on well-researched evidence of potential outcomes, and evaluating the results of their interventions. A recent NASW study found that child welfare social workers, both older and younger social workers, were regularly using mobile technology, sometimes including e-mail access. Digital cameras and laptop computers were also among the technology used in the field (Pace, 2011).

Online groups dealing with specific issues such as breast cancer or children who are school phobic are now being used and are likely to be further developed rapidly. They are inexpensive for clients with computer access, and they usually function within a time frame that fits today's hectic lifestyles. In other countries, too, technology is increasingly used to improve communication.

Russian social workers, for example, are using the Internet to help incarcerated youths to stay in touch with their families (Malamud, 2010).

Social action, advocacy, and policy research also benefit dramatically from the availability of shared databases, from programs that permit statistical analysis of massive amounts of statistical data, and from the ease of computer-assisted international communication. Online databases available through the Internet are rich sources of data for social workers. Technological advances in computers, fax transmission, and long-distance telephone access will continue to affect the way social workers "do business" each day. These tools are fostering globalization at a rapid rate, and for creative social workers, their potential uses in organizational, community, and even international change efforts are nearly unlimited.

Biomedical Technology

Technological advances in medicine continue to startle the world—and to bring both hope and havoc to the lives of patients and their families. Social workers in health care settings very quickly encounter the ethical and personal dilemmas precipitated by advances in medicine, but across social work settings all social workers can anticipate working with people whose lives are affected by advances in medical technology.

Across social work settings, all social workers can anticipate working with people whose lives are affected by advances in medical technology.

Regenerative Medicine

Organ transplantation, an area that continues to evolve, involves social workers as key members of the medical team. Social workers are called upon to bridge the communication gap between the highly specialized medical professionals and the persons so vitally affected—such as organ recipients and family members of the potential organ donor. Social workers help family members understand the medical situation, the decisions that need to be made, and the potential ramifications. Simultaneously, they help people deal with the overwhelming emotions of such health crisis situations.

Many lives could be saved today if organ donors could be found, but only a small fraction of donors are found in countries like Canada or the United States, where reluctance to consent to organ donation seems especially strong. Futurists like James Canton predict that stem cell technology will generate these organs and more. By 2030, Canton (2006) suggests stem cell treatment may be able to offer:

1. New organs, including hearts and lungs
2. New bone growth for legs, arms, and backs
3. New sensory functions and optic nerves to restore eyesight
4. New cancer treatments
5. New nerves to heal muscles and to restore movement
6. New cells to offset the aging brain (p. 136)

Regenerative medicine is the name given to the promising new field that utilizes the science of chemistry, medicine, engineering, computer science, biology and other areas (including stem cell research) to restore damaged tissue and organs. Much of this exciting new technology is just now being implemented. Progress has been made, for example, with the creation of replacement human bladders grown from the patient's own cells. This has been used so far primarily for children and adolescents whose birth defect of spina bifida left them with nonfunctioning bladders. But tissue engineering can also design and grow new organs using a mold and biomaterials (not the patient's own cells) to grow into a replacement organ, a heart valve, for example. In addition, stem cells from a newborn baby can now be collected and retained for a future time when that child or adult needs these highly potent cells to repair or heal when there has been major tissue damage from disease, trauma, or from a lifetime of wear and tear (McGowan Institute for Regenerative Medicine, 2010).

Tissue engineers are making progress in research with stem cells that can be manipulated to develop the capacity to reproduce or heal organs. In Scotland, for example, scientists have learned to reproduce from stem cells the cells that are found in the brain and central nervous system. It is believed that this discovery could lead to the development of new cell-based drugs that could be used to treat Parkinson's and Alzheimer's diseases. In London, researchers converted stem cells into the type of cells that line a critical functioning portion of the human lungs. This could lead to cell therapy for lung tissue destroyed by cancer or even eventually generate entire replacement lung organs. Bone marrow transplants, one of the cell-based therapies, are already in use (Tucker, 2006).

Ethical issues regarding human embryo stem cell research have been intensely debated in the media for the past several years. In considering the arguments for and against the use of stem cells, it is important to understand the difference between embryonic and adult stem cells. A fertilized human egg is made up of cells, pluripotent cells, that are not yet differentiated into distinct, separate body organs; that occurs beginning in the 9th week following conception. If placed in a laboratory culture dish and provided the right environment, they will continue to divide and produce more pluripotent cells, but they are not able to form organs without further treatment. These are the **embryonic stem cells** that have greatest potential for research. Multipotent cells, which are known as **adult stem cells,** are taken from various parts of the human body, but the most useful sources are from bone marrow or from the umbilical cord or placenta.

In the United States, there is opposition to use of embryonic cells because this use destroys the fertilized egg that would otherwise have potential to develop into a human being. Until 2009, the U.S. government did not outlaw stem cell research, but it placed considerable restrictions on it. In 2009 the Obama administration eased some of these restrictions and in 2010 Amendments to the National Academies' Guidelines for Human Embryonic Stem Cell Research were issued. These guidelines permitted federal funding for research but only for the use of embryonic lines that had been created from fertility clinic embryos that were not going to be saved, and only as long as they had been obtained ethically and from couples who had received no financial incentive (Stein, 2009; National Academy of Sciences, 2011). Meanwhile, other countries, notably the United Kingdom, are aggressively moving ahead with stem cell research aimed at advancing treatment for cancer, Alzheimer's disease, and other human organ malfunctions (Wagner, 2007).

Biomedical ethics groups are engaged in serious and deeply emotional considerations of myriad difficult questions engendered by stem cell research, questions such as when human life begins, when it becomes sacrosanct, whether an embryo has different value as a living being than a fetus or a newborn child, and whether one human life can ethically be sacrificed to save the life of another. These are tough questions!

Genetic Research

Significant advances have also been made in genetics, thanks to the **Human Genome Project.** The Human Genome Project was an international effort, initiated in 1990, to seek significantly greater understanding of human genetics that could ultimately cure diseases and promote health and longevity. A **genome** is an organism's DNA that contains the genetic instructions responsible for developing and directing the activities of that organism. It is made up of 3 billion twisted strands of chemicals that exist in the 23 pairs of chromosomes within human cells (National Human Genome Research Institute, 2006). The Human Genome Project was completed in 2003.

It was an amazing feat involving the collaboration of researchers around the world, and it was possible only because of information technology that enabled large computers and robots to analyze massive amounts of data. Its findings are being explored but have already led to the development of more than 1,000 genetic tests that aid diagnostic studies or reveal specific genetically linked risk factors. There are already genetic tests to determine the potential for such conditions as cystic fibrosis, Huntington's disease, sickle-cell anemia, and certain kinds of cancer (some forms of ovarian, colon, and breast cancer). Genomics can also guide decisions about prescription medication. HIV-infected patients' antiretroviral abacavir medications are now routinely genetically guided prescriptions. Genetic testing is increasingly guiding prescriptions, too, for Plavix (used for anxiety), tamoxifen (cancer treatment), and warfarin (a blood thinner) (Malone, 2011).

As genetic information becomes increasingly available, it raises difficult spiritual, emotional, and ethical questions.

As genetic information becomes increasingly available, it raises difficult spiritual, emotional, and ethical questions, "such as whether to go ahead with a pregnancy or whether to inform existing children and siblings of their risk" (Dahinden et al., 2006, p. 24). Because the meaning of genetic risk carries such significance and potentially involves multiple generations of family members, social workers and other allied health professionals often become involved.

The ethical and social quandaries of women seeking genetic testing for breast or ovarian cancer were studied back in 1998 by Tovia Freedman, a social worker. The two segments from her research interviews reveal the emotion experienced by these women and, one would suspect, these emotions might be mirrored in women as well today:

- I do not want to carry on another generation of cancer. Should my daughter be told not to have children? It feels like a death sentence. There is uncertainty and the never knowing.
- There is tyranny involved because the technology is available. I feel that it would be stupid of me not to avail myself of it. If there is anything that I can do to assure myself that I do not have to share my mother's fate, that I won't die a horrible death from ovarian cancer, I will do it. I don't want to be in the position down the road of beating my head against the wall and saying, "Why didn't I do this?" (pp. 216–217)

Social workers help people understand what genetic testing means, the kinds of information that can come from the tests, and how it can be used. They help family members resolve the issues that testing results bring, the multigenerational consequences of information suggesting susceptibility to disease.

The social worker is not usually the actual genetics counselor—that person is a medical specialist. But social workers provide the supportive relationship, assist with panic or psychological crises that result, and assist families after the information is given to them. The genetic testing that is commercially available is costly. Its current lack of availability to all socioeconomic groups raises ethical questions, too, for social workers.

Completion of the Human Genome Project is only the beginning of extensive research by government as well as education, business and private research organizations around the world. Pharmaceutical corporations' clinical trials for drugs that will effectively target individuals' specific genetic makeup are increasingly guiding drug therapy. New modes of delivery of drugs will enable them to take effect very quickly and be more effective than medications that are currently available. Box 13.1 reflects the possibilities that may be realized in the next 50 years as a result of the Human Genome Project and related research.

Related to regenerative medicine and genomics are two additional areas of technology that are revolutionizing medicine: nanotechnology and neurotechnology. Nanotechnology refers to the creation and utilization of materials and devices that are too small to be seen by the naked eye, barely the size of molecules. Testing is well underway with implementation expected shortly, while some other nanotechnology techniques are currently in use. Briefly, just a few examples of nanotechnology applied to medicine include nanoparticles used to speed the delivery of chemotherapy drugs to cancer cells, or to reduce severe bleeding by absorbing the watery fluids in blood and helping it to clot quickly. Z-Medica, a manufacturer, has already produced a medical gauze that utilizes an aluminum nanoparticle product. A cream made of nanoparticles containing nitro oxide gas has been shown to kill staph infections in laboratory tests. Nano tools are being developed to be used by nanorobots to repair diseased cells, implant medical devices, and conduct surgery (UnderstandingNano.com, n.d.).

Neurotechnology, the set of tools and functions capable of influencing the human brain, evolved out of nanotechnology. Lynch (2004) anticipates

Box 13.1 The Next 50 Years of Medical Science: The Impact of the Human Genome Project

Individualized analysis based on each person's genome will lead to a very powerful form of preventive medicine. We'll be able to learn about risks of future illness based on DNA analysis. Physicians, nurses, genetic counselors, and other health care professionals will be able to work with individuals to focus efforts on the things that are most likely to maintain health for a particular individual. That might mean diet or lifestyle changes, or it might mean medical surveillance. But there will be a personalized aspect to what we do to keep ourselves healthy. Then, through our understanding at the molecular level of how things like diabetes or heart disease or schizophrenia come about, we should see a whole new generation of interventions, many of which will be drugs that are much more effective and precise than those available today.

We are entering a new age of discovery that will transform human health. Our eventual knowledge about the workings of the genome has the potential to fundamentally change our most basic perceptions of our biological world. It is difficult to predict what will be learned and how future knowledge will be applied, but there can be little doubt that understanding the genome will revolutionize our concept of health and improve the human condition in remarkable ways.

Source: National Human Genome Research Institute. (2006, December). *The Human Genome Project completion: Frequently asked questions.* Retrieved from: http://www.genome.gov/11006943

that China and India will provide the human testing environment necessary to generate the technology that will dramatically improve memory and learning, emotional stability, and such sensory experiences as hearing, taste, and sight. Lynch projects that "by 2020, biochips will have radically altered the drug development process, reducing the time to develop new therapies from 15 to 2 years," (Neurotechnology section, para. 2). Already the U.S. government spends $6 billion on neuroscience funding. In a 2010 Congressional Hearing exploring the future of neurotechnology, "expert witnesses agreed that the promise for a scientifically principled approach to preventing, treating, and curing brain disease has never been greater" (Reppas, para. 3).

Human Reproductive Technology

The area of human reproduction continues to evolve through changes in reproductive technology and future advances may result in quite complex moral and ethical issues. Currently multiple for-profit organizations exist (many are advertised on Internet websites) that offer infertile persons alternatives for parenthood. Among the alternatives are surrogate parenting, human egg donation (or sale), and embryo transfer. In **surrogate parenting,** a woman agrees to be impregnated and to release the baby that she delivers to the person(s) who contracted with her for this purpose. In human **egg donor programs,** the egg, also called ovum, of a donor is surgically implanted in another woman who is unable to produce her own ovum; she may then be able to conceive a baby through sexual intercourse. **Embryo transfer** involves surgical implantation in a woman of another woman's egg that has been fertilized by her husband's, partner's, or a donor's sperm (*Glossary of terms*, 2001).

As of 2006 (most recent available data), more than 3,000,000 babies had been born as a result of one or more forms of assisted reproductive technology (Rathode, 2006). Most infertility is successfully treated with medication or surgery; therefore, people seeking more involved procedures, such as in vitro fertilization using sperm banks or human egg donors, are likely to have to pay large fees (generally not covered by insurance). Fees in excess of $5,000 for an egg (oocyte) donor are not uncommon. Often people are not aware that egg donation is painful and risky for a woman. It involves repeated injections of hormones over several weeks, followed by surgery and the possibility of severe pelvic pain, bleeding, cysts, and some forms of cancer. Low-income women, especially in the United States where this procedure is not legally regulated, are at greatest risk of exploitation.

Cloning is an asexual, as compared with a sexual, form of reproduction. Animals have been cloned, so why not humans? That, at least, is a question asked by futurists. In human cloning, an embryo grows from either a male or female stem cell and then is implanted in a woman so that it can be brought to term and delivered as a newborn infant. This "clonal embryo" does not carry the genetic makeup of two persons; it consists of the genes of only the person who donated the stem cell. Obviously these genes could also be scientifically engineered or altered so that the child will not carry a predisposition to known diseases. There could potentially also be alterations to determine sex of the child, hair color, intelligence, body type, and numerous other traits. Or the child might be a true clone, identical to the "parent." Therapeutic cloning occurs when stem cell tissue is used to replace organs or held indefinitely to permit future creation of future organs, should there be a need. Box 13.2 suggests some of the arguments that are inevitable as cloning possibilities draw near. What a strange and fascinating future awaits us!

Box 13.2

Proposal: In the future, humans should be cloned the way animals are now.

Yes	No
Children would not be born with inheritable diseases or defects.	Cloning may not totally prevent defects and may, in fact, result in tragic malformations.
Regulating human reproduction has so many benefits to humankind that it should be mandatory.	Moral and spiritual values that view God as the creator should prevail over procedures that science makes possible.
Cloning should be allowed in order to obtain the most perfect human specimen.	Who is to determine the "perfect" human? Is the perfect human a mighty warrior or a peace maker, an intellectual giant, or a nurturer?
The health, longevity, and economic benefits of cloning are obvious.	Human variety and diversity are such valuable traits that they should be cherished, not obliterated

ENVIRONMENTAL SUSTAINABILITY

Environmental sustainability is a major concern for futurists. Canton, for example, lists among his "top ten threats that could kill America's future" the possibility of an environment so damaged that it could cause significant reduction to the quality of life and even the public health and well-being of Americans (2006). The earth, even today, is being increasingly overwhelmed by pollutants of various kinds. Around the world, carbon is currently being produced in twice the amount that oceans and forests can absorb. Global climate change is likely to threaten both coasts of the United States as well as coastlines in many other countries with flooding. Blythe is one of several futurists who contemplate a post-petroleum world, where there will not be sufficient gasoline to fuel even hybrid cars and where some communities that rely on petroleum products to fuel their cars, farm implements, and other industries will become ghost towns. Some small communities in Arizona, for example, are viewed as too dependent on automobiles to survive (2006).

The earth's inherent self-regulating mechanisms, however, do not have to be totally overwhelmed by pollutants and chemicals of modern living. Efforts are increasing worldwide to save the planet. The European Union has assumed a remarkable leadership role with its precautionary principle that holds all nation-members of the EU to regulations that will not permit "economic activity, regardless of how lucrative or beneficial it might be, [to] be allowed to compromise the integrity of the life-support systems that make up the indivisible biosphere in which we all dwell, and from which we draw our sustenance" (Rifkin, 2004, p. 338). Nations that wish to become EU members, too, must clean up their environments and initiate earth-friendly ecological practices.

Both the United Nations, through its Millennium Development Goals, and the GAO Strategic Plan of the United States forcibly address environmental needs as vital to the future of humankind. The United Nations is especially concerned for developing nations, which are expected to be hardest hit by drought, deforestation, flooding, and degradation of cropland resulting from climate change. Legal empowerment of the poor to their land is viewed by the United Nations as a potential tool to fight degradation of the land, decrease greenhouse gases, and reduce poverty (United Nations Development Programme, 2010).

This would require legal protections by governments as well as involvement of transnational corporations to ensure land rights to native people or at least access to land needing rehabilitation after deforestation or other use by the transnational corporations.

The GAO Strategic Plan of the United States recognizes that some of the nation's natural resources are increasingly stressed. Of special concern is energy as the citizens of the United States, which comprise 4.5 percent of the world population, are currently consuming approximately 20 percent of the world's energy resources. Development of oil resources existing on federally owned land could increase production of energy but a competing demand is the preservation of natural resources and wildlife habitat. Already "about 44 percent of the nation's 3.5 million miles of rivers and streams are impaired" by pollutants (U.S. Government Accountability Office, 2010, p. 99). Cleanup of hazardous and radioactive waste sites that pose potential health issues is another critical and perplexing challenge facing the GAO as it seeks to assist Congress in addressing these environmental concerns.

The profession is awakening to the enormous impact of current and past environmental degradation on humanity. Increasingly, there are calls for a fresh generation of leaders who will revitalize the social work literature and enrich social work practice with a holistic, planetary view of practice (Besthorn & Canda, 2002; Holland, 2005). A future for the profession is envisioned where the ecological, social, and spiritual dimensions of practice will be merged and strengthened. Increased involvement with the environment, possibly including planned experiences with natural and wilderness areas, will be built into social work education and practice.

Today social work environmental advocates believe that "we are an interdependent planet and share responsibility for sustainable growth and the development of new technologies for future generations. Thus, human future on the earth means valuing our connection to our habitat" (Link & Ramanathan, 2011, p. 196). The social work profession, including students, must assume increasing responsibility for practice, social policy development, and research that supports environmental sustainability.

In acknowledging the interdependence of all living things, people are viewed as connected to each other and to the life of the planet. When people or the environment is endangered, nurturing and care are needed. Social workers can help others develop capacity to care for other people and other living things. As social workers help their clients and communities to assume greater responsibility in nurturing the environment so, too, can social workers experience a new emergence as we become actors in the work of creating an environment that truly respects and nurtures all people and all living beings.

Practice Contexts

Practice Behavior Example: Social workers keep informed, resourceful, and proactive in responding to evolving organizational, community, and societal contexts at all levels of practice

Critical Thinking Question: How might students at your school proactively respond to environmentally degraded areas in your community?

THE FUTURE OF THE SOCIAL WORK PROFESSION

Throughout this chapter, we explored several powerful forces—demographic, political, and economic trends, technological and biomedical advances, and issues of environmental sustainability—that will affect life on the planet in the next 5, 10, 20 years, or more. We now narrow our focus and briefly look at the future for the social work profession.

The organization that undoubtedly has the greatest amount of data on which to build future employment projections for social work or any other profession or occupation is the U.S. Department of Labor's Bureau of Labor Statistics (BLS). If BLS statistics are one criterion of predictability, then the profession of social work is likely to remain healthy and in existence for a long time. In its most recent report, the BLS noted: "Employment for social workers is expected to grow *faster than the average* for all occupations through 2018" (Bureau of Labor Statistics, 2009, Job Outlook section, para. 1). The BLS publication, the *Occupational Outlook Handbook*, is a good source of information on trends in employment. According to this publication, changing demographics in the United States and technological advances are creating new and expanding existing niches for social work employment. Services to older adults will need to expand as the U.S. population ages. The BLS predicts that growth will take place in home health care, in assisted living, and within nursing homes and hospice programs. Similarly, in an *NASW News* article, Carolyn Messner, the president of the Association of Oncology Social Work, expressed grave concern about an impending workforce shortage of social workers skilled in work with cancer patients and their families ("Social Work in the Public Eye," 2010). Other areas that are expected to expand include mental health and substance abuse services, school social work, and child and family services. Detailed information from the BLS as well as NASW's manpower survey can be found in Chapter 1 of this book.

While opportunities will continue to exist for social workers, there is a clear need for the profession to define itself much more clearly for the public. Nurses, teachers, librarians, dentists, and accountants all have clear, if not always correct, images in the public. Social work is not well understood, nor is occupational therapy, psychology, or professional counseling. One of the reasons people have difficulty understanding social work is that the social work profession is, in Leon Ginsberg's terms, "a mammoth occupation" (2005, p. 8). The profession functions across a very diverse array of fields of practice. The breadth of social work as a profession is truly both a strength and an exciting challenge.

The future of the profession depends greatly on its ability to attract students who identify with the mission, values, and ethics of the social work profession. This new generation of social workers will help the profession to evolve and become even more committed to social and economic justice, equality, and social change. To make change happen, social workers need to add the dimension of policy practice to their intervention roles. This means that while working with individual persons, families, or groups, social workers are simultaneously seeking to create or improve policies or programs. To do so, they may actively support legislation or organizational policies that will result in the resources and programs that are needed to ensure a good quality of life for clients and, indeed, for all Americans.

To prepare for the exciting challenges of the future, social work education will need to retain a firm hold on its values and ethics but change some parts of the curriculum. Social work courses will need to broaden the human diversity content they incorporate, paying increased attention

Professional Identity

Practice Behavior Example: Social workers serve as representatives of the profession, its mission, and its core values

Critical Thinking Question: What personal qualities will students need to acquire in order to represent the social work profession well?

to spirituality, economic differences, ability/disability, gender identity, new immigrant and refugee populations, and evolving family systems. Fluency in Spanish may become a requirement in some social work programs as Spanish-speaking populations become a larger presence in many parts of the United States. Computer and technology skills will expand students' access to information. The social work curriculum will develop students' ability to organize, analyze, and effectively use information as well as the technology tools that will increasingly be used to deliver services. Social work courses of the future will also increasingly incorporate global content and will build upon multi-cultural, international, and historical content from courses taken in the liberal arts. As military might is built in many parts of the world and security technology is developed to defend against possible biological and chemical terrorists, the social work curriculum may add a new dimension of study. Peace studies—alternatives to the use of violence to resolve conflict in families, communities, and worldwide—could become a focus for social work education of the future.

The profession of social work is probably one of the most difficult to practice. It is demanding and frustrating. It is not always well understood. Sometimes it is poorly paid. But it is potentially the most rewarding and enriching profession that anyone could choose. It also provides a unique opportunity to participate in the creation of a future society, one that we would choose for ourselves as well as for the people we serve.

PRACTICE TEST The following questions will test your knowledge of the content found within this chapter. For additional assessment, including licensing-exam type questions on applying chapter content to practice behaviors, visit **MySearchLab.**

1. Which of these statements BEST reflects John Naisbitt's view of the future?

   a. The synthesis of new ideas, trade, communications and collaboration will promote global prosperity, freedom, and opportunity.

   b. There is a growing sense of exclusion from the rapidly interconnected and modernizing world.

   c. People have always changed locations and now this movement fosters an exchange of ideas and values that create global communities.

   d. America is changing more dramatically than America is actually changing the world.

2. Which of the following is NOT a United Nations Goal for 2015?

   a. Respond to changing security threats and the challenges of global interdependence.

   b. Eradicate extreme poverty and hunger.

   c. Ensure environmental sustainability.

   d. Reduce child mortality.

3. By the year 2050 Caucasians are expected to make up _____percent of the U.S. population.

   a. 38

   b. 46

   c. 62

   d. 85

4. Which of the following statements BEST reflects an "ethnoconscious" approach to provision of social services?

   a. Social workers include ethnic sensitivity and empowerment approaches that promote appreciation for the strengths of ethnically diverse communities.

   b. Services are provided by social workers with the same ethnic background and national origin as the clients that are served.

   c. Social workers are focused on bringing about social change through providing empowerment services to clients.

   d. Social workers understand culture and social class differences.

5. Which set of skills and knowledge are most critical for future social workers to cultivate?

   a. Spanish language, willderness hiking, and texting.

   b. Child development, counseling, and ethics.

   c. Computer/Internet navigation, biomedical understanding, and environmental sustainability.

   d. Security strategies, immigration, and financial management.

6. Identify the social work value that Rachel, the student intern, was demonstrating in her work with James.

   a. Competence

   b. Integrity

   c. Dignity and worth of the person

   d. Social justice

7. Rachel learned that in order to truly help people social workers often need to facilitate change at the larger system level. Identify two larger systems described in the case study that should be priorities for political action and intervention. Provide examples to justify your priorities. Identify the anticipated outcomes if these systems were improved.

MySearchLab CONNECTIONS

Reinforce what you learned in this chapter by studying videos, cases, documents, and more available at **www.MySearchLab.com**.

Watch and Review

Watch these Videos

*Managing Personal Values: The Code of Ethics

*Advocating for Human Rights and Social and Economic Justice

*Intervention

*Evaluation

Read and Review

Read these Cases/Documents

Δ Adventures in Budgets and Finances

Δ Community to Community

Δ Professional Decision Making in Foster Care

Δ The Boyds

Δ The Morgan Family

Explore and Assess

Explore these Assets

Lawrence Berkeley National Laboratory, U.S. Department of Energy—http://www.lbl.gov/

Canadian Heritage—http://www.pch.gc.ca/eng/1266037002102/1265993639778

World Watch Institute—http://www.worldwatch.org/

International Forum on Globalization—http://www.ifg.org/

Assess Your Knowledge

Assess your knowledge with a variety of topical and chapter assessment.

Conclude your assessment by completing the chapter exam.

* = CSWE Core Competency Asset

Δ = Case Study

References

Chapter 1

American Association for Marriage and Family Therapy. (2002). *FAQs on MFTs*. Retrieved from http://www.aamft .org/faqs/index_nm.asp

Association of Social Work Boards. (2006). *Licensing requirements*. Retrieved from http://www.aswb.org/lic_reqs.html

Biggerstaff, M. A. (1995). Licensing, regulation, and certification. In R. L. Edwards & J. G. Hopps (Eds.), *Encyclopedia of social work* (19th ed., Vol. 2, pp. 1616–1624). Washington, DC: NASW Press.

Buchan, V., Hull, G. H., Mather, J., Pike, C., Ray, J., Rodenhiser, R., et al. (2010). *BPD Baccalaureate Education Assessment Project (BEAP) total reports*. Retrieved from http://beap.socwk.utah.edu

Bureau of Labor Statistics, U.S. Department of Labor. (2009a). *Occupational outlook handbook, 2010–11 edition: Counselors*. Retrieved from http://www.bls.gov/oco/ocos067.htm

Bureau of Labor Statistics, U.S. Department of Labor. (2009b). *Occupational outlook handbook, 2010–11 edition: Overview of the 2008–18 projections*. Retrieved from http://www.bls .gov/oco/oco2003.htm

Bureau of Labor Statistics, U.S. Department of Labor. (2009c). *Occupational outlook handbook, 2010–2011 edition: Psychologists*. Retrieved from http://www.bls.gov/oco/ ocos060.htm

Bureau of Labor Statistics, U.S. Department of Labor. (2009d). *Occupational outlook handbook, 2010–11 edition: Social workers*. Retrieved from http://www.bls.gov/oco/ocos060 .htm

Community Action. (2005, May 23). *UK has social worker shortage, recruitment campaigns failing*. Retrieved from http://www.findarticles.com/p/articles/mi_mOLVZ/is_9_20/ ai_n13800696

Council on Social Work Education. (2008). *Council on social work education: Educational policy and accreditation standards*. Alexandria, VA: Author.

Council on Social Work Education. (2010). *About CSWE: Mission*. Retrieved from http://www.cswe.org/About.aspx

Harvey, D. (2001). Social worker shortage: Illusion or reality? *Social Worker Today, 1*(7), 10–12.

Hooyman, N. (Ed.). (2009). *Transforming social work education: The first decade of the Hartford Geriatric Social Work Initiative*. Alexandria, VA: Council on Social Work Education.

International Federation of Social Workers. (2005, November 11). *About: Aims*. Retrieved from http:/www.ifsw.org

Lee, N. (2006, May 16). *Social worker shortage slams state*. Retrieved from KGMB 9Local News website: http://kgmb/ display.cfm?storyID=8183

Morales, A. T., & Sheafor, B. W. (2002). *The many faces of social workers*. Boston, MA: Allyn & Bacon.

Nadelhaft, A., & Rene, D. (2006, March 8). *Landmark study warns of impending labor force shortages for social work profession* [Press release]. Washington, DC: National Association of Social Workers.

National Association of Black Social Workers (NABSW). (n.d.). *Code of ethics and history*. Retrieved from http://www .nabsw.org/mserver

National Association of Puerto Rican/Hispanic Social Workers. (2010). *Membership; mission*. Retrieved from http://www .naprhsw.org

National Association of Social Workers [NASW]. (n.d.). *About NASW*. Retrieved from https://www.socialworkers.org/nasw/ default.asp

National Association of Social Workers [NASW]. (2006, March 8). *Landmark study warns of impending labor force shortages for social work profession*. Washington, DC: Author.

National Association of Social Workers [NASW]. (2009). Environment: Policy statement. In J. J. Kelly & E. J. Clark (Eds.), *Social work speaks: National Association of Social Workers policy statements 2009–2012* (8th ed., pp. 121–126). Washington, DC: NASW Press.

National Association of Social Workers [NASW]. (2010a). *NASW code of ethics* (Rev. 2008). Retrieved from https:// www.socialworkers.org/pubs/code.asp

National Association of Social Workers [NASW]. (2010b). *NASW credentials and specialty certifications*. Retrieved from http://www.socialworkers.org/credentials/list.asp

National Organization for Human Services. (2009). *Certification*. Retrieved from www.nationalHumanservices.org/mc/ page.do?sitePageId=89287&orgId=ohs

News 24. (2006, March 28). *Social worker shortage critical*. Retrieved from News 24.com website: http://www.news24.com/ News24/South_Africa/News/0,2–7–1442_1906277,00.html

Popple, P. R. (1995). Social work profession: History. In R. L. Edwards (Ed.), *Encyclopedia of social work* (19th ed., Vol. 3, pp. 2282–2291). Washington, DC: NASW Press.

SNP: It's Time. (2005, November 3). *Hyslop: Shortage of social workers is putting children at risk*. Retrieved from http:// www.snp.org/press-releases/2005/HYSLOP/

Thyer, B. A., & Biggerstaff, M. A. (1989). *Professional social work credentialing and legal regulation: A review of critical issues and an annotated bibliography*. Springfield, IL: Charles C. Thomas.

Whitaker, T., Weismiller, T., & Clark, E. (2006). *Assuring the sufficiency of a frontline workforce: A national study of licensed social workers, executive summary*. Washington, DC: National Association of Social Workers.

Whitaker, T., & Wilson, M. (2010). *National Association of Social Workers 2009 compensation and benefits study: Summary of key compensation findings prepared for the 2010 Social Work Congress, April 2010.* Washington, DC: National Association of Social Workers.

Whitaker, T., Wilson, M., & Arrington, P. (2009). *The results are in: What social workers say about social work.* Washington, DC: NASW Press.

Chapter 2

Abbott, A. (1999, October). Measuring social work values. *International Social Work, 42*(4), 455–470.

Abramovitz, M. (2000). *Under attack, fighting back: Women and welfare in the United States.* New York: Monthly Review Press.

Bauerlein, M. (2006, July/August). Every breath you take: Air pollution kills tens of thousands of Americans each year. It doesn't have to be that way. *Sierra,* pp. 56–62.

Berg-Weger, M. (2005). *Social work and social welfare: An invitation.* Boston, MA: McGraw-Hill.

Closing press briefing. (2009, December 19). Retrieved from the official website of the UN Climate Change Conference in Copenhagen: http://unfccc.int/meetings/cop_items/5257.php

Compton, B., & Galaway, B. (1999). *Social work processes* (6th ed.). Pacific Grove, CA: Brooks/Cole.

Council on Social Work Education. (2008). *Educational policy and accreditation standards.* Alexandria, VA: Author.

Dubois, B., & Miley, K. K. (2011). *Social work, an empowering profession* (7th ed.). Boston, MA: Allyn & Bacon.

Figuera-McDonough, J. (2007). *The welfare state and social work.* Thousand Oaks, CA: Sage Publications Inc.

Franklin, C., & Warren, K. (1999). Advances in systems theory. In C. Franklin & C. Jordan (Eds.), *Family practice: Brief systems methods for social work* (pp. 397–425). Pacific Grove, CA: Brooks/Cole.

Germain, C. B., & Gitterman, A. (1995). Ecological perspective. In R. Edwards (Ed.), *Encyclopedia of social work* (19th ed., pp. 816–822). Washington, DC: NASW Press.

Ginsberg, L. (1998). *Conservative social welfare policy, a description and analysis.* Chicago, IL: Nelson-Hall.

Glicken, M. D. (2004). *Using the strengths perspective in social work practice.* Boston, MA: Allyn & Bacon.

Guralnik, D. (Eds.). (1984). *Webster's new world dictionary of the American language* (2nd ed.). New York: Simon and Schuster.

Johnson, M. J., & Rhodes, R. (2005). *Human behavior and the larger social environment.* Boston, MA: Pearson.

Karger, J. K., & Stoesz, D. (2005). *American social welfare policy: a pluralist approach* (4th ed.). Boston, MA: Allyn & Bacon.

Karger, J. K., & Stoesz, D. (2010). *American social welfare policy* (6th ed.). Boston, MA: Allyn & Bacon.

Kirst-Ashman, K., & Hull, G. (2006). *Understanding generalist practice* (4th ed.). Pacific Grove, CA: Wadsworth.

Lampman, J. (2006, November 9). New sermon from evangelical pulpit: Global warming. *The Christian Science Monitor,* pp. 13, 14.

Lerner, M. (2006). Surviving the great dying. In M. Schlitz, T. Amorok, & M. S. Micozzi (Eds.), *Consciousness and healing.* St. Louis, MO: Elsevier.

Lum, D. (2007). *Culturally competent practice, a framework for understanding diverse groups and justice issues* (3rd ed.). Pacific Grove, CA: Wadsworth.

Nadakavukaren, A. (2006). *Our global environment.* Long Grove, IL: Waveland Press, Inc.

Norlin, J., Chess, W., Dale, O., & Smith, R. (2006). *Human behavior and the social environment: Social systems theory* (5th ed.). Boston, MA: Allyn & Bacon.

O'Driscoll, P. (2006, June 5). Spate of lawsuits target e-voting. *USA Today,* p. 1.

Popple, P. R., & Leighninger, L. (2005). *Social work, social welfare and American society* (6th ed.). Boston, MA: Allyn & Bacon.

Popple, P. R., & Leighninger, L. (2008). *Social work, social welfare and American society* (7th ed.). Boston, MA: Allyn & Bacon.

Popple, P. R., & Leighninger, L. (2011). *The policy based profession: An introduction to social welfare policy analysis for social workers* (5th ed.). Boston, MA: Allyn & Bacon.

Poulin, J. (2005). *Strengths-based generalist practice* (2nd ed.). Pacific Grove, CA: Wadsworth.

Robbins, P., Chaterjee, P., & Canda, E. (2006). Systems theory. *Contemporary human behavior theory: A critical perspective for social work* (2nd ed.). Boston, MA: Allyn & Bacon.

Rothman, J. C. (2005). *From the front lines, student cases in social work ethics* (2nd ed.). Boston, MA: Allyn & Bacon.

Saleebey, D. (2006). *The strengths perspective in social work practice* (4th ed.). Boston, MA: Allyn & Bacon.

Schriver, J. M. (2004a). Global perspectives and theories. *Human behavior in the social environment, shifting paradigms* (4th ed., pp. 542–567). Boston, MA: Allyn & Bacon.

Schriver, J. M. (2004b). Paradigm thinking and social work knowledge for practice. *Human behavior in the social environment, shifting paradigms* (4th ed., pp. 105–166). Boston, MA: Allyn & Bacon.

Segal, E., & Brzuzy, S. (1998). *Social welfare policies, programs, and practice.* Itasca, IL: Peacock.

Shaefor, B. W., Horejsi, C. R., & Horejsi, G. A. (2000). *Tactics and guidelines for social work practice* (5th ed.). Boston, MA: Allyn & Bacon.

Sommer, V. L. (1995). The ecological perspective. In M. J. Macy, N. Flax, V. L. Sommer, & R. Swaine (Eds.), *Directing the baccalaureate social work program, an ecological perspective* (pp. 1–15). Jefferson City, MO: Association for Baccalaureate Social Work Program Directors.

Stoessen, L. (2004, July). Collaborating with faith-based services. *NASW News,* p. 4.

Talking financial reform to death. (2010, March 1). *The Washington Spectator, 36*(4), 1, 2.

Trumbull, M. (2007, May 16). Corporate concern on climate rises. *The Christian Science Monitor,* pp. 1, 10.

Tucker, M. E., & Grim, J. (2009). *Overview of world religions and ecology.* Retrieved from the Forum on Religion and Ecology website, Yale University: http://fore.research.yale.edu/religion/

Tyuse, S. W. (2003). Social justice and welfare reform: A shift in policy. In J. Stretch, E. Burkemper, W. Hutchinson, & J. Wilson (Eds.), *Practicing social justice.* New York: Hayworth Press.

Weissman, R. (2010, January/February). Shed a tear for democracy. *Public Citizen News,* p. 3.

Wells, C. (1998). *Stepping to the dance: The training of a family therapist.* Pacific Grove, CA: Brooks/Cole.

Wheatley, M. (2009). *Leadership and the new science.* San Francisco, CA: Berrett-Koehler Publishers, Inc.

Wheatley, M. (2010, January). *Community leadership*. Paper presented at the Milwaukee Community Leadership Conference, Marquette University, Milwaukee, WI.

Zastrow, C. H. (2007). *The practice of social work, applications of generalist and advanced content* (8th ed.). Pacific Grove, CA: Brooks/Cole.

Chapter 3

Anti-torture efforts on Capitol Hill. (2006, June). *FCNL Washington Newsletter, 708,* pp. 6, 8.

Bernstein, R. (2007, May 17). *Minority population tops 100 million*. Retrieved from U.S. Census Bureau News: http://www.census.gov/Press-Release/www/releases/archives/population/010048.html

Brown, N. (2010, January). The state of America's children is deteriorating. Retrieved from http://www.healthline.com/blogs/teen_health/2009/01/state-of-americas-children-is.html

Butler, R. (1994). Dispelling ageism: The cross-cutting intervention. In R. D. Enright Jr. (Ed.), *Perspectives in social gerontology* (p. 5). Boston, MA: Allyn & Bacon.

Caldera, S. (2009). Social security: Ten facts that matter. *AARP Public Policy Institute*. Retrieved from www.aarp.org/ppi

Civil liberties and human rights. (2004, September). *FNCL Washington Newsletter*, 8.

Dumhoff, G. W. (2009, October). *Who rules America? Wealth, income, and power*. Retrieved from http://sociology.ucsc.edu/whorulesamerica/power/wealth.html

Eisler, R. (1987). *The chalice and the blade*. San Francisco, CA: Harper.

Farrell, M. B. (2010, January 24). Trial raises stakes in gay-marriage debate. *The Christian Science Monitor,* pp. 19, 20.

Federal minimum wage increase for 2007. Retrieved from www.laborlawcenter.com/federal-minimum-wage.asp

Feldmann, L. (2006, June 6). GOP targets gay marriage. *The Christian Science Monitor,* pp. 1, 10.

Fisher, G. M. (1998, Spring). Setting American standards of poverty: A look back. *Focus, 19*(2), 47–51.

FY 2009/2010 Federal poverty guidelines. (2009, September 24). Retrieved from http://www.liheap.ncat.org/profiles/povertytables/FY2010/popstate.htm

Gabriel, P., & Schmitz, S. (2007, June). Gender differences in occupational distributions among workers. *Monthly Labor Review*, 19–23.

General information on social security. (2005, April). Retrieved from American Association of Retired Persons website: http://www.aarp/research/social security/ general/aresearch-import-352-FS39R.html

Goldberg, G. (2002). More than reluctant: The United States of America. In G. Goldberg & M. Rosenthal (Eds.), *Diminishing welfare, a cross-national study of social provision* (pp. 33–71). Westport, CT: Auburn House.

Grier, P. (2001, December 13). Fragile freedoms, which civil liberties, and whose, can be abridged to create a safer America? *The Christian Science Monitor,* pp. 1, 8, 9.

Heining, A. (2010, August 16 & 23). Gay marriage, to a national stage? *The Christian Science Monitor,* p. 19.

Hidden pockets of elderly said to be in poverty. (2009, September 4). *AARP Bulletin Today*. Retrieved from http://bulletin/aaro/org/yourmoney/personalfinance/articles/hidden_pockets_of_eelderly_said_to_be_in_poverty.html

Hodge, D. R. (2007, April). Social justice and people of faith: A transnational experience. *Social Work, 52*(2), 139–147.

Huang, C. (2007, April 19). The House of Representatives in Oregon passed a bill Tuesday to recognize same sex couples. *The Christian Science Monitor,* p. 3.

Hunger in the U.S. (2009, November). Retrieved from Food Research and Action Center website: http://www.frac.org/html/hunger_in_the_us/hunger_index.html

Income, poverty and health insurance coverage in the United States: 2008. (2009, September). Retrieved from http://www.census.gov/Press-Release/www/releases/archives/incomewealth/014227.html

Income, poverty and health insurance in the United States 2009: Highlights. (2009). Retrieved from http://www.census.gov/newsroom/releases/archives/income_wealth/cb10-144-html

Irons, J. S. (2009, September 30). *Economic scarring: The long term impacts of the recession*. Retrieved from the Economic Policy Institute website: http://www.epi/publications/entry/bp243/

Karger, H. J., & Stoesz, D. (2010). *American social welfare policy, a pluralist approach*. Boston, MA: Allyn & Bacon.

Kozol, J. (1996). *Amazing grace*. New York: HarperCollins.

Kramer, S. (2004, August 5). Same sex marriage takes a hit. *The Christian Science Monitor,* pp. 1, 10.

Lilly Ledbetter Fair Pay Act. (2009). Retrieved from the National Women's Law Center website: http://www.nwlc.org/fairpay/ledbetterfairpayact.html

Lum, D. (2007). *Culturally competent practice, a framework for understanding diverse groups and justice issues* (3rd ed.). Pacific Grove, CA: Wadsworth.

Marks, A. (2000, April 27). Vermont launches revolution by allowing same-sex unions. *The Christian Science Monitor*, p. 2.

May-Chahal, C., Katz, I., & Cooper, L. (2003). Social exclusion, family support and evaluation. In I. Katz & J. Pinkerton (Eds.), *Evaluating family support, thinking internationally, thinking critically* (pp. 45–65). West Sussex, UK: John Wiley.

Native Americans still poorest in United States. (2006, August 30). Retrieved from Indianz.com website: http://64.38.12.138/News/2006/015687.asp

Navetta, J. M. (2005, Spring). Gains in learning, gaps in earning. *Outlook, 99*(1), 11–13.

Nine million uninsured children need a solution now. (2007). Retrieved from http://childrensdefense.org/site/PageServer

Oliver, R. (2007, April 25). *Women short-changed—still*. Retrieved from The Institute for America's Future website: http://www.tompaine.com/articles/2007/04/25/women_shortchanged_still.php

Over 13 million children face food insecurity. (2005, June). Retrieved from http://www.childrensdefense.org/family income/food security 2005.pdf

Pagels, E. (1979). *The gnostic gospels*. New York: Random House.

Pagels, E. (2003). *Beyond belief*. New York: Random House.

Paulson, A., & Stern, S. (2003, November 19). Landmark ruling on gay marriage. *The Christian Science Monitor,* pp. 1, 10.

Poverty among individuals by the official poverty measure. (2005). Retrieved from Institute for Research on Poverty website: http://www.irp.wisc.edu/faqs/faq3/ table1.html

Poverty thresholds for 2009 by size of family and number of related children under 18 years. (2010). Retrieved from http://www.census.gov/hhes/www/poverty/data/threshold/thresh09.xls

Racuya-Robbins, A. (2010, September 22). *Poverty up for American women and children: Census 2009 data released.* Retrieved from http://www.results.org/blog/poverty_up_for_american_women_and_children_census_2009_data_released/

Richey, W. (2007, June 29). Court rejects diversity plans. *The Christian Science Monitor,* pp. 1, 10.

Richey, W., & Feldman, L. (2006, June 12). Many perils at Guantanamo—for Bush, too. *The Christian Science Monitor,* pp. 1, 10.

Rocha, C. J., & McCarter, A. K. (2003/2004, Fall/Winter). Strengthening economic justice content in social work education. *Arete, 27* (2), 4–14.

Scherer, R. (2006, July 7). Two states say "no" to gay marriage. *The Christian Science Monitor,* p. 3.

Segal, E., & Brzuzy, S. (1998). *Social welfare policies, programs, and practice.* Itasca, IL: Peacock Publishers.

Sheirholz, H. (2009, September 10). *New 2008 poverty, income data reveal only tip of the recession iceberg.* Retrieved from the Economic Policy Institute website: http://www.epi.org/publications/entry/income_picture_20090910

State by state: The legal battle over gay marriage. (2009, December 15). Retrieved from http://www.npr.org/templates/story/story.php?storyId=112448663

Terzieff, J. (2007, June 1). *Maloney and Ginsberg parry high court ruling.* Retrieved from http://www.womensnews.org/article/cfm?aid=3190

The state of America's children 2008: Highlights. (2008). Retrieved from The Children's Defense Fund website:http://www.childrensdefense.org/child-research-data-publications/state-of-America-children-2008-highlights.pdf

United Nations. (1948). *Declaration of human rights.* Retrieved from http://www.un.org/overview/ rights/html

Women Appointees Celebrated. (2010, January). *NASW News, 55*(1), pp. 1, 6.

You can't save what you don't earn. (2008). *Older Women's League.* Retrieved from http://www.owl-national.org.Policy_Issues_files/Equal%20Pay%Day202008.doc

Chapter 4

Annual summary of food and nutrition service programs. (2010, January 8). Retrieved from http://www.fns.usda.gov/pd/annual/htm

Association joins global coalition. (2005, February 1). *NASW News, 50*(2), 1.

Bane, M. J. (2003). A Catholic policy analyst looks at poverty. In M. J. Bane & L. M. Mead (Eds.), *Lifting up the poor* (pp. 12–52). Washington, DC: Brookings Institution Press.

Bartkowski, J. P., & Regis, H. A. (2003). *Charitable choices: Religion, race and poverty in the post-welfare era.* New York: New York University Press.

Brieland, D. (1995). Social work practice: History and evolution. In R. L. Edwards (Ed.), *Encyclopedia of social work* (19th ed., Vol. 3, pp. 2250–2255). Silver Spring, MD: NASW Press.

Bryner, G. (1998). *The great American welfare reform debate, politics and public morality.* New York: W. W. Norton.

Champagne, A., & Harpham, E. (1984). *The attack on the welfare state* (pp. 97–105). Prospect Heights, IL: Waveland.

Democracy and the death tax. (2006, June 12). *The Christian Science Monitor,* p. 17.

Federico, R. (1984). *The social welfare institution* (4th ed.). Lexington, MA: Heath.

General information on social security. (2005, April). Retrieved from American Association of Retired Persons website: http://www.aarp/research/social security/general/aresearch-import-352-FS39R.html

Goldberg, G. (2002a). Diminishing welfare: Convergence toward a liberal model? In G. Goldberg & M. Rosenthal (Eds.), *Diminishing welfare, a cross-national study of social provision* (pp. 320–372). Westport, CT: Auburn House.

Goldberg, G. (2002b). More than reluctant: The United States of America. In G. Goldberg & M. Rosenthal (Eds.), *Diminishing welfare: A cross-national study of social provision* (pp. 33–71). Westport, CT: Auburn House.

Goldberg, G., & Rosenthal, M. (Eds.). (2002). *Diminishing welfare: A cross-national study of social provision.* Westport, CT: Auburn House.

Harrington, M. (1962). *The other America: Poverty in the United States.* New York: MacMillan.

Heilprin, J. (2009, June 22). *Obama administration seeks to join U.N. Rights of the Child Convention.* Retrieved from http://www.huffingtonpost.com/2009/06/23/obama-admininstration-seek_n_219511.html

How America ranks among industrialized countries. (2008). Retrieved from http://childrensdefense.org/child-research-data-publications/america-ranks-among-industrialized-countries.htm

Johnson, N. (2000, November 2). *A hand up, how state earned income tax credits help working families escape poverty in 2000: An overview.* Retrieved from the Center on Budget and Policy Priorities website: http://www.cbpp.org/11–2–00sfp.htm

Karger, H. J., & Stoesz, D. (2010). *American social welfare policy: A pluralist approach* (6th ed.). Boston, MA: Allyn & Bacon.

Kim, R. Y. (2001). The effects of the earned income tax credit on children's income and poverty: Who fares better? *Journal of Poverty, 5*(1), 1–22.

Lieby, J. (1987). History of social welfare. In R. L. Edwards (Ed.), *Encyclopedia of social work* (18th ed., Vol. 1, pp. 761–765). Silver Spring, MD: NASW Press.

McSteen, M. (1989). Fifty years of social security. In I. Colby (Ed.), *Social welfare policy: Perspectives, patterns, insights* (pp. 172–174). Chicago, IL: Dorsey.

National Coalition on Health Care. (2007). *Facts on health insurance coverage.* Retrieved from http://www.nchc.org/facts/coverage.html

Nomura, M., & Kimoto, K. (2002). Is Japanese-style welfare society sustainable? In G. Goldberg & M. Rosenthal (Eds.), *Diminishing welfare: A cross-national study of social provision* (pp. 296–319). Westport, CT: Auburn Press.

Paulson, A. (2006, June 12). A tighter rein on faith-based initiatives. *The Christian Science Monitor,* p. 3.

Popple, P. R. (1995). Social work profession: History. In R. L. Edwards (Ed.), *Encyclopedia of social work* (19th ed., Vol. 3, pp. 2250–2255). Silver Spring, MD: NASW Press.

Press conference by world food programme on hunger and financial food crises. (2009, May 28). Retrieved from United Nations website: http://www.un.org.News/briefings/docs/2009/090528_WFP.doc.htm

Quadagno, J. (1982). *Aging in early industrial society: Work, family and social policy in 19th century England* (p. 95). New York: Academic Press.

Rocha, C. J., & McCarter, A. K. (2003/2004, Fall/Winter). Strengthening economic justice content in social work education. *Arete, 27*(2), 4–14.

Segal, E., & Brzuzy, S. (1998). *Social welfare policies, programs, and practice.* Itasca, IL: Peacock Publishers.

Stoessen, L. (2004, July). Collaborating with faith-based services. *NASW News,* p. 4.

The state of America's children. (2005). Retrieved from Children's Defense Fund website: http://www.childrens-defense.org/publications/greenbook/defalut.aspx

The state of America's children 2008, key data findings. (2008). Retrieved from the Children's Defense Fund website: http://www.childrensdefense.org/child-research-data-publications/data/state-of-America's-children-2008-report-key-data-findings-pdf

Thompson, R. A., & Raikes, H. A. (2003). Children and welfare reform. In R. Gordon & H. Walberg (Eds.), *Changing welfare.* New York: Kluwer Academic/Plenum.

Trattner, W. I. (1999). *From poor law to welfare state* (6th ed.). New York: The Free Press.

Trumbull, M. (2007, July 24). Rising food prices curb aid to global poor. *The Christian Science Monitor,* pp. 1, 2.

Tyuse, S. W. (2003). Social justice and welfare reform: A shift in policy. In J. Stretch, E. Burkemper, W. Hutchison, & J. Wilson (Eds.), *Practicing social justice.* New York: Hayworth Press.

Where do our income taxes go? (2010, February). Retrieved from the Friends Committee on National Legislation website: http://www.fcnl.org/09taxchart

Whitaker, W., & Federico, R. (1997). *Social welfare in today's world* (2nd ed.). New York: McGraw-Hill.

Whittle, D., & Kuraishi, M. (2009, August 16). Small doners, big impact. *The Christian Science Monitor,* p. 27.

WIC program participation and costs, 2009. (2010, January 8). Retrieved from http://www.fns.usda.gov/pd/wisummary.htm

Wilensky, H., & Lebeaux, C. (1965). *Industrial society and social welfare* (pp. 138–139). New York: Free Press.

Wyers, N. (1987). Income maintenance system. In R. Edwards (Ed.), *Encyclopedia of social work* (18th ed., p. 888). Silver Spring, MD: NASW Press.

Chapter 5

Abramovitz, M. (2000). *Under attack, fighting back: Women and welfare in the United States.* New York: Monthly Review Press.

Adoption and Safe Families Act clarifies child welfare commitments. (1998, February). *Partnerships for Child Welfare, 5*(5), 3.

African Americans by the numbers. (2008). Retrieved from http://www.infoplease.com/spot/bhmcensus1.html

Allen, M., Kakavas, A., & Zalenski, J. (1994, Spring). Family preservation and support services. *The prevention report* (p. 2). Iowa City, IA: National Resource Center on Family Based Services, University of Iowa School of Social Work.

Appleby, G., Colon, E., & Hamilton, J. (2001). *Diversity, oppression and social functioning.* Boston, MA: Allyn & Bacon.

Axinn, M., & Levin, H. (1992). *Social welfare: A history of the American response to need* (3rd ed.). New York: Longman.

Belsie, L. (2001, March 14). Ethnic diversity grows, but not integration. *The Christian Science Monitor,* pp. 1, 4.

Bernstein, R. (2007, May 17). *Minority population tops 100 million.* Retrieved from U.S. Census Bureau News: http://www.census.gov/Press-Releases/www/releases/archives/population/010048.html

Bourne, J. K. (2009, June). The end of plenty; special report, the global food crisis. *National Geographic, 215*(6), 38–59.

Campbell, K. (2004, June 23). Welfare reform hasn't led to more marriage—yet. *The Christian Science Monitor,* p. 11.

Carter, B., & McGoldrick, M. (2005). *The expanded life cycle, individual, family, and social perspectives.* Boston, MA: Allyn & Bacon.

Casey, T. (2009, December 9). *New data reveals TANF caseload declines in twenty two states over the first sixteen months of the recession.* Retrieved from http://www.legalmomentum.org/assets/pdfs/tanf-caseload-down-in-over-22.pdf

Collins, C. (2005, January). N.H. adoptees gain access to records. *The Christian Science Monitor,* p. 14.

Delgado, M., Jones, K., & Rohani, M. (2005). *Social work practice with refugee and immigrant youth in the United States.* Boston, MA: Allyn & Bacon.

Diller, J. V. (1999). *Cultural diversity: A primer for the human services.* Pacific Grove, CA: Brooks/Cole.

Dossey, L. (1989). *Recovering the soul: A scientific and spiritual search.* New York: Bantam Books.

Dossey, L. (2003). *Healing beyond the body: Medicine and the infinite reach of the mind.* Boston, MA: Shambhala.

Dossey, L. (2008). Compassion and healing. In D. Goleman (Ed.), *Measuring the immeasurable: The scientific case for spirituality* (pp. 47–60). Boulder, CO: Sounds True, Inc.

Economic Inequality. (2009, July). Retrieved from http://www.newsbatch.com/econ.htm

Eighty-one years of paving the way, a history of family planning in America. (1997, Fall/Winter). *Planned Parenthood Today, 4,* 5.

Engbur, A., & Klungness, L. (2000). *The complete single mother.* Holbrook, MA: Adams Media Corporation.

Erickson, J. (2006a, Fall). FDA finally acts on emergency contraception with plan B approval. *National NOW Times,* p. 16.

Erickson, J. (2006b, Fall). NOW scores with U.N. Human Rights Report. *National NOW Times,* p. 17.

First nationwide estimate of homeless population in a decade announced. (2007, January). Retrieved from National Alliance to End Homelessness website: http://www.endhomelessness.org/content/article/detail/1443

Ford, P. (2005, June 2). Europe's balancing act. *The Christian Science Monitor,* pp. 1, 10.

Francis, D. R. (2006, July 3). How to slow the population clock. *The Christian Science Monitor,* p. 15.

Gardner, M. (2006, July 31). The problem of a pregnant pause. *The Christian Science Monitor,* pp. 13–14.

Guarino, M. (2010, February 14). Poverty's new face: suburbs. *The Christian Science Monitor,* p. 18.

Gustavsson, N. S., & Segal, E. A. (1994). *Critical issues in child welfare.* Thousand Oaks, CA: Sage Publications.

Hays, S. (2007). Flat broke with children. In S. Shaw & J. Lee (Eds.), *Women's voices feminist visions* (3rd ed., pp. 641–648). New York: McGraw-Hill.

Heilprin, J. (2009, June 22). Retrieved from http://www.huffingtonpost.com/2009/06/23/obama-administration-seek_n_219511.html

Home at last. (2007). Retrieved from PBS website: http://www.pbs.org/now/shows/305/index.html

How many people experience homelessness? (2009, July). Retrieved from http://www.nationalhomeless.org/factsheets/How_Many.html

Hunger in America: 2010 key findings. (2010). Retrieved from http://feedingamerica.org/faces-of-hunger/hunger-in-america-report-2010/key-findings.aspx

Income, poverty, and health insurance in the United States: 2009 – Highlights. Retrieved from http://www.census.gov.hhes/www/poverty/data/incpovhlth/2009/highlights.html

Jonsson, P. (2007, February 21). The homeless get counted. *The Christian Science Monitor,* pp. 2, 4.

Kadushin, A., & Martin, J. (1988). *Child welfare services* (4th ed.). New York: Macmillan.

Karger, J., & Stoesz, D. (1998). *American social welfare policy: A pluralist approach* (3rd ed.). New York: Addison Wesley Longman.

Karger, J., & Stoesz, D. (2010). *American social welfare policy: A pluralist approach* (6th ed.). Boston, MA: Allyn & Bacon.

Kaufman, M. (2007, January 11). Climate change causes warmest year in 2006. *The Christian Science Monitor,* p. 2.

Key data findings. (2008). Retrieved from http://www.child-rensdefense.org/child-research-data-publications/data/state-of-america's-children-2008-report-key-data-findings.pdf

Ki-moon, B. (2009). Forward, *Millennium Development Goals Report.* Retrieved from http://un.org/millenniumgoals/pdf/MDG_Report_2009_ENG.pdf

Kirchheimer, S. (2005, April). *The credit card sinkhole.* Retrieved from AARP Bulletin Online: http://www.aarp.org/bulletin/consumer/ec_sinkhole.html

LeShawn, L. (2009). *A new science of the paranormal, the promise of psychical research.* Wheaton, IL: Theosophical Publishing House.

Lindsay, R. (2002). *Recognizing spirituality: The interface between faith and social work.* Crawley, Western Australia: Western Australia Press.

Llana, S. M. (2010, February 7). Women leaders on rise in Latin America. *The Christian Science Monitor,* p. 7.

Loeb, P. R. (1999). *Soul of a citizen, living with conviction in a cynical time.* New York: St. Martin's Griffin.

Logan, S. M. L., Freeman, E. M., & McRoy, R. G. (1990). *Social work perspective with black families: A culturally specific perspective.* New York: Longman.

Lum, D. (1992). *Social work with people of color: A process-stage approach* (2nd ed.). Pacific Grove, CA: Brooks/Cole.

Macdonald, G. (2004, February 4). Is having a home a right? *The Christian Science Monitor,* pp. 15–16.

McKenzie, J. K., & Lewis, R. (1998). Keeping the promise of adoption and safe families act. *The Roundtable, 12*(1), 1–9.

Meyers, M., Han, W., Waldfogel, J., & Garfinkel, I. (2001, March). Child care in the wake of welfare reform: The impact of government subsidies on the economic well-being of single-mother families. *Social Service Review, 75*(1), 30–59.

Miks, J. (2006, December 20). Growing income inequality troubles Japanese. *The Christian Science Monitor,* p. 4.

Miller, S. (2005, August 22). Rise in homes with multiple generations. *The Christian Science Monitor,* p. 2.

Mink, G. (1998). *Welfare's end.* Ithaca, NY: Cornell University Press.

Nadakavukaren, A. (2006). *Our global environment* (6th ed.). Long Grove, IL: Waveland Press.

National Coalition on Health Care (2007). *Facts on health insur-ance coverage.* Retrieved from National Coalition on Health Care's website: http:// www.nchc.org/facts/coverage.shtml

Ornes, S. (2007, February). The hole story. *Discover, Science, Technology and the Future,* 60–65.

Pardess, E. (2005). Pride and prejudice with gay and lesbian individuals. In C. L. Rabin (Ed.), *Understanding gender and culture in the helping process* (pp. 109–128). Belmont, CA: Thompson Wadsworth.

Quarles, B. (1987). *The Negro in the making of America* (3rd ed.). New York: Macmillan.

Radin, D. (2006). *Entangled minds: Extrasensory experiences in a quantum reality.* New York: Simon & Schuster.

Ramanathan, C. S., & Link, R. J. (1999). *All our futures: Principles and resources for social work practice in a global era.* Belmont, CA: Science and Behavior Books.

Reich, J. (2005). *Fixing families, parents, power, and the child welfare system.* New York: Routledge.

Richey, W. (2007, April 19). Court allows late-term abortion ban. *The Christian Science Monitor,* pp. 1, 2.

Ross, J. (2006, September 12). In Chile, free morning-after pills to teens. *The Christian Science Monitor,* pp. 1, 10.

Roth, C. (2006, Summer). War against reproductive rights surges through states. *National NOW Times,* pp. 1, 3.

Samantrai, K. (2004). *Culturally competent public child welfare practice.* Pacific Grove, CA: Brooks/Cole-Thompson Learning.

Savin-Williams, R., & Esterberg, K. G. (2000). Lesbian, gay, and bisexual families. In D. Demo, K. Allen, & M. A. Fine (Eds.),*Handbook of family diversity* (pp. 197–215). New York: Oxford University Press.

Schlitz, M. (2005). Consciousness beyond death. In M. Schliz, T. Amorok, & M. Micozzi (Eds.), *Consciousness and healing: Integral approaches to mind body medicine* (pp. 221–223). St. Louis, MO: Elsevier.

Schwartz, G., Simon, W., & Chopra, D. (2002). *The afterlife experiments.* New York: Atria Books.

Segal, E., & Brzuzy, S. (1998). *Social welfare policy, programs, and practice.* Itasca, IL: F. E. Peacock Publishers.

de Silva, E. C. (2006, June). Human rights and human needs. *NASW News,* p. 3.

Smith, M. K. (1998, January). Utilization-focused evaluation of a family preservation program. *Families in Society: The Journal of Contemporary Human Services, 76*(1), 11–19.

Soss, J., Schram, S., Vartanian, T., & Obrien, E. (2004, Winter). Welfare policy choices in the states: Does the hard line follow the color line? *Focus, UW Madison Institute for Research on Poverty, 23*(1), 9–15.

Steinberg, D. (2006, November 17). When war and children collide. *The Christian Science Monitor,* p. 9.

Stoessen, L. (2005, March). Court reverses foster care decision. *NASW News,* p. 6.

Stoessen, L. (2007, March). Children said at higher risk in red states. *NASW News,* p. 11.

Tart, C. T. (2009). *The end of materialism: How evidence of the paranormal is bringing science and spirit together.* Oakland, CA: New Harbinger Publications, Inc.

Trattner, W. I. (1999). *From poor law to welfare state: A history of social welfare in America* (6th ed.). New York: The Free Press.

Trumbull, M. (2007, February 2). Washington takes aim at C.E.O. pay. *The Christian Science Monitor,* pp. 1, 10.

United States fails to meet key health goals for infants and mothers. (2006, May 17). Retrieved from The Children's Defense Fund website: http://www.childrensdefense.org/site/News2?page=NewsArticle& id=6669

US & world population clock. (2010, February 9). Retrieved from http://www.census.gov/population/www.popclockus.html

USA news in brief. (2006, November 17). *The Christian Science Monitor,* p. 3.

Van Gelder, S. (2010, Spring). America: The remix. *Yes, 53,* 18–23.

Van Wormer, K. (1997). *Social welfare: A world view.* Chicago, IL: Nelson Hall Publishers.

Vives, O. (2007, Winter). NOW opposes anti-marriage ballot measures. *National NOW Times,* p. 3.

Yule, R. (2006, May/June). Super-wealthy families try to repeal estate tax. *Public Citizen News,* pp. 1, 11.

Watkins, S. A. (1990, November). The Mary Ellen myth: Correcting child welfare history. *Social Work, 35*(6), 501–503.

World POPClock projection. (2010, February 9). Retrieved from http://www.census.gov/ipc/www.popclockworld.html

Wright, J., Rubin, B., & Devine, J. (1998). *Beside the golden door: Policy, politics, and the homeless.* New York: Aldine de Gruyter.

Chapter 6

American Psychiatric Association. (2000). *Diagnostic and statistical manual of mental disorders* (4th ed., text revision). Washington, DC: Author.

American Psychiatric Association. (2010a). *Classification issues under discussion.* Retrieved from http:www.dsm5.org/ProposedRevisions/Pages/ClassificationIssuesUnderDiscussion.aspx

American Psychiatric Association. (2010b). *Definition of a mental disorder.* Retrieved from http://www.dsm5.org/Proposed Revisions/Pages/proposedrevision.aspx?rid=465

American Psychiatric Association. (2010c). *Schizophrenia and other psychotic disorders.* Retrieved from http://www.dsm5.org/ProposedRevisions/Pages/SchizophreniaandOtherPsychoticDisorders.aspx

Beers, C. (1908). *A mind that found itself.* New York: Longmans, Green, & Co.

Bentley, K. J., & Walsh, J. (2001). *The social worker and psychotropic medication: Toward effective collaboration with mental health clients, families, and providers* (2nd ed.). Belmont, CA: Brooks/Cole.

Brave Heart, M. Y. H. (2004). Incorporating native historical trauma content. In L. Gutierrez, M. Zuniga, & D. Lum (Eds.), *Education for multicultural social work practice: Critical viewpoints and future directions* (pp. 201–211). Alexandria, VA: Council on Social Work Education.

Callicutt, J. W. (1987). Mental health services. In A. Minahan (Ed.), *Encyclopedia of social work* (18th ed., Vol. 2, pp. 125–135). Silver Spring, MD: National Association of Social Workers.

Davis, K. (2008). The mental health field of practice. In K. Sowers & C. Dulmus (Eds.), *Comprehensive handbook of social work and social welfare* (Vol. I, pp. 253–266). Hoboken, NJ: John Wiley & Sons.

Eng, A., & Balancio, E. F. (1997). Clinical case management with Asian Americans. In E. Lee (Ed.), *Working with Asian Americans: A guide for clinicians* (pp. 400–407). New York: The Guilford Press.

Franklin, C., & Lagana-Riordin, C. (2009). The social worker in a behavioral health care setting. In A. R. Roberts (Ed.), *Social workers' desk reference* (2nd ed.). New York: Oxford University Press.

Gelman, C. R., & Mirabito, D. M. (2005). Practicing what we teach: Using case studies from 9/11 to teach crisis intervention from a generalist perspective. *Journal of Social Work Education, 41*(3), 479–494.

Hollis, F. (1964). *Casework: A psychosocial therapy.* New York: Random House.

Humes, K. R., Jones, N. A., & Ramirez, R. R. (2011). *Overview of race and Hispanic origin: 2010; 2010 Census briefs.* (Report No. C2010BR-02). Retrieved from United States Census Bureau website: http://www.census.gov/prod/cen2010/briefs/c2010br-02.pdf

Johnstone, M. (2007). Disaster response and group self-care. *Perspectives in Psychiatric Care, 43*(1), 38–40.

Kelly, J. J., & Clark, E. J. (2010). Mental health policy statement approved by the NASW Delegate assembly, August 2002. In J. J. Kelly & E. J. Clark (Eds.), *Social Work Speaks: National Association of Social Workers policy statements 2009-2012* (pp. 234-235). Washington, DC: NASW Press.

KEN Publications/Catalog. (n.d.). *Final report: Consumer bill of rights and responsibilities.* Retrieved from http://www.mentalhealth.org/consumersurvivor/billofrights.htm

Lerner, M. D., & Shelton, R. D. (2001). *How can emergency responders help grieving individuals? and How do people respond during traumatic exposure? Trauma response infosheet.* Retrieved from the American Academy of Experts in Traumatic Stress website: http://www.aaets.org

Lum, D. (1992). *Social work with people of color: A process-stage approach* (2nd ed.). Pacific Grove, CA: Brooks/Cole.

Lum, D. (1999). *Culturally competent practice: A framework for growth and action.* Pacific Grove, CA: Brooks/Cole.

Lum, D. (2007). *Culturally competent practice: A framework for understanding diverse groups and justice issues.* Belmont, CA: Thomson, Brooks/Cole.

Mankiller, W., & Wallis, M. (1993). *Mankiller: A chief and her people.* New York: St. Martin's Press.

Meyer, C. (1987). Direct practice in social work: Overview. In A. Minahan (Ed.), *Encyclopedia of social work* (19th ed., Vol. 1, pp. 409–422). Silver Spring, MD: National Association of Social Workers.

National Alliance on Mental Illness. (2010). *About NAMI.* Retrieved from http:www.nami.org

National Association of Social Workers. (2010a). *NASW credentials & specialty certifications.* Retrieved from www.socialworkers.org/nasw//default.asp

National Association of Social Workers. (2010b). *Social workers and the Mental Health Parity Act of 2008.* Retrieved from www.socialworkers.org/1df/legal_issue/2009/200901.asp

Pace, P. R. (2007). New York parity law signed. *NASW News, 52*(3), 7.

Perlman, H. H. (1957). *Social casework: A problem-solving process.* Chicago, IL: University of Chicago Press.

Red Horse, J. (1988). Cultural evolution of American Indian families. In C. Jacobs & D. D. Bowles (Eds.), *Ethnicity and race: Critical concepts in social work* (pp. 86–102). Silver Spring, MD: National Association of Social Workers.

Reynolds, B. C. (1934). *Between client and community.* Silver Spring, MD: National Association of Social Workers.

Reynolds, B. C. (1935). *Social work and social living: Explorations in philosophy and practice.* New York: Citadel Press.

Reynolds, B. C. (1942). *Learning and teaching in the practice of social work.* Silver Spring, MD: National Association of Social Workers.

Richmond, M. E. (1917). *Social diagnosis.* New York: Russell Sage Foundation.

Richmond, M. E. (1922). *What is social casework? An introductory description.* New York: Russell Sage Foundation.

Social work in the public eye. (2002). *NASW News, 47*(1), 15.

Social work in the public eye. (2006). *NASW News, 51*(9), 11.

Susser, E., Schwartz, S., Morabia, A., & Bromet, E. J. (2006). *Psychiatric epidemiology: Searching for the causes of mental disorders.* New York: Oxford University Press.

Taft, J. (1933). *The dynamics of therapy in a controlled relationship*. New York: The Macmillan Co.

U.S. Department of Health and Human Services. (2010, January 29). *News release: Obama administration issues rules requiring parity in treatment of mental, substance use disorders.* Retrieved from http://www.hhs.gov/news/press/2010pres/01/20100129a.html

Vastola, J., Nierenberg, A., & Graham, E. H. (1994). The lost and found group: Group work with bereaved children. In A. Gitterman & L. Shulman (Eds.), *Mutual aid groups, vulnerable populations, and the life cycle* (2nd ed., pp. 81–96). New York: Columbia University Press.

Wilson, D. C. (1975). *Stranger and traveler: The story of Dorothea Dix, American reformer.* Boston, MA: Little, Brown & Co.

World Health Organization. (2007). *Quantifying environmental health impacts.* Retrieved from http://www.who.int/quantifying_ehimpacts/global/en/

Wortsman, P. (2006). Alumni profile Ezra Susser: A life in epidemiology. *Alumni News and Notes: The College of Physicians & Surgeons of Columbia University, 26*(2). Retrieved from http:cumc.columbia.edu/news/journal/journal/-o/spring-2006/alumni.html

Chapter 7

Bab, I. A., & Yirmiya, R. (2010). Depression and bone mass. *Annals of the New York Academy of Sciences, 1192*(1), 170–175.

Barnes, F. (1994, August 15). A White House watch: Left out. *New Republic, 211*(7), 15–17.

Berger, R. M. (1995). Habitat destruction syndrome [Op. Ed]. *Social Work, 40*(4), 441–443.

Besthorn, F. H. (2002). Radical environmentalism and the ecological self: Rethinking the concept of self-identity for social work practice. *Journal of Progressive Human Services, 13*(1), 53–72.

Bureau of Labor Statistics, U.S. Department of Labor. (2010). *Career information: Social worker* (2010-2011ed.). Retrieved from http://www.bls.gov/k12/help05.htm

Cannon, I. M. (1952). *On the social frontier of medicine: Pioneering in medical social service.* Cambridge, MA: Harvard University Press.

Center for Medicare Advocacy. (2007). *Center for Medicare Advocacy testifies regarding Medicare Part D and Medicare Managed Care.* Retrieved from http://www.medicareadvocacy.org/PtDTestimony/PartD_07_05.03.Testimony.htm

Cizza, G., Primma, S., Coyle, M., Gourgiotis, L., & Csaka, G. (2010). Depression and osteoporosis: A research synthesis with meta-analysis. *Hormone and Metabolic Research, 42*(7), 467–482.

Cizza, G., Primma, S., & Csaka, G. (2009). Depression as a risk factor for osteoporosis. *Trends in Endocrinology and Metabolism, 20*(8), 367–373. doi:10.1016/j.tem.2009.05.003

Commission on Social Determinants of Health, World Health Organization. (2008). *Closing the gap in a generation.* Retrieved from http://wholibdoc.who.int/pblications/2008/97892415637

Csikai, E. L., & Chaitin, E. (2006). *Ethics in end-of-life decisions in social work practice.* Chicago, IL: Lyceum Books.

Davidson, T., Davidson, J. H., & Keigher, S. M. (1999). Managed care: Satisfaction guaranteed . . . Not! *Health & Social Work, 24*(3), 163–168.

Devore, W., & Schlesinger, E. G. (1987). *Ethnic sensitive social work practice* (2nd ed.). Columbus, OH: Merrill.

Dziegielewski, S. F. (2004). *The changing face of health care social work: Professional practice in managed behavioral health care* (2nd ed.). New York: Springer.

Galambos, C. M. (Ed.). (2003). Building healthy environments: Community- and consumer-based initiatives. *Health & Social Work, 28*(3), 171–173.

Germain, C. B., & Gitterman, A. (1980). *The life model of social work practice.* New York: Columbia University Press.

Gorin, S. H. (2000). Progressives and the 2000 election. *Health & Social Work, 25*(2), 139–143.

HealthCare.gov. (2010). *The Affordable Care Act: Overview; Affordable Health Care for America: Health insurance reform at a glance, implementation timeline.* Retrieved from http:www/healthcare.gov/law/introduction/index.html

Henry, H., & Kaiser Family Foundation. (2010). *Kaiser health tracking poll—June 2010* (Publication Report No. 8082). Retrieved from http:www/kff.org/kaiserpols/8082.cfm

Hoff, M. D., & McNutt, J. G. (Eds.). (1994). *The global environmental crisis: Implications for social welfare and social work.* Brookfield, VT: Avebury.

Karger, H.J. & Stoez, D. (2010). *American social welfare policy: A pluralistic approach* (6th ed.). Boston: Pearson Education.

Keigher, S. M. (2000, February). Knowledge development. *Health & Social Work, 25*(1), 3–8.

Kelly, J. J., Clark, E. J., & National Association of Social Workers [NASW]. (2009a). Environment: Policy statement. J. J. Kelly & E. C. Clark (Eds.), *Social work speaks: National Association of Social Workers policy statements 2009–2012* (8th ed., pp. 121–126). Washington, DC: NASW Press.

Kelly, J. J., Clark, E. J., & National Association of Social Workers [NASW]. (2009b). Health care: Policy statement. J. J. Kelly & E. C. Clark (Eds.), *Social work speaks: National Association of Social Workers policy statements 2009–2012* (8th ed., pp. 167–170). Washington, DC: NASW Press.

Kelly, J. J., Clark, E. J., & National Association of Social Workers [NASW]. (2009c). Hospice care: Policy statement. J. J. Kelly & E. C. Clark (Eds.), *Social work speaks: National Association of Social Workers policy statements 2009–2012* (8th ed., pp. 180–191). Washington, DC: NASW Press.

Kelly, J. J., Clark, E. J., & National Association of Social Workers [NASW]. (2009d). Mental health: Policy statement. J. J. Kelly & E. C. Clark (Eds.), *Social work speaks: National Association of Social Workers policy statements 2009–2012* (8th ed., pp. 234–235). Washington, DC: NASW Press.

Malamud, M. (2010). Health care reform measure celebrated. *NASW News, 55*(5), 4.

McGinn, F. (1996). The plight of rural parents caring for adult children with HIV. *Families in Society, 77*(5), 269–278.

Mizrahi, T., Fasano, R., & Dooha, S. N. (1993). National health line: Canadian and American health care: Myths and realities. *Health & Social Work, 18*(1), 7–8.

Moniz, C., & Gorin, S. (2010) *Health and mental health care policy: A biopsychosocial perspective* (3rd ed.). Boston: Allyn & Bacon.

Munch, S., & Shapiro, S. (2007). Osteoporosis as the silent thief in women of all ages. *Health Section Connection, 1*(1), 3–6.

National Association of Social Workers [NASW]. (2003). *NASW standards for social work services in long-term care facilities.* Retrieved from http://www.socialworkers.org/practice/standards/NASWLongTermStandards.pdf

National Association of Social Workers [NASW]. (2006). Environmental policy. In E. C. de Silva & E. J. Cark (Eds.), *Social work speaks: National Association of Social Workers policy statements 2006–2009* (7th ed., pp. 136–141). Washington, DC: NASW Press.

National Association of Social Workers [NASW], (n.d.). *Social work services in nursing homes: Toward quality psychosocial care.* Retrieved from http://www.socialworkers.org/research/naswresearch/0605Psychosocial/default.asp

National Osteoporosis Foundation. (2007). *Fast facts.* Retrieved, from http://www.nof.org/osteoporosis/index.htm

New Rules Project. (n. d.). *Canadian healthcare system.* Retrieved from the Institute for Local Self-Reliance website: http://www.newrules.org/equity/rules/singlepayer-and-universal-health-care/cnandian-healthcare-system

Rehr, H. (Ed.). (1994). *Medicine and social work: An exploration in interprofessionalism.* New York: Prodist Press.

Rehr, H., & Rosenberg, G. (1982). *Advancing social work practice in the health care field.* New York: Haworth Press.

Rehr, H., & Rosenberg, G. (2006). *The social work-medicine relationship: 100 years at Mount Sinai.* New York: Haworth Press.

Richman, J. M. (1995). Hospice. In R. L. Edwards (Ed.), In R. L. Edwards (Ed.), *Encyclopedia of social work* (19th ed., pp. 1358–1365). Washington, DC: NASW Press.

Rural Assistance Center. (2010). *Rural health disparities: Introduction.* Retrieved from http://www.raconline.org/info_guides/disparities/

Saleebey, D. (2004). The power of place: Another look at the environment. *Families in Society, 85*(1), 7–16.

Skocpol, T. (1997). *Boomerang: Health care reform and the turn against government.* New York: W. W. Norton.

Susser, E., & Morabia, A. (2006). The arc of epidemiology. In E. Susser, S. Schwartz, A. Morabia, & E. V. Bromet (Eds.), *Psychiatric epidemiology: Searching for the causes of mental disorders* (Ch. 2). New York: Oxford University Press.

UNAIDS; Joint United Nations Programme on HIV/AIDS. (2009). *2009 AIDS epidemic update: Global facts and figures.* Retrieved from http://data.unaids.org/pub/FactSheet/2009/20091124_fs_global_en.pdf

U.S. Department of Health and Human Services, Centers for Medicare & Medicaid Services. (2009). *Medicare enrollment reports: Overview.* Retrieved from https://www.cms.gov/MedicareEnrpts

U.S. Department of State. (2010). *Trafficking in persons: Ten years of partnering to combat modern slavery.* Retrieved from http://www.state.gov/r/pa/scp/fs/2010/43115.htm

Weiss, L. (1997). *Private medicine and public health: Profit, politics, and prejudice in the American health care enterprise.* Boulder, CO: Westview Press.

Wolfe, S. M. (2006). Outrage of the month: Massachusetts' mistake. *Public Citizen Health Research Group Health Letter, 22*(5), 10, 12.

World Health Organization. (2010). *World health statistics: Health expenditures 2007* (pp. 48–56); *Mortality and burden of disease 2008* (pp. 130–137). Retrieved from http://www.who.int/whosis/whostat/2010/en/index.html

World Health Organization. (n.d.). *Linkages between health and human rights.* Retrieved from http://www.who.int/hhr/HHR%20linkages.pdf

Chapter 8

Bernstein, R. (2007, May 17). *Minority population tops 100 million.* Retrieved from U.S. Census Bureau News: http://www.census.gov/Press-Release/www/releases/archives/population/010048.html

Bishop, K. (2006). Family-centered services to infants and toddlers with or at risk for disabilities: IDEA 2004, Part c. In R. Constable, C. Massat, S. McDonald, & J. Flynn (Eds.), *School social work* (6th ed., pp. 189–204). Chicago, IL: Lyceum Books.

Boyle-Del Rio, S., Carlson, R., & Haibeck, L. (2000, Fall). School personnel's perception of the school social worker's role. *School Social Work Journal, 25*(1), 59–75.

Burt, M., Resnick, G., & Novick, E. R. (1998). *Building supportive communities for at-risk adolescents.* Washington, DC: American Psychological Association.

Button, J., & Rienzo, B. (2002). *The politics of youth, sex, and health care in American schools.* New York: The Hayworth Press.

Caple, F. S., & Salcido, R. M. (2006). A framework for cross-cultural practice in school settings. In R. Constable, C. Massat, S. McDonald, & J. Flynn (Eds.), *School social work* (6th ed., pp. 299–320). Chicago, IL: Lyceum Books.

Constable, R. (2006). The role of the school social worker. In R. Constable, C. Massat, S. McDonald, & J. Flynn (Eds.), *School social work, practice, policy, and research* (6th ed., pp. 3–27). Chicago, IL: Lyceum Books.

Constable, R., & Kordesh, R. (2006). Policies, programs, and mandates for developing social services in the schools. In R. Constable, C. Massat, S. McDonald, & J. Flynn (Eds.), *School social work, practice, policy, and research* (6th ed., pp. 123–144). Chicago, IL: Lyceum Books.

Constable, R., & Thomas, G. (2006). Assessment, multidisciplinary teamwork, and consultation: Foundations for role development. In R. Constable, C. Massat, S. McDonald, & J. Flynn (Eds.), *School social work, practice, policy, and research* (6th ed., pp. 283–320). Chicago, IL: Lyceum Books.

Costin, L. (1987). School social work. In A. Minahan (Ed.), *Encyclopedia of social work* (18th ed., pp. 536–539). Silver Spring, MD: National Association of Social Workers.

Current population trends in the Hispanic population. (2006). Retrieved from http://www.census.gov/population/www/socdemo/hispanic/files/Internet_Hispanic_in_US_2006.ppt#11

Dupper, D. R. (2000). The design of social work services. In P. Allen-Meares, R. O. Washington, & B. L. Welsh (Eds.), *Social work services in schools* (3rd ed., pp. 243–272). Boston, MA: Allyn & Bacon.

Dupper, D. R. (2003). *School social work, skills and interventions for effective practice.* Hoboken, NJ: John Wiley & Sons.

Elias, M. J. (2003). *Academic and social-emotional learning.* Brussels, Belgium: International Academy of Education.

Fast facts. (2009). Retrieved from the National Center for Educational Statistics website: http://nces/gov/FastFacts/display.asp?id=16

Franklin, C. (2000). The delivery of school social work services. In P. Allen-Meares, R. O. Washington, & B. L. Welsh (Eds.), *Social work services in schools* (3rd ed., pp. 273–298). Boston, MA: Allyn & Bacon.

Freeman, E. M. (1995). School social work overview. In R. L. Edwards (Ed.), *Encyclopedia of social work* (19th ed., pp. 2087–2097). Washington, DC: NASW Press.

Freeman, E. M., Halim, M., & Peterson, K. J. (1998). HIV/AIDS policy development and reform: Lessons from practice, research, and education. In E. M. Freeman, C. G. Franklin, R. Fong, S. G. Shaffer, & E. M. Timberlake (Eds.), *Multisystem skills and interventions in school social work practice* (pp. 371–377). Washington, DC: NASW Press.

Gardner, W. (2009, August 30). Grade for charter schools? "Needs improvement." *The Christian Science Monitor*, p. 27.

Ginorio, A., & Huston, M. (2001). *Si, se puede! Yes, we can, Latinas in school.* Washington, DC: AAUW Educational Foundation.

Hancock, B. (1982). *School social work.* Englewood Cliffs, NJ: Prentice Hall.

Hare, I., Rome, S., & Massat, C. (2006). The developing social, political, and economic context for school social work. In R. Constable, C. Massat, S. McDonald, & J. Flynn (Eds.), *School social work, practice, policy, and research* (6th ed., pp. 145–170). Chicago, IL: Lyceum Books.

Harris Interactive. (2001). *Hostile hallways, bullying, teasing, and sexual harrassment in school.* Washington, DC: AAUW Educational Foundation.

High school dropout and completion rates in the United States: 2007. (2009). Retrieved from the National Center for Education Statistics website: http://nces.ed.gov/PUBSEARCH/pubsinfo.asp?pubid=2009064

Hinkelman, J. M. (2005). Triple oppression. In C. L. Rabin (Ed.), *Understanding gender and culture in the helping process* (pp. 167–185). Belmont, CA: Thompson Wadsworth.

Hobbins, W. (2007, April 16). *Personal communication. Madison, WI.*

Idea Funding Gap. (2010, February 1). Retrieved from the National Education Association website: http:www.nea.org.specialed

Jayson, S. (2009, January 1). Teen birth rates up in 26 states. *USA TODAY.* Retrieved from http://www.usatoday.com/news/health/2009-01-07-teenbirths_N.htm

Jolly, E. J. (2004, Spring). *Mosaic, an EDC report series.* Retrieved from the Mosaic Home/Educational Development Center, Inc. website: http://main.edc.org/Mosaic/Mosaic9/beneath.asp

Khadaroo, S. (2009, April 19). Schools are learning how to foil attacks. *The Christian Science Monitor*, p. 21.

Khadaroo, S. (2009, August 23). Online school is cheaper than a bricks-and-mortar one. *The Christian Science Monitor*, p. 18.

Koch, K. (2000). School violence, are American schools safe? In D. Bonilla (Ed.), *School violence* (pp. 5–33). New York: H. W. Wilson.

Kopels, S. (2000). Securing equal educational opportunity: Language, race, and sex. In P. Allen-Meares, R. O. Washington, & B. L. Welsh (Eds.), *Social work services in schools* (3rd ed., p. 216). Boston, MA: Allyn & Bacon.

Kronick, R. F. (2005). *Full service community schools.* Springfield, IL: Charles C. Thomas.

Llana, S. M., & Paulson, A. (2006, June 13). Bilingualism issue rises again. *The Christian Science Monitor*, pp. 1, 11.

Lum, D. (1992). *Social work with people of color: A process-stage approach.* Pacific Grove, CA: Brooks/Cole.

Mann, E., & Reynolds, A. (2006, September). Early intervention and juvenile delinquency prevention: Evidence from the Chicago longitudinal study. *Social Work Research, 30*(3), 153–167.

Martin, J. A., Hamilton, B. E., Sutton, P. D., Ventura, S. J., Menacker, F., Kirmeyer, S., et al. (2009, January 7). Births: Final data for 2006. *National Vital Statistics Reports, 57*(7), 1–6.

Matuszek, T., & Rycraft, J. (2003). Using biofeedback to enhance interventions in schools. In B. Pahwa (Ed.), *Technology-assisted delivery of school based mental health services* (pp. 31–56). New York: Hayworth Press.

Mercola, J. (2001, January 21). *Chemical contamination linked to early puberty.* Retrieved from Dr. Mercola's website: http://cmsadmin.mercola.com/2001/jan/21/chemicalspuberty.htm

National Campaign to Prevent Teen Pregnancy. (2007). *New survey of Latino teens shows that there is still work to do and foster care youth.* Retrieved from The National Campaign to Prevent Teen Pregnancy website: http://www.teenpregnancy.org

O'Driscoll, P. (2007, April 20–22). Teen rant reminiscent of Columbine: Shooters in both spewed contempt in recordings. *USA Today*, p. 1.

Openshaw, L. (2008). *Social work in schools: Principles and practice.* New York: The Guilford Press.

Paulson, A. (2005, March 25). Schools using many lessons from Columbine. *The Christian Science Monitor*, pp. 1, 10.

Paulson, A. (2006, September 5). Push to win back dropouts. *The Christian Science Monitor*, pp. 1, 11.

Paulson, A. (2007, January 8). Next round begins for No Child Left Behind law. *The Christian Science Monitor*, pp. 1, 10.

Paulson, A. (2009, November 1). Why Johnny stays in school till 5 p.m. *The Christian Science Monitor*, p. 23.

Paulson, A. (2010, January 10). At US high schools, good news is scarce. *The Christian Science Monitor*, p. 22.

Pawlak, E., Wozniak, D., & McGowen, M. (2006). Perspectives on groups for school social workers. In R. Constable, C. Massat, S. McDonald, & J. Flynn (Eds.), *School social work: Practice, policy, and reseach* (6th ed., pp. 559–578). Chicago, IL: Lyceum Books.

Politics & Opinion. (2002). *National survey of Latinos.* Retrieved from the Hispanic Publishing Group/HispanicOnline.com website: http://www.hispaniconline.com/pol&opi/02_nat_survey_latinos.html

Poverty among individuals by the official poverty measure. (2008). Retrieved from http://www.irp.wisc.edu/faqs/faq3/table1.htm

Respect for charter schools. (2009, October 11). *The Christian Science Monitor*, p. 26.

Rose, S. (1998). *Group work with children and adolescents, prevention and intervention in school and community systems.* Thousand Oaks, CA: Sage Publications.

Sappenfield, M. (2001, June 22). For more students, summer means–more school. *The Christian Science Monitor*, pp. 1, 9.

Sossou, M., & Daniels, T. (2002). School social work practice in Ghana: A hope for the future. In M. Huxtable & E. Blyth (Eds.), *School social work worldwide* (pp. 93–108). Washington, DC: National Association of Social Workers.

Special education and the Individuals with Disabilities Education Act. (2007). Retrieved from the National Education Association website: http://www.nea.org/specialed/index.html?mode=print

Stoessen, L. (2006, July). Health focus of LGBQ workshop. *NASW News*, p. 5.

Students who serve, graduate. (2009, November 15). *The Christian Science Monitor*, p. 26.

Study: Safe-sex programs don't increase sexual activity [West Bend, WI]. (2001, May 30). *The Daily News, West Bend, WI*, p. A 10.

Sunderman, G. L., Kim, J. S., & Orfield, G. (2005). *NCLB meets school realities: Lessons from the field.* Thousand Oaks, CA: Corwin Press.

Thomas. (2009, January 5). *Abstinence-only sex education statistics–final nail in the coffin.* Retrieved from http://www.openeducation.net/2009/01/05/abstinence-only-sex-education-statistics-final-nail-in-the-coffin

Twemlow, S. W., & Sacco, F. C. (2008). *Why school antibullying programs don't work.* New York: Jason Aronson.

Tyre, P. (2006, January). *The trouble with boys.* Retrieved from Newsweek website: http://www.msnbc.msn.com/id/10965522/site/newsweek/

Chapter 9

The A,A. Grapevine. (n.d.). *Information on A.A., Alcoholics Anonymous.* Retrieved from http://www.aa.org/lang/en/subpage.cfm?pa

Alcoholics Anonymous. (2009). *A.A. around the globe.* Retrieved from http://www.aa.org/lang//en/en_pdfs/smf-165.en

Allen, J. P. (1998). Project MATCH: A clarification. *Behavioral Health Management, 18*(2), 42–44.

American Psychiatric Association. (2000). *Diagnostic and statistical manual of mental disorders* (4th ed., text revision). Washington, DC: Author.

Anderson, S. C. (1995). Alcohol abuse. In R. L. Edwards (Ed.), *Encyclopedia of social work* (19th ed., pp. 203–215). Washington, DC: NASW Press.

AVERT.org. (2010). *Needle exchange and harm reduction.* Retrieved from http://www.avert.org/needle-exchange.htm

Babor, T. F., Higgins-Biddle, J. C., Saunders, J. B., & Monteiro, M. G. (2001). *AUDIT, The Alcohol Use Disorders Identification Test: Guidelines for use in primary care* (2nd ed.). World Health Organization (WHO/MSD/MSB/01.6a). Retrieved from http://whqlibdoc.who.int/hq/2001/WHO_MSB_01.6a.pdf

Brown, P. (2006). Drinking for two? *New Scientist, 191*(2558), 46–49.

Butcher, J. N., Mineka, S., & Hooley, J. M. (2008). *Abnormal psychology: Core concepts.* Boston, MA: Pearson Allyn & Bacon.

Center for Disease Control and Prevention (CDC). (2007). *HIV/AIDS Surveillance Report, 2007 (19).* Atlanta, GA: Center for Disease Control and Prevention.

Center for Substance Abuse Treatment. (2010). *Substance abuse specialists in child welfare agencies and dependency courts considerations for program designers and evaluators* (HHS Pub. No. (SMA) 10-4557). Rockville, MD: Substance Abuse and Mental Health Services Administration.

Crape, B. L., Latkin, C. A., Laris, A. S. & Knowlton, A. R. (2002). The effects of sponsorship in 12-step treatment of injection drug users. *Drug and Alcohol Dependence, 65*(3), 291–301.

DiNitto, D. M., & McNeece, C. A. (2009). Guidelines for chemical abuse and dependency screening, diagnosis, and treatment. In A. R. Roberts (Ed.), *Social workers' desk reference.* New York: Oxford University Press.

Emrick, C. D. (1987). Alcoholics anonymous: Affiliation processes and effectiveness as treatment. *Alcoholism: Clinical and Experimental Research, 11*(5), 416–423.

Gibbs, L. E., & Hollister, C. D. (1993). Matching alcoholics with treatment: Reliability, replication and validity of a treatment typology. *Journal of Social Science Research, 17*(1/2), 41–72.

Gillespie, W., & Blackwell, R. L. (2009) Substance use patterns and consequences among lesbians, gays, and bisexuals. *Journal of Gay & Lesbian Social Services, 21,* 90–108. doi: 10.1080/10538720802490758

Hannon, L., & Cuddy, M. M. (2006). Neighborhood ecology and drug dependence mortality: An analysis of New York City census tracts. *American Journal of Drug and Alcohol Abuse, 32,* 453–463.

Harrison, L., & Straussner, L. (2002). Introduction. In L. A. Straussner & L. Harrison (Eds.), *International aspects of social work practice in the addictions* (pp. 1–5). New York: Haworth Press.

Icard, L., & Traunstein, D. M. (1987). Black, gay, alcoholic men: Their character and treatment. *Social Casework, 68*(5), 267–272.

Kinney, J., & Leaton, G. (1995). *Loosening the grip: A handbook of alcohol information* (5th ed.). St. Louis, MO: Mosby.

Kisthardt, W. E. (2009). The opportunities and challenges of strengths-based, person-centered practice. In D. Saleebey (Ed.),*The strengths perspective in social work practice* (5th ed.). Boston, MA: Pearson Allyn & Bacon.

Knittel, A., Wren, P. A., & Gore, L. (2010, April 29) Lessons learned from a peri-urban needle exchange. *Harm Reduction, 7,* 1–7. doi: 10.1186/1477-7517-7-8

de Koning, P., & de Kwant, A. (2002). Dutch drug policy and the role of social workers. In L. A. Straussner & L. Harrison (Eds.), *International aspects of social work practice in the addictions* (pp. 49–68). New York: Haworth Press.

Krimmel, H. (1971). *Alcoholism: Challenge for social work education.* New York: Council on Social Work Education.

Lacerte, J., & Harris, D. L. (1986). Alcoholism: A catalyst for women to organize: 1850-1980. *Affilia, 1*(2), 41–52.

Loebig, B. J. (2000). *European alcoholism and drug abuse perceptions.* Retrieved from http://www.geocities.com/bourbonstreet/2640/topic.htm

Logan, S., McRoy, R. G., & Freeman, E. M. (1987). Current practice approaches for treating the alcoholic client. *Health and Social Work, 12*(3), 176–186.

Major victory for cocaine sentencing reform. (2010, Fall). *Sentencing times* (pp. 1, 3). Washington, DC: The Sentencing Project.

Masis, K. B., & May, P. A. (1991, October 8). A comprehensive local program for the prevention of fetal alcohol syndrome. *Public Health Reports, 106*(5), 484–489.

McNeece, C. A., & DiNitto, D. M. (2005). *Chemical dependency: A systems approach* (3rd ed.). Boston, MA: Pearson Allyn & Bacon.

Murphy, B. C., & Dillon, C. (2011). *Interviewing in action in a multicultural world* (4th ed.). Belmont, CA: Brooks/Cole.

National Center for Health Statistics. (2010). Table 65 Lifetime alcohol drinking status among adults 18 years of age and over, by selected characteristics: United States, selected years 1997–2007 and Table 66 Heavier drinking and drinking five or more drinks in a day among adults 18 years of age and over, by selected characteristics: United States, selected years 1997-2007. *Health, United States, 2009: With special feature on medical technology.* Hyattsville, MD.

National Center for Health Statistics. (2011). Table 64 Lifetime alcohol drinking status among adults 18 years of age and over, by selected characteristics: United States, selected years 1997-2009; Table 65 Heavier drinking and drinking five or more drinks in a day among adults 18 years of age and over, by selected characteristics United States, selected years 1992-2009.*Health, United States, 2010: With special feature on death and dying* (pp.242-247). Hyattsville, MD.

National Institute on Drug Abuse (NIDA). (2010a). *Addiction science: From molecules to managed care.* Retrieved from http://www.drugabuse.gov/pubs/teaching/Teaching6/ Teaching2.html

National Institute on Drug Abuse (NIDA). (2010b). *Commonly abused drugs.* Retrieved from http://www.drugabuse.gov/ DrugPages/DrugsofAbuse.html

National Institute on Drug Abuse (NIDA). (2010c). *Prescription drug abuse chart.* Retrieved from http://www.drugabuse.gov/ DrugPages/PrescriptionDrugsChart.html

National Women's Health Information Center. (2000, October 23). *Alcohol abuse and treatment.* Retrieved from http:// www.4woman.gov/faq/sa_alcoh.htm

O'Connor, M. J., & Whaley, S. E. (2007). Brief intervention for alcohol use by pregnant women. *American Journal of Public Health, 97*(2), 252–258.

Osman, M. M. (2002). Drug and alcohol addiction in Singapore: Issues and challenges in control and treatment strategies. In L. A. Straussner & L. Harrison (Eds.), *International aspects of social work practice in the addictions* (pp. 97–117). New York: Haworth Press.

Pagano, M. E., Krentzman, A. R., Onder, C. C., Baryak, J. L., Murphy, J. L., Zywiak, W. H., et al. (2010). Service to others in sobriety (SOS). *Alcoholism Treatment Quarterly, 28*(2), 111–127. doi: 10.1080/07347321003656425

Peltenberg, C. (1956). Casework with the alcoholic patient. *Social Casework, 37*(2), 81–85.

Rapp, R. (1997). The strengths perspective and persons with substance abuse problems. In D. Saleebey (Ed.), *The strengths perspective in social work practice* (2nd ed., pp. 77–96). New York: Longman.

Rapp, R. C., & Lane, D. T. (2009). Implementation of brief strengths-based case management. In D. Saleebey (Ed.), *The strengths perspective in social work practice* (5th ed., pp. 147–160). Boston, MA: Pearson Allyn & Bacon.

Rhodes, R., & Johnson, A. D. (1994). Women and alcoholism: A psychosocial approach. *Affilia, 9*(2), 145–154.

Richmond, M. E. (1917). *Social diagnosis.* New York: Russell Sage Foundation.

Robertson, N. (1988). *Getting better: Inside alcoholics anonymous.* New York: Ballantine.

Roffman, R. A. (1987). Drug use and abuse. In A. Minahan (Ed.), *Encyclopedia of social work* (18th ed., pp. 477–487). Silver Spring, MD: NASW Press.

Sapir, J. V. (1957). The alcoholic as an agency client. *Social Casework, 38*(7), 355–361.

Shulman, L. (2011). *Dynamics and skills of group counseling.* Belmont, CA: Brooks/Cole.

Singapore Anti-Narcotics Association (SANA). (2008). *Services: Preventive education.* Retrieved from http://www .sana.org.sg/ourservices.shtml

Smith, M. J. W., Whitaker, T., & Weismiller, T. (2006). Social workers in the substance abuse treatment field: A snapshot of service activities. *Health & Social Work, 31*(2), 109–115.

Smyth, N. (1995). Substance abuse: Direct practice. In R. L. Edwards (Ed.), *Encyclopedia of social work* (19th ed., Vol.3, pp. 2328–2339). Washington, DC: NASW Press.

Steiker, L. K. H., & MacMaster, S. A. (2008). Substance abuse. In K. M. Sowers & C. N. Dulmus (Eds.), *Comprehensive*

handbook of social work and social welfare: The profession of social work (Ch. 11, pp. 227–252). Hoboken, NJ: John Wiley & Sons, Inc.

Substance Abuse and Mental Health Services Administration. (1998). *Table 11: Percentages reporting past month use of any illicit drug, by age group, race/ethnicity, and sex: 1979–1997* [Online]. Retrieved from http://www.samhsa.gov/oas/nhsda/ hnsda97/97tab.htm

Substance Abuse and Mental Health Services Administration. (2006). *Results from the 2005 National Survey on Drug Use and Health: National findings. Office of Applied Studies* (NSDUH Series H-30, DHHS Publication No. SMA 06–4194). Rockville, MD.

Substance Abuse and Mental Health Services Administration, Office of Applied Studies. (2008). *The National Study on Drug Use and Health Report: Alcohol use among pregnant women and recent mothers, 2002 to 2007.* Rockville, MD.

Substance Abuse and Mental Health Services Administration, Office of Applied Studies. (2009a). *The NSDUH Report: Illicit drug use among older adults.* Rockville, MD.

Substance Abuse and Mental Health Services Administration, Office of Applied Studies. (2009b). *Results from the 2008 National Study on Drug Use and Health Report* (NSDUH Series H-36, HHS Publication No. SMA 09-4434). Rockville, MD.

Substance Abuse and Mental Health Services Administration, Office of Applied Studies. (2011). *Results from the 2010 National Study on Drug Use and Health: Survey of national findings, detailed tables*, NSDUH Series H-41, HHS Publication No. (SMA) 11-4658. Rockville, MD.

Szlemko, W. J., Wood, J. W., & Thurman, P. J. (2006). Native Americans and alcohol: Past, present, and future. *Journal of General Psychology, 133*(4), 435–451.

Teo, M. (2010, June 5). *Singapore's policy keeps drugs at bay. Guardian.* Retrieved from http://www.guardian.co.uk/ commentisfree/2010/jun/05/Singapore-policy-drugs-bay/print

The Sentencing Project. (2007, December 11). *United States Sentencing Commission approves crack reform for federal prisoners.* Retrieved from http://www.staf.org/prevention/ needlesexchange/

Traub, J. (2010, April 9). Africa's drug problem. *New York Times.* Retrieved from http://www.nytimes.com/2007/10/21/ magazine/21wwln-idealab-t.html

Turnbull, J. E. (1988). Primary and secondary alcoholic women. *Social Casework, 69*(5), 290–297.

U.S. Department of Health and Human Services, National Institute on Drug Abuse. (n.d.). *Commonly abused drugs.* Retrieved from http://www.drugabuse.gov/DrugPages/Drugs ofAbuse.html

U.S. Sentencing Commission. (2007, May). *Cocaine and federal sentencing policy.* Retrieved from http://www.ussc .gov/r_congress/cocaine2007.pdf

U.S. Sentencing Commission. (2010, Nov. 1). *Supplement to the 2010 guidelines manual.* Retrieved from http://www .ussc.gov/2010guid/PDF_Supplement_2010_guidelines_ Manual.pdf

van Wormer, K. (1995). *Alcoholism treatment: A social work perspective.* Chicago, IL: Nelson-Hall Publishers.

van Wormer, K., & Davis, D. R. (2008). *Addiction treatment: A strengths perspective* (2nd ed.). Belmont, CA: Thomson, Brooks/Cole.

Vogt, I. (2002). Substance use and abuse and the role of social workers in Germany. In L. A. Straussner & L. Harrison (Eds.),

International aspects of social work practice in the addictions (pp. 69–83). New York: Haworth Press.

Walsh, D. C., Hingson, R. W., Merrigan, D. M., Levenson, S. M., Cupples, L. A., Heeren, T., et al. (1991). A randomized trial of treatment options for alcohol-abusing workers. *New England Journal of Medicine, 325*(11), 775–782.

World Health Organization. (2010). *HIV/AIDS: Injecting drug use and prisons.* Retrieved from http://www.who.int/hiv/topics/idu/en/index.html

Chapter 10

A mortgage in retirement? (2010, November). *AARP Bulletin, 51*(9), 20.

A profile of older Americans: 2009. (2010). Retrieved from the Administration on Aging Website: http://www.aoa.gov/aoaroot/aging_statistics/profile/2009/docs/2009profile_508.pdf

About ALFA. (2007). Retrieved from Assisted Living Federation of America website: http://www.alfa.org/alfa/About_ALFA.asp

About Bernard Nash. (2006). Retrieved from the American Association for Retired Persons (AARP) website: http://www.aarp.org/money/careers/employerresourcecenter/bestemployers/bernardnash

Administration on Aging. (2010, May 11). *Frequently asked questions (FAQs).* Retrieved from the Administration on Aging website: http://www.aoa.gov/aoaroot/aoa_programs/oaa/resources/Faqs.aspx#Resource

Aire, S. (2004, September 23). A lonely Italian retiree puts himself up for adoption. *The Christian Science Monitor,* pp. 1, 4.

Alzheimer's facts and figures. (2010, December 6). Retrieved from the Alzheimer's Association website: http://www.alz.org/alzheimers_disease_facts_and_figures.asp

Austin, C. D., & McClelland, R. W. (2003). Case management practice with the elderly. In M. J. Holosko & M. D. Feid (Eds.), *Social work practice with the elderly* (3rd ed., pp. 175–202). Toronto, ON: Canadian Scholars Press.

Barry, P. (2006, June). Medicare Part D: In and out of the doughnut hole. *AARP Bulletin,* 16–18.

Bellos, N. S., & Ruffalo, M. S. (1995). Aging: Services. In R. L. Edwards (Ed.), *Encyclopedia of social work* (19th ed., Vol. 1, pp. 165–171). Washington, DC: NASW Press.

Benson, H. (1996). *Timeless healing: The power and biology of belief.* New York: Scribner.

Brown, B. (2004, November). Communes for grownups. *AARP Bulletin,* 22.

Butler, S., & Kaye, L. W. (2004). Rurality, aging, and social work: Setting the context. In S. Butler & L. W. Kaye (Eds.), *Geronological social work in small towns and rural communities* (pp. 1–18). New York: The Haworth Press.

Caregiving in the U.S., 2009. (2009). Retrieved from the American Association of Retired Persons website: http://www.aarp.org/research/surveys/care/ltc/hc/articles/caregiving_09.html

Conner, K. A. (2000). *Continuing to care.* New York: Palmer Press.

Cox, C. B. (2005). *Community care for an aging society.* New York: Springer.

Cox, E., & Parsons, R. (1994). *Empowerment-oriented social work practice with the elderly.* Pacific Grove, CA: Brooks/Cole.

Dunkel, R. E. (1987). Protective services for the aged. In A. Minahan (Ed.), *Encyclopedia of social work* (18th ed., Vol. 2, pp. 393–395). Silver Spring, MD: NASW Press.

Edmonson, B. (2010, November/December). Just ask the lonely. *AARP Magazine,* 68–69.

Edwards, M. (2004, November/December). As good as it gets; what country takes the best care of its older citizens? *AARP Magazine,* 47–53.

Elderly people were abused in almost one-third of the U.S.'s nursing homes. (2001, July 31). *The Christian Science Monitor,* p. 20.

Eustis, N., Greenberg, J., & Patton, S. (1984). *Long term care for older persons: A policy perspective.* Monterey, CA: Brooks/Cole.

Ex, C., Gorter, K., & Janssen, U. (2004). Providing integrated health and social care for older persons in the Netherlands. In K. Leichsenring & A. Alaszewski (Eds.), *Providing integrated health and social care for older persons* (pp. 415–445). Burlington, VT: Ashgate.

Facts and figures: Statistics on minority aging in the U.S. (2006). Retrieved from Administration on Aging website: http://www.aoa.gov/prof/Statistics/minority_aging/facts_minority_aging.asp

Fischer, M. (2010, March & April). Love is (not) all you need. *AARP Magazine,* 29–33.

Freeman, M. S. (1998, December 2). Sharing a roof and a way of life. *The Christian Science Monitor,* pp. 11, 14–15.

Hodge, G. (2008). *The geography of aging: Preparing communities for the surge of seniors.* Quebec, CA: McGill-Queen's University Press.

Gardner, G. (2006, June 21). Independent but alone. *The Christian Science Monitor,* pp. 13–14.

Green, A. (2006, December 26). A flap over recouping costs of Medicaid. *The Christian Science Monitor,* p. 3.

Greene, R. R. (2000). *Social work with the aged and their families* (2nd ed.). New York: Aldine de Gruyter.

Healy, T. C. (2003). Ethical practice issues in rural perspective. In S. Butler & L. Kay (Eds.), *Gerontological social work in small towns and rural communities* (pp. 265–285). New York: The Hayworth Social Work Practice Press.

Hinden, S. (2010, December). Top questions and answers on Social Security. *AARP Bulletin, 51*(10), 21–24.

Hodge, D. R. (2003/2004). Points of spiritual congruence and dissimilarity: A comparative study. *Arete, 27*(2), 17–33.

Hong, L. (2006, June). Rural older adults' access barriers to in-home and community-based services. *Social Work Research, 30*(2), 109–118.

Hopkins led nation's relief effort. (1998). Retrieved from NASW website: http://www.socialworkers.org/profession/centennial/hopkins.htm

Hospice Services of America. (2006). *Hospice services and expenses.* Retrieved from http://www.hospicefoundation.org/hospiceInfo/services.asp

Huttman, E. (1985). *Social services for the elderly.* New York: Free Press.

Income, poverty and health insurance coverage in the United States. (2010, September 20). Retrieved from the U.S. Census Bureau website: http://www.census.gov/newsroom/releases/archives/income_wealth/cb10-144.html

Karger, H. J., & Stoesz, D. (1998). *American social welfare policy: A pluralist approach* (3rd ed.). New York: Addison Wesley Longman.

Karger, H. J., & Stoesz, D. (2010). *American social welfare policy: A pluralist approach* (6th ed.). Boston, MA: Allyn & Bacon.

Kochman, A. (1997). Gay and lesbian elderly: Historical overview and implications for social work practice. In J. K. Quam (Ed.), *Social services for senior gay men and lesbians* (pp. 1–10). New York: Haworth Press.

Kosberg, J. I., & Nahmiash, D. (1996). Characteristics of victims and perpetrators and milieus of abuse and neglect. In L. A. Baumhover & S. C. Beall (Eds.), *Abuse, neglect, and exploitation of older person* (pp. 31–45). Baltimore, MD: Health Professions Press.

Kropf, N. P., & Wilks, S. (2003). Grandparents raising grandchildren. In B. Berkman (Ed.), *Social work and healthcare in an aging society* (pp. 177–200). New York: Springer.

Kubler-Ross, E. (1969). *On death and dying.* New York: Macmillan.

Lamb, G. M. (2004, November 9). In some nations, the rise of "shortgevity." *The Christian Science Monitor*, pp. 13, 14.

Llana, S. M. (2006, September 8). Seniors raising their grandkids get a new boost. *The Christian Science Monitor*, pp. 1, 2.

Mackelprang, R. W., & Mackelprang, R. D. (2005, October). Historical and contemporary issues in end-of-life decisions: Implications for social work. *Social Work, 50*(4), 315–323.

Magnusson, P. (2006, June). Today's do-it-yourself pension. *AARP Bulletin,* 22–23.

Malamud, M. (2010, November). NASW board approves family caregiver standards. *NASW News,* p. 9.

Marsh, J. C. (2005, April). Bush plan takes security out of social security. *Social Work, 50*(2), 99.

Metz, P. (1997). Staff development for working with lesbian and gay elders. In J. K. Quam (Ed.), *Social services for senior gay men and lesbians* (pp. 35–45). New York: Hawthorn Press.

Miller, K. (2010, August 6). *Ten things you should know about social security.* Retrieved from the American Association of Retired Persons' website: http://aarp.org/work/social-security-info-08-2010-/10-things-you-need-to-know-about-social-security.html

Moody, R. A. (1976). *Life after life: The investigation of a phenomenon—survival of bodily death.* Harrisburg, PA: Stackpole Books.

Mui, A. C., Choi, N. C., & Monk, A. (1998). *Long term care and ethnicity.* Westport, CT: Auburn House.

Nadelhaft, A. (2005). *NASW launches "Understanding aging, the social worker's role."* Retrieved from the National Association of Social Worker's website: www.socialworkers.org

Nadelhaft, A. (2006). *NASW launches new aging credential for social workers.* Retrieved from the National Association of Social Worker's website: www.socialworkers.org

Naleppa, M. J., & Reid, W. J. (2003). *Gerontological social work: A task centered approach.* New York: Columbia University Press.

Nathanson, I. L., & Tirrito, T. T. (1998). *Gerontological social work: Theory into practice.* New York: Springer.

National Association of Social Workers. (1994). *Social work with older people: Understanding diversity.* Washington, DC: NASW Press.

National Shared Housing Resource Center. (2006). *Shared housing, more than just a place to live.* Retrieved from http://www.nationalsharedhousing.org/index.html

Newberg, A., D'Aquili, E., & Rause, V. (2001). *Why god won't go away: Brain science and the biology of belief.* New York: Ballentine Books.

NHPCO facts and figures: hospice care in America. (2009). Retrieved from the National Hospice and Palliative Care Organization website: http://www.nhpco.org/files/public/Statistics_Research/NHPCO_facts_and_figures.pdf

Nursing homes, business as usual. (2006, September). *Consumer Reports,* 38–41.

Older Americans Act. Retrieved from Administration on Aging website: http://www.aoa.gov/ about/legbudg/oaa/legbudg_oss.asp

Olson, L. K. (2003). *The not so golden years: Caregiving, the frail elderly, and the long term care establishment.* Lanham, MD: Rowman & Littlefield.

Our fight: Keeping social security strong. (2007). Retrieved from AARP website: http://www.aarp.org/money/social_security/a2004–10–22-ss_strong.html

Popple, P. R., & Leighninger, L. L. (1999). *Social work, social welfare, and American society.* Boston, MA: Allyn & Bacon.

Poverty among individuals by the official poverty measure. (2005). Retrieved from the Institute for Research on Poverty website: http://www.irp.wisc.edu/faqs/faq3/table1.htm

Providing care for another adult a second job for many, National Alliance for Caregiving/AARP study shows. (2004, April 6). Retrieved from AARP website: http://www.aarp.org/research/press-center/presscurrentnews/2004–03–30-caregiving.html

Radin, D. (2006, September–November). Becoming mindful of consciousness. *Shift: At the Frontiers of Consciousness, 12,* 40–41.

Rose Dobrof, DSW. (2001). Retrieved from Next Age website: http://nextagespeakers.com/rdobrof.htm

Rosengarten, L. (2000). *Social work in geriatric home health care.* New York: Hayworth Press.

Schlesinger, R. (2006, June). An expert's view of ageism: Things aren't any better. *AARP Bulletin,* 6.

Schope, R. (2005). Who's afraid of growing old? Gay and lesbian perceptions of aging. *Journal of Gerontological Social Work, 45*(4), 23–39.

Schroeder-Sheker, T. (2001). *Transitus: A blessed death in the modern world.* Missoula, MT: St. Dunstan's Press.

Schwartz, K. (2010, October 12). *Unemployment among older adults stuck near record highs.* Retrieved from the National Council on Aging website: http://www.ncoa.org/press-room/press-release/unemployment-among-older.html

Sebelius, K. (2010). *Medicare and the new health care law—what it means for you.* Washington, DC: Centers for Medicare and Medicaid Services, Department of Health and Human Services.

Seeber, J. (1995). Congregational models. In M. Kimble, S. McFadden, J. Eilor, & J. Seeber (Eds.), *Aging, spirituality, and religion* (pp. 253–269). Minneapolis, MN: Fortress Press.

Segal, E., & Brzuzy, S. (1998). *Social welfare policy, programs, and practice.* Itasca, IL: Peacock Publishers.

Small, G.W., Rabins, P. V. B., Patricia, P. B., Neil, S. D., Steven, T. F., Steven, H. F., et al. (1997, October 22). Diagnosis and treatment of Alzheimer disease and related disorders: Consensus statement of the American Association for Geriatric psychiatry, the Alzheimer's Association, and the American Geriatrics Society. *Journal of the American Medical Association, 278*(6) (electronic version). Retrieved from http://www.alz.org/Resources/FactSheets/Diagnosistreatment.pdf

Smoothing the way to retirement pay. (2006, July 28). *The Christian Science Monitor,* p. 8.

SNAP/Food Stamps. (2010). Retrieved from the Food Research and Action Center (FRAC) website: http://frac.org/federal-foodnutrition-programs/snapfood-stamps/

Stoessen, L. (2006, June). Legal articles cover CIGNA case, end-of-life choices. *NASW News*, p. 10.

Stoessen, L. (2007, January). Stress on women studied. *NASW News*, pp. 1, 8.

The new Medicare (Part D) drug "benefit." (2006, January). *Health Letter, Public Citizen Research Group*, pp. 14–16.

The Social Services Block Grant Plan. (2009–2010). Retrieved from http://www.ncdhhs.gov/dss/publications/docs/SSBG_2010.pdf

Toedtman, J. (2010, October). The great recession's next wave. *AARP Bulletin, 51*(8), 3.

Torres-Gil, F. M., & Puccinelli, M. A. (1995). Aging: Public policy issues and trends. In R. L. Edwards (Ed.), *Encyclopedia of social work* (19th ed., Vol. 1, pp. 159–164). Washington, DC: NASW Press.

Trumbull, M. (2006, August 18). Reform erodes future of pensions. *The Christian Science Monitor*, p. 2.

Yeoman, B. (2010, March, April). Living on the edge. *AARP Magazine*, 45–75.

What is Alzheimers? (2007). Retrieved from the Alzheimer's Association website: http://www.alz.org/alzheimers_disease_what_is_alzheimers.asp

Chapter 11

Aging inmates prompt creation of assisted living center at Washington prison. (2010, August 16). FOX News.com. Retrieved from http:www.foxnews.com/us/2010/08/16/aging-inmates-prompt-creation-assisted-living-center-washington-prison-FoxNews.com

Amnesty International. (2000, May). *A briefing for the UN Committee against torture.* Retrieved October 30, 2001, from http://www.web.amnesty.org/ai.nsf/indes/ AMR510562000

Amnesty International USA. (2010). *Lesbian, gay, bisexual and transgender human rights.* Retrieved from http://www.amnestyusa.org/print/php

Ashford, J. B. (2009). Overview of forensic social work: Broad and narrow definitions. In A. R. Roberts (Ed.), *Social workers' desk reference* (pp. 1055–1060). New York: Oxford University Press.

Barker, R. L. (2003). *The social work dictionary* (5th ed.). Washington, DC: NASW Press.

Barker, R. L., & Branson, D. M. (2000). *Forensic social work: Legal aspects of professional practice* (2nd ed.). New York: Haworth Press.

Bartollas, C., & Schmalleger, F. (2011). *Juvenile delinquency* (8th ed.). Boston, MA: Prentice Hall.

Brown, G. (2010). *The intersectionality of race, gender, and re-entry: Challenges for African-American women.* Washington, DC: American Constitution Society.

Chiu, T. (2010). *It's about time: Aging prisoners, increasing costs, and geriatric release.* New York: Vera Institute of Justice.

Dickerson, J. G. (2001). Margaret Murray Washington: Organizer of rural African American women. In I. B. Carlton-LaNey (Ed.).*African American leadership: An empowerment tradition in social welfare history.* Washington, DC: NASW Press.

Farr, K. A. (2000). Classification for female inmates: Moving forward. *Crime & Delinquency, 46*(1) 3-15.

Fiorenze, J. A. (1999). *Statement: national Conference of Catholic Bishops.* Retrieved from http://www.usccb.org

Galaway, B. (1981). Social service and criminal justice. In N. Gilbert & H Specht (Eds.), *Handbook of social services.* Englewood Cliffs, NJ: Prentice Hall.

Greene, J., & Mauer, M. (2010). *Downscaling prisons: Lessons from four states.* Washington, DC: The Sentencing Project.

Hoffman, J. (2007, October 21). Criminal element. *New York Times.* Retrieved from http;//www.nytimes.com/2007/10/21/magazine/21wwln-idealab-t.html?ref=magazine

Human Rights Watch. (n.d.). *Did you know?* Retrieved from http://www.hrw.org

Hutchison, E. D. (1987). Use of authority. *Social Service Review, 61*(4), 581–598.

Isenstadt, P. M. (1995). Adult courts. In R. L. Edwards (Ed.), *Encyclopedia of social work* (19th ed., pp. 68–74). Washington, DC: NASW Press.

Jensen, J. M., & Howard, M. O. (1998). Youth crime, public policy, and practice in the juvenile justice system: Recent trends and needed reforms. *Social Work, 43*(4), 324–334.

Knox, K. S., & Roberts, A. R. (2009). The social worker in a police department. In A. R. Roberts (Ed.), *Social workers' desk reference* (pp. 85–94). New York: Oxford University Press.

Leveille, V. (2008, October 20). *Bureau of Prisons revises policy on shackling of pregnant inmates [Web log post].* Retrieved from ACLU Blog of Rights: http://www.aclu.org/2008/10/20/bureau-of-prisons-revises-policy-on-shackling-of-pregnant-inmates.

Lyons, K., Manion, K., & Carlsen, M. (2006). *International perspectives on social work: Global conditions and local practice.* New York: Palgrave Macmillan.

MacKenzie, D. L. (2000). Evidence-based corrections: Identifying what works. *Crime & Delinquency, 46*(4), 457–471.

Maguire, K., & Pastore, A. L. (Eds.) (2001, February 2). Figure 6.1, Sentenced prisoners under jurisdiction of state and federal correctional authorities on December 31; Table 6.27, Rate (per 100,000 resident population) of sentenced prisoners under jurisdiction of state and federal correctional authorities on December 31. *Sourcebook of criminal justice statistics 2000.* Retrieved from http://www.albany.edu/sourcebook

Malone, D. (2005). Cruel and inhumane: Executing the mentally ill. *Amnesty International, 31*(3), 20–23.

Maschi, T., Hatcher, S. S., Schwalbe, C. S., & Rosato, N. S. (2008). Mapping the social service pathways of youth to and through the juvenile justice system: A comprehensive review. *Children and Youth Services Review, 30*(12), 1376–1385. doi:10.1016/jchildyouth.2008. 04.006

Mauer, M. (1994). *Americans behind bars: U.S. and international use of incarceration, 1992–1993.* Washington, DC: The Sentencing Project.

McNeece, C. A. (1995). Adult corrections. In R. L. Edwards (Ed.), *Encyclopedia of social work* (19th ed., pp. 61–68). Washington, DC: NASW Press.

Mears, D. P., & Kelly, W. R. (1999). Assessments and intake processing: Emerging policy considerations. *Crime & Delinquency, 45*(4), 508–529.

Messerli, J. (2010). *Should the death penalty be banned as a form of punishment?* Retrieved from http://www.balanced-politics.org/death_penalty.htm

Misleh, D. J., & Hanneman, E. U. (2004). Emerging issues: The faith communities and the criminal justice system.

In E. H. Jucah & M. Bryant (Eds.), *Criminal justice: Retribution vs. restoration* (pp. 111–131). New York: Haworth Press.

Moon, M. M., Sundt, J. L., Cullen, F. T., & Wright, J. P. (2000). Is child saving dead? Public support for juvenile rehabilitation. *Crime & Delinquency, 46*(1), 38–60.

Myers, D. L. (2005). *Boys among men: Trying and sentencing juveniles as adults.* Westport, CT: Praeger Publishers.

National Association of Social Workers. (2008). *Code of ethics of the National Association of Social Workers.* Washington, DC: Author. Retrieved from http://www.naswdc.org/pubs/code/code.asp?

Netherland, W. (1987). Corrections system: Adult. *Encyclopedia of social work* (18th ed., pp. 351–360). Silver Spring, MD: NASW Press.

Newport, F. (2010). *In U.S., 64% support death penalty in cases of murder.* Retrieved from http://www.gallup.com/poll/144284/Support-Death-Penalty-Cases-Murder.aspx?version= print

O'Neil, J. V. (2003). Forensic field broader than most think. *NASW News,* 48(10).

Pastore, A. L., & Maguire, K. (Eds.). (2005). Table 4.26.2005; Table 6.41.2005. *Sourcebook of criminal justice statistics* [online]. Retrieved from http:www//albany.edu/sourcebook/

Pinard, M. (2010). Collateral consequences of criminal convictions: Confronting issues of race and dignity. *New York University Law Review, 84,* 457–534.

Pray, K. (1945). Place of social casework in the treatment of delinquency. *Social Service Review, 19*(2), 235–248.

Puzzanchera, C. (2009). Juvenile arrests 2008. *Juvenile Justice Bulletin.* U.S. Department of Justice, Office of Justice Programs. Retrieved from http://www.ncjrs.gov/pdffiles1/ojjdp/228479.pdf

Ritter, J. A., Vakalahi, H. F. O., & Kiernan-Stern, M. (2009). *101 careers in social work.* New York: Springer Publishing Company.

Robinson, B. A. (2001, February 16). *Capital punishment: The death penalty.* Retrieved from http:// www.religioustolerance.org/ecute.htm

Saleebey, D. (Ed.). (2006). *The strengths perspective in social work practice* (4th ed.). Boston, MA: Pearson Allyn & Bacon.

Schiller, L. Y., & Zimmer, B. (2005). Sharing the secrets: The power of women's groups for sexual abuse survivors. In A. Gitterman & L. Shulman (Eds.), *Mutual aid groups, vulnerable & resilient populations, and the life cycle* (pp. 290–319). New York: Columbia University Press.

Scott, E. S., & Grisso, T. (1998). The evolution of adolescence: A developmental perspective on juvenile justice reform. *Journal of Criminal Law and Criminology, 88*(1), 137–189.

Sentencing Report. (2010, December 21). *New BJS report show first decline in correctional populations in decades.* Retrieved from http://sentencingproject.org/detail/news.cfmnews_id=1050&id=167

Siefert, K., & Pimlott, S. (2001). Improving pregnancy outcome during imprisonment: A model residential care program. *Social Work, 46*(2), 125–134.

State of Wisconsin Department of Corrections. (2007). Form DOC-10 (Rev. 12/2006): Rules of community supervision. Form DOC-10SO (Rev. 12/2006): Standard sex offender rules. Form DOC-502 (Rev. 1/03): Admission to adult field caseload: Assessment of offender risk. Wisconsin Administrative Code. Madison, WI: Author. Provided by Peggy Kendrigan, Division of Community Corrections.

Travis, J. (2004). Building from the ground up: Strategies for creating safe and just communities. In E. H. Judah & M. Bryant (Eds.), *Criminal justice: Retribution vs. restoration* (pp. 173–195). New York: Haworth Press.

Trimble, D. (2005). Uncovering kindness and respect: Men who have practiced violence in intimate relationships. In A. Gitterman & L. Shulman (Eds.), *Mutual aid groups, vulnerable & resilient populations, and the life cycle* (pp. 352–372). New York: Columbia University Press.

UNICEF. (2009). *Child protection from violence, exploitation and abuse: Child trafficking.* Retrieved from UNICEF website: http://www.unicef.org/protection/index_exploitation.html

U.S. Department of Justice, Bureau of Justice Statistics. (2009a). *Criminal victimization, 2009, bulletin NCJ 231327.* Retrieved from http://www.albany.edu/sourcebook/pdf/t3212009.pdf

U. S. Department of Justice, Bureau of Justice Statistics. (2009b). *Sourcebook of Criminal Justice Statistics Online.* Table 6.13.2009 Number and rate (per 100,000 U.S. residents) of persons in State and Federal prisons and local jails. Retrieved from http://www.albany.edu/sourcebook/pdf/t6132009.pdf

U. S. Department of Justice, Bureau of Justice Statistics. (2009c). *Sourcebook of Criminal Justice Statistics Online.* Table 6.33.2009 (per 100,000 resident population) of sentenced prisoners under jurisdiction of State and Federal correctional authorities on December 31. Retrieved from http://www.albany.edu/ sourcebook/pdf/t6292009.pdf

U.S. Department of Justice, Bureau of Justice Statistics. (2010a). *Capital punishment.* Retrieved from http:bjs.ojp.usdoj.gov/index.cfm?ty=tp&tid=18

U.S. Department of Justice, Bureau of Justice Statistics. (2010b, December). *Probation and parole in the United States, 2009.* Washington, DC: U.S. Department of Justice. Retrieved from http://bjs.ojp.usdoj.gov/index.cfm?ty=pbdetail&iid=2233

U.S. Department of Justice, Bureau of Justice Statistics. (2010c). *Sourcebook of criminal justice statistics online 2009.* Table 4.25 juveniles taken into police custody. Retrieved from http://www.albany.edu/sourcebook/pdf/t4252009

van Wormer, K. (2004). *Confronting oppression, restoring justice: From policy analysis to social action.* Alexandria, VA: Council on Social Work Education.

van Wormer, K. (2010). *Working with female offenders: A gender-sensitive approach.* Hoboken, NJ: John Wiley & Sons, Inc.

van Wormer, K., Roberts, A., Springer, D. W., & Brownell, P. (2008). Forensic social work: Current and emerging developments. In K. M. Sowers & C. N. Dulmus (Eds.), *Comprehensive handbook of social work and social welfare: The profession of social work* (pp. 315–342). Hoboken, NJ: John Wiley & Sons.

Walmsley, R. (2009). *World prison population list* (8th ed.). London: King's College, International Centre for Prison Studies. Retrieved from http://www.kel.ac.uk/depsta/law/Research/icps/downloads/wppl-8th_41.pdf

Wills, C. (2011, March 9). *Illinois Gov. Pat Quinn abolishes death penalty, clears death row.* Retrieved from http:// www.wasingtonpost.com/wp-dyn/content/article/2011/03/AR2011030900319_pf.html

Wright, V. (2010, November). *Deterrence in criminal justice: Evaluating certainty vs. severity of punishment.* Washington, DC: The Sentencing Project.

Chapter 12

Americans with Disabilities Act of 1990. Section 2, Findings and Purposes. Public Law 101–336.

Asch, A., & Mudrick, N. R. (1995). Disability. In R. L. Edwards (Ed.), *Encyclopedia of social work* (19th ed., Vol. 1, pp. 752–760). Washington, DC: NASW Press.

Autism. (2007). Retrieved from the March of Dimes website: http://www.marchofdimes.com/printableArticles/4439_10110.asp

Bagenstos, S. R. (2009). *Law and the contradictions of the disability rights movement.* New Haven, CT: Yale University Press.

Barnwell, D. A., & Day, M. (1996). Providing support to diverse families. In P. Beckman (Ed.), *Strategies for working with families with disabilities* (pp. 47–65). Baltimore, MD: Paul H. Brookes.

Baroff, G. S. (1991). *Developmental disabilities: Psychosocial aspects.* Austin, TX: ProEd.

Bishop, K. (2006). Family-centered services to infants and toddlers with or at risk for disabilities: IDEA 2004, Part C. In R. Constable, C. Massat, S. McDonald, & J. Flynn (Eds.), *School social work* (6th ed., pp. 189–204). Chicago, IL: Lyceum Books.

Cerebral palsy. (2007, December). Retrieved from the March of Dimes website: http://www.marchofdimes.com/baby/birthdefects_cerebralpalsy.html

Christensen, C. (1996). Disabled, handicapped, or disordered: What's in a name? In C. Christensen & F. Rizvi (Eds.), *Disability and the dilemmas of education and justice* (pp. 63–78). Buckingham, UK: Open University Press.

Convention on the rights of persons with disabilities. (2007, June 7). Retrieved from the American Association for Intellectual and Developmental Disability (AAIDD) website: http://www.aamr.org/unresolution.shtml

Council on Social Work Education. (2001). *Educational policy and accreditation standards.* Alexandria, VA: Author.

Devitt, T. (2010, August 3/Fall). Study by Sigan Hartley, PhD, and Marsha Mailick Seltzer, PhD, details autism's heavy toll beyond childhood on marriages. *Autism Society Wisconsin, 10*(3), 2.

DeWeaver, K., & Kropf, N. (1992, Winter). Persons with mental retardation: A forgotten minority in education. *Journal of Social Work Education, 28*(1), 38–40.

Disability characteristics data set: 2009 American Community Survey. Retrieved from U.S. Census Bureau website: http://factfinder.census.gov/servlet/STTTable?bm=y&qr_name=ACS_2009

Donovan, S. (2010). *The 2009 annual homeless assessment report.* Retrieved from http://kiwinc.itgo.com/mwc/intercity.html

Dossey, L. (2003). *Healing beyond the body, medicine and the infinite reach of the mind.* Boston, MA: Shambala.

Drinking alcohol during pregnancy. (2007). Retrieved from the March of Dimes website: http://www.marchofdimes.com/printableArticles/14332_1170 asp

Emotional disturbance, fact sheet 5. (2010, June). Retrieved from The National Dissemination Center for Children with Disabilities website: http://www.nichcy.org/Disabilities/Specific/Pages/EmotionalDisturbance.aspx

Epilepsy and seizure statistics. (n.d.). Retrieved from the Epilepsy Foundation website: http://epilepsyfoundation.org/about/statistics/cfm

Fact sheet: Self advocacy. (2005). Retrieved from the American Association on Intellectual and Developmental Disabilities (AAIDD) website: http://www.aamr.org/Policies/faq_movement.shtml

Fetal alcohol syndrome. (2008, June). Retrieved from the KidsHealth website: http://kidshealth.org/parent/medica/brain/fas.html

Flagel, R. (2007). *Raven's guide to special education, summary.* Retrieved from http://www.seformmatrix.com/raven/raven2.htm

Freedman, R. (1995). Developmental disabilities: Direct practice. In R. L. Edwards (Ed.), *Encyclopedia of social work* (19th ed., Vol. 1, pp. 721–728). Washington, DC: NASW Press.

Genetic counseling. (2007). Retrieved from the March of Dimes website: http://www.marchofdimes.com/printableArticles/4439_15008.asp

Gilson, S. F. (1998). Choice and self-advocacy: A consumer's perspective. In P. Wehman & J. Kregel (Eds.), *More than a job: Satisfying careers for people with disabilities* (pp. 3–23). Baltimore, MD: P. H. Brookes.

Gold, S. (2005, February 20). *2003 census data for persons with disabilities.* Retrieved from the National Association for the Mentally Ill (NAMI) website: http://namiscc.org/Research/2004/2003-CensusData.htm

Habilitation plan administrator. (2001). Retrieved from the Washington State Department of Personnel website: http://hr.dop.wa.gov/lib/hrdr/speca/50000/56980.htm

Hall, J. & Parker, K. (2010, September 10). *Federal programs to assist the unemployed are failing job seekers with disabilities.* Center for Research on Learning, University of Kansas. Retrieved from http://www.disabled-world.com/disability/employment/unemployment-programs.php

Hearing impairment. (2010, March). Retrieved from the March of Dimes website: www.marchofdimes.com/baby/birthdefects_hearing.html

Hearing loss. (2004). Retrieved from http://www.marchofdimes.com/printableArticles/4439_1232.asp

Hooyman, N. R., & Gonyea, J. G. (1995). Family caregiving. In R. L. Edwards (Ed.), *Encyclopedia of social work* (19th ed., Vol. 1, pp. 951–957). Washington, DC: NASW Press.

Illicit drug use during pregnancy. (2006, November). Retrieved from the March of Dimes website: http://search.marchofdimes.com/cgi-bin/MsmGo.exe?grab_id=0&page_id=480&query=coc

Johnson, A. B., & Surles, R. C. (1994). Has deinstitutionalization failed? In S. A. Kirk & S. D. Einbinder (Eds.), *Controversial issues in mental health* (pp. 213–216). Boston, MA: Allyn & Bacon.

Learning disabilities. (2010, August 11) Retrieved from the MedicineNet website: http://www.medicinenet.com/learning_disability/article.htm

Lift every voice: Modernizing disability policies and programs to serve a diverse nation (p. 50). (1999, December 1). Washington, DC: National Council on Disability.

Liu, G. Z. (2005). Best practices: Developing cross-cultural competence from a Chinese perspective. In J. Stone (Ed.), *Culture and disability: Providing culturally competent services* (pp. 65–85). Thousand Oaks, CA: Sage.

Mackelprang, M., & Saisgiver, R. (1999). *Disability: A diversity model approach in human service practice.* Pacific Grove, CA: Brooks/Cole.

Mannes, M. (1998). *The new psychology and economics of permanency. The prevention report #2.* Iowa City, IA: The

University of Iowa National Resource Center for Family Centered Practice.

May, G. E. (2005). Changing the future of disability: The disability discrimination model. In G. May & M. B. Raske (Eds.), *Ending disability discrimination: Strategies for social workers* (pp. 82–98). Boston, MA: Allyn & Bacon.

May, G. E., & Raske, M. (Eds.). (2005). *Ending disability discrimination: Strategies for social workers*. Boston, MA: Allyn & Bacon.

McDonald-Wikler, L. (1987). Disabilities: Developmental. In A. Minahan (Ed.), *Encyclopedia of social work* (18th ed., Vol. 1, pp. 423–431). Silver Spring, MD: NASW Press.

Meekosha, H., & Jakubowicz, A. (1996). Disability, participation, representation and social justice. In C. Christensen & F. Rizvi (Eds.), *Disability and the dilemmas of education and justice* (pp. 9–95). Buckingham, UK: Open University Press.

Mendez, T. (2004). A special compromise on education. *Christian Science Monitor*, pp. 11, 12.

Morrison-Orton, D. J. (2005). The use of religion and spiritual strategies in rehabilitation. In J. Murphy & J. Pardeck (Eds.), *Disability issues for social workers and human services professionals in the twenty-first century* (pp. 5–41). New York: Hayworth Press.

Murphy, J. W., & Pardeck, J. T. (Eds.). (2005). *Disability issues for social workers and human service professionals in the twenty-first century*. New York: Hayworth Press.

National Association of Social Workers. (1996). *NASW code of ethics*. Washington, DC: NASW Press.

NINDS traumatic brain injury information page. (2010, November 19). Retrieved from the National Institute of neurological Disorders and Stroke website: http://www.ninds/nih/gov/disorders/tbi.htm

Oliver, M., & Sapey, B. (2006). *Social work with disabled people* (3rd ed.). New York: Palgrave Macmillan.

Pardeck, J. T. (1998). *Social work after the Americans with Disabilities Act*. Westport, CT: Auburn House.

Pardeck, J. T. (2005). An analysis of the Americans with Disabilities Act (ADA) in the twenty-first century. In J. Murphy & J. Pardeck (Eds.), *Disability issues for social workers and human services professionals in the twenty first century* (pp. 121–151). New York: Haworth Press.

Parent, W. S., Cone, A. A., Turner, E., & Wehman, P. (1998). Supported employment: Consumers leading the way. In P. Wehman & J. Kregel (Eds.), *More than a job: Securing satisfying careers for people with disabilities* (pp. 149–166). Baltimore, MD: P. H. Brooks.

Parkinson, C. B., & Howard, M. (1996). Older persons with mental retardation/developmental disabilities. In M. J. Mellor (Ed.), *Special populations and systems linkages* (pp. 91–101). New York: Haworth Press.

Patton, J. R., Blackbourn, J. M., & Fad, K. (1996). *Exceptional individuals in focus* (6th ed.). Englewood Cliff, NJ: Prentice Hall.

Petr, C., & Barney, D. (1993, May). Reasonable efforts for children with disabilities: The parents' perspective. *Social Work, 38*(3), 252–255.

Putnam, M. (2007). Moving from separate to crossing aging and disability service networks. In M. Putnam (Ed.), *Aging and disability: Crossing network lines* (pp. 5–17). New York: Springer.

Raske, M. (2005). The disability discrimination model in social work practice. In G. May & M. Raske (Eds.), *Ending disability*

discrimination strategies for social workers (pp. 106–107). Boston, MA: Allyn & Bacon.

Richey, W. (2002, January 9). In workplace, tougher standards on job-related injuries. *Christian Science Monitor*, p. 2.

Richey, W. (2004, May 18). Court boosts civil rights law for disabled. *The Christian Science Monitor*, pp. 1, 10.

Richmond, M. (1917). *Social diagnosis* (p. 26). Philadelphia, PA: Russel Sage Foundation.

Rothman, J. C. (2003). *Social work practice across disability*. Boston, MA: Allyn & Bacon.

Schlitz, M., & Amorok, T. (2005). *Consciousness and healing, integral approaches to mind-body medicine*. St. Louis, MO: Elsevier.

Segal, S. P. (1995). Deinstitutionalization. In R. L. Edwards (Ed.), *Encyclopedia of social work* (19th ed., Vol. 1, pp. 704–711). Washington, DC: NASW Press.

Self advocates becoming empowered. (2010). Retrieved from the SABE website: http://www.sabeusa.org

Smart, J. (2001). *Disability, society, and the individual*. Gaithersburg, MD: Aspen.

Snyder, R., & Ne'eman, A. (2007, July 10). *Autism from autistics*. Retrieved from the Autism Self Advocacy Network website: http://www.autisticadvocacy.org

Special education and the Individuals with Disabilities Education Act. (2007). Retrieved from the National Education Association website: http://www.nea.org/specialed/index.html?mode=print

Stites, S. (2001). *Allyse*. Unpublished paper, Smith College, Northampton, MA.

Stoessen, L. (2005, March). Children with disabilities: A family affair. *NASW News*, p. 4.

Stone, J. H. (Ed.). (2005). *Culture and disability, providing culturally competent services*. Thousand Oaks, CA: Sage.

Switzky, H., Dudzinski, M., Van Acker, R., & Gambro, J. (1988). Historical foundations of out-of-home residential alternatives for mentally retarded persons. In L. Heal, J. Haney, & Amado A (Eds.), *Integration of developmentally disabled individuals into the community* (2nd ed., pp. 19–35). Baltimore, MD: P. H. Brooks.

Talbott, R. E. (1992). Communication disorders. In P. J. McLaughlin & P. Wehman (Eds.), *Developmental disabilities: A handbook for best practices* (pp. 98–100). Boston, MA: Andover Medical.

Torres-Gill, F. (2007). Translating research into program and policy changes. In M. Putnam (Ed.), *Aging and disability* (pp. 245–262). New York: Springer.

Understanding epilepsy. (2007). Retrieved from the Epilepsy Foundation website: http://www.epilepsyfoundation.org/about/

U.S. Census Bureau. (2007, May). *Asian/Pacific American Heritage Month*. Retrieved from the IM Diversity website: http://www.imdiversity.com/Villages/Asian/reference/census_asian_american_heritage_2007.asp

Weathers, R. R. II. (2005). *A guide to disability statistics from the American Community Survey*. Retrieved from the Employment and Disability Institute Collection website: http://digitalcommons.ilt.cornell.edu/edicollect/129

Wehman, P. (2006). *Life beyond the classroom*. Baltimore, MD: Paul H. Brookes.

Wehman, P., Inge, K., Revell, W. G., Jr., & Brooke, V. (2007). *Real work for real pay: Inclusive employment for people with disabilities*. Baltimore, MD: Paul. H. Brookes.

Welcome to L'Arche USA. (2008). Retrieved from the L'Arche USA website: http://www.Larcheusa.org

What causes autism? (2009, March 11). Retrieved from http://autism.about.com.od/whatisautism/p/autismcauses.htm

Willer, B., & Itagliata, J. (1984). *Promises and realities for mentally retarded citizens.* Baltimore, MD: University Park Press.

Wolfe, P. S. (1992). Challenges for service providers. In P. J. McLaughlin & P. Wehman (Eds.), *Developmental disabilities: A handbook for best practices* (pp. 125–130). Boston, MA: Andover Medical.

Chapter 13

Acs, G., & Loprest, P. (2007). *TANF caseload composition and leavers synthesis report.* Retrieved from http://www.acf.hhs.gov/programs/opre/welfare_employ/tanf_caseload/reports/tanf_caseload_comp/tanf_caseload_final.pdf

Benard, B. (2006). Using strengths-based practice to tap the resilience of families. In D. Saleebey (Ed.), *The strengths perspective in social work practice* (4th ed., pp. 197–220). Boston, MA: Pearson Allyn & Bacon.

Besthorn, F., & Canda, E. R. (2002). Revisioning environment: Deep ecology for education and teaching in social work. *Journal of Teaching in Social Work, 22*(1/2), 79–101.

Blythe, M. (2006). Will wind and biofuels be enough? *The Futurist, 40,* 28.

Brown, G. W. (2008). Globalization is what we make of it: Contemporary globalization theory and the future construction of global interconnection. *Political Studies Review, 6,* 42–53.

Bruno, A. (2006). *Refugee admissions and resettlement policy. CRS report for Congress* (Congressional Research Service; the Library of Congress). Retrieved from http://www.ilw.com/immigdaily/news/2006.0215-crs.pdf

Bureau of Labor Statistics, U.S. Department of Labor. (2009). *Occupational outlook handbook: 2010–2011 edition, social workers.* Retrieved from http://www.bls.gov/oco/ocos060.htm

Canton, J. (2006). *The extreme future: The top trends that will reshape the world for the next 5, 10, and 20 years.* New York: Dutton.

Chideya, F. (1999). *The color of our future.* New York: William Morrow.

Dahinden, U., Lindsey, N., Chatjouli, A., Diego, C., Fjaestad, B., Matias, M., et al. (2006). Dilemmas of genetic information. In G. Gaskell & M. W. Bauer (Eds.), *Genomics and society: Legal, ethical and social dimensions.* London: Earthscan.

Devore, W., & Schlesinger, E. G. (1999). *Ethnic-sensitive social work practice* (5th ed.). Boston, MA: Allyn & Bacon.

Fadiman, A. (1997). *The spirit catches you and you fall down: A Hmong child, her American doctors, and the collision of two cultures.* New York: Farrar, Straus and Giroux.

Freedman, T. G. (1998). Genetic susceptibility testing: Ethical and social quandaries. *Health & Social Work, 23*(3), 214–222.

Ginsberg, L. (2005, Spring). The future of social work as a profession. *Advances in Social Work,* 5–16.

Glossary of terms. (2001). Retrieved from the Fertility Institutes website: http://www.fertility-docs.com/glossary.html

Grew, R. (2006). Global history and globalization. In S. Hewa & D. Stapleton (Eds.), *Globalization, philanthropy, and civil society: Toward a new political culture in the 21st century* (pp. 15–32). New York: Springer.

Gutierrez, L., & Nagda, B. A. (1996). The multicultural imperative in human services organizations: Issues for the twenty-first century. In P. R. Raffoul & C. A. McNeece (Eds.), *Future issues for social work practice* (pp. 203–213). Boston, MA: Allyn & Bacon.

Hewa, S., & Stapleton, D. H. (2006). Structure and process of global integration. In S. Hewa & D. Stapleton (Eds.), *Globalization, philanthropy, and civil society: Toward a new political culture in the 21st century* (pp. 3–13). New York: Springer.

Holland, J. (2005). The regeneration of ecological, societal, and spiritual life: The holistic post modern mission of humanity in the newly emerging planetary civilization. *Journal of Religion and Spirituality in Social Work, 24*(1/2), 7–25.

Holody, R. (1999). Toward a new permanency planning: How kinship care can revitalize the foster care system. *Areté, 23*(1), 1–10.

Ki-Moon, B. (2007). *The millennium development goals report 2007.* New York: United Nations.

Larsen, L. J. (2004). *The foreign-born population in the United States: 2003.* Retrieved from http://www.census.gov/prod/2004pubs/p20-551.pdf

Lee, J. (2011). *Annual flow report, U.S. Naturalizations: 2011.* Retrieved from the Office of Immigration Statistics, U.S. Department of Homeland Security website: http://www.dhs.gov/assets/statistics/publications/natz_fr_2010.pdf

Link, R. J., & Ramanathan, C. (2011). *Human behavior in a just world: Reaching for common ground.* Lanham, MD: Rowman & Littlefield Publishers, Inc.

Lynch, Z. (2004). *Neurotechnology and society (2010-2060).* Retrieved from http://lifeboat.com/ex/neurotechnology.and.society?background=white

Lyons, K., Manion, K., & Carlsen, M. (2006). *International perspectives on social work: Global conditions and local practice.* New York: Palgrave Macmillan.

Malamud, M. (2010, November). In Russia, discovering a new view of social work. *NASW News, 55*(10), 1, 12.

Malone, B. (2011). 10 years after the human genome project: Will the DTC genetic test debate shape the future of genomics? *Clinical Laboratory News, 37*(4). Retrieved from http://www.Aacc.org/publications/cln/2011/April/Pages/10YearsAftertheHumanGenomeProject.aspx

McGoldrick, M. (2009). Using genograms to map family patterns. In R. Roberts (Ed.), *Social workers' desk reference* (2nd ed., pp. 409–423). New York: Oxford University Press.

McGowan Institute for Regenerative Medicine. (2010). *What is regenerative medicine.* Retrieved from http://www.regenerativemedicine.net/What.html

McKinley, B. (n.d.). *Editorial: Looking at the bigger picture in migration.* Retrieved from the International Organization for Migration website: http://www.iom.int/jahia/jsp/index.jsp

Miller, J., & Garran, A. M. (2009). The legacy of racism for social work practice today and what to do about it. In A. R. Roberts (Ed.), *Social workers' desk reference* (2nd ed., pp. 928–933). New York: Oxford University Press.

Naisbitt, J. (2006). *Mind set! Reset your thinking and see the future.* New York: HarperCollins.

National Academy of Sciences. (2011). *Appendix A: National institutes of health guidelines for research using human embryonic stem cell research (2010).* Retrieved from http://search.nap.edu/nap-cgi/skimchap.cgi?recid=12923&chap=9-16&act=nap

National Association of Social Workers. (2008). *Code of ethics of the National Association of Social Workers.* Washington, DC: NASW Press.

National Association of Social Workers. (2011). *Social workers in Congress (112th Congress).* Retrieved from http://www.socialworkers.org/pace/swCongress/SW_InCongress.pdf

National Committee on Pay Equity. (2010). *The wage gap over time: In real dollars, women see a continuing gap.* Retrieved from http://www.pay-equity.org/info-time.html

National Committee on Pay Equity. (2011). *Wage gap statistically unchanged.* Retrieved from http://www.pay-equity.org

National Human Genome Research Institute. (2006, December). *The Human Genome Project completion: Frequently asked questions.* Retrieved from http://www.genome.gov/11006943

Olzak, S. (2011). Does globalization breed discontent? *Journal of Conflict Resolution, 5*(1). doi: 10.1177/002200271038366

O'Neil, J. V. (2002). EAPs offer multitude of internet services. *NASW News, 47*(1), 14.

Pace, P. R. (2011, January). Attitudes on technology studied: Generational data yield some surprising results. *NASW News, 56*(1), 7.

Questions and answers on pay equity. (1998). Retrieved from http://www.Feminist.com/fairpay.htm

Rathode, B. (2006, June 22). *Over 3 million babies born through IVF in 3 decades.* Retrieved from http://www.earthtimes.org/articles/show/7288.html

Reppas, J. (2010). *Congressional hearing explores the future of neuroscience research and development.* Retrieved from http://www.neurotechindustry.org/congressionalhearing.html

Rifkin, J. (2004). *The European dream: How Europe's vision of the future is quietly eclipsing the American dream.* New York: Jeremy P. Tarcher/Penguin.

Social work in the public eye. (2010). *NASW News, 55*(10), 11.

Stein, R. (2009). U.S. set to fund more stem cell study. *The Washington Post.* Retrieved from http://www.washingtonpost.com/wp-dyn/content/article/2009/12/02/AR2009120201955_pf.html

Tucker, P. (2006). Technology: Embryonic stem cells promise new cures. *The Futurist, 40*(2), 16–17.

UnderstandingNano.com. (n.d.). *Nanotechnology in medicine: Nanomedicine.* Retrieved from http://www.understandingnano.com/medicine.html

United Nations. (2010). *The millennium development goals report 2010.* New York: United Nations.

United Nations Development Programme. (2010). *Beyond the midpoint: Achieving the millennium development goals.* New York: United Nations Development Programme.

U.S. Bureau of Labor Statistics. (2010, July 26). *TED: The editor's desk: Usual weekly earnings in second quarter 2010 by education.* Retrieved from http://www.data.bls.gov/cgi-bin/print.pl/opub/ted/2010/ted_20100726.htm

U.S. Bureau of the Census. (1950). *Census of population: 1950* (Vol. II, Pt. 1, U.S. Summary, Table 38, pp. 90–91 & Table 61, pp. 109–111) and *U.S. census of population: 1950* (Special Reports: Nonwhite Population by Race, Table 2, p. 16, Table 3, p. 17, Table 4, p. 18, and Table 5, p. 19).

U.S. Census Bureau. (2004). *Table 2a. Projected population of the United States, by age and sex: 2000 to 2050.* Retrieved from http://census.gov/ipc/www/usinterimprojtab02a.pdf

U.S. Census Bureau. (2008). *Newsroom: An older and more diverse nation by midcentury.* Retrieved from http://www.census.gov/newsroom/releases/archives/population/cb08-123.html

U.S. Census Bureau. (2009). *Newsroom: As baby boomers age, fewer families have children under 18 at home.* Retrieved from http:/www.census.gov/newsroom/releases/archives/families/_households/cb09-29.html

U.S. Census Bureau. (2010a). *United States S2501 occupancy characteristics, American factfinder.* Retrieved from http://factfinder.census.gov/servlet/STTable?bm=y&-geo_id=01000US&-qr_name=ACS

U.S. Census Bureau. (2010b, September). *American Community Survey Briefs. Poverty: 2008 and 2009.* Retrieved from http://www.census.gov/hhes/www/poverty/poverty.html

U.S. Census Bureau. (2011, March 24). *2010 census shows America's diversity, U.S. Census Bureau News.* Retrieved from http:2010.census.gov/news/releases/operations/cb11-cn125.html

U.S. Department of Homeland Security. (2011). *Proposed refugee admissions for fiscal year 2011: Report to the Congress.* Retrieved from http://www.state.gov/documents/organization/148671.pdf

U.S. Government Accountability Office. (2010). *U. S. Government Accountability Office Strategic Plan: Serving the Congress and the nation 2010-2015.* Retrieved from http://www.gao.gov/new.items/d105559sp.pdf

Vincent, G. K., & Velkoff, V. A. (2010, May). Appendix Table A-1. Projections and distribution of the total population by age for the United States: 2010 to 2050, The Next Four Decades: The Older Population in the United States: 2010 to 2050, p. 10. U.S. Census Bureau. Retrieved from http: // www.census.gov/prod/2010pubs/p25-1138pdf

Wagner, C. (2007, January-February). Values conflicts in stem-cell research. *The Futurist, 40*(1), 8-9.

Wall, C. D., Proctor, B. D., & Smith, J. C. (2010, September). *Income, poverty, and health insurance coverage in the United States: 2009. Current population reports, consumer income.* Retrieved from http://www.census.gov/prod/2010pubs/p60-238.pdf

Walsh, D. (2010, September 29). *2009 income gap in the US highest on record.* Retrieved from the World Socialist website: http://www.wsws.org/articles/2010/sep2010/cens-s29.shtml

Walsh, F. (2009). A family resilience framework. In R. Roberts (Ed.), *Social workers' desk reference* (2nd ed., pp. 423–428). New York: Oxford University Press.

Wolff, R. (2010). *LA progressive: Does welfare work?* Retrieved from http://www.laprogressive.com/economic-equality/welfare-work

World Future Society. (2007). *Forecasts: Top 10 forecasts from Outlook 2007; World trends & forecasts.* Retrieved from http://www. wfs.org/forecasts.htm

Photo Credits

Index